Imagine No Religion

Imagine No Religion

How Modern Abstractions Hide Ancient Realities

Carlin A. Barton and Daniel Boyarin

FORDHAM UNIVERSITY PRESS

NEW YORK 2016

Library of Congress Cataloging-in-Publication Data

Names: Barton, Carlin A., 1948– author.
Title: Imagine no religion : how modern abstractions hide ancient realities / Carlin A. Barton and Daniel Boyarin.
Description: First edition. | New York, NY : Fordham University Press, 2016. | Includes bibliographical references and index.
Identifiers: LCCN 2016013979| ISBN 9780823271191 (cloth : alk. paper) | ISBN 9780823271207 (pbk. : alk. paper)
Subjects: LCSH: Religion.
Classification: LCC BL48 .B3665 2016 | DDC 200—dc23
LC record available at https://lccn.loc.gov/2016013979

Printed in the United States of America

18 17 16   5 4 3 2 1

First edition

to Carole and Fred, Karen and Norman

CONTENTS

Religio

Part I.   Mapping the Word

Part II.   Case Study: Tertullian

Thrēskeia

Part I.   Mapping the Word

Part II.   Case Study: Josephus

This book is written in one scholarly voice but two authorial voices. Hence, we have chosen to write in the first-person singular throughout.

I want to understand you: I study your obscure language.

—ALEXANDER S. PUSHKIN

Imagine No Religion

Introduction: What You Can See When You Stop Looking for What Isn't There

> When one encounters the word "religion" in a translation of an ancient text: First, cross out the word whenever it occurs. Next, find a copy of the text in question in its original language and see what word (if any) is being translated by "religion." Third, come up with a different translation: It almost doesn't matter what. Anything besides "religion."
>
> —EDWIN JUDGE[1]

We laughed when we came upon this wonderful apothegm of Judge's while coming close to the end of writing this book and composing the introduction.[2] Judge's remarks reflected conclusions to which we had come early on when we discovered that we needed to "untranslate" *religio* and *thrēskeia* to return them to their original contexts, and to allow the contexts to convey the range of their meanings. This book, generated by semantic studies of Latin *religio* and Greek *thrēskeia*, has as its project to see what it was possible to see when we ceased to look for what was not there, when we ceased to rely on the anachronistic word "religion" and instead, attempted to study, in the most nuanced way that we were able, these conceptual networks and the cultures from which they came "on their own terms," integrated back into the endless depths and complexities of mundane existence.

Brent Nongbri writes that, "[I]f we follow Judge's dictum and do not allow ourselves to invoke the concept of religion in our descriptive accounts, we will force ourselves to think outside our usual categories."[3] Aligning our aspirations to his, we hope that our study of *religio* and *thrēskeia* might encourage the production of books, not on "Athenian religion," the "Jewish religion," or "Roman religion," but rather books that will link what was conjoined in ancient cultures, and will explore the question of *why* the categories and boundaries of other cultures were drawn differently from our own. We hope to encourage books "that will encapsulate and thoroughly rearrange those bits and pieces of what we once gathered together as 'ancient religions.'"[4]

Close Encounters of the Lexicographical Kind

> The meaning of a word is its use in the language.
>
> Wittgenstein, *Philosophical Investigations* 20

What we identify as different senses of a word are merely, C. P. Jones has observed, "... possible translations in light of the fact that English lacks a simple equivalent."[5] There are no simple English equivalents of *religio* or *thrēskeia*. The uses of these words, it transpired, could be understood metonymically rather than metaphorically, by association rather than by distillation, and we had no possibility in advance of predicting the chains of association. It was not possible to abstract a covering "soul of the word" from either term. Rather, meanings developed out of other meanings by a series of transformations (the intermediary steps often being occluded). And so we tried, as far as we were able, to disentangle and distinguish the various relationships of one usage to another, to map the semantic ranges of *religio* and *thrēskeia*, attending to the varieties and range of their specific and pragmatic functions, their denotations and connotations.[6]

In the end, to translate *religio* or *thrēskeia* in any context, we needed many English words—and even then, we have been able only to approximate, if that, the world of nuance and ambiguity conveyed by the Latin and Greek terms. These words functioned in the semantics of a different cultural world, a different "form of life," one that we can only approximate by using lots and lots of words—hence, this book.

We can listen to and imagine people living in an ancient culture more precisely and richly when we begin with the assumption that we don't know what their key words mean, especially if they are "false friends" of our own words. In translating both *religio* and *thrēskeia*, "religion" has often been used as a shortcut—a "worm hole"—to carry the reader quickly and safely from an often very alien ancient world back into our own. But we have lingered on the rich history and complexity of *religio* and *thrēskeia* in the hope that time spent on and with these words would enable us to make these words into "true friends"—an aid to expanding our conceptual universe. We hoped to imagine more richly the ancient "forms of life" that they evinced. "The history of a word," as Richard Reizenstein asserts, "when it deepens into the history of a concept, can always give us rich information about problems that we cannot approach by any other means."[7]

While there have been some researchers who have striven to bring the gorilla into our world and teach her sign language so that she might live with us and communicate with us in our terms, we aspire to be like those researchers who have been willing to submerge themselves in the lives and language of the gorillas in the hope of learning a very different way of understanding and negotiating the world.

J. Z. Smith writes:

> Giving primacy to native terminology yields, at best, *lexical* definitions that historically and statistically, tell how a word is used. But lexical definitions are almost always useless for scholarly work. To remain content with how "they" understand "magic" may yield a proper description but little explanatory power. How "they" use a word cannot substitute

for the *stipulative* procedures by which the academy contests and controls second-order specialized usage.[8]

Intellectuals and academics in the contemporary world are cosmopolites who are tossed together, from a variety of backgrounds, into a kaleidoscopic variety of situations. They are like the relativist and essentialist Xenophanes who boasted of travelling the "world" for 67 years. Scholars who study the ancient world, in particular, "travel" far in time (as well as in space). They are pressed hard to find ways of ordering and reconciling the great diversities in human experience. We scholars, like all cosmopolites, like the ancient Ionian thinkers, cope with and harmonize our often discordant, interrupted, and discontinuous experience by creating covering abstractions. And like the "pre-Socratics," we tend to see abstractions not only as necessary for establishing a "critical distance," but we pride ourselves on them as characterizing and elevating the person who uses them. For Western scholars, it is above all the Greek philosophers with their covering abstractions, rather than the Romans (with their persistent attachment to the concrete), who seem to us to have found a useful language to embrace the intricacies of culture.

Cultures with elaborate divisions of labor and with the developed hierarchical structures needed to coordinate and rationalize the activities of the participants in that culture often rely for unity on highly simplified covering ideas and symbols. It is exactly the abstraction that sacralizes these ideas, that sets them apart. Each word becomes, so to speak, the head of a hierarchy. Like the inhabitants of the vast Roman Empire, of any vast, artificial and imaginary unity, we feel the need for these condensed ideas and symbols to unite us (e.g., *logos*, *theos*, race, class, gender, religion, politics, economics). The more distilled and simplified the language, the greater power to "cover" a multitude of distinct individual cases. Like Plato's "Truth," "Beauty," "Goodness," and "God," one can often draw an equal sign between all the abstractions, and they enable us to embrace almost anything. "Everything is politics." "Everything is economics." While all language relies on categories and abstractions, in complex cultures, particular prestige and faith is put not only in language over direct experience of the world, but particularly in the reification of deductively drawn abstractions even over generalizations derived from observation of particulars.

While scholars (not excepting ourselves) have the irresistible tendency, as they read, to use the literary work to symbolize and finally, to replicate themselves,[9] we have tried to the best of our ability not to let the scales of custom blind us to those aspects of the texts that are unfamiliar and difficult to comprehend. We both chose to work, in the second parts of each part of the book, on authors who were far from our "comfort zone," convinced that an important project of the humanities is to describe and understand, as well as possible, the myriad ways that humans have chosen to live their humanity with the disciplines of anthropology, history, literary criticism, archaeology, and religious studies and so forth *serving* that grand endeavor by accessing very different kinds of evidence and deploying different strategies of analysis.

Our resulting study is divided into two, with each half containing a close semantic study followed by an attempt to place the word in the broad context of a particularly pertinent author's language and life world. The book begins with an analysis of Latin republican and early imperial *religio*, followed by a reading of Tertullian, the (second- to third-century C.E.) African writer who did the most to mold Latin to the new Christian movement. The second half of the book treats of Greek *thrēskeia* in its earlier usages and in the Christian apologists, followed by a study of its functions in the world of Josephus, the (first-century C.E.) Judaean historian and writer who made the greatest and most complex use of this word. We have also made the acquaintance of many of the Latin and Greek words in the general semantic fields of *religio* and *thrēskeia*: *pudor, conscientia, fides, scrupulus, superstitio, therapeia, sebomai, eusebeia, deisidaimonia, pistis, timē*, although we have not given them nearly the attention they deserve.

WHAT DOES "NO RELIGION" MEAN?

When we make the claim that there is "no religion" as we know it in the cultures we are describing, we can hear readers objecting: But that culture has gods and temples, holy days and priestly rules, so how can we say they have "no religion"? The point is not, as Nongbri emphasizes, that there weren't practices with respect to "gods" (of whatever sort), but that these practices were not divided off into separate spheres from eating, sleeping, defecating, having sexual intercourse, making revolts and wars, cursing, blessing, exalting, degrading, judging, punishing, buying, selling, raiding and revolting, building bridges, collecting rents and taxes. We are not arguing that "religion" pervaded everything in those cultures or that people in those times and climes were uniquely "religious," but that, as Nongbri makes clear, "[A]ncient people simply did not carve up the world in that way."[10] Timothy Fitzgerald has made the point in another way: "When [an] author points out that 'religion' permeates the whole of life, the reader can wonder what is the difference between saying that and saying that the concept has no distinct meaning, because nothing is picked out by it."[11] It is in the disembedding of human activities from the particular contexts and aggregations found in many societies into one concept and named entity or even institution that we find the genealogy of the modern western notion of "religion." Just as people had intercourse of more or less the same varieties as today (if the pictorial evidence from antiquity can be relied on) and made babies (or not) but did not organize these practices and experiences into a category of "sexuality,"[12] so too people sacralized and desacralized/desecrated, feared and revered and loved,[13] made bonds and oaths, performed rituals, and told stories about gods and people without organizing these experiences and practices into a separate realm.

"Imagining no religion" does *not* mean that we imagine that people did not make gods or build temples, praise and pray and sacrifice, that they did not ask metaphysical questions or try to understand the world in which they lived, conceive of invisible beings (gods, spirits, demons, ghosts), organize forms of worship and festival, invent cosmologies and mythologies, support beliefs, defend morals and ideals, or imagine other worlds. But, as Daniel Dubuisson points out:

[I]t was the West that made from this collection of attitudes and ideas an autonomous, singular complex, profoundly different from everything surrounding it. And it conferred on this distinct complex a kind of destiny or essential anthropological vocation: humans are held to be religious in the same way as they are omnivorous, that is, by nature, through the effects of a specific inborn disposition.[14]

Nongbri notes that, "What is modern about the ideas of 'religions' and 'being religious' is the isolation and naming of some things as 'religious' and others as 'not religious.'"[15] And Fitzgerald remarks: "The symbolic links between rituals directed toward ghosts, kami, ancestors, and bodhisattvas and those directed toward the Emperor, the boss, foreigners, animals such as monkeys, and special status people are as interesting as the differences formulated in terms of unseen beings. Relations with the vague term 'superhuman' do not *a priori* guarantee any distinct semantic field."[16]

Many readers may feel that "religion" provides a perfectly comprehensible English translation of *religio* or *thrēskeia* even while not conveying the nuances of the ancient context. But the "perfectly comprehensible" English translation often occludes the interesting or pertinent differences between our concepts and the Latin or Greek. It is as if someone, wanting to understand Chinese culture, is given a Chinese cookbook. The ingredients might be obscure and unfamiliar to her. Every time she came to ingredients or a set of instructions that she was not familiar with, she could translate it by "food": "Gather the food." "Put the food in the bowl." "Grind some food and mix it with the other food." These perfectly good and comprehensible English sentences, if not deliberately censoring the text, would not teach her much about Chinese cuisine. Her impression might be, in the end, that there was little new to learn—and she might as well throw the cookbook out. We suggest that translating *religio* and *thrēskeia* as "religion" gives us about as much information about ancient Roman and Hellenistic cultures as "food" used to translate the ingredients in a Chinese cookbook gives us about Chinese cuisines. We have tried to show what we miss describing and misdescribe when we use the particular modern terminology of "religion" and how much there is to be gained in nuance and depth by treating the sources in a different way.[17]

J. Z. Smith is one of the scholars who have done the most to problematize the category of "religion." Nonetheless he concludes his essay, *"Religion, Religions, Religious"* with the declaration:

> "Religion" is not a native term; it is a term created by scholars for their intellectual purposes and *therefore is theirs to define*. It is a second-order, generic concept that plays the same role in establishing a disciplinary horizon that a concept such as 'language' plays in linguistics or 'culture' plays in anthropology. *There can be no disciplined study of religion without such a horizon.* [our emphasis][18]

Many readers may feel that "religion," *even if it is a modern construct*, serves important disciplinary, theoretical, or explanatory roles (especially those enabling cultural comparisons). *There can be no disciplined study of religion without such a horizon.* Indeed, there cannot be. But is it self-evident that the "disciplined study of religion" is a salutary procedure for understanding human beings if it results in consistent significant distortion in our descriptions/redescriptions of ourselves and others? Smith writes in another essay:

> [E]xplanation is, at heart, an act of translation, of redescription, a procedure where the unknown is reduced to the known by holding that a second-order conceptual language appropriate to one domain (the known, the familiar) may, with relative adequacy, translate the language appropriate to another domain (the unknown, the unfamiliar).[19]

We grant (emphatically) that the understanding of one human by another is dependent on the possibility of translation. But the question remains of how far one can "reduce the unknown to the known" before one loses the irreducible difference of "the unknown."[20] Smith suggests that:

> While the adequacy of any translation proposal may be debated, the only grounds for rejecting such a procedure *tout court* is to attack the possibility of translation itself, most often attempted through appeals to incommensurability. Such appeals, if accepted, must entail the conclusion that the enterprise of the human sciences is, strictly speaking, impossible.[21]

But much is systematically occluded when the categories of analysis that are mobilized are not produced inductively but simply deployed without being subject to constant revision in face of the words and categories of the cultures being studied. We are hoping, in this work, to do the "impossible" work of making an incommensurable thought world comprehensible without resorting to the pre-sorted categories produced in the scholar's study.

Fitzgerald formulates another question that will be raised by many of the readers of this book: "Surely . . . the study of other people's religions brings the student face to face with alternative non-western forms of faith and worship?" Fitzgerald responds:

> [I]t ("religion") imposes on non-western institutions and values the nuance and form of western ones, especially in such popular distinctions as those between religion and society, or between religion and the secular, or religion and politics, or religion and economics. In addition, and in pursuit of this constructed image of the other religions, it draws up typologies of Judaeo-Christian monotheistic categories such as worship, God, monasticism, salvation, and the meaning of history and tries to make the material fit those categories.[22]

Fitzgerald demonstrates in his book (with greater success in some cases than others[23]) what is missed when one imposes on a given culture (in particular, modern India and Japan) analytic categories drawn, even very knowingly so, from the outside.

The abstract category "religion" most certainly allows the scholar to search for, arrange, and compare a preselected set of cultural characteristics, but it is in the way that the picture on the cover of a jigsaw puzzle facilitates the search for, comparison, and fitting together of a thousand separate pieces. But that picture also predetermines what one will look for and find in the pieces. The seeker often finds what he or she is looking for. ("In a field, a cow looks for grass, a dog for a hare, a stork for a lizard.") But if the cover picture was not in place before the pieces were cut, if the pieces were arbitrarily put in the box and never corresponded to the picture on the cover—and if, moreover, most of the pieces are missing—the scholar might be better served by the (admittedly laborious) examination of each piece of the puzzle from every angle and trying by continual comparative experiments to fit the pieces together, even if they never form a beautifully clear and comprehensible picture. We assert that the necessity and potential for comparisons is increased, not decreased, by abandoning as many of the predetermined abstract categories of the scholar as possible. A concept of "culture"—in the broad sense of "the way we do things around here"—is, perhaps, sufficiently capacious to allow for multivariate comparison without the imposition of a category as culture-specific as "religion."

To comprehend another people in another time or place, it is important to be as self-conscious as we are able to be concerning our own categories and conceptions and not to give our categories and conceptions any more epistemological privilege than we simply cannot help doing, not to impose them any more than we cannot help ourselves from doing. This self-critical consciousness helps us not only to stretch our imagination but also to understand how our concepts and categories organize and configure our own world. We know how very hard this is to do. The work of the great sociologist of the last century, Emile Durkheim, illustrated how his use of categories often undermined his own project of getting away from them. In his classic work, *The Elementary Forms of the Religious Life*, Durkheim renders the following opinion:

> The *really religious beliefs* are always common to a determined group, which makes profession of adhering to them and of practicing the rites connected with them. They are not merely received individually by all the members of this group; they are something belonging to the group, and they make its unity. The individuals which compose it feel themselves united to each other by the simple fact that they have a *common faith*. A society whose members are united by the fact that they think in the same way in regard to *the sacred world* and its relations with *the profane world*, and by the fact that they translate these common ideas in common practices, is what is called a *Church*. In all history, *we do not find a single religion without a Church*. Sometimes *the Church* is strictly national, sometimes it passes the frontiers; sometimes it embraces an entire people (Rome, Athens, the Hebrews), sometimes it embraces only a part of them (the Christian societies since the advent of Protestantism); sometimes it is directed by a corps of priests, sometimes it is almost completely devoid of any official directing body. But wherever we observe *the religious life*, we find that it has a definite group as its foundation [emphases ours].[24]

Durkheim had carefully dismantled all previous (and most subsequent) definitions of "religion" as a universal by showing that these definitions depended on theism or the recognition of the supernatural, which restricted them to certain traditions and not others. He wished to construct a universal human category in order precisely to distance any definition of "religion" from a particularly Christianizing model. But in the definition just quoted, as can be seen, he effectively defines "religion" as Christianity.[25] It is telling that he had to append the adjective "really" to "religious," suggesting, as "really" always does, an important and frequently highly ideological intervention into the meaning of a word. We make this point not to disparage so fine and important a scholar of over a century ago but to emphasize how bound up the very project of defining "religion" *understood as a project of redescription* is in Christian concepts and categories—and how difficult it is for a Western scholar to escape those concepts and categories.

A counter-example may suffice. As Benson Saler points out,[26] Louis Dumont, in his classic work, *Homo Hierarchicus*,[27] attempted to understand India in terms of its "holism" and "hierarchy," and noted that what westerners "intuitively call religion" could not usefully be distinguished from "social structure" (i.e., caste) in the Indian case. Dumont contrasted India with the West, "in terms of a distinction between Indian holism on the one hand, and Western individualism and differentiated domains on the other." Dumont developed "comparative analytic categories which cross-cut our usual distinction between 'religion' and other domains," analytic categories that help us to clarify and map the concomitants of Western categorical distinctions (for example, the ways that domain distinctions "religion, politics, economics," are necessary for our individualism).[28] Had Dumont been looking to compare entities of the genus "religions," he would not have made his discoveries. Similarly for our own work: not looking for "religion" in Tertullian and Josephus has enabled comparisons of their multifaceted strategies for coping with life in the Roman Empire that would be missed were we worrying that one is a "Christian" and the other a "Jew." Dumont tried to interrogate not only our particular categories and abstractions but our very propensity to make them. Our project in this book has been inspired by all of these scholars and critical discourses around the concept "religion."

Wittgenstein said that, "Uttering a word is like striking a note on the keyboard of the imagination."[29] If, as he also remarked, "to imagine a language is to imagine a form of life,"[30] our task now is to imagine the form of life that attended the language of the ancient Romans (including those called Christians) and Greeks and (Greco-Roman) Judaeans, to accept their languages with their own aggregations and disaggregations, paradoxes and obfuscations, and thus to "imagine no religion."

GENEALOGY OF THE GENEALOGY OF "RELIGION"

> In the academic field of religious studies, the claim that religion is a modern invention is not really news.
>
> Brent Nongbri

In the scholarly literature as it stands today, there are two almost directly opposed stances to the category "religion" and especially of religion as a form of identity. On the one hand, we find still many—if not most—writers writing as if "religion" were something as essentially human as language, or walking, and the only relevant questions being what kind of religion any given human group or human individual "had" or adhered to, usually expressed in terms of his "beliefs" or "faith."[31]

On the other hand, we find too a growing consensus that "religion" and especially the notion of "*a* religion" is a historical and thus "historicizable" category, a particular kind of institution, something like literature or science and, as such, not found before the Enlightenment[32] (or in variations, not before the fourth century,[33] or the nineteenth century,[34] or the Peace of Westphalia,[35] etc.). The two most outstanding exponents of the latter view (with major variations between them) are William Cantwell Smith and Talal Asad, both of whom demonstrated how much of an imposition this invention was on the various cultures which Christian Europe met with in modernity.[36]

Building on their work—but especially on that of Asad, Brent Nongbri contributed a work entitled *Before Religion: A History of a Modern Concept*,[37] in which he attempted to work out a more detailed genealogy of the modern concept of "religion," locating it in particular historical conditions. He traces the "pre-history" of the term, including the words that donated their phonetic shape and some of their semantic substance to the words that in modern European languages signify "religion"—namely, Latin *religio* (in Romance and Germanic languages), and Greek *thrēskeia* (in modern Greek)—showing that in no case does the word in antiquity function like its modern reflexes. Our work expands considerably the sketchy (but not inaccurate) treatments by Nongbri, attempting to discover what work these words did and what we can learn from them about antique cultural forms.

Nongbri has observed that despite decades of problematization of the notion of "religion," "[I]t is still common to see even scholars using the word 'religion' as if it were a universal concept native to all human cultures. In . . . the study of the ancient Mediterranean world, every year sees a small library's worth of books produced on such things as 'ancient Greek religion.'"[38] Indeed, the number of scholars who begin their books on "Roman Religion" by asserting that they know that the term doesn't fit Roman culture, but they will continue using it anyway "for convenience" is remarkable.[39] Nongbri goes on to suggest that the reason for such self-contradiction is the lack of a coherent narrative of the development of the concept of religion, a lack that his book proposes to fill.[40] Fitzgerald forthrightly argues that, "[R]eligion cannot reasonably be taken to be a valid analytical category since it does not pick out any distinctive cultural aspect of human life," as opposed, for instance, to ritual that does but that also crosses boundaries between that which we habitually call "religion" in our culture and that which we habitually call the "secular."

Yet religion is still widely if somewhat loosely used by historians and social scientists as if it were a genuine cross-cultural category. Typically such writers treat religion as one among a number of different kinds of sociocultural phenomena whose institutions can be studied historically and sociologically. This approach may seem to have some obvious validity in the context of societies (especially western Christian ones) where a cultural and juridical distinction is made between religion and nonreligion, between religion and the secular, between church and state. We shall argue, however, that in most cross-cultural contexts, such a distinction, if it can be made at all, is at best unhelpful and at worst positively misleading because it imposes a superficial and distorting level of analysis on the data.[41]

Religio

PART I

Mapping the Word

Religio without "Religion"

> [I]t can be somewhat anachronistic and misleading to talk about "religion" in
> the Roman world, although, for the sake of convenience, I will continue to do so.
>
> —JAMES RIVES[1]

In the following chapters, I am going to try, with as much patience as I am capable of, to remove a mountain—one spoonful at a time. The mountain I will be attempting to remove is the word "religion" used to translate Latin *religio*. Like an archaeologist, my goal is to show that this huge "tell" covers a wonderfully interesting world that can only be revealed by its removal. My purpose is to uncover a way of life occluded by our conceptions and translations and to reconceptualize a particular set of phenomena in a way that will enhance our understanding of them.

Introduction

The ancient Roman *religiones* involved motives and movements evoked by and servicing the array of bonds and obligations embedded in every aspect of everyday life. The emotions and behaviors of *religio* guided and directed attention, but they did not demarcate nor were they limited to a particular sphere of experience. They were not generated or regulated by, nor did they necessarily concern, gods or priests, magistrates or kings. I will argue in the first of the following chapters that if the English word "religion" can be set aside (if only momentarily), Latin *religio* can reveal an economy of ideas and emotions otherwise obscured: a homeostatic system of reciprocities moving back and forth across a boundary or bond—an emotional economy closely related to and reflecting the self-regulating "government of shame" of cultures without powerful centralized institutions and means to enforce their claims to authority and legitimacy.[2]

In this chapter, I want to bring to light the pattern and logic of the sometimes bewildering and contradictory range of meanings of *religio* in the literature of the Republic and early Empire. I will argue that the ancient Roman *religiones* were part of a system of equilibrations, of weighing and balancing. Like *pudor*, the Roman "sense of shame" (which it often closely resembles),[3] *religio* operated as a homeostatic system of psychological and emotional restraints and adjustments on every level and in every situation of Roman life. *Religio* did concern the "sacred" in so far as the "sacred" embraced the words, things, people, persons, places, and times set apart, removed, bounded—but *religio* did not require and was not evidence for a transcendent reality: A Roman had *religiones* that had nothing to do with gods.[4]

I will argue that it is exactly the flexible, undefined, and less formalized powers and play of emotions exercised in Latin *religio* that will be suppressed in an increasingly defined, disciplined, regimented system of government legitimated by reference to a notion of an ultimate authorizing power.

I will argue that it took a very long time for our notions of religion to congeal. Their development had its seeds in the war band in agricultural societies, but that it was, above all, the advocates for a strong and stable Roman *civitas*, a powerful centralized *res publica*, who claimed for its leaders the authority to define and formalize, to solidify and electrify the boundaries of "the sacred"—and that it was this standing sphere, when combined with the failure of the old and more flexible systems of self-regulation that, in the civil war period, elicited the creation of a set of deliberately conceived and self-consciously defined notions of *religio* that turned the ancient notions on their heads, evolving into our "religion" on several distinct trajectories. When the ancient *religiones* could no longer govern the Romans, Ciceronian *religio* would move in, discipline and educate from the top down, from the outside in. The movement from *religio* to "religion" went hand and hand with the movement from *honor/pudor* to *honestas* (from "honor" to "honesty"),[5] from poise to submission, from anxious wariness to trust, "faith," and obedience.

"Roman Religion"

Marcus Tullius Cicero, like the Pontifex Maximus Quintus Mucius Scaevola and the scholar and antiquarian Marcus Terentius Varro, and like many members of the senatorial aristocracy from the second century B.C.E. on, asserted the legitimacy and necessary primacy of the city cult and its regulatory instruments. Scholars like Joachim Marquardt, Theodor Mommsen, Numa Fustel de Coulanges, William Warde Fowler, Georg Wissowa, Franz Altheim, Franz Cumont, George Szemler, Arnaldo Momigliano, Jörg Rüpke, and John Scheid, to name just a few, followed suit in giving a privileged ontological status to the cult of the ancient Roman city-state, its hierarchy, institutions, and claims.[6] The centralized and collective institutions possessed, for them, a heightened and compelling interest. When Robert Schilling says, "*[L]es pontifes et les augures constitutent pour les*

Anciens les piliers fondamentaux de la religion romaine," he accepts the perspective of Cicero and Varro and the preponderance of nineteenth- and twentieth-century scholars.[7] For these scholars, "religion" is a useful, an essential analytic category, and the collective institutions of the city-state its most characteristic,[8] if not its only manifestation.[9]

Robert Schilling,[10] Herbert M. Howe,[11] Henri Bouillard,[12] Michel Despland,[13] Huguette Fugier,[14] J. H. W. G. Leibeschuetz,[15] John Sheid,[16] Clifford Ando,[17] and Johannes Irmscher,[18] for example, elide or rapidly pass over earlier uses of the word *religio* to concentrate on Cicero and authors who came after him, in whose works they can occasionally find examples of the use of *religio* that seem to fit with our modern notions of "religion". To quote Schilling, "*[L]aisser le soin d'une définition à Cicéron lui-même. Qui entend-il par religio? deorum cultu pio continetur.*"[19] Schilling's reliance on Cicero is justified by a few select oft-cited passages like the following (attributed to Cicero's Academic spokesman Cotta in *De natura deorum*):

> You [the Stoic Balbus] exhorted me to remember that I am both a Cotta and a *pontifex*. By this I believe you meant that I ought to uphold the *opiniones* about the immortal gods that we have received from the *maiores*, and defend the *sacra*, the *caerimoniae* and the *religiones*. Indeed I will always defend them and always have, and no *oratio* learned or unlearned will ever move me from the *opinio* I have inherited from the ancestors concerning the *cultus* of the immortal gods. When it is a matter of *religio* I am guided by the *pontifices maximi* Titus Coruncanius, Publius Scipio or Chrysippus and not by Zeno or Cleanthes or Chrysippus. And I have Gaius Laelius, both an augur and wise man, who, when speaking of *religio* in that notable oration I would prefer to listen to than any leader of the Stoics (3.2.5).[20]

For Cicero's Cotta, at issue is the authority of the magisterial priests of the Republic. Adherence to the *sacra*, *caerimoniae*, and *religiones* cannot, he argues, finally be a matter of reasoning, preference, or choice, nor a matter of bargaining with a myriad of all too easily made and manipulated conceptions of the forces outside one's control. Rather, it should be a matter of unquestioning deference to the *auctoritas* of the ancestors and the pontiffs who keep order within the *civitas*.[21]

It is not the least bit coincidental that those who wish to trace historical links between the *religio* of the Romans and Christian "religion" start off with or quickly move their discussion to Cicero—indeed, to a very particular set of Ciceronian passages in which the word seems most easily translatable by our word "religion." When, for instance, Cicero says, "Every city, Laelius, has its own *religio* and we have ours" (*Sua cuique civitati religio*) (*Pro Flacco* 41), it is not difficult to translate Cicero's *religio* here into English "religion" if and when "religion" is thought of as (1) a universal aspect of every society, (2) a distinct and bounded sphere of human behavior, and (3) a set of behaviors and ideas that needs to be generated and regulated by the polity.[22] Cicero asks, after returning from exile:

> Would you transfer the most vicious vices of the ignorant multitude: fickleness and inconstancy, and a mind as changeable as the weather to those men (i.e. the *pontifices*) whose *gravitas* deters them from *inconstantia*, and who are deterred from wanton shifts of view (*libidinosa sententia*) by the *certum et definitum ius religionum*, by the *vetustas* of *exempla*, and by the *auctoritas* of the literature and records? (*De domo sua* 2.4).[23]

Cicero expresses his desire in this passage that the *religio deorum* be an anchor set and fixed by the sober *pontifices* and held in place by the heavy weight of tradition. The *ancora religionis* would prevent the ship of state from being wrecked by the storms engendered by the inconstant Clodius and the fickle and fluctuating mob. Here it is easy to see Cicero's *religio* as both an institutionalized and hierarchical aspect of a society, and a power structure demanding and eliciting submission and obedience.

In his essay *On the Laws*, Cicero says:

> So from the very beginning *we must persuade our citizens* that the gods are the masters and regulators of all things (*dominos omnium rerum ac moderatores*), and that what is done is done by their *iudicium* and *numen*; that the race of humans are greatly indebted to them (*eosdemque optime de genere hominum mereri*). They observe the character of every individual: what he does (*quid agat*), what wrong he perpetrates/is guilty of (*quid in se admittat*), and with what intentions and with what pietas he fulfils his *religiones* (*colat religiones*); and that they take note (*habere rationem*) of the pious and impious (*De legibus* 2.7.15).

Cicero here makes clear his desire for the Roman people to believe that the "immortal gods" are the ends and ultimate sources of the authority of the Roman priests and magistrates, and hence, the Roman *religiones*, and the censors and enforcers of the behavior of the citizen.[24] He wants the eye of god to replace the eye of the Roman's fellow citizens.[25]

It is possible to conclude from this very limited selection of the passages that for Cicero, the word *religio* was (1) a universal; (2) a distinct and bounded sphere of human behavior; (3) an institutionalized and hierarchical aspect of a *civitas*; (4) a power structure demanding submission and obedience; and finally, (5) an order instituted, authorized and enforced both by all-powerful, all-knowing gods and the magistrates and priests of the state. These Ciceronian notions are compatible with many ancient and modern Christian notions of "religion" and so appear to justify the use by modern scholars of "religion" as both a covering category and to translate Roman *religio*.

When Cicero was writing, during the sporadic but protracted civil wars, he was (like Lucretius and Varro) struggling to articulate a new set of emotional and psychological remedies for the disequilibrations of the Republic: on the one hand, to debilitating fear and anxiety, and on the other, to insufficient fear and respect for the authority and legitimacy of the senatorial aristocracy. Cicero, throughout his adult life, like Plato before him—and for similar reasons—was grasping for a new way to sufficiently authorize and legitimate the regulatory institutions of the republic so that they could replace the homeostatic self-regulating systems of *religio* and *pudor*. At one point, Cicero praises his contemporary Varro for his systematic revelations and definitions of the laws (*iura*) of *sacra* and *sacerdotes*, the civil and military disciplines (*domesticum . . . bellicam disciplinam*) of the Republic (*Academica posteriora* 1.3.9). Both Cicero and Varro were engaged in an effort to slow down what felt to them like a runaway train. They were most concerned with the Three D's: Discipline, Discipline, Discipline.[26]

Mary Beard is right to ascribe to Cicero "the definition of 'religion' for the first time as an independent subject of discourse."[27] But the first self-conscious definitions of a word that has a long and unself-conscious history are often attempts to alter its meaning.[28] Cicero's *religio* was perhaps his most lasting and original contribution to the thought world of the Empire. Cicero's *religio*, however, could be, at times, the inversion of the older *religiones* of the republic. He began, on occasion, to use the word *religio* in a way that was meant to "cover" and overturn republican *religio* (not being broader, but simpler and more abstract). Cicero sometimes used *religio* in exactly the way and for the same reason that American capitalists use the word "business" to cover both Lehman Brothers global investment firm and Tommy's hot dog stand. If we get our definition of "religion" from Cicero, we also get its confusions and obfuscations right from the start.

I will return again to treat Cicero's notion of *religio* in greater detail, but I want to make clear from the beginning that the Ciceronian web of ideas acts for us as a filter, and often as a blinder to older and deeper psychosocial ways of ordering the world. Scholars who privilege "Roman religion" (especially as envisaged by Cicero) have difficulty—or simply do not bother—reconciling it with the older complex of notions that were the *religiones* of ancient Rome, notions developed out of and as a reflection of a way of negotiating the world formed prior to the evolution of a hierarchical state system and which way of negotiating the world continued to function in an increasingly submerged manner in the *res publica* and its cult.[29]

All ideologies are simplifications, superstructures, but not hiding a reality" of "economic" relations, but hiding an undifferentated, categorically undivided unity of being, a world without "politics," "economics," and "religion." The problem—indeed, the impossibility—of understanding something called "Roman religion" is exacerbated by the discontinuities between the bewildering complex of meanings attached to republican *religio* and Ciceronian *religio*, and by the even greater disjunction between the ancient Roman *religiones* and our "religion." Otto pointed out this incompatibility a century ago: "*Das Wort religio war weder von Anfang an auf die Sphäre dessen, was wir Religion nennen, beschränkt, noch ist es später ausschliesslich in dieser Einschränkung verwendet worden.*"[30] I hope, in some small part, to conceptualize and so bridge these disjunctions.

Maurice Sachot believed that the *religio* of the republic "*ne désigne qu'un aspect subjectif et somme toute assez réduit de la réalité religieuse romaine.*"[31] I would assert, on the contrary, that there was firstly, no such *réalité religieuse romaine* as he imagines, and that the ancient *religiones* covered, in fact, a much more capacious and complex set of relations of humans to the world than is covered by our notion of "religion."

The Sentiments of Religio

Religio was most often (and still long after Cicero) used by the Romans to describe *not* an institution or set of institutions but rather a range of emotions arising from heightened attention: hesitation, caution, anxiety, fear—feelings of being bound, restricted, inhibited, stopped short. The emotional aspects of Roman *religio* have been frequently observed by scholars. Eduard Zeller described *religio* as "*jenes Gefühl der Gebundenheit.*"[32] Among the meanings that William Warde Fowler, Walter Otto, Émile Benveniste, and P. G. W.

Glare[33] attribute to *religio* were doubt, hesitation, constraint, scrupulousness, conscientiousness, carefulness, anxiety, awe, fear, and dread.[34] Stanley Pease believed that one of the central meanings of *religio* was a "sense of uneasiness."[35] J. B. Kätzler lists, among the emotions associated with *religio*: *timor, pudor, metus, Gewissensangst, Furcht, Zaghaftigkeit, Skrupel, Bedenklichkeit.*[36]

There *are* scholars—such as Dario Sabbatucci, Georg Wissowa, Robert Schilling, and Robert Turcan—who, although they recognize *religio* as an emotion, make the assumption, like the Christian Lactantius, that the source of that anxiety or fear was necessarily "the divine" or "the gods." For Sabbatucci, *religio* was "*un sentimento di paura del divino.*"[37] For Wissowa, *religio* was the "*Gefühl der Abhängigkeit*" on the gods and their solicitude.[38] For A. Ernout and A. Meillet, *religio* was "*obligation prise envers la divinité.*"[39] For Jean Bayet, "*religio . . . signifiait l'ensemble des liens reconnus qui rattachaient l'activité humaine aux dieux.*"[40] "For Schilling, "*expressions telles que mihi religio est . . . établissent le sens de liens entres les hommes et les dieux.*"[41] For Nicole Belayche, "Care for the gods [is] the very meaning of *religio.*"[42] For Huguette Fugier, John Scheid, Robert Turcan, Jörg Rüpke, and James Rives Roman, *religio* and Roman "religion" are both inseparable from a communal relationship to the gods.[43] All of these scholars are working backward from the emphatically theistic and Christian notion of religion—not unlike the third-to-fourth–century Christian apologist Lactantius who linked *religio* etymologically to *religare*, and to the humans' bonds to God.[44]

There are other scholars who do not sense the emotional aspects of *religio* at all. J. H. W. G. Liebeschuetz ignores the evidence of *religio* as an emotion, perhaps because for him, the emotions of *religio* are not the ones that he associates with "religion" (such as awe, love, ardent devotion, and longing for completion). Speaking of religion in Livy, Liebeschuetz makes the statement, "[R]eligion is unemotional. . . ."[45] For Theodor Mommsen, Roman cultic life lacked "the mysterious awe after which the human heart has always a longing."[46] For Franz Cumont, "[T]here never was a religion so cold and prosaic as the Roman," which "looked suspiciously at the abandonment of the soul to the ecstasies of devotion."[47] The love envisaged by these scholars is for the god who completes, the complement, and so the one who heals, who saves, who offers salvation. The individual whose wholeness and completion depends on the group, the nation, the king or the god, will love that object (or rather, the concept of that object). But Roman farmers were not looking to their gods for completion, or for the sense of vicarious fullness of being. On the contrary, they suspected that the gods were envious of their life, their energy, their honor, their fullness of being. The farmer valued relative independence and competence and was less likely to value this yearning, this "love." He or she did not want so much transcendence or completion as a little help—but a farmer who desperately needed help or protection might, indeed, "love" a brigand or a king or a god.

The feelings central to *religio* were not those of love but of being bound. Even Cicero, who links *religio* etymologically with *relegere* (retrace, pick out again, reread) (*De natura deorum* 2.72),[48] continually used *religio* with verbs of binding such as *alligare, adstringere, continere, impedire, ligare, obligare, obstringere, solvere, exsolvere.*[49] And the bind, as I will stress repeatedly, is not generally or necessarily to the gods. Indeed, gods need not be anywhere in the picture. In its earliest preserved appearances, Latin *religio* was the feeling that "gave one pause," "made one stop in one's tracks," or caused one to reverse one's course. In the *Mercator* of Plautus [d. 184 B.C.E.], young Charinus is despondent and wants to leave home (881). His friend Eutychus, in order to try to change his mind, compares Charinus' proposed flight to a stormy and hazardous voyage on the sea attended by many forbidding horrors. He urges him to look on the port side (*ad sinistrum*) where the sky is bright with promise. Spoken as an aside by Charinus: "That man (Eutychus) causes me to have second thoughts / makes me pause and ponder; I'll turn around and go over to him." (*Religionem illic (mi) obiecit: recipiam me illuc.*)[50]

Plautus' parasite Curculio, in the play of that name, has been sent by the young man Phaedromus to secure for him the maiden Planesium. In the market place, he meets a soldier who tells him that he had paid a sum of money to the banker Lyco to be used to purchase a girl from the pimp Cappodox. Instructions were given to Lyco that the purchased girl should be turned over to whomever should bring a request for her signed by the soldier and sealed with a ring. The soldier apparently intended to ask Curculio to do this errand for him. However, he had made no such request at the time Curculio turned to go away, whereupon the soldier calls him back (*revocat me ilico*) and invites him to dinner. Curculio tells the story to Phaedromus:

> "After he [the soldier] recounted this, I leave him but he calls me back and invites me to dinner. It was a *religio* (*religio fuit*) [i.e., "This made me think twice." "This gave me pause."] I felt I had to be polite to the man, and didn't want to say no."
>
>   *Postquam hoc mihi narravit, abeo ab illo, revcat me ilico, vocat me ad cenam; religio fuit, denegare nolui* [349–50].

Wilt points out that in both the *Curculio* and the *Mercator,* someone is called back, and something is pointed out to him or offered to him, which makes him reverse his course of action, turn to the opposite direction (*Religio* 61–62).

Religio, throughout the Republic and well into the Empire, was experienced as a hindrance (Plautus, *Mercator* 881),[51] an impediment (Cicero, *Pro Flacco* 10), an obligation (Cicero, *De legibus* 2.58), or a restraint (Livy 27.23.1). Marcus Lurco gave evidence when he was angry with Valerius Flaccus: [But] "he said nothing to harm Flaccus, although he longed to do so, because he was impeded by *religio* (*impediebat religio*). And what he did say, with what *pudor* he said it!—with what trembling and ashen pallor!" (Cicero, *Pro Flacco* 10).[52] Publius Septimius, according to Cicero, was also angry at Lucius Valerius Flaccus, "Yet he kept hesitating and *religio* repeatedly resisted / fought back against his anger." (*Tamen haesitabat, tamen eius iracundiae religio non numquam repugnabat* [*Pro Flacco* 11].) There was something that restrained his antagonists, despite their anger, from attacking Valerius Flaccus. This restraining thought/emotion is conceived of as *religio.* Acting in violation of this inhibition caused one to feel *pudor*—whose symptoms, in this case, are those of high anxiety: quaking pallor.

In 391 B.C.E., the Gallic tribes hesitated to cross the roadless Alps and invade Italy because of fear of the Massiliotes:

> While the Gauls were fenced in, as it were, by the lofty mountains, and were looking about to discover where they might cross, over heights that reached to the skies, into another world, *religio* held them back (*religio tenuit*) because it had been reported to them that some strangers seeking lands were beset by the Salui (i.e., Massiliotes) (Livy 5.34.7).[53]

In 216 B.C.E., according to Livy, the general Varro was eager to fight Hannibal at Cannae. The other general, Paulus, was not so eager:

> Paulus himself wished to delay; and when the sacred chickens had refused their sanction (i.e., refused to eat), he gave orders to notify his colleague, who was just setting forth with the standards from the gate of the camp. Varro was greatly vexed at this hindrance, but the recent disaster of Flaminius and the memorable defeat of the consul Claudius in the first Punic War struck his *animus* with *religio* (*religionem animo incussit*) (22.42.8–9).

The thought of the previous military disasters at Trasimene occasioned by Claudius' and Flaminius' failure to observe negative omens causes the general Varro to stop in his tracks, to hesitate, to think twice.

A modern man or woman might approach and fondle a Maltese lapdog or a cocker spaniel casually and without second thoughts but might hesitate before petting a Doberman pinscher or a pit bull. That person might, without "thinking twice," ask for the hour from a harmless-looking old woman carrying a shopping bag but approach a tattooed and shaven-headed teenager with extreme caution. Just so, Roman *religio* was evoked in dealing with the risky adventures of everyday life, but it was especially the perilous, the untoward, the uncanny, and the unprecedented that evoked the emotions of *religio* and caused the Roman to behave with particular circumspection, with awe or reverence. No fear of magisterial authority or divine judgment was necessary.

> If a cave, made by the deep crumbling of the rocks, holds up a mountain on its arch, a place not built with hands but hollowed out into such spaciousness by natural causes, it will strike your spirit with a certain presentiment of *religio*. (. . . *animum tuum quadam religionis suspicione percutiet*) (Seneca, *Epistulae* 41.1–3).[54]

Religio was especially evoked by highly charged boundaries and limitations and the fear of transgressing "taboos," such as those surrounding the oath, the treaty, the *domus* or *fanum*. The Romans approached such boundaries as we might approach an electrified fence.[55] But it is important to notice that the gods were not the inhibiting or disciplining forces in any of these instances of *religio*. Rather, the inhibitions of Roman *religio*, like those of Roman *pudor*, are generated internally and psychologically by the particularities of each situation.

RELIGIO AND SCRUPULUS

Religio was often closely associated with or equated to the *scrupulus*—a small sharp or pointed stone, the smallest weight that could move the pan of a scale. The *scrupulus* could also be thought of as the little irritant, the stone on which one stubbed one's toe or the pea under the princess' mattress. The *homo scrupulosus*,[56] the *homo religiosus*,[57] was someone who, like the peasant farmer (or the pilot of a ship), was alert, cautious, circumspect. Anyone who has read Hesiod, Cato, or Columella, or the georgic poetry of Virgil, comes away with the sense of the vigilance with which the farmer observed and policed his universe: the ways in which the world presented to him a vast array of symptoms and signals and omens that he had to read and interpret for the sake of himself, his family, his flocks and crops. ("I will teach you the causes and *signa* of diseases. . . ." [*Georgica* 3.440].) This attentiveness extended to everything that affected the farmer and his family and flocks, crops, and land, including to use the lists of Victor David Hanson: drought; hail; frosts; unseasonable rain; gusting winds; fungal, viral, and bacterial pathogens; insect outbreaks; animal and human attack; infestations of noxious, perennial weeds; idiopathic crop failure; human error ". . . a March hail, an April frost, an August rain, and October spate of unusual heat; never-ending quarrels over boundaries, water, borrowing . . ."[58] "The farmer was constantly apprehensive, continually examining plants and animals for some clue, some help in warding off disaster."[59] The viticulturalist was engaged in "constant decisions, endless searching for the precise but elusive equilibrium between multifarious choices, the need for constant attention and labor, and reverence for ancestral practice."[60] The farmer had to determine, in every case, what was the proper response, as well as the degree of control and expertise he would be able to bring to bear in each situation. Like the pilot of a ship, the farmer would attempt to maximize his autonomy and effective energy. Dependence on or obedience to the gods or magisterial authorities was very far from practicable, and far from what one finds in Cato or Columella or Pliny the Elder.[61] The farmer, like the pilot of a small boast, had to drive and determine the ends and means, as best he could, of his own world. As Virgil explains, when a sheep has an ulcer, one must lance its mouth with a knife instead of "doing nothing and praying to the gods that things will get better" (*Georgica* 3.454–456). Compare Plutarch's description of the pilot of the ship: He may pray to Castor and Pollux, but while he prays, he turns into the wind and lowers the yard and furls the sails (*De superstitione, Moralia* 169B). Hesiod's farmer prays to chthonian Zeus and Demeter before plowing and sowing—all the while holding on to the plow (Plutarch, op. cit. 169B; Hesiod, *Opera et dies* 465–68).[62] The farmer's and villager's attitude could be described with the phrase, "Praise the Lord, and pass the ammunition." Turcan describes this *observantia*, this *vigilantia assidua*:[63] He is mistaken only in thinking that the attentiveness of *religio* was only or even primarily focused on human relations *with the gods* and so a version of piety *to the gods*.[64] The adverbs *religiose* and *scrupulose* described all actions performed with vigilant care and concentration.[65]

The Roman youths who were sent to the defeated town of Veii in 396 B.C.E. to bring to Rome the Veian statue of Juno Regina, after reverently entering her temple, "approached her *religiose* with their hands because this image was one that according to Etruscan practice only a priest of a certain family was wont to touch" (Livy 5.22.4–5), cf. Cicero, *Pro Balbo* 24.55. Note that Aulus Gellius can, in the second century of the Empire, still use *religiose* to mean "extremely precisely" "scrupulously" (11.18.19). Interestingly, this is the most ancient usage of *religio* still in wide circulation in English: We still say, "She flosses her teeth religiously." "He does his homework religiously."

The substantive *scrupulus* could, like *religio*, describe *both* the inhibited and focused attention and also the impediment, hindrance, obstruction that elicited that attention.

In the *Melanippus* of Accius [ca. 170–85 B.C.E.] appears the line:

> You cast from yourself *religio*; would you then impose a *scrupea* on yourself? (*Reicis abs te religionem; scrupeam imponas tibi?*) (fr. 421 Warmington)[66]

After having rid yourself of one sort of stumbling block, would you impose another one on yourself?

In the *Andria* of Terence [195–159 B.C.E.] appears the following dialog:

> **Davus:** Mysis, I want all your ready cunning and wits for this job.
> **Mysis:** What's your scheme?
> **Davus:** Take the baby, quick, quick and lay it on our doorstep.
> **Mysis:** No, I beseech you, on the ground?
> **Davus:** Take a bough or two from the altar there and make a bed of them.
> **Mysis:** Why don't you do it yourself?
> **Davus:** Because if I happened to have to swear to my master that I didn't put it there I would be able to swear "transparently" (*liquido*).[67]
> **Mysis:** I see. A novel *religio* to have gotten into your brain/to have occurred to you. Hand over the kid (722–30).[68]

Davus expresses his fear, his anxiety lest he be forced to forswear himself. Mysis considers this a surprising inhibition for Davus to have; nevertheless, he respects Davus' scruple and performs the act himself.

Compare this dialog also from the *Andria*:

> **Simo:** I'm extremely delighted that she turns out to be your daughter.
> **Pamphilus:** I'm sure you are her father.
> **Chremes:** There's just one small doubt left (*at scrupulus mi etiam unus restat*).
> **Pamphilus:** Confound you and your *religio*, wretch! You look for knots in a bulrush (939–41).[69]

Here, *scrupulus* and *religio* are synonyms and both evoke hesitation. It is clear from this passage that one character's scruple is not necessarily that of another's. Chremes' *religio*, his *scrupulus*, is not that of Pamphilus. The *religiones* did not respond to any formal or covering laws. They were the result of the individual's doubts, fears, and anxieties. To Pamphilus, Chremes' *religio* is ridiculous.

In Terence's *Heautontimorumenos*, the young Clitipho, without funds, cannot bring himself to admit to his greedy and demanding mistress Clinia that he has nothing. In acquiescing to her demands, he declares: "It is a *religio* for me to say I have no money." (*Nam nil esse mihi religiost dicere* [228].)[70] *Religio* causes one to have "scruples." It evokes his or her sense of shame; it causes him or her to act with hesitation.

In Plautus' *Assinaria*, the parasite has drawn up an excessively long and hilarious contract that the young aristocrat Diabolus hopes to impose on his mistress, Philaenium. It would surround his mistress with more taboos than the Flamen Dialis. Among the endless restrictions: "Let her call upon any goddess she pleases for favors, but upon no male god; if she is anxiously concerned / if this offends her sense of scrupulousness (*si magis re-ligiosa fuit*), let her tell you and so you make the prayer for his favor in her stead" (781–83).

Livy tells the following story:

> Valerius the consul, having marched an army against the Aequi, was unable to entice the enemy into a battle, and directed an assault upon their camp. This plan was foiled by a terrible storm that descended upon them [the Roman soldiers] with hail and thunder. Their amazement was soon increased by the reappearance, on the signal for retreat being given, of so tranquil and cloudless a sky, that, as though some *numen* had defended the camp, there was a *religio* [i.e., they scrupled] to attack it a second time, and so directed all their hostility toward devastating the fields (2.62.1–2).[71]

Here it is important to note that the *religiones* of the soldiers, their anxious hesitations occasioned by the extraordinary and ominous weather, took no consideration of but indeed overrode the will of their commander. *Religio* did not necessarily imply obedience to figures of authority.[72]

In 390 B.C.E., the Gallic invaders of Rome agreed to evacuate in return for a large sum of gold. The Romans agreed to the shameful terms, but they scrupled to touch any of the gold deposited as offerings in their shrines:

> [T]he *religio* of the city had been made apparent when there was not enough gold in the public coffers to make up the sum demanded by the Gauls. They accepted what the matrons got together in order that they might abstain from touching the sacred gold (*sacrum aurum*) (Livy 5.50.7).[73]

In this passage, the close relationship of the notion of *religio* to the sense of shame, *pudor*, is again made apparent.[74]

This notion of *religio* as "scruple" continued into the Empire:

> A *religio* then arose: In what temple were the equestrians to place the offering vowed to Equestrian Fortune for the recovery of Augusta (*pro valetudine Augustae*)? For though there were many shrines to Fortune in the city, none, however, carried the *cognomen Equestris* (Tacitus, *Annales* 3.71).[75]

> Before we leave off our description of Scythia, it would be a *religio* [we might say, "it would be a shame"] to pass over the peculiarities of the fauna of Scythia. . . . (Gaius Iulius Solinus, *Collectanea rerum memorabilium* 19.9 [early–third century C.E.]).[76]

Mommsen remarked on the Roman's "mercantile punctuality" in the absence of the "sense of awe in the presence of an all-controlling nature or of an almighty God." The Romans' *religiones*, linked so closely with their sense of honor, could be even more demanding, more punctilious than Mommsen's "Roman religion."

RELIGIO AND "TABOO"

The changes in the meanings of the word *religio* after Cicero entailed the loss of many of its ancient meanings. As a result, modern scholars have had to borrow the word *taboo* to fill the catachresis, the hole—and, paradoxically, to describe *religio*.[77] Many of the ideas that we associate with the Polynesian word *taboo* were essential elements of ancient *religio*.

Because it was once used to start a fatal fire, a cellar filled with salt set on the table was a *religio* for a potter (*figulis religioni habetur* [Festus p. 468 Lindsay]).[78] "Such *religio* was felt concerning graves that it was not considered permissible (*fas*) to bury in them corpses that did not belong to the clan or to those who participated in its rites (*sacra*)" (Cicero, *De legibus* 2.22.1).[79] The phallus, the eye-catching "fascinator" (*fascinus*) that hung under the chariot of the general or over the cradle of the infant, protected it with inhibiting *religio* (Pliny, *Naturalis Historia* 28.7.39). Dangerous things and persons, times and places set apart and surrounded with *taboo* were particularly liable to elicit the hesitations— the "second thoughts" of *religio*.[80] Caesar remarks that when the Germans unexpectedly attacked a Roman fortification located on a site that many of the defending Romans already deemed unlucky, it caused widespread panic among the soldiers, most of whom conjured up new *religiones*, new *taboos* with regard to the spot (*plerique novas sibi ex loco religiones fingunt* [*De Bello Gallico* 6.37*].*) Cato the Elder, as censor (ca. 185 B.C.E.), gave a speech lambasting the Romans for *not* feeling any inhibition at the appropriation and casual use of the images of the gods of the defeated:

> I am amazed that they dare—and are not held back by *religio* (*religione non teneri*)—from setting up statues of the gods, the models of their appearance (*exempla facierum*), in their houses as if they were furniture (Cato Maior, *Oratio uti praeda in publicum referatur*).[81]

> No *religio* is an obstacle to the dredging of a stream (*rivos deducere nulla religio vetuit*) (Virgil, *Georgica* 1.269).

It is not possible to know whether Virgil is thinking of a formalized prohibition. I suspect he is referring to a tradition. But the later texts allow at least the possibility of a *religio* being a magisterial decision. According to Livy:

> The censors who were chosen (*creati*) were Gaius Sulpicius Camerinus and Spurius Postumius Regillensis [380 B.C.E.], and they had already set about their task when it was interrupted by the death of Postumius because it was a *religio* to replace the colleague of a censor. [5] So then Sulpicius resigned, and other censors were elected, but, owing to a defect in the election, did not serve. *Religiosum fuit* for the senators to proceed to a third election, being persuaded that the gods would permit no censorship (Livy 6.27.4–5).[82]

The expression *religio esse* seems to be a synonym for *nefas esse* and could refer to either a tradition or an explicit decision of, for instance, the augural college. Tacitus' Otho went forth to meet the forces of Vitellius coming south from Gaul:

> As he set forth, there were those who presented to Otho—as a reason for delay and *religio* (*moras religionemque*) that the sacred shields [of the Salii] had not yet been restored to their place (*Historiae* 1.89).[83]

Aulus Gellius, relying on *De sacerdotibus publicis* and the first book of Fabius Pictor, addressed the prohibitions and taboos surrounding the *flamen dialis*:

It is *religio* for the Flamen Dialis to ride a horse. Likewise it is *religio* for him to see the *classes* (i.e., the army arrayed for battle) outside the *pomerium*. . . . (. . .) He never enters a place of burial, he never touches a dead body; [25] but *non est religio* to attend a funeral (*Noctes Atticae* 10.15.3–4+24–25).[84]

I believe that the heightened anxiety evoked by the transgression of highly sacralized boundaries, traditions, regulations, and laws will be one of the paths from *religio* to "religion."

THROUGH THE LOOKING GLASS OF *RELIGIO*: *RELIGIO* PROJECTED ONTO AND REFLECTED BACK BY THE WORLD

Servius, commenting on Virgil's *religio*, explains, "*Religio* is fear arising from whatever binds the mind—which fear is also called *religio*" (*ad Aeneidem* 8.349).[85] In the Romans' system of psychological reciprocities, *religio* was, like *pudor*, projected onto and reflected back by any object that evoked the emotions of *religio*. Festus preserves a line of Cato the Elder: "Is there anyone more uncultivated, more *religiosus*, more desolate and repulsed from public intercourse? ("*Ecquis incultior, religiosior, desertior, publicis negotis repulsior?*" [*Contra Cornelium ad populum* fr. 194 Kienast].)[86] The repulsive person fills Cato with a feeling of repulsion.

We are ourselves so deeply accustomed to such hypallage that we hardly notice it. We project an emotion onto any object, event, and so forth that seems to call forth that emotion. We say: "What a curious object." "He made his weary way." "We watched a horror movie." "She had a restless night." "What they did to her is a crying shame." "The budget is an outrage." "His sense of balance is a wonder." Just so, for the Romans, the person who aroused distrust was *suspiciosus*, the thing or person or behavior that provoked envy was *invisus*,[87] the one who aroused gratitude was *gratiosus*, the person or behavior that elicited honor or praise was *dignus*, the person who aroused contempt was *contemptus*, and so on.

And so the emotions of *religio* could be attributed to anything that inspired fear, anxiety, caution, and care.

Paternal and maternal blood has great restraining/constraining force (*necessitas*), great *religio*; a single drop of this blood produces a stain, which not only cannot be washed out, but penetrates even to the heart, to be succeeded by the height of frenzy and madness (Cicero, *Pro Sexto Roscio Amerino* 24.66).[88]

Notice in the preceding passage the reflexive link between the emotion and the bonds and obligations that elicit that emotion.[89] (In a similar way, beginning with Cicero, the emotions of *veritas* would later be attributed to anything that inspired confidence and trust.[90]) And so anything—any bond or boundary, any oath, prodigy or omen, any law or tradition or prohibition: indeed, any thought that called one's bonds and obligations to mind—could be a *religio*.[91] Pliny, speaking of the plant Cure-All (*Panaces*) that alleviated many illnesses:

After [the plant] has been pulled up, filling the resulting hole with various cereals is a *religio* and an expiatory offering (*piamentum*) to the earth (*Naturalis historia* 25.11.30).[92]

Praecordia is the comprehensive name we use for the vital organs of the human body. When any one of them is in pain, the application of a suckling puppy pressed close to that part of the body is said to transfer the malady to the puppy. They add that, if the organs of the puppy are taken out and washed with wine, by observation of the diseased aspect of those organs it is possible to detect the source of the patient's pain; but the subsequent burial of an animal so used *religio est* (*obrui tales religio est*) (Pliny, *Naturalis historia* 30.14.42).[93]

It is in this context that the obligations and strictures of cultic behaviors could be *religiones* for a Roman. When Ennius talks of Jupiter establishing the *religio* of his own *cultus* (*Euhemerus* 116 Warmington), he is referring to the obligations for attention and cultivation that he is imposing on mankind. In establishing altars on which his name is joined to that of his allies and hosts, he secures for himself and his hosts divine honors and an everlasting name, with cultic obligations, with *religio* (*Euhemerus* 108 Warmington).[94]

THE CRIME OF *RELIGIO*

Religio, like *pudor*, had two faces: a negative as well as a positive valance. In the way that *pudor*, the "sense of shame" that inhibited the Roman from transgressing was mirrored by the *pudor*, the "shame" that resulted from transgression, the *religio* that restrained was mirrored by the *religio* that resulted from and punished transgressions. Roman *religio* was not only the anxiety that caused one to "think twice" before breaking a bond—and the bond itself—but also the guilt, shame, and high anxiety evoked by the *scelus*, the breaking of a highly charged bond.[95] *Religio* could be the feeling of being tainted, indebted, doomed, imperiled, cursed—liable to punishment. Because this negative aspect of *religio* is the most difficult for someone accustomed to translate *religio* as "religion" to grasp, I will offer several examples:

Tiberius Gracchus, then consul for the second time, was holding the election of his successors. The first returning officer, in the very act of reporting the persons named as elected, suddenly fell dead. Gracchus nevertheless proceeded with the election. Perceiving that the matter involved *religio* for the people (*rem illam in religionem venisse populo*), he referred the matter to the Senate. (. . .) Tiberius, a man of the greatest wisdom and distinction of character preferred to make public confession of an offence that he might have concealed than that a *religio* should cling to the commonwealth (Cicero, *De natura deorum* 2.10–11).[96]

No one has ever, in the process of dedication, laid a hand upon the door-post of a promenade; and if you have dedicated any statue or altar contained within a promenade, it can be removed from its position without incurring *religio* (*sine religione*) (Cicero, *De domo sua* 46.121 [57 B.C.]).[97]

Whoever is present at the auspices, if he should announce something falsely, the *religio* pertains to him (Livy 10.40.11).

The Latin festival was repeated (*Latinae instauratae*) because the share of the meat which was due to be given to the Laurentes was not given to them. There was also a *supplicatio* on account of these *religiones* (Livy 37.3.5).[98]

Lest a *religio* should contaminate the god with impunity, he caused a tomb which one of his freedmen had built for his son with stones intended for the temple of Capitoline Jupiter to be destroyed by his soldiers and the bones and ashes in it to be thrown into the sea (Suetonius, *Domitianus* 8.4).[99]

It is impossible to understand the emotional economy of the ancient Romans without fully grasping that *religio* could adhere to a person or the city, a god, or a temple in the manner of a curse. Transgression set apart, "electrified," "tabooed," cursed. A *religio* could render a man *sacer*. "A man," Festus tells us, "is *sacer* whom the people have convicted of a crime."[100] As a result, he informs us, "Any bad or shameless man is accustomed to be called *sacer*" (Festus, s.v. *sacer mons*).[101] The Romans used the expression *sacer esto!* "Let him be sacred!" to effect the *consecratio capitis*, the setting apart or cursing, the devotion of the enemy or the person who was so highly charged, so dangerous that he could no longer be tolerated within the community.[102] Similarly, the author of a *religio* was the one, so to speak, "charged with the crime"; he was *sons*, "the one," "the real one," the one with an excessively heightened charge. He was "ɪᴛ," as we said as children playing "Tag."[103] Livy tells the story of the attempt, in 173 B.C.E., of the censor Quintus Fulvius Flaccus to roof his new temple of Fortuna Equestris with tiles stripped from the temple of Juno Lacinia in Bruttium:

> The magistrate to whom had been given the duty of enforcing the repair of public
> shrines and of contracting for their maintenance was himself roving through the cities of
> the allies plundering the temples and stripping off the roof of sacred edifices. (. . .)
> [He was] binding the Roman people with *religio* (*obstringere religione populum Romanum*)
> (42.3.5–9).

Whenever possible, attempts were made to expiate the transgression, to remove the *religio*. In this case, the senate decreed that the tiles should be restored and that the *religio* committed by Quintus Fulvius Flaccus should be carefully expiated (*quae ad religionem pertinebant cum cura facta*) (42.3.11).

Livy's Lucius Atilius, in 168 B.C.E., encouraged the people of Samothrace to bring Evander, the agent of King Perseus and would-be assassin of King Eumenes, to judgment for having brought the unclean hands of a homicide into the temple of Samothrace—and thereby liberate the temple from *religio* (*liberaret religione templum*) (45.5.8).

A *religio*, like an unpaid debt, hung over one like a curse, binding one and causing one anxiety. On the day he last fought with the Celtiberians in 179 B.C.E., according to Livy, Quintus Fulvius had vowed to offer games to Jupiter Optimus Maximus and a temple to Fortuna Equestris. Having purchased his victory with a vow, a sort of ɪᴏᴜ, he was *reus voti*, "guilty" of his promise, of his as yet unpaid debt:

Quintus Maximus the consul said that before he brought up any matter of public business he wished to free himself and the republic from *religio* by fulfilling his vows (*liberare et se et rempublicam religione votis solvendis*) (40.44.8).[104]

The goal of the Roman was to balance the books to once more be "in the black." To liberate or purify one of *religio* was to alleviate the terror, anxiety, and the sense of doom that came with guilt. Cicero imagines a thief, who, "terrified in his spirit" after despoiling temples, "stimulated by dreams or *religio*, consecrated an altar on a deserted strand, . . . compelled to appease by his prayers the *numen* whom he had violated with his crime" (*De domo sua* 55.140).[105]

But a crime of commission or omission could be so great that the resulting *religio* could not be relieved; it could be inexpiable. Cicero objects to a decision of the senate to commingle a *supplicatio* for a victorious general with rites in honor of the dead:

> Do you think I would have supported the decree . . . by which *inexpiabiles religiones* would be introduced into the republic? (*Philippicae* 1.6.13).

Our "religion" never describes guilt or shame, a crime or a curse. Usages of *religio* like that in the immediately preceding passage of Cicero are among the scores that are obscured by and next to impossible to see given our conception of "religion." But in the ancient Roman psychological and emotional economy of *religio*, there could be inexpiable *religiones*.

THE CURSE OF *RELIGIO*

Fearful associations such as those evoked by the *parentalia* (the February "Days of the Dead") could render those days, in the words of Lucilius (second century B.C.E.), "horrible, miserable and *religiosi*" (*tetri miseri ac religiosi* (fr. 838–39 Warmington).[106] "Nigidius [Figulus (first century B.C.E.)] labeled infamous and unlucky days *religiosus*." (*Religiosus quoque dies infames vel infaustos . . . Nigidius appellavit* [*Commentariorum Grammaticorum* XI fr. 4 = Nonius Marcellus, ed. Lindsay p. 604].)[107] Ovid explains that among the positive ritual prescriptions involved in the Parentalia, are the following negative imperatives:

> While these rites are being performed, do not marry—you widowed young women. (. . .) Oh god of marriage, hide your torches, and from these somber fires bear them away! (. . .) Screen too, the gods, by shutting up the temple doors; let no incense burn upon the altars, no fire upon the hearths. Now unsubstantial souls and buried dead wander about, now the shades feed on the food left for them (*Fasti* 2.557–570).[108]

"Those days are *religiosi*," according to Festus, "on which it is considered forbidden (*nefas*) to do anything except that which is necessary." (*Dies autem religiosi, quibus nisi quod necesse est, nefas habetur facere* [s.v. "*Religiosus*" p. 348 Lindsay].)[109]

A disaster or defeat associated with a particular day could render that day *religiosus*:

> Our ancestors maintained that the day of the battle of the Allia was *funestior* [more infected with the stench of death] than that day on which the city was taken [by the

Gauls] because the latter disaster was the result of the former. Therefore the day of the battle of the Allia is even now *religiosus*, while the other is unknown to the general public (Cicero, *Ad Atticum* 9.5.2).[110]

In the cult of the city-state, *dies religiosi* were days on which *one feared to make offerings or open the doors of the temples*.[111] *Dies religiosi* were set apart and tabooed but were the antitheses of what we would call "religious" or "holy" days! The *dies religiosi* were days on which one did *not* offer sacrifice!

> Those days are called *religiosi* which are ill-famed and hampered by evil omen, so that on them one must refrain from offering sacrifice or beginning any new business whatever; they are the days the ignorant multitude call *nefasti* (Aulus Gellius, *Noctes Atticae* 4.9.5).[112]

After the departure of the Gauls from Rome in 389 B.C.E., Livy described the attempts of the Tribunes with Consular Power to repair the fabric of Roman life:

> Then the Roman senate took up the matter of the *dies religiosi*. The eighteenth of July was notable (*insignem*) for a double misfortune, since it was on that day that the Fabii were massacred at the Cremera and that subsequently the rout at the Allia occurred, which resulted in the destruction of the city. From the latter disaster they named it the Day of the Allia (*Alliensem*) and forbade any public or private business to be done that day (6.1.11).[113]

Notice that in this passage, the *dies religiosi* existed prior to any senatorial acknowledgment or legitimization.[114] The fixing and formalizing of a taboo, the setting apart, definition, and sanctioning of the sacred by the senate, was part of the institutionalizing, the bureaucratization of *religio*.[115]

RELIGIO AND ENERGY

Religio operated similarly to and in conjunction with the "sense of shame" as sensitivity to bonds and boundaries and to the dangers of transgressing those bonds and boundaries. The emotions of *pudor* and *religio* operated like dams on a stream, concentrating, channeling and directing the Roman's attention and energy. Without such restraints, the energies and attentions of a person or group were dissipated, etiolated. Those who voluntarily bound themselves were, by that very restraint, positively set apart, sanctified (*sanctus, purus, castus, intemeratus, integer, incolumnis*).[116] There could be no feeling of poise or elegance or grace, no *fides*, no *ius*, no *libertas*, no *comitas* without *religio*.[117] The constraints of *religio*, closely related to those of *pudor* and *pietas*, were prerequisite for and aspects of self-discipline and so important components of Roman notions and emotions of honor, of the fullness of being. *Religio*, then, acted as an essential part of the homeostatic system of the culture of the agriculturally based Republic, an essential part of the government of shame. "Marcellus," Cicero remarks, "though everything was profaned by his victory, was obstructed by *religio* from laying hands (on the paintings in the temple of Minerva at Syracuse)." (*Cum omnia victoria sua profana fecisset tamen religione impeditus non attigit* [*In Verrem* 2.4.122].)

John Sheid states, "It ['Roman religion'] was a religion with no moral code."[118] According to Robert Turcan, *"La religion des Romains n'a rien à voir non plus avec une morale personelle ou sociale. . . ."*[119] The *religiones* of the Romans did not, emphatically, constitute a moral *code*, but rather the system of emotional restraints that governed and directed Roman behavior. *Religio*, in guiding the energy and will of the Romans, deflected them from perilous and inexpiable transgressions, kept them back from the edge of the precipice.[120] Functioning in every aspect of their lives, *religio* set the Romans apart from other peoples and encouraged them to fulfill their obligations, to expiate transgressions, to lustrate defilements.[121] Persons who did not feel *religio*, like persons who did not feel shame, were dangerous to themselves and to others.[122] Gaius Flaminius Nepos was famously defeated and slain in 217 B.C.E. by Hannibal at Lake Trasimene with the loss of 15,000 troops. Cicero remarks:

> Did not Gaius Flaminius by his neglect of premonitory signs in his second consulship in the Second Punic War cause great disaster to the republic? For, after the *lustratio* of his army, he had moved his army and was marching toward Arretium to meet Hannibal, when his horse, for no apparent reason, suddenly fell with him just in front of the statue of Jupiter Stator. He did not consider/feel it as a *religio* (*nec enim habuit religioni*) what seemed to those learned in interpreting signs to be a sign not to join battle (*De divinatione* 1.77 [44 B.C.E.]).[123]

After his defeat, some of his fellow Romans decided that Flaminius *should* have felt *religio*. His fall in front of the statue of Jupiter Stator ("Jupiter who stays the rout") *should* have triggered hesitation, awe, alarm; it should have caused him "to think twice" before going into battle.

As an aside, it is interesting that when in the early second century C.E., the Greco-Roman Plutarch tells of the story of Flaminius, the gods have moved to the center. Plutarch's Fabius Maximus attributes Flaminius' defeat by Hannibal at Lake Trasimene (217 B.C.E.) to Flaminius' *oligoria*: "Fabius Maximus showed the people that the recent disaster was due to the neglect and scorn with which their general Flaminius had treated matters concerning the gods (*oligoria kai periphronesei pros to daimonion*), and not to the cowardice of those who fought under him. He, Fabius, thus induced the Roman people to propitiate and honor the gods rather than fear their enemies. It was not that he filled them with *deisidaimonia* but rather that he emboldened their valor with piety, allaying and removing the fear which their enemies inspired, *with hope of aid from the gods*" (Plutarch, *Fabius Maximus* 4.3–4). Plutarch's very different version is evidence for the application of Greek conceptions to a Roman story.

I shall attempt to translate the whole complex that I have observed so far into the language of someone living in West in the twenty-first century: An American waiter, having used the toilet, is about to exit the lavatory with hands unwashed. The recollection that he has forgotten to wash his hands (or a glimpse of the sign reading *Employees Must Wash Hands*) acts as a *religio*, causing him to think twice—to turn back and wash his hands. Washing his hands, he might feel further *religiones*: "Am I washing them with enough soap? For long enough? With enough hot water?" The scrupulous fulfillment of what he believes as his duty will free him from his *religiones* and restore his sense of honor and purity. But if he leaves the lavatory without washing his hands, he will carry the *religio* with him in the form of a kind of guilt or pollution. The *religio* might cling to him like a debt or curse, adhere to him, *and heighten his anxiety* until—and perhaps even after—he washes his hands very thoroughly.

Another scenario: A young New Yorker is passing a Sunday in May and realizes (or notices on her calendar) that it is Mother's Day and that she has failed to write or call her mother. She stops short with a twinge of *religio* and goes to call her mother. It is possible that she might feel still further *religiones*: Did her mother notice that she didn't send a card? Should she have sent flowers? Should she have arranged to take her mother out to dinner? The more scrupulously she fulfills her obligations, the more she will feel clear, honorable, righteous, and pure. If she decides to ignore Mother's Day, the *religio* will cling to her, a sort of debt crime. Perhaps only a profusion of apologies and treating her mother to an especially nice dinner in a fine restaurant might relieve her of the *religio*. It will, without a doubt, take much greater effort, attention and expense to expiate, to atone for the *religio* than to observe the inhibitions. (Note also that if her mother does not accept her apologies, the anxiety of *religio* may become unbearable, and the daughter may grow to hate and rebel against her mother and Mother's Day.)

PARALYZING *RELIGIO* = *SUPERSTITIO*

Georges Dumézil asserted that "*religiones, religio* . . . originally expressed . . . not a flight of the spirit or any form of activity but a halt. . . ."[124] Benveniste believed that *religio* was "*pas un sentiment qui dirige vers une action*. . . ."[125] But, I would assert that the emotions of *religio*, like a dam on a stream, generally had a positive role in facilitating—*by directing and channeling*—action. Like the emotions of honor/*pudor*, to which they were closely related, they were the prerequisites of effective action. Only the *excess* of *religio*, in the form of terror, choked and paralyzed—something dreaded by a people whose souls were made by and for action. The anxious attention of *religio*, unrelieved, could become terrorizing *superstitio*, the culmination and inversion of *religio*. *Religio* carried to the point of crippling anxiety was a kind of altered state, a sort of frenzy or *furor*. "*Superstitio*," according to Servius, "is fear that is superfluous and crazy." (*Superstitio est timor superfluens et delirus* [*Ad Aeneidem* 8.187].)[126]

> Each virtue will be found to have a vice bordering upon it . . . as temerity borders on self-confidence, or stubbornness borders on perseverance, or *superstitio* which is akin to *religio* . . . (Cicero, *De inventione* 2.54.165).[127]

The word *superstitio* makes its first appearance in Cicero, but the adjective *superstitiosus* goes back as far as Plautus.[128] Cicero, at first, used *superstitio* like republican *supersitiosus*, as a synonym for *religiosus*: Cicero attacked Verres in 70 B.C.E. for having despoiled the temple of Ceres in Sicilian Henna while acting as governor:

> The rights of our wronged allies, the authority of our laws, the reputation and honor of our courts are here at stake; and all these are all very great matters. But the most important issue is that the whole province of Sicily is seized by such *religio* (*tanta religio*

obstricta)—such *superstitio* has overtaken the minds of the whole population in Sicily (*tanta superstitio mentes occupavit*) that every public or private misfortune that befalls them is believed to come about as the result of his crime (*scelus*) (*In Verrem* 2.4.51.113).

Here, for Cicero, *superstitio* and *religio* are synonymous; both characterize the heightened anxiety of the Sicilians produced by the violation of their temple.[129]

The *religiones* that concentrated and channeled the will could paralyze that same will. Excessive scrupulousness could be a form of debilitating weakness. The restraint that channeled and directed the energies of the Romans had the potential to incapacitate them. *Religio* might cease to facilitate action and begin, like excessive shame, to cripple it. It was *religio* that caused the Gauls, in Livy's account of their siege of the Capitol in 390 B.C.E., to stand stupefied while Fabius Dorsuo walked through their lines unchallenged (*seu attonitis Gallis miraculo audaciae seu religione etiam motis* [Livy 5.46.3].)[130]

Calvus was, as Cicero tells us:

> . . . an orator much more erudite than Curio, and who presented a style of speaking more meticulously elaborated and carefully detailed. Though he handled it with knowledge and discrimination, yet from excessive self-examination, self-consciousness, and fear of committing an error, his speech was exsanguinated. His language, thus, was weakened through too much *religio*. . . . (*Brutus* 82.283).[131]

Calvus, with his excessive refinement and restraint, went beyond the *sanitas* and *integritas* that, Cicero asserts, should be the *religio* and *verecundia* of every orator (ibid. 82.284). Too much *religio*, like too much shame, incapacitated him. Quintilian uses the adverb *supersitiose* to characterize the behavior of students of rhetoric who adhere blindly and "superstitiously" to the rules instead of creatively learning from them (e.g., *Institutio Oratoria* 4.2.85; 10.6.5; 12.10.14).

Superstitio and *religio*, then, are often closely related and equally negative in the Roman sources. Livy's warlike ancient Roman King Tullus Hostilius (seventh century B.C.E.) contracted a lingering disease:

> Those violent spirits [of Tullus] were so broken with the breaking of his health, that the man who had hitherto thought nothing less worthy of a king than to devote himself to sacred rites, suddenly became prey to all sort of *superstitiones* great and small and filled even the minds of the people with *religiones* (Livy 1.31.5).[132]

When the anxious scrupulosity of *religio* was carried to excess, it became the crushing weight or debilitating fetter from which Lucretius wished to free the Roman (*De natura rerum* 1.62–79; 1.931).[133] Cicero, addressing the college of pontiffs, mocks Clodius' pretentions to scrupulousness in preserving the consecration of Cicero's property:

> Act as good pontiffs should, and admonish him that there is a certain measure to be applied to *religio*. . . . (*De domo sua* 29.105 [57 B.C.E.]).[134]

He goes on to mock the "*superstitiosa dedicatio*" of Clodius the "*castissimus sacerdos*" (39.103).

There were those, according to the Roman senator Nigidius Figulus [first century B.C.E.], who bound themselves by an excessive and *superstitiosa religio*. In the words of Gellius:

Nigidius Figulus, in my opinion the most learned man after Marcus Varro, in the
eleventh book of his *Grammatical Commentaries* quotes a truly remarkable line from an
ancient poem: "Best to be *religens* (restrained), lest one be *religiosus*" (*religentem esse oportet,
religiosus ne fuas*)[135] . . . and in the same connection Nigidius adds: "The suffix *-osus* in
words of this kind, such as *vinosus, mulierosus, religiosus*, always indicates an excessive
amount of the quality in question. Therefore *religiosus* is applied to one who has bound
himself by an extreme and *superstitosa religio* (*nimia et superstitiosa religione sese alligaverat*)
which was regarded as a fault" (Aulus Gellius, *Noctes Atticae* 4.9.2).[136]

Just as a Roman could feel too much shame, he or she could be too inhibited, too anxious, too careful.[137]

Our ancestors distinguished *religio* from *superstitio*.[138] Persons who spent whole days in
prayer and sacrifice to ensure that their children should outlive them were termed
superstitiosi (Cicero, *De natura deorum* 2.71–72).[139]

Here, again, *superstitio* is not the antithesis but the excess of *religio*.

In times of great danger, such as the war with Hannibal, the terror of *religio* could be
hard to moderate. Excessive fear could result in shameless temerity.

The longer the war dragged on and success and failure altered the spirits of men no less
than their fortunes, such a great *religio* invaded the republic, for the most part from
outside, that either men or gods suddenly seemed changed. [The Romans began to
practice strange and foreign rites openly, to consult *vates* and *sacrificuli*. Livy attributes
the disorder in part to the influx into the city of panicked rustics.] Now that the disorder
appeared to be too strong to be quelled by the lower magistrates, the senate assigned to
Marcus Aemilius, the city praetor, the task of freeing the people from these *religiones*
(Livy 25.1.6+11 [213 B.C.E.]).[140]

In Livy's account, the extreme *religio*, the anxiety of the Roman people, is thought of as
a debilitating disorder that first the lower magistrates and then the higher magistrates feel
the need and responsibility to address. The spontaneous attempts of the people to respond
to and alleviate these fears, these *religiones*, are considered inadequate or even dangerous
by the senate. The senators feel the need to regulate, orchestrate, and hopefully, free the
people from their *religiones*.

In 207 B.C.E., according to Livy, the anxious Romans received a whole series of threatening omens and prodigies to which the pontifices felt compelled to respond:

These prodigies were attended to (i.e., averted, expiated [*procurata prodigia*]) with
full-grown victims, and a single day of prayer (*supplicatio*) was observed by decree of the
pontiffs. (. . .) Their minds relieved of *religio* (*liberatas religione mentes*), they were
troubled again by the report that at Frusino there had been born a child as large as a
four-year-old and . . . it was uncertain whether male or female (27.37.1–5).

The pontifical expiations succeed in calming the populace only momentarily. Heightened sensitivity to hostile omens was symptomatic of fear/*religio*.

If *religio* might cause a man to carefully wash his hands with soap under hot running
water, the man who washed his hands continually would be *religiosus*=*supersitiosus*. His

exceeding anxiety would cause him to be obsessed, "fixated."[141] We, having our own ways of labeling an excess of debilitating anxiety as a sickness, might diagnose him as having "obsessive-compulsive disorder." Standing or walking close to a precipice might cause a woman to step with particular and deliberate care and hesitation, but if it caused paralysis and panicked terror, we might diagnose her as having acrophobia.[142] When Lucretius declared that his purpose in writing was "to free the spirit from the knots/bonds of *religio*" (*religionum nodis animos exsolvere* [*De natura rerum* 1.931]), the *religio* that he wishes to dispel was this excessive and debilitating terror (*De natura deorum* 1.42.117).

Distorted, irregular, *prava religio* might cause one to give excessive and fearful attention to matters of very little importance. For example, when it was announced as a prodigy from Cumae that the mice had gnawed at the gold in the temple of Jupiter, Livy remarks in exasperation, "To that extent *prava religio* involves the gods in even the smallest matter" (27.23.2).[143]

> Nothing is more deceptive in its appearance than *prava religio*. When the *numen* of the gods is put forward as a pretext for evil acts, a fear enters the spirit lest, in punishing human transgressions, we might violate the province (*iuris aliquid*) of the gods. Innumerable decrees of the pontifices should have liberated you from this *religio* (Livy 39.16.6–7).[144]

The author of *Ad Herennium* 2.21.34 lists *religio* as one of the motivations for evildoing (*maleficia*)—along with luxury and greed: "What about love? *religio*? fear of death? desire for power? (*Quid amor? . . . quid ambitio? quid religio? quid metus mortis? quid imperii cupiditas?*) In *De domo sua*, Cicero talks at length about the use made by Publius Clodius of the *nomen sanctissimum religionis* to commit his crimes (47.123). He goes on to mention Gaius Atinius Labeo, who, as *tribunus plebis* 133 B.C.E., with brazier duly placed on the rostra and with flute player in attendance, devoted the property of Quintus Metellus Macedonicus—the man who, as censor, had previously ejected Labeo from the senate. Lucretius is aware, however, that in attacking *religio* as a motivation for *scelera*, he might be seen as guilty of attacking the regulating mechanisms of his culture.

> I fear one thing in this matter—that you may perhaps reckon approaching the *elementa rationis* to be impiety and entering the path of *scelus*; whereas, on the contrary, too often it is that very *religio* which has brought forth wicked and impious deeds (*scelerosa and impia facta*).

He proceeds to retell the story of the slaying of Iphianassa (= Iphigeneia) by her father Agamemnon, ". . . all in order that a fair and fortunate release might be given to the fleet. So potent is *religio* in urging men on to evil deeds." (*Exitus ut classi felix faustusque daretur. Tantum religio potuit suadere malorum* [*De rerum natura* 1.80–101].)

Superfluous anxiety was often associated, in the literature composed by members of the Roman upper classes, with the peasant, the unsophisticated, the woman—especially the old woman. The weak spirit, the *imbecillus animus* was *religiosus/superstitiosus*.[145] Livy talks about the *simplices et religiosi homines* who are wont to be credulous and anxious concerning prodigies (24.10.6). Terence's Sostrata confesses to her husband Chremes that she did not expose their infant girl herself as he had ordered her, but had instead instructed a trusted old woman to dispose of the baby. She adds the fact that she removed a ring from her hand and asked the old woman to place it with the child. Sostrata begins this part of her apology with the words:

> As all us foolish and miserable women are *religiosae*, when I gave the baby to the old woman to be exposed I took a ring off of my finger and told her to expose it with the child (*Heautontimorumenos* 649–650).[146]

In the first satire of Horace, the peregrinating poet depicts himself besieged by a shameless and importuning would-be client who wants the poet to introduce him to the great Maecenas. The poet encounters a sly acquaintance, the friend who, he earnestly hopes, will save him from the parasite. Instead, the friend gets sadistic pleasure in leaving miserable Horace with his *garrulus*:

> "Surely," ['Horace' asks his acquaintance hopefully] "you said there was something you wanted to tell me in private."
> "I remember it well, but I'll tell you at a better time. Today is the thirtieth sabbath. Would you affront [*oppedere*—the only appearance of this word] the circumcised Jew?"
> Horace replies "*Nulla mihi religio est.*"
> "But it is for me [*at mi*];—I am somewhat weaker—one of the many. You will pardon me; I'll talk another day" (1.9.69–73[33–30 B.C.E.]).[147]

To paraphrase: the friend asks, "Would you affront the Jews on the sabbath?" Horace replies, "I have no hesitation, no scruple, no *religio*. I am not afraid of the consequence of insulting the Jews." His friend cleverly protests, "But I *do* have such a *religio*—I am somewhat weaker." Horace's friend declares himself afraid to affront the Jews—simultaneously confessing that such a *religio* is a fault that he shares with the feeble multitude. Note that the *religio* of excessive scrupulosity is here an unnecessary, a personal, and a superfluous fear—and this excess of *religio* is simultaneously the characteristic, in the poem, of the man who indeed has no shame! In the way that an excess of *pudor* could be construed as a form of shamelessness, an excess of *religio* could be a form of no *religio* at all—and so the equivalent of *superstitio*.[148]

It is impossible to understand Roman *religio*—and its transformations—without understanding its equivocal and negative aspects, that is, the possibility of there being excessive, shameful, and inexpiable *religiones*.

Conclusions

The Romans of the Republic were like sailors who sometimes ran with the wind and the currents, but who most often negotiated these forces, tacking back and forth—always carefully observing and utilizing the wind and weather, tide and currents—but not necessarily acting in consonance with them, and often against them. The *religiones* of the Romans were a matter of constant conscious and careful adjustments and manipulations. The goal of these negotiations was to facilitate one's own motions, fulfill and facilitate one's desires and designs, concentrate and direct one's own and the effective energies of those forces that one had influence over. The rules, such as they were, were like the "Cider House rules" of John Irving's novel: landmarks by which one directed and oriented one's actions; one attended to and considered them rather than obeyed them.

When modern scholars complain that the ancient Roman "religion" was not "moral," they are reacting against the lack of (divinely sanctioned) codified law that they perceive as the foundation of morality. (The ethics of *pudor* and *religio* were "situational" ethics and so seem to many moderns to be no ethics at all—the ethics of the uncivilized.) Rather, the ancient way of operating in the world produced a heightened alertness and hesitant (and usually uncomfortable) self-consciousness, like that produced in an American driver at a four-way stop or a British driver entering a roundabout.[149] It was, I assert, a more subtle and complex set of notions and emotions that the ones that would replace it.

The Latin word *religio* embraced and expressed a balancing system so sensitive that it trembled.[150] *Aurea mediocritas* was not produced by a set of restrictions but rather by a set of reverberations, of transgressions and expiations. There was a boundary to be kept always in sight, but the assumption was always that a Roman would cross and recross that boundary, that he or she would get dirty to be cleansed, cleansed to get dirty. The social, psychological, and physical worlds of the Romans of the republic were all based on reciprocal resonations. As inhibiting *pudor* disposed a Roman to avoid behavior that could evoke the *pudor* that was shame, so inhibiting *religio* disposed the Romans to avoid the *religio* that was anxious guilt. But, like that purposeful poise created by fear of the vendetta, after the balance was lost, after the fluctuations became too extreme, the poise of *religio* was difficult, sometimes impossible, to recover.

The Romans were moving from heightened self-consciousness to "conscience," from *religio* to "religion," from the old Volkswagen (with its Idiot's Manual, spare tires, hairpins, and Band-Aids) to the jet plane (with its tickets, passports, and security checks) to a way of travelling through the world where one strapped oneself in and left the flying to the pilot and his crew.

The Ciceronian Turn

> *Religio* is that which brings men to serve and worship a higher order of nature which they call divine.
>
> —CICERO, *De inventione* 2.53.161[1]

> *Religio*, that is, the cult of the gods.
>
> —CICERO, *De natura deorum* 2.3[2]

The tense self-regulating mechanisms of the ancient *religiones*—doubt, hesitation, inhibition, and anxiety—governed most effectively in the house and village and small face-to-face culture. The ancient balancing systems of *religio* ceased adequately to discipline the increasingly complex, urbanized, and cosmopolitan Roman empire. Both the growing centralized and hierarchical state powers as well as the disruptions of those powers in the century of civil wars overwhelmed and undermined the informal, flexible, and often arbitrary system of the ancient *religiones*.[3] The century of intermittent but escalating civil wars, in particular, that brought an end to the Republic produced profound and paralyzing disequilibrations, excesses of *religio/superstitio*. The ancient balancing systems of the Roman *religiones* will continue to function—sometimes under other names and in sublimated manner—but they will be augmented by and subordinated to a simpler ideological structure that will help to lay the foundation for the cult of the emperor and Latin Christendom.

Religio, in the civil war and after, was consistently in the Empire associated with fear rather more than just hesitation or inhibition. *Religio: metus vel sollicitudo* (Nonius 604 Lindsay); *Connexa sunt timor et religio* (Servius, *Ad Aeneidem* 2.75; cf. 12.139). *Religio: id est metus* (ibid. 8.349); *Religio est timor cum veneratione* (*Corpus glossariorum latinorum* ed. Goetz, vol. 5.659). It was also in this period that fear became an explanation for the creation/existence of the gods:

Human life lay for all to see foully grovelling upon the ground, crushed beneath the weight of *religio* which displayed her head in the regions of heaven, threatening mortals from on high with horrible aspect. . . . (Lucretius, *De rerum natura* 1.62–79).[4]

[I must show] in what ways that fear of gods crept into the heart which in our earth keeps holy their shrines and pools and groves, their altars and images (Lucretius, *De rerum natura* 5.73–75).[5]

It was fear first made gods in the world, when the lightning fell from high heaven, and the walls were rent with flame, and Athos was struck and blazed (Petronius, *poemata* 3 Warmington).[6]

It was fear, first made gods in the world (Statius, *Thebaid* 3.661).[7]

Cicero, like Lucretius, was inclined to pair the fears of *religio* to the careful attention to, and observance of, the bonds and obligations that tie humans, particularly, to the gods:

They call that *religio* which manifests itself in the *metus* and *caerimonia* of the gods. (*Religionem eam quae in metu et caerimonia deorum sit appellant* [De inventione 2.22.66].)[8]

I want to return to the idea that fear of the gods, when exaggerated, could be debilitating and counterproductive.[9] It was while the Samnites were busy with their *superstitiones* (*operati superstitionibus*) that the consul Spurius Carvilius Maximus was able to seize their town of Amiternum and slay 2,800 Samnite men (Livy 10.39.1–2). The Jews' excessive scrupulosity, which involved an unwillingness at times to fight on the Sabbath, seemed to Pliny unnecessarily self-destructive, even suicidal (*Epistulae* 10.96.9).[10] Horace depicts a mother whose fear of the gods is a threat to her and her sick child, causing her to behave in a self-destructive way:

"O Jupiter who gives and takes away sore afflictions," cries the mother of a child that for five long months has been ill in bed, "if the quartan chills leave my child, then on the morning of the day on which you appoint a fast he shall stand naked in the Tiber." Should chance or the doctor raise the sick lad up from his peril, his crazy mother will kill him by planting him on the cold bank and bringing back his fever. What is the malady that has stricken her mind? *timor deorum* (Satirae 2.3.288–295).[11]

Seneca critiques the self-destruction of the ecstatic followers of Magna Mater:

One man cuts off his virile parts, and another slashes his arms. What can they fear from the wrath of the gods, when they use such means to win their favor? (. . .) So great is the frenzy of a disordered and unsettled mind that means are used to placate the gods that have never been employed even by the most horrible men whose cruelty is recorded in myth and legend. Tyrants have mutilated the limbs of some of their victims, but have ordered no one to mutilate his own limbs. Some have been castrated to serve the lust of a king, but no one has unmanned himself with his own hands at a master's order. They slash themselves in temples and make supplication with their own bleeding wounds. If anyone has leisure to view what they do and what they suffer, he will find practices so indecent for honorable men, so unworthy of free men, that if their number were fewer no one would have any doubt that they were demented (*De Superstitione*=Augustine, *De civitate dei* 6.10–11).[12]

Ovid described the stricken Vestals, the *attonitae ministrae* who, when wildfires burned the temple of Vesta in 241 B.C.E., were so confounded by fear that they lost the ability to act (*abstulerat vires corporis ipse timor*). "It is not by prayers but by deeds that they (the *sacra*) can be saved!" the *pontifex maximus* Lucius Caecilius Metellus admonished the disabled priestesses (*Fasti* 6.437–54). It was only his willingness to transgress into the tabooed space of the temple that enabled Metellus to rescue the sacred fetishes contained in the holy of holies of the Roman state.

Lucretius provided some of the most vivid descriptions of the paralysis that resulted from fear. For Lucretius, there could be way too much anxiety, too much *religio*:

> When the intelligence is deeply moved by vehement fear, we see the whole spirit through-
> out the frame share in the feeling, sweating and pallor hence arise over the whole body,
> the speech falters, the voice dies away, blackness comes before the eyes, a sounding is in
> the ears, the limbs give way beneath, in a word we often see men fall to the ground for
> mental terror (*De rerum natura* 3.152–158).[13]

Lucretius wished to release those who read his poem from the fetters of that terror. In part, he did this by urging the human to surrender to the operations of an automatic and atomistic universe in which human control and influence was impossible and the Powers That Be indifferent.[14]

Both the frenzy and paralysis of excessive *religio* were of concern to members of the senatorial class. They were intolerant of altered or enthused states, of being "out of one-self" or "above oneself" except when that enthusiasm was, like the soldier's *furor*, in the service of the Republic. It was, I believe, association with altered, excessive, and unbal-anced states that caused the early Jesus movement to be described by the Roman Pliny as a *superstitio prava, immodica* (*Epistulae* 10.96.8; cf. 9), by Suetonius as a *superstitio nova ac malefica* (*Nero* 16.2), by Tacitus as an *exitiabilis superstitio* (*Annales* 44.5). The participants in this movement were seen as extremists—not unlike the excited *vates* and *harioli* and *sacri-ficuli* that one met in every village and on every city street, not unlike the prophet and wonder-worker Eunus who lit the conflagration of the First Sicilian Slave War, or the Bacchic enthusiasts or the despised Galli, all of whom went overboard in their enthusiasms and fears.[15] They were, at least at first, ecstatics: prophesying, speaking in tongues, and so forth. The failures of the members of this movement in the Empire to respect the Roman *sacra* and to signal their loyalty to the Emperor—and especially their unwillingness to allow the Emperor to determine the direction in which the energies of his subjects was to be released—seemed absurdly destructive both to themselves and to the state.

Externalized Regulation

In Livy's history, the rebellious Latins revolt from their treaty with the Romans and burn down the town of Satricum (377 B.C.E.):

> They applied the torch without discrimination both to sacred and profane buildings, and
> not one escaped destruction except the temple of Mater Matuta; from this they were kept

away, according to the story, neither by their own *religio*, nor by their *verecundia* (respectful shyness) for the gods,—but by an awe-inspiring voice that issued from the temple and threatened dire retribution if they did not remove those *nefandos ignes* far from the walls of the *delubrum* (Livy 6.33.4–5).[16]

In this passage, Livy clearly remarks on the ineffectiveness of the inner emotional restraints of *religio* and *verecundia*, and in contrast, the success of the terrifying threats issued by a voice inside the temple. In this passage, Livy carefully distinguishes *religio* from obedience to an externalized command with its threats of punishment.

Livy, writing at the end of the civil wars, is also my source for the story of the terrible drought that in 429 B.C.E. caused the Romans almost unendurable suffering. The bodies of dead cattle lined the parched stream beds. Those not carried off by thirst were stricken with the mange, which spread from the afflicted animals to human beings, first in the country and then in the city. Like a disease, all manner of fearful *religio*—mostly foreign— invaded their spirits (*animos multiplex religio et pleraque externa invasit*); the spirits of the country men were seized by *superstitio* (*sunt capti superstitione animi*) fostered by individuals who, in order to enrich themselves, introduced through divination unknown forms of sacrifices into their homes, until the news and sight of the "public shame" (*publicus pudor*) reached the ears and eyes of the leading citizens. Seeking to suppress the novel and foreign rites with which the people were attempting to placate the gods (*peregrina atque insolita piacula pacis deum exposcendae*), the senate commissioned the aediles to see to it that only Roman gods might be worshipped, and only in the ancestral manner (*ne qui nisi Romani di neu quo alio more quam patrio colerentur*) (4.30.8–11).

In Livy's story, the excessive anxiety of the people (their *religio/superstitio*) causes them to act shamelessly in the eyes of the senators. *Religio* and *pudor* were no longer considered adequate by the senators to restrain and moderate the behaviors of the Roman people. The magistrates step in to harness, focus, and direct their energies.[17] Gordon points out that Livy is presaging, in this passage, his treatment of the senate's reaction to the Bacchants in 186 B.C.E., where the senators stepped in to quell what they saw as the uncontrolled and dangerous excesses of the *religiosi/superstitiosi* ("*Superstitio*" p. 88).

In a passage of the *Bellum Civile* wherein he imagined his generals, Petreius and Afranius, discussing the dangers of engaging his troops in night battles during the civil wars, Julius Caesar, like Livy, determined that the intervention of the magistrates was necessary to quell the fears of the soldiers.

> Night battles should be avoided . . . because the soldiers in their terror of civil strife are likely to consider their fears rather than their *religio*. But, in daylight *pudor*, when the eyes of all are looking on, contributes much as does the presence of military tribunes and centurions, and that it was by such considerations that troops are wont to be restrained and kept in allegiance (*Bellum civile* 1.67).[18]

In this passage, *religio* is the *antidote* to fear and the equivalent of the *pudor* the soldiers felt in regard to their bond to their officers, which needed to be supplemented and reinforced by the visible presence and observation of the officers. In Caesar's mind, the cure for the shamelessness occasioned by great fear is (1) the daylight in which the soldiers' sense of shame, their sensitivity to the eyes and opinions "of all" will be brought into play, and (2) fear and shame produced by the authority of the military tribunes and centurions. The fear of shame will trump their fear of the night and of killing their fellow citizens.

Divinae Religionis *Ratio: The Ciceronian Conversion*

> There is nothing more agreeable to the pre-eminent god who rules the whole world . . .
> than the councils and societies of humans associated by law, which are called *civitates*.
>
> Cicero, *De republica* 6.13.13[19]

I cannot sufficiently emphasize that Cicero, even while modifying the meaning of *religio* in several passages, continued to use the word in the entire array of its ancient and customary usages (inhibition, scruple, fear, and the object that evoked those emotions: *taboo*, bond, obligation, oath, treaty, transgression, guilt of transgression, curse, etc.). Nevertheless, from his earliest surviving works, there is a consistent attempt to respond to the disarray and excessively heightened—or excessively lowered—anxiety he associated with these *religiones* and to formulate certain cures. Like most conversions, Cicero's was a long time coming.

In the early work *De inventione* (before 81 B.C.E.), the young Cicero described a kind of pre-state Hobbesian war of all against all where brute strength prevailed over *ratio animi*. Men wandered like beasts and lived on wild food. These foragers were in urgent need of discipline and the ordering and regulating of life—something, he believed, they could not do for themselves. Cicero, given that his entire life was lived amidst the disorders of civil war, could not imagine (any more than Hobbes) that an effective "government of shame" had long preceded (as it did among all populations of mammals) any government of laws and punishments. For the young Cicero, the only alternative to a world of perpetual civil war seemed to be one governed by the *divinae religionis ratio* (1.2.1).

What could control the people if their inner balancing systems were poorly functioning or non-existent? For Cicero, *religio*, as an emotion that bound and obliged (like *pietas*, *gratia*, and v*eritas*) was instilled into humans by *natura* or the "pre-eminent God who rules the whole world."[20] This "natural" *religio* obliged humans to fear the gods as rulers and to show that fear in *caerimoniae deorum* (2.22.66).[21] For Cicero, the doctrines of the atheists Diagoras and Theodorus and the agnostic Protagoras

> . . . abolish not only *superstitio* which implies a groundless fear of the gods (*timor inanis deorum*), but also *religio* which consists in the pious cult of the gods (*cultu pio deorum*) (*De natura deorum* 1.42.117).[22]

For Cicero, this fear of the gods was wholesome—provided it be disciplined, regulated, instructed by the collective Fathers.

There were certain *habitus animi* that came, by their utility and advantages for humans, to be institutionalized, to be sanctified by fear of the laws and *religio* (*legum metus et religio sanxit* [*De inventione* 2.30.92]).[23]

But it was only in Cicero's darkest and paralyzed days that he had the leisure for the philosophical ruminations "necessary for moderating *religio*" (*ad moderandam religionem necessaria* [*De natura deorum* 1.1.1]).[24] His exile from the centers of power allowed him to write and speak in the greatly abstracted language of Greek philosophy.[25] Even when—or especially when—he does not explicitly adhere to any of the positions taken by his speakers in his philosophical dialogs, he is nevertheless still engaged in the process of simplifying, magnifying, and focusing attention on the category of "the god" with whose remote authority he wishes to identify his words, his will, and his judgments. He is in the process of creating the stripped-down ideology that will be necessary to survive in and to serve the Roman Empire and Christendom.

Cicero, *at times*, makes compliance with the will or *auctoritas* of god and the magistrate–priests into *religio*. In *De divinatione*, Cicero declares that when Lysander desired to alter the laws established in accordance with the *auctoritas* of the Delphic oracle by the Spartan Lycurgus, he was prevented from doing so by *religio* (1.43.96). The Roman kings, he asserts, and later the augurs ruled by *religionum auctoritas* (1.41.90). The senate, at the height of its *imperium*, added the Etruscan discipline of interpreting lightning to the *religionis auctoritas* (1.41.92). "The god," at times, becomes the ultimate state authority and the holders of magisterial priesthood, particularly the college of augurs (to which he himself belonged),[26] become those authorized to access the will of this god. (Cicero quotes the lines of Ennius, which declared that, "Romulus perceived that he had gained a throne and land made firm through augury" [*De divinatione* 1.48.109].)[27] The senators with their divinatory monopoly would have the sole right to discern this divine will,[28] which right would allow them to engage and funnel the collective power of the citizens in the directions they chose.

Cicero both reinforced (and reinterpreted) the *religiones* of the Romans as a disciplinary code based on authoritative strictures—with the gods operating both as the ultimate authors and as the ultimate enforcers, rewarding the good citizen with eternal life, and punishing rebels and the lawbreakers (like Catiline) with eternal torments.[29]

> You Jupiter, whom Romulus established (*es constitutus*) with the same auspices as this city, whom we justly call the supporter (*stator*) of this city and empire, will keep Catiline and his confederates from your temple and those of the other gods, from the houses and walls of the city, from the lives and fortunes of all her citizens. And these men, the foes of loyal citizens, public enemies of their native land, plunderers of Italy, men who are joined together in an evil alliance and companionship of crime, these men alive or dead you will visit with eternal punishment (*aeternis suppliciis vivos mortuosque mactabis* [*In Catilinam* 1.33]).[30]

> The spirits of those who . . . violate the laws of gods and men . . . after leaving their bodies, fly about close to the earth, and do not return to this place except after many ages of torment (*De republica* 6.26.29).[31]

Cicero, at times, wanted to change the main source of disciplined self-restraint from fear of shame to fear of punishment. It were as if while continuing to urge his fellows to exercise care and caution when crossing a busy city street, the mayor of Greenfield emphasized that jaywalking would be punished with a jail sentence. The fear of being observed by a policeman might replace and exceed the fear of being hit by a car. Or, it were as if the nervous attention elicited by the four-way stop or the traffic circle was being replaced not only by a traffic light but also a surveillance camera. These reinforcing mechanisms could *simplify* the demands made on the driver by ending ambiguity and, perhaps, ease the tension of the driver at the crossroads—which might have the results that one's behavior at the crossroad would be governed less by attentive inhibition and more by fear of being observed and punished for "breaking the law."[32]

What Cicero, like Varro, wanted to retain of the traditional practices were their predictable formalism, their rules and regularities, their hierarchies, authorities, and disciplines. He wanted to retain those elements he believed would contribute to the stability and hierarchical structure of the state. The small-scale improvisations, the bargaining, the negotiations, the reciprocity of the ancient sacrificial system were, often, irrelevant for Cicero. From *De natura deorum*:

> The whole of the *religio* of the Roman people is divided into *sacra*, *auspicia*, and the third additional division consisting of all such predictions as the interpreters of the Sybil or the *haruspices* have derived from portents and prodigies. Well I have always thought that the *religio* of these are not to be despised, and I have held the conviction that Romulus by his auspices and Numa's constitution of the *sacra* laid the foundations of our state, which assuredly could never have been as great as it is without the fullest placation of the immortal gods.
>
> There, Balbus, is the opinion of a Cotta and a *pontifex*. You are a philosopher and I ought to receive from you a systematic justification of *religio* (*ratio religionis*) (3.2.5).[33]

Even in matters of *religio domestica*, in Cicero's mind, the *pontifices* needed to be consulted and their opinions prevail (*De domo sua* 51.132). He would limit or eliminate the anxious attention paid to *vates*, *Chaldaei* and *haruspices*, soothsayers, dreams, omens, prodigies, sacrifices, the flight of birds, thunder and lightning—all things that prevented Romans from preserving "a tranquil state of mind" (*quieta mens*) and that, more importantly, usurped and obscured the increasingly essential and threatened power of the priests and magistrates of the republic to set the future agenda, determine the goals and purposes of the people, to harness, augment, focus, and direct the energies of the Romans.[34]

> Out of respect both for the *opinio* of the masses and on account of their great usefulness to the republic, we maintain the tradition (*mos*), discipline (*disciplina*), *religio*, law (*ius*), and authority (*auctoritas*) of the augural college (*De divinatione* 2.33.70).[35]

At the same time as Cicero wanted to obliterate the weak and womanly terrors of *religio*, he wanted to *increase* the necessary and effective fear of the people for the priests and magistrates of the state—and, in particular, for augurs, the interpreters of the will of Jupiter Optimus Maximus (*De legibus* 2.20).[36] To do that, he would have to increase their fear of the all-knowing, all-powerful ruler of the universe who authorized these priests. The people must respect the gods whose will they, the augurs, were authorized to interpret and transmit.[37] Cicero, in *De legibus*, went so far as to make disobedience to the augurs a capital offense. ("Whatever an augur shall curse as unjust, *nefas*, pernicious or ill-omened let that be null and void; and whosoever does not obey let it be considered as guilty of a capital offense." [*Quaeque augur iniusta, nefasta, vitiosa dira defixerit, inrita infectaque sunto; quisque non paruerit, capital esto* (2.21).]) The consuls Publius Claudius and Lucius Iunius, he declared, deserved capital punishment for setting sail, contrary to the auspices, in the First Punic War (*De divinatione* 2.71). Like Momigliano's Nigidius Figulus, Cicero "had left behind the traditional ways of bargaining with the gods and was trying to discover safer rules for the interplay between men and gods."[38]

Cicero was induced, in the civil war period, to formulate an alternative to the malfunctioning systems of self-regulation and to advocate and justify its substitution with a system of discipline coming from the top down in which god-fearing would be critical. Like Plato, his inspiration, he had spent most of his life caught in the dread confusion of civil war and could see no other way.

It was Cicero's philosophical works—and especially that book of Cicero's that will be most widely read by Christians, *De natura deorum* (likely completed just a few months before the assassination of Caesar)—that gave Tertullian, Minucius Felix, Lactantius, and Ambrose the version of the word *religio* that would eventually evolve into our "religion."[39]

Superstitio *Opposed to* Religio

> Superstitious people thought that the gods were evil, jealous and tyrannical, and this distressed them. This "ill-controlled fear" of the immortals drove them to excess.
>
> John Scheid[40]

It was Cicero who, in the course of the sometimes violent fluctuations of his life, attempted to articulate what Herbert Howe thought of as "an orderly scheme codified and informed by rational explanation," a disciplined and regulated *religio* that would be the antithesis and antidote to an extreme, unreasonable, outlandish, shameless, unauthorized, and illegitimate *superstitio*.[41] By the time Cicero delivered the *Pro Cluentio* in 66 B.C.E., he was beginning to use the word *superstitio* as the antonym of *religio* (194).[42] Cicero attempted to free *religio* from its negative aspects and associations. It was as if he was peeling a soft and rotten fruit to get to a clean, hard nut.

> Speaking frankly, *superstitio*, which is widespread among the nations, has taken advantage of human weakness to cast its spell over the mind of almost every man. (. . .) I thought that I should be rendering a great service both to myself and to my countrymen if I could tear up this *superstitio* by the roots. *But I want it distinctly understood that the destruction of* superstitio *does not mean the destruction of* religio.
>
> For it is the part of the wise man to preserve the institutions of our forefathers by retaining their sacred rites and ceremonies. Furthermore, the celestial order and the beauty of the universe compel me to confess that there is some eternal and excellent being who deserves the respect and homage of men.
>
> Wherefore, just as it is a duty to extend the influence of *religio*, which is conjoined with the knowledge of *natura*, so it is a duty to weed out every root of *superstitio*. For *superstitio*

is ever at your heels to urge you on; it follows you at every turn (Cicero, *De divinatione* 2.148–149.)[43]

Here Cicero employs the word *superstitio* for the very same emotions that Lucretius employed the word *religio*.[44] Cicero wanted to rid the Republic of what he understood to be the common, vulgar, vain, ineffectual "old-womanly" weakness, the agitated anxiety that pursued the Romans, overtaking them and possessing them like evil spirits.[45]

> How often do you find anyone who pays attention to dreams or who understands or remembers them? On the other hand, how many disdain and consider that to be a *superstitio* of a weak and haggish mind/spirit (*animi anilis*)! (*De divinatione* 2.60.125 [44 B.C.E.]).[46]

Cicero mocks Publius Clodius' pretended scrupulousness recalling the latter's scandalous behavior at the Bona Dea festival:

> Where was the necessity, fanatic man (*homo fanatice*), of being so haggishly superstitious (*anili superstitione*) as to attend a sacrifice that was taking place at the house of another man? What was the feebleness of mind (*mentis imbecillitas*) that led you to think that the gods could not be satisfactorily appeased unless you too should be tangled up in women's *religiones* (*nisi muliebribus religionibus te implicuisse* [*De domo sua* 40.105]).[47]

Gordon believes that Cicero's use of the word *superstitio* expresses "confidence" and so indicates that the meanings he gives to that word must have already been in circulation.[48] Gordon is right in that *superstitiosus* had been used negatively for a long time—but so had *religiosus*! I would argue that the meanings of both *superstitio* and *religio* are evolving radically—but very inconsistently—in Cicero's thought. It seems to me likely that Cicero chose the word *superstitio* to be the antithesis of his developing notion of *religio* for two reasons: first, because of the associations of *superstitio* with heightened anxiety, altered states, inspiration, frenzy, and mantic prophecy, all of which had been discouraged in the developing Roman city-state, and which Cicero himself saw as characteristic of an unbalanced and undisciplined mind; and second, that he wanted *religio* to be able to translate Greek *eusebeia*, which could express the notion of a sane, safe, and salutary fear. Servius will later express very nicely the dichotomy that Cicero is beginning to develop:

> *Superstitiosi* is used to signify those who are perpetually and vainly apprehensive . . . ; the *religiosi* are those who fear out of reverence (Servius, *Ad Aeneidem* 6.596).[49]

Many Latin and Latin Christian authors after Cicero, adopting Cicero's distinction, distinguish *religio* from *superstitio*, the *religiosi* from the *superstitiosi*:

> They are said to be *religiosi* who have chosen what to do and what to omit doing of divine matters *in accordance with the traditions of the city*, and who do not involve themselves in *superstitiones* (Festus p. 366 Lindsay.)[50]

Pietas and *verecundia*, piety and reverence, forms of mild and limited fear (the kind that one has for a father), will be the models for the positive emotional content of the city-state cult for Varro as well as for Cicero. According to Augustine:

[Varro] makes a distinction between *religiosus* and *superstitiosus*, saying that the *superstitiosus* fears the gods, whereas the *religiosus* does not fear them as if they were enemies but reveres them as if they were parents (*Antiquitates* 1.47 Cardauns = Augustine, *De civitate dei* 6.9).[51]

The same modulated, regulated fear will be advocated by the Greco-Roman Plutarch, who in his essay on *deisidaimonia*, explains that fear of the gods, when excessive, makes men into the slaves of hideous tyrants—when they could be the children of gentle saviors (*De superstitione, Moralia* 166C-D).

The modern scholars L. F. Janssen and, following him, Maurice Sachot, both working backward from the perspective of the Christian sources—but, importantly, only back as far as Cicero—understand *religio* and *superstitio* as a simple and severe dichotomy:

Superstitio, en tant qu'opposé à *religio*, n'était pas seulement incompatible avec *religio*, comme l'était *religio* avec *superstitio*; ils s'excluaient mutuellement; l'un refusait totalement l'existence à l'autre et chacun ne pouvait considérer l'autre que comme ennemi mortel. . . . [52]

This dichotomy, to which modern westerners are the proud heirs, was the product of a particular historical moment.

Cicero desired a radical pruning of the collective consciousness. After the amputation of the infected parts, something would be left that he *sometimes* called *religio*, which would entail a moderated and regulated fear of the highest state gods and priests. Cicero wanted to distinguish a positive discipline, the *publicum vinculum religionis* (*Pro Balbo* 15.34), the strictures of a sanguine and utilitarian state cult, from unnecessary, extraneous, and ineffectual fear.

Much later, when Lactantius (240–320 C.E.) argued that it was not possible to have too much *religio*, he was not so far from Cicero in the latter's darkest days. Fear, even greatly heightened fear, could be positive when it led to *confessio* and *deditio*, confession and submission on the part of the governed—the confession of defeat and surrender, resignation into the *fides* of the Powers That Be. Fear could trigger the prerequisite surrender, the voluntary *deditio*, and result in reliance on, trusting in, faith in "the Powers That Be," which trust could, simultaneously, assuage and limit the fear. Paradoxically, as the Roman Stoics understood so well, submission could produce a sense of heightened will and effectiveness, an "infantile omnipotence" in those who surrendered. Linking one's gears with the powerful made one feel powerful, like swimming with the current. Those very abstract powers that inspired the fear would also inspire the confidence and trust—and so acquire a heightened sense of firmness, reality, *veritas*.

Interestingly, when in the Christian Empire, *superstitio* becomes the negative antithesis of a positive *religio*, the word "scruple" will step in to fill part of the lexical vacancy left by negative *religio*. In Catholic moral theology, "scruple" becomes the word to express what the ancient Romans meant by excessive *religio*. The *Oxford Dictionary of the Christian Church*, Third Edition (1997) explains that:

[Scruples are] often the outcome of nervous disturbances. (. . .) [Scrupulosity] may . . . err with regard to duties which it is prone to see where they do not exist. Scrupulosity, which often inclines the penitent to refuse submission to the judgments of his confessor, may lead to the sins of obstinacy and despair, or conversely, to self-indulgence. *The scrupulous, who are discouraged from making minute confessions, are usually counseled to disregard their scruples and to act in obedience to the advice of a prudent spiritual director* (p. 1475, emphasis mine).

Note that the personal sensitivity, the "scruples" of individuals, are assumed to be either excessively rigorous (and so debilitating) or less rational/sensible/useful than those of the "legitimate" disciplinary system of the clerical authorities. It is the priest who can "manage" the fear.

The *"Useful"* Religio

In *De republica*, Cicero explicitly articulated his *ratio* for the ideal Roman *religio*: It was *useful* to have the people believe that there were *benevolent* gods, and that the authority of the lawmakers comes from them, and that the gods are witnesses to and enforcers of the laws, oaths, treaties, and cultic obligations. These gods vigilantly scrutinize and record all the behaviors of men.

> So from the very beginning we must persuade our citizens that the gods are the masters and guides (*dominos omnium rerum ac moderatores*), and that which is done is done by their *iudicium* and *numen*; that humans are greatly indebted to them (*eosdemque optime de genere hominum mereri*). The gods observe the character of every individual: what he does (*quid agat*), what wrong he perpetrates / is guilty of (*quid in se admittat*), and with what intentions and with what piety (*qua pietate*) he fulfils his *religiones* (*colat religiones*); and that they take note (*habere rationem*) of the pious and impious.
>
> *Who will deny that such beliefs are useful* when he remembers how often oaths are used to confirm agreements, how important to our well-being are the *religiones* of treaties, how many persons are deterred from crime by the fear of divine punishment, and how sacred an association of citizens becomes when the immortal gods are made members of it, either as judges or as witnesses? (*De legibus* 2.7.15–16).[53]

The notion of the utility of evoking *religiones* in the people appears frequently in Cicero's works, especially in his later works. Before he delivered his scathing attacks on divination, Cicero puts these words into the mouth of his own skeptical *persona*:

> I will begin with *haruspicina* which I judge should be cultivated *causa rei publicae communisque religionis* (*De divinatione* 2.12.28).[54]

In the first book of *De divinatione*, we are told that when Cicero was consul, the augur Appius Claudius Pulcher divined that civil war was at hand. According to "Quintus Cicero," the other senators (who did not give any credit to the divination of the augurs) laughed at him, and said that such predictions were *religiones* invented to influence the ignorant (*ad opinionem imperitorum esse fictas religiones*) (1.47.105). Cicero himself, famously, twice quoted the remark of the elder Cato: "'I wonder,' he said, 'that a *haruspex* doesn't laugh when he sees another *haruspex*.'" (*qui mirari se aiebat quod non rideret haruspex harus-picem cum vidisset* [*De divinatione* 2.24.51; *De natura deorum* 1.26.71].) Cicero's personal skepticism was not a crucial factor in this ideal governing system, in his new *religio*.

The exceptional men, the good men, the leaders, the aristocrats in spirit, like the pilot of a ship, would not and should not be bound by the same restrictions as others.[55] (Indeed, they operated—indeed were compelled to operate by their inner sonar and their most ancient and internalized *religiones*.) Cicero, leader and governor, needed freedom from the strictures and sanctions with which he would bind others. Let anxiety adhere to the fickle mob, the lawbreakers and rebels, to the *improbi*. As a professed Academic skeptic, the augur Cicero—like his skeptic and *pontifex* Cotta in *De natura deorum*, (like Plato,[56] Polybius,[57] Quintus Mucius Scaevola,[58] and Varro[59])—believed that the leader, like the point of a compass or the pilot of a plane, needed to be free; he should not be censored and disciplined, should not be restricted in the same way as the people. Indeed Cicero, in the last almost unbearably stressful years of his life, not so surprisingly, wanted *for himself* (not unlike Lucretius or Seneca in his later years) relief from fear: "The lives of good men," he declares wistfully, "are free from fear, care, anxiety, danger. In contrast, some *scrupus* always adheres to the spirit of the *improbus*" (*De republica* 3.16.26).[60]

At the same time that Cicero advocated his version of the "pious falsehood," he also warned his fellow aristocrats against revealing its existence:

> Those who have asserted that the entire notion of the immortal gods is a fiction invented by wise men in the interest of the state, to the end that *religio* might lead in the path of duty those whom reason could not, . . . do they not overturn *religio* from the bottom up? (*De natura deorum* 1.42.118).[61]

It is most important to point out that neither the ancient gods nor the ancient rites were at the center of Cicero's thought any more than they were the center of Varro's. As Ursula Heibges points out, Cicero otherwise paid very little attention to the gods and goddesses of the state cult.[62] Indeed, he would radically revise the pantheon. Away with *Febris* and *Mala Fortuna*! Let's hear it for *Salus* and *Honor*, *Victoria*, *Fors*! (*De legibus* 2.11.27 ff.)

Cicero's *religiones* were the means to the end of preserving the state, as the ancient *religiones* were the means to the end of preserving the family, the flocks and herds and fields. Varro, who also saw the cult as secondary to and subordinate to the *urbs*, began his discussion of *res divinae* with the pontiffs and augurs, and from there proceeded to temples, festivals, and rites. Only three of his sixteen books discussed the gods. (These latter books were the ones that Augustine, not surprisingly, found most compelling.[63])

The energy wasted in the strife and disunity produced by individuals and small groups pursuing their own aims and strategies needed to be subordinated to the greater *collective* goals and purposes as determined by the senate, its magistrates and priests. The wild and errant humans needed to be domesticated, their energies corralled and directed. Claiming a monopoly on the ability to predict and determine the future goals of human behavior was an extremely important way of focusing the attention of humans, of giving a meaning: a goal and purpose to their lives and deaths.[64]

Conclusions

Cicero's ideal world would not be one of calculated bargaining and deceit, a ninth-day market where every purchase was a test, a contest, and an ordeal. Nor would it be an exotic bazaar with a myriad of confusing options and possibilities. There would be no need for careful weighing, tricking, manipulating. The rules would be set and streamlined, authorized by the highest powers, policed by priestly/magisterial edicts and enforced by the threat of eternal punishments. The active and willful behaviors of the ancient *religiones* would be strictly limited. What Cicero was struggling toward is to make all good citizens purchase their well-being at one Big Store where both the stock and the prices were fixed from above. For Cicero, this vision of *religio* was the necessary means to the end of social order.

Consciously or unconsciously, Cicero—like Varro and Nigidius Figulus—was preparing the way for the imperial divine king. Momigliano makes the point that Varro dedicated his *Antiquitates rerum divinarum* to Caesar and asserts that Cicero and Varro and Nigidius Figulus wrote "their most important work on *religio*" when they were at peace with Caesar. According to Suetonius, it was the same Nigidius Figulus who prophesied to the father of the future Augustus that his son would rule the world (*Augustus* 94).[65]

The abstraction of the source of fear and anxiety into a god and/or or a divinized king, allowed for the creation of a strong hierarchical system.[66] After Cicero, the god-king would serve as the one to whom one *could* surrender, and who would supply the simplified focus and enforce the discipline and order necessary to have "truth" and security. Firm, fixed, unwavering faith/fidelity could *not* come without there being a person or power or body of law to whom one surrendered;[67] one *needed* a dangerous disciplinarian to whom one totally submitted for the psychological strategy to work.[68]

It was Cicero's assertion of the right of a limited group within the Republic to define "the sacred" that caused *religio* to be made into a particular and separate sphere of life. Only if one accepts that there are those who are authorized to limit and define the sphere of "the sacred" could there ever be some sphere of the "nonsacred," some "secular" or "political" sphere. That there are historians who accept such a distinction is evidence for the success of Cicero's endeavor.

Why, finally, did Cicero choose the word *religio* for the whole of his disciplinary system? *Religio* was not a word that had had any traditional or formal cultic function. Indeed, there was no word in Latin that came even close to the Platonic/Ciceronian conception. Indeed, there was no word . . . *sacrificia, caerimoniae* have few of the emotional or disciplinary connotations he wished his concept to embrace. But perhaps it was exactly the lack of sacralization, of fixing and defining of the word *religio*, that may have allowed Cicero to coax it in a new direction. Perhaps *religio* seemed to him the most likely candidate for the new meanings that he was to give it because it had always been, throughout its history, associated with (1) *observatio*, mental focus and attention to bonds and boundaries; (2) the restraining emotions of inhibition and fear; and (3) the observation of "taboos" through ritualized and regulated behaviors.

PART II

Case Study: Tertullian

THREE

Preface to Tertullian

In the large body of the surviving works of the African Christian Tertullian [ca. 160 C.E.–ca. 220 C.E.], the first major Latin Christian writer, the language of the ancient Romans went through many changes. In reading slowly through these works, I sought to discover whether and how and why the Latin word *religio* changed its contexts and purposes. What I discovered, which I will try to articulate in the following chapters, was that Tertullian preserved many of the ancient meanings of *religio*, eliminated many others, and pressed the word to serve new functions with new companions along several trajectories that will lead, in the third, and particularly the fourth century, to resemble (some of) our notions of "religion."

I found, in addition, other deeper and more profound continuities that concerned the functioning, in Tertullian's thought, of the emotions of fear and the ways in which that fear might serve to harness, focus, and direct the attention and energies of Tertullian and his fellow Christians. In particular, I found that Tertullian advocated, in most instances (although, as I will explain, not all) a greatly heightened and intensified fear, a riveting fear, a terror that would both render one helpless and fasten the attention of Tertullian and his fellow Christian soldiers on a set of (thereby) highly sacralized bonds and obligations to the greatest power, the greatest help of which he could conceive—his King of Kings, his god. He was learning how to adjust to, to conceive of an empire.

Human beings have devised a large but limited spectrum of adaptations to the conditions created by densely populated, highly complex hierarchical cultures with elaborate divisions of labor. Caught in these tightly woven cultural nets of armies and states and empires, there is no person or group that does not have to weigh endlessly, sometimes exhaustively, often discordant desires and needs against the advantages, demands, and strictures of the powers and institutions that affect their ability to care for themselves, their families, possessions, and traditions, and that could enhance or destroy their honor and well-being. Every person and group has to decide whether and how to flee, to fight, to negotiate, or to submit. The radiated circumspection, diversified skills, and relative self-sufficiency of the hunter or farmer or pastoralist must be replaced with the focused attention and disciplined expertise of the dependent urban dweller. The problem of adaptation to a hierarchically structured society was particularly acute when the Powers That Be were perceived as unpredictable, terrible, and terrifying; it could be intensified to the point of anguish, when one perceived oneself or one's group as impossibly outmatched, the game rigged, the dice loaded.

The Roman Seneca [4 B.C.E.–65 C.E.], living in acute insecurity in the early Empire, imagined the array of strategies deployed by the captive Andromache in her battle of will and wits against the might of the victorious Achaean kings in her attempt to save the life of her child Astyanax.[1] The African Apuleius [ca. 125 C.E.–ca. 180 C.E.] depicted all the tactics employed by the pathetically poor market gardener struggling alone against the Roman centurion who requisitioned his ass, trying in every way he could think of to keep possession of the animal upon which his meager living depended.[2] Seneca's mother and Apuleius' market gardener tried feigning ignorance, hiding, deceiving, persuading, cajoling, flattering, shaming, cursing, supplicating, submitting, violently rebelling, and fleeing. Both of these acutely self-conscious authors, not tormented by the hobgoblin of consistency, added to the array of strategies in their repertoire the "strategy to end all strategies": that is, total and willing submission to and collaboration with the Powers That Be.[3]

Tertullian (sometimes) rejected the patterns of thought and behavior expressed in the ancient Roman *religiones*; he was usually impatient of the nervous mental, emotional, and behavioral strategies whose aim was the preservation and protection of the life and well-being of self and family. Mundane existence and family and possessions were found wanting when weighed in the balance against his personal integrity, his personal majesty, his personal god. Nevertheless, the endless transgressions and inhibitions, balancings and bargainings, deceits, manipulations, and compromises of the ancient Roman *religiones* are reflected in the writing of the skilled and crafty rhetorician—particularly in his "apologetic" or "negotiatory" mode. But words were often, for Tertullian the rhetor, a sort of banquet of abstemiousness, a xerophagy: Words were, at best, the fuel of his fasts. His desire for existence absolute could be impeded only by words. He seemed to be set on the road to self-annihilation, to "martyrdom"; but unlike Lucan, Thomas More, or Yukio Mishima—all of whom were torn between collaboration and resistance—the conflicted Tertullian, for all we know, died in bed, vainly or maliciously nursed by his undoubtedly long-suffering wife.

I will be distinguishing two frameworks of Tertullian's thought, but they will not be the "orthodox" versus the "heretical" (or "Montanist"). It is inaccurate and anachronistic to think of him as rebelling against "The Church." Unlike Cyprian in the third century, Tertullian was not much interested in authorizing an institutional *ecclesia*.[4] An abstract *ecclesia* played a part in Tertullian's thought as the imaginary, transcendent, and longed for unity and harmony of Christians,[5] but *mater ecclesia* never had the authority or disciplinary weight given to the *spiritus sanctus* (the *Paracletus*), the initiatory oath (*sacramentum*), the *scriptura*, or the *apostoli*—in that order.[6] The *haeretici* were those who subverted and destroyed the harmony. Despite his deep affection for the word *hairesis*, Tertullian did not have a word for "orthodoxy."[7] *Veritas* was the word that came closest to Tertullian's notion of correct teaching or doctrine—and *veritas* was something Tertullian had direct and independent access to (through the help of the *spiritus sanctus*). Tertullian was able to recognize, to apprehend *veritas* when he saw or heard it, just as he did *hairesis*. At the same time, Tertullian continually weighed and assessed all possible sources of influence and authority: temporal precedence, tradition, innovation, *ekstasis*, *natura*, the respect due to *confessores*, *ordines*, and *prophetae*—strategically marshaling sources of *veritas* differently in the service of each of his myriad arguments. When he moved in the direction of the New Prophecy, it was never as a rebel against "the Church" but against the *diabolus* and the *imperator* and those who aided and abetted them (the *infideles*, both Christian and non-Christian).

The broadest distinctions I will be making in the thought of Tertullian are between (1) those passages and works in which Tertullian revealed his willingness to accommodate the existing *saeculum* with its power structures; and (2) those passages and works where accommodation, collaboration was adjudged traitorous and demoralizing, and where being a Christian became, for Tertullian, a fight to death against the Roman world.[8] The first of these modes—the "negotiatory mode"—is perhaps the most familiar, largely owing to the great fame of the *Apologeticum*. The psychologically and emotionally complex, flexible, and inconsistent strategies of thought deployed by Tertullian in his negotiatory modes (like those of Lucan and Josephus and More and Mishima) were similar to those expressed in the ancient systems of the Roman *religiones*. These conciliatory strategies, however, played a relatively minor role in the totality of the surviving writings of Tertullian. In his "segregationist" or "insurrectionary" moods, the complex thought patterns of his more compliant moods were rejected for simpler and more static principles that resemble the sometimes fixed and god-centered *religio* of Cicero.

Some of Tertullian's ideas are, I think, so overly familiar to modern Westerners that his strangeness, his particularity—and his Romanness—can be obscured. It is as if the listener were to start singing, "He wants his shirt, he wants his shirt . . ." at the first notes of Bizet's "Habanera," or "Hot diggity, dog diggity, boom! what you do to me!" at the first notes of Chabrier's "España."[9] The listener has the simplest version so ready at hand that the more interesting complexities of the music are all but blocked from perception.) Our work is to make Tertullian's thought patterns once again a bit difficult and unfamiliar— a bit more Roman, I hope, by shining a light from an odd angle to throw into relief some dimensions of a subject that might otherwise be difficult to see.

A Few Words on Tertullian's Religio

My goal in the chapters on Tertullian is to demonstrate a way of analyzing and discussing his thought that is not reliant on or limited to notions of "religion" (or that distinguish such a field from "politics" or "economics," etc.). I will highlight the spaces occupied by *religio* in the often tortured and tumbled landscape of Tertullian's thought alongside of his ideas of *timor* and *metus*, *disciplina* and *fides*, *constantia*, *patientia*, *conscientia*, *misericordia*, and *compassio*. With regard to *religio*, I hope to demonstrate first that Latin *religio* played a minor and relatively unself-conscious role in Tertullian's thought (when compared, for instance, with *disciplina* and *fides*); and second, that *religio* was given an array of particular roles in Tertullian, some of them consonant with ancient Latin usage but with some notable shifts.

It is possible to trace, in the extant works of the first major Latin Christian author and in the other surviving early Latin Christian texts, the beginnings of two basic trajectories of development of the notion of *religio* that will continue to evolve in the following millennia. In one trajectory—the negotiatory or "apologetic" trajectory, in which the Christian *must* serve at least two masters[10]—*religio* comes to be conceived of as occupying a separate and distinct (or rather, as will be shown, "distinctly nebulous") sphere coordinate to or subordinate to the Roman imperial government; in this trajectory, *religio* is some subordinate but indigestible aspect of the Roman Imperial social body.[11] In the other trajectory—that of the separatist or segregationist, in which the Christian Tertullian refuses to serve two masters—*religio is* used, on the Platonic/Ciceronian model, to describe a monarchical and hierarchical governing system in its totality, whose system has at its summit a single god/king competing with the Roman Emperor.

The notion of *religio* as a separate sphere or dimension of life compatible with and capable of surviving under the umbrella of the Roman imperial government made its appearance in Tertullian's negotiatory writings; it was in this context that *religio* was pressed into use to translate Greek *thrēskeia*, linking it closely to god-centered cultic behaviors. The Ciceronian/Platonic notion of *religio* as a comprehensive and hierarchical government headed by a god-king, structured by fixed laws and reinforced by heaven and hell will play an important role in Tertullian's separatist, segregationist mode. Neither of these trajectories have completed their arch in Tertullian. The meanings of *religio* in Tertullian are still very unsettled.

Among the ancient meanings and connotations of Latin *religio* retained by Tertullian are: (1) those relating to the array of emotions of fear and inhibition, respect and veneration; and (2) those relating to the notion of scrupulous attention, restraint, hesitation, and continence evoked by the emotions of fear and inhibition.

But even while Tertullian used *religio* in *some* of its ancient Latin senses, there were important differences. Tertullian was not comfortable with the ancient Roman systems of reciprocal complementarities and paradoxes that appeared in so many important Latin concepts, and this discomfort affected his use of many ancient Latin words.[12] In Tertullian's mind, human attempts at controlling, at governing themselves and their worlds, at securing health (*salus*) by their own efforts must, necessarily, come to nothing. The sensitive balancing and bargaining systems of the semi-autonomous farmer and pastoralist, expressed in the Roman *religiones* and in the whole of the sacrificial system, illustrated for Tertullian a battle of wits and wills that the human could only lose. All Tertullian's linguistic expertise and skill was not enough. He needed a supremely powerful and dangerous patron and master in whose devoted service he would rise to supremacy. He needed to link gears with the greatest powers of the universe. He was willing to be the slave, but only the slave of the greatest of kings. And so he accepted (as had many of the educated in the Roman world) an ideal of a unitary, univocal monarchical government of the world; this was necessarily a dichotomous vision of the world.[13] He privileged the One against the Many. As a result, he was ill at ease with the elaborate complementarities of ancient Roman thought (and the sacrificial system) and also with the ancient balancing of conceptions within *religio* (accursed and salvific, transgression and inhibition, guilt and reverence). And so, like many modern translators of paradoxical Latin words (*religio, sacer, fides, conscientia*, etc.), Tertullian deprived those words of their multidimensional depth and interest. He tended to limit *religio* to positive notions, especially to veneration of, scrupulous observance of, and attachment to particular authorities, especially to his divine *imperator*.

One finds in Tertullian a sort of apocalyptic utopianism. Tertullian had been trained to persuade and negotiate, but he knew that could take him only so far; to turn slavery into freedom, the incapacitation and miniaturization of the human into glory, he would need to go to the tipping point, the point of inversion. To effect this miracle, Tertullian needed, like many of the urban educated of the Empire (not to mention modern academics), to create a mental physics independent of the often intractable world outside his head. To do this, he had to begin where he wanted his chains of cause and effect to end: with abstractions like *veritas, ratio, natura, deus* that were—emphatically—not inductively derived, not distilled from his own attention to, recognition of, or observations of the particulars of the world. He did not want to be a farmer. He wanted to be a king.

Segregated by a Perfect Fear

> This is the main reason why the people of Maui worshipped sharks—in order to
> be saved from being eaten by a shark when they went fishing. The worship of
> some sharks makes it possible to reverse their value. Instead of devouring those
> who worship them, they protect them against ordinary sharks. Instead of
> stealing fish from such men, "the *akua mano* [shark gods] would lead fishes right
> to them."
>
> —SAMUEL KAMAKAU[1]

> The primary form of social control is the manipulation of sentiments. The most
> powerful sentiment is fear.
>
> —VALERIO VALERI[2]

If tension, anxiety, hesitation, and inhibition were the motive forces of the ancient Roman *religiones*, a greatly intensified, focused, and sacralized fear is central to understanding Tertullian's strategies of thought in his separatist or segregationist mode. "Fear," Tertullian says, "is the foundation of salvation." (*Timor fundamentum salutis est* [*De cultu feminarum* 2.2.2].) Like the light of the sun captured and concentrated by a pinhole lens, Tertullian's *timor*, his *metus*, sufficiently focused and intensified, turned the world upside down producing the cauterizing fire through which the Christian passed to the looking-glass world of power and love.

Tertullian was acquainted with fear. In the *Scorpiace*, he conjures up the paralyzing horror experienced by the man or woman forced to an unwilling death:

> Immediately all the former senses become dull, the blood of the mind turns to ice, the
> spirit fades away from the flesh. . . . Now the mind seeks for itself a place where it might
> vomit; and so the weakness, once it has smitten, breathes out wounded *fides* (*sauciatam
> fidem*)[3] either in heresy or in *saeculum* (1.10).[4]

This description of nauseating fear is not far from that formulated by the "soul-killing" Epicurean,[5] the Roman Lucretius, writing in the civil war period:

> Truly, when the intelligence is deeply moved by vehement fear, we see that, throughout
> the limbs, the whole spirit shares in the feeling; hence sweatings and pallor arise over the
> whole body, the speech falters, the voice dies away, blackness comes before the eyes, a

ringing in the ears, and the limbs give way beneath. In a word, we often see men fall to the ground for mental terror (*De rerum natura* 3.152–158).[6]

Tertullian shared Lucretius' dread of the confusion, doubt, nausea, and paralysis caused by fear.[7] But the two men formulated very different solutions to the problem of the heightened and crippling fear evoked by a world that had become unconditionally hostile, unnavigable. Both were urban and urbane denizens of the vast Roman Empire, and so devised strategies of adjustment very different from the "taboos" and *religiones* of semi-autonomous foragers and farmers in their huts and villages. Lucretius wanted to assuage the fear, while Tertullian wanted to concentrate and intensify it. While Lucretius (like Horace,[8] Petronius,[9] and Tertullian's arch-foe Marcion) took comfort in abandoning all hope of controlling the indifferent and perilous forces of the universe, Tertullian (like Cicero, Lucan, the Roman Stoics, and love poets) determined to make a ferocious effort to construct a world in which he could feel dynamic and fearless. He would build a fortress in a prison.[10]

Pushing the World to the Tipping Point

> Once, in the course of general conversation someone quoted the line: "When I am dead, may fire consume the earth." But Nero said that the first part of the line should read: "While I yet live. . . ."
>
> Suetonius, *Nero* 38[11]

In one of few relatively unguarded moments, Tertullian declared himself "a most miserable man, ever sick with the red tempests of impatience" (*Miserrimus ego semper aeger coloribus inpatientiae* [*De patientia* 1.4].) In that same treatise, he declared that he could endure his suffering were the world destroyed: "Let the whole world perish, so long as I can make patience my gain!" (*Totum licet saeculum pereat dum patientia lucrifaciam!* [7.8].) But until the world perished, until that final and much anticipated overturning of everything, Tertullian suffered from a corrosive impatience, a yearning and desire so extreme as to be explosive. While the world existed, Tertullian, like his evil twin, the "Prince of the World,"[12] suffered from frustrated desire, envy, and malice—what Albert Camus (after Max Scheler) called "the evil secretion in a closed vessel of prolonged impotence."[13] Tertullian was as angry as his god, as frustrated as the devil, as impotent as an emperor. He did not want the equilibrations of the ancient *religiones*; he would push his desires to the tipping point so that the order of the world might invert, that the ship of state might capsize, that the last might be first. When Tertullian wanted to topple the world, the sensitive balancing systems of the Roman *religiones* served no purpose.

No Step Backward

> The City of God utterly denounces doubt as madness. (. . .) We walk without hesitation.
>
> Augustine, *De civitate dei* 19.18[14]

The Roman proconsul Saturninus, in his interrogation of the Scillitan Christians in 180 C.E., urged them to be cautious and to deliberate (*Numquid ad deliberandum spatium vultis?*). The Christian Speratus replied: "In a cause so just there is no deliberation" (*Passio Sanctorum Scillitanorum* 10).[15] Caecilius, the spokesman for the non-Christians in Minucius' *Octavius*, advocated the maintenance of doubt and hesitation:

> To my mind things that are doubtful, as they are, should be left in doubt, and where so many and such great minds differ, rash and hasty votes should not be cast on either side for fear of introducing the *superstitio* of old women, or of destroying all *religio* (13.5).[16]

To preserve *religio* and avoid *anilis superstitio*, Caecilius advised the preservation of a cautious doubt. But the Christian Octavius derided the wavering hesitation of Caecilius. Caecilius was like a lost man who did not know the right road: If he knew the path, he would go straight on without doubt or hesitation.

Tertullian, like Minucius and Speratus, did not want his energies arrested with doubt. The calculated and careful measures of the ancient *religiones* were (as I will try to show in Chapter 5) not unknown to Tertullian, but they could not weather the tempests of his impatience. He rejected, finally, vacillation; he did not want to be ever poised and trembling on the edge.[17] In this aspect of Tertullian's thought, all movement, all energy was to be directed at a final reckoning—simple, settled, supreme.

> We say that the judgment of God must be believed, first of all, to be plenary, then absolute, so as to be final, and therefore irrevocable (*De resurrectione carnis* 14.10).[18]

The ultimate goal of thinking and speaking was, for Tertullian, to get past thought and words. "Seek and you shall find" (*Quaerite et invenietis*) was, for Tertullian, an unacceptable—indeed, a heretical—statement.[19] "There is no need of *curiositas* after Christ Jesus, no inquisition after the gospel! When we believe (*credimus*) we have no need to believe anything further. When we believe in this to begin with, there is nothing additional we should believe" (*De praescriptione haereticorum* 7.12–13).[20] The "*veritatis integritas . . .* never changes its decision, never wavers in its judgment. What is truly good cannot be anything but good; nor what is evil anything but evil. All things are fixed within God's truth (*veritatem dei*)" (*De spectaculis* 20).[21] Tertullian condemned the Marcionite practice of burdening their arguments against the resurrection of the body with "scruples" (*scrupuli*) (*De resurrectione carnis* 2.9). Elsewhere, he condemns the over-nice, the "persnickety" person (*De virginibus velandis* 11).

The fury of Tertullian's hopes and expectations would, with the blasting power of a rocket engine, hurtle him beyond the barrier of words and thought, beyond the abrading gravity of doubt. He would be pitched by his surpassing fervor to a consummate and perfect power in a new kingdom ruled by his good twin, his *deus* whom he projected into the sky like a Brocken specter.[22] Tertullian hoped to feel, as a human being, the kind of complete and certain power that he imagined that someone, somewhere must have, power that had somehow escaped him or been stolen from him—and that, with a cosmic revolution, would fall again to him, its rightful possessor. In his angriest ruminations, far from blessing the Romans for postponing the Day of Destruction,[23] Tertullian gleefully awaited the conflagration that would burn the spectacle of the Roman *saeculum* like a circus tent coated with paraffin and white gasoline.

To turn his nervous hybridity into a righteous and rigorous purity, Tertullian needed to disentangle himself from the seductive embrace of the emasculating harlot dressed in scarlet and gold who presided over the seven mountains and many waters (*De cultu feminarum* 2.12.2). To fortify and so purify himself for his triumphal entry into the city that *his* god built upon a mountain (ibid. 2.13.1), he would have to do the impossible: extract himself not only from the Roman *saeculum* but from the modes of speech and action that he had learned to employ in negotiating with her. But, as Peter Berger and Thomas Luckman remark in describing the enthusiastic "convert": "[T]o forget completely is notoriously difficult."[24] Even while his complex and cosmopolitan education informed every sentence he wrote, I believe that Tertullian, like Apuleius' Lucius, came to experience his very survival skills, the panoply of his mind and his tongue, as impediments that could be overcome only in the absolute, ultimate, and altered state in which all paradoxes are resolved.[25] Only when possessed by the Spiritus Sanctus could the conflicts of his world and his person dissappear.

Shameless Christians

> No [Christian] is ashamed, none feels regret. (. . .) What sort of evil can it be that has none of the natural marks of evil: fear, shame, hesitations, regrets, lamentation?
>
> Tertullian, *Apologeticum* 1.12–13[26]

The inhibiting emotions of the ancient Romans' *religiones* had operated hand in hand with the inhibiting emotions of *pudor*, the Roman sense of shame, an acute sensitivity to and respect for the eyes and opinions of others.[27] But, Tertullian's Christians *could not be shamed* by the eyes of non-Christians.

> By now even the common people know the name of Christ, taking him to be some man (as the Jews also thought), so that it is easy for anybody to think of us as worshippers of a man (*hominis cultores*). But we do not blush for Christ, since it delights us to be reckoned under, and to be condemned under his name. . . . (*Apologeticum* 21.2).[28]

> "If you are exposed to public infamy," he says,[29] "it is for your good," for he who is not exposed to dishonor among men is sure to be so before the Lord. Do not be ashamed; righteousness brings you forth into the public gaze. Why should you be ashamed of gaining glory? (*De fuga* 9.3).[30]

The Christian Athenagoras [late–second century c.e.] asserted that Christians despised the insults leveled at them by non-Christians (*Legatio* 1.4).[31] Minucius Felix declared that the accused Christian did not blush or fear (*Christianus reus nec erubesceret nec timeret* [*Octavius* 28.2, cf. 6–7]).[32] Cyprian will ask, "How can he be one with Christ who either blushes or fears to belong to Christ?" (*Quomodo potest esse cum Christo qui ad Christum pertinere aut erubescit aut metuit?* [*De lapsis* 28].)

In one of the most famous (and famously misquoted) passages of Tertullian (*De carne Christi* 5.4), in the midst of a long dissertation aimed at Marcion—who rejected the idea of Christ suffering the physical indignities of being born and dying (not to mention, being crucified) as a human being[33]—Tertullian declared himself contemptuous of shame (*contemptus ruboris*). Inverting the definitions of *stultitia* and *sapientia*, as Paul had before him,[34] Tertullian declares:

> The son of God was crucified; I am not ashamed—because one *ought* to be ashamed of it. And the son of God died; it is credible because it is *ineptus* (stupid, silly, awkward). And having been buried he rose again; it is certain because impossible.

> *Crucifixus est dei filius; non pudet, quia pudendum est. Et mortuus est dei filius; credibile est quia ineptum. Et sepultus resurrexit; certum est quia impossibile* (*De carne Christi* 5.4).

The emphasis here, for Tertullian, was twofold. First, if the most important axioms of his thought could not be approached by any of the postulates of common sense, he was not dismayed or embarrassed.[35] There were convictions (such as the resurrection of the body) that Tertullian could not reach by any path of reasoning or common consent, and of which he refused to feel shame.[36] (What he could not reach by limping, he would reach by flying.) Second, although there were those who thought it shameful to sacralize a man who had been publically executed, Tertullian was not ashamed.[37]

While in republican Latin, *pudor* and *religio* were closely related and embraced the whole spectrum of honor and shame, Tertullian often opposed *pudendus* to *religiosus*. Marcion had made everything to do with human procreation and birth shameful and unworthy of a god,[38] but what was *pudendus* for this "heretic" was *religiosus* for Tertullian:

> You [Marcion] inveigh now . . . against the *pudor* itself of a woman in travail, which, however, ought to be honored (*honorandum*) in consideration of her peril, or considered *religiosum* in respect of nature.

> *Invehere iam et in ipsum mulieris enitentis pudorem, vel pro periculo honorandum, vel pro natura religiosum* (*De carne Christi* 4.1).

In overturning his own consternation at the human condition, Tertullian was willing to upset the values of the larger Mediterranean world in which he lived.[39] It was the Romans and other devils who were liable to blush. The Romans, he asserted, prayed with their heads covered because they felt ashamed; Tertullian's Christians did not feel shame and so prayed with their heads uncovered:

> Looking up to heaven with hands outspread, the Christians, because innocent, pray with head bared because we do not blush. . . . (*Apologeticum* 30.4).[40]

The rejection of *pudor*, the most ancient and important governing emotion, was also the rejection of the greatest source of anxiety. While even the Epicureans, according to Plutarch, continued to attend communal rituals out of "fear of the many" (*dia phobon tōn pollōn*),[41] Tertullian, like Cyprian, and many Christians, imitating the Cynics, made it a "point of honor" to be shameless before the eyes of non-Christians.[42] Tertullian had climbed so far up the ladder of humility that he could easily look down his nose at his enemies and detractors. Like Seneca's captive Astyanax who met the fatal malice of the Achaean conquerors with a bold and ferocious face,[43] the Christian Perpetua refused to lower her eyes in shame at her entrance into the arena, and instead, stared down the crowd of spectators with the fierceness of her gaze, *vigore oculorum deiciens omnium conspectum* (*Passio Perpetuae* 18).[44]

Tertullian chastised persons reluctant to undergo the humiliations of confession and supplication (*exomologesis*) for putting their sense of shame (*pudor*) before their salvation (*salus*) (*De paenitentia* 10.1). These abasements, embraced and carried to extremes, would invert to glory:

> He who is not exposed to dishonor among men is sure to be so before the Lord. Do not be ashamed; righteousness brings you forth into the public gaze. Why should you be ashamed of gaining glory?[45]

After three weeks of a semi-fast, the humiliation and xerophagy of the Daniel of scriptures is rewarded with prophetic inspiration:

> An angel was sent out (from God) addressing him in this way: "Daniel you are a pitiable man (*homo miserabilis*); fear not, since, from the first day on which you gave your soul to recognition and to humiliation before God, your word has been heard, and I am entered in your word." [4] Thus the pitiableness and the humiliation of xerophagies expel fear and attract the ears of God, and put men in control of secrets (*De ieiunio* 9.3).[46]

While in his more conciliatory moods, "turning the other cheek" could be used to affirm the harmless docility of Christians,[47] the same behavior could, in Tertullian's fiercer moods, express the Christian's refusal to be shamed.[48] Here is Tertullian's version of what psychologists call the "snub gambit":

> Every injury, whether inflicted by tongue or hand, while it aims at offending patience, will be cancelled out (*dispungetur*) with the same outcome as a weapon launched against and blunted on a rock of the most steadfast hardness. For it will fall to the ground then and with vain and fruitless labor; and sometimes it will recoil and spend its rage with retorted impetus on him who sent it out. No doubt the reason why anyone hurts you is so that you might feel pain; therefore, when you avert the fruits of his actions by not being pained, he himself must feel pain at the loss of his enjoyment. Then you not only go away unhurt (which alone is satisfaction for you), but gratified, into the bargain, by your adversary's frustration, and revenged by his pain (*De patientia* 8.7–9).[49]

It was not that the Christians had no shame in their eyes, but they refused to see themselves in the eyes of non-Christians.[50] According to Minucius Felix, Christians reserved their *pudor* for one another (*Octavius* 37.11, 38.2). Tertullian's version of The Golden Rule was that one must love those similar or near to oneself "as oneself" (*diliges proximum tibi tamquam te ipsum* [*Adversus Iudaeos* 2.3]).[51] The version of the Pseudo-Cyprianic *De centesima, sexagesima, tricesima* was "to love the *dominus* with all your heart and those *like you* as yourself" (*amare Dominum ex omnibus praecordiis tuis et similem tibi quasi te ipsum* [58.10–13]).[52] For Tertullian the rigorist, there could be only bad Samaritans.

Selective shamelessness required erecting strong fortifications between oneself and "The Other," refusing to see oneself in others' eyes, refusing to recognize him or her as a being like oneself. There are moments when Tertullian cannot abide even being tolerated by the non-Christian:

> Let us suppose that a man is found who tolerates *nostra* without complaint. Right here, then, there is a fault (*delictum*) in that the *gentiles* come to know *nostra*; we are in the consciousness (*conscientia*) of the "unjust," and it is only through their kindness that we are allowed to do our duty (*Ad uxorem* 2.5.1; cf. 2.6).[53]

> Would that we did not have to live in the same world with them! (*Utinam ne in saeculo quidem simul cum illis moraremur* [*De spectaculis* 15].)

In the essay addressed to his wife, Tertullian prefers secrecy and segregation even to tolerance; tolerance would compel the Christian to be indebted to non-Christians—and to fear the loss of that acceptance. The devil was working through the Roman authorities and trying, by offers of inclusion, to "overthrow our *constantia*" (*Apologeticum* 27.3). Toleration—indeed, any offer of *salus* by the Romans—should be met with the brazen-face of *obstinatio*. Let Christianity be a secret *mysterium* (*Ad nationes* 1.7.13).

The lines between Christians and non-Christians needed to be more firmly drawn when The Other was in the immediate vicinity, when one dwelt in the same city with him or her, when one shared one's life with him or her.

> Who could doubt that *fides* (loyalty/commitment) is weakened every day by commerce with the infidel? (*Quis dubitet obliterari quotidie fidem commercio infideli?* [*Ad uxorem* 2.3.3].)[54]

> It is evident that *fideles* who enter into marriage with *gentiles* are guilty of *stuprum* and are to be kept away from any *communicatio fraternitatis*, in accordance with the letter of the Apostle who says that with such a one we must not even consume food (*Ad uxorem* 2.3.1).[55]

The Romans of the Republic had not, as a rule, hated their enemies until the period of the civil wars. When they began treating their enemies with shamelessness, it was, of course, their fellow Romans whom they "bestialized."[56] Demonization (or what Berger and Luckman call "nihilation"[57]) of non-Christians and other heretical Christians reaches grotesque levels in Tertullian and Cyprian and Tatian.[58]

Rejection of Compassion

> If God were not so full of compassion there would have been compassion in the world not just in him.
>
>   Yehudah Amichai[59]

It is as a lost and degraded ass that Apuleius' Lucius revealed the sorrows and sufferings of his fellow two-footed and four-footed creatures. The conversion of Lucius seemed as effective as that of Augustine in saving him from the burden of compassion and creature-liness. Similarly, Tertullian's desire to emerge from the mess of his Romanness pushed him toward stripping himself of empathy. The notions of *misericordia* and *compassio* play as restricted a role for Tertullian as they do for Perpetua, the strength of whose will and com-mitment was demonstrated by her rejection of both her tormented father and her infant child.[60] Tertullian fumed against the less rigorous Christians, the *psychici*, who gave too easy absolution to those who had committed sexual transgressions. No amount of suffer-ing, even if it moved other Christians to tears, should result in the reintegration of the infidel into the group. In an odd and interesting passage of the *De pudicitia*, he argued that it was not the place of the Christian to grant absolution to those who committed inexpi-able crimes, such as adultery, fornication, marriage outside the *ecclesia*, or remarriage. Let the unforgiven penitent, by his hopeless misery, serve as a negative example to other Chris-tians. It should be left to God to be merciful even if the suffering of the excommunicated might incite *compassio*.[61]

> He stands before her doors, and by the example of his stigma admonishes the others, and at the same time calls out for himself his brother's tears, and returns having negotiated something more than communion (*communicatio*)—that is, *compassio* (3.5).

The intransigence of the *fratres* would, ultimately, constitute a greater gift to the sinner than readmission into the community. The tears of the *fratres* might help to elicit God's mercy—but only after the criminal's death:

The fetters of common humanity needed to be overcome. While Tertullian seems to have coined the word *compassio* ("suffering with"), he did not greatly value "suffering with."[62] The clearest and least-problematical use that Tertullian makes of the notion comes in *De carnis resurrectione* where he speaks positively of the shared sufferings of spirit and flesh with one another and with Christ (40.12–14). But in that same treatise, Tertullian asserts that *compassio sententiae*, the common feeling that served as the basis of *communes sensus*, was to be contrasted with—and trumped by—the *ratio divina* (3.6).

Similarly, *pietas* in the sense of "pity" played a small role in Tertullian's thought. (Our English "pity" evolved from Latin *pietas*, the bonds of mutual obligation that bound parent and child being extended, in the imperial period, to include a general notion of the bonds binding together all humans.[63]) Tertullian commends Socrates, at the approach of death, for resisting the terrors evoked by the *lex pietatis* that bound him to wife and children:

> Even if it [Socrates' mind] was placid and tranquil, and remained inflexible lest it be moved, in this commotion, by the law of *pietas*, at the tears of his wife so soon to be his widow and at the sight of his thenceforward orphan children. His *constantia* must, however, have been shaken in his struggle against the disturbance of inconstancy around him (*De anima* 1.1).[64]

What *pietas* Tertullian sanctioned was, like the sense of shame, limited to other (ap-proved) Christians. Tertullian's "work of love" (*dilectionis operatio*) was the fund by which Christians helped care for orphans, widows, the poor, and those held in the mines, pris-ons and islands—"for the sake of God's sect" (*ex causa dei sectae*).[65]

"Look how they love one another (*se diligant*)!" the enemies of the Christians remark (*Apologeticum* 39.7). The amity that the Christians showed one another was often understood as a form of enmity to those outside the *ecclesia*. Non-Christians, Tertullian tells us, are indignant at Christians, calling one another *frater* (*Apologeticum* 39.8). (*Frater* must have sounded the way "comrade" did to many Americans during the period of the Cold War between the United States and Soviet Russia, or "brother" in the period of acute national racial tensions in the 1960s and 1970s.) Combined with their shameless spite for non-Christians, this solidarity caused non-Christians to experience the Christians as hateful.[66] The Scillitan "martyrs" had to defend themselves against the charges of cursing others ("We never cursed anyone but, rather, while suffering harm from others, we gave thanks" [*Numquam malediximus, sed male accepti gratias egimus*]).[67]

In Tertullian's apologetic or negotiatory moods, Christians love all men.[68] But in Tertullian's segregationist mode, there is no such love for humanity. Despite talk about *dilectio*, his list of enemies, like that in the Gospels, is a very long one. They include, but are not limited to, the *diaboli* and *daemones* and their wicked angels, the *aemuli* and *adversarii*, the *nationes* and *ethnici*, the *haeretici* (especially Marcionites and Valentinians), *antichristi*, *negatores*, and *desertores*, the *psychici*, *philosophi* (especially Epicureans and Cynics), the *poetae*, the *athletae*, the *profani*, *the vulgus*, the non-Christian *prophetae*, *haruspices*, *augures*, *mathematici*, *circulatores*, *Magi*, and frequently the *domestici*, *servi*, *feminae*, and other members of one's own family.[69] Despite assertions to the contrary, Tertullian's Christians were most certainly cursing (*maledicere*) and anathematizing their enemies—and one another—exactly like contemporary non-Christians.[70] In a *jeremiad* from *De spectaculis*, Tertullian does not try to hide his hate; he relishes the incineration of his enemies:

> What a spectacle is already at hand . . . that day which the *gentiles* never believed would come, that day they laughed at, when this old world and all its judgments would be consumed in one fire. How vast the spectacle that day! How wide! What sight shall wake my wonder, what my laughter, my joy, my exaltation?—as I see all those kings, those great kings, un-welcomed in heaven, along with Jove, along with those who told of their ascent, groaning in the depths of darkness! And the magistrates who persecuted the name of Jesus liquefying in fiercer flames than they kindled in their rage against Christians!—those sages too, *the philosophers blushing before their disciples* as they blaze together, the disciples whom they taught that god was concerned with nothing, that men have no souls at all, or that what souls they have shall never return to their former bodies! And, then, the poets *trembling* before the judgment seat—not of Rhadamanthus, not of Minos, but of Christ whom they never expected to see! And then there will be the tragic actors to be heard, more vocal in their own tragedy; and the players to be seen, lither of limb by far in the fire; and then the charioteer to watch, red all over in the wheel of flame; and next the athletes to be gazed upon, not in their gymnasiums but hurled in the fire. . . . What praetor, consul, quaestor, priest, will ever give you of his bounty such sights, such exultation? And yet all these, in some sort, are ours, pictured *per fidem spiritu imaginante*. . . . I believe things of greater joy than circus, theater, amphitheater, or any stadium (30).[71]

Stripping Off the Family

To turn from the fragility of a prey animal to the vigor and intense motivation of the predator required the rejection of the ancient Roman *religiones*. The ancient *religiones* functioned,
above all, to protect oneself, one's children, one's household and family, one's flocks and
herds and crops. The person encumbered with spouse and children would, however, in
Tertullians' view, be less able to meet the challenge of persecution; he would be less steadfast *in martyriis* (*De exhortatione castitatis* 12.3). Commitment to spouses and/or children
would be a disability on The Last Day (*Ad uxorem* 1.5.2–3; *De exhortatione castitatis* 9.5; *De
anima* 1.1).[72] The burial of a father took too long for *fides*. The death of a spouse was a sort
of *seisachtheia*, a shaking off of the heavy burden of mutual indebtedness.

> [You (the widower or widow) are the more powerful the more autonomous you are. Then
> it can be just you and your inner God:] "What if you come to feel that what we called a
> loss is a gain (*lucrum*)? For *continentia* will be a means to amass a great wealth of *sanctitas*.
> Being parsimonious to the flesh you will acquire spirit. For let us ponder over our *conscientia*
> itself, to see how different a man feels himself when he chances to be away from his wife.
> He savors spiritually. If he makes a prayer to the Lord, he is nearer heaven. If he is
> applying himself to the scriptures, he is wholly in them.[73] If he is singing a psalm he
> satisfies himself (*placet sibi*). If he is adjuring a demon, he is confident in himself (*confidit
> sibi*) (*De exhortatione castitatis* 10.1–2).[74]

Like Virgil, Seneca, and Epictetus, Tertullian understood that the greatest threat to
one's total commitment/surrender was one's love for spouse and children; attachments rendered you fearful and vulnerable. Anything and anyone you felt bound to could be and
would be lost; anything and anyone you felt responsible for would reveal your powerlessness. To forestall these terrors, Tertullian employs the logic so dear to Epictetus and the
Roman Stoics:

> Even what seems to be ours belongs to another; for nothing is ours, since all things are
> God's—to whom we ourselves also belong. (. . .) [G]rieving at the loss of what was not
> our own, we shall be detected as bordering on *cupiditas*. We are seeking for what is
> another's when we bear with difficulty losing what is another's. He who is disturbed with
> impatience of a loss, by giving things earthly precedence over things celestial, sins
> directly against God (*De patientia* 7.5–7).[75]

Because of his willingness to sacrifice his son, Abraham became, for Tertullian, the ex-
emplum of *fides* and the precept that *fides* should hold no pledges of affection dearer than
God (*ne qui pignora deo cariora haberet* [*De oratione* 8.3]). The lonely widower's desire to re-
marry was proof of the weakness of his *fides* (*Ad uxorem* 1.1–2). In the end, the most demonic
enemies were those found among one's family members and slaves. The apostles, Tertullian
asserts, were not betrayed by family members—but many of us have been (*Scorpiace* 9.4–5).

Not only family, but all means of livelihood must be expendable:

> If parents, wives and children have to be left on account of God (*propter deum*),—do you
> doubt this in the case of crafts, trades and professions—even [those engaged in] for the

sake of your children and parents? Already it was shown to us that *pignora* [literally, "hostages": i.e., husbands, wives and children, the guarantee of the public bond][76] and handicrafts and businesses are to be left behind *propter dominum* (*De idololatria* 12.3).[77]

When James and John were called by the *dominus*, they left behind both father and ship. Matthew was roused from the tollhouse (*de telonio*).[78] For Tertullian, bodily and emotional *necessitas carnis* was the enemy of the fidelity of the Christian. Forget about food. *Fides* did not fear hunger (*fides famem non timet* [*De idololatria* 12.3–4]).[79] *Propter deum*, the *fidelis* despised hunger.

Like the Stoicism of Cato the Younger, the Christian commitment admitted of no degrees:

> The *status fidei* admits no plea of necessity.[80] (. . .) Even if one is pressured to sacrifice and the denial [of one's commitment to Christ] by the direct necessity of torture or punishment . . . *disciplina* does not connive even at that necessity because there is a higher necessity to fear denying and to undergo martyrdom, rather than to escape from suffering and perform the [in this case, military] duties required. In fact, an excuse of this sort overturns the entire substance of our *sacramentum* (*substantia sacramenti*). . . . (*De corona* 11.6–7).[81]

All of Chapter 12 of *De idololatria* concerns the need to renounce attachment to anything, including life itself, that might lure one to set aside the baptismal oath of loyalty, to abjure all those things that are "dangers to the *fides*" (*fidei periculosa* [*Ad uxorem* 1.5.2; cf. 2.3]). Tertullian imagines the makers of idols and images protesting that they cannot be asked to abandon the trade by which they earn their ability to live. Tertullian replies:

> So [you claim], "you have to live." What have you to do with God, if you live according to your own laws? (*De idololatria* 5.1)[82]

The Christian, stripped of all encumbrances, like the Cynic or Tacitus' Fenni, needed nothing.[83] He was godlike in his autonomy. In his address to his wife is an elegant description of the Christian, who, trusting in the promises of his god, makes no provision for food or clothing, spouse or children. "Take it for granted that you will need nothing if you serve the *dominus*; indeed you have everything if you have the *dominus*" (*Ad uxorem* 1.4.8).[84]

Nothing to Lose

> The missing all prevented me from missing lesser things.
>
> Emily Dickinson[85]

As it was for Siddharta Gautama, Diogenes of Sinope, the Qumranites, John the Baptist, or Mohandas Ghandi, the setting apart and sacralization of Tertullian's Christian would not be by the usual method of setting apart and decorating up, but by setting apart and stripping down. Like the IRA prisoners in Long Kesh prison who in their Blanket Protest refused all clothing and comforts, self-sacralization was a sort of *via negativa*.[86] Enlistment in the *militia Christi* required that one first peel away and cast aside the enemy's signifiers of honor. Tertullian encouraged the *fratres* to cast away the titles, positions, honors, and ornaments of the Roman *saeculum*.[87] They should embrace the role of alien, eunuch, and slave, to take up the burden and ignominy of the cross. A great part of the appeal of the New Prophecy movement to the increasingly more rebellious Tertullian was its extreme ascetic rigor.[88]

> There are those who think that Christians, a race of men ever freed up for death, are trained in that *obstinatio* of theirs by the renunciation of pleasures, in order that they might find it easier to despise life, when once its tentacles, as it were, are amputated and they no longer crave what they have already emptied of meaning for themselves (*De spectaculis* 1).[89]

The Romans were accustomed to fight to the "confession" of their enemy; it was the bending of the will, the echoing, the repetition of the formula dictated by another that signaled submission and allowed for a *pax* to be imposed.[90] The Romans liked to distinguish the broken-spirited *confessio* of the defeated opponent from the defiant *professio*, but Tertullian willingly embraced the word *confessio*, as he did the cross, as an act of *sacralizing by inversion*.[91] At the same time, Tertullian's confession had less to do with *what* was confessed than the opportunity that such contumacious obstinacy provided the Christian to set himself or herself apart, to draw a line in the sand, to declare himself or herself a rebel, to provoke a contest of wills.

> Our triumph over them is never greater than when we are condemned on account of our faithful *obstinatio* (*Apologeticum* 27.7).[92]

There is a wonderful and justly famous scene in the *De corona* (ca. 208 C.E.). It is one of very few dramatic set pieces in Tertullian. I will be returning to this remarkable story (in Chapter 5, "Segregated by a Perfect Fear. The Terrible War Band of the Anti-Emperor"), where Tertullian imagined the Roman *imperatores* dispensing donatives to the honored soldiers, the *milites laureati*. A Christian soldier ostentatiously rejects the crown offered to him by his commander:[93]

> A certain one of the soldiers approached—one who was more of a soldier of God (*dei miles*), more constant than the rest of his [Christian] brothers (*constantior fratribus*)—who assumed that they could serve two masters—his head alone uncovered, the useless crown in his hand. And by this *disciplina* he was known as a Christian and he shone forth (1.1).[94]

This soldier of god, *constantior* than his Christian brothers (who had wrongly supposed that they could serve their god and the emperor), is mocked and abused by the other Roman soldiers, questioned by the tribune, and finally brought before a higher tribunal to be questioned by the prefects. It is there that he begins the rebel's self-sacralization by stripping down:

> The tribune at once put the question to him, "Why are you so different in your attire?" He asserted that he was not allowed [to wear the crown of victory given him by the Roman commander] with the rest. Being urgently asked for his reasons, he answered,

"I am a Christian." Oh soldier boasting in God! There was an outburst; . . . and the
offender was conducted to the prefects. At once he put away the heavy cloak, and his
"disburdening" commenced; he loosened from his foot the military shoe, beginning to
stand upon holy ground (*terrae sanctae insistere incipiens*). He gave up the sword, which was
not necessary, either, for the protection of our *dominus*; from his hand likewise dropped
the laurel crown; and now purple-clad with the hope of his own blood, shod with the
preparation of the *euangelium*, girt with the sharper word of God, completely equipped in
the apostle's armor, to be crowned more worthily with the shining white crown of
martyrdom, he awaits in prison the donative of Christ (1.2–3).[95]

It was the Christian Soldier's voluntarily and publically stripping himself of all those
marks of service to the Emperor that sacralized him, glorified him. There would be a second
crowning as a reward for the soldier's courage and constancy, but this crowning would be
by the "true" king in the new kingdom.[96]

Having rejected all the emotional and psychological bases of the government of *religio*
and *pudor*, what could take their places?

Discipline, Discipline, Discipline

Are we not also soldiers? Soldiers, indeed, subject to all the more strict *disciplina*, as we are
subject to so great an *imperator*?

   Non enim et nos milites sumus—eo quidem maioris disciplinae, quanto tanti imperatoris?

                              Tertullian, *De exhortatione castitatis* 12.1

In Tertullian's more rebellious mode, his model for Christian *fraternitas* is much more
the military than the philosophical schools or cultic associations. Every reader of Tertullian is aware of the overwhelmingly important role played in his thought by the notion
of *disciplina*. In his apologetic moods, *disciplina* is, above all, education: the behaviors and
doctrines inculcated by the Spiritus Sanctus through the inspired Christian teacher.[97] But
in his more rebellious moods, *disciplina* beats its martial rhythm. That drumbeat grew
louder and more insistent with the passage of time, allowing and informing the metaphors through which Tertullian conceived militant Christianity.

For Tertullian the rebel, *disciplina* and *religio* are often synonymous, and Tertullian's
superstitio (in contrast with ancient Latin *superstitio*) is not an excess of anything, but rather
an insufficiency of ascetic discipline.[98] While Tertullian often uses *religio* as a synonym
for *disciplina*, he was more apt to use *disciplina*—or *fides*—than *religio* in describing Christians
for the following reasons.[99]

First, many of the ancient meanings of Latin *religio* were incompatible with his notion
of the *obstinatio disciplinae* (*De spectaculis* 1). Latin *religio* still carried echoes of the flexible
responsive adjustments, the cunning intelligence and deceptions required by the kind of
life led by the relatively autonomous hunter, the farmer, the shepherd, the fisherman—or
the trader, *rhetor*—or leader.[100] The ancient *religiones* were basically the emotions and

behaviors of the prey animal: Tertullian wanted to feel the focused attention and energy of the predator.[101]

Second, Tertullian was aware that the ancient Roman *religiones* inhibited more than they directed or channeled action. There had been nothing teleological, nothing prophetic about Latin *religio*. The *religiones* that stopped one in one's tracks did not necessarily impel or direct subsequent action, whereas *disciplina* implied for Tertullian (as it did for the Romans) not only the restraining but also the focusing and channeling of one's energies, enabling one to act with will and force. "[D]*isciplina est . . . ce qui . . . s'oriente vers l'action, la pratique: règles, morales, attitude prescrite à l'égard de la vie." Disciplina "fait la force principale des armées"* (Henri-Irenée Marrou).[102] Tertullian's *Spiritus Sanctus* was the general who would augment and direct the energies of the Christians.

Third, Tertullian preferred to describe the Platonic/Ciceronian hierarchical-monarchical universe as *disciplina* on account of the word's martial overtones. Tertullian's *disciplina*, is, above all, the soldier's *disciplina*. An army could, and frequently did, unseat or supplant an emperor.

Finally, *religio* had been, for centuries in the Republic, a highly particularized response to circumstances; it could reflect a group or a very personal response to circumstances. What was a *religio* to one might or might not be experienced as a *religio* by another person. But Tertullian's Christian *disciplina* involved fixed and universal rules and regulations: Tertullian's Christianity had its *regula fidei*.[103] (Tertullian is often frustrated by what he thinks of as the lack of *disciplina* of the simple, uneducated Christians, the Christian *plebs*, who did not have a clear idea of what it means to be a Christian and needed to be instructed by the *spiritus sanctus* through him.[104])

FIVE

Segregated by a Perfect Fear. The Terrible War Band
of the Anti-Emperor: The *Coniuratio* and the *Sacramentum*

It is I who ordained that nothing should be more feared than an oath.

—"ISIS"[1]

The non-Christian Caecilius of Minucius Felix offered a famous description of the Christians in terms highly reminiscent of Livy's description of the *coniuratio* of the Bacchants: They were a hateful and spiteful rabble, a *plebs profanae coniurationis* composed of ignorant men and credulous women who met in secret at night for strange fasts and "inhuman" meals, ridiculing the *sacra*, despising the temples, the gods, and the priesthoods along with the marks of honor and purple robes of the magistrates. These sociopaths could not be governed even by threats of coercion (*Octavius* 8.3–5). In his commentary on the *Octavius* of Minucius Felix, G. W. Clarke dismissed the characterization of the Christians made by Minucius' non-Christian Caecilius as a *plebs profanae coniurationis* as "*almost standard jargon*" to describe contemptuously any clandestine *religious* sect . . . [which jargon] reflected the Roman attitude toward such apparently subversive *religious* groups outside *official religion* [emphases mine]."[2] Regardless of whether the Christians were, indeed, morally innocent and worthy of being tolerated within the Roman empire, Clarke has totally misrepresented the Roman conceptual framework.

The Romans had a very old notion of *coniuratio*—a "swearing together"—and of the power of the oath to weld together a disparate group. They would have been able to identify a *coniuratio* many centuries before they had a concept of "religion."[3] In my effort to show not only what *was not* in the ancient sources but also what *was* there, I would give a few pages to the Roman conception of the oath and the *coniuratio* and how deeply this influenced Tertullian and integrated him into spheres of behavior that cut across our notions of "religious" and "political" (or "secular").

An oath was a *religio* in one of its ancient Latin senses: a bond—indeed, *the most power-ful bond* that the Romans knew. ("For a sworn oath is an *adfirmatio religiosa*." [*Est enim ius iurandum adfirmatio religiosa* (Cicero, *De officiis* 3.29.104.)])[4] The oath was the *sacramentum* ("the thing that made sacred"—that bound or set apart), the *auctoramentum* ("the thing that augmented," "the thing that authorized"). For the Romans, the voice was the spirit speaking, the spirit realized in the world. The oath set apart, augmented, and channeled the energies of the one who professed. Important oaths of all kinds (treaties, contracts, marriage bonds, inaugurations, initiations, etc.) were further sanctioned by blood. The fiercest oaths were sanctioned by human blood.

A "swearing together"—a *coniuratio*—could be for *any* purpose. ("Note that the word *coniuratio* can be used of good things, for *coniuratio* is a 'neutral' word." [*nota de re bona coniurationem dici posse: nam coniuratio* τῶν μέσων *est* (Servius, *Commentarius ad Aeneidem* 8.5)].)[5] The purpose of a *coniuratio* was to heighten the energies and create a powerful *religio* that would cause the professors to fear deserting the group—and to make their enemies fear such a powerfully augmented and sacralized common will.[6] The famous and fatal war of the Roman clan of the Fabii against the Veians was, according to Servius, a *coniuratio* (*coniuratio . . . ut inter Fabios fuit* [*Commentarius Ad Aeneidem* 7.614]). According to Livy, a *coniuratio* was traditionally and voluntarily made by Roman soldiers, either before the imposition by the senate of a compulsory oath (*sacramentum*) or over and above the oath the soldiers swore to their commanding officer (22.38.1–5).[7] According to Servius, the Roman forces hastily assembled to respond to the sudden incursions of the *bellum Italicum* and *Gallicum* were *coniurationes* (ibid. 8.1).

Jochen Bleicken suggested that a *coniuratio* was the only possible way of uniting in pur-pose people who did not possess any common coercive or centralized institutions.[8] The oath could be used—as it was in the Roman army—to forge bonds between people who did not necessarily share *communitas* or *societas*. The institution of an oath administered by the magistrates of the state to its soldiers made it an important tool for arousing in the soldiers a sense of solidarity and loyalty to their general. It made their obedience and total commitment to him a point of honor.[9]

Great oaths were foundational events. The senatorial Republic, in Livy's account, was founded in the late–sixth century B.C.E. upon the oath of Brutus, who raising high the knife dripping with gore (*manentem cruore*) from the body of Lucretia, exclaimed, "By this blood (*per hunc*) . . . I swear (*iuro*) and take you gods as witnesses, that I will pursue Lucius Tar-quinius Superbus and his wicked wife and children with sword, fire and whatever violence I may . . . and I will not suffer them or another to be king in Rome."[10] The plebeian gov-ernment, like the senatorial *res publica*, was instituted and authorized by a powerful oath sanctioned by a curse/blood sacrifice: the mutinous plebeian soldiers climbed the Mons Sacer, created their own assembly (the *concilium plebis*), and declared that henceforth the decisions, the laws (*leges*=bonds) made by the assembly of the plebs (the *plebiscita*), should be binding on all Romans, patrician and plebeian alike (Livy 2.33).[11] At this insurrection-ary congregation, the plebs declared their leader, the tribune of the plebs *sacrosanctus*. Dio-nysius of Halicarnassus, although writing in Greek in the time of Augustus, described this *ecclesia* in a way that reflects the understanding of a *coniuratio*:

Brutus,[12] summoning [the plebeians] to their assembly (*ecclesia*), advised them to render this magistracy (the tribunate of the plebs) sacred (*hieros*) and inviolable (*asulos*), insuring its security by both a law (*nomos*) and an oath (*horkos*). (. . .) If anybody should [violate the sacrosanctity of the tribunate] let him be sacred/accursed (*exagistos estō* = Latin *sacer esto*) and let his goods be consecrated (*hiera*) to Demeter/Ceres; and if anybody should kill one who has done any of these things, let him be pure/guiltless of murder (*phonou katharos*). And to the end that the people might not even in the future be able to repeal this law, but that it might remain forever unalterable, it was ordained that all the Romans should solemnly swear (*omosai*) over the sacrificial victims to preserve it for all time, both they themselves and their descendants; and a prayer was added to the oath that the *theoi* of the sky and the *daimones* of the earth might be propitious to those who observed it, and that the displeasure of the gods and daemons might be visited upon those who violated it, as being guilty (*enochoi*) of the greatest sacrilege. From this arose the custom among the Romans of regarding the body of the tribunes as "sacrosanct" (*hiera*), which custom continues to this day. After they had passed this vote they erected an altar upon the summit of the mountain where they had encamped and named it . . . the altar of "Jupiter the Terrifier" (6.89.2–4; 90.1).[13]

Octavian in 32 B.C.E. used the oath to unite the peoples of the Roman Empire behind him personally. "The whole of Italy of its own free will (*sponte sua*) swore an oath of allegiance to me *in mea verba*,[14] and demanded me as the leader in the war in which I was victorious at Actium. The Gallic and Spanish provinces, Africa, Sicily and Sardinia swore the same oath of allegiance."[15] Oaths of loyalty were subsequently sworn by the consuls, leading equestrian officials, senate, soldiers, and people at the death of Augustus and accession of Tiberius (Dio 57.3.2; Tacitus, *Annales* 1.7+34), and at the accession of emperors until after 38 C.E., when it was renewed annually by both civilians and soldiers as an *ad hoc* test of loyalty. P. A. Brunt and J. M. Moore have reconstructed this fierce oath of loyalty from an inscription of the oath taken by both Roman residents and natives in Gangra (Paphlagonia), and from that taken by the Cypriots and in Portugal, Asia, and, perhaps, Italy:

I swear by Zeus, Ge, Helios, and all gods and goddesses and by Augustus himself that I will be loyal to Caesar Augustus and to his children and descendants all the days of my life in word, deed and mind, accounting as friends whomsoever they account as friends and regarding as personal enemies (ἐχθροί) whomsoever they judge to be such, and that *on their behalf I will spare neither spirit* (ψυχή) *nor life nor children*, but in every way I will endure every danger in their interest. Whatsoever I may learn or hear that is said or planned or done adverse to them, that I will reveal, and I will be the personal enemy of any one who says, plans or does any such thing. Whomsoever they judge to be their personal enemies, these I will pursue and resist by land and sea with arms and iron. *But if I should infringe this oath or not act in accordance with its terms, I invoke on my body, spirit, life, children, and my whole race and interest utter and total destruction down to the last of my line and all who descend from me, and may the bodies of my family or issue not be received by land or sea nor enjoy their fruits.*[16]

This fierceness of this oath of loyalty placed the life (*and afterlife*) of oneself and one's children on the line. As in the Christian Gospels, this new loyalty required the displacement of one's loyalties to one's family and children (loyalties that needed no oath to cement them). This was the *religio* to replace all *religiones*.

A *coniuratio*, then, was not a plot against the state, but might, like any guild, school, sect, war band—*or the Roman army itself*—have a purpose and a collective identity not necessarily in harmony with the interests and purposes of the Roman senate, its magistrates and military. Common and collective oaths had, for instance, been widely used to cement the insurrectionary forces during the civil and Italian wars.[17] It was as swearers of a joint oath that, aroused by the murder of their champion Marcus Livius Drusus, the Italians rose in revolt against the Romans in the bloody Social War early in the first century B.C.E.[18] The disparate Italiote peoples of the Italian peninsula, in their hatred of the Romans, had bound themselves together by a great sacrificial oath, a *sacramentum* in which they devoted themselves to Drusus in 91 C.E.:

> I swear by Jupiter Capitolinus and the Vesta of Rome and by Mars . . . and by the Sun, etc. that I will hold the friend and enemy of Drusus to be my friend and enemy and that *I will not spare possessions or the life of my children or of my parents if it be to Drusus' advantage and to the advantage of those who have taken this oath* (Diodorus Siculus 37.11D [17B]).[19]

In professing this oath, the Italians declared their determination to collect and direct their will to the ends determined by Drusus, loyalty to whom they placed before that to their children and parents. On the reverse of the denarius (struck by Drusus' *hospes*, Q. Pompaedius Silo), a youth is represented about to sacrifice a pig; eight warriors point their swords toward the victim.[20] Another coin issued ca. 91–88 B.C.E. shows on the reverse of a denarius two groups of four warriors pointing with their swords toward a pig held by a kneeling youth between them in front of a standard,[21] a depiction of a blood oath or *foedus*.[22]

The Roman senate and emperor feared secret, unauthorized, and unsupervised cabals that signaled to them the existence of hostile slaves, plebeians, women, foreigners, and other nonprivileged groups or subject "nationalists." A *coniuratio* became particularly dangerous in the eyes of the senate or emperor when those who had sworn together, sacralizing themselves and confirming their mutual loyalty and commitment, turned their energies in a direction not chosen by the senate (or later emperor).[23]

Out of fear of dangerous *coniurationes*, meetings at night (*coetus nocturni*) had been outlawed by the earliest codified laws of the Romans (the "Twelve Tables" [450/1 B.C.E.]). (The negative sanction in these early laws being sacralization [cursing] and devotion [condemning] to a god.[24]) The transgressor was put under the ban to be killed by anyone who was able—without incurring blood guilt—as an offering (along with his wealth) to a god. Indeed, any assembly without the presence and direction of a senatorial magistrate were met with intense suspicion by the senators. Such unsupervised congregations, when accelerated by a fierce *sacramentum*, were considered dangerous in the extreme.

Modern scholars have frequently compared the Roman repression of the Christians with that of the Bacchants in 186 B.C.E. (described by Livy as a *coniuratio intestina* [39.8.1+3, 39.17.6]).[25] This has seemed an apt comparison to many scholars because both these movements appeared to them as "religious" as opposed to "political" movements.[26] But any reading of Livy's account should quickly dissolve these categories. The *coniuratio* of the Bacchants involved *sacrificuli, vates, sacra, sacraria,* and *sacerdotes*; it also involved secret and nightly meetings in which mingled Romans and foreigners, males and females, slaves, freedmen, and free Romans. "Their number," the informant Hispala said, "was very great, almost a *populus*" (39.13.14).[27] "A great panic," according to Livy, "seized the *patres* (*patres pavor ingens cepit*) . . . lest these *coniurationes* and gatherings by night (*coetus nocturni*) might produce something of hidden treachery or danger. . . ." (39.14.4). "Not yet have they revealed all the crimes (*facinora*) to which they have conspired (*coniurarunt*). Their impious compact still limits itself to private crimes, since *as yet it does not have strength to crush the state (nondum ad rem publicam opprimendam satis virium est)*. Daily the evil grows and creeps abroad. It is already too great to be a purely private matter; *its objective is control of the state (ad summam rem publicam spectat)*" (39.16.3) [emphasis mine]. In the preserved *senatus consulta de Bacchanalibus* of 186 B.C.E., the senators, addressing the issue of the "confederated" Bacchants (the *foideratei* [line 2]) expressly forbid them from making oaths, exchanging vows or promises, or pledging their faith (*fides*) to one another. (*Neve . . . inter sed coniourase neve comvovise neve conspondisse neve conpromesise velet, neve quisquam fidem inter sed dedise velet* [lines 13–15].)[28] The inscription demonstrates decisively that the *coniuratio* that the senate feared was precisely the confederation by oath. Both the iteration of the prohibition against binding themselves by oaths and the injunction to apply for permission from the senate to meet (in small numbers) in the inscription emphasize the concerns that the senators thought were vital.[29]

Livy, describing the Bacchants, had already written of the terrible and violent struggles occasioned by the revolts of their own plebeians, peasants, and slaves. The leader of the First Sicilian Slave War, which subjected the Roman Republic to some of its greatest military tests, had been a fire-breathing, wonder-working charismatic slave, prophet, and elected "King of Syria" Eunus, with his faithful general Cleon.[30] The Second Sicilian Slave War had been led by the mantic slave and elected "King" Salvius.[31] In the time of Tertullian and Minucius, the *coniurationes* of Catiline against the senate and of Piso against the Emperor Nero were still in the Roman memory. To modern scholars, these might seem to be different sorts of movements from Christianity (i.e., "political" vs. "religious" movements), but such distinctions would not have been conceivable to the Romans. When Dio Cassius, a contemporary of Tertullian, had "Maecenas" advise "Augustus" to revere the god according to ancestral tradition (*sebou to theion kata ta patria*) and to compel others to do the same, it was because *sunomosiai, sustaseis,* and *hetaireiai* were dangerous to monarchs and liable to advocate changing the traditions: that is, to be revolutionaries. He very specifically includes philosophers in his warning (55.35–36).

Listen to the language of the following passages:

> It was said at that time that Catiline, after finishing his address, compelled the participants in his crime to take an oath, and that he passed around bowls of human blood mixed with wine. [It was said that] after uttering a fierce curse (*exsecratio*) upon traitors, and after all had tasted it, as is usual in solemn rites, he disclosed his project. His end in so doing was, they say, that they might be more faithful to one another because they shared the *conscientia* of so dreadful a deed (Sallust, *Catilina* 22).[32]

Catiline's followers had proved tenaciously loyal. Wherever the Romans found such fidelity, they assumed a ferocious blood oath:[33] hence, the similar charges of clandestine human sacrifices (the so-called blood libel) made against the Bacchants, the Catilinarians, Jews, and Christians. Secret and unauthorized meetings (especially nocturnal ones), a heterogeneous and disparate membership (including slaves, peasants, women, or foreigners), an ecstatic, prophetic, or cultic component—and above all, "kings"—were wont to draw the attention and excite the fears of Romans (and not just the authorities).[34]

The Romans knew very well that all wars (hot or cold) were "holy wars": All rebellions and resistance movements were cultic associations.[35] Rebellious associations authorized their own revolts against the Powers That Be by calling on the still-greater Powers To Be; all rebels were involved in breaking and re-establishing boundaries, deeply engaged in desecrating and resacralizing behaviors. The Romans nervously anticipated the inevitable overturning of their *imperium sine fine* by the Powers That Will Be. Still, they were less afraid of "gods" *per se* than humans; the gods of even those of their most adamant enemies could always be evoked, appropriated, "turned."[36] Even the most powerful war gods were available for the taking. Greco-Roman Christians were busy appropriating both the "high" god of Greek philosophers and that of the Jews, even while they were separating themselves off from the latter and making them into rivals and enemies. Just so, the Roman emperors would eventually appropriate the "high" god of the Jews and Christians along with that of Greek philosophy. When the senate went after the Bacchants, it was never Bacchus/Liber whom the Roman senators feared. (It goes without saying that the Romans paid little or no attention to the homely little gods of farmers and pastoralists.[37]) Nor did the Romans ever express the slightest fear of Christus, but they were especially sensitive to king gods and to the type of assemblies that adopted such gods. What the ruling Romans feared was disloyalty by humans,[38] and so they were *very* attuned to the kind of prophetic language and god-talk used by rebels to justify their challenge to Roman authority. To servants of the imperial state, Christians might seem not unlike the followers Judas of Galilee, "the formidable teacher" and founder of Josephus' Fourth Philosophy, who reproached the Jews for recognizing the Romans as masters when they already had God (and whose followers therefore refused to pay taxes to the Romans)—the "philosophical" movement that begot the ferocious rebellion of the Jews in 66–70 and the resistance unto death of the Sicarii at Masada led by a grandson of this same Judas and at Alexandria.[39]

Tertullian's *fratres*, coming from disparate backgrounds, and having no effective centralized or coercive powers were, like the Italiotes (or the subjects and soldiers of the Empire), effectively united, set apart, sacralized by a common *sacramentum*, the initiatory oath taken at the time of baptism. The Christian's oath, the *fides Christiana* played a central role in Tertullian's thought. There was no infant baptism in Tertullian—infant baptism being a kind of "naturalization" that would make Christianity, like Judaism, into a kind of state. For Tertullian, it was the voluntary oath made by the confessing adult that was the solemn bond of the new Christian.[40] It was a bond enforced by and reinforcing the *disciplina*, the *religio* of those who swore. A "pledge of allegiance" was used by Tertullian's Christians in just the way it was used by the emperor of Rome or the Congress of the United States:[41] to articulate and cement the devotion of a very heterogeneous population.[42]

It was the Christians' voluntary baptismal oath, the *fides christiana*, that in Tertullian's mind set up the condition of the Christians' glory and the endless tests of their fidelity. The words of this *fides*, this sacralizing oath, this *sacramentum* that the Christian swore at his initiation into the Camp of Light were, "to renounce the devil, his angels and all of his pomps:"

> When he enters the water, he professes the *fides christiana* in the words of its law: with our mouth we swear to renounce the devil and his pomps and his angels.
>
> *Cum acquam ingressi christianam fidem in legis suae verba profitemur, renuntiasse nos diabolo et pompae et angelis eius de ore nostro contestamur (De spectaculis 4.1).*

This oath appears very frequently in Tertullian.[43] (Oddly, it is nowhere in the treatise *De baptismo!*[44])

"Faith," for modern Christians and many modern scholars, is a synonym for "religion,"[45] implying "belief in," "trust in," either a god or a set of propositions about a god. But Tertullian continued to use Latin *fides* (cognate with *foedus*, the Latin word for a covenant) primarily as "loyalty" in the sense of being voluntarily bound to one's word or oath. In his tirades against the *haeretici*, the object eliciting Tertullian's *fides* might be a set of propositions, a doctrine, or teaching (*disciplina*) to which Tertullian felt the Christian should be unstintingly and uniformly committed.[46] (Tertullian usually resorted to the verb *credere* when he wanted to express "believing in," "trusting in," something or someone or in the propositions of a "creed" [e.g., *De carne Christi* 2.4–5; *Adversus Marcionem* 3.2.4].) For Tertullian, *fides* was less about trusting and more about being steadfast, unwavering, dedicated, consecrated, fiercely, fervently loyal. That loyalty, however, could be encouraged by confidence and trust (*Adversus Marcionem* 3.2.4).

It is to be noted that Tertullian has several versions of a "creed" that, with its public profession, was another form of such a loyalty oath, a pledge of allegiance to a set of propositions. These creeds formed, for him, a part of the *regula fidei* to which all Christians had to bind themselves without reserve (e.g., *De praescriptione haereticorum* 13.1–6; *De virginibus velandis* 1.3–4). These "creeds" were *not*, however, the words of Tertullian's *sacramentum*. The initiatory *sacramentum* remained the oath against the demonic forces. These different sorts of loyalty oaths were aimed at different enemies and had different purposes. The anti-demonic oath was aimed against the Romans and non-Christians, the creedal oath against the "heretics."

In the separatist or insurrectionary framework of his thought, Tertullian's Christians both swear and hope together, forming exactly a *coniuratio* and a *conspiratio* that he hopes will result in the replacement of the Roman Empire with one of its own—in which the cult of the king-god will be all-embracing and saturate every aspect of the safe and eternal life. In this aspect of Tertullian's thought, the Christian is not an example of a *philosophus* or of a *cultor*, but rather a *miles sacratus*, set apart and sacralized by his oath in exactly the way how the Roman soldier, the Roman *miles sacratus* was bound and sacralized by his *sacramentum*, his *auctoramentum*.[47] The *sacramentum* of the *miles dei* was a competing and more extreme version, an inversion and a rejection of the oaths of loyalty to the Emperor and his ministers, with their offices, honors, and symbols of power: their *purpurae*, *fasces*, *vittae*, *coronae*, *contiones*, *edicta*, and so forth:

> Now the question at issue is whether the *fidelis* may enlist and whether men serving in the [Roman] military may be admitted to the *fides*—even if he were to be a private soldier of lower rank, one for whom there is no necessity to sacrifice or to pass capital judgment. The divine *sacramentum* and the human *sacramentum* are incompatible (*non convenit sacramento divino et humano*), the standard (*signum*) of Christ and the *signum* of the devil, the camps (*castrae*) of light and that of dark. One soul cannot serve two masters: God and Caesar (*De idololatria* 19.1–2).

The *dei miles*, the soldier of God who "disburdened" himself of the vestments of the Roman *miles sacratus*, was Tertullian's model of the Christian breaking his ties with the powerful forces of "this age" and defining a simplified, purified, more homogenous self.[48] This desire to strip down, to purge oneself of divided and conflicting—and so disabling— obligations, loyalties, and desires attracted those who longed for an energized and clari- fied vision of one's self in the world.[49] Freed from complexity, guilt and confusion could be washed away.[50] The greatest problem for the person who would attune his or her will to that of the Powers That Be was if those powers were divided or conflicted—in which case, then there was, alas, no possibility *not* to will, *not* to make decisions. That is why, for Tertullian's separatist strategy to work, one could not serve two *imperatores* or tolerate *haeresis*.

In this framework of Tertullian's thought, he spurns the "quibbling," the *cavillatio* in which the Christians who served in the armed forces of the Roman emperor must inevi- tably have engaged (*De corona* 11.4). How could a Christian take the soldier's *sacramentum* that directly competed with the Christian *sacramentum*? Would they be required to guard a temple? Participate in a triumph? Worship the standards or the *tropaea*?

The solemn oath of loyalty formed the center of the initiatory *mysterium* of the *miles dei*:

> We were called to serve in the army of the living God, at the moment we answered with the words of the *sacramentum*. *Vocati sumus ad militiam Dei vivi iam tunc, cum in sacramenti verba respondimus* (*Ad martyras* 3.1).

> Soldiering under this *sacramentum*, I am challenged/provoked by the enemy. I am like him unless I fight him. In defending [this oath], I fight it out on the line, am wounded, hewn in pieces, slain. Who wished this fatal issue to his soldier, but he who sealed him by such a *sacramentum*? (*Scorpiace* 4.5)[51]

For Tertullian, the baptismal oath was an oath *against* "the devil and his pomps."[52] For Cyprian, it will be an oath *against* "the devil and the *saeculum*" (*De lapsis* 8), and an oath of loyalty *to* Christ, having strong and deliberate martial overtones; it was the *divinae militiae sacramenta* (*Epistulae* 74.8; cf. *De lapsis* 7). "I wished" [says the broken *confessor*] "to contend bravely, and remembering my *sacramentum*, I took up the arms of *devotio* and *fides*" (*certare quidem fortiter volui et sacramenti mei memor devotionis ac fidei arma suscepi* [*De lapsis* 13]).

Cyprian's "soldiers of Christ" are the *confessores* armed to endure suffering, imprisonment and death who offer a *spectaculum gloriosum* to God.[53]

Christians who saw themselves as soldiers were better able to inure themselves to the shaming behaviors of their enemies. Soldiers were accustomed to be provoked and taunted by their enemies and to taunt and shame in turn. We have wonderful examples of the kind of insults soldiers hurled at one another inscribed on the *"Perusinae glandes,"* the "bullets" launched at one another by opponents at the battle of Numantia during the civil wars between Octavian and Antony. Livy also describes such taunting behavior in his stories of the single combats of Torquatus with a Gaul and his with a Latin.[54]

Tertullian's oath was as ferociously anti-Roman as that of his fellow Carthaginian Hannibal, as much a vow of undying hatred as it was of loyalty.[55] Christian *disciplina* and *fides* required what the Romans called the *metus hostilis*, the annealing fear of the enemy. Hatred was the necessary correlative of loyalty. It was this oath, this seal of faith, this *signaculum* that according to Tertullian, prevented the Christian from attending any of the Roman spectacles or serving in the Roman army (*De spectaculis* 4, 24; *De corona* 11.4).

The difference in the Christian oath as described by Tertullian from that described by Pliny in his letter to Trajan is telling. According to the Roman Pliny, the Christians he interviewed while serving as the Roman governor of Bithynia and Pontus [between 110–112 C.E.] ". . . meet before dawn on a fixed day to chant verses alternately among themselves, in honor of Christ as if to a god, and also *to bind themselves by oath (se sacramento obstringere)*—not for any *scelus*—but to abstain from theft, robbery and adultery, to commit no breach of trust and not to deny a deposit when called upon to restore it" (*Epistles* 10.96.7). But when Tertullian describes this letter of Pliny, it reads differently in an important way: "Asserting that apart from an *obstinatio* that refused to sacrifice, he [Pliny] had learned nothing about the Christian *sacramenta* apart from their meeting before dawn to sing to Christ and to God, and *for the purpose of confederating their disciplina*, forbidding murder, adultery, dishonesty, treachery, and the other crimes." (*Adlegans praeter obstinationem non sacrificandi; nihil aliud de sacramentis eorum conperisse quam coetus antelucanos ad canendum Christo et Deo, et ad confoederandam disciplinam: homicidium, adulterium, fraudem, perfidiam et cetera scelera prohibentes* [*Apologeticum* 2.6].) In Tertullian's account, the moral restraints are elements of the *disciplina* and *not the words specified in or contents of the oath*. Tertullian's oath is much more militant than that implied in Pliny's account.

For Tertullian, the Christian can take no other oath apart from the initiatory baptismal *sacramentum* (*De idololatria* 11.1). Because of the ban on all other oaths (*praescribit Christus non esse iurandum* [ibid. 23.2]),[56] those making contracts or marriage bonds with non-Christians were guilty of the crime of "idolatry." As Tertullian makes abundantly clear in this treatise, the transactions of the battlefield, the bedroom, or the marketplace are not to be placed in categories of human behaviors distinct from the cultic; in this separatist aspect of Tertullian's thought, there can be no complementary or even opposed "secular" sphere to Christianity. (Again, our modern notions of a "religious" domain versus a "secular" or "political" one are totally inappropriate for describing the ideal of Christian life for Tertullian, the separatist.)

Tertullian's Christian soldiers, devoted to their Lord in death, often sound (with good reason) like the warrior of the German war band of Tacitus' *Germania* devoted to death to his *princeps*, or like the thanes of King Hrothgar in *Beowulf*, or like the ideal samurai of the *Hagekure* devoted to death to his *daimyo*.[57]

> I have been enjoined . . . not to honor or in any way show reverence to another than to him who commands me, whom I am both bid to fear so that I may not be forsaken by him, and love with my whole being, that I may die for him. Soldiering under this *sacramentum*, I am challenged/provoked by the enemy. (. . .) In defending [this oath], I fight hard in battle, am wounded, hewn in pieces, slain. Who wished this fatal end to his soldier, but he who sealed him by such a *sacramentum*? (*Scorpiace* 4.4–5).[58]

It is in the rebellious "segregationist" context of Tertullian's thought that the appearance of the word *religio* can be understood in the report of the Scillitan Martyrs. In this text, the *religio* of the Romans is in direct conflict with that of the martyrs. Either in response to remarks by the Christians not recorded in the transcript, or to the claim by the Christians that they behaved scrupulously (neither malefactors/sorcerers in their actions nor malevolent in their thoughts), Saturninus the Roman proconsul is reported to have replied:

> We also are *religiosi* and our *religio* is *simplex*, and we swear by the *genius* of our *dominus* the *imperator* and we perform supplications on behalf of his *salus*, which things you should do as well.
>
> *Et nos religiosi sumus et simplex est religio nostra, et iuramus per genium domni nostri imperatoris et pro salute eius supplicamus, quod et vos quoque facere debetis* (*Passio sanctorum Scillitanorum* 3).[59]

Notice here two ancient meanings of *religio* and *religiosus*: *religio* as the oath or bond, and *religiosus* as scrupulous behavior. The oaths and loyalties of the Christians and the Roman proconsul are irreconcilable because they are in direct contest with one another: They are incompatible because they occupy the same space.

The Soldier's Askēsis

> See how much more zealous valor is to embrace peril than cruelty is to inflict it.
>
> Seneca, *Epistulae* 24.5

> The greatest fruit of suffering is . . . . fearlessness.
> *Malorum maximum fructum . . . nihil timere.*
>
> Seneca, *Troades* 422–23

Being harder on oneself than your enemy was (and is) a strategy of gaining power often adopted by those who feel powerless.[60] The power offered by ascetic self-torture was to gain the upper hand. It was a way of losing one's fear of those who terrify you. Embracing, encouraging, enacting the frightful, shameful things that non-Christians might do to them deprived the non-Christians of the ability to frighten them.[61]

Tertullian bids the Christian woman anticipate chains and tortures and death:

> Let us meditate on the things that are very hard to bear, and we shall not feel them. Let
> us abandon the things that are more pleasant and we will not miss them. Let us stand
> ready to endure every violence—having nothing that we fear to leave behind. [The things
> we fear to leave behind] are the nets impeding our hope (*De cultu feminarum* 2.13.5).[62]

> [We are] enjoining every form of *tapeinophronēsis* (humiliation, humble-mindedness) since
> we must become familiar with the prison, and we must practice hunger and thirst (. . .) so
> that the Christian may enter into prison as he would emerge from it;—he will suffer there
> not punishment but *disciplina*, not the world's tortures, but his own dutiful observances;
> and to go forth from the prison to the *certamen* with more confidence, having nothing of
> the flesh about him, so that the tortures might not even have material to work on, since he
> is cuirassed in a mere dry skin, and cased in horn to meet the claws, the succulence of his
> blood already sent on before him like the baggage of the soul—the soul herself hastening
> now after it, which already, by frequent fasting, knows death up close! (*De ieiunio* 12.2)[63]

The extreme of humiliation, of ascetic self-denial, the sacrifice of one's own will, resulted in a powerful inversion: in enthusiasm, possession by the Spiritus Sanctus, in self-
deification. As it was for the Stoic Epictetus, willing not to will was the ultimate test and
proof of will, of *animus*, of spirit over flesh.[64] The destruction of self, then, is strategic.
Tertullian calculated that, like Job, he would get everything back in the end with interest.
The more he submitted to the strictest regulation, the more he experienced these trials
and tests and ordeals as purgative and curative. Patience and suffering were the precondi-
tions of mercy, the precondition of both self-absolution and the absolute.[65]

When Tertullian defends the prolongation of the *stationes* (the vigilant fasts held by adherents of the ascetic New Prophecy) from the anniversary of the crucifixion of Jesus
until late in the day of the anniversary of his resurrection, he does so on the model of the
steadfast watches of the Roman soldier. "[T]he *statio* has received its name from the example of military life—for we are God's *militia*" (*statio de militari exemplo nomen accepit—
nam et militia dei sumus* [*De oratione* 19.5]).[66]

> If this [prolonged vigil] savors more of Christian *religio* [here a synonym for *disciplina*] (*hoc
> si magis ad religionem sapit Christianam*), then one will protract the hours of the *statio* until
> the time when the body of the *dominus* was entombed.[67]

He explains his logic:

> It is *irreligiosus* [i.e., undisciplined] for the flesh of the slaves (*famuli*) to be refreshed
> before that of their *dominus*.
>   *Inde et irreligiosum est ante famulorum carnem refrigerari quam domini* [*De ieiunio* 10.8].

The Loyal and Voluntary Slave

> The will of God is our sanctification.
>   *Voluntas dei est sanctificatio nostra.*
>
> Tertullian, *De exhortatione castitatis* 1.3

The concomitant of Tertullian's total and shameless insubordination to the Emperor is his total and willing subordination to his god.[68] The notion of the Christian as *servus* (voluntary slave) soldiering, like a voluntary gladiator (also, in this capacity, a slave), under his fierce *sacramentum* ranked with the *fidelis* ("the loyal one") as Tertullian's most frequently used designations for the ideal Christian (especially in his parables and metaphors).[69] Modern translators are often reluctant to translate Tertullian's *servi* as "slaves" and prefer the milder "servant"—but Tertullian used the word *servi* advisedly, as he does the word *dominus*, slave-master.[70]

> When we see all slaves of probity and good intention shaping their conduct to their master's disposition (*ingenium dominicum*) the art of deserving favor (*obsequii disciplina*) being compliant subjection (*morigera subiectio*)—how much more obliged are we to be found to have our behavior molded in accordance with our *dominus*—slaves of the living god (*servi dei vivi*), whose judgments on those who belong to him (*suos*) is not a matter of a fetter or a cap of freedom, but of an eternity either of punishment or of salvation. The shunning of which severity or the courting of which liberality requires diligence in obedience (*obsequii diligentia*) in proportion to the warnings of this *severitas*, or the promises of this *liberalitas*. And yet we exact obedience not from men only, who have been bound into servitude or bound by whatever right of debt, but even from cattle, even from the beasts; understanding that they have been provided and delivered for our uses by the *dominus*. Shall, then, creatures which God makes subject to us be better than we are in the *disciplina* of obedience? . . . Do we hesitate to listen diligently to him to whom alone we are subjected—that is, the *dominus*? (*De patientia* 4.1–3).[71]

> Repent of having loved what God does not love, when even we ourselves do not permit our slave boys not to hate the things which are offensive to us; for the *ratio* of voluntary obedience (*obsequium*) consists in similarity of minds (*De paenitentia* 4.4).[72]

Like the Roman gladiators serving under a fierce oath (*sacramentum*), he meant to show Christians to be inspired, exalted by an equally terrible (and so fearless) commitment.

One can compare Tertullian's psychological strategies with those of Apuleius of Madauros, who puts into the mouth of Isis the emotions experienced by Lucius at his final collapse and submission to the all-powerful goddess:

> You have suffered many different toils and been driven by Fortune's great tempest and mighty storm winds; but finally, Lucius, you have reached the harbor of Peace and the altar of Mercy (*portum Quietis et aram Misericordiae*). Not your birth, nor even your position, [nor your fine education] has been of any help to you whatever. . . . Nevertheless the blindness of Fortune, while torturing you with the worst of perils, has brought you in its random wickedness to this holy state of happiness. Let her be gone now! Let her rage in all her fury and hunt some other object for her cruelty, for hostile chance has no opportunity against those whose lives the majesty of our goddess has emancipated into her own servitude. (. . .) Let the *irreligiosi* see and recognize the error of their ways. Behold! Lucius, set free from his tribulations of old and rejoicing in the providence of great Isis, triumphs over his Fortune. But to be safer and better protected, enlist in this holy army to whose oath of allegiance you were summoned not long ago. Dedicate yourself today to obedience to our *religio* and take on the voluntary yoke of her servitude;

for as soon as you become the goddess's slave you will experience more fully the fruit of your freedom (*Metamorphoses* 11.15).[73]

Apuleius' Lucius embraced the voluntary yoke of servitude as—if not even more—consciously than Tertullian. Apuleius' ass had tried to negotiate the Roman world on his own. He attempted, with avoidance, hesitation, deceptions, and a hundred maneuvers to manage his fears and anxieties, to avoid the worst abuse and beatings. All his strategies were in vain. After exhausting every possibility, he turned in his despair to Isis who, in return for his salvation, demanded total focus and commitment, willing servitude. Isis admonishes Lucius:

> Only remember and keep the remembrance fast in your heart's deep core, that all the remaining days of your life must be dedicated to me, and that nothing can release you from this service but death (*Metamorphoses* 11.5).[74]

For Apuleius' Lucius, the unendurable subjection was to the human slavemasters, to Stone-blind Fortune, and to the witches and sorceresses; for Tertullian, it was to "the devil and his pomps."

When it came to servility, Tertullian's devotees of Christus and Apuleius' devotees of Isis had the Jews beaten hands down.[75] Indeed, for Tertullian and Minucius Felix, the Jews were a warning. Their disobedience and disloyalty had cost them the blessings of their *dominus* and caused them, like Apuleius' ass, to be subject to cruel and alien powers. Minucius' god devoted/cursed the Jews for being deserters of his discipline (*sed a deo ut disciplinae transfugas deditos* [*Octavius* 32.5]),[76] refuting the argument of the non-Christian Caecilius, who asserted that the defeat of the Jews by the Romans was proof, rather, of their god's impotence (ibid. 10.4; cf. Tertullian, *Apologeticum* 21.5).

For Tertullian, a highly focused and intensified fear of the enemy was a proper *antiperistasis*—the annealing opposition that excited and invigorated the Christian, concentrating and directing his or her energies.[77] Provided the devotion and submission was complete and voluntary, and that the Christian incorporated the fearful power of god into his or her own mind and identified that power with one's own will and well-being, the fear could turn upside down and be experienced as an elation, a liberation, as exuberant loyalty and love. As in Roman Stoicism, the love depended upon the completeness of the identification of one's will and that of the powers with the potential to terrify you. The more complete the identification, the more likely the "possession" would be experienced as a positive ecstasy.[78] Fear causes hate ("fear . . . breathes forth hate" [*odium . . . timor spirat* (*Apologeticum* 27.6)]),[79] but fear could be exciting and pleasurable if and when raised to the point of forgetting one's self (and the burdensome *religiones*: anxieties, and sometimes impossible obligations, to protect family, farms, flocks, etc.). Fear of God, for Tertullian, is pleasurable and salvific if and when it trumps all other obligations, all other *religiones*, all other loves.

For those for whom one's life, one's children and spouse, one's flocks, herds, and land were precious, Tertullian's enthusiasm for fatal confrontation with the Romans might seem incomprehensible; but for Tertullian, this renunciation of life and all that was generally considered most precious in life revealed not insanity but exhilarating enthusiasm:

When challenged to sacrifice, we stand immobile (*obstruimus gradum*) in the confidence of our shared knowledge (*pro fide conscientiae nostrae*), by which we are certain to whom those services are directed [i.e., the (Roman) devils]. . . . But some think it insanity that while we could sacrifice at that moment (*in praesenti*) and go away unhurt, preserving a reservation/scruple in one's mind (*propositum apud animum*), we prefer *obstinatio* to *salus* (*Apologeticum* 27.1–2).[80]

The nervous anxiety of *religio* and *pudor* could be inverted and replaced by total submission to the oversight of God.

A Sterner, More Vigilant Eye in the Sky

All things are plain in the sight of heaven.

Gospel of Thomas, Logion 6

Christians like Tertullian who did not feel it a *religio* to swear by the *genius* of the emperor rejected the notion that the eye of the emperor could be their witness and judge: that the eye of the emperor could inhibit or shame them. And if the eye of the emperor could not make them blush, what human eye could? The deliberate and self-conscious shamelessness of the Christians, like that of the Cynics, resulted in their being seen as despisers of mankind. Tertullian, in his separatist mode, would not deny the charge:[81]

The first [charge against us of] *obstinatio* concerns that *religio*—coming second after that felt for the gods (*secunda a deis religio*)—due to the majesty of the Caesars, on account of which we are said to be *irreligiosi* towards them since we neither propitiate their images nor swear by their *genius*. [3] *We are called enemies of the people (hostes publicae). Well, so be it!!*

[2] *Prima obstinatio est, qua secunda a deis religio constituitur Caesarianae maiestatis, quod inreligiosi dicamur in Caesares neque imagines eorum repropitiando neque genios deierando.* [3] *Hostes publicae nuncupamur. Ita vero sit!* (*Ad nationes* 1.17).

According to the Roman Pliny, governor of Bithynia, it was not the contents of the Christians' "confession" (*Epistulae* 10.93.3) but this shameless and nonnegotiable opposition, this implacable hostility, this *inflexibilis obstinatio* (that caused them to be *irreligiosi* toward the emperor) that needed to be punished (*debere puniri*).[82] Refusing to feel shame before the emperor was perceived as an impertinence antithetical to the *religio* due to the *maiestas* of the Emperor, an insupportable insult.[83] Saying, like the African Christians from Scilla, that they honored the emperor but feared only god,[84] would seem, to a Roman, at best a form of *dissimulatio*—"double-speak"—not just disloyal, but insulting.

As Tertullian's strategy of overcoming debilitating fear involved not less but more fear, so his rejection of shame involved not less but more shame. The eye of one's neighbors and the eye of the emperor needed to be replaced by a much more fearful, penetrating and relentless eye. "The eyes of the Lord are upon those who fear him." (*Oculi enim domini super timentes* [*Adversus Marcionem* 2.19.4; Psalm 33.18].) It was heightened fear of the eye of his god, reinforced by the Christian's great baptismal oath, that allowed the little *ecclesiae* of Tertullian's day to be communities, ironically, policed *almost* entirely by shame. Tertullian does not have a word for a formalized *excommunicatio*, but he supports the ample use, nevertheless, of forms of ostracism and shaming (as revealed, for instance, in his treatises *De pudicitia*, *De monogamia* and *De virginibus velandis*). Cyprian, in the next century, will call on God to punish those who, without being tortured into submission, had agreed to sacrifice or sought certificates of sacrifice from Imperial authorities at the command of the emperor Decius. Meanwhile, he will do everything he can to shame them (*De lapsis, passim*). Relentless vigilance was essential for preserving discipline within the *ecclesia*.

In the balancing systems of the Roman republic, there had been a pulsing of heightened and subsiding attention, tension and relaxation. But for Tertullian, the ebb of attention, the lapse of inhibition effected by Roman festivities and spectacles was incompatible with the need to be inexorably on guard against oneself, to imagine God as one's own vigilant inner eye.[85] Speaking of attendance at the Roman games, the *ethnici* mistakenly argue:

> Such great external solace of eye and ear cannot clash with *religio in animo et in conscientia*; god is not offended by a man's enjoying himself; provided that the fear and honor of god are preserved, it is no *scelus* to avail oneself of such enjoyment in its proper time and place.
>
> *Ethnici . . . qui in ista causa adversus nos ita argumentari consuerunt: nihil obstrepere religioni in animo et in conscientia tanta solacia extrinsecus oculorum vel aurium nec vero deum offendi oblectatione hominis, qua salvo erga deum metu et honore suo in tempore et suo in loco frui scelus non sit* (*De spectaculis* 1).

These non-Christians, according to Tertullian, are under the illusion that their *religiones* are compatible with enjoyment of the shows. But for Tertullian, being "off guard" was antithetical to the stubborn and steadfast vigilance, scrupulous inhibitions, and total obedience of "true" *religio*:

> [The pleasure of attendance at the spectacles] is not compatible with *vera religio* and *verum obsequium* towards the true god.[86]
>
> *Non competant verae religioni et vero obsequio erga verum deum* (*De spectaculis* 1).

For Tertullian, *religio* and *solacia*, vigilance and *voluptas* were irreconcilable. He brands the games of the Greeks as attempts to put these two incompatible states together; they are, in fact, "contests of *religio* with *voluptas*." In his mind, the *voluptas* of the games cancels out *religio* and renders the Greek games *certamina superstitiosa*. (*Agonas istos, contentiosa sollemnia et superstitiosa certamina Graecorum et religionum et voluptatum, quanta gratia saeculum celebret iam et Africae licuit* [*Scorpiace* 6.2].)

The Roman censors, in Tertullian's mind, had not been censorious enough. He observes that the Roman censors had long disapproved of building permanent theaters; they would destroy them out of concern for the *mores* of the people (*destruebant moribus consulentes*). But in the civil war period, the warlord Pompey built a permanent theater surmounted with a chapel of Venus. "So, a structure condemned and deservedly condemned, he disguised with the title of 'temple,' and 'humbugged' *disciplina* with *superstitio*." (*Ita damnatum et damnandum opus templi titulo praetexit et disciplinam superstitione delusit* [*De spectaculis* 10].) Tertullian feels that two wrongs were committed by Pompey: First, he abandoned the ancient and severe *mores* by building a standing theater with permanent (if not exactly comfortable) seats. Second, he gave the fair name of Temple of Venus to the building built as a breach of those *mores*. For Tertullian, "pleasure (luxury and laxity) and *superstitio* (absence of discipline) gained ground together" in the course of Roman history (*De spectaculis* 9). In his essay on fasting, Tertullian remarks:

> How many are mindful of *religio* when the seats of the memory are occupied [by food and drink], the limbs of wisdom impeded? No one will suitably, fitly, usefully remember [to fear] god at that time when it is customary for a man to destroy his own self. Food either slays or else wounds all *disciplina* (*De ieiunio* 6.2).[87]

Tertullian espies, in the virgin's lowering of her guard within the Christian community, her perfidy. In *De virginibus velandis*, Tertullian censors those young women who, while veiling themselves outside the *ecclesia*, removed the veil and relaxed their vigilance within the protected confines of the *ecclesia*. ("For it is *aemulatio* [zeal, eagerness], not *religio* which impels them" [*aemulatio enim illas, non religio producit*].) They are looking to please and attract the men (16); they are inviting attention, poised to slide down the slippery slope of sexual promiscuity. As in the case of the theater, all relaxation leads to *delicta*. The virgin should be terrified of herself:

> Firm and absolute and pure virginity fears nothing more than herself. She does not wish to suffer the gaze of even female eyes. She [*virginitas*] *has other eyes* [i.e., the eyes of god]. She takes refuge in the veiling of the head as if a helmet, as if a shield, to protect her *bonum* against the blows of temptations, against the darts of scandals, against suspicions and whispers and emulation; against envy (*livor*) itself.

The virgin's terror of the eye of God and her terror of herself are equated. The unrelenting rigor of the true Christian is not negative and excessive but commendable and positive: an intrusive eye that does not feel shame to pry into one's own deepest and shameful secrets.[88] He goes on to compare God's eye to the Roman *fascinum*—both the evil eye of malice and its cure:

> For there is something to be feared even among the *ethnici* which they call *fascinum*, the too unhappy result of excessive praise and glory. This [*fascinum*] we sometimes ascribe to the devil for his is hatred of the good; sometimes we attribute it [the *fascinum*] to God, for his is the judgment of haughtiness (*superbia*), exalting, as he does, the humble and depressing the elated. And so the more holy virgin will fear, even under the name of *fascinum*, on one hand The Adversary, on the other God; the envious disposition (*lividum ingenium*) of the former, the censorial light (*censorium lumen*) of the latter, and will take pleasure in being known to herself alone and to God.
>
> But even if she has been recognized by any other person, she is wise if she has blocked the path to temptations. For who will dare to intrude with his eyes upon a closed face, a face without feeling, a face, so to say, morose. Any evil thought will be broken by this severity (15.1–3).

The shameless, staring, intrusive *fascinum* could be, in typically Roman fashion, part of a system of complements: the source of danger (because it fascinated, captivated, and paralyzed) and the protection against it (the eye, the phallic amulet, the third finger, spitting, etc.).[89] Here Tertullian distinguishes an evil *fascinum*, the "evil eye" of envy, from a good *fascinum*, the uninhibited gaze of God that levels the haughty (in the way that Apuleius' jealous Venus reduced the too beautiful and too sacralized Psyche, or his Isis leveled the arrogant *curiosus* Lucius). Tertullian used the hugely magnified and unblushing eye of God both to exaggerate the shame within the community and to pre-empt, to trump the shaming eyes of non-Christians, spies, and informers. Tertullian accepts his god as the *fascinum*, the penetrating eye that *should* fascinate, that *should* transfix you. Fixation by the eye of god would turn shameful paralysis to honorable *obstinatio*.

For the Romans, the eye (including the inner eye) could be too vigilant and intrusive, but Tertullian would give total license to the censoring eye of his god. For Tertullian, the critical issue was *whose* eye was the staring eye. Fascination by anything and anyone *but* his god was a form of license. Under Tertullian's god and king, there could be no release of tension, no "steam valve," no Saturnalia, no Wednesday night Bingo, no jokes about Jesus. There could be little festive, playful, or pleasurable, little left to whimsy. The *ecclesia* of *tristis* Tertullian was a pressure cooker, a disciplinary regime of constant and consistent weightiness. Like those Romans of the early Empire who sought refuge from what had, for them, become a perpetual and terrifying Saturnalia, *gravitas* offered Tertullian relief from the harrowing confusion, a "Saturnalia from the Saturnalia."[90] Only by being harder on themselves than their enemies could Tertullian's Christians experience their superior power.

One of the main purposes of greatly concentrating fear of the judgmental surveillance of a supreme and all-powerful king god was to consume, to drive out all other fears; the pain that cured pain could act as a medicine. The narrowly focused and intensified fear could eclipse all other fears, in the way that terror of an approaching tornado can drive out anxiety about one's dentures.

The notion that the penetrating, staring, intrusive and unblushing eye of god was positive was bound up with the history of the development of the Latin word *conscientia*. *Conscientia* was an old word whose long and complex development was ongoing—like that of *religio*—in the time of Tertullian and Cyprian. *Conscientia* had been the alienated consciousness or acute self-consciousness (the "guilt") of the ancient Romans. Tertullian and Cyprian both still used *conscientia* as "guilt," but occasionally they used it as the equivalent to the critical, censorious, and penetrating Inner Eye, which, being identified with the Eye of God, turned/inverted *conscientia* from being one's personal torturer to one's dependable moral guide, from one's inner demon to one's Jiminy Cricket.[91] "No evil act is exempt from fear, because none is exempt from consciousness of itself." (*Nullum maleficium sine formidine est, quia nec sine conscientia sui* [*Adversus Marcionem* 4.17.12].) Self-alienation as perpetually heightened self-consciousness became the condition of self-transcendence. To transform guilt into righteousness (the *pura conscientia* of *Adversus Marcionem* 4.1.9), the self-criticism had to be relentless.

The Consecration of Fear

[Christ] reminds them that they must consecrate their fear to him (*illi metum consecrandum*).

Tertullian, Scorpiace 9.6–7[92]

For Tertullian, "There is nothing apart from *contumacia* that can subvert fear." (*Neque enim timorem alia res quam contumacia subvertit* [*De paenitentia* 5.4].) To the suggestion made by the Roman proconsul that the Scillitan *confessi* show their loyalty to the Emperor—and so earn his *indulgentia*—the Christian Cittinus replied:

We have none other to fear, save only our *dominus deus*, who is in the skies.

Nos non habemus alium quem timeamus nisi domnum deum nostrum qui est in caelis (*Passio Sanctorum Scillitanorum 8*).

We fear . . . God, and not the proconsul.

nos . . . deum non proconsulem timentes (*Apologeticum* 45.7).[93]

The injunction is given me . . . not to worship or in any way show reverence to another than to him who thus commands me, whom I am both bidden to fear so that I may not be forsaken by him, and love with my whole being, that I may die for him (*Scorpiace* 4.4–5).[94]

For Cyprian of Carthage, the collaboration of Christians with the Roman emperor Decius' requirement of universal sacrifice (249–51 C.E.) was a form of "desertion" motivated by insufficient fear of God. Many Christians, he complains, feared the Romans more than they feared God. If they had sufficient *timor* of God, they would have considered resistance as a necessary *probatio fidei* and endured the wrath of the Romans with patience and courage (*De lapsis* 7).

Marcus Aurelius had expressed his admiration for the person prepared for a death that could come at any instant, but he believed that "this resolve . . . must arise out of a specific decision, not out of sheer unreasoned opposition as that of the Christians (*kata psilēn parataxin hos hoi Christianoi*). The chosen death should come after reflection and with dignity, and so as to convince others, without histrionic display" (*Meditations* 11.3). The emperor's words reveal his frustration with what seemed to him the irrational *contumacia* of those Christian subjects who sought the *ambitiosa mors* decried by Tacitus (*Agricola* 42.4) and Lucian (*De morte Peregrini* 21). He could not comprehend why those for whom he suffered so much should take such pride in defiantly resisting him. What more could they ever ask of a king?[95] But Tertullian believed that the Christians' fearless and self-annihilating *obstinatio* was finally the greatest attraction and recruiting tool of the movement (*semen est sanguis Christianorum* [*Apologeticum* 50.13]):[96]

Many of you preach the endurance of pain and of death, such as Cicero in his *Tusculanae*, Seneca in his *Fortuita*, Diogenes, Pyrrho, Callinicus. And yet their words never find so many disciples as the Christians who teach by deeds. That very *obstinatio* with which you taunt us, is your teacher. For who that beholds it is not stirred to inquire, what lies indeed within it? Who, on inquiry, does not join us? (*Apologeticum* 50.14–15)[97]

As long as the Christian's death could be represented as voluntary and without fear, it testified to, it "witnessed" the will and power, the *fides* of the Christian.[98] Like the brave gladiator, Tertullian was prepared to run headlong into the embrace of the greatest causes of his fear.[99] Tertullian's god was, like the Vedic Prajapati, "the Lord of Death whose shade is Immortal Life." And Tertullian's embrace of that god is expressed, above all, in *amor mortis*.

In this framework of Tertullian's thought, so far from being avoided, suffering and persecution are useful—indeed, necessary disciplinary exercises for the potential soldier-slave of the Kingdom of God (as they were to Apuleius' Lucius)—and so these sufferings originate, at times in Tertullian's thought, not with the evil Romans but Tertullian's good god (as Lucius' sufferings, which appeared to be inflicted by Stoneblind Fortune, turned out to be, finally, ordained by Isis Fortuna):

> And when is God more believed in (*deus magis creditur*) than when there is a greater fear of him—than in times of persecution? (. . .) Then is *fides* both more zealous in preparation, and better disciplined (*disciplinatior*) in fasts and *stationes*, in prayers and humility, in diligence and love, in sanctity and sobriety. There is no room, in fact, for anything but fear and hope. So even by this very thing it is clearly shown to us that that [suffering] cannot be imputed to the devil which improves the slaves of God (*De fuga in persecutione* 1.5–6).[100]

In one of the many "slippages" in the *Apologeticum*, Tertullian asks his fellow Christians why they complain about persecution when *they wish to suffer*? "You ought to love those who guarantee that you suffer what you wish!" (50.1.), he says.

In his treatise *De fuga in persecutione*, there is (as there is in *Ad martyres* 3.1–5) an extended metaphor where Tertullian's god is pictured as the *agōnothetēs*, the *editor* of the *agōn* in which the *servi* are tested and the proven *martyres* separated from the *negatores*:

> Persecution may be viewed as a contest. By whom is the conflict proclaimed, but by him by whom the crown and the rewards are offered? You will find in the Apocalypse [of John] its proclamation, setting forth the rewards by which he incites to victory those, above all, who have the distinction of conquering in persecution, in very deed contending in their vicarious struggle not against flesh and blood, but against spirits of wickedness. So, too you will see that the judging of the contest belongs to the same glorious one who, as *agōnothetēs*, calls us to the prize (1.5).[101]
>
> For the sake of the contest God had appointed *martyria* for us, that thereby we might make trial with our opponent. . . . (. . .) He wished to make man, now plucked from the devil's throat through *fides*, trample upon him likewise by *virtus*, that he might not merely have escaped from, but also completely vanquished his enemy (*Scorpiace* 6.1).[102]

And yet, as many have noted, Tertullian, finally, did not embrace the voluntary death that he so admired. Perhaps it was for the same reason that he seems desperate to hold onto his education, his body, and the wife whose very presence must hold him hostage in the Roman *saeculum*.

Through Tertullian's Looking Glass

In Tertullian's topsy-turvy world, Christians, enthused, energized by their great and powerful King of Kings, are the ones to be feared.[103] They are able, even before the trumpet's blare, to turn the tables and terrorize the gods and powers of non-Christians:

> O Christian, do you fear man?—you who ought to be feared by the angels, since you are to judge angels; you who ought to be feared by evil spirits, since you have received power also over evil spirits; you who ought to be feared by the whole world, since by you, too, the world is judged (*De fuga* 10.2).[104]

The Christian has the power to coerce the possessing demons (i.e., the gods of non-Christians); he compels them to confess, against their wills, in blushing shame, that they are really no gods at all. These demons and false gods are terrified of the Christians' power to call upon the greatest powers of the universe. The most powerful forces of the non-Christians are subject to the will of the slaves of God:

> They are subjects to the slaves of God and Christ. At a touch, a breath from us, they are seized by the thought of, the foretaste of that fire, and they leave the bodies of men at our command, all against their will, in pain, blushing to have you witness it (*Apologeticum* 23.15).[105]

Perpetua treads on the head of the "dragon" who behaves *quasi timens me* (4.7). She is feared by the *immundus spiritus* (10.10).

In this mode of his thought, far from denying that Christians have formed a *coniuratio*, Tertullian describes the Christians as a sort of "Fifth Column": You Romans are lucky that our *disciplina* encourages us to die rather than kill—for we have infiltrated, no—filled up the whole Roman world—including the army![106]

> If we wished to play the part of open enemies and not merely hidden avengers (*vindices occulti*), would we lack the power that numbers and resources give? (. . .) We are but of yesterday, and we have already filled the world and everything you have—cities, *insulae*, small settlements (*castella*), towns, *conciliabula*, the camps themselves, tribes, decuries, palace, senate, forum. All we have left to you is the temples. For what war should we not have been fit and ready even if unequal in forces—we who are so glad to be butchered— were it not, of course, that in *ista disciplina* we are given greater allowance to be killed than to kill? (*Apologeticum* 37.4–5)[107]

In the upside-down, the extreme and capsized world of Tertullian, the Christians are in position of the imperial conquerors, and it is the Romans who are the rebel slaves:

> For though all the power of demons and spirits . . . is subject to us, still, like worthless slaves, they mingle insolence with their fear, and delight in injuring those whom at other times they fear/respect (*verentur*) (for fear also is a source of hate). And, besides, their desperate condition of being condemned already causes them to consider it a consolation to gratify their spite while their punishment is delayed. And yet, when recognized, they are subdued and succumb to their condition; hostile to us from afar, face to face they entreat us. So when, like rebels breaking out of slave-jails, prison or mines, or that sort of

penal servitude, they break out against us (in whose power they are)—though they well
know they are no match for us and are only so much the more damned for it (*Apologeticum*
27.5–7).[108]

In a passage that would have delighted James C. Scott, the role of rebels and slaves has
shifted onto the Roman devils.[109] Tertullian illustrates the "slave's mentality" very well—
the obsequiousness and submissiveness up close and the hatred at a distance, the hatred
caused by fear. Non-Christians, in Tertullian, are always the envious *aemuli* of the Christians, never the other way around.[110] The cancellation of fear allows the reversal of roles.

At the inquisition held by the Proconsul Saturninus in July, 180 c.e., the Christian Speratus responded to the proconsul's advice that he and his fellow confessed Christians
demonstrate their loyalty and submission to the Emperor (and so earn his pardon, his *indulgentia*) by swearing by his *genius*. Speratus answered the Proconsul with the following
words:

> The empire of this *saeculum* I do not recognize; but rather I serve that god, whom no man
> hath seen . . . because I know my *dominus* is the emperor of kings and of all peoples (*Passio
> Sanctorum Scillitanorum* 6).[111]

Speratus insisted that the Christians were not malevolent or malefactors, but that their
King is the *dominus* of the Romans' king. Rejection of the Roman imperial order, then,
was emphatically not, in the rebellious or separatist realm of Speratus or Tertullian's
thought, rejection of monarchical government or hierarchical chains of commands. In this
looking-glass world, "emperor" and "god" were not incompatible ideas—only "*Roman
emperor*" and "god."

What did the notion of "king" mean to Tertullian? Like other humans in complex cultures, Tertullian could think of no greater title or honor.[112] What made a "king" by any
name was exactly his being very set apart and highly sacralized (i.e., made "unnatural":
surrounded with *taboo/religio*; highly praised, decorated, honored; given a raised seat or dais,
a headdress, titles, a stick).[113] At the same time, for Tertullian, the human "king" and his
world (where the rules of the game were fragile, execrable, or non-existent) could only be
the *aemulus*, the demonic imitator, the twisted mirror of the true and original ruler of the
true kingdom and the supreme *deus/dominus* of the Christians. Every universalism is a form
of topsy-turvydom: Tertullian's "universal" order could only be in opposition to the
Roman "particular universalism."

For Tertullian, there needed to be one king at the top of one pyramid of authority. In
De praescriptione haereticorum, Tertullian rails against the democratic and egalitarian ten-
dencies of the *haeretici* whom he brands, as he does the Romans, as *rebelles*. These *rebelles*
have no strictly derived or apportioned *auctoritas* and so lack *disciplina*. They have, for Tertullian, many of the faults that the Bacchants or the Catilinarians had for the senators of
republican Roman:

> Nowhere is promotion easier than in the camp of the rebels (*in castris rebellium*) where the
> mere fact of being there is the cause of their advancement. And so today one man is their
> *episcopus*, tomorrow another; today a man is a *diaconus* who tomorrow is a *lector*, today one

is a *presbyter* who tomorrow is a *laicus*. For (among them) sacerdotal duties (*sacerdotalia munera*) are given even to *laici* (41.7–8).[114]

A government headed by the most fearful and majestic *imperator* Tertullian could imagine was the ultimate source of the discipline and restraint necessary for the orderly government of humans. Such fear and majesty was undermined, for Tertullian, by the casual way the Romans and Greeks depicted even their most powerful gods. For Tertullian, like Minucius Felix, the playful familiarity shown to the gods in Varro's *fabulae* or the *rationes* of the poets, disqualified such gods for the role of moral enforcers.[115] In *Ad nationes*, he calls non-Christians *irreligiosi* (1.10.20); they dishonored their gods by casually putting their images up for sale. Indeed every single object of cult is on the market (1.10.20). For Tertullian, involving the gods in the bargains, exchanges, oaths, and contracts in the daily reciprocities of life demeaned and desecrated them. The King God must be more carefully set apart and shielded from the casual touch of the humans lest his unassailable majesty be worn away by friction like right hands of the bronze statues set up by ancient gateways, or the big toe of the Vatican's bronze Peter.[116]

S I X

Governed by a Perfect Fear

> Rabbi Hanina . . . said "Pray for the peace of the government, for except for fear
> of that, we should have swallowed each other alive."
>
> —MISHNA AVOT 3.2[1]

The Roman historian Tacitus (56–117 C.E.), believed that there had once been a time when
humans did not need to be governed by fear (*metus*). The most ancient mortals (*vetustis-
simi mortalium*) had been restrained by *pudor* and *modestia* and had sought nothing discon-
sonant with the *mores*. But when equality (*aequalitas*) was replaced with self-serving ambition
(*ambitio*) the government of shame (*pudor*) and self-restraint (*modestia*) were replaced by
coercion (*vis*) and fear (*metus*) (*Annales* 3.26).[2]

The Greco-Roman Plutarch (before 50 C.E.–after 120 C.E.) took exception to Epicurus'
insistence that the mechanisms of shame and guilt were sufficient to terrify the transgressor
even if he escaped detection. For Plutarch such self-control might characterize the aristocrat,
but the dregs of humanity must be terrified by hell and lured by hope of a pleasant afterlife.
While the absence of fear and hope in the Epicurean universe may have assuaged *deisidaimonia* (*Non Posse Suaviter Vivi Secundum Epicurum, Moralia* 1090C-D; 1100F), the absence
of fear and hope put humans on the level with "the brutes" (ibid. 1092A-C). Shame and fear
(*aidos* and *phobos*) *directed only at the god/s* would be the price of hope (*elpis*) (1101C).[3]

Pudor and *religio* were most effective in governing the behavior of humans in cultures
with a high degree of socialization, and as Peter L. Berger and Thomas Luckmann point
out, "Maximal success in socialization is likely to occur in societies with very simple division of labor and minimal distribution of knowledge."[4] This was emphatically *not* the case
in the Roman Empire which elicited visions of human governance consonant with its
often chaotic complexity. Paradoxically, Tertullian more often saw the world from the
point of view of the rulers rather than the ruled, imagining himself as the spokesman,

slave and vicar of the Spiritus Sanctus.[5] From this perspective, Tertullian, like Cicero, saw the world as spiraling inexorably downward, slipping away from the discipline and self-constraint (the *pudor* and *religio*) in which the moral life of humans had been anchored into the maelstrom of confusion and impurity. The more complex the culture, the simpler but firmer the ideology needed to whip the world into order. Tertullian was one of many minds engaged in formulating the ideology of empire.

A world without cities, kings and hierarchical structures of government, empires and kings was as remote to Tertullian as it was to Ovid.[6] While the Romans of the civil war period and the empire and the Christians of the empire could (just barely) imagine a time before kings, elaborate hierarchies and divisions of labor, laws and punishments, they imagined that the mechanisms of self-government had either never worked or that they had long ago ceased to work.[7] Savage, untamed humans, living in perpetual civil war, had to be set apart, domesticated, controlled—their energies enhanced but harnessed and directed.[8]

When in the heterogeneous and cosmopolitan Roman Empire *pudor* and *religio* became inadequate governing forces, Tertullian, like Cicero (and unlike the Cynics and Epicureans) felt that the moral structure, the regulation of human behavior needed to be authorized and dictated from without, standardized, and fortified with fear of a powerful king god. Unlike systems of reciprocity, which seem all but "hard-wired" into human social networks,[9] this imposed order (Tertullian's *disciplina*) required that the human undergo a radical *re*-education, indoctrination into the new order, and, particularly, into the fear that is central to maintaining that order.

The Christian Athenagoras asserted that Marcus Aurelius and Commodus allowed every *ethnos* and *dēmos* to have their own gods, but he felt it imperative that every people fear some god, in order that "through fear of god they might be kept from wrongdoing" (*Legatio pro Christianis* 1.2). Lactantius will assert that it was hard to build a kingly government on a benign god; such a god could have no *administratio*, no *mundi gubernatio* worthy of a god "to whom all lands are subject" (*cui omnia terrena subiecta sunt*) (*De ira* 4). It was fear that inspired the behaviors and attitudes upon which these Christians would build Tertullian's ideal government of the world. The government of Tertullian's New Kingdom required not a gentler or more compassionate king, but a fiercer one. *De praescriptione haereticorum* (43.3–5) and the five books of the *Ad Marcionem* were the bloody fields in which Tertullian waged perhaps his fiercest battle (cf. the battle metaphors in *Adversus Marcionem* 3.5.1, 4.5.7), that against the "heretical" position that there had to be a good and gentle god above and beyond the awful creator god of the Jews, one "with no fire warming up in hell and no outer darkness in which there is shuddering and gnashing of teeth."[10]

> If he [God] displays neither hostility or wrath, if he neither condemns nor *vexat*, if, that is, he never makes himself a judge, I cannot see how the *ratio disciplinarum* . . . can have any stability (*Adversus Marcionem* 1.26.1).[11]

> They [the Marcionites] say that god is not to be feared . . . . Where, however, is god not feared, except where he is not? Where god is not, there is no *veritas* (firmness, certainty).

Where there is no *veritas*, then, naturally enough, there is also such *disciplina* as theirs!
But where god is, there exists 'the fear of God, which is the beginning of wisdom.'[12]
Where the fear of God is, there is an honest/consistent gravity (*gravitas honesta*), a
thunderstruck diligence (*diligentia attonita*), as well as an anxious carefulness (*cura sollicita*)
and a well-considered admission to the group (*adlectio explorata*) and thoughtful commu-
nion (*communicatio deliberata*), promotion after good service (*promotio emerita*), and a
scrupulous submission (*subiectio religiosa*),[13] a devout service (*apparitio devota*) and a
modest gait (*processio modesta*), a united *ecclesia*, and God in all things (*De praescriptione
haereticorum* 43.3–5).[14]

There are those who, while they do not deny the existence of God, hold that he is neither
inquisitor (*dispector*) or judge, and treat with particular disdain those of us who go over to
this *disciplina* out of fear of a coming judgment, as they think they are honoring God in
freeing him from the cares of keeping watch, and the trouble of taking note—not even
regarding him as capable of anger. For if God, they say, gets angry, then he is susceptible
of corruption and passion; but that which passion and corruption can be affirmed may
also perish,[15] which God cannot do (*De testimonio animae* 2.3–5).[16]

Under the Marcionites' good and gentle god, *disciplina* could only be a *phantasma* given
that those who commit offences are free from fear (*secura delicta*) (*Adversus Marcionem*
1.27.1).[17] Tertullian's god might be loved as a *pater—propter pietatem*—but he should also be
feared like a father: *propter potestatem*. He might be loved like a legitimate *dominus*, but
he should also be feared like a *dominus: propter disciplinam* (ibid. 1.27.3). The seductively
mild god who elicited only affection could never effectively curb the appetites of his
pleasure-seeking subjects. Christians with insufficient fear of god would attend the race
course, the wild beast shows, and the theater (ibid. 1.27.5). Tertullian was very clear on the
kind of god that his government needed.

After aligning himself with the New Prophecy movement, he was even more strident in
his insistence on an angry and judgmental God. In the second chapter of *De pudicitia*, Tertullian quoted many of the scriptural passages that the despised *psychici* and their excessively
clement leader (whom he derisively labels "Pontifex Maximus"[18]) proffered to prove the
mercifulness of God. In response, he was able to fire back a tidal wave of quotations from
the prophets to confirm that God was angry, judgmental, and jealous (*zēlōtēs*), and not easily
induced to be merciful. The *psychici*, by advocating mercy, were "effeminizing rather than
invigorating *disciplina*" (*effeminantia magis quam vigorantia disciplinam* [*De pudicitia* 2.3]). He
wanted, finally, an angry judge rather than a merciful father (2.12–16). He wanted a father
with a whip.[19]

God's anger, like that of The Apostle—and unlike that of the emperor and his agents—
was always, by definition, rational and just. The purpose of his indignation was, in all cases,
the maintenance of *disciplina* (*Rationalis et indignatio quae ex affectu disciplinae est* [*De anima*
16.5–6]).[20] The fear of god encouraged obedience and fidelity (*De paenitentia* 5.3, 6.14).

While the sovereignty, universalism, and unity of Tertullian's conception of god owed
much to the remote and abstract god of urban cosmopolitan Greek philosophy,[21] he was
aware that a characterless and emotion-free god could not inspire sufficient awe and
terror to focus the attention and tame the wanton impulses of lusty virgins and other

wayward men.[22] The generic god of many Greek philosophers did not have the ferocious personality that Tertullian needed and wanted. He needed the dangerous god of the Hebrew prophets—the universal *imperator*—in order to combat the inveterate and (for Tertullian) anarchic, human practice of sacralizing, making gods of every and any force that could help or hurt them. The absolute and abstract god of Greek philosophy, freed from all boundaries and definitions was emasculated, as terrifying as an empty jelly jar in a cobwebbed basement.

Tertullian rejected the Marcionites, Valentinians, and Epicureans for many of the same reasons that Cicero rejected the Epicureans; no matter how ascetic and self-abnegating they might be individually, their teachings, by undermining fear of god(s), undermined the order and authority of government. Epicurus' indifferent and Marcion's benign gods were of no use to Tertullian.[23] A benign god encouraged *anomia*.[24] *Anomia* might encourage a different kind of morality—one based on compassion[25]—but compassion blurred all the boundaries between oneself and others that Tertullian was desperate to draw, and made one feel vulnerable and weak. Tertullian preferred the brazen halo of righteous indignation to the disarming fragility and pollution of compassion.[26]

Tertullian rejected the myriad of Roman gods because they seldom acted like magnificent kings; they were not the source or the enforcers of human moral order. For Tertullian, their failure to play the commanding and kingly role (or their doing so without sufficient *maiestas* and *gravitas*) vitiated their very claim to godliness. Tertullian either cannot understand or simply will not grant that gods, in cultures governed by shame, by *pudor* and *religio*, were not and did not need to be consistently kings or policeman. But Tertullian feels they *should*, they *must* play the role of kings and generals and governors— that was what a *real* god did! For Tertullian, that the Roman *dei* did not have those disciplinary functions (apart from their most important state functions) undermined their authority and seriousness. For Tertullian, the gods of the non-Christians simply could not fulfill their proper and princely functions; they could not inspire sufficient fear and the respect—and Tertullian's purpose was to make them still less worthy of respect.

And so, inevitably, the most formidable and dangerous rival to Tertullian's god was *never* the Roman *dei* but always the Roman *imperator.*

> You watch Caesar with greater fear and shrewder timidity than you do Olympian Jove himself. (. . .) In this, too, you will be found *irreligiosi* to those gods of yours when you show more fear for the rule of a man.[27] In fact, among you perjury by all the gods together comes quicker than by the genius of the single Caesar (*Apologeticum* 28.2–3).[28]

Minucius Felix made a similar complaint about the excessive respect that Romans have for their emperors:

> Men invoke their *numen*, make supplication to their images, pray to their *genius*, that is, their *daemon*; and think it safer to swear falsely by the genius of Jupiter than by that of their king (*Octavius* 29.5).[29]

Tertullian and Minucius Felix profess to be astonished that the subjects of the Roman Empire feared the emperor more than the gods and tried to propitiate him with more cleverness.[30] Are these Christian authors actually surprised by this? I think not! But Tertullian, at least, needed to argue that the very *religio* they show to the emperors causes them to be *irreligiosi* to the gods!

Like Cicero, Tertullian wanted both the legislator and the laws of his *politeuma* to be super-sacralized. They should be electrified, backed up with eternal, inexorable, and painful physical punishments. Respecting the fixed, highly charged, and dangerous boundaries should be rewarded by greatly magnified and eternal life and power.[31]

> Think over all this, remembering how short is any punishment that does not continue after death (*Apologeticum* 45.6).[32]

> There is no real fear (*timor iustus*) if the peril is in doubt. On the . . . resurrection [of the body] both the reward and the danger hang (*De resurrectione carnis* 21.4).[33]

In ancient Roman tradition, the boundary had been the pivot; every line was crossed and re-crossed in an elaborate and interminable series of transgressions and expiations. But, for Tertullian, boundaries should be at the edge, firmly fixed and unbreachable. "Merely human" laws and traditions could be evaded:

> How much authority can human laws have, when a man has the chance to evade them, and being so often invisible in his guilt, and by breaking the laws by choice or by necessity finally feeling contempt for them? (*Apologeticum* 45.5).[34]

"That is why," he goes on to say, "Epicurus makes light of all torture and pain; if it is slight, he says, you may despise it, if it is great it will not last long."[35]

Cicero helped Tertullian conceptualize and find words for an ideal world government as part of a fixed and ordered monarchical hierarchy, whose laws were divinely authorized, fixed, and very, very strictly enforced. The divine king god was as central to Tertullian's Christians as it was to the Romans of the Empire, and had the potential to set him (as did the Sicilian rebels' King Eunus) into direct conflict with the Roman *imperator*.

Conclusions: Through the Imperial Looking Glass

Tertullian's desire for self-determination—to be the author of the rules by which he lived—was the fiercer the more the vast cosmopolitan and hierarchical Empire moved toward an increasingly sacralized universality, toward legal uniformity and common citizenship.[36] Tertullian is facilitating an imperial vision of the world.

In the increasingly dominant rebellious and separatist thought of Tertullian, his idealized *ecclesia* was a kingdom.[37] Christians—provided that they quarantined themselves from the pollution of contact with non-Christians—could be their own *natio* or *genus*.[38] Tertullian's segregated world was not unlike that of the author of the *Epistle of Diognetus* where *eusebeia, thrēskeia, deisidaimonia, basileia, politeuma* all share the same mental universe.[39] In Tertullian's "utopia," there is no distinct cultic sphere, no possible separation of anything like our "religion" and "politics" and "economics" any more than there could be for the Amish, the Tibetans, the Navaho, the authors of the Mishna, the *umma* of

Muhammad, or the inhabitants of More's Utopia. When Tertullian (as later *mutatis mu-tandis* Cyprian) is most rebellious in his rejection of the Roman Empire and its authorities ("the devil and his pomps"), he creates a divinely authorized hierarchical system that mirrors and competes with a Ciceronian idealized, essentialized, comprehensive state *religio*.[40] He imagines a complete and heavily fortified Empire of God possessing its own king and royal family, its *imperator Christus*, its own magisterial hierarchy, its own army, its own laws, its own system of sacralizing and desecrating, its eternal rewards and punishments. This kingdom, already existing *in potentia*, will eventually exist *in substantia*, supplanting the Roman one. Tertullian's Kingdom of God will be the perfect, the real *imperium sine fine*, ruled over by the real and perfect Emperor.[41] In his separatist frame of mind, Tertullian distinguished the Christian from the slaves of the devil in every way possible; eating, dressing, speaking, marrying, dying must all set the Christian apart. He was an ardent "narcissist of minor differences."[42] If the non-Christians passed on the right, the Christians must pass on the left; if "heretics" cut short their fasts, "true" Christians would prolong them. Compare the author of the *Didache*: "Do not fast with the hypocrites, for they fast on the second and fifth days of the week (Mondays and Thursdays), but fast, rather,[43] on the fourth and sixth days (Wednesdays and Fridays)" (8.1). The exaggeration of differences does not hide the mirroring. In the words of Anton Blok, "Social identity lies in difference, and difference is established, reinforced and defended against what is closest—and what is closest (in several senses of the word) represents the greatest threat."[44]

But the myriad of minor distinctions by which the community of Christians was sacralized mattered much less to Tertullian, finally, than *who* was doing the sacralizing. In this looking-glass universe, what was most significant was *who* did the binding and separating off, *who* performed the critical acts of sanctifying and authorizing.[45] It was not the functions or offices of government that were nonnegotiable but whether *Christians* filled them that mattered. It made no difference to Tertullian that Christians purified and initiated with water like myriad other groups known to him: What mattered was *who* was doing the initiating and *who* stipulated the conditions. It didn't matter that other groups sacralized marriage bonds: It was *who* could sacralize the marriage bond and *who* determined its conditions. Tertullian had a strong desire to legislate the conditions of marriage, divorce, remarriage, the days and lengths of fasts. He asserted the right of Christians to sacralize and desecrate and not to accept or respect the distinctions made by others.[46]

> I consider it audacity to dispute the goodness of a divine precept; for *it is not the fact that it is good which binds us to obey, but the fact that God has enjoined it.* The majesty of divine power has the paramount right to exact the rendering of obedience; the authority of he who commands is prior to the utility of he who serves (*De paenitentia* 4.6).[47][emphasis mine]

The *utilitas* of the *serviens* is trumped by the *auctoritas* of the *imperans*; by this decree, Tertullian negates the purpose of the ancient *religiones*.

It mattered less what a god prescribed than *whose* god prescribed it. Even in his apologetic modes, Tertullian made it clear that while the Scythian Diana's demand for human blood was revolting, such bloodshed would not be disgusting were it required by the Christian's god:

> This *saeculum* allowed Diana of the Scythians, or Mercury of the Gauls, or Saturn of the Africans to be appeased by human *victima*, and in Latium to this day Jove has human blood given him to taste in the middle of the city; and no one thinks it is a matter of debate, or imagines that it occurs without reason, or without the incalculable/precious will of his god (*inaestimabilis dei voluntas*). If our God, too, for the purpose of having victims of his own should require *martyria* for himself, should anyone reproach him for the mournful (*funesta*) *religio*, and the lugubrious rites (*lugubres ritus*), and the altar which was a pyre (*ara rogus*), and the undertaker who was priest (*pollinctor sacerdos*)—and not, rather, have counted as blessed those whom god would have eaten?
>
> *Sed enim Scytharum Dianam aut Gallorum Mercurium aut Afrorum Saturnum hominum victima placari apud saeculum licuit, et Latio ad hodiernum Iovi media in urbe humanus sanguis ingustatur, nec quisquam retractat aut non rationem praesumit aliquam aut inaestimabilem dei sui voluntatem. [7] Si noster quoque deus propriae hostiae nomine martyria sibi depostulasset, quis illi exprobrasset funestam religionem et lugubres ritus et aram rogum et pollinctorem sacerdotem, et non beatum amplius reputasset quem deus comedisset?* (*Scorpiace* 7.6–7)[48]

Sacralizing and desecrating, blessing and cursing were behaviors shared by Tertullian's Christians with the "idolaters"—but when performed by non-Christians, these similar behaviors were derivative, mocking diabolical imitations. Non-Christian *castitas* was, for instance, a Satanic mocking emulation of the Christian (*Ad uxorem* 1.7.5):

> The *diabolus* by the mysteries of idols (*idolorum mysteriis*) emulates/competes with the *res* of the divine *sacramenta*. He, too baptizes (*tingit*) some, that is, of his own *credentes* and *fideles*; he promises the putting away of sins by a *lavacrum* (of his own); and if my memory still serves me, Mithra there sets his marks on the foreheads of his soldiers; celebrates the oblation of bread, and introduced an image of resurrection and before a sword wreathes a crown (*De praescriptione haereticorum* 40.2–4).[49]

The World Upside Down: Fear Begets Love

> How will you love unless you fear not to love?
>   *Quomodo diliges, nisi timeas non diligere?*
>
> Adversus Marcionem 1.27.3[50]

> He who is not afraid to suffer will be perfect in love, without a doubt, of God.
>   *Qui pati non timet, iste erit perfectus in dilectione utique Dei.*
>
> Tertullian, De fuga 14.2

The fear that was so heightened and intensified that it could overturn the fear of death could be experienced as love. The man who is not afraid to suffer will be perfect in love.

> John exhorts us to lay down our lives—even for our brethren—affirming that there is no fear in love (*negans timorem esse in dilectione*): "For perfect love (*perfecta dilectio*) casts out

fear (*timor*), since fear has punishment; and he who fears is not perfect in love (*non est perfectus in dilectione*)."[51] (. . .) What love (*dilectio*) does he assert to be perfect, but that which puts fear to flight, and motivates confession (*animatrix confessionis*)? What penalty (*poena*) will be appointed as the punishment of fear (*timorem puniat*), but that which "He Who Denies" (the *negator*) is about to pay, who has to be slain, body and soul, in *gehenna*: and if he teaches that we must die for the brethren, how much more for the *dominus*? (*Scorpiace* 12.4–5)

Notice that fear of anything other than God will result in the emotion of fear dominating that of love, and was, for Tertullian, a crime that would be punished in Gehenna. Similarly love of anything or anyone except God would prevent you from having the complete surrender to/identity with God necessary for your *theōsis*.[52]

The Culmination

How could the effort at self-sublimation possibly be worthwhile?

I believe that the crushing frustration and disappointment of standardization and miniaturization that takes place in complex cultures with their often steeply graded hierarchies and elaborate divisions of labor, with the concomitant disempowerment and loss of autonomy, and with the necessity to accept sometimes endlessly deferred gratification, ceases to feel like deprivation and more like *theōsis* when carried to the extreme of self-annihilation.[53]

Embrace it [*paenitentia*] as a shipwrecked man embraces the *fides* of some plank. It will draw you forth when sunk in the waves of sins, and bear you forward into the port of divine clemency. Seize the chance for the unexpected felicity that you, who were nothing to God but a drop in a bucket and dust of the threshing floor and a potter's vessel become that tree which planted by the waters, perennially in leaf, bearing fruit in its season, and which will see neither fire not the axe (*De paenitentia* 4.2).[54]

To live as much as possible in his imaginary or potential world, Tertullian had to radically reduce the role played by both the dangers and the attachments that inspired the *religiones* of the ancient Romans: the illnesses and storms and floods and famines, the brigands and soldiers, the landlords, tax collectors and officials who threatened one's family and flocks. The kind of fears and dangers that inspired the *religiones* of the Roman farmer are almost invisible in the thousands of pages of Tertullian's work. The system of wily diversions and substitutions, the calculated bargaining of the sacrificial system, was to be replaced by total sacrifice, "spiritual sacrifice": the sacrifice of one's *animus*, one's will.

Needless to say, the fight that Tertullian and his fellow Christians had to engage in would be lifelong, and they could not finally prevail without the weight of powerful coercive hierarchical institutions. The deepest and most ancient ties and concerns, like all elemental bonds and obligations, tend to reassert themselves. These primary attachments could only be sublimated.[55]

The satisfactions of relative competence and independence that motivated the ancient farmer's *religiones* with all its squirrel-like fears and tensions would be replaced, in Tertullian, by the ecstasy of focused and fanatic loyalty and loss of the anxious and alienated self in a united and collective (even if often imaginary) Royal We. What one loses in one sphere would be made up for in the other. The ultimate in joy and simplicity is that of the militant martyr, the self-confessing and self-sacrificing soldier/citizen of the alternative world.

Tertullian grew weary of trying to sail without a compass and began, as best he could, to block his ears to the voice of the sirens luring this *saeculum* onto the rocks.[56] He longed to pass safely through the narrow straits that led to the harbor of the New Kingdom. He attuned his radio crystal to the voice of the *spiritus sanctus* and relayed its directives to the passengers of his own little vessel, his *ecclesia*. There could be, for him, a homecoming—but only to a city that, like New Orleans after Hurricane Katrina, would require an enormous expenditure of energy to renew and protect. The vigor of his *fides* and the relentless efforts of his *disciplina* would raise the ramparts and dams and levees of the new City of God. But this resplendent new world, like a second childhood, could only be erected over the slimy mess of an adult's complexity and responsibilities that hung like radioactivity in the air, like mildew in the walls, like typhus in the lungs. Like the golden outer sarcophagus of Tutankhamen, the dazzling splendor of the New Kingdom would have, at its core, a blackened corpse. The adult Tertullian's righteousness could act only as a purifying firewall or breakwater against the demonic forces of impurity that lay in ambush on every side. Tertullian's bitter rages had to hold back the riptides of desire and guilt—not to mention compassion—that threatened to overwhelm him as they did Jesus in the wilderness, Hermas in the countryside, or Antony in the desert. The simplicity and righteous innocence and purity of the adult would always be under threat not only from without but even more from within. For his dream to survive at all, he would have to reinforce it with towering fortifications, carefully identifying and excluding the enemy without; sniffing out, with a vigilant and ferocious hate, the enemy within—his anxious, inadequate, weak, soft-hearted, doubtful and fearful human self.[57] Like the Roman Stoics, and for the same reason, Tertullian would carry the plague-infected rats with him into the port of salvation in the hold of his own ship.

SEVEN

Precarious Integration. Managing the Fears of the Romans: Tertullian on Tenterhooks

At the beginning of his first treatise against Marcion, Tertullian evoked the world of the nomadic Scythians. He was endeavoring to arouse the shuddering horrors of his reader for the "Pontic" heretic who, like Diogenes the Cynic, emerged from the wastes of the Black Sea (*Adversus Marcionem* 1.3). Otherwise, there is little in the way of landscape in Tertullian.[1] The evolution that Tertullian desired—for farms to replace forest and wilderness, herds to replace wild beasts, cities to replace isolated farmsteads (*De anima* 30)—was all but accomplished on the pages of his books. The world of the first major Latin Christian writer whose work we possess was emphatically a world of cities conglomerated into an empire.[2] It was all he knew, all he cared to imagine. When he imagined working, it was as an advocate, artisan, athlete, a slave, servant, philosopher, teacher, or tax collector. Nor was there room in his mind for other creatures apart from humans.[3] The only lamb was Christ.[4]

Even or especially when he was repulsed by them, the city-state and the empire were the negative mirror images and chief competitors, the envious and demonic *aemuli* of his *regnum*, his *imperator*, his *ecclesia*.[5] His was a world not of competing "religions" but of vying *imperia*.[6] Tertullian's god was an *imperator* who from his throne issued judgments and edicts, bestowed donatives and crowns, dispatched messengers and *procuratores*. Tertullian's *princeps generis* (*Adversus Marcionem* 1.24.7) had his *plebs* and his *milites sacrati*, his *servi*, his games and shows, his own exclusive cult. Tertullian was, first of all, the *miles sacratus* to his *imperator*, and only secondarily a *servus* to his *dominus*, or (more rarely) a *filius* to his *pater*.

Tertullian's enemies were not "pagans" or "heathens" but *nationes* and *ethnici*.[7] The *saeculum* of Tertullian was not "secular" as opposed to "sacred," but rather "this age" or "this world" as opposed to the world to come, the empire of god, "our time."[8] *Saeculum* suggested temporal revolution to Tertullian, one age replaced by another. (Eternity, for Tertullian, was the cycle of the ages, the *saecula saeculorum* [*Ad uxorem* 1.1.3].[9]) There was—*for certain*—a *saeculum* to come.[10] (He preferred *saeculum* to *mundus* precisely because the *mundus* was the fixed axis, the "navel" or *omphalos*, of a spatial dimension and the spatial dimension itself.[11])

Tertullian's Kingdom To Come was *not* molded from the clay of ancient Israel. The ancient scriptures spoke to Tertullian about Christ, and even more, about Tertullian and his immediate and urban imperial milieu. While Tertullian was steeped in the prophetic texts of the Greek Septuagint, he tended to read the prophets as the Qumranites read them: allegorically.[12] He was not interested in finding the physical, emotional, and psychological worlds in the books of the Hebrews; rather than expanding his own world with them, he used *scriptura* (like many a modern Christian for the same reasons) as a quarry of figures and signs that he could raid for any purpose.[13] His use of these highly charged words could give his own words authority with other educated Christians, even if most Christians and other Greeks and Romans might be insensitive to them.[14] For the same reason that Plato and many of the Athenian elite emulated the Spartans, the urbane and cosmopolitan "pseudo-alien" Tertullian (to use Meek's phrase) will use his universalizing and essentializing education to construct a very limited and localized counter-culture universe that resembled that of the isolated Montanists of Phrygia or the Amish of Pennsylvania.

In the *De corona* (written after 208 C.E., at a time when he had determined on a policy of outright resistance to the Roman Emperor), Tertullian wrote his extended and justly famous narration of the rebellion of a single Christian soldier. But the aspect of this account that I want to bring to the attention of my reader at this point is that Tertullian allowed that there were Christians in the Roman army who were greatly disturbed by this soldier's calling attention to his identity as a Christian. Written while in a profoundly rebellious frame of mind, Tertullian was reluctant even to grant the name of Christian to these critics (*nescio an Christianorum; non enim aliae ethnicorum*). But, the *fratres* who were serving the Emperor rebuked the confessing Christian soldier:

> . . . as headstrong and rash, and too eager to die, because, when interrogated on a mere matter of attire, he brought trouble to the bearers of The Name. [They berated] the only brave man among so many brethren soldiers—the only Christian (*solus scilicet fortis inter tot fratres commilitones, solus Christianus*). It is plain that they also intend to reject *martyria*. . . . So they murmur that a peace so good and long is endangered for them.[15] Nor do I doubt that some are already moving away from the Scriptures, packing their bags, equipping themselves for flight from city to city (for that is all of the *evangelium* they care to remember)! I know, too, their *pastores* are lions in peace, deer in the fight! (*De corona* 1.4–5).[16]

This is one of the innumerable passages (many pointed out by Eric Rebillard[17]) where early Christian writers revealed their awareness of the ways in which Christians were deeply enmeshed in the life of the empire, and had many-layered and conflicted notions of themselves and their roles within it. Tertullian mapped out in the *De idololatria* the myriad of ways in which Christians were entangled in the demonic world around them. Only those who chose death could break free altogether.[18]

Highly trained in Latin and Greek literature and rhetoric, inhabiting a Roman colony with family bonds to (at least) a wife and brother,[19] it would have been almost as difficult for a man like Tertullian as it was for Seneca or Tacitus to extract himself from the web of attachments, obligations, duties, and loyalties of the Roman Empire.[20] And Tertullian undeniably still wanted something from the world he saw as implacably hostile. Like Minucius Felix and Justin Martyr, Tatian, Athenagoras, Origen, and others, Tertullian still hoped for something in return for his often flamboyant displays of erudition in Greek and Roman literature, lore, and philosophy—some degree of honor and respect, of leverage with the educated of the Mediterranean.[21] (Consider the almost pathetic self-appreciation of Minucius Felix in *Octavius* 39.) Tertullian wanted and desired non-Christians to recognize his intellect—and respect the movement that could attract such qualities of intellect (cf. *De cultu feminarum* 2.13).

We cannot know what made Tertullian so hostile to the Greco-Roman world. He may have suffered some disappointment or insult. He may simply have been frustrated with the human condition and felt, as so many humans do, that "the world as it is" was fundamentally unendurable, and that in some other world he would be at the center and apex—where he belonged.[22] Tertullian, like other highly trained Christians in the first centuries, suffered acutely from an inversion of the "subaltern's dilemma": Even while thinking of himself as a spokesman for and voluntary member of an oppressed group, he adopted and adapted the urban and imperial worldview, the language and class attitudes of the dominant Greco-Roman culture. Only in his perfect and imaginary *regnum* could the world be stripped of all its entangled and unsettling confusions, its terrifying uncertainties—only in the divine kingdom could he find the pristine ideology of monarchical rule. Tertullian was, paradoxically but most emphatically, helping to formulate and advance the program of sacralizing, centralizing, rationalizing, and justifying an intensely monarchical, hierarchical, hegemonic system,[23] one that would find its earthly and regal fulfillment in another *saeculum* that Tertullian could not have imagined in his wildest nightmares.

Stayin' Alive

> Domitian, though prone by nature to anger . . . was pacified by the moderation and discretion of Agricola, in whom there was no *contumacia*, no vain and pompous display of freedom inviting both renown and ruin. Let those whose tendency it is to admire only what is forbidden learn from him that great men can live even under bad rulers; and that *obsequium* and *modestia*, if industry and energy go with them, can reach the same height of fame, to which, more often, men have climbed by precipitous paths, and have earned their glory by an ostentatious death, but with no profit to the state.
>
> Tacitus, *Agricola* 42.3–4[24]

Tertullian's main goal, then, in his negotiatory moods,[25] was to allay his fear of the Romans by allaying the fears of the Romans. Tertullian set up his revival tent within the gates of the devil's own circus. He found himself in the position of a concessionary who had to maintain tolerable relations with and allay the suspicions of the management that he was diverting the loyalty of the audience from the Big Top. At the same time, he had to bark loudly and persuasively enough to lure the attention of the public away from the main show. To the degree that he feared being ejected from the only venue in which he could recruit his community, he had to allay the fears of the men in the front office. Allaying his fears depended on allaying their fears. He had to prove to them that he was not plotting a hostile takeover—that his movement was not a Fifth Column, not a dangerous *coniuratio*—even while, in his mind, it was exactly that.

Tertullian's Christians were exactly a *coniuratio*, a swearing together, in the Roman sense. The *sacramentum*, the oath of loyalty, was absolutely central to Tertullian's conception of the Christian *fraternitas*. Nevertheless, Tertullian scrupulously avoided using the word *coniuratio* of the Christians, knowing that this word would cause the Romans to watch them even more *religiose*, to fasten on them an eye as penetrating and critical as that of their own God.

Tertullian does not want Christians to be seen as *rebelles* any more than he wants them to be seen as criminals. The Romans applied the term *rebelles* to those who, having surrendered into the Roman *fides*, lived at the mercy of the Romans. Having been defeated and allowed to live by the clemency of the Romans, *rebelles* were in the position of slaves who dared to take up arms against their masters. There was, in Latin, no ideal or romanticized type of the rebel as there is in English. The word *martyr* ("witness") was a euphemism that Tertullian and other Christians used to avoid *rebellis*. (It should be remarked that Christians also had no positive word for rebels against anything but Rome. When Tertullian brands the Marcionites as *rebelles* in *De praescriptione haereticorum* [41.7], he means to excoriate—not to idealize them.[26])

Caught in the Devil's Tentacles

> You must always fear, when you desire to be safe.
>   *Metuendum est semper, esse cum tutus velis.*
>
>   Publilius Syrus (359 Friedrich)

Even while loathing the *saeculum* in which he lived, in his more conciliatory moments (and I want to emphasize that they are never more than moments), Tertullian presented his movement as compatible with, or even complementary to, the Roman *saeculum*; even when not serving in the legions, the Christians were the emperor's very best auxiliary forces. When still willing to negotiate with the Roman world (as in the *Ad nationes*, *Apologeticum*, *Ad scapulum*) or as a philosopher (as often in the *De anima*, *De baptismo*, and *De pallio*), Tertullian's thought showed the greatest complexity and tactical ingenuity. In these moments, Tertullian was closest in his patterns of thought to the delicate balancing systems, the bargaining, reciprocities, manipulations, and deceptions of the ancient sacrificial system and to the *religiones* of the ancient Romans. Indeed, there are even passages in which Tertullian urged a cautious balance: for example, in Tertullian's very philosophical *De anima*:

> Nature should be an object of reverence, not of blushes. It is lust, not natural usage, which has brought shame on the intercourse of the sexes. It is the excess, not the normal state, which is immodest and unchaste: the normal condition has received a blessing from God and is blest by Him: "Be fruitful and multiply" (and replenish the earth). Excess, however, he has cursed, in adulteries and wantonness, and whorehouses.[27]

Whereas Tertullian was wont to be a rigorist, in his more conciliatory moods, Tertullian was as moderate, modulated, astute, and flexible as he could stand to be, speaking like Plautus' slaves or Tacitus' aristocrats.[28] In this mode of Tertullian's thought, he was still willing to respect, to fear the Romans because he did not fear them over-much.

It was in this propitiatory mode that Tertullian presented his group not as a bounded, segregated, complete, and alternative universe, but rather as a particular aspect, sphere, or dimension of the Roman world. His models for co-existence were other associations, communities, and subgroups (households, towns, cities, philosophical schools, and cultic associations) that had preserved for themselves and their institutions some degree of coherence in the Empire.[29] In this mode, Tertullian likened his movement at different times to a *gens*,[30] a *natio*,[31] a *populus*,[32] a *nomen*,[33] a *philosophia*, a *secta*[34]—and, above all, a *disciplina*.[35]

Tertullian worked the wonderfully ambiguous word *disciplina* to exhaustion precisely because of its broad range of meanings and useful ambiguity. In the milder strains of his thought, *disciplina* was not the *askēsis* of the camp but the teaching of the schools.[36] While in particular passages Tertullian treats the Greek philosophical schools with contempt,[37] in his "apologetic" mode, he suggests that the Christians should be afforded the same tolerance. The Christians should have the title, the position, and the privileges of the philosophic schools:

> The freedom is openly given to philosophers of transgressing from you (*transgrediendi a vobis*) and attaching themselves to any *secta*, bearing its founder's name as their own; and nobody stirs up any hatred against them, although both in public and private they bark out their bitterest eloquence against your *mores, ritus, cultus,* and *victus* (manner of life) with so much contempt for the laws, and so little respect for persons that they even flaunt their freedom of speech against the emperors themselves with impunity (*Ad nationes* 1.4.4).[38]

While our *veritas* is manifest to everyone, nevertheless even while convinced of the goodness of our *secta*, incredulity does not reckon us a "divine business" (*divinum negotium*) but rather a species of philosophy (*philosophiae genus*). "The philosophers," he says, "teach the same things, make the same professions: innocence, justice, patience, sobriety, chastity." If, so far as *disciplina* goes, we are compared with them why are we not put on an equality with them in freedom and impunity of *disciplina*? (. . .) Who compels a philosopher to sacrifice or to take an oath, or to set out silly lamps at mid-day? . . . [The philosophers] openly destroy your gods and attack your *superstitiones* in their treatises and you applaud.

Yes, and many of them also bark against the emperors, and you sustain them. You are more ready to reward them with statues and stipends than to condemn them to the beasts (*Apologeticum* 46.2–4).[39]

In *De anima*, Christian *veritas* is the "wisdom from the school of the sky . . ." (*sapientia de schola caeli* [1.6]). In *Scorpiace*, he speaks of the "school of Christ" (*Christi schola*) whose students (*discipuli*) were chosen and informed on all points (12.1).[40]

> I confer on the *pallium* (the philosopher's gown) a fellowship with a divine *secta* and *disciplina*. Rejoice, *pallium*, and exult! A better *philosophia* has now deigned to honor thee, ever since you have begun to be a Christian vesture! (*De pallio* 6.2)[41]

Tertullian speaks of Christianity as a *cultus* (and sometimes, significantly, uses *religio* as a synonym for *cultus*). The outlandish Jews and the even more outlandish Egyptians are allowed their *cultus*, so why shouldn't we be allowed ours?[42] The Roman Empire, he argued, had and could continue to embrace a great diversity of cults. In the following quotation, the first party referred to in each of the parallel examples is the Christian, the second the non-Christian:

> Let one man cultivate (*colat*) God, another Jove; let this man raise suppliant hands to heaven, that man to the altar of *Fides*; let one (if you so suppose) count the clouds as he prays, another the panels of the ceiling; let one dedicate his own life spirit (*anima*) to his god, another that of a goat. Look to it, whether this also may form part of the accusation of *irreligiositas*—to do away with freedom of *religio* (*libertas religionis*), to forbid a man choice of deity, so that I may not cultivate (*colere*) whom I would, but am forced to cultivate (*colere*) whom I would not. No one, not even a man [i.e., the emperor] will wish to be cultivated by an unwilling man (*ab invito coli*) (*Apologeticum* 24.5–6).[43]

While in speaking to his fellow Christians, Tertullian might be belligerently intolerant, in negotiations with the Romans he suggested—15 centuries before the Enlightenment—that the Roman governors should not impair the *libertas religionis*. What he was requesting was the freedom NOT to revere, honor, or cultivate Jove or the emperor. If even the *vana superstitio* of the Egyptians is tolerated, Tertullian complains, with some bitterness, why not ours?

> Why! to the Egyptians is permitted the power of their empty *superstitio* to consecrate birds and beasts, and to condemn to death any who might kill a god of that sort (*Apologeticum* 24.7–9).[44]

In that same chapter of the *Apologeticum*, he went on to say that every *provincia*, every *urbs* had its own *deus*. Syria had Astartes, Arabia had Dusares, the Norici had Belenus, Africa had Caelestis, Mauretania its *reguli* (its "little" divine kings—like Juba).[45] There were municipal gods in Italy not cultivated by the Romans: Casinum had Delventinus. Narnia had Visidianus. Asculum had Ancharia. Volsinii had Nortia. Ocriculum had Valentia. Sutreium had Hostia. Among the Faliscans, Juno took the cognomen Curis in honor of Pater Curis.[46]

> We alone are forbidden a *religio* of our own. We injure the Romans, because we do not worship the god of the Romans. (. . .) Among you it is lawful to worship anything at all

so long as it is not the true god. We alone are kept away from our own particular *religio*. (*Sed nos soli arcemur a religionis proprietate* [*Apologeticum* 24.9].)

It is while pursuing this trajectory of thought that Tertullian whittled Latin *religio* (under the influence of Cicero's definition of *religio* as the cult of the gods) to fit one of the niches occupied by *thrēskeia* as it appeared in the Greek Jewish and Christian apologetic writers.[47] In this passage, one can see the origin of a notion of *religio* as occupying a distinct, separate (and privileged) dimension of life that could exist within and still be distinguished from the government of the Empire. This use of Tertullian's *religio* appears to be original with him. While *religio* in Tertullian preserved its association with scrupulous attention and reverence, *religio* here does not seem to be associated with any of the emotions of fear. This *religio* is, rather, a synonym for *disciplina* and for the acts and obligations that made up that *disciplina*: that is, the sacralizing behaviors, the *sacramenta* or *sacra* of the myriad of peoples and subgroups within the Empire. Tertullian classified among the *religiones* of the Iudaei the *sabbata*, *cena pura*, *ritus lucernarum*, *ieiunia cum azymis*, and *orationes litorales* (*Ad nationes* 1.13.4). Sacrifices and offerings were *officia*, *munera* of the *religio dei* (*Adversus Marcionem* 2.18.3, 2.23.4). Baptism was the *religio* of water (to be classified among the *sollemnia disciplinae* [*De baptismo* 9.1]). The "dry meal" (*xerophagia*) of the adherents of the New Prophecy was a *religio* as ancient as it was effective (*tam antiquissima quam efficacissihma religio* [*De ieiunio* 9.1]). "You charge us with the crime of incest in the *sacramenta* of our *religio* (*de sacramentis nostrae religionis*)," but, Tertullian complains, there are similar charges to be made against you for behaviors not even connected with your *sacramenta* (*Ad nationes* 1.16.20).

After a long discourse on the "idols" that were honored in the circus, Tertullian admonished his fellow Christians: "Mark well . . . how many unclean names have possessed the circus. Alien to you is a *religio* which so many spirits of the devil have occupied." (*Animadverte, Christiane, quot nomina inmunda possederint circum. Aliena est tibi religio, quam tot diaboli spiritus occupaverunt* [*De spectaculis* 8].) He spoke of the *religio* of the Roman military camp (*religio castrensis*) in which the standards and trophies of victory were cultivated (*Ad nationes* 1.12.14). A Jew, a "deserter from his *religio*" (*suae religionis desertor*), having hired himself out as a *bestiarius* in the arena, carried about an image of a Christian or of Christ with the label *onocoetes* [meaning uncertain, from *onos*, ass] (*Ad nationes* 1.14.1–2).[48] Tertullian explained: Tacitus, in his account of the *bellum Iudaicum* in the fifth book of his *Historiae*, had discoursed on the *nomen et religio gentis* (*Apologeticum* 16.2). There he described the Jews, expelled from Egypt, guided to water by wild asses. And as "we are near to the *religio* of the Jews (*nos ut Iudaicae religionis propinqui . . .*) we are thought to cultivate the same image" (*Ad nationes* 1.11.3; *Apologeticum* 16.3). Pompey, when he took Jerusalem, "visited the temple to look into the *arcana* of the *religio Iudaica*." (. . . *templum adisset speculandis Iudaicae religionis arcanis . . .* [*Apologeticum* 16.3].)

In a passage of the *Apologeticum* that has elicited a great deal of wrangling among scholars, Tertullian says:

Perhaps some question may be raised as to the standing of the *secta* [of the *Christiani*] on the ground that, under cover of a very famous *religio*, *certe licita* the *secta* insinuates quietly certain claims of its own.

fortasse an hoc nomine de statu eius (sectae) retractetur, quasi sub umbraculo insignissimae religionis, certae licitae, aliquid propriae praesumptionis abscondat. . . . (21.1)[49]

As I hope to have shown Chapter 1, "*Religio* without 'Religion,'" the word *religio* never had a legal or cultic function in Roman life.[50] Indeed, Tertullian, when and where he used the word *religio* to mean "cult," was much more likely than the Romans to make distinctions between legitimate and illegitimate *religio*. (He was, after all, a heretic hunter.) Sometimes practices that Tertullian judged to be illicit were labeled *superstitio* and contrasted with *religio*. In speaking of the refusal of the Christians to acknowledge or respect the gods of the Romans, Tertullian affected to speak from the Romans' point of view:

> In this matter we [Christians] are guilty not merely of forsaking the *religio* of the community but of introducing a monstrous *superstitio*.
>
> *Nec tantum in hoc nomine rei desertae communis religionis, sed superductae monstruosae superstitionis* (*De spectaculis* 8).

Tertullian, in his negotiatory mode, wanted to carve out, according to an array of models, a separate sphere in which Christians could be seen as some variety of already existent and tolerated association within the Empire. He (like the Romans themselves!) was prepared to operate with a complex, layered, hybrid identity. It is in this framework that Tertullian (like most of the Roman soldiers who were Christians; or like Paul, or Apuleius or Josephus) lived with sometimes conflicting sets of laws and loyalties, serving two masters.

> So as regards *honores* to kings or emperors, we have been sufficiently enjoined [by Paul] that we are to be in complete obedience (*in omni obsequio*), being, according to the precept of the apostle, submitted (*subditos*) to magistrates, princes and powers, but within the limit of the *disciplina* of our *familia* (*sed intra limites familiae nostrae disciplinae*), that is, as long as we keep at a distance from idolatry. For it is for this reason, too, that the famous example of the three brothers precedes us, who, though in other respects obedient to king Nebuchadnezzar, refused with the utmost firmness to do homage to his image (*honorem imaginis eius constantissime respuerunt*), thus showing that everything must be regarded as idolatry which elevates someone beyond the measure of human honor unto the likeness of divine sublimity (*probantes idololatrian esse quicquid ultra humani honoris modum ad instar divinae sublimitatis extollit*).[51] Thus Daniel too, who in other respects subjected himself to Darius, functioned in this way only as long as he was free from endangering his *disciplina* (*quamdiu a periculo disciplinae vacaret*). For in order not to be exposed to this danger, he feared the king's lions as little as the three brothers feared the king's fire [Daniel 6.5–7] (*De idololatria* 15.8–10).

Like Plato's Socrates, Tertullian expressed his willingness to be obedient and submissive to the authorities of the Roman state, *provided* they did not require him to act or speak in contradiction to the *dei disciplina*. Like Daniel, Shadrach, Meshach, and Abednego, Tertullian would cooperate with the king if and only when the king permitted him to place his *disciplina* first. Plato's Socrates famously declared to a jury of his fellow Athenians, "Gentlemen, I am your very grateful and devoted servant—*but* I owe a greater obedience to god than to you" (*Apologia* 29d). Therein lay the rub. The conditions of obedience set by Socrates' "little inner voice" were exactly those of Tertullian. In both cases, the escape clause that they attached to their contract with the state had the effect of cancelling the debt of obedience. I am more afraid of my king than yours. Tertullian refused, in all cases, to be terrified of the Roman king, and he knew that all the imperial honors in the world without the terror that they were meant to inspire reduced the king's power to nothing.

In *Scorpiace* 14, Tertullian again rephrased Paul's admonitions to be subject to all power. Indeed, both Paul and the author of 1 Peter said that the king must be honored.[52] Such submission was required of the Christian because all governing power ultimately came from God. But Tertullian would strictly limit the degree to which the Roman emperor was set apart, authorized, sacralized, abstracted from and exalted over other human beings. He would limit the Roman emperor's *imperium*, his *dominium*, his *maiestas*.[53] Submission to and cooperation with the Roman emperor did not mean that a Christian would place him at the summit of the hierarchy. That place was reserved for the King of Kings: his own emperor of the universe to whom his ultimate loyalty, his *fides*, was fixed.

> Though a king is supremely great on his own throne, next after God, yet he is inferior to God, and when brought into comparison with God must be deposed from his supreme greatness (*Adversus Marcionem* 1.4.3).[54]

In this extended comparison of the king with the god, Tertullian's god becomes the *rex regum* (1.4.4–6), an emperor ruling on account of his victory (*ex victoria*), from the "pinnacle of domination" (*culmen dominationis*) over all other kings. And so, where and when Tertullian accepted the necessity of living a conflicted and confusing existence under both Christian and Roman laws, he was forced to create order and clarity through hierarchy.[55] While not insulting the emperor outright, Tertullian often put him, as a human, on a level even lower than the non-existent/dangerous and demonic gods.[56]

Tertullian was aware that he was in less immediate danger from the demonic gods of the Romans than from the Emperor or his representatives.[57] And so the strategy of Tertullian, when and to the degree that he was willing to haggle with the hated Roman authorities, was to whip the saddle rather than the ass; his "evil gods" and "demons" were often *vicarii* for the Emperor and his agents. Similarly, Minucius Felix avoided attacking the cult of the Emperor but attacked, instead, the ancient Egyptian tradition of divinizing the Pharaoh (*Octavius* 29.4).[58]

Tertullian went so far as to phrase attacks on the cult of the emperor as defenses of the emperor's honor. When the festivals (*sollemnia*) in honor of the Roman Emperor, the obligations of the imperial *disciplina*, were made the occasion for lewd lawlessness, Tertullian asked:

> Does such conduct befit the festal days of princes, when it ill befits other days? Are men who maintain *disciplina* out of consideration for Caesar, to desert it for Caesar's sake? Shall their good feeling for him be their license to follow bad ways? Shall *religio* be reckoned as an occasion for *luxuria*?
>
> *Haecine sollemnes dies principum decent, quae alios dies non decent? Qui observant disciplinam de Caesaris respectu, hi eam propter Caesarem deserunt, et malorum morum licentia pietas erit, occasio luxuriae religio deputabitur?* (*Apologeticum* 35.3)

Other Ways of Soft-pedaling Christianity in Tertullian

To illustrate what one does *not* find in Tertullian, I will divert the reader briefly back to the Roman sources, to the type of stories (of which there are numerous examples in Roman literature) that would have been available to Tertullian—and that might have been very attractive to him—but which he and the other Christian "apologists" studiously avoided. He does not touch the story, for example, of the slain "savior of the people" Marcus Manlius Capitolinus. According to Livy, Marcus Manlius gained fame and his *cognomen* in 390 B.C.E. when during the Gallic sack of Rome, he heroically and almost single-handedly protected the Capitol of Rome with its great temple of Jupiter, Juno, and Minerva. Manlius' spirit was, according to Livy, *inflatus* by the adulation of the Roman people, and he became their champion. In an extraordinary act of generosity, he sold his own property to pay the debts of all those citizens and soldiers who were threatened with debt slavery (*nexum*, a common but horrendous fetter for the plebs of the early Republic). One Roman centurion, who although renowned for his military prowess had been bound into slavery by debt, solemnly devoted himself (*devovere*, to vow/promise/condemn to death) for Manlius as his savior and *parens* "with all his remaining strength and life and blood" (6.14.8). The senate, alarmed, appointed a dictator to deal with the threat that Capitolinus posed to their *libertas*. When the dictator cast Capitolinus into the little underground prison that served as "death row" in Rome, the people put on mourning, let their hair and beards grow, and besieged the entrance to the prison night and day. "Would they suffer one whom they had all but made a god . . . to be confined, to be shut up, in prison, and to draw his breath in darkness, at the mercy of the executioners?" (Livy 6.16.5). The senate, intimidated by the plebs and the reputation and accomplishments of Manlius, released him. According to Livy, the spirit of Manlius was not broken by the insult of his imprisonment but inflamed, and he now openly professed his advocacy and patronage of the plebs. The senate was able, finally, to bring the rebellious Capitolinus to trial, and despite the 400 men who came forward as witnesses to testify for him, he was condemned and flung from the Tarpeian rock. After the execution of Manlius, according to Livy, a plague and a famine struck Rome "that many people attributed to the murder of Manlius":

> The capitol had been polluted by the blood of its savior, and the gods had not been pleased that the man who had rescued their temples from the enemy would be punished under their very eyes (6.20.16).[59]

The followers of Marcus Manlius Capitolinus, like the followers of Drusus in the Social War, the followers of Ben Yair in the Jewish rebellion were, for the Roman senatorial aristocracy, mixed in the same putrid contagion. The job of the Christian apologists was to cleanse themselves of association with all such *rebelles* and paint themselves as occupying a distinct, wholesome, nonthreatening sphere. That is why in his negotiatory mode, Tertullian cautiously avoided stories like that of Marcus Manlius Capitolinus, Spurius Maelius, Spurius Cassius, Tiberius and Gaius Gracchus, Marcus Livius Drusus or Lucius Sergius Catilina—all of whose movements formed closer parallels to their own than the ones they do use. What famous Roman heroes do the Christian apologists repeatedly compare themselves to? Mucius Scaevola and Atilius Regulus—those self-sacrificing *exempla* of *loyalty to the state*, or to Lucretia by whose blood the senatorial state was founded. (When Christians looked for positive figures of *insubordination* to the state, they were careful to use *exempla* unfamiliar to the Romans: Moses, the suffering servant in Isaiah, the Maccabean Jewish resistance against the Greeks. The only Greco-Roman model of resistance that was considered "safe" was Socrates.)

In his conciliatory moods, one detects the damper with which Tertullian tried (not always successfully) to mute the most strident themes of his thought.[60] He softened or omitted reference to Christians who might harness and channel the energies of the Emperor's subjects in other directions: prophets of the future, messianic or eschatological texts and oracles, generals who would fight their own private wars, and all other helmsmen who would hijack the ship of state and steer it in a different direction, renegades, pirates, or brigands. And so, in his apologetic works, Tertullian's Paraclete does not issue so many directives. Indeed, Tertullian is always safe, in this context, to belittle divinators, astrologers, prophets, and magi (of other movements and cultures).[61]

In Tertullian's apologetic mode, he minimized the most dangerous of his conceptions: that of the Christian soldier and his voluntary commitment to death, that which I have discussed extensively in the preceding three chapters.

Useful Ambiguities

Another important strategy used by Tertullian in his negotiatory mode (as it was by Josephus; see Chapter 11, "A Jewish Actor in the Audience: Josephan Doublespeak") was indefinition. Tertullian's language is much less distinctly Christian than that used by modern translators of his works who feel safe to "disambiguate" many of his most important words (like *ecclesia*, *fides*, *colere*, *deus*—and of course, *religio* and *disciplina*). Modern scholars often translate the word *ecclesia* by the word "church," in which case it ceases to be an "assembly" (like that of any Greek town [or the congregation of Dio's Roman plebs]) and becomes a specifically set-apart Christian and God-centered institution. But in the time of Tertullian, it was still easy to leave it sounding like any assembly—and there were times when Tertullian wanted it to sound as innocuous as the first and not the second.

Fides is often translated by modern scholars as "faith" (i.e., belief/trust in God or a series of propositions and the organized institutional structure to promote and express this "belief"). But, with a few exceptions, there was nothing particularly Christian or god-centered in Tertullian's use of *fides* (even while he sometimes uses it as the equivalent of *disciplina nostra* or of Greek *pistis*). Otherwise, Tertullian's *fides* is very close to old Roman *fides* (without its more complex and paradoxical aspects).

Modern scholars are wont to translate *colere* by "worship" rather than "cultivate"—to give the word a particular regal and god-centered meaning. (Even avid gardeners are rarely described as "worshipping" their perennials.) But *colere* was still easy in Tertullian's day—and still in Augustine's—to recognize as the same word one used of the solicitous attention one might give to plants or children.[62]

Modern scholars translate *deus* by the Germanic (generic) "god" and capitalize it, thus making it into a name/title, thus separating it out from the generic and giving it both a higher status and a very particular Christian flavor. Needless to say, reading or speaking aloud the Latin text, there was absolutely no distinction in sound or appearance between the Christian *deus* and the non-Christian *deus*. Moreover, importantly, there were many times when Tertullian used *deus* ambiguously to refer to either his god or a generic god, especially when he wanted to claim that his concept of *deus* was "natural" to mankind and shared with even his enemies outside of the *fraternitas*.

> But you concede, do you not, on the basis of common consent (*de aestimatione communi*), that there is something more sublime and more potent, the *princeps*, as it were, of the world, of perfected/complete power and majesty (*potentia et maiestas*)? For that is how most men apportion divinity; they hold that the *imperium* of the supreme *dominatio* is under the control of one. (. . .) the title of *deus*, like the title of Emperor, belongs to one supreme over all (*Apologeticum* 24.3–4).[63]

Compare *De corona* 6.2: "We need nothing more than *natura* to inform us that *deus* is the *iudex*." *De testimonio animae* 2.2: "You [non-Christians] are liable to say '*deus bonus*' and '*deus benefacit*' which proves that the human's 'natural soul' tells them that god is good."[64] *De paenitentia* 3.2: "It is generally agreed that *deus* is some great thing of good. . . ." (*cum deum grande quid boni constet esse . . .*). *De resurrectione carnis* 2.8: "the creator of the world who is known to all men by the testimony of his works."[65] In the course of telling the reader that neither Marcion or Valentinus, the *vulgus*, the philosophers, the poets or the painters would admit to it, Tertullian supplies the definition of god, "[T]he *conscientia* of all acknowledges: that god is the *summum magnum* . . . [upon which] there is universal agreement" (*cum de isto conveniat apud omnes*). . . . (*Adversus Marcionem* 1.3.2–3; cf. 1.4.5).

Almost eighteen hundred years of linguistic development has set apart, sacralized, and calcified words that were very much homely and ambiguous in the time of Tertullian—and whose mundanity he often put to his own strategic purposes. It is necessary to "untranslate" many of Tertullian's words to arrive at a more nuanced understanding of his thought world.

Indeed, in this negotiatory mode, Tertullian looked to find common ground with the Romans and other non-Christians. In this passage, Tertullian was answering the charge that the Christians worshipped the cross:

> You also adore victories, and in all trophies the cross is the inner structure of the trophy. The whole of the Roman *religio* of the camp (*religio castrensis*) venerates (*veneratur*) the standards (*signa*), swears by the *signa*, sets the standards before all the gods. All those rows of images on the standards are but ornaments hung on crosses. Those hangings of your standards and banners are but robes upon crosses. . . . You did not wish to consecrate crosses naked and unadorned (*Apologeticus* 16.7).[66]

While elsewhere in his thought, the wisdom of the world was foolishness (e.g., *De resurrectione carnis* 3.3), in this mode of Tertullian's thought, he deliberately emphasized the words and images shared with non-Christians.

Finally, Tertullian's strongest bargaining position was that there were reciprocal benefits of co-existence for Christians and Romans. In an extraordinary passage, Tertullian asserted the gratitude of Christians to the Roman Empire for postponing the miseries of the end time:

> There is another and greater necessity for us to pray for the Emperors, and for the whole estate of the empire and the interests of Rome: We know that the great force which threatens the whole world, the end of the age itself with its menace of hideous suffering, is delayed by the respite which the Roman empire means for us.[67] We do not wish to experience all that; and when we pray for its postponement we are helping forward the continuance of Rome (*Apologeticum* 32.1).[68]

In return for sustaining the *saeculum* and averting the cosmic disaster, the Emperor benefitted from the prayers that Christians made for him to a really powerful and effective god, solicitations infinitely more valuable than those made by non-Christians to their own vain and powerless gods. Even while non-Christians might attribute every disaster to the Christians, Tertullian argued that things were actually much better now that there was *innocentia* in the world and intercessors (*deprecatores*) for the Emperor and the Empire. He complained that the Romans did not recognize the Christians' successful interventions. If there had been a prolonged summer heat and anxiety over the crops, well-fed non-Christians—indulging in all their vices (like eating!)—enjoined a barefoot procession to supplicate Jupiter. Meanwhile,

> We, parched with fasting, pinched with every austerity (*continentia*), abstaining from all life-sustaining food, sweltering in sackcloth and ashes, assail heaven in malice, touch God—and then, when we have wrung *misericordia* from him—Jupiter gets all the honor! (*Apologeticum* 40.15).[69]

In still another attempt to establish common ground with the educated classes of the empire Tertullian confessed the need, for the sake of governing the *plebs*, of the "necessary lie," the "pious falsehood":

> Now suppose what we maintain is false and really a presumption; still it is necessary: silly but *useful*! since those who believe in it are driven to be better men by fear of eternal punishment and hope of eternal refreshment. So it is in no one's interest that those ideas should be judged silly which it is in the interests of all to presume to be true. What is beneficial cannot be condemned on any grounds. It is with you that the presumption lies—in condemning what is useful. (. . .) even if they [our ideas] are false and silly, they are harmful to no one. For they are just like many other tenets on which you lay no penalties, vain tenets, and sheer fable, but exempt from punishment because harmless (*Apologeticum* 49.2–3).[70]

In this extraordinary passage Tertullian identified himself with and assumed the voice of the Greek and Roman governing class, of both Plato and Cicero (and so many members of governing elites of every age) and acknowledged that the leader (like the physician or the pilot of the jet plane) could not operate in the world of *veritas*. The leader/king, like the good physician—or the peasant farmer—was compelled to pay attention to a great and endless variety of threats and anxieties, boundaries and limitations—the world not of absolutes but of practical utility.[71] (The pilot could not announce over the plane's loudspeaker that he is "leaving everything in the hands of God.") Here Tertullian urges not the *veritas* but the *utilitas* of his *disciplina* for governing the *plebs*.

In his negotiatory mode, then, far from being poor, propertyless, envious, dangerous, insubordinate and immoral malefactors, rebels, sorcerers and atheists, Christians are the most useful of subjects offered the very best moral *exempla* not only for one another, but for the Romans. Compare Minucius Felix:

> Just because we reject your *honores et purpuras* does not mean (!) that we are composed of the dregs of the *plebs*; we are not factious (*nec factiosi sumus*). If we are united in knowledge of the one good; we gather together, quietly, singly (Minucius Felix, *Octavius* 31.6).

Conclusions

The operation, in Tertullian's thought, of both "modes" or "moods"—that of resistance and collaboration—reflect his inner struggles, struggles that he must have shared with many thousands of other subjects of the Roman Emperors. Despite the great complexity of his thought, there was only so much he could do, only so many strategies he could come up with. In examining the fate of the Greek *thrēskeia* in the next five chapters of this book—and especially its vicissitudes as it, like its cousin, *religio*, enters into Jewish and Christian thought worlds—the reader will find these two strategies recurring, albeit with some fascinating differences as well.

Thrēskeia

PART I

Mapping the Word

EIGHT

Imagine No *Thrēskeia*: The Task of the Untranslator

If *religio* is traditionally given as the Latin word for "religion," *thrēskeia* is cited as the ancient Greek one (and indeed, in Modern Greek, that is its meaning). In this regard, the Greek word is as much a false friend as the word *religio* is itself. In other ways, however, the two aren't quite compatible in that the Latin word is attested much more widely and richly than the Greek. Moreover, as has been shown in earlier chapters, studying *religio* in the earlier periods gives access to an entire cultural system that has been named here the "balancing system." *Thrēskeia* is a different kettle of fish. Only very, very sparsely attested at all in classical Greek, it appears primarily and increasingly widely from the later Hellenistic period onward. Its usages, moreover, suggest only a partial semantic overlap with *religio* until quite late in late antiquity when it is adopted as the translation equivalent of a reconfigured *religio*, or (alternatively put) when *religio* acquires new values partly by being used as a translation equivalent of *thrēskeia*.[1] Nonetheless, the analogy of *religio* will provide some heuristic value in the study of this word as well.

A contextual study of the usages of *thrēskeia* in antiquity demonstrates a world of nuance that simply does not map onto the abstraction "religion" as used in modern folk (and to a lesser extent, scholarly) language. This is much easier to carry out than the parallel study of *religio*, owing simply enough to the relative paucity of ancient usages. I have conducted here a fresh and fairly exhaustive collection of literary contexts in which the term is used, starting with Herodotus and ending in the Hellenistic period, including Jewish authors such as Philo. To this a partial study of epigraphic evidence has been added as well. I have found ambiguity and even ambivalence in these uses—or better put, while each individual context can be fairly well specified (at least I hope so and have tried to demonstrate so), the aggregate does not permit one or even a set of clear definitions. Rather, it is important to realize that the word always has the potential for communicating overtones of meaning that cannot be captured in a definition, and certainly not—it should be unnecessary to say by now—by using the term "religion" in any form while glossing and discussing these usages.

I have found, indeed, that the contexts in which *thrēskeia* functions within the textual corpus just specified involve a range of usages that one might be inclined to see as opposites. *Thrēskeia* is used, on the one hand, by writers to indicate excessive, extravagant, and even harmfully distracting practices of others; but, on the other hand, can be used by participants to indicate their own cultic practices, thus presumably with a positive valence and not the negative charge associated with the first set of usages. It is as if a single word in Greek incorporates both our modern English "religion" and "superstition," usually taken as opposites.[2] Although, to be sure, many in our culture regard religion negatively, but even they, nonetheless, distinguish lexically between the denotation of "superstition" and "religion." Thus, even a sentence, which we might imagine in the mouth of a Richard Dawkins—"All religion is mere superstition"—nonetheless, makes the semantic distinction that *thrēskeia* does not, as I shall show here. In fact, the preceding sentence could not be expressed in ancient Greek. Carlin Barton has pointed out that "[T]he Latin noun *pax*, like the Latin nouns *fides, pudor, religio, purgamen, piaculum, lustrum, flagitium*, and like the Latin verbs *sancire, sacrare, mactare*, had two complementary valences, poised, as it were, on the two opposite poles of a balance beam."[3] This kind of nuance, in which a word functions in such seemingly divergent ways, which ultimately reveals an entirely other semantic, cultural world is completely obscured when one uses a covering abstraction as a shortcut for translation. In this chapter, I will suggest, too—very hypothetically—a possible historical context for these double, and nearly opposite, meanings.

Thrēskeia *and the Thracian Women*

Plutarch (ca. 46–120 C.E.) writes of ideal wifely behavior:

> A wife ought not to make friends of her own, but to enjoy her husband's friends in common with him. The gods are the first and most important friends. Therefore it is seemly for a wife to fear [*sebesthai*] and to know only the gods that her husband honors [*nomizei*][4], and to shut the outer door against all *periergoi thrēskeiai* and *xenai deisidaimoniai*.

> Ἰδίους οὐ δεῖ φίλους κτᾶσθαι τὴν γυναῖκα, κοινοῖς δὲ χρῆσθαι τοῖς τοῦ ἀνδρός· οἱ δὲ θεοὶ φίλοι πρῶτοι καὶ μέγιστοι. διὸ καὶ θεοὺς οὓς ὁ ἀνὴρ νομίζει σέβεσθαι τῇ γαμετῇ καὶ γιγνώσκειν μόνους προσήκει, περιέργοις δὲ θρησκείαις καὶ ξέναις δεισιδαιμονίαις ἀποκεκλεῖσθαι τὴν αὔλειον. [Plutarch *Coniugalia praecepta* 140d].

This is a particularly rich passage given that it explicitly draws a contrast between proper *sebas* (*sebomai* = to show awe, fear, revere, with respect to gods, persons, and objects) and improper *thrēskeia* and *deisidaimonia*, both of which are associated explicitly with negative adjectives; *thrēskeia* is with *periergo*s (taking needless trouble; useless) and *deisidaimonia* with *xenos* (alien, strange, unusual), an opposition that I will discuss again herein.[5] This is a common enough pattern to show that Greek culture had a certain similarity to the Roman culture explored thus far in this book in the form of a balancing system in which the mid-point between extremes is seen as the ideal, one in which too much fear of the god was as negative a moment as too little. Moving along, one will frequently find the word *eusebeia*—literally "good fear": that is, that which is appropriate and within measure, not over the top or otherwise useless—in contrast to *deisidaimonia* and *thrēskeia*. *Thrēskeia* frequently functions in Greek much like *superstitio* in Latin. *Deisidaimonia* and *thrēskeia* in this text are the disdained extremes of proper *sebas* of good fear, or appropriate piety/reverence.

For another clear indication of the close semantic affiliation of *deisidaimonia* and *thrēskeia*, one need look no further than Soranus, the gynecologist of late–first and early–second centuries Alexandria and Rome. In Soranus' gynecological writings, we find the following among the qualifications for a midwife: "She will be free from *deisidaimonia*[6] so as not to overlook salutary measures on account of a dream or omen or some customary mystery or vulgar *thrēskeia*."[7] ἀδεισιδαίμονα χάριν τοῦ μὴ δι' ὄνειρον ἢ διὰ κληδόνας ἢ σύνηθές τι μυστήριον καὶ βιωτικὴν θρησκείαν ὑπεριδεῖν τὸ συμφέρον (Book 1, chapter 1, section 4). The good midwife has to be free of vain and popular beliefs and practices—LSJ even gives "superstition" here—because if she is not, she might be so busy with them that she ignores salutary ones.[8] Here, even more explicitly than in the texts already cited, both the correlation of *thrēskeia* with *deisidaimonia* and the negative marking of both as excessive and distracting from what must be done are as clear as a bell.[9]

Deisidaimonia nearly always carries the negative sense of excessive ardor or scrupulousness (in the negative sense found in Roman Catholic moral theology), fear of taboos. For this negatively marked sense of *deisidaimonia*, see the following already from the fourth century B.C.E. Theophrastus' *Characters*:

> *Deisidaimonia*, I need hardly say, would seem to be a sort of cowardice with respect to the divine; and your *deisidaimōn* is one who if he happens upon a funeral processions, washes off his hands and sprinkles himself (with water) from a shrine, puts bay-leaf in his mouth, and walks about all day like that. And if a weasel/cat should cross his path he will not proceed on his way until someone else has gone by, or he has cast three stones across the street.

> [ΔΕΙΣΙΔΑΙΜΟΝΙΑΣ Ιc (1.) Ἀμέλει ἡ δεισιδαιμονία δόξειεν ἂν εἶναι δειλία πρὸς τὸ δαιμόνιον], ὁ δὲ δεισιδαίμων τοιοῦτός τις, (2.) οἷος ἐπιτυχὼν ἐκφορᾷ ἀπονιψάμενος τὰς χεῖρας καὶ περιρρανάμενος ἀπὸ ἱεροῦ δάφνην εἰς τὸ στόμα λαβὼν οὕτω τὴν ἡμέραν περιπατεῖν. (3.) καὶ τὴν ὁδὸν ἐὰν ὑπερδράμῃ γαλῆ, μὴ πρότερον πορευθῆναι, ἕως διεξέλθῃ τις ἢ λίθους τρεῖς ὑπὲρ τῆς ὁδοῦ διαβάλῃ.[10]

It is clear, at least from the preceding context, that *deisidaimonia* had a range of meanings that partly overlapped with *superstitio* in its Latin sense; thus, excessive zeal for the gods > scrupulosity > *superstitio* and partly with something like "superstition" in its modern sense as well. The aforementioned established nexus between *deisidaimonia* and *thrēskeia* indicates that the latter may carry a similar range of acceptations.

Another author slightly older than Plutarch, but writing in a very different milieu, paints the same picture. I speak of Philo (ca. 20 B.C.E.–ca. 50 C.E.), the Jewish intellectual from Alexandria. In a crucial text, for Philo, *eusebeia* itself is a perfect mid-point between *asebeia* and *deisidaimonia*, being overly fearful with respect to god: what a Latin writer would call *superstitio*. He writes in the *Special Laws*:

> In the same fashion, if one adds anything small or large to the queen of the virtues, *eusebeia*, or takes anything away, in either way he will change and transform its entire form [in the Platonic sense]. Adding will beget *deisidaimonia*, and taking away, *asebeia*. *Eusebeia* will, moreover, disappear, that for which everyone should pray that it may be permanent and shining, since it is the cause of the greatest of the goods, producing knowledge of the *therapeia* of god, which one must deem more sovereign and more kingly than any dominion or authority.

> τὸν αὐτὸν μὲν τρόπον κἂν τῇ βασιλίδι τῶν ἀρετῶν, εὐσεβείᾳ, προσθῇ τις ὁτιοῦν μικρὸν ἢ μέγα ἢ τοὐναντίον ἀφέλῃ, καθ' ἑκάτερον ἐπαλλάξει καὶ μεταμορφώσει τὸ εἶδος·γεννήσει γὰρ ἡ μὲν πρόσθεσις δεισιδαιμονίαν, ἡ δ' ἀφαίρεσις ἀσέβειαν, ἀφανισθείσης αὖ τῆς εὐσεβείας, ἣν ἀνίσχειν καὶ ἐπιλάμπειν εὐκταῖον ἀγαθόν, ἐπειδὴ τοῦ μεγίστου τῶν ἀγαθῶν αἰτία καθέστηκεν, ἐπιστήμην ἐμποιοῦσα θεραπείας θεοῦ, ἣν πάσης ἀρχῆς καὶ ἡγεμονίας ἀρχικωτέραν καὶ βασιλικωτέραν εἶναι νομιστέον [Special Laws IV, 147].

We learn a few things from this citation. First, for Philo, as presumably for other Greek-writing Judaeans, *eusebeia* is identified as the keeping of the commandments, as in the context [143], he has written, "that one must not add anything to, or take anything away from the law." He then produces an analogy to "courage" and argues that adding to courage produces audacity, while taking away leads to cowardice.

And then, in a brilliant exposition of this very verse, Deut. 4:2:

> Thus shalt not add to that which I command you nor subtract anything from it, in keeping the commandment of The Lord your God which I command you, . . .

> לא תספו על הדבר אשר אנכי מצוה אתכם ולא תגרעו ממנו לשמר את מצות ה' אלהיכם
> אשר אנכי מצוה אתכם:

Philo gives a philosophical explanation indicating that keeping of the commandments is equivalent to *eusebeia*, while adding to them produces *deisidaimonia* and subtracting from them destroys *eusebeia* and produces *asebeia*. For such a Hellenophilic author (even a Jew such as Philo), much as for a Roman, too much scrupulousness or fear of god turns into a highly undesirable condition, referred to in Greek as *deisidaimonia* and in Latin as *superstitio* (which is not worship of the wrong god but too much, or wrongheaded, worship of even the right ones.)[11] Nor is this view in any way confined to Philo. Exactly the same sentiment is observed once again in Plutarch, who remarks that one who tries too hard to avoid *deisidaimonia* risks "leaping over" *eusebeia*, "which lies between," and landing in atheism [Superstition 171 f]. Rather than, as one would think, *eusebeia* and *deisidaimonia* being opposites, they are on a quantitative scale, Goldilocks-style,[12] with *deisidaimonia* being too much of a good thing. *Eusebeia* is, therefore, the "just right" of cultic behavior, while too much or too little are negatively marked qualities. I have already presented more than one instance in which *deisidaimonia* and *thrēskeia* are treated as virtual synonyms or at the very least close congeners. It follows that *thrēskeia* can defensibly be said to represent the excessive pole as well in contrast to *eusebeia*.

Plutarch makes this point about the semantics of *thrēskeia* in a highly fanciful etymology of the word that, for all its whimsy, nonetheless—or even more so—reveals how the word functioned in his lexicon. This is, for instance, explicit in Plutarch's *Life of Alexander* 2. 5–6:

> But concerning these matters there is another story to this effect: all the women of these parts were addicted to the Orphic rites and the orgies of Dionysus from very ancient times (being called Klodones and Mimallones), and imitated in many ways the practices of the Edonian women and the Thracian women about Mount Haemus, from whom, as it would seem, the word "*thrēskeuein*" [θρησκεύειν] came to be applied to the celebration of immoderate and *periergoi* [overwrought, taking needless trouble, superfluous][13] ceremonies.

> πολλὰ ταῖς Ἠδωνίσι καὶ ταῖς περὶ τὸν Αἷμον Θρήσσαις ὅμοια δρῶσιν, ἀφ' ὧν δοκεῖ καὶ τὸ θρησκεύειν ὄνομα ταῖς κατακόροις γενέσθαι καὶ περιέργοις ἱερουργίαις.[14]

So clear and explicit is it for Plutarch that *thrēskeuein* connotes the excessive that he derives its etymology from those very Thracian women [*thrēssai*] proverbial for their excesses of ecstasies.

For another passage in which *thrēskeia* is given the same Thracian etymology again, van Herten observes:

> Θρησκεία was more often regarded as a strange, unusual service, as is shown by the scholion on Euripides Alc. 968 (ed. Schwartz) [Orpheus first handed over the mystery of the gods, whence the mystery is called θρησκεία, after the Thracian Orpheus].

> πρῶτος Ὀρφεὺς μυστήρια θεῶν παραδέδωκεν. ὅθεν καὶ θρησκεία τὸ μυστήριον καλεῖται, ἀπὸ τοῦ Θρακὸς Ὀρφέως.[15]

Once more, as in Plutarch, the word *thrēskeia* is associated with the foreign and exotic: in this case, via connections with the Thracian Orpheus (rather, in the scholiast's view, than those women who tore him apart). We learn once more of the strong association of the word with Thrace, as well as carrying the semantic load of wild, undisciplined practice, such as the Orphic rites (analogous more to Latin *superstitio* than *religio*). At least for some late-Hellenistic writers, *thrēskeia*, like *deisidaimonia*, indicates the extreme pole of a spectrum of emotion and practice that extends from the one pole, *asebeia* (not enough fear) to the other, *thrēskeia* and *deisidaimonia* (too much fear), with the eponymous *eusebeia* in the middle as just the right amount of fear: hence, piety. Ancient Greek culture seemingly has an economy of characters, emotions—more like the Roman balancing system than one might have imagined, although, of course, not identical to it.

Thrēskeia *and the Excessive*

Perhaps the most common usage of *thrēskeia* in the earlier Greek literature is with reference to the practices of others. In pre-Hellenistic Greek, the word shows up only in Herodotus. Here is the first case from the historian. In this passage, the inhabitants of an area on the borders of Libya balk at being required to observe prohibitions that belong to the Egyptians:

> The inhabitants of the cities of Mareia and Apis, of Egypt on the border of Libya, considering themselves as Libyans and not as Egyptians, and aggrieved at the *thrēskeia* about sacred things, wishing not to be constrained from eating cows, sent to Ammon saying that since they had nothing in common with the Egyptians, living outside of the Delta and not agreeing with them, they desired to be allowed to eat everything.

> Οἱ γὰρ δὴ ἐκ Μαρέης τε πόλιος καὶ Ἄπιος οἰκέοντες Αἰγύπτου τὰ πρόσουρα Λιβύῃ, αὐτοί τε δοκέοντες εἶναι Λίβυες καὶ οὐκ Αἰγύπτιοι καὶ ἀχθόμενοι τῇ περὶ τὰ ἱρὰ θρησκηίῃ, βουλόμενοι θηλέων βοῶν μὴ ἔργεσθαι, ἔπεμψαν ἐς Ἄμμωνα φάμενοι οὐδὲν σφίσι τε καὶ Αἰγυπτίοισι κοινὸν εἶναι· οἰκέειν τε γὰρ ἔξω τοῦ Δέλτα καὶ οὐδὲν ὁμολογέειν αὐτοῖσι, βούλεσθαί τε πάντων σφίσι ἐξεῖναι γεύεσθαι [2.18].

These people wish to prove themselves non-Egyptians so that they won't be subject to the restriction against eating the "Holy Cow." In the eyes of these aspiring Libyans (non-Egyptians), these restrictions are *thrēskeia* and not, for instance, *therapeia* or *eusebeia*. Here is a word that means rules and regulations or prohibitions/taboos.[16] It is not that these Libyans consider themselves free of Egyptian *thrēskeia* and committed only to their own (as it ought to be were *thrēskeia* an unmarked word for cult) but rather that they do not want any part of *thrēskeia* at all: They want to be able to eat anything and not be inhibited from any food. Otherwise, they would have said "aggrieved at the *Egyptian thrēskeia*" and not *thrēskeia* simpliciter. In this usage, *thrēskeia* is not entirely different from ancient Latin *religio* in the sense of the inhibiting prohibition. What is, moreover, in common with the Latin is the ever-present possibility of the inhibition turning into a hyper-inhibition. The balancing system does not provide the structure of binary opposition but of a sliding scale in which too much of a good thing, as it were, turns into a bad thing. Once again, to make the point clear, such a semantic range does not exist with other Greek words that roughly inhabit this semantic field—namely, *eusebeia* or *therapeia*—where the positive sense is always present in the word; the very sense of these terms ("good fear" and "care, attention," respectively) excludes excess *a priori* from their semantic scope. It is, therefore, significant when writers choose *thrēskeia* over one of those.

The sense of *thrēskeia* as profligate can be suggested from another Herodotean usage where, of the Egyptian priests, Herodotus remarks "They complete infinite numbers of other *thrēskeiai*, so to speak" (ἄλλας τε θρησκείας ἐπιτελέουσι μυρίας ὡς εἰπεῖν λόγῳ [2.37]).[17] The connotation of overabundance is supported as well by the same context in which Herodotus has remarked that the Egyptians "are the most excessively [*perrissōs*] god-fearing of all humans" (Θεοσεβέες δὲ περισσῶς ἐόντες μάλιστα πάντων ἀνθρώπων [2.37]).

In another Herodotean usage from this lexical item, the participle *thrēskeusantes* is found being used in a context in which it means something like those bound by an inhibition with respect to the sacred. (It also could, in this context, support a sense more like those engaged in cultic performances.) This is an instance in which Herodotus identifies fully with the practice of the Egyptians and even cites it as the origin of a Hellenic practice of which he thoroughly approves:

> And they [the Egyptians] were the first *thrēskeusantes* not to have intercourse with women in temples and not to go into temples from [intercourse with] women without washing. For nearly all people, except for the Egyptians and the Greeks, have intercourse in temples, and rising up from women unwashed enter into temples, thinking that humans are all like the other beasts, for we see the other beasts and birds have sex in those precincts of the gods and in those sacred places; were this unliked by the god, the beasts would not behave thus. Those people, now, explain thus [by this example of the animals], their doing of that which to me, myself, is unacceptable.

> καὶ τὸ μὴ μίσγεσθαι γυναιξὶ ἐν ἱροῖσι μηδὲ ἀλούτους ἀπὸ γυναικῶν ἐς ἱρὰ ἐσιέναι οὗτοι εἰσὶ οἱ πρῶτοι θρησκεύσαντες. οἱ μὲν γὰρ ἄλλοι σχεδὸν πάντες ἄνθρωποι, πλὴν Αἰγυπτίων καὶ Ἑλλήνων, μίσγονται ἐν ἱροῖσι καὶ ἀπὸ γυναικῶν ἀνιστάμενοι ἄλουτοι ἐσέρχονται ἐς ἱρόν, νομίζοντες ἀνθρώπους εἶναι κατά περ τὰ ἄλλα κτήνεα: [2] καὶ γὰρ τὰ ἄλλα κτήνεα ὁρᾶν καὶ ὀρνίθων γένεα ὀχευόμενα ἔν τε τοῖσι νηοῖσι τῶν θεῶν καὶ ἐν τοῖσι τεμένεσι: εἰ ὦν εἶναι τῷ θεῷ τοῦτο μὴ φίλον, οὐκ ἂν οὐδὲ τὰ κτήνεα ποιέειν. οὗτοι μέν νυν τοιαῦτα ἐπιλέγοντες ποιεῦσι ἔμοιγε οὐκ ἀρεστά [2.64].

It is not entirely clear what *thrēskeusantes* means here: Something like "devotees" might be in order. In this case, at any rate, far from considering this an unnecessary scruple, Herodotus remarks that he, himself, approves of this prohibition and associates it with the Greeks and the Egyptians, uniquely among all peoples. (He probably had not read the Hebrew prophets!)

In the continuation of this very passage:

> But the Egyptians *thrēskeuousi* excessively in these and other sacred matters/matters to do with the Temple.

> Αἰγύπτιοι δὲ θρησκεύουσι περισσῶς τά τε ἄλλα περὶ τὰ ἱρὰ καὶ δὴ καὶ τάδε.

yielding a sense something akin to, "But the Egyptians are excessively scrupulous in matters to do with the sacred." It would seem that even when Herodotus approves of the particular practice in question—refraining from sex in Temples—he nonetheless remarks by using the verb from *thrēskeia* that the Egyptians are somehow excessive in the scrupulosity. The general sense of the root as carrying overtones of the foreign and the excessive remains, therefore, intact even in this one seemingly contradictory passage.

It is remarkable that after making an appearance on the stage in fifth century B.C.E., the word *thrēskeia* disappears from the Greek lexicon entirely until well into the Hellenistic period. It seems never to have been used in Attic Greek at all (an important point for the elaboration of which, see upcoming discussion). It is difficult, if not impossible, to determine why suddenly the word reappeared when it did, becoming eventually a fairly common word within the literary and inscriptional lexicon. It is possible, of course, even probable, therefore, that *thrēskeia* had been functioning in non-Attic dialects all along.[18] In upcoming discussion, I will conjecture that it is precisely the strangeness of the word, as well as its apparent localization in the strange, wild Northeast that lent it the sense of *deisidaimonia* that I have been documenting for it.

As already noted, the sense of excess, of superfluous fervor and over-scrupulosity, that for which both the noun *superstitio* and the adjective *religiosus* are used in ancient Latin, remains one important component to the semantics of *thrēskeia* in Greek as the word resurfaces in the Hellenistic period as well.

After *thrēskeia* does reappear in literature—for example, in Strabo, the first-century (B.C.E. and C.E.) geographer—it retains the overtones of "otherness" in one sense or another found in Herodotus. Strabo has made the point that it is necessary to carefully examine the complete inventory of the "muthologia" of the ancients because at least some of them are enigmas [*ainigmata*]: that is, allegorical representations of physical realities. These allegories, he suggests, cannot be decoded exactly by themselves because in them, fables are mixed with the "science"; but by examining many of them, some consistent and some contradictory with each other, one can discern something of the physical opinions of the ancients. He then exemplifies this point:

> For example, probably they mythologize about those zealous for the gods and the gods themselves, as roaming over the mountains and their frenzies, for the same reason that they considered the gods as dwelling in the sky, and taking care of all things and prognostications. Mining, hunting, and a search after things useful for the purposes of life, appeared to have a relation to the mountain-roaming, but *enthousiasmos*, *thrēskeia*, and *mantikē* are connected with *agurtikos* and *goēteia*. And such also were the devotion to the Dionysiac and Orphic arts. But enough of this subject.

> οἷον τὰς ὀρειβασίας τῶν περὶ τὸ θεῖον σπουδαζόντων καὶ αὐτῶν τῶν θεῶν καὶ τοὺς ἐνθουσιασμοὺς εἰκότως μυθεύουσι κατὰ τὴν αὐτὴν αἰτίαν καθ' ἣν καὶ οὐρανίους νομίζουσι τοὺς θεοὺς καὶ προνοητικοὺς τῶν τε ἄλλων καὶ τῶν προσημασιῶν: τῇ μὲν οὖν ὀρειβασίᾳ τὸ μεταλλευτικὸν καὶ τὸ θηρευτικὸν καὶ ζητητικὸν τῶν πρὸς τὸν βίον χρησίμων ἐφάνη συγγενές, τῶν δ' ἐνθουσιασμῶν καὶ θρησκείας καὶ μαντικῆς τὸ ἀγυρτικὸν καὶ γοητεία ἐγγύς. τοιοῦτον δὲ καὶ τὸ φιλότεχνον μάλιστα τὸ περὶ τὰς Διονυσιακὰς τέχνας καὶ τὰς Ὀρφικάς. ἀλλ' ἀπόχρη περὶ αὐτῶν [10.3.23].

Strabo observes that in mythological stories about the gods and their devotees there are frequently two narrative elements: mountain-roaming and *enthousiasmos*, frenzy. The first is taken as an allegorical representation of the arts of mining and metallurgy; the second, together with two added elements *thrēskeia* and *mantikē*, is taken as a representation of *agurtikos* and *goēteia*. Some lexical work is necessary for the usual translation of *agurtikos* here as "jugglery" falls far short of the mark. In his study of Greek magic, Fritz Graf analyzed this term and its congener here, *goēteia* in some detail. Defining the latter term as "witchcraft,"[19] he shows that the former refers to wandering night priests, who practiced "divination, initiation, healing, and magic."[20] Given that, and given that the counterparts of *thrēskeia* here are frenzy and oracle-meddling, it must refer as well to something on the order of the emotionally intemperate, the disorderly—or at any rate, disordered.

What Strabo seems, then, to be saying is that representing the gods as wandering over mountains represents allegorically the useful arts. Representing them as frenzied, on the other hand, signifies an entirely different kind of behavior, the behavior of wandering priests and the practitioners of witchcraft. One learns two things from this text, therefore: On the one hand, *thrēskeia* goes into the same category of the psychic states of frenzy and the mantic; on the other hand, all these are associated in Strabo's mind with sorcery and its concomitants. In accord with Plutarch, moreover, is an association with the Orphic and Dionysiac. In this sense, *thrēskeia* overlaps some of the territory of Latin *superstitio* as well, including especially such readings of that word that incorporate *superstitio* as excessive *religio* and *superstitio* as spirit possession and finally *superstitio* as referring to foreign cults and interdictions. The synchronic semantic mechanism of the Greek—whatever the etymological origins—seems not entirely unlike the Latin analogy, in which appropriate inhibition, when exaggerated, turns into fear and then fear into a kind of ecstasy. *Thrēskeia* as inhibitions/prohibitions becomes *thrēskeia* as excessive fearfulness and thence turns to frenzy, while *eusebeia* then comes to fit the semantic spot of appropriate and measured strictness in observance. One might compare the semantic range of "scrupulous" in English, where generally "scrupulousness" as meticulousness, painstaking behavior is a good thing and appropriate, but the same vocable in the form "scrupulosity" can indicate hyperfastidiousness bordering on the superstitious, and a Catholic website offers to "reduce and even eliminate the hold scrupulosity has on your heart."[21]

The term shows up in a context where it clearly refers to the practices of others in a fragment of the historian Aristodemos, who has, it seems, been dated anywhere between the fourth century B.C.E. (when the events took place) and the second century C.E. (when they may have been recorded). The Spartan tyrant Pausanias has run into a Temple for sanctuary from those who would kill him:

> While the Spartans were at a loss as to what to do because of the [*dia tēn*] *eis ton theon thrēskeian*, Pausanias' mother carried in a brick and placed it at the entrance of the sanctuary, and she was the one who began the punishment of her son.

> (8.4) τῶν δὲ Λακεδαιμονίων ἐν ἀπόρωι ὄντων διὰ τὴν εἰς τὸν θεὸν θρησκείαν, ἡ μήτηρ τοῦ Παυσανίου βαστάσασα πλίνθον ἔθηκεν ἐπὶ τῆς εἰσόδου τοῦ τεμένους, προκαταρχομένη τῆς κατὰ τοῦ παιδὸς κολάσεως.[22]

Eis ton theon thrēskeian means *thrēskeia* with respect to the god, probably the emotion of inhibiting reverence (not unlike *religio*). Given what I have shown so far, it would also not be impossible to understand this here as the interdiction of the god (against killing in the Temple). There is, one would think, at least an overtone of fearfulness in this reverence as well (and even perhaps of the ridiculous). It would not be impossible to imagine here something like ancient Roman *religio* in the sense of a fearful thing that one avoids, an inhibition, in this Greek case (but not always even in Greek; see upcoming discussion), however, with respect to a god.

In the middle of the first century C.E., in the earliest Hellenistic novel, *Chareas and Callirhoe*, is the following:

> An Egyptian soldier who had been given the job of guarding the people in the building discovered that the Queen was inside. Given the innate *thrēskeia* of the barbarians towards the royal title, he could not bring himself to approach her.[23]

> Αἰγύπτιος στρατιώτης, ὁ πεπιστευμένος φυλάττειν τοὺς ἐν τῷ οἰκήματι, γνοὺς ἔνδον εἶναι τὴν βασιλίδα, κατὰ τὴν ἔμφυτον θρησκείαν τῶν βαρβάρων πρὸς τὸ ὄνομα τὸ βασιλικὸν ἐγγὺς μὲν αὐτῇ προσελθεῖν οὐκ ἐτόλμησε.

Here, *thrēskeia* clearly is an emotion of reverence, fearful honoring, once again reminiscent of ancient Latin *religio*. In any case, as shall be seen over and over (especially in Josephus), the emotions of *thrēskeia* always issue in particular acts and disciplines. The foreignness here is marked explicitly. It is very important, moreover, that here the emotion of *thrēskeia* is directed toward a "royal title" instead of a god. The correct generalization seems not to be, as found in the literature, that these barbarians deified their queen but rather that the practice of *thrēskeia* did not know of this distinction at all.

The "Others" Talk Back: Epigraphic Thrēskeia

As noted earlier, *thrēskeia* in pre-Christian writers very often means emotional inhibitions, prohibitions, "taboos," similar (albeit not identical) to Latin *religio*. Although Latin *religiosus*, the adjective, can refer to one who shows too much *religio*, Latin has no noun from this root that refers to that state and uses for that *superstitio*. In Greek, on the other hand, the sense of too much *thrēskeia* being referred to as *thrēskeia* also, as well as *deisidaimonia*, is present in the texts, leaving examples of, therefore, foreign, strange, and especially excessive, unnecessary ritual practice in the contexts of this word.[24] In both of these languages, the sense is that balance is good: Too much of a good thing leads to a bad thing. When *thrēskeia* is used negatively, in sum, it is of the sacralizing behaviors of others, including others within, which the observer sees as dangerous, subversive, or foreign, motivated by nervous or excessive fear (*deisidaimonia*) with or without altered states (*goēteia*).

What is fascinating is to observe that at least some of those "others" seem to use *thrēskeia* to refer without pejorative tone as the name of "our" cult and practices. Such usages are limited largely, but not completely, to epigraphic evidence and to non-Attic Greek use. It is important to note that epigraphically, the word appears only in inscriptions from Asia Minor, Thrace, and adjoining (and ethnically closely related) Bythinia—nearly never from Attica, the Peloponnese, or Thessaly.[25] Louis Robert provides inscriptional evidence that *thrēskeia* may refer simply to "our own" cult, and, therefore, in such contexts can have no negative connotation.[26] Thus, the "*thrēskeia tou Apollōnos*" SIG 801 D (Delph., i C.E.)[27] needs surely to be understood as the rites due to Apollo or the service of Apollo although reverence for Apollo cannot be entirely excluded. In her article on the subject of *thrēskeia*, Laurence Foschia has adduced, as well, a second-century (C.E.) inscription [from Macedonia?] in which appears the collocation "sacrifices and *thrēskeiai* of our ancestral gods," where surely the only sense possible of *thrēskeiai* is interdictions or rites that must be observed.[28] (What precisely those were, we do not know other than that they were distinct from the sacrificial cult itself, as seen from the structure of the sentence.) Moreover, also from the second century, there is a series of inscriptions in which *thrēskeia* refers in a very positive way to the observance of rites in honor of one's god or gods.[29] One index of the different semantics of *thrēskeia* in this group of texts is that here, frequently enough, *thrēskeia* goes along with *eusebeia* as a virtual synonym rather than being its antonym.[30]

Finally, once again, its usage in this sense of prescribed rites can refer to the honoring of humans as well as gods, as pointed out by van Herten:

> An inscription from the first century C.E., originating from Amorion [Phrygia], refers to θρησκεία as the duty of those initiated in the Zeus mysteries. These initiated honored the memory of Cyrilla, an untimely deceased daughter of Antipater Caius, by devoting an altar to her and by buying a vineyard εἰς τὴν θρησκείαν τοῦ μνημείου αὐτῆς. The produce of this vineyard had to serve for the annual festival of Mithras. The initiated had to participate in this festival as well as their descendants and heirs. Antipater Caius also gave a vineyard to the initiated in order to let its produce be used by the participants in the annual festivals in honor of his deceased daughter. Excluded from this is ἐὰν δέ τις μὴ συνέλθη ἢ μὴ συνθρησκεύῃ αὐτός. This θρησκεία τοῦ μνημείου consisted, according to Poland, in wreathing the monument and in having a festive meal in its neighborhood.[31]

Several things are evidenced from these remarkable citations. First of all, as noted earlier, in this inscription the object of the *thrēskeia* is the memory of a deceased human and secondly: It is not only not a prohibition or something overdone but an obligation—something to be performed.

Even though it is indeed striking the extent to which this highly positive usage is found in epigraphic sources, it is not entirely restricted to them. In the first century B.C.E., Dionysius of Halicarnassus (where Herodotus came from!), shows such usage as well. In his *Roman Antiquities*, referring to the law-giver Numa, Dionysius uses *thrēskeia* seemingly in a wholly positive (in both senses of positive) context. Dionysius describes the activities of Numa and then concludes:

> and enacting laws concerning purifications, *thrēskeiai*, expiations and the other *therapeiai* and *timai* in their multitude.
>
> ἀγνείας τε καὶ θρησκείας καὶ καθαρμοὺς καὶ τὰς ἄλλας θεραπείας καὶ τιμὰς πάνυ πολλὰς νομοθετῶν [Roman Antiquities, Book 2 ch. 63.1].

Now whatever the precise differences between purifications, expiations, and *thrēskeiai*, it is clear that they are all subcategories of *therapeiai* (services) and *timai* (honors) due, it would seem, the gods and not the catch-all term for all such observance.[32] In other words, *thrēskeia* refers here to a specific species of service practice.

Similarly, in Athenaeus' *Deipnosophistae*, is the following ethnographic comment:

> Among the Persians, the queen accepts a multitude of concubines, for the king rules his wife like a despot, but also for another reason: the queen—as Dino says in his "The Persians"—is *thrēskeuesthai* by the concubines; at any rate, they perform obeisance to her.

παρὰ δὲ Πέρσαις ἀνέχεται ἡ βασίλεια τοῦ πλήθους τῶν παλλακίδων διὰ τὸ ὡς δεσπότην
ἄρχειν τῆς γαμετῆς τὸν βασιλέα, ἔτι δὲ καὶ διὰ τὸ τὴν βασιλίδα, ὥς φησιν Δίνων ἐν τοῖς
Περσικοῖς, ὑπὸ τῶν παλλακίδων θρησκεύεσθαι· προσκυνοῦσι γοῦν αὐτήν [Athenaeus,
Deipnosophistae, XIII. 556].

It would seem most plausible here to understand the verb *thrēskeuesthai* as referring to the
emotion of reverence: That is, they reverence their queen, or at any rate, whatever their
emotional state, perform obeisance to her. It will not do to remark that the Persians considered their royals as gods, which completely begs the question, as it were.[33] The point is
surely that there is no distinction in Greek between *thrēskeia* directed at so-called gods
and at so-called humans (similar in this sense to *eusebeia*, which of course, can be directed
at humans as well as gods).

A Conjecture

Following the discussion to this point, one might propose that the word *thrēskeia* (for which
no Greek etymology has been successfully advanced) was restricted originally to dialects of
Greek from the Northeast and down into Ionia (given that Herodotus knows of it) while
unknown in mainland Hellas. It might even have been a loan word in those Thracian climes
from some otherwise unknown non-Greek language: perhaps Thracian itself. Regardless of
whether it is a foreign loan word into Greek, its apparent absence from Attic Greek could
certainly explain its foreignness to later Greek writers who might very well associate it with
the people and practices of the dialect areas where they encountered it. The adducing of it as
a near synonym of *deisidaimonia* by several Hellenistic writers could be explained as the encounter between those writers and others who used *thrēskeia* (as shown in the epigraphic
evidence) for their own practices and emotions that were seen by our authors (notably Strabo
and Plutarch, but not only them) as wild and extravagant and "oriental," explaining the etymologies connecting it with barbarous Thracian practices. A fine analogy to this is the way
that the word *magus*—Zoroastrian priest—was taken up in Greek to mean "sorcerer" owing
to the picture that the Greeks had of Zoroastrians. This conjecture has the advantage of
explaining what seem to be contradictory senses of a single word within a single language
without forcing us to regard the word itself as neutral[34] although synchronically, whatever
its origins, according to its usage, we find this a rich example of cultural patterning in which
too much of a good thing becomes a bad thing.

What will be most crucial moving forward in this study of Greek and Greco-Judaic
usages of *thrēskeia* is to remember the double sense in which it is found in earlier Greek
texts, as frequently positive in usage: that is, referring to "our practices," but as frequently,
or even more so perhaps, as negative in connotation, referring to the practices of others
that are marked as in some sense excessive.

NINE

The *Thrēskeia* of the Judaeans:
Josephus and The New Testament

In this chapter, I propose to look at Palestinian Judaean writers of the period of the first century c.e. to see how *thrēskeia* functions in their texts and thought. In Greek-writing Judaean authors are several instances of the use of *thrēskeia* that are seemingly unambiguously positive in interpretation. First is Josephus: first, in part because (as discussed later herein and also in the next two chapters of this book) the richest attestation of *thrēskeia* in antiquity is in his works. Although I will be treating him extensively in the next two chapters, I would like to introduce his usage of *thrēskeia* at this juncture to observe how it fits into a larger picture. Josephus, the first-century Palestinian historian, uses the term frequently with positive connotation. Whether drawing on the resources of "eastern" *koinē* as attested in the inscriptions or not, Josephus' usage of *thrēskeia* seems often to match them much more closely than the usage in other Greek authors. Josephus' usages of *thrēskeia* in the sense of cultic activity, of service to the deity, thus matching the epigraphic usage, can be documented specifically. In Antiquities 9:133:

> Jeous called to him to mount the chariot and accompany him to Samaria, saying that he would show him, how he would spare no evil person and would punish the false prophets and the false priests and those who mislead the people such that they abandon the *thrēskeia* of the greatest god and bow down [*proskunein*] to foreign ones.

> Ἰηοῦς δὲ ἀναβάντα ἐπὶ τὸ ἅρμα συνεισελθεῖν αὐτὸν εἰς Σαμάρειαν παρεκάλει λέγων ἐπιδείξειν, πῶς οὐδενὸς φείσεται πονηροῦ, ἀλλὰ καὶ τοὺς ψευδοπροφήτας καὶ τοὺς

ψευδιερεῖς καὶ τοὺς ἐξαπατήσαντας τὸ πλῆθος, ὡς τὴν μὲν τοῦ μεγίστου θεοῦ θρησκείαν ἐγκαταλιπεῖν τοὺς δὲ ξενικοὺς προσκυνεῖν.

Here is a virtual synonymy between *thrēskeia* and *proskunein*, to bow down, prostrate one-self, pay obeisance, enabling us a more precise delineation of our target lexeme as cultic acts. The point is not, of course, that *thrēskeia* refers in any way to bowing down but rather that *proskunein* has become a synecdoche for veneration (in action) of a deity.[1]

A similar instance can be found at Ant. 9:138:

> Achabos wishing to gratify his father-in-law Ithobal, King of the Tyrians and the Sidonians, built a temple for him in Samaria and appointed prophets and honored him with all *thrēskeia*.

> Ἄχαβος δὲ τῷ πενθερῷ βουλόμενος χαρίσασθαι Εἰθωβάλῳ Τυρίων ὄντι βασιλεῖ καὶ Σιδωνίων ναόν τε αὐτῷ κατεσκεύασεν ἐν Σαμαρείᾳ καὶ προφήτας ἀπέδειξε καὶ πάσης θρησκείας ἠξίου.

The point is surely that the human king is being treated as a god, with a temple to him in which all manner of cultic acts are performed in his honor/worship. *Thrēskeia* here seems clearly to refer to those practices or acts although one might read *thrēskeia* here as the emotion: thus, "with all devotion/reverence." It is perhaps worth comparison here to Tertullian's usage of *religiones* in a similar sense.[2]

Another similar instance in which *thrēskeia* appears as service of the deity and exactly correlated to ancestral customs is the following:

> When, however, those on the other side heard that those whom they had just dismissed had erected an altar, not for the purpose for which they had set it up, but rather with intent to change and as an introduction of strange gods, they were unwilling to disbelieve this. Rather, thinking this slander about their *thrēskeia* convincing, they took up arms, doing so in order to inflict vengeance on those who had erected the altar by crossing the river and punishing them for their deviation from the ancestral customs [*tōn patriōn ethōn*].

> ἀκούσαντες δὲ οἱ πέραν βωμὸν ἱδρῦσθαι τοὺς ἀπολυθέντας οὐ μεθ' ἧς ἐκεῖνοι γνώμης ἀνέστησαν αὐτόν, ἀλλ' ἐπὶ νεωτερισμῷ καὶ ξενικῶν εἰσαγωγῇ θεῶν, οὐκ ἤθελον ἀπιστεῖν, ἀλλὰ περὶ θείαν θρησκείαν τὴν διαβολὴν πιθανὴν νομίζοντες ἐν ὅπλοις ἦσαν ὡς ἐπ' ἀμύνῃ τῶν τὸν βωμὸν ἱδρυσαμένων περαιωσόμενοι τὸν ποταμὸν καὶ κολάσοντες αὐτοὺς τῆς παρατροπῆς τῶν πατρίων ἐθῶν [Ant. 5:101–102].[3]

The two-and-one-half tribes who had been left behind at their request on the other side of the Jordan to worship God there, apparently reneged on that commitment, setting up an altar to worship "foreign" gods and not the god of Israel. Their allegedly "foreign" cult is referred to by *thrēskeia* and a deviation from the ancestral *nomoi*. Josephus, himself, however refers to this as a slander, apparently disbelieving that which he suggests the Israel-ites had too readily believed.[4] The levels of ambiguity are so palpable and subtle that it is almost impossible to work out the precise nuance of *thrēskeia* here, but it is clear that it refers to service of a god via observance of *nomoi*.

The story goes on to have a happy ending when the Trans-Jordanians successfully argue against the slander by demonstrating that they are not changing the worship or introducing foreign gods:

> When Phinees had said these things, the heads of the assembly and the entire crowd itself began to make a defense regarding the things alleged against them. They said that they would neither apostatize [*apostēsesthai*] from their kinship with them, nor had they set up their altar with revolutionary [*neōterismon*] intent. They knew that there is one God, common to all the Hebrews, and that sacrifices were to be made to him on the bronze altar in front of the tent. They had erected the one [altar] they had set up—and on account of which they had become suspect—not for *thrēskeia* but that it might be a symbol and a token of our everlasting relationship with you and of the necessity of thinking prudently and abiding by the ancestral [customs] [*tois patriois*], rather than as a beginning of transgression, as you surmise. May God be a credible witness for us that we constructed the altar for this very purpose. May you then have a better opinion of us and not condemn us for these things, for which all those belonging to the race of Abraham who adopt revolutionary ways, contrary to customary practice [*tou sunēthous tropou*], would justly be wiped out.

> Τοσαῦτα τοῦ Φινεέσου διαλεχθέντος οἱ προεστῶτες τῆς ἐκκλησίας καὶ τὸ πλῆθος αὐτὸ πᾶν ἤρξαντο περὶ τῶν ἐγκεκλημένων αὐτοῖς ἀπολογεῖσθαι, καὶ μήτε συγγενείας τῆς πρὸς αὐτοὺς ἀποστήσεσθαι μήτε κατὰ νεωτερισμὸν ἀναστῆσαι τὸν βωμὸν λέγειν, ἀλλὰ θεόν τε ἕνα γινώσκειν τὸν Ἑβραίοις ἅπασι κοινὸν καὶ τὸν πρὸ τῆς σκηνῆς βωμὸν χάλκεον, ᾧ τὰς θυσίας ποιήσειν· τὸν μέντοι γε νῦν ἀνασταθέντα, δι' ὃν καὶ ὕποπτοι γεγόνασιν, οὐ κατὰ θρησκείαν ἱδρῦσθαι, σύμβολον δὲ ὅπως εἴη καὶ τεκμήριον εἰς τὸν αἰῶνα τῆς πρὸς ὑμᾶς οἰκειότητος καὶ ἀνάγκη τοῦ σωφρονεῖν καὶ τοῖς πατρίοις ἐμμένειν, ἀλλ' οὐχὶ παραβάσεως ἀρχήν, ὡς ὑπονοεῖτε. μάρτυς δ' ἡμῖν τοῦ ἐπὶ τοιαύτῃ τὸν βωμὸν αἰτίᾳ κατασκευάσαι γένοιτο ὁ θεὸς ἀξιόχρεως, ὅθεν ἀμείνονα περὶ ἡμῶν ἔχοντες ὑπόληψιν μηδὲν καταγινώσκετε τούτων, ἐφ' οἷς ἐξώλεις εἶναι δίκαιοι πάντες ὅσοι τοῦ Ἀβράμου γένους ὄντες νεωτέροις ἐπιχειροῦσιν ἔθεσι καὶ τοῦ συνήθους τρόπου παρηλλαγμένοις.

The Trans-Jordanians defend themselves successfully by claiming that they have not built the altar for the purpose of *thrēskeia* but as a symbol and marker of kinship. *Thrēskeia* here clearly signifies the sacrificial order—what you normally do with an altar—and is almost palpably here a translation equivalent of Hebrew ʿavoda or the Aramaic equivalent *pulḥana*. Although the Septuagint uses *latreia* in this sense, Josephus nearly always prefers *thrēskeia*, perhaps for the reasons I will suggest shortly. But again note the collocation of *thrēskeia* with *tois patriois* [the ancestral ways; the *mos maiorum*], producing an almost perfect coordination of Roman and Israelite usages and values. *Sumbolon* is very precisely chosen here. In ancient Greece, it was an object, a bone or sherd of pottery for instance, broken in two of which two people who were about to be separated would each take half. Upon being reunited sometimes years or more later, the match of the two halves of the *sumbolon* would be the guarantee of identity (not infrequently that of siblings). The two identical [?] altars are not for the purpose of setting up a competing cult which would be revolution but as the two halves of a *sumbolon* for marking and guaranteeing close relationship.

That *thrēskeia* does not mark in Josephus a sphere of the religious as opposed to the secular is demonstrated further by the following text which, at first glance, seems to argue the opposite case from what I show to be the case. Thus [Ant. 4:74]:

> It is necessary for those who slaughter at home for the sake of feasting and not as a *thrēskeia* to provide for the priests the stomach and the cheeks and the right foreleg of the victim.

> εἶναι δὲ καὶ τοῖς κατ᾽ οἶκον θύουσιν εὐωχίας ἕνεκα τῆς αὐτῶν ἀλλὰ μὴ θρησκείας ἀνάγκην κομίζειν τοῖς ἱερεῦσιν ἔνυστρόν τε καὶ χελύνιον καὶ τὸν δεξιὸν βραχίονα τοῦ θύματος.

Josephus is working here from a Hebrew category and distinction. Hebrew maintains a clear linguistic opposition between קדשים versus חולין, *Qodashim* versus *Ḥullin*, which I might translate, at least provisionally, as "sacralized things" and "unsacralized things." According to Deuteronomy (but not the older Leviticus!), this distinction applies to the slaughter of animals for food as opposed to the slaughter of animals (only in the Temple, again according to Deuteronomy) as an offering.[5] It must be remembered, however, that even outside the Temple, this slaughter of animals is not neutral: It must be done in a certain fashion, the animal must be kosher, and certain portions are reserved, nonetheless, for the priests. Indeed, this is Josephus' entire point. Even the slaughter of animals just for an ordinary feast remains within the sacred precincts, if not of the Temple, then of the *nomos*. We manifestly do not have a distinction between the religious and the secular in distinguishing between *thrēskeia* and *euōkhia*, a point almost certainly to be missed were one to understand "religion" by *thrēskeia*. This distinction is maintained so clearly within the post-biblical tradition that the Mishna contains an entire order devoted to *Qŏdoshim* (holy matters, sacrifices) within which there is a tractate called *Shḥitat ḥullin* (slaughter of unsacralized animals), which alone may be carried out at home, outside the Temple, but certainly cannot be described as secular or even quite profane unless keeping in mind that the Latin profanum, meaning "in front of the Temple," is also a relative matter, not a binary opposition. Josephus' point here precisely is to inform that in that latter case—that is, in relatively less-sacralized slaughter—the slaughterer is, nonetheless, obligated to provide certain parts of the animal for the provision of the priests. For this Hebrew opposition, Josephus uses *euōkhia//thrēskeia*, in which the first term means "feasting." Interestingly, for Josephus, *thuō*—normally in Greek used for sacrifice—can be used for any slaughter, whether devoted in the Temple or not; but it is *thrēskeia* that marks it as highly sacralized (Temple-sacrificial) slaughter. This provides very important support, in my estimation, for the hypothesis that Josephan values and even the turns of his usages of words need to be related to his background as a Judaean as much or even more than to the ancient Greek lexicon. Cultural difference seems as much at work as lexical differences, rendering this usage even more important. The most important lesson to be learned, however, from this passage is how dangerous it is to use terms like "secular" or "profane" with respect to cultures that do not make such distinctions. Rather than an opposition between the sacred and the profane, let alone the secular, speaking of degrees of sacrality is paramount here, a very common usage within rabbinic discourse for sure, as seen from the following in Mishna Kelim, Chapter 1:

Mishna 6. There are ten grades of holiness: the Land of Israel is holier than all other lands. And what is the nature of its holiness? That from it are brought the *'omer*, the first fruits and the two loaves, which may not be brought from any of the other lands. Mishna 7. Cities that are walled are holier, for lepers must be sent out of them and a corpse, though it may be carried about within them as long as it is desired, may not be brought back once it has been taken out. Mishna 8. The area within the wall is holier, for it is there that holy things of a minor degree and second tithe may be eaten. The Temple Mount is holier, for neither *zabs* [men with a genital flux] nor *zabahs* [women with a genital flux] nor menstruants nor women after childbirth may enter it. The rampart is holier, for neither idolaters nor one who contracted corpse uncleanness may enter it. The court of women is holier, for no *tebul yom* [one who has immersed for purification but the sun has not set yet] may enter it, though no sin-offering is thereby incurred. The court of the Israelites is holier, for a man who has not yet offered his obligatory sacrifices may not enter it, and if he enters he incurs thereby a sin-offering. The court of the priests is holier, for no Israelites may enter it except when they are required to do so in connection with the laying on of hands, slaying [a sacrifice] or waving [the offering of wheat]. Mishna 9. The area between the *ulam* and the altar is holier, for men afflicted with blemishes or with a wild growth of hair may not enter it. The *hekal* is holier, for no one whose hands or feet are unwashed may enter it. The Holy of Holies is holier, for only the high priest, on the Day of Atonement, at the service, may enter it.

One sees here a structure in which there is no binary opposition between sacred and profane but in which sacrality is explicitly relative. This is identical to the Roman system in which *profanum*—that which is in front of the *fanum* (roughly, Temple)—is sacralized as well, just not as much as the *fanum* itself. Similarly, even though Josephus clearly marks the difference between a particular form of sacred slaughter and daily eating, this does not render everyday slaughter outside the realm of the Law and Temple, either. The ordinary slaughter is constrained and sacralized as well, and this is, actually, Josephus' very point here.

In this section, I have explored the range of usages in Josephus of *thrēskeia* to refer to his own Judaean cult and behavior with respect to God. It seems plausible to suggest that Josephus here is using the word as attested in the epigraphic material from Thrace and Bithynia. Of course, I am not suggesting that he had access to such epigraphic material, but presumably the word was available in some version of a *koinē* that Josephus had to draw on. Further evidence for this usage in Palestinian *koinē* can be adduced from the group of documents belonging to the various followers of Jesus that we have come to call the New Testament.

In the Judaean writings collected as the New Testament, *thrēskeia* is used with very positive connotations. In a somewhat mysterious passage in Colossians, this locution is used in accord with at least one of its usages noted earlier.

Let no one seduce you, into voluntary self-abasement and the *thrēskeia* of the angels . . . [2:18].

(18.) μηδεὶς ὑμᾶς καταβραβευέτω θέλων ἐν ταπεινοφροσύνῃ καὶ θρησκείᾳ τῶν ἀγγέλων, ἃ ἑόρακεν ἐμβατεύων, εἰκῇ φυσιούμενος ὑπὸ τοῦ νοὸς τῆς σαρκὸς αὐτοῦ,

I don't think that anyone quite understands this verse, but it is clear enough that the "*thrēskeia* of the angels" is negatively marked; it is what one is not supposed to be seduced into. It would seem to fit best into the semantic category shown earlier in which "θρησκεία τοῦ Ἀπόλλωνος" means, as I explain earlier, the cult of Apollo. This usage matching with the epigraphic evidence fits nicely with the roughly contemporaneous Palestinian Josephus, as I have just shown.

A second context in which one finds this word in the New Testament is in the Epistle of James:

If anyone appears to be *thrēskos* without bridling his tongue but rather is cheating in his heart, his *thrēskeia* is worthless. Pure and undefiled *thrēskeia* before our God and father is this, to visit orphans and widows in their affliction, and to guard oneself stainless from the world.

Εἴ τις δοκεῖ θρησκὸς εἶναι, μὴ χαλιναγωγῶν γλῶσσαν αὐτοῦ ἀλλὰ ἀπατῶν καρδίαν αὐτοῦ, τούτου μάταιος ἡ θρησκεία. θρησκεία καθαρὰ καὶ ἀμίαντος παρὰ τῷ θεῷ καὶ πατρὶ αὕτη ἐστίν, ἐπισκέπτεσθαι ὀρφανοὺς καὶ χήρας ἐν τῇ θλίψει αὐτῶν, ἄσπιλον ἑαυτὸν τηρεῖν ἀπὸ τοῦ κόσμου [1:26–27].

Traditionally, these usages are translated by "religious" and "religion." In verse 27, however, that meaning is actually excluded (or virtually so). What could "pure and undefiled religion before our God" possible mean? This has been realized by many commentators already. One would be, I think, on much stronger grounds to understand *thrēskos* as devoted or pious and the noun form as exactly semantically matched to the adjective: that is, piety or the like.

In the Acts of the Apostles, however, find:

[The Judaeans], having known me from the first, if they are willing to testify, I have lived, as a Pharisee according to the most exact sect[6] of our *thrēskeia*.

προγινώσκοντές με ἄνωθεν, ἐὰν θέλωσι μαρτυρεῖν, ὅτι κατὰ τὴν ἀκριβεστάτην αἵρεσιν τῆς ἡμετέρας θρησκείας ἔζησα Φαρισαῖος [Acts 26:5].

This is going to be, in my view, a critical text. To be sure, Luke might very well have meant the most exact party of our discipline, without the meaning of *thrēskeia* as that full complex of ideas, emotions, and practices that we call a "religion" having developed yet; nevertheless, it is surely from ambiguous instances as this that the latter meanings develop.

One might be tempted to conclude that *thrēskeia* is an unmarked term in itself, and the negative (or positive) connotation appears only in and through the context. Close reading of texts, however, suggests that this is not the case, and that in specific writers and literary types, it manifests distinctly different undertones. The trick is to perceive with which other terms in its general semantic field it appears and how it is differentiated or coordinated with them.

Judaean-Greek Thrēskeia *with Negative Connotations*

In contrast to the usage in Josephus, in many Judaean-Greek texts of the first century, especially from outside Palestine, *thrēskeia* is used as in Plutarch and other Greek writers with distinct negative contexts. The first two passages to be considered are from Chapter 14 of the *Wisdom of Solomon*, a first century Jewish Greek text (probably from Alexandria). The context of the following sentence is a remarkable etiology for "idol worship," which explains that because people could not honor the king in his presence because he was far away, they had images of the king made which they honored in his absence. Now:

> The love of honor of the artificer urged forward the ignorant into an increase in intensity of *thrēskeia*.

> (18.) εἰς ἐπίτασιν δὲ θρησκείας καὶ τοὺς ἀγνοοῦντας ἡ τοῦ τεχνίτου προετρέψατο φιλοτιμία.

The narcissism of the artificer made him make the statue so beautiful that the ignorant were fired up to intense *thrēskeia* by its beauty. Here is a clear example in which *thrēskeia* signifies an emotion. There is, I think, no internal necessity to understand the term *thrēskeia* here as in itself pejorative given that it is the misplaced object of this devotion that is the problem, not the nature of devotion itself, but, of course, it is also highly plausible to assume that the term *thrēskeia* evokes here its negative contexts as well. Moreover, as one piles up contexts in which *thrēskeia* is used with such negative associations, it becomes clearer and clearer that the negative associations (explicitly marked by Plutarch and other writers cited in the preceding chapter) seem to stick to the word. It is hard, for instance, to imagine *eusebeia* or *therapeia* being used here. The people, seduced by the beauty of the semblance of the king, now reckoned him an object of worship (νῦν σέβασμα ἐλογίσαντο), whom they had previously just honored (*timaō*), although, once again, it must be emphasized it is only in the Jewish text that such a distinction is made at all. Further on, in the same context, in verse 27:

> For the *thrēskeia* of anonymous images is the beginning and the cause and the perfection of all evil.

> ἡ γὰρ τῶν ἀνωνύμων εἰδώλων θρησκεία παντὸς ἀρχὴ κακοῦ καὶ αἰτία καὶ πέρας ἐστίν.

Either it is the *thrēskeia* that is the cause of evil or the fact that it is directed at images; in either case, it would seem to refer to the emotion of reverence/devotion, as well as the practices that issue from that. Once again, the point is precisely that one doesn't have to decide—nor can one, nor did the ancient Greek writer—precisely what connotations are intended here, but rather that the connotations, including the bad odor that frequently attended *thrēskeia* throughout its history, were certainly available for writer and readers here. To make the point clearer, it is not that *thrēskeia* always carries somehow in its soul or essence the senses of *superstitio* or the like, but that it very frequently—in many authors exclusively—appears in such contexts and is, therefore, available for referring negatively to the cults of others, while *therapeia* or *eusebeia* are not.

An elegant example of this semantic ambivalence in yet another Hellenistic Jewish text, the Sybilline Oracles Book 8:

> They decree an image, fashioned of wood, to be mine, and shaping it with their hands, a speechless idol; they honor it with prayers and unholy *thrēskeiai*. Abandoning the Creator, they *elatreusan* [from *latreia*] licentiousness [*aselgeiai*].[7] All have gifts from me but give them to useless things, and they think all these things useful, like my honors, making burnt offerings at meals, as to their own dead. For they burn flesh and, sacrificing bones full of marrow on altars, they pour blood to demons and light lamps for me, the giver of light. Mortals pour libations of wine as if to a thirsty god, getting drunk to no purpose for useless idols. I have no need of your sacrifice or libation or polluted burnt offerings or most hated blood. For they will do these things to the memory of kings and tyrants, for dead demons, as if they were heavenly beings, performing a godless and destructive *thrēskeia*.[8]

> εἰκόνα θεσπίζουσιν ἐμὴν πλασθεῖσαν ἀφ' ὕλης, χερσί τε μορφώσαντες ἑαῖς εἴδωλον ἄναυδον δοξάζουσι λιταῖς καὶ θρησκείῃσιν ἀνάγνοις. τὸν κτίστην προλιπόντες ἀσελγείαις ἐλάτρευσαν †πάντες δ' αὐτοῦ† ἔχοντες ἀχρήστοις δῶρα διδοῦσιν †καὶ ὡς ἐμᾶς† τιμὰς τάδε χρήσιμα πάντα δοκοῦσιν θοίνῃ κνισσοῦντες, ὡς τοῖς ἰδίοις νεκύεσσιν. σάρκας γὰρ καίουσι καὶ ὀστέα μυελόεντα θύοντες βωμοῖς καὶ δαίμοσιν αἷμα χέουσιν καὶ λύχνους ἅπτουσιν ἐμοὶ τῷ φῶτα διδόντι, χὸς διψῶντι θεῷ θνητοὶ σπένδουσι τὸν οἶνον εἰς οὐδὲν μεθύοντες ἐπ' εἰδώλοισιν ἀχρήστοις. οὐ χρῄζω θυσίης ἢ σπονδῆς ὑμετέρηφιν, οὐ κνίσσης μιαρῆς, οὐχ αἵματος ἐχθίστοιο· ταῦτα γὰρ ἐς μνήμην βασιλήων ἠδὲ τυράννων δαίμοσι ποιήσουσι νεκροῖς, ὡς οὐρανίοισιν, θρησκείαν ἄθεον καὶ ὀλέθριον ἐκτελέοντες [Book 8, lines 390–94].

It is difficult (actually impossible, for good theoretical reasons) to determine denotation and connotation here. In any case, this seems the wrong question to ask. The historical record of usages suggests that the "meaning" of *thrēskeia*, understood, once again as simply the aggregate of its usages within the language, allows it to function in highly negative contexts as well as neutral or (in epigraphic and Josephan contexts) positively marked ones. Such would certainly follow, for instance, from Plutarch's virtually explicit definition. Given, however, other contexts that I have shown (especially in the epigraphic witnesses) in which *thrēskeia* is used with entirely positive valence, one could also think that like *litai* [prayers] with which it is matched here, it carries no negative evaluation in this text. To bring out this point more sharply (that *thrēskeia* incorporates in its usage *à la* Wittgenstein the markedly negative usages), I remark again that it is nearly impossible to imagine that the last sentence would incorporate *eusebeia* or *therapeia* in place of *thrēskeia*. Neither of the first two appears in negative contexts of usage, while *thrēskeia* clearly does.

To get some further sense of how this semantic character operates, I adduce the following text from Philo:

> Further, if anyone going under the name and guise of a prophet and appearing divinely inspired and possessed lead us to the *thrēskeia* of the locally established gods, I should not heed him and be deceived by the name of prophet. For he is a *goēs* and not a prophet, since he has lied and made up the oracles.

Κἂν μέντοι τις ὄνομα καὶ σχῆμα προφητείας ὑποδύς, ἐνθουσιᾶν καὶ κατέχεσθαι δοκῶν, ἄγῃ πρὸς τὴν τῶν νενομισμένων κατὰ πόλεις θρησκείαν θεῶν, οὐκ ἄξιον προσέχειν ἀπατωμένους ὀνόματι προφήτου·γόης γὰρ ἀλλ᾽ οὐ προφήτης ἐστὶν ὁ τοιοῦτος, ἐπειδὴ ψευδόμενος λόγια καὶ χρησμοὺς ἐπλάσατο [De specialibus legibus 1.315].

One possibility here is that *thrēskeia* itself has neutral meaning, and the heavily negative indications here are only because it is the wrong gods, as it were, that are being revered and served. Indeed, frequently enough, it would seem that precisely what marks the negative space of *thrēskeia* is the fact that the "wrong" folk—barbarians, Egyptians, women—are doing the sacralizing! On the other hand, it is striking that it is precisely with respect to such wrong folk that this very word is so often used. (Notice the association with *goēs* noted earlier for Strabo.) The other (and in some ways, more attractive) possibility is, therefore, that by using precisely *thrēskeia* here and not *therapeia*, Philo is mobilizing the potentially highly negative usages and intertexts of *thrēskeia* and implying that these are not truly service of any god, even the false ones, but only outward lip service. An example may help. Although the English word "cult" means service of a god (or even of a human), it has come to have highly negative charges in modern usage: A cult is something somehow illicit, conspiratorial, improper, false, not properly "religious." Except, therefore, in scholarly writing, one would be hard-pressed to use "cult" with reference, shall I say, to Judaism or Islam—and if one were to do so, the strong aura of negativity would attend it. This is what I suggest is happening for *thrēskeia* in Philo.

Thrēskeia *in the Second and Third Centuries* C.E.

In the second and third centuries C.E., one finds *thrēskeia* much more commonly as a neutral descriptor of cultic activities in both positive and negative narrative contexts. *Thrēskeia* is used in contexts that are unambiguous and simply denote prohibitions and services or practices enjoined by the gods: indeed, "our gods" or "our god." These literary usages match up more closely with Josephus in the first century and with the epigraphic contexts of *thrēskeia* than with earlier literary usage. *Thrēskeia* certainly is not always used for the exaggerated, overwrought, but can refer to the rites and prohibitions that are accepted within a given collective, even in "ours." Like *religio*, however, *thrēskeia* can also signify obligations that must be followed and not just interdictions. For an analogy, perhaps think of the word "enjoin" in English[9] or "sanction."[10]

A nice example can be cited from Sextus Empiricus, the second/third-century C.E. theoretician of scepticism. He offers us a discussion in which he has listed the food taboos of myriad peoples: The Jews and Egyptians would rather die than eat swine, the Libyans don't eat sheep, while the Syrians no doves; "we" eat no dogs, but "the Thracians are reported to be dog eaters" [Outlines of Pyrrhonism III. 222–25]. Then in summing this paragraph, he concludes, "Yet if the *thrēskeia* and the *athesma* existed by nature, all would observe them equally" [ibid. 226]. In this context, *thrēskeia* would seem to be the positive enjoinments, *viz.* the command to eat dogs on the part of the Thracians, while the *athesmon* is that which it is forbidden to eat, although it is possible as well that both mean prohibitions in a kind of hendiadys. Both, however, are being stigmatized by the skeptic as something less than piety and more like what one would call "superstitions."

In Aelian, a Greek writer roughly contemporaneous with Sextus, one finds the term, once again "ethnographically," as it were, referring to someone else's ceremonies, not his. Some Egyptians worship donkeys:

> But those who with respect to *thrēskeia* hold that of Serapis, hate the donkey [ἀλλὰ καὶ ὅσοι περὶ τὴν θρησκείαν ἔχουσι τὴν τοῦ Σαράπιδος μισοῦσι τὸν ὄνον; i.e., more idiomatically: Those who hold to the *thrēskeia* of Serapis hate the donkey].[11]

Notwithstanding the fact that it still refers to the rites of others, it would seem that one sees here a distinct variance in meaning from strange, excessive, Orphic to the ordinary rites of devotees, perhaps the "cult of Serapis." Thus one finds again in Sextus Empiricus, in a similar vein to Aelian: "Ὅθεν καὶ τὰ περὶ θυσιῶν καὶ τῆς περὶ τοὺς θεοὺς θρησκείας ὅλως πολλὴν ἀνωμαλίαν ἔχει. ἃ γὰρ ἔν τισιν ἱεροῖς ὅσια, ταῦτα ἐν ἑτέροις ἀνόσια." Translating this as literally as possible, one arrives at, "Hence, also the matters concerning sacrifices and the *thrēskeiai* of the gods in general are very varied. For things that are holy [*hosia*] for some cults [*hierois*] are for others unholy [*anosia*]."[12]

When turning to Herodian, a third-century Roman historian, it becomes a bit difficult, if not impossible, to see *thrēskeia* as neutral in affect. In the first instance in the corpus, it does seem to be so. Thus, after great victories in the East, Severus returns to Rome in triumph:

> As one victorious, he was received by the Roman people with great acclamations and *thrēskeia*; he provided the people with sacrifices, and holidays, spectacles, and feasts.
>
> νικηφόρος ὑπὸ τοῦ Ῥωμαίων δήμου μετὰ μεγάλης εὐφημίας τε καὶ θρησκείας ὑπεδέχθη, θυσίας τε καὶ ἑορτὰς θέας τε καὶ πανηγύρεις τῷ δήμῳ παρέσχε·[Herodian 3.10].[13]

It is difficult to say quite what *thrēskeia* signifies in this context, but it certainly has not even a whiff, I think, of negativity. It presumably means some forms of obeisance. Note, however, that were we tempted to see *thrēskeia* as a cult of Severus, it would be passing strange that he is the one providing the sacrifices and not receiving them.

Interestingly enough, in all other usages of *thrēskeia* in the corpus of Herodian's writings, it is always associated with hypocritical behavior. The first such context is the sly behavior of one prefect Plautianus. Plautianus sought the purple upon the Emperor, Severus having become old. Not entirely surprisingly, the latter was not well pleased with this intention. Far from elevating Plautianus, Severus engaged in a process of lowering his power and prestige. He turned to his military tribune, Saturninus. At this point is the following description of the latter:

> Although all of them [the other tribunes] behaved alike, he [Saturninus] endeavored to ingratiate himself with [Plautianus] with more *thrēskeia*.
>
> καὶ πάντων μὲν τοῦτο ποιούντων, ἐκεῖνος δὲ πλείονι θρησκείᾳ ᾠκείωτο αὐτόν [3.11].[14]

Plautianus sends the faithful Saturninus to murder Severus. Saturninus ends up tricking his erstwhile master who, of course, suffers a just downfall: execution by the sword and having his body thrown into the gutter. *Thrēskeia* can mean here only something like the devotion, ardor that is observed elsewhere herein in Josephus' usages. This devotion is, to be sure, hypocritical, and there is at least a suggestion of over-the-topness in his devotion (bordering on obsequiousness as the Loeb translator renders it).

In the next passage, Herodian is describing the obsequies of a dead emperor. After stating that dead emperors underwent apotheosis, he remarks:

> All over the city sorrow is displayed, combined with a festival and *thrēskeia*.
>
> μεμιγμένον δέ τι πένθος ἑορτῇ καὶ θρησκείᾳ κατὰ πᾶσαν τὴν πόλιν δείκνυται [IV. 1].[15]

A cultic observance is the only possible interpretation in this context, but it is difficult to determine the historian's attitude toward this—perhaps—incongruous mixture.

Be that as it may, in the next instance, the odor of hypocrisy is once more explicit. Caracalla sets off from Antioch to Alexandria to see the city founded in honor of his hero, Alexander, and also to sacrifice there to the special god of the place:

> There were two surpassing [reasons], he pretended: the *thrēskeia* of the god and the memory of the hero.
>
> δύο γὰρ ταῦτα ὑπερβαλλόντως προσεποιεῖτο, τήν τε τοῦ θεοῦ θρησκείαν καὶ τὴν τοῦ ἥρωος μνήμην [IV. 8].[16]

Given that in a virtual doublet of the sentence just before it, sacrifice to the god is given as the reason for the trip, and thus one would be hard pressed not to see the same activity denoted here. It is interesting but perhaps not entirely significant that this is the second case of what is, after all, only a handful of usages in Herodian, where *thrēskeia* is attended by hypocrisy. In the end, Caracalla ends up massacring more Alexandrians than the numbers of animals sacrificed by him in lulling them.

In another instance of *thrēskeia* in Herodian, one finds it in the ordinary sense of "the cult," something that a priest can be in charge of [Book 5, Chapter 3]. But even in this very context, hypocrisy is possible, for that same priest was, it seems, a very personable young man:

> The soldiers were therefore frequent visitors in the city and went to the temple on the pretext of *thrēskeia*; there they delighted in watching the boy.
>
> φοιτῶντες οὖν οἱ στρατιῶται ἑκάστοτε ἐς τὴν πόλιν, ἔς τε τὸν νεὼν ἰόντες θρησκείας δὴ χάριν, τὸ μειράκιον ἡδέως ἔβλεπον [V.3].[17]

Although clearly *thrēskeia* here does not in itself carry the sense of hypocrisy or improper worship, after all that is what they were pretending to be about, nonetheless it seems hardly coincidental that in nearly all of the usages of this word in Herodian, it occurs in contexts of hypocrisy. The sense that *thrēskeia* more often than not carries a overtones of the dubious in Herodian is borne out explicitly by the final instance of the word in his text. Here's the fascinating story. Elagabalus, having been promoted to the purple owing to the manipulations of his grandmother, Maesa, disappointed (*litotes*) her through his dissolute behavior. The grandmother became quite worried, thinking that he would be deposed by the army and "she would again be reduced to the status of an ordinary person." She accordingly develops a plan. She persuades the feckless young man to adopt and appoint as Caesar his cousin, another grandson of hers:

> She persuaded him saying that it was necessary for him to be free for the priesthood and the *thrēskeia* of the god,

> εἰποῦσα αὐτῷ κεχαρισμένα, ὡς ἄρα χρὴ ἐκεῖνον μὲν τῇ ἱερωσύνῃ καὶ θρησκείᾳ σχολάζειν τοῦ θεοῦ

while the other grandson would engage himself in vulgar temporal power of course. Once again: Now, to be sure, there is nothing in any of these usages to suggest that *thrēskeia* itself implies something false or hypocritical, but nonetheless it seems more than coincidental that in so many of the cases within a small set within which Herodian uses the term, nearly all refer to trickery or hypocrisy of one sort or another. Indeed, the grandmother herself refers to his practices as "ecstatic [Bacchic] and secret mysterious [orgiastic]" rites (βακχείαις καὶ ὀργίοις) in the very next clause. I would tentatively suggest that older meanings having to do with the extravagant, the extreme, the overdone still clung to the word, making the word available so easily for these usages by Herodian.

Here then are two well-attested sorts of usage for *thrēskeia*: one that tends toward the neutral or praiseworthy, and one that tends toward the negative and critical, the latter certainly being quite dominant in certain kinds of documents (*viz.* Plutarch). It will not do, moreover, to find an abstraction sufficiently general enough that it incorporates both meanings. Wittgenstein once remarked: "Imagine someone saying: 'All tools serve to modify something. Thus the hammer modifies the position of the nail, the saw the shape of the board, and so on.'—And what is modified by the rule, the glue-pot, the nails?— 'Our knowledge of a thing's length, the temperature of the glue, and the solidity of the box.'—Would anything be gained by this assimilation of expressions?—."[18] Definitions of religion seem frequently, if not always, to function like this definition of "tools" so effectively disposed of by Wittgenstein. The range of usage of the word *thrēskeia* incorporates both the highly negative and positive senses in one, in a way that simply cannot be mapped onto any English word. A comparison may help to clarify the point further: Old English *smearcian*, related to Germanic words for "contempt," means in that language both to smile and to smirk. In the literature of Old English, moreover, there are passages in which this doubling or ambiguity of meaning functions productively and richly. These effects cannot be reproduced in Modern English in which the two words, "smile" (incorporated into Middle English from North-Germanic) and "smirk," are so clearly marked in usage as different from each other. Similarly with *thrēskeia*, its positive and negative connotations cannot be distinguished clearly, giving it the possibility of semantic effects that are impossible to reproduce in English. (In Chapter 11, "A Jewish Actor in the Audience: Josephan Doublespeak," I shall hypothesize how an actual author, Josephus, makes use of these ambiguities).

Interestingly, as I have shown, *thrēskeia*, owing to the economy of balance that governs early Greek thought, similarly but differently, from early Roman thought, can easily shade into the too much where it flips from being a good thing to being a bad thing—and, moreover, very frequently does so to the extent of that meaning becoming an explicit component of its invented etymologies. In that sense, it contrasts with *eusebeia*, while in its sense of prohibitions and obligations that are ours and appropriate, it congenes with *eusebeia*.

THRĒSKEIA IN PHILO

Philo Judaeus was the most famous Judaean in Alexandria, author of philosophical tracts and allegorical interpretations of the Bible. As opposed to his Palestinian contemporary Josephus, in Philo's lexicon, *thrēskeia* is opposed to *eusebeia*. There is, moreover, frequently in this writer, a kind of negative tinge to the use of the term—or, at least, and better put, he uses it in contexts that have a negative charge. Thus, within Philo's writings, are instances in which *thrēskeia* is more marked with the overtones of the useless sort of observances. Thus, I find the following context in which it is clearly and explicitly marked as nearly the opposite of *eusebeia*. Note well, moreover, the sense of extravagance here. Philo speaks of one "who has more money than he knows what to do with" and founds a temple and sacrifices unceasingly, providing expensive votive offerings with all manner of rich furnishings, nonetheless:

> Let him not be inscribed with the *eusebeis*, for he has wandered from the way of *eusebeia*; thinking it [*eusebeia*] *thrēskeia* as opposed to *hosiotēs* [*anti hosiotētos*], and giving gifts to the unbribable one who will never take them and flattering the unflatterable, the one who welcomes [all] that which belongs to the genuine class of *therapeia*—the genuine class being the soul bearing simply and solely truth—while he rejects counterfeit ones.

> μετ' εὐσεβῶν ἀναγεγράφθω πεπλάνηται γὰρ καὶ οὗτος τῆς πρὸς εὐσέβειαν ὁδοῦ, θρησκείαν ἀντὶ ὁσιότητος ἡγούμενος καὶ δῶρα τῷ ἀδεκάστῳ διδοὺς οὐδέποτε ληψομένῳ τὰ τοιαῦτα καὶ κολακεύων τὸν ἀκολάκευτον, ὃς γνησίους μὲν θεραπείας ἀσπάζεται—γνήσιοι δ' εἰσὶν αἱ ψυχῆς ψιλὴν καὶ μόνην θυσίαν φερούσης ἀλήθειαν—, τὰς δὲ νόθους ἀποστρέφεται·[Quod deterius potiori insidiari soleat 21].[19]

This unrighteous person has been led to his hypocrisy by mistakenly thinking that proper reverence [*eusebeia*] is *thrēskeia*, glossed here explicitly as sacrifices, offerings, and the like, rather than as opposed to appropriate *hosiotēs*, glossed, once more, explicitly as a movement of the soul bearing truth. There are here several clear semantic contrasts. *Thrēskeia* is defined as not *eusebeia* nor *therapeia* ("proper" divine service), and especially not *hosiotēs*, but rather as that which is only external and hence "counterfeit," as he is not bringing truth from his soul as his sacrifice.[20] For Philo, it would seem, as I learn by unpacking the sentence as I have, that the notoriously difficult to define *hosiotēs* refers as well to inner dispositions. In any case, the text could not be clearer or more explicit than it is in its valuation of *thrēskeia* as the inferior or even negative term. The negative affect associated with the term *thrēskeia* from classical Greek writers is thus continued in this usage by Philo.

Retaining, once again, an ancient sense of the extraordinary (but not the negative), one finds the following in the same author:

> For the best prize for humans is the *therapeia* of the only God.[21] Therefore whenever we have arrived at the courts of *therapeia* not yet completely purified, but thinking only to have washed off . . . , rather than approach (lit. sooner than approach), we have run away from it [*therapeia*], not bearing its austere way of living and the sleepless *thrēskeia* and the unremitting and inexhaustible, unbearable toil [*ponos*].

> ἀνδρῶν δὲ ἄριστον ἆθλον ἡ θεοῦ μόνου θεραπεία. τοιγαροῦν ἐπειδὰν μήπω τελείως καθαρθέντες, δόξαντες δὲ αὐτὸ μόνον ἐκνίψασθαι τὰ καταρρυπαίνοντα ἡμῶν τὸν βίον, ἐπ' αὐλὰς τῆς θεραπείας ἀφικώμεθα, θᾶττον ἢ προσελθεῖν ἀπεπηδήσαμεν, τὴν αὐστηρὰν δίαιταν αὐτῆς καὶ τὴν ἄυπνον θρησκείαν καὶ τὸν συνεχῆ καὶ ἀκάματον πόνον οὐκ ἐνεγκόντες [*De Fuga et inventione* 41].

The ministering or caring for God (in the soul, as Philo has argued in the preceding passage) is the highest prize for humans, but seeking to fulfill that before we are ready, we come to the courts in which this soulful cult takes place, but then flee after we realize the hardships which it demands, among them *thrēskeia* without sleep closely associated with *ponos*, painful and torturous labor. This usage, not indicating a negative attitude toward *thrēskeia*, clearly signposts some form of arduous practice that is a *part* of or propaideutic for *therapeia*, and certainly does imply a restricted sense for this term, not as *therapeia* but necessary for it. It is not entirely clear here of what this *thrēskeia* consists, but it is arduous and marked positively as part of *therapeia* and not more or less as its opposite as shown in the passages discussed in this chapter.

The best proof, however, for the pejorative sense inhering to the word *thrēskeia* comes from a text approximately contemporaneous with Philo, 4 Maccabees.

THRĒSKEIA IN 4 MACCABEES

Indeed, one of the richest texts for exploring the interpretative profit from a nuanced account of the semantics of *thrēskeia* that avoids rendering it with anachronistic abstractions is the first-century (either one) Jewish text, 4 Maccabees.[22] This work, which is a philosophical tract in the form of narrative of the martyrdoms of various Judaeans in the Hasmonean period, consists of an attempt to demonstrate that the Judaean commitment to the Torah even until a martyr's death constitutes the victory among them of reason over passion and not the triumph of passion over reason as others might see it. To be sure, *Ioudaismos* appears in the text at 4:26, but it has been long established that it is mistaken to translate there "Judaism," as if the name of a "religion" since the term coined on the model of Greek *Hellēnismos* (loyalty to the Greek culture and language), *Mēdismos* (acting like a Persian—and thus disloyal to the Greek cause and culture) must mean loyalty to the Judaean cause and culture.[23] But this has nothing to do with *thrēskeia*, which appears in another context and at another place in the text.

The Seleucid king Antiochus considers the Judaeans' absolute inflexibility and willingness to die for what he takes as small points of the law the very opposite of reason defeating passion. This point is vitally important for the interpretation of the text, a small fragment of which I will present here.

In this incident, Antiochus is trying to persuade Eleazar, the elderly leader of the Judaeans, to eat pork and abandon the foolish prohibitions of the Judaeans/Jews:

> "For I respect your age and your gray hair; although you have had it for a long time, you don't seem to me a philosopher, holding [as you do] to the *thrēskeia* of the Judeans."

> αἰδοῦμαι γάρ σου τὴν ἡλικίαν καὶ τὴν πολιάν, ἣν μετὰ τοσοῦτον ἔχων χρόνον οὔ μοι δοκεῖς φιλοσοφεῖν τῇ Ἰουδαίων χρώμενος θρησκείᾳ [4 Maccabees 5:7].

Although one might be tempted (as various interlocutors have been) to interpret here that it is the *thrēskeia* of the Judaeans that is under condemnation here and not *thrēskeia* simpliciter, I hope to make a defensible and plausible case otherwise.

While David deSilva, author of a most authoritative and very recent commentary on 4 Maccabees translates "the Jewish religion," he himself clearly remarks that "inventing derogatory explanations of the Jews' adherence to food laws, Sabbath laws, and circumcision enabled Greek and Latin authors to marginalize Judaism as a superstition rather than a dignified religion or philosophy . . . Antiochus speaks as though Eleazar and the Judeans are trapped in the barbaric and dishonorable form of slavery described by Dio Chrysostom (Or. 14.18) as 'ignorance of what is allowed and what is not allowed.'"[24] Given that point, which he makes in a comment to this very passage and as an explanation thereof, it would seem that "religion" is precisely the wrong translation here. The entire context of the passage, in fact, does not suggest that the tyrant is trying to get Eleazar to abandon Judaean belief and practice tout court but rather that he is arguing for a rational response to the compulsion of the tyrant himself, one that will not leave him tortured and dead. He goes so far as to argue that surely God would forgive transgression "arising on account of compulsion." It is the exaggeration of holding on to prohibitions that are otherwise irrational and doing so to the point of death that qualifies Eleazar as no philosopher but the adherent of a *thrēskeia*, thus rendering the text consistent with deSilva's own interpretation (and not his translation).[25] Here, given the context, is a quite clear instance of the odor of the derogatory that occurs so frequently in context with *thrēskeia*. It is not the cultic practice of the Jews, per se, that makes it a *thrēskeia* but their boundless (and irrational) devotion to that practice even unto martyrdom that makes it so.

There are further arguments for understanding that it is *thrēskeia* simpliciter that the tyrant considers irrational and not the Judaean *thrēskeia* particularly and as opposed to, say, the Athenian one. Just a bit later, the same tyrant further remonstrates, referring now to Eleazar's Jewish practices as "foolish philosophy":

> Will you not awaken from this foolish philosophy of yours and dispel your futile reasonings and taking up a mind appropriate to your age, philosophize according to the beneficial truth.

> οὐκ ἐξυπνώσεις ἀπὸ τῆς φλυάρου φιλοσοφίας ὑμῶν καὶ ἀποσκεδάσεις τῶν λογισμῶν σου τὸν λῆρον καὶ ἄξιον τῆς ἡλικίας ἀναλαβὼν νοῦν φιλοσοφήσεις τὴν τοῦ συμφέροντος ἀλήθειαν [v. 11].

That *thrēskeia* of the Jews is now defined as foolish philosophy and futile reasonings: that is, as matters that avail nothing, inappropriate to one whose wisdom matches his gray hairs. One could argue, once again, that it is not *thrēskeia* that is negatively marked but only Jewish *thrēskeia*, just as there is philosophizing that is foolish and philosophizing that is truthful. I prefer, for the following reasons, to consider "foolish philosophy" the virtual semantic equivalent of *thrēskeia*.

It has not been noted before that only Antiochus uses the term *thrēskeia* at all in the text. The Jewish respondent to Antiochus never uses the word *thrēskeia* with reference to the Judaeans' practice and loyalties, but only *eusebeia* or *nomos*, "our law." For instance, in responding to the very same challenge by Antiochus, Eleazar at one point declares, "For you will terrorize *asebeis* [people without *eusebeia*], but you will not have power over my reasonings on behalf of *eusebeia* either by words or actions" [5:38]. And again, addressing as it were the other Jews, "You, on the one hand, O children of Abram, die nobly for the *eusebeia* of God" [6:22]. *Eusebeia*, not *thrēskeia*. Finally, when the old man is about to die in the fire, he says, "You know, God, that though I had the opportunity to save myself, I am dying by fiery torments on account of the *nomos*" [6:27]. *Nomos* not *thrēskeia*. This suggests a strong contrast in meaning in this text as in Philo between *thrēskeia* and *eusebeia*, a contrast that lies precisely at the heart of the entire text: That which Antiochus refers to as foolish and extravagant as *thrēskeia*, the willingness of Judaeans to be martyred for food prohibitions, the Judaeans themselves see as *eusebeia*, the very mark of rational self-control. (Extremism in the defense of Torah is no *thrēskeia*!) Antiochus argues that given the opportunity to save himself, to accept fiery torments and to die is *thrēskeia*. In other words, the very dispute between Antiochus and the old Jew is whether willingness to die for the Law is *thrēskeia* or *eusebia*, irrational fanaticism (one might say) or rational piety!

I recall as witnesses the texts cited earlier from Plutarch and Philo in which *eusebeia* is marked as the just right of a Three Bears semantics in which *asebeia* is too little, and *deisidaimonia/thrēskeia* is too much: a usage that is borne out precisely by referring to the Judaean willingness to die for the law as *thrēskeia*, while the Judaeans themselves call it *eusebeia*. (Imagine a modern context in which an accuser refers to a cult, and alleged cult members respond by describing themselves as a religion or a church.)

We can now decode from within its own context Antiochus' use of *thrēskeia*, as well as the fact that the Judaeans never use the word in 4 Maccabees to refer to their own commitments and practices, but only *eusebeia*. It is as if Eleazar and his fellows say: No, Antiochus, our practices and even our willingness to die for them, are not in any way excessive; they are not *thrēskeia* but *eusebeia*, the correctly balanced measure. Antiochus, at this moment in the discourse, for rhetorical purpose, is not so much condemning the practices and beliefs of the Judaeans so much as marking their extravagant nature, their ignoring the flexibility built into any rational system on his view and thus being willing to die. The Judaeans, themselves, of course, refer to their own ways as *eusebeia* and *nomos*: that which is just enough devotion—or one might say that for them, absolute devotion to the Law is *eusebeia* and never too much. Indeed, when toward the end of the book, even Antiochus and his minions come to admire the martyrs, it is as "athletes of the divine law," not of the Judaean [or any other] *thrēskeia* (17:16). "What may appear to you, O tyrant, as giving in to emotion and running amok" precisely proves, as the author repeats over and over in Chapter 7, Eleazar's ability to conquer the emotions with reason. This is not *thrēskeia* but *eusebeia* and *theosebeia*. deSilva, by translating *thrēskeia* as "religion" and by even not noticing that the Judaeans use quite another word, *theosebeia* (7:6, which he also translates blithely as "religion"), has totally obscured a realm of subtle meaning in the text.

At the very end of 4 Maccabees is a passage that nails down, as it were, the absence of "religion" from that text:

> If it were proper for us to paint the story of your piety [*eusebeia*] upon something, would not those viewing it shudder, seeing a mother of seven children enduring, for the sake of piety [*eusebeia*], their diverse torments [leading to death]?

> εἰ δὲ ἐξὸν ἡμῖν ἦν ὥσπερ ἐπί τινος ζωγραφῆσαι τὴν τῆς εὐσεβείας σου ἱστορίαν οὐκ ἂν ἔφριττον οἱ θεωροῦντες ὁρῶντες μητέρα ἑπτὰ τέκνων δι' εὐσέβειαν ποικίλας βασάνους μέχρι θανάτου ὑπομείνασαν [7:17, translation following de Silva].

The NRSV translates here "the history of your religion," an absurd translation on the face of it because it is a picture of the particular incidents of martyrdom that is in question and not a history of an imaginary "Judaism." One can see here how misleading it is to assume that there is "Judaism," any Judaism at all, religion or not, in the minds of the authors of these texts. However, in this case, one need not rely on semantic taste alone, as the text itself glosses *eusebeia* only a verse later:

> Here an elderly priest and elderly woman and seven children lie buried on account of the violence of a tyrant wishing to destroy the polity.

> Ἐνταῦθα γέρων ἱερεὺς καὶ γυνὴ γεραιὰ καὶ ἑπτὰ παῖδες ἐγκεκήδευνται διὰ τυράννου βίαν τὴν Ἑβραίων πολιτείαν καταλῦσαι θέλοντος.

The martyrs were defending the polity of the Hebrews with their piety, nothing more, nothing less.

Moving forward in our exploration of the semantics of *thrēskeia*, one will find the ambiguities and ambivalences of its usages productive of complex resonances in a variety of cultural contexts and rhetorical situations not even suspected (and that earlier readers have not suspected) if glossed with the anachronistic abstraction "religion." The next two chapters of this book hold deeper investigation of the writer who uses it more than anyone else before the fourth-century C.E. Josephus. It is no wonder that this writer, more than all others, it seems, exploits the multiple connotations of the word to express his own equivocations and ambiguities.

Case Study: Josephus

Josephus without Judaism: *Nomos, Eusebeia, Thrēskeia*

In Chapters 8 and 9, I have shown the complexity of the semantic range of the Greek word *thrēskeia*. It is especially important to recapitulate the point that this word refers to "cult" in both very negative and positive valuations, and these nuances are fairly neatly divided in the archive between two corpora—literary and epigraphic—with the literary material tending strongly toward the pole of associating *thrēskeia* with *deisidaimonia* and therefore the excessive, useless, and untrammeled in cultic behavior as opposed to *eusebeia*. The inscriptional material (from Thrace and its eastern neighbor, Bithynia) treats it more neutrally as "our own cultic behavior," separating it from *deisidaimonia* and associating it semantically with *eusebeia*. On the other hand, in the previous chapters, I introduce literary writers who use *thrēskeia* in the aforesaid "positive" sense: notably, the first-century Judaean historian, Josephus.

In this chapter, I continue to explore this writer who used this word *thrēskeia* more than any other writer of antiquity. I propose to show how it is possible and distinctly advantageous to describe Josephus' world entirely without using the concept of "religion" at all. Josephus, the son of Mattias, was one of the generals of the revolt of the Jews of Palestine against Rome in the first century. At a certain point in the war, he changed his mind and his colors,[1] and attempting to convince his fellows of the hopelessness of the war and the likelihood of total destruction, he became a client of Vespasian the Roman general (later to be emperor) and of his son Titus (also a future emperor), spending the rest of his days (20 years) in Rome in a palace provided by the former and writing all his books there. He not only changed his mind but also his name: the new nomen, Flavius, honoring his new patrons.[2] Josephus is always in a cultural situation of negotiation or mediation between loyalties, writing apologetically, as it were, to both his Judaean and Roman audiences at one and the same time.

I argue that abandoning the very notion that there is such a thing as "religion" within Josephus' cultural or imaginative world opens up possibilities for reading him complexly and understanding him richly that are foreclosed when we anachronistically separate different spheres.

When Josephus speaks of the ideas, thoughts, ideologies of the Torah, he does not call them *Ioudaismos* or the Judaean *thrēskeia*: Rather, he calls them "the philosophy of the sacred books." When he refers to the enjoined and proscribed practices encoded in those books as well as in Judaean custom, he calls them "ancestral laws/customs," and as I show, he calls the whole complex *Nomos/nomoi*. As does ancient Greek, Josephus, however, does have words that mean "cult," "reverence," "prohibitions," especially—but not exclusively—with respect to God. One of these is *thrēskeia*. In the previous chapters, I show that no English word can possibly be used to translate Greek *thrēskeia*. There, I map the semantic range or occasions of usage of this word within a corpus of Greek texts stretching from Herodotus through the writings of such authors as Strabo and Plutarch to the writings of Hellenistic Jews, such as Philo, and Josephus, as well as observing its usage in a somewhat different sense in epigraphical materials from Thrace and Bithynia. I note in those chapters, moreover, a well-known gap in the attestation of this word from Herodotus until the first century B.C.E., and even then it is first attested in Strabo, from Pontus, and not in peninsular Greek.

In this chapter, I would like to show that the word *thrēskeia* enters into complex semantic relations in Josephus' corpus with other words within its semantic field. The reason why it would seem—with one important exception—that such a study has not been undertaken until now is that on the assumption that *thrēskeia* means "religion," and that we know what "religion" is (even if "we" somehow can't agree on a definition), what remains to investigate?[3] Being released from the apprehension that there is a concept/word, "religion" in all (or even most, or even many) cultures, and having begun to see how complex a word *thrēskeia* is semantically, the opportunity but also the *desideratum* of an expansive study in the Josephan corpus becomes apparent.

As Josephus scholar, Steve Mason, has written, "Although the word θρησκεία hardly occurs outside of Judaean or Christian Greek before Josephus, Josephus has it a remarkable 91 times."[4] This provides an incredible opportunity, of course, to study the semantics of this crucial word in one author, but also raises a riveting question: Why Josephus? Why so much there? The potential to learn a great deal about Josephus and his world from such an inquiry is palpable, if once again, one doesn't paper it over with an anachronistic abstraction or beg the question. Josephus' writings provide one of the best places to observe the multiple and shifting semantics of the word. One must consider, moreover, the possibility that a Greek word with a somewhat different or varying set of associations and connotations has been adapted as well as adopted to speak of a different culture's (Israelite) conceptual world.[5]

Why, then, does Josephus suddenly use such a rare word in Greek literature with such frequency and range of nuance? Mason has offered an explanation: "Josephus also favours a noun that integrates 'divine worship, ritual, cult, and piety' (*thrēskeia*) and its cognate verb 'to worship'. Though rarely used by non-Judaean writers the word group had some currency among other Judaean authors before Josephus picked it up. He found it singularly convenient for his claims about the Judaean disposition toward piety and worship."[6] Mason is careful not to confuse that integration with the production of a concept anything like modern "religion." I shall show here, building on Mason and adding to his conclusions, that the word *thrēskeia*, even in Josephus, signifies a much more interesting complex of ideas that would be obscured by that covering abstraction, "religion."[7] Agreeing with Mason by and large in his interpretations of *thrēskeia* in Josephus, I would like to essay a somewhat different explanation for its deployment by him: namely, that the word was not just employed by the historian to make claims about "the Judaean disposition toward piety and worship," but to do work for him that was even more freighted than that. The heuristic question of this chapter will be why Josephus, among all the users of Hellenistic Greek up to and around his time, used the word *thrēskeia* so frequently. The question is sharpened by connecting it with the results of the previous chapters in which it has been shown that *thrēskeia* itself quite frequently carries negative connotations (or even denotations). The answer to this question—a question that reveals itself only when one "imagines no religion"—will, I reckon, reveal much about Josephus and his world that we would not have perceived otherwise.

Josephus without Religion

Mason has written:

> Josephus has often been criticized for presenting his teacher Bannus as well as the Pharisees, Sadducees, and Essenes as *philosophical schools*,[8] because of our modern assumption that they were obviously *religious* groups. But there was no such terminology available to Josephus that would be intelligible to his audiences. He *could* say that these groups or individuals were concerned with piety, simple living, contempt for suffering and death, and expectation of a certain afterlife, and that is what he does. But these were what philosophical schools did, and that is why he calls them philosophies. There was no genus called *religion*, of which any of these could be a species [Mason, ms.].

This revealing point made by Mason exposes perfectly what is at stake in this investigation. As Mason shows, the application of anachronistic categories and abstractions leads to a fundamental misapprehension of Josephus' very text and results in him being accused of a flaw in understanding his own culture, as it were. Such accusations by historians of category error on the part of Josephus—anatomized by Mason—remind one of nothing so much as the repeated historians' critiques directed at the Romans for not distinguishing clearly enough between the sacred and the profane, or between religion and politics, as if these were real entities, Platonic forms, and not the constructs of particular cultures and always different in configuration. "There is nothing more difficult, in writing about the Palestine of this period, than to form an adequate conception of the relation between religion and other spheres of life," writes Tessa Rajak.[9] Perhaps, I would suggest, the difficulty lies in the fact that there is no such distinction made by the people in the culture—least of all, Josephus. As Rajak herself notes elsewhere, "What is even more interesting is that prayer could be converted on the instant into a political meeting: 'We were proceeding with the ordinary service and engaged in prayer, when Jesus rose and began to question us about the furniture and uncoined silver . . .' (295; Thackeray's translation)."[10] So much for separate spheres!

NOMOS AND NARRATION: *AGAINST APION*

Without any covering term such as *Ioudaismos* and without a term that means "religion," how did a Greek-writing Jew (or for that matter, a Hebrew or an Aramaic-writing Jew) such as Josephus refer to the Judaean way of life? More precisely put, how does Josephus translate the terms of art of Judaean language/culture into Greek terms? The burden of argument in this chapter is that Josephus presses *thrēskeia* into service (along with some allies) to cover two different Hebrew/Aramaic terms—*Torah* and *'avoda*—and that his usage of the Greek words is also a mode of negotiation of two languages, two identities, and two sets of cultural commitments.

To begin to make this argument, I undertake what will appear at first glance to be a digression, a look at an entirely different word than *thrēskeia* in Josephus: namely, *nomos* and its plural *nomoi*. These terms are usually translated into English as "law" and "laws," but I will try to show that that translation also significantly misses the point in Josephus. In his remarkable defense of the Judaean way of life in *Against Apion*, the only term used to describe that way of life is *nomos*. This chapter begins, therefore, with an examination of what Josephus means by *nomos*, a task easily and profitably accomplished given that he tells us exactly what it comprises for him. In Josephus—as I dare say, in ancient writers in general—the abstractions and categories of law, politics, and religion are not useful analytic categories. The following narrative will begin to show how what one calls "law"—*nomos* in Greek—is imbricated in these complex lexical usages and thus conceptual fields. I submit that the term for Josephus that embraced the Book and the entire Judaean way of life was *nomos*, and that it was equivalent to Hebrew *Torah* and Aramaic *'orayta*. On one level, this point is trivial given that already in the LXX, the regular translation of Torah is *nomos*, but the point here is not that the Greek translators misunderstood the import of Torah with this translation but that rather the word *nomos* in Greek was resignified by being used among Judaeans as the equivalent of Torah.

The best way to see this is to follow his description and defense of the Judaean *nomos* in his *Against Apion*, a text in which Josephus explicitly defends the Judaean *nomos* from attacks on the part of several "pagan" authors, including one Apion. Here, he gives as full an account as could be desired of what *nomos/Torah* means for him.

An excellent sense of what the Torah comprises can be found in the following passage:

> But since Apollonius Molon and Lysimachus and certain others, partly out of ignorance,
> but mostly from ill-will, have made statements about our legislator Moses and the laws

[*nomoi*] that are neither just nor true—libeling Moses as a charlatan and fraudster, and claiming that the laws are our teachers in vice and not a single virtue—I wish to speak briefly, as best I can, about the whole structure of our constitution [*politeuma*] and about its individual parts.

For I think it will become clear that we possess laws that are extremely well designed with a view to piety, fellowship with one another, and universal benevolence, as well as justice, endurance in labors and contempt for death.

I appeal to those who will peruse this text to conduct their reading without envy. For I did not choose to write an encomium of ourselves, but I consider this to be the most just form of defense against the many false accusations against us—a defense derived from the laws in accordance with which we continue to live.

Ἐπεὶ δὲ καὶ Ἀπολλώνιος ὁ Μόλων καὶ Λυσίμαχος καί τινες ἄλλοι τὰ μὲν ὑπ᾽ ἀγνοίας, τὸ πλεῖστον δὲ κατὰ δυσμένειαν περί τε τοῦ νομοθετήσαντος ἡμῖν Μωσέως καὶ περὶ τῶν νόμων πεποίηνται λόγους οὔτε δικαίους οὔτε ἀληθεῖς, τὸν μὲν ὡς γόητα καὶ ἀπατεῶνα διαβάλλοντες, τοὺς νόμους δὲ κακίας ἡμῖν καὶ οὐδεμιᾶς ἀρετῆς φάσκοντες εἶναι διδασκάλους, βούλομαι συντόμως καὶ περὶ τῆς ὅλης ἡμῶν καταστάσεως τοῦ πολιτεύματος καὶ περὶ τῶν κατὰ μέρος ὡς ἂν ᾧ δυνατὸς εἰπεῖν. οἶμαι γὰρ ἔσεσθαι φανερόν, ὅτι καὶ πρὸς εὐσέβειαν καὶ πρὸς κοινωνίαν τὴν μετ᾽ ἀλλήλων καὶ πρὸς τὴν καθόλου φιλανθρωπίαν, ἔτι δὲ πρὸς δικαιοσύνην καὶ τὴν ἐν τοῖς πόνοις καρτερίαν καὶ θανάτου περιφρόνησιν ἄριστα κειμένους ἔχομεν τοὺς νόμους. παρακαλῶ δὲ τοὺς ἐντευξομένους τῇ γραφῇ μὴ μετὰ φθόνου ποιεῖσθαι τὴν ἀνάγνωσιν· οὐ γὰρ ἐγκώμιον ἡμῶν αὐτῶν προειλόμην συγγράφειν, ἀλλὰ πολλὰ καὶ ψευδῆ κατηγορουμένοις ἡμῖν ταύτην ἀπολογίαν δικαιοτάτην εἶναι νομίζω τὴν ἀπὸ τῶν νόμων, καθ᾽ οὓς ζῶντες διατελοῦμεν [2:145–47].

Although, to be sure, Josephus uses here *politeuma*—something like "constitution," and thus a term that modern speakers would use to refer to politics, government—to refer to the Torah of Moses, the *nomoi* are that which makes up the *politeuma*. Moreover, as I shall demonstrate shortly, he frequently uses *nomos* in this very sense of the whole unified object: the *politeuma*.[11] Within the *politeuma* are laws, but take note of what the laws consist: piety, fellowship, universal love of humans, justice, perseverance in labor, and contempt for death. Unpacking this, one sees that the whole—by whatever name he refers to it, and he has several—consists of what we might call "ritual laws," structures of governance that lead to fellowship and benevolence, but also laws in the strict sense (justice) as well as prescribed practices to inculcate personal moral characteristics. Neither could one extract one piece of this whole and call it law, politics, or religion, nor could the whole be nominated with such a covering term. Note that the term *nomoi* includes all these categories and practices, as well, and even more, as I shall show.

In a lengthy passage, Josephus argues for the totality of the Judaean code of laws as well as its accessibility to all Judaeans. Referring to Greek philosophers, including Plato and the Stoics, who are all recognized by Josephus as followers of the true god, he writes:

These, however, confined their philosophy to a few and did not dare to disclose the truth of their doctrine to the masses, who were in the grip of opinions. But our legislator, by putting deeds in harmony with words, not only won consent from his contemporaries but also implanted this belief about God in their descendants of all future generations, [such that it is] unchangeable.

The reason is that, by the very shape of the legislation, it is always employable by everyone, and has lasted long. For he did not make piety a part of virtue, but recognized and established the others as parts of it—that is, justice, moderation, endurance, and harmony among citizens in relation to one another in all matters.

For all practices and occupations, and all speech, have reference to our piety towards God; he did not leave any of these unscrutinized or imprecise.

ἀλλ' οἱ μὲν πρὸς ὀλίγους φιλοσοφοῦντες εἰς πλήθη δόξαις προκατειλημμένα τὴν ἀλήθειαν τοῦ δόγματος ἐξενεγκεῖν οὐκ ἐτόλμησαν, ὁ δὲ ἡμέτερος νομοθέτης ἅτε δὴ τὰ ἔργα παρέχων σύμφωνα τοῖς λόγοις οὐ μόνον τοὺς καθ' αὑτὸν ἔπεισεν, ἀλλὰ καὶ τοῖς ἐξ ἐκείνων ἀεὶ γενησομένοις τὴν περὶ θεοῦ πίστιν ἐνέφυσεν ἀμετακίνητον. αἴτιον δ' ὅτι καὶ τῷ τρόπῳ τῆς νομοθεσίας πρὸς τὸ χρήσιμον πάντων ἀεὶ πολὺ διήνεγκεν· οὐ γὰρ μέρος ἀρετῆς ἐποίησεν τὴν εὐσέβειαν, ἀλλὰ ταύτης μέρη τἆλλα, λέγω δὲ τὴν δικαιοσύνην τὴν σωφροσύνην τὴν καρτερίαν τὴν τῶν πολιτῶν πρὸς ἀλλήλους ἐν ἅπασι συμφωνίαν.

ἅπασαι γὰρ αἱ πράξεις καὶ διατριβαὶ καὶ λόγοι πάντες ἐπὶ τὴν πρὸς θεὸν ἡμῖν εὐσέβειαν ἀναφέρουσιν·οὐδὲν γὰρ τούτων ἀνεξέταστον οὐδὲ ἀόριστον παρέλιπεν [2:169–71].

Several things are of note. First, the ideas of Plato and the Stoics are designated as "philosophies," not in contrast to the Torah of Moses but as members of the same class. The legislation of the Torah, as opposed to that of the worthy Greeks, is so perfectly designed as to inculcate in all its receivers correct doctrine about god as well, which the others fail to do owing to their esotericism. Second, the very esotericism of such thinkers as Plato was guaranteed by the fact that they spoke about ideas only, while the Torah also prescribes a whole way of life for all the people. The practices and the ideas thus reinforce each other, not only for the intellectual elite but also for everyone.

In this passage, Josephus begins a wide-ranging comparison of the Torah of Moses with the practices of other peoples with regard to inculcating merit according to their lights. Josephus has already designated the form of Judaean government [*politeuma*], via an apparent neologism, as a theocracy [*theokratia*], rule by God [2. 165]: that is, God as he has expressed himself in the Torah.[12] Josephus here explains how the theocracy works by elaborating a theory in which virtues are inculcated by the Torah via combination of "words" and "practices," thus rendering it superior to those cultures that seek to transmit their values either by words alone (Athens) or deeds alone (Sparta). Josephus makes the point as well that for the Judaeans *eusebeia*—reverence—toward God is not a virtue among the other virtues but is the master virtue that incorporates and inculcates all the others: hence, *theokratia*. "Words," here, it should be emphasized, means precisely the written "laws," which one studies (but which are, as we are seeing, so much more than what we call "law") as it is glossed in the next sentence,[13] while "deeds" is glossed in the next Josephan sentence as "instructing through customs, not words" [ἔθεσιν ἐπαίδευον, οὐ λόγοις] [2.172]. Josephus is clearly relating to the dual practice, so characteristic of later rabbinism, of lives dedicated both to the study of the Torah, *logoi*, and to the practice of the commandments, *erga*.[14]

As Barclay points out, Josephus here is mobilizing ancient topoi and stereotypes; thus, with respect to Roman virtue, Dionysius of Halicarnassus writes, "[N]ot by words is it taught but inculcated through deeds."[15] Josephus goes on in the next sentences to write explicitly:

> But our legislator combined both forms with great care: he neither left character-training mute nor allowed the words from the law to go unpracticed. Rather, starting right from the beginning of their nurture and from the mode of life practiced by each individual in the household, he did not leave anything, even the minutest detail, free to be determined by the wishes of those who would make use of [the laws], but even in relation to food, what they should refrain from and what they should eat, the company they keep in their daily lives, as well as their intensity in work and, conversely, rest, he set the law as their boundary and rule, so that, living under this as a father and master, we might commit no sin either willfully or from ignorance.
>
> He left no pretext for ignorance, but instituted the law as the finest and most essential teaching-material; so that it would be heard not just once or twice or a number of times, he ordered that every seven days they should abandon their other activities and gather to hear the law, and to learn it thoroughly and in detail. That is something that all [other] legislators seem to have neglected.

> Ὁ δ᾽ ἡμέτερος νομοθέτης ἄμφω ταῦτα συνήρμοσεν κατὰ πολλὴν ἐπιμέλειαν· οὔτε γὰρ κωφὴν ἀπέλιπε τὴν τῶν ἠθῶν ἄσκησιν οὔτε τὸν ἐκ τοῦ νόμου λόγον ἄπρακτον εἴασεν, ἀλλ᾽ εὐθὺς ἀπὸ τῆς πρώτης ἀρξάμενος τροφῆς καὶ τῆς κατὰ τὸν οἶκον ἑκάστων διαίτης οὐδὲν οὐδὲ τῶν βραχυτάτων αὐτεξούσιον ἐπὶ ταῖς βουλήσεσι τῶν χρησομένων κατέλιπεν, ἀλλὰ καὶ περὶ σιτίων, ὅσων ἀπέχεσθαι χρὴ καὶ τίνα προσφέρεσθαι, καὶ περὶ τῶν κοινωνησόντων τῆς διαίτης ἔργων τε συντονίας καὶ τοὐμπαλιν ἀναπαύσεως ὅρον ἔθηκεν αὐτὸς καὶ κανόνα τὸν νόμον, ἵν᾽ ὥσπερ ὑπὸ πατρὶ τούτῳ καὶ δεσπότῃ ζῶντες μήτε βουλόμενοι μηθὲν μήθ᾽ ὑπ᾽ ἀγνοίας ἁμαρτάνωμεν.
> οὐδὲ γὰρ τὴν ἀπὸ τῆς ἀγνοίας ὑποτίμησιν κατέλιπεν, ἀλλὰ καὶ κάλλιστον καὶ ἀναγκαιότατον ἀπέδειξε παίδευμα τὸν νόμον, οὐκ εἰσάπαξ ἀκροασομένοις οὐδὲ δὶς ἢ πολλάκις, ἀλλ᾽ ἑκάστης ἑβδομάδος τῶν ἄλλων ἔργων ἀφεμένους ἐπὶ τὴν ἀκρόασιν ἐκέλευσε τοῦ νόμου συλλέγεσθαι καὶ τοῦτον ἀκριβῶς ἐκμανθάνειν·ὃ δὴ πάντες ἐοίκασιν οἱ νομοθέται παραλιπεῖν [2. 173–75].

So far is Josephus here from identifying the Torah with "religion," that Moses is described as a law-giver. (Of course, Josephus has not forgotten his description of the polity as a *theokratia*.) Even more striking, the primary purpose for the Sabbath rest here is precisely the opportunity for study of the Torah. Moses combined into a perfect whole the instruction of Israelites in virtue by not leaving any required practices unexpressed (so correctly, Barclay) nor by leaving any words to be theoretical or unpracticed. The *nomos* is thus the perfect expression and teaching mechanism for all Judaean merit. The combination of constant hearing of the words and practicing the deeds inscribed in those words achieves excellence:

> For us, who are convinced that the law was originally laid down in accordance with God's will, it would not be pious to fail to maintain it.

> Ἡμῖν δὲ τοῖς πεισθεῖσιν ἐξ ἀρχῆς τεθῆναι τὸν νόμον κατὰ θεοῦ βούλησιν οὐδ᾽ εὐσεβὲς ἦν τοῦτον μὴ φυλάττειν·[2:184].

Josephus goes on at this point to detail the merits and virtues inculcated by the *nomos*. Among the values and orders inculcated by the *nomos* are some that we in our modern thought world might identify as "political," some as "religious," and others as "legal," without any distinction of these three latter-day abstractions being made by Josephus. Thus, the *nomos* has led to concord among all Judaeans [hah!] in their conception of God. Moreover, their commonly held life-style [*bios*] leads them to concord, as well.

The *nomos* organizes the world with god at the top, as governor of the universe, who designates the priests as managers, as overseers, and judges in disputes [187], in this respect not at all unlike Tertullian's *disciplina*. Josephus follows this with what might appear as a *non sequitur:* namely, that one of the merits of the Judaean people is that their very *politeia* is organized like a "mystery" [188–89]:

> For the whole constitution is organized like a mystic rite [*teletē*].

> ὥσπερ δὲ τελετῆς τινος τῆς ὅλης πολιτείας οἰκονομουμένης [188].

Everything in the Torah, including the civil law, the rules for government, the rituals, the morals and ethics, the whole "constitution" [*politeia*] is organized like an initiation ritual into the Mysteries. This passage requires some exegesis. The Mysteries were a vitally important part of Athenian and more generally Hellenic life. Although not a great deal is known about the details of the initiation—precisely for this reason, they are, after all, Mysteries—we do indeed know that these rituals consisted of doings and sayings together, precisely that which Josephus is vaunting as the special characteristic of the Torah, the Judaean constitution over those of Hellenic poleis. What Josephus seems to be saying, then, is that while the Athenians, in their Mysteries (especially the Eleusinian in which great numbers of Athenians participated) teach, transform by a practice that involves saying and doing, the Athenian constitution as a whole does not (the point made by Josephus). The Judaean constitution, however, incorporates such doing and saying at every point in its existence; it is, therefore, organized like a Mystery initiation (but for all).

The details are then given: There are the commandments that speak about God and prohibit other gods, make it illegal to make images of him. Following them, Josephus talks about sacrifices and the rules of sacrifice, prayer, and purification rites. Josephus completes this section by emphasizing that all this is part and parcel of the *nomos* [198].[16] There follows a discussion of sexual practices and marriage rules, purification practices, funerary rites, and honor of parent. Then follows [2:207] that the law prescribes how to behave with friends and the requirements for judges. Next are laws having to do with the treatment of enemies in battle [212] and animal welfare [213]. Then follows honest business practice [216], and the list goes on. By the time Josephus is done, he has certainly encompassed what we call government, ritual, religion, politics, and law under the one rubric: *nomos*.

I could not nail this point down better than by citing Josephus' own summary:

> Concerning the laws, there was no need of further comment. For they themselves have been seen, through their own content, teaching not impiety but the truest piety, exhorting not to misanthropy but to the sharing of possessions, opposing injustice, attending to justice, banishing laziness and extravagance, teaching people to be self-sufficient and

hardworking, deterring from wars of self-aggrandizement, but equipping them to be courageous on their behalf, inexorable in punishment, unsophisticated in verbal tricks, but confirmed always by action; for this we offer [as evidence] clearer than documents.

Thus, I would be bold enough to say that we have introduced others to an enormous number of ideals that are, at the same time, extremely fine. For what could be finer than unswerving piety? What could be more just than to obey the laws?

What could be more profitable than concord with one another, and neither to fall out in adverse circumstances, nor in favorable ones to become violent and split into factions, but in war to despise death, and in peace to be diligent in crafts and agriculture, and to be convinced that God is in control, watching over everything everywhere?

Περὶ τῶν νόμων οὐκ ἐδέησε λόγου πλείονος· αὐτοὶ γὰρ ἑωράθησαν δι᾽ αὐτῶν οὐκ ἀσέβειαν μὲν εὐσέβειαν δ᾽ ἀληθεστάτην διδάσκοντες, οὐδ᾽ ἐπὶ μισανθρωπίαν, ἀλλ᾽ ἐπὶ τὴν τῶν ὄντων κοινωνίαν παρακαλοῦντες, ἀδικίας ἐχθροί, δικαιοσύνης ἐπιμελεῖς, ἀργίαν καὶ πολυτέλειαν ἐξορίζοντες, αὐτάρκεις καὶ φιλοπόνους εἶναι.

διδάσκοντες, πολέμων μὲν ἀπείργοντες εἰς πλεονεξίαν, ἀνδρείους δὲ ὑπὲρ αὐτῶν εἶναι παρασκευάζοντες, ἀπαραίτητοι πρὸς τὰς τιμωρίας, ἀσόφιστοι λόγων παρασκευαῖς, τοῖς ἔργοις ἀεὶ βεβαιούμενοι· ταῦτα γὰρ [ἀεὶ] ἡμεῖς παρέχομεν τῶν γραμμάτων ἐναργέστερα.

διόπερ ἐγὼ θαρσήσας ἂν εἴποιμι πλείστων ἅμα καὶ καλλίστων ἡμᾶς εἰσηγητὰς τοῖς ἄλλοις γεγονέναι· τί γὰρ εὐσεβείας ἀπαραβάτου κάλλιον, τί δὲ τοῦ πειθαρχεῖν τοῖς νόμοις δικαιότερον.

ἢ τί συμφορώτερον τοῦ πρὸς ἀλλήλους ὁμονοεῖν καὶ μήτ᾽ ἐν συμφοραῖς διίστασθαι μήτ᾽ ἐν εὐτυχίαις στασιάζειν ἐξυβρίζοντας, ἀλλ᾽ ἐν πολέμῳ μὲν θανάτου καταφρονεῖν, ἐν εἰρήνῃ δὲ τέχναις ἢ γεωργίαις προσανέχειν, πάντα δὲ καὶ πανταχοῦ πεπεῖσθαι τὸν θεὸν ἐποπτεύοντα διέπειν [2:291–94].

Contrary to the frequent stereotype that Greek Judaean writers reduced the Torah to "law," it is clear from Josephus that he, at any rate, understood *nomos* in a way far more expansive than our notion of "law" would predict. For him, it incorporates civil and criminal law, the organization of government, plus cultic practice including Temple and private observance, and also beliefs about god, much more than "law," "politics," or "religion," incorporating (one might fairly say) all of them and thus demonstrating the falseness of all these terms as categories for describing his world.

THRĒSKEIA AS *NOMOS*

I hope that the preceding discussion has been enough to warrant understanding *nomos* in Josephus as almost the exact equivalent of *Torah* in Hebrew and its Aramaic cognate *'orayta*. In this section, I wish to establish that often in Josephus, *thrēskeia* can be seen to be functioning in this sense as well. There are texts in the *Antiquities* in which *thrēskeia* functions almost exactly as *nomos* does in the passages from *Against Apion* just discussed, but never in *Against Apion* itself, where the term *thrēskeia* does not appear even once. (Indeed, one could adduce this as one of the arguments for Josephus' sensitivity to the frequently negative sense of *thrēskeia* in other writers!) One can demonstrate the virtual synonymy of *nomos* and *thrēskeia* in those contexts by showing that the two nouns occur in the same collocations. To be sure, as I show in the preceding chapter, Josephus' usage of *thrēskeia* frequently closely matches how it is used in that epigraphical material; but given the negative associations that *thrēskeia* bears in various Greek texts from around the time of Josephus, the question arises as to why he uses it at all when referring to the Judaean way of life when he is writing in defense of that way of life itself. It is one thing, as I shall show in Chapter 11, "A Jewish Actor in the Audience: Josephan Doublespeak," to employ this word precisely in order to produce willed ambiguity but less clear why he would use it when he does not in any apparent way want to produce anything but a positive impression. It is, on this perception of things, not surprising that Josephus never uses *thrēskeia* in *Against Apion*, the most directly and literally apologetic of all his texts. Any ambiguity of reference to the Judaean way of life in that text would be entirely counterproductive given that the whole point of that exercise is, of course, to unequivocally defend that way of life, the Torah over-against both Roman and Greek ways of life. But why risk such ambiguity elsewhere, especially in the *Judaean Antiquities*? The answer to this question will prove—I reckon (and hope)—very illuminating.

Just as *nomos* functions for Josephus as an equivalent to Hebrew Torah, so one finds *thrēskeia* also, as for example, in Ant. 2:211–12. The Pharaoh has just declared that all Judaean male infants should be drowned in the Nile. One very concerned Jew, Amarames (Amram in the Hebrew), feared for the future of the entire race but especially for the unborn child in his wife's womb (who would grow up to be Moses):

> So he turned to supplication of God, imploring him to take pity at length on men who had not turned aside from his *thrēskeia* at all and to grant release to them from the misfortunes from which they were suffering at that time and from the expectation of the demise of their clan.

> ἐν ἀμηχάνοις ἦν, πρὸς ἱκετείαν τοῦ θεοῦ τρέπεται παρακαλῶν οἶκτον ἤδη τινὰ λαβεῖν αὐτὸν ἀνθρώπων μηδὲν τῆς εἰς αὐτὸν θρησκείας παραβεβηκότων δοῦναί τ' ἀπαλλαγὴν αὐτοῖς ὧν παρ' ἐκεῖνον ἐκακοπάθουν τὸν καιρὸν καὶ τῆς ἐπ' ἀπωλείᾳ τοῦ γένους αὐτῶν ἐλπίδος.

Because "god" here is the grammatical subject and the owner of "his" *thrēskeia*, as it were, one would not be transgressing to see here *thrēskeia* as Josephus' equivalent for "Torah"—Torah in the sense of all that is required by god of a human being, the affective and cognitive commitment as well as the practice. The Torah of God in Hebrew [Torat H'] is the teaching of god, the *nomos* in the expansive sense that I identified earlier herein. In a sense, what I am suggesting is that some (at least) of Josephus' key words—his cultural buzzwords, as it were—need to be referred to two lexica: Roman-Greek, of course, and Judaean-Hebrew as well. Understanding *thrēskeia* as only formal practice of the cult will not capture the totalizing sense of *thrēskeia* as a way of life and a character of mind found here. Consider that this same verb *parabainō*—"to step out, to transgress"—is also used with *theou nomos* [the *nomos* of God] or *dikē* (justice). *Thrēskeia* can be concatenated with both *dikaiosunē* and *dikē*—and more to my purpose here, it is the same kind of thing as *theou nomos*, the Torah of God. Tellingly, in Thucydides, it is used in almost identical contexts with ancestral traditions, another common synonym in Josephus for Torah/Nomos: The Plataeans are accused of "transgressing their ancestral traditions" "παραβαίνοντες τὰ πάτρια" (Thucydides 3.61.2).[17] Josephus, however, does not write here *Torah* or *nomos*, and refers to the keeping of the commandments alone as *ta patria ethē*. *Thrēskeia*, for Josephus, is clearly greater (semantically) than just "cult" but represents the entire array of human obligation toward God, including then all the things that Josephus identified as part and parcel of *nomos*: piety, fellowship [*koinōnia*], good order of government.[18]

Here is an example of how this works in a not untypical passage of Josephus [Ant. 9: 95]. With respect to Joram, the King of Jerusalem, Josephus remarks that "[H]e did not differ in any way from the earlier Kings of Israel,"

> who first transgressed the ancestral customs of the Hebrews and the *thrēskeia* of God.

> οἳ πρῶτοι παρηνόμησαν εἰς τὰ πάτρια τῶν Ἑβραίων ἔθη καὶ τὴν τοῦ θεοῦ θρησκείαν.

It would not be unwarranted to see in *thrēskeia* here a reflection of the Hebrew *Torah*, an interpretation supported in this case by the verb *paranomeō*, literally to step outside/transgress the law, which I have already shown used with *nomos*.[19] *Thrēskeia of God* would mean the *thrēskeia* owned by and given by God, just as the Hebrew collocation *Torat H'* refers to the Torah given by God. It is beyond, moreover, the mere living according to Judaean ways, for that is encompassed in the first phrase *ta patria ethē*. At the same time, however, I have gathered ample evidence that *thrēskeia* comprises an attitude of mind or the emotional character of a human being, as, for instance, in passages to be discussed shortly in which *thrēskeia* is coordinated with such terms as *dikaiosunē*, as dispositions of particular individuals. I would suggest that Torah, with its entire behavioral and emotional load in Judaean parlance, might frequently be the best rubric under which to understand Josephus' *thrēskeia*.

In further support of this interpretation, I offer the following:

> In the third year of his reign, calling together the leaders of the country and the priests, he [Jehoshafat] directed them to go round the entire country and teach the people in it, city by city, the Mosaic laws, both to keep these and to be zealous [*spoudazein*] about the *thrēskeia* of God.

> Τρίτῳ δ' ἔτει τῆς βασιλείας συγκαλέσας τοὺς ἡγεμόνας τῆς χώρας καὶ τοὺς ἱερεῖς ἐκέλευε τὴν γῆν περιελθόντας ἅπαντα τὸν λαὸν τὸν ἐπ' αὐτῇ διδάξαι κατὰ πόλιν τοὺς Μωσείους νόμους καὶ φυλάσσειν τούτους καὶ σπουδάζειν περὶ τὴν θρησκείαν τοῦ θεοῦ [Ant. 8: 395].

Here again, it would seem that keeping the laws and being eagerly engaged in the *thrēskeia* are neither quite the same thing nor covered one by the other (unless the latter is an explanatory gloss, as it were on the former), but they do run closely together. It is important, once again, to pay attention to the verb *spoudazein* (to be serious, earnest, zealous) found here, as elsewhere, used together with *thrēskeia*. I think it would not be going too far to see here the *thrēskeia* as incorporating the heightened emotions attendant upon this keeping of the Torah, the discipline, the militant commitment. No wonder, then, that the people were (as Josephus reports in the next sentence) filled with enthusiasm for this project. It is not, moreover, inapposite to remember as well that in other Greek writers, such as

Plutarch and even Philo, it is that very *enthousiasmos* that leads to *thrēskeia* in the sense of too much zeal, too much fear of God—but not, it seems, for Josephus. It is also not inapposite here to remark Josephus' own instances of "ecstasy," leading to prophetic insight [War 3:353]. The very term that Josephus uses there is *enthous*, clearly marked as a highly desirable state; while for Greeks, as shown already, *enthousiasmos* was negatively marked. No wonder, then, that Josephus chooses the "hot" *thrēskeia* as his favored term to describe Judaean life (but not, as aforementioned, ever in *Against Apion*).

I can further support the identification of *thrēskeia* with Torah in yet another passage in Josephus. The passage is long, and a look at its context will be necessary. The narrative is of righteous King Hezekiah:

> In the fourth year of the reign of Osēos, Hezekiah assumed the kingship in Jerusalem; he was the son of Achaz and Abia, a citizen of that country [*genos*]. His nature was kindly, and just [*dikaia*], and *eusebēs/theosebēs*.[20] Therefore, he supposed nothing to be more necessary or profitable upon his first coming to the kingship for himself and those he ruled than supporting *to thrēskeuein* God. Therefore, he called together the people and the priests and the Levites and addressed them, saying:
> "You are not ignorant that it was owing to the sins of my father, transgressing against the divine *hosia* and *timē*, that you have had experience of many great evils having been corrupted in mind by him to make obeisance to those who seemed to him to be gods. I exhort you [to forget . . .], now that you have learned by experience that being *asebēs*/behaving with *asebeia* is a terrible thing."

> ἔτει δὲ τετάρτῳ Ὠσήου τῆς βασιλείας ἐβασίλευσεν Ἐζεκίας ἐν Ἱεροσολύμοις Ἀχάζου υἱὸς καὶ Ἀβίας ἀστῆς τὸ γένος. φύσις δ᾽ ἦν αὐτῷ χρηστὴ καὶ δικαία καὶ εὐσεβής: οὐδὲν γὰρ ἄλλο πρῶτον εἰς τὴν βασιλείαν παρελθὼν οὐδ᾽ ἀναγκαιότερον οὐδὲ συμφορώτερον αὐτῷ τε καὶ τοῖς ἀρχομένοις ὑπέλαβε τοῦ θρησκεύειν τὸν θεόν, ἀλλὰ συγκαλέσας τὸν λαὸν καὶ τοὺς ἱερεῖς καὶ τοὺς Ληουίτας ἐδημηγόρησεν ἐν αὐτοῖς λέγων:
> ʼοὐκ ἀγνοεῖτε μέν, ὡς διὰ τὰς τοῦ πατρὸς ἁμαρτίας τοὐμοῦ παραβάντος τὴν πρὸς θεὸν ὁσίαν καὶ τιμὴν πολλῶν ἐπειράθητε καὶ μεγάλων κακῶν, διαφθαρέντες ὑπ᾽ αὐτοῦ τὴν διάνοιαν καὶ ἀναπεισθέντες οὓς αὐτὸς ἐδοκίμαζεν εἶναι θεοὺς τούτοις προσκυνεῖν:ʼ
> παραινῶ δὲ ὑμῖν ἔργῳ μεμαθηκότας, ὡς ἔστι δεινὸν τὸ ἀσεβεῖν [Ant. 9: 260–62].

This passage gives us a rich set of semantic data. First, *eusebeia/theosebeia* is coordinated as a character of a person with *dikaia* but also with *chrēstē*, generosity or kindness. Second, the result of those three characteristics—being generous, just, and reverent—is support for the *thrēskeia*, namely the Torah of God. Third, *asebeia* consists of worshipping other gods than the one in Jerusalem, and this is defined as transgressing against divine *hosia* and *timē*. The latter term is best glossed as "honor," whether to king or god. *Hosia* is a more complex semantic term, meaning (very roughly) "holiness."[21] The net result is that *thrēskeia* here, far from being the too much pole in the Three Bears arrangement of *thrēskeia*=too much, *asebeia*=not enough, *eusebeia*=just right, is now allied with the just right pole. Too much is now just enough.

This same righteous Hezekiah proceeds to engage in many restorations of the ancient cult, allegedly departed from by his immediate ancestors, including restoring the Pesaḥ sacrifice and observance, and then:

They likewise cleansed the city of every idolatrous pollution. The king arranged that the daily sacrifices be offered from his own [property] in accordance with the law. He fixed the tithes to be given to the priests and Levites by the crowd, as well as the first fruits, so that they [the priests and Levites] might always persevere in their *thrēskeia* and be single-minded in their *therapeia* of God. The crowd collected every sort of fruit for the priests and Levites. The king constructed storehouses and chambers for these and made a distribution to each of the priests and Levites, along with their children and wives. Thus they returned again to their ancient *thrēskeia*.

καὶ τὴν πόλιν δὲ παντὸς ἐκάθηραν μιάσματος εἰδώλων, τάς τε καθημερινὰς θυσίας ὁ βασιλεὺς ἐκ τῶν ἰδίων ἐπιτελεῖσθαι διέταξε κατὰ τὸν νόμον, καὶ τοῖς ἱερεῦσι καὶ Ληουίταις τὰς δεκάτας ὥρισε παρὰ τοῦ πλήθους δίδοσθαι καὶ τὰς ἀπαρχὰς τῶν καρπῶν, ἵν' ἀεὶ τῇ θρησκείᾳ παραμένωσι καὶ τῆς θεραπείας ὦσιν ἀχώριστοι τοῦ θεοῦ. καὶ τὸ μὲν πλῆθος συνεισέφερε παντοδαπὸν καρπὸν τοῖς ἱερεῦσι καὶ Λευίταις, ἀποθήκας δὲ καὶ ταμιεῖα τούτων ὁ βασιλεὺς κατασκευάσας ἑκάστῳ διένειμε τῶν ἱερέων καὶ Ληουιτῶν καὶ παισὶν αὐτῶν καὶ γυναιξί· καὶ οὕτω πάλιν εἰς τὴν ἀρχαίαν θρησκείαν ἐπανῆλθον [Ant. 9:273–27].

Given that the final sentence is the summary of a series of reforms, from the purification of the city, the giving of the tithes, the observance of the Passover, it seems best to understand the *thrēskeia* here as referring to the entire complex of practices enjoined by the Torah, or even to the Torah *simpliciter*.

For another text that helps illuminate the precise sense of *thrēskeia* in Josephus as the Torah of the deity, I adduce:

For seeing his kingdom augmented in this way, Roboam turned aside into unjust and impious practices and disdained the *thrēskeia* of God.

τὴν γὰρ βασιλείαν αὐξανομένην οὕτω βλέπων Ῥοβόαμος εἰς ἀδίκους καὶ ἀσεβεῖς ἐξετράπη πράξεις καὶ τῆς τοῦ θεοῦ θρησκείας κατεφρόνησεν. [Ant. 8:251].

The Torah of God would work perfectly in this context. Note that the opposite of the Torah of God are practices that are *adikoi*, as well as practices that are *asebeis*: Or better put, these are the same practices, piety and justice being so fully identified. As a result of this malfeasance, when threatened, this same king turned to God only to be informed by the deity that he would not support them, just as they τὴν θρησκείαν αὐτοῦ κατέλιπον "had abandoned his Torah [*thrēskeia*]" Ant. 8: 256: the Law, indeed, but so much more than law. It is not the case, then, for Josephus, that the Torah has been reduced to Law but rather that the terms *nomos* and (sometimes) *thrēskeia* are close equivalents of Hebrew *Torah*, Aramaic *'orayta*. Sometimes, however, Josephus uses *thrēskeia* in a more restricted sense: namely, in the sense of Hebrew *'avoda*, more properly the *latreia* (cultic activity) in the Temple.

THRĒSKEIA AS 'AVODA

Josephus also can use *thrēskeia* in this other sense, one in which a different Hebrew term would have been appropriate: namely, in the specific sense of cult, of ritual, as performed especially in the Temple. While this seemingly matches the usage of the epigraphic sources, the fact that Josephus also employs *thrēskeia* in the broader sense that I have been documenting suggests that even in this more limited acceptation, the Temple cult is seen as a kind of synecdoche for the whole Torah:

> [Jeroboam] reasoned that if he allowed the crowd to go to *proskunēsai* God in Jerusalem and celebrate the feast there, they might perhaps repent and, captivated by the sanctuary and the *thrēskeia* of the god within it, would abandon him and go over to their first king.

> λογισάμενος, ὡς ἐὰν ἐπιτρέψῃ τῷ πλήθει προσκυνῆσαι τὸν θεὸν εἰς Ἱεροσόλυμα πορευθέντι καὶ ἐκεῖ τὴν ἑορτὴν διαγαγεῖν, μετανοῆσαν ἴσως καὶ δελεασθὲν ὑπὸ τοῦ ναοῦ καὶ τῆς θρησκείας τῆς ἐν αὐτῷ τοῦ θεοῦ καταλείψει μὲν αὐτόν, προσχωρήσει δὲ τῷ πρώτῳ βασιλεῖ. [Ant. 8:225].

It seems fairly clear that *proskuneō* refers here to the proceedings in the Temple, especially around the Festival, so the magnificent sacrifices and other rituals that are carried out there. It seems also fairly clear that *thrēskeia* here functions as a virtual synonym for Temple service. Josephus could have used *therapeia*, but I hypothesize that *thrēskeia* is chosen here by him precisely to convey that sense of excitement, of enthusiasm that would "captivate" the participants. Rehoboam is, therefore, concerned that if he lets the folks go to Jerusalem, they will be charmed by the Temple and by the service that goes on there; and because that Temple and that service are within, of course, the Southern kingdom of Jeroboam (his great rival), they will go over to him, their former king, and reject Rehoboam. If there were ever an example to prove the mistake made in applying the modern categories of politics and religion to antiquity, this is it. To lose the folks to another cult and cult center is to lose their loyalty for the king entirely.

Then, having argued that there is no reason for the cult to be localized and restricted to Jerusalem, Rehoboam's efforts at directing the people to offer sacrifice at his sanctuary meet with success, and, then, in Josephus' judgment,

> In saying these things, he misled the people and turning away from their ancestral *thrēskeia*, he made them transgress the laws.

> ταῦτ' εἰπὼν ἐξηπάτησε τὸν λαὸν καὶ τῆς πατρίου θρησκείας ἀποστάντας ἐποίησε παραβῆναι τοὺς νόμους [Ant. 8:229].

"Torah" here gives excellent sense for *thrēskeia*. Josephus could be said, then, to be playing on two meanings (not contradictory ones as in the next chapter but one more specific and one more general); it is the turning away from the ritual that leads the people away from the Torah—confirming Josephus' notion in *Against Apion* that the observance of the physical commandments is an integral part of the inculcation of values. What is most important to note, however, is that in this passage *thrēskeia* clearly implies the keeping of the laws. The maintenance of the ancestral practice or service is called *thrēskeia*. We are very far, indeed, from a modern culture where "Law, so the story goes, withdraws from the worlds of religion and politics."[22] With none of these "worlds" differentiated at all, all of them "mean" something substantially, crucially different about the culture in study here.

A passage from Antiquities makes much clearer precisely of what abandoning the *thrēskeia* of God consists:

But you disregarded these things and forsook my *thrēskeia*, and having constructed gods of cast metal, it is them that you [now] honor.

σὺ δὲ τούτων ἠμνημόνησας καὶ τὴν ἐμὴν θρησκείαν καταλιπὼν χωνευτοὺς θεοὺς κατασκευάσας ἐκείνους τιμᾷς [Ant. 8:270].

Whatever its precise referent, the opposite of the *thrēskeia* of God is the honoring of "idols." In Hebrew, it is, of course, the Torah that one forsakes, even "My Torah." Why did you lose the land?, asks Jeremiah [9:13], and God answers, על עזבם את תורתי אשר נתתי לפניהם *'al 'ozvam et torati 'asher natati lipnēhem* "because they forsake my Torah which I gave before them." The Septuagint translates: καὶ εἶπεν κύριος πρός με διὰ τὸ ἐγκαταλιπεῖν αὐτοὺς τὸν νόμον μου ὃν ἔδωκα πρὸ προσώπου αὐτῶν καὶ οὐκ ἤκουσαν τῆς φωνῆς μου, using, of course, *nomos*. It becomes clearer and clearer that *thrēskeia* in Josephus is the Greek equivalent of biblical Torah meaning the worship-doctrine-practice of God but also all that is encompassed under the rubric Torah as well, justice, kindliness, good government. The question of why Josephus prefers here *thrēskeia* to *nomos* becomes only sharper and sharper.

THRĒSKEIA AS *EUSEBEIA*: JOSEPHUS AGAINST 4 MACCABEES AND PHILO

In Josephus' texts, which read almost as a double apology, of the Judaeans to the Romans, on the one hand, and of the Romans to the Judaeans on the other,[23] we thus find the word itself moving in a subtly different semantic direction from the ways seen in much contemporaneous literary usage in the preceding two chapters. Corresponding, in part, to Louis Robert's Thracian-Asiatic epigraphic attestations of *thrēskeia* seen there, the term seems not, in Josephus, generally to refer to the foreign, excessive, extreme, "superstitious." It is, moreover, very frequently the case in Josephus that the term *thrēskeia* is used to refer to "our": that is, the Judaean cult, the Torah, as in some of the Josephan stories already adduced here. Furthermore, *thrēskeia* is used to refer to the quality, the ethical, affective, or emotional quality of the people engaged in cultic behavior. How does such transformation take place? An example from Josephus' usage shows how it is not so much that the word *thrēskeia* has changed or developed in meaning in Josephus but that a kind of transvaluation of values imbues it with different affect in different historical situations or in the eyes of different cultural actors/speakers.

In Book 6 of the Antiquities:

The entire people during that time while the ark was in the city of the Kariathiarimites, turned to God with prayer and sacrifice and exhibited much *thrēskeia* and *philotimia* towards him.

Τοῦ δὲ λαοῦ παντὸς ἐκείνῳ τῷ χρόνῳ, καθ' ὃν εἶχεν ἡ τῶν Καριαθιαρειμιτῶν πόλις τὴν κιβωτόν, ἐπ' εὐχὰς καὶ θυσίας τραπέντος τοῦ θεοῦ καὶ πολλὴν ἐμφανίζοντος τὴν περὶ αὐτὸν θρησκείαν καὶ φιλοτιμίαν [Ant. 6: 19].

The interesting interpretive problem here is that the term *philotimia* literally means "love of honor" or "distinction." It can have quite negative connotations in Greek: "vainglory," "overweening ambition," and the like: πάντων δ' αὐτῶν αἴτιον ἀρχὴ ἡ διὰ πλεονεξίαν καὶ φιλοτιμίαν, "The cause of all of these [evil] things was power [pursued] on account of greed and *philotimia*" [Thuc. 3:82]. It can, however, carry positive meanings as well, thus ἐπὶ δὲ τοῖς καλοῖς φιλοτιμίαν: in Plato's Symposium, 178d, to be translated something like "ambitiousness for the noble things." It is this latter, but rarer, acceptation that is being mobilized by Josephus. Assuming that it is semantically close to its congener in the list here, *thrēskeia*, we see not so much a semantic shift in the denotation of the word—of both of these words!—as a cultural shift in its connotation; "naked ambition" for this Judaean writer when it is for god is only a good thing. That same "ambition," which might have been negatively evaluated under a Roman value system, receives an entirely positive valence in the Judaean cultural context. *Thrēskeia*, so frequently in Hellenistic literature appearing as the superfluous, the hyper fear of the gods and superstitious practice, now appears in Josephus as the highly valued utmost militance of devotion to God. From fanaticism, I might say, to zeal.

Referring to the gap in education and culture between Josephus and a Greek-educated non-Jew (to which I would add, a Greek-educated Jew as well), Rajak has written compellingly, "The fact that he still found it necessary, towards the end of his life, to define his relationship to the language of his adoption, is in itself revealing of the gap. And he came, as he said, from a people which, in the end, could fully endorse only the contemplation of its own law. Most of those with whom he had associated in Judaea would probably not have approved of his travelling as far as he did along a dangerous path. And he himself, unlike the Jew from Asia Minor whom Aristotle was said to have met, would never wish to become truly 'Greek in his soul.'"[24] Philo's situation, as an Alexandrian Jew whose education and native culture were thoroughly Greek, is quite a different kettle of fish from Josephus'; perhaps he would not have wanted his "soul" to be Greek, but his intellect certainly was. It was this cultural gap, I propose, that led at least in large part to their different value judgments with respect to *thrēskeia*.

The most dramatic way to demonstrate the difference in the semantics of *thrēskeia* as used by Josephus and that of Philo is to observe the relation between *thrēskeia* and *eusebeia* (proper reverence), which I began to explore in the last part of the previous chapter. As I show there, in Philo and in 4 Maccabees, these two terms were contrasted. In Philo also the way of *eusebeia* is explicitly defined as *not thrēskeia*. Philo defines *eusebeia* rather as *hosiotēs*, defining the latter as "the soul's bringing of truth [to the altar]." *Thrēskeia* and *eusebeia* are, for Philo and the author of 4 Maccabees, opposites or near opposites. For Josephus, the precise contrary is the case. The two terms probably are not synonyms but belong, for sure, on the same side of any value equation.[25] Observing Josephus' usages of *thrēskeia*, for instance, on the background of Philo's much rarer use of the word, please observe very important different nuances as well:

> But even enjoying [these blessings] from God, you have neglected *thrēskeia* and *eusebeia*.

> (90.) καὶ τούτων ἀπολαύσαντες ἐκ τοῦ θεοῦ προδεδώκατε τὴν θρησκείαν καὶ τὴν εὐσέβειαν [Ant. 6.90].

One cannot tell here the precise nuances of the two nouns—whether one refers more to practice and the other to emotion, or whatever subtle differences might obtain—but what is certain here is that the two terms are clearly coordinated and not in opposition. The sense of *thrēskeia* as the too much of *eusebeia*, as virtually *deisidaimonia* (hyper fear of the gods, superstition), is entirely absent. Thus, Josephus manifests the same transvaluation of values observed in 4 Maccabees in the previous chapter where willingness even to die for the Law is named *eusebeia* and not *thrēskeia*. While the author of the martyrology, however, retains the lexicographical opposition—our practice is not *thrēskeia* but *eusebeia*—the historian has gone one further and taken up the positive acceptations of the term (*perhaps* from the dialectal resources found in the epigraphic materials) and mobilized them. *Thrēskeia* itself, devotional fervor and high emotion, is now a good thing.

In yet another very telling passage, *thrēskeia* is used in prophetic style to refer to "true" service of the deity as opposed to the "mere" offering of sacrifices:

> From those who do not obey and do not *thrēskeuein* the true *thrēskeia* which alone is gratifying to God.

> παρὰ δὲ τῶν οὐχ ὑποτασσομένων οὐδ’ ἀληθῆ καὶ μόνην τῷ θεῷ κεχαρισμένην θρησκευόντων θρησκείαν [Ant. 6.148].

Here we see both the verb and the object of the verb together, so it must mean something on the order of those who perform the correct services, or observe the correct disciplines, that are alone pleasing to god. Note, once again, to what extent Josephus’ usage of *thrēskeia* seems (nearly) opposite to that of Philo. Where in Philo, *thrēskeia* could be used precisely for insincere (or improper) external practice not matched with the proper attitude of mind or even for the overdone and excessive, in Josephus, the proper *thrēskeia* is exactly what God wants. The proper service for God according to that Hellenistic-Platonistic-Stoic Egyptian Jew is called *eusebeia*, *hosiotēs*, and *therapeia*. For Josephus, however, it is the true service that is named as *thrēskeia*: that is, that service that includes not only sacrifice but appropriate behavior and ardor.

One more example underlines the same point about the coordination of *thrēskeia* and *eusebeia* in Josephus:

> These are proofs of your impiety and not your *thrēskeia*.

> ἃ δείγματα τῆς ἀσεβείας ἐστὶν ὑμῶν ἀλλ’ οὐχὶ τῆς θρησκείας; [Ant. 8:279].

Here, clearly *thrēskeia* is the opposite of *asebeia* and thus a virtual synonym of *eusebeia*, while in Philo, *thrēskeia* is in contrast with *eusebeia*, not *asebeia*! Something else is learned from this passage: namely, that in Josephus, *thrēskeia* is not only a name for practice (approved or disapproved) but also for a quality of a human being or an emotion. A person or a collective can possess *thrēskeia*. It is, moreover, in Josephus a highly laudable character. For Josephus, such exceeding zeal is, in this Josephan modality, not excessive, while the very same text being read by Romans through their value system could very well be taken negatively. A nice analogy for this is afforded by the different value given to *obstinatio* by Roman writers or by a Christian like Tertullian; if for ancient Romans, *obstinatio* is always a negative character, for Tertullian it is one of the highest goods.[26]

On the Good of Enthousiasmos: *Josephus against the Balancing System*

My first answer, then, to the question of why Josephus uses *thrēskeia* as a virtual equivalent of *nomos*, Torah is that he desires to express a positive orientation to forms of enthusiasm generally disdained by Greco-Roman cultures. One of the reasons, indeed, that *thrēskeia* has so often carried negative associations in those texts is that it has functioned semantically in a cultural context in which excess was highly disapproved of, cultures of the balancing system including even such Greek-Judaeans as Philo and especially the Stoic author of 4 Maccabees. Josephus is much less enamored of the balancing system. As a Palestinian Judaean, however much "acculturated," his is a more biblical sensibility of admiration for the extremes, as I shall document further shortly. If for our Greek writers cited in the previous chapter, *enthousiasmos* is associated with *thrēskeia* and disparaged, for Josephus *enthousiasmos* is a positively marked quality and thus also *thrēskeia*.

For a very rich example of this positive evaluation of over-the-top enthusiasm, see:

> But each individual, having the internal witness of the conscience, has come to believe—as the legislator prophesied and as God provided firm assurance[27]—that to those who keep the laws and, should it be necessary to die for them, meet death eagerly, God has granted renewed existence and receipt of a better life by turn. I would hesitate to write this now, were it not evident to all from the facts that, to date, many of our people on many occasions have nobly undertaken to suffer anything rather than utter even a single word in contravention of the law.

> ἀλλ' αὐτὸς ἕκαστος αὑτῷ τὸ συνειδὸς ἔχων μαρτυροῦν πεπίστευκεν, τοῦ μὲν νομοθέτου προφητεύσαντος, τοῦ δὲ θεοῦ τὴν πίστιν ἰσχυρὰν παρεσχηκότος, ὅτι τοῖς τοὺς νόμους διαφυλάξασι κἂν εἰ δέοι θνήσκειν ὑπὲρ αὐτῶν προθύμως ἀποθανεῖν ἔδωκεν ὁ θεὸς γενέσθαι τε πάλιν καὶ βίον ἀμείνω λαβεῖν ἐκ περιτροπῆς. ὤκνουν δ' ἂν ἐγὼ ταῦτα γράφειν, εἰ μὴ διὰ τῶν ἔργων ἅπασιν ἦν φανερόν, ὅτι πολλοὶ καὶ πολλάκις ἤδη τῶν ἡμετέρων περὶ τοῦ μηδὲ ῥῆμα φθέγξασθαι παρὰ τὸν νόμον πάντα παθεῖν γενναίως προείλοντο [*Against Apion*, 218–19].

Barclay remarks on this passage, "This additional comment seems gratuitous: the reward is presumably for all who keep the laws, not only for those who die for them. But the addition serves a number of functions. First, it highlights the Judaean 'contempt of death' (2.146) and simultaneously helps refute Apollonius' double charge of cowardice and recklessness (2.148): Judaeans are prepared to die, but for a noble cause (for the laws), not in sheer stupidity. Secondly, it repeats a theme already announced in 1.42–43, 191–92 (the language here very closely matches that of 1.42) and sets up the full-scale discussion of this topic in 2.219–35; again Josephus uses a phrase at the end of one paragraph to announce the theme of the next."[28] Josephus is surely more of a Palestinian Judaean than a stoic.

Let me close this section with one evocative Josephan text that illuminates the transvaluation of *thrēskeia* in his writing and that best educes the difference in his thinking from the "balancing system" still manifest in Philo and Plutarch. Perhaps the most dramatically affirmative use of *thrēskeia* in Josephus can be found in his account of the so-called sacrifice of Isaac. In the first book of the Antiquities, we read of Isaac:

His father Habramos exceedingly loved Isakos, who was his only child and who had been born to him on the threshold of old age, as a gift from God. And the child, practicing every virtue and showing attention to his ancestors and eager [*espoudakōs*] for the *thrēskeia* of God, won even more the affection and the love of his parents. And Habramos put his own happiness solely on the hope that on departing from life he should leave behind his son unscathed. He attained this, to be sure, by the will of God, who, wishing to make trial of his *thrēskeia* toward himself, appeared to him and after enumerating all the things that he had granted, how he had made him stronger than his enemies and how he had his present happiness and his son Isakos owing to his benevolence, asked him himself to offer this one as a sacrifice and victim to himself, and he bade him to lead him up Mount Morion, build an altar, and offer him as a burnt-offering. For thus he would demonstrate his *thrēskeia* toward him if he valued what was pleasing to God above the preservation of his child.

Ἴσακον δὲ ὁ πατὴρ Ἄβραμος ὑπερηγάπα μονογενῆ ὄντα καὶ ἐπὶ γήρως οὐδῷ κατὰ δωρεὰν αὐτῷ τοῦ θεοῦ γενόμενον. προεκαλεῖτο δὲ εἰς εὔνοιαν καὶ τὸ φιλεῖσθαι μᾶλλον ὑπὸ τῶν γονέων καὶ αὐτὸς ὁ παῖς ἐπιτηδεύων πᾶσαν ἀρετὴν καὶ τῆς τε τῶν πατέρων θεραπείας ἐχόμενος καὶ περὶ τὴν τοῦ θεοῦ θρησκείαν ἐσπουδακώς. Ἄβραμος δὲ τὴν ἰδίαν εὐδαιμονίαν ἐν μόνῳ τῷ τὸν υἱὸν ἀπαθῆ καταλιπὼν ἐξελθεῖν τοῦ ζῆν ἐτίθετο. τούτου μέντοι κατὰ τὴν τοῦ θεοῦ βούλησιν ἔτυχεν, ὃς διάπειραν αὐτοῦ βουλόμενος λαβεῖν τῆς περὶ αὐτὸν θρησκείας ἐμφανισθεὶς αὐτῷ καὶ πάντα ὅσα εἴη παρεσχημένος καταριθμησάμενος, ὡς πολεμίων τε κρείττονα ποιήσειε καὶ τὴν παροῦσαν εὐδαιμονίαν ἐκ τῆς αὐτοῦ σπουδῆς ἔχοι καὶ τὸν υἱὸν Ἴσακον, ᾔτει τοῦτον αὐτῷ θῦμα καὶ ἱερεῖον αὐτὸν παρασχεῖν ἐκέλευέ τε εἰς τὸ Μώριον ὄρος ἀναγαγόντα ὁλοκαυτῶσαι βωμὸν ἱδρυσάμενον· οὕτως γὰρ ἐμφανίσειν τὴν περὶ αὐτὸν θρησκείαν, εἰ καὶ τῆς τοῦ τέκνου σωτηρίας προτιμήσειε τὸ τῷ θεῷ κεχαρισμένον.[29]

The nuances of the different usages of *thrēskeia* within the passage help confirm its range of Josephan acceptation.[30] In the first instance, *thrēskeia* belongs to god. As shown in the preceding chapter, this concatenation refers to the cult. Thus, as also shown in the preceding chapter, the epigraphic *thrēskeia tou Apollōnos* (*SIG* 801 D [Delph., i C.E.]) refers to the rites due to Apollo or the service of Apollo, and this is precisely the syntactic string found here in Josephus' *peri tēn tou theou thrēskeian*. This last collocation, however, surely also refers to transgression of *Torat Hashem* (the Torah of God) at the same time that it does to its Greek intertexts. Isaac is zealous for the Torah of God. I must note the continuation in which Abraham's *thrēskeia* toward God *peri auton thrēskeia* is emphasized. The shift in the syntax here must be noted. In the first usage God, as it were, is the subject of the *thrēskeia*; while in the latter two usages, Abraham is the subject, and God the object. Abraham would demonstrate his *thrēskeia* toward God, were Abraham to show that he is willing to slaughter his child at God's demand. I think that one would not be straying far were one to understand it as both the rules and regulations that he demands that we keep and the human zeal for observing those rules in order to capture the nuances of the word within this single context. I would suggest that the antecedents for such shifts in Josephus' diction *vis-à-vis* the older *koinē* involve two factors: the (hypothesized) impact of the type of Greek manifested in the inscriptions in which *thrēskeia* is used in this fashion; and the Judaean/Josephan transvaluation of values in which a word redolent of ardor, enthusiasm, even excess in devotion, has been imbued with the positive values ascribed to such characters within Judaean culture in contrast with the older cultures of Greece and Rome (continued even in Philo) in which moderation in such matters was considered the ideal.[31] It is precisely that range of emotions, I hypothesize, that drew Josephus to *thrēskeia* as a lexical supplement to *nomos*.

THRĒSKEIA: EMOTION AND PRACTICE

Thrēskeia indeed frequently is used by Josephus to refer to a form of practice that is generated by or at any rate deeply connected with an emotional state, with both designated as *thrēskeia*.[32] Perhaps one of the clearest examples of all for the interpretation of *thrēskeia* as discipline, fidelity in the sense of obedience to the practices in this case of Sabbaths and Festivals, appears in Josephus' War at Book 2: 517:

> When the Judaeans realized that the war was already coming near to the mother-city, they quit the festival and went to their weapons; taking great confidence in their mass, in disarray with a yell they leapt forward into the fight, taking no cognizance of the seventh-day rest, though indeed the Sabbath was certainly their paramount *thrēskeuomenon*.

> Οἱ δὲ Ἰουδαῖοι κατιδόντες ἤδη πλησιάζοντα τῇ μητροπόλει τὸν πόλεμον, ἀφέμενοι τὴν ἑορτὴν ἐχώρουν ἐπὶ τὰ ὅπλα, καὶ μέγα τῷ πλήθει θαρροῦντες ἄτακτοι μετὰ κραυγῆς ἐξεπήδων ἐπὶ τὴν μάχην μηδὲ τῆς ἀργῆς ἑβδομάδος ἔννοιαν λαβόντες· ἦν γὰρ δὴ τὸ μάλιστα παρ' αὐτοῖς θρησκευόμενον σάββατον.[33]

The Sabbath was obviously their paramount practice, their paramount prohibition, but also their paramount observance (in the positive sense).[34] It needs to be noted that the Sabbath rest is the most frequent observance noted in the Hebrew Torah itself, as well as one of the three most prominent distinctions of Jews in the ancient world, the other two being their practice of circumcision and refusal to eat pork. The theme of war on Sabbath was, moreover, nearly ubiquitous in Judaean writings of the Second-Temple period. It could certainly be said, then, of the Sabbath that it is the paramount observance of the Judaeans.

Supporting this interpretation is another passage:

> For it fell out indeed that they did this slaughter on Sabbath, on which owing to the *thrēskeia*, they hold a truce[35] from *hosios* acts.

> καὶ γὰρ δὴ σαββάτῳ συνέβη πραχθῆναι τὸν φόνον, ἐν ᾧ διὰ τὴν θρησκείαν καὶ τῶν ὁσίων ἔργων ἔχουσιν ἐκεχειρίαν [War 2. 456].

The *thrēskeia* here is obviously the rule, the discipline, the prohibition. This usage, it needs to be said, hearkens back to the earliest occurrences of *thrēskeia* in Herodotus. *Hosios* can mean holy (and so Mason), but it can also mean mundane in the sense of unsacralized but normally permitted, every day, which yields here better sense, for it is from those that Jews refrain on Sabbath, not, of course, from holy acts.

Here is another example in which *thrēskeia* refers to the observance of the rites of sacralized days:

With the onset of the "Fiftieth" [Pentecost]—so the Judaeans call a certain festival
that occurs seven weeks past, taking its name from the number of days—it was not the
customary [*sunēthēs*] *thrēskeia* that brought the populace together, but their ire
[War Book 2:42].

[42] ἐνστάσης δὲ τῆς πεντηκοστῆς, οὕτω καλοῦσίν τινα ἑορτὴν Ἰουδαῖοι παρ' ἑπτὰ
γινομένην ἑβδομάδας καὶ τὸν ἀριθμὸν τῶν ἡμερῶν προσηγορίαν ἔχουσαν, οὐχ ἡ συνήθης
θρησκεία συνήγαγεν τὸν δῆμον, ἀλλ' ἡ ἀγανάκτησις.[36]

Even though the people come together on a festival, it was not really the observance of
their customary *thrēskeia*, rites for that festival or even observance of the festival that
brought them together but their ire. Although one might be inclined to think of this as
hypocrisy, it seems that that is not Josephus' intent at all, for this passage is illuminated by
comparison to War I. 88, in which it is related by Josephus that most seditious rebellions
and conspiracies took place at festival gatherings. He is not indicating the reason for their
coming together but rather the emotion that moved them on that occasion. It wasn't so
much their ardor but their ire. For the people, at least, there seems to have been little (or
no) distinction between so-called political and so-called religious motivations.

WHY *THRĒSKEIA*: WHAT *NOMOS* DOESN'T DO

Finally, it was in my view, the wide semantic range of *thrēskeia*, incorporating practice,
character, and emotion that made it available to Josephus to bear so much of the weight of
Torah in the Semitic-Judaean semantic system. There are many passages in Josephus' work
in which *thrēskeia* goes beyond *nomos* in that it encompasses a range of powerful emotive
force, ardor, and devotion. As I discuss in the preceding chapter, it is the "barbarians'"
thrēskeia toward their queen that prevented the soldier in Chareas and Callirhoe from
approaching her, thus their reverence or the like. As suggested there, as well, there is an
element of the fearful, the over-scrupulous encoded frequently in the word as it appears in
the literature. In Josephus, it seems, the heightened emotional component is retained, but
rather than seeing this emotion as negative, as fearfulness, it is reversed in value and carries
the sense of a highly ennobled reverence, ardor, and devotion.

For an example of *thrēskeia* as a state, a character, or an emotional quality of a human
being (leading, to be sure, to practice but not naming the practice itself), the following is
a clear and simple case. The following example sharply demonstrates the positive valence
of the term:

Since there dwelt there a certain Aminados of the Levite by genos who had a reputation
for righteousness [*dikaiosunē*] and *thrēskeia*, they brought the ark into his house.

ἔνθα τινὸς Λευῖτου τὸ γένος Ἀμιναδάβου δόξαν ἔχοντος ἐπὶ δικαιοσύνῃ καὶ θρησκείᾳ
καταβιοῦντος εἰς οἰκίαν τὴν κιβωτὸν ἤγαγον [Ant. 6: 18].

It is clear that *thrēskeia* refers to a human quality, not an institution or a practice (although
faithfulness to a practice is surely possible). Among the options are "devotion," "zeal," "ardor," "faithfulness." The important point to remember is that ultimately we will not choose

between the translation options just offered (fortunately, we are not bound to) but observe these different semantic components in action, as it were. Given the coordination between *dikaiosunē* (righteousness, justice) and *thrēskeia* as well as the narrative context, there can be no ambiguity as to the positive valence of the latter term at all in this case.

Not infrequently in Josephus, the term *thrēskeia* refers to an emotion, something in the semantic field of ardor, devotion (in the sense of abnegation of the self to the other), or militant commitment. For another clear example of *thrēskeia* as an emotional state of a human being (leading, as earlier, to practice but not naming the practice itself), the following is a clear and simple case:

> [praying, εὐχομένους] that their minds would be guarded pure of all evil in righteousness [*dikaiosunē*] and *thrēskeia* and in the keeping of the abiding the commandments God had given them through Moses.

> καὶ τὴν διάνοιαν αὐτοῖς καθαρὰν ἀπὸ πάσης φυλάττεσθαι κακίας ἐν δικαιοσύνῃ καὶ θρησκείᾳ καὶ τῷ τὰς ἐντολὰς τηρεῖν ἃς διὰ Μωυσέος αὐτοῖς ἔδωκεν ὁ θεὸς διαμενούσας· [Ant. 8:120].

Once again, *thrēskeia* here is coordinated with *dikaiosunē*. It is absolutely certain here that *thrēskeia* refers to a quality of mind, as it is the product of attentiveness, a guarding of the mind. Here is the additional collocation with keeping of the commandments in addition to righteousness/justice and *thrēskeia*. This gives a clue, perhaps, to the way that *thrēskeia* as habits of the heart is related semantically to *thrēskeia* as habits of the body given that we see explicitly the mental state of purity from evil, issuing in the characters of righteousness and *thrēskeia*, resulting in persistence in keeping the commandments of God. It is easy to see how *thrēskeia* could be used to refer to both the emotional state and the result of that emotional state in practice. Fidelity leading to militant commitment.

Based, at least, then, on the documentation before us, it would seem that Josephus began to use *thrēskeia* to represent a different culture's (his own) values, not the ancient balancing systems of both Greek and Roman cultures in which the moderate was the heroic point but rather a more biblical axiology in which the extremes of devotion and militance were highly treasured. Where both ancient Greek and Roman cultures tended to imagine a too-muchness of devotion and practice with respect to gods and to denote it with such words as *superstitio*, *deisidaimonia*, and frequently *thrēskeia*, Judaean culture, as represented by Josephus, seems to consider no amount of zeal excessive. Note that for Greek thinkers and writers, "nothing in excess" was a watchword; and in Latin, *mediocritas* is the ideal, not the flaw: It is, in fact, that entity that we habitually refer to, calquing the Latin, as the golden mean. It is, I think, not until Maimonides that such an ideal is articulated in Judaean circles. One can observe, as it were, the sources of that usage in the semantic map developed in the previous chapter. A word that carried overtones of the excessive (*periergos*, *perieimi*) related to cultic practice has had those overtones modulated from a minor into a major key. Another semantic element of the same word, *thrēskeia* that seems to have referred to a sort of fearful reverence (the reverence of those others for their queen, or the Spartan reverence for the Temple) has been translated by Josephus—to be sure, not at all necessarily by him alone—into superlative and militant commitment. The ever-present, at least slightly, negative sense, thus, of the extravagant commitment that the term carried with it in those usages has also been shifted tonally into the quality of being militantly, enthusiastically dedicated to obedience to the law of God. This serves, I reckon, to help Josephus negotiate his position, his very delicate position, in Flavian Rome as defender of the Jews and, at the same time, loyal Flavian client (see the discussion in the next chapter). Building up the Judaeans, on the one hand, makes them a more worthy enemy for Rome to have subdued but also renders Judaeanness a more honorable position, *in Roman eyes*, for Josephus to be occupying. It also ameliorates, one might imagine, his own sense of disloyalty (in both directions). The expansion of usage of *thrēskeia* thus reveals/conceals a world of personal politics. For Josephus, however, *thrēskeia* seems largely to replace both Septuagintal *latreia* and *therapeia* in the sense of service of God: The Septuagint itself knows not of the word *thrēskeia* although some of the later apocryphal Greek works incorporated do. I suggest that it might have been precisely the emotional aspect associated (for him positively as ardor, devotion) that stimulated this shift in his lexicon, or perhaps that led him to use *thrēskeia* in the sense that we find it otherwise in the early period only in the Thracian and Asian inscriptions.

ELEVEN

A Jewish Actor in the Audience: Josephan Doublespeak

Abandoning religion as an analytic category enables one also to see how consonant Josephus is in spirit and tone with other Roman writers of his time and place, negotiating their lives and dignity under conditions of Imperial tyranny. Like Tacitus and many others, Josephus was able to mobilize facility with language and rhetoric to produce a studied ambiguity within his writing. To see how *thrēskeia* functions within that discursive project, I first spend time on establishing the grounds of Josephan ambiguity per se. As Shadi Bartsch has demonstrated, it is in the very nature of such ambiguity to be unprovable,[1] but neither does it seem implausible to posit it, especially given the culture of speech in the Rome in which Josephus lived and wrote for the last 20 years of his life, much of it under the tyrant Domitian, as bad as Nero or Caligula.

The slant on Josephus being offered here provides a different approach to the age-old scholarly "attempt to find out to what extent Josephus can be considered a Jewish apologist or a Flavian propagandist,"[2] to which my answer is "both."[3] As Tessa Rajak has put it, Josephus was playing a "double-game."[4] For Josephus, one must abandon any notion, I think, of a false outer versus a true inner self and place both sides of the "painful conflict" within himself as two contradictory internal voices, to use a contemporary metaphor. Josephus is convinced that his counsel and choice to abandon the conflict was right and just for himself and for Israel, but somewhere within him another voice cries out in admiration of those who gave all for the integrity of Judaean life and independence even when it was a lost cause. As I shall show presently, that other voice cries out within the text as well. It is necessary, once again, to emphasize that such double voicing or double game does not mark Josephus as utterly different from other Roman intellectuals and writers. Seneca and Tacitus, at least, are as marked by ambivalence and doubt as is Josephus: His is rather a particular variant of Roman self-adjustment and self-fashioning in the early Empire. There was no time in which the Romans were writing in which these elaborate strategic adjustments were not being made by themselves and their subjects. The slaves of Plautus' and Terence's plays flattered, manipulated, deceived, cajoled, or submitted to their masters. Livy's peasant soldiers, incorporated into the ranks of the Roman army, continually debated whether their interests were better off served by being separated/segregated off from or integrated into the *res publica*. Seneca and Tacitus endlessly considered the best tactics in coping with the dangerous powers so near to them. Every person and group has to ask themselves: To what extent do we want and need to collaborate or to resist the Powers That Be? To what extent can we actually cooperate with those who are perceived to have important powers? To what extent, and at what cost, can we resist? If we wanted to, could we actually withdraw or flee from, hide from those powers? If so how and to where? Josephus was involved in a project of constant self-adjustment.

In some ways parallel to Tertullian and in other ways quite different, Josephus' works throughout, I would suggest, are marked by ambivalence: an ambivalence that is much harder to see when one works with the analytical concept of "religion," even one that is avowedly "the product of the scholar's study." To start with, I would claim that precisely the world-simplifying strategy of such rationalized analytic categories makes it more difficult to perceive the multiple levels and layers of contradiction that pervade all of culture.[5]

Josephus' Divided Mind

In his classic book, *Seven Types of Ambiguity*, William Empson carefully and with great nuance analyzed and articulated seven ways in which ambiguous meanings in poetry (and artistic prose) relate to each other semantically. The seventh type of ambiguity classified by him "occurs when the two meanings of the word, the two values of the ambiguity are the two opposite meanings defined by the context so that the total effect is to show a fundamental division in the writer's mind."[6] This section attempts to lay bare (or perhaps, more modestly put, to contribute something to the laying bare of) the uses that the seventh type of ambiguity may have played in the composition of Josephus' *Jewish War*, or perhaps, once again, more modestly put, the uses that the concept may play in interpretative assays on that great work of narrative prose.[7]

I just cited Empson's seminal insight that the seventh type of ambiguity occurs when the two meanings of the word, the two values of the ambiguity, are the two opposite meanings defined by the context so that the total effect is to show a fundamental division in the writer's mind.[8] This situation is perhaps best described with the classic psychoanalytic concept of ambivalence. As Laplanche and Pontalis have defined it:

> The novelty of the notion of ambivalence as compared to earlier evocations of the
> complexity of emotion and the fluctuations of attitudes consists on the one hand in the

maintenance of an opposition of the yes/no type wherein affirmation and negation are simultaneous and inseparable, and, on the other hand, in acknowledgment that this basic opposition is to be found in different sectors of mental life.[9]

And so I am suggesting now to read the ambiguity in Josephus' texts as a sign of ambivalence. Indeed, such equivocation may be the perfect linguistic representation of ambivalence. One certainly cannot predict or know what Josephus' psychology was during the war or after it, but I can show that he retained a great deal of admiration for even the most extreme of rebels, even when he was in Rome, so it would be perverse to deny that he held such sentiments when he was in Palestine, leading the revolt, even if, then too, one can hardly know what else he felt. Whatever the emotional or other charge of the division, Josephus can very plausibly be said to provide evidence of a divided mind.

One can see the enormous tensions within Josephus' mental life by observing the contradictions between his sentiments in the work.[10] It bears emphasizing once again that of course, this is all written by Josephus after his great turn from rebel leader against Rome to Flavian court historian, as it were, so that one cannot simply render these differences as chronological within his biography but as the synchronic conflicts that remain within him in Flavian Rome—and even more to the point, they seem likely to have been conflicts within him even as he led the Galilean rebels. Indeed, as already mentioned, these very contradictions render him not atypical but entirely typical of Roman intellectuals of his time and place—with, of course, a difference. His divided mind can be exhibited by attending to the sharp apparent divisions in his affect toward the rebels of Palestine, sometimes portraying them as fanatical troublemakers, sometimes as heroes for God and country.

THE REBELS EXCORIATED

The dominant voice in the Josephus writing in Rome at any rate is condemnatory of the Zealots and of the rebellion, and blames them, in fact, for all the disasters that befell his country and countryfolk, including the destruction of the Jerusalem Temple itself. This is illustrated in the following text. Josephus himself has been sent by Titus to speak to the forces defending the city. He is attempting to persuade the rebels to surrender rather than see Jerusalem and the Temple destroyed:

> To be sure, it might be proper to have contempt for low masters, not those under whose hand was everything. For what [place] had escaped the Romans, except that either through heat or cold was unprofitable? For fortune had passed over to them from all sides, and God bringing around to each nation the rule, was now with the Italians. There is indeed an ordained law most powerful among animals and humans: Give way to those who are stronger and the command is for those who are at the acme with arms. That was why their ancestors, who were in soul and body and also in other resources better, gave way to the Romans, which had they not known God was with them [the Romans], they would not have dared.[11]

δεῖν μέντοι καὶ δεσπότας ἀδοξεῖν ταπεινοτέρους, οὐχ οἷς ὑποχείρια τὰ πάντα. τί γὰρ
Ῥωμαίους διαπεφευγέναι, πλὴν εἰ μή τι διὰ θάλπος ἢ κρύος ἄχρηστον; μεταβῆναι γὰρ πρὸς
αὐτοὺς πάντοθεν τὴν τύχην, καὶ κατὰ ἔθνος τὸν θεὸν ἐμπεριάγοντα τὴν ἀρχὴν νῦν ἐπὶ τῆς
Ἰταλίας εἶναι. νόμον γε μὴν ὡρίσθαι καὶ παρὰ θηρσὶν ἰσχυρότατον καὶ παρὰ ἀνθρώποις,
εἴκειν τοῖς δυνατωτέροις καὶ τὸ κρατεῖν παρ' οἷς ἀκμὴ τῶν ὅπλων εἶναι. διὰ τοῦτο καὶ τοὺς
προγόνους αὐτῶν καὶ ταῖς ψυχαῖς καὶ τοῖς σώμασιν ἔτι δὲ καὶ ταῖς ἄλλαις ἀφορμαῖς
ἀμείνους ὄντας εἶξαι Ῥωμαίοις, οὐκ ἂν εἰ μὴ τὸν θεὸν ᾔδεσαν σὺν αὐτοῖς τοῦθ' ὑπομείναντας
[War 5.365–68].

This is a passionate, both reasoned and theological (but also equivocal), call to abandon arms and the struggle against the Romans since clearly God had ordained them to rule over Israel at this time. Zealotry, martyrdom, abandoning oneself entirely to the cause of Judaean independence, risking life and limb, wife, children, and home (not to mention the Temple) seem nothing but foolish and even sacrilegious in this speech and passim in the *War*.

Just before this passage, indeed, Josephus brings out a theme that recurs several times within the *War*: namely, the responsibility of the Rebels for the destruction of the Temple:

> Josephus, accordingly circled the wall and, striving to keep out of the range of their missiles but within hearing, at different positions, appealed to them repeatedly to spare their country and their Temple, and not to show themselves more indifferent to their fate than were the aliens. The Romans, he urged, though they had no share in them, yet respected the holy places of their enemies, and until now had kept their hands off them; while those who had been brought up in them and—if they were kept safe from injury— would be the only ones to enjoy them, were actually determined to destroy them.

> Οὗτος περιιὼν τὸ τεῖχος καὶ πειρώμενος ἔξω τε βέλους εἶναι καὶ ἐν ἐπηκόῳ, πολλὰ κατηντιβόλει φείσασθαι μὲν αὑτῶν καὶ τοῦ δήμου, φείσασθαι δὲ τῆς πατρίδος καὶ τοῦ ἱεροῦ μηδὲ γενέσθαι πρὸς ταῦτα τῶν ἀλλοφύλων ἀπαθεστέρους.

> Ῥωμαίους μέν γε τοὺς μὴ μετέχοντας ἐντρέπεσθαι τὰ τῶν πολεμίων ἅγια καὶ μέχρι νῦν τὰς χεῖρας ἐπέχειν, τοὺς δ' ἐντραφέντας αὐτοῖς κἂν περισωθῇ μόνους ἕξοντας ὡρμῆσθαι πρὸς ἀπώλειαν αὑτῶν [V: 362–63].

Not only, then, do the rebels—and especially the Zealots—risk their own life and limb and their families and countrymen in continuing this war, but they also are the ones who will be responsible for the ultimate burning of the Temple itself. Josephus repeats this accusation against the leaders of the revolt even more forcefully a few paragraphs later:

> It was they [the Zealots] who overthrew the city and compelled the unwilling Romans to be credited with so melancholy a triumph, and almost drew the tardy flames to the Temple!

> τὴν μέν γε πόλιν ἀνέτρεψαν αὐτοί, Ῥωμαίους δ' ἄκοντας ἠνάγκασαν ἐπιγραφῆναι σκυθρωπῷ κατορθώματι καὶ μόνον οὐχ εἵλκυσαν ἐπὶ τὸν ναὸν βραδῦνον τὸ πῦρ. [V: 444].

It is, paradoxically, the very defenders of the liberty of the City and its inviolability who bring down, according to Josephus, the destruction and burning of the Temple.

If this were all we had of Josephus, it would be easy to understand him as simply and unequivocally blaming the rebels for all the evil that befell Judea and the Judaeans and especially as responsible for the destruction of their own holy of holies, the Temple of Jerusalem. The rebels who do not give in, in this Josephan mood, are unequivocally wicked and evil, as they are explicitly so described in this very passage.

THE REBELS ADMIRED

Josephus can, however, appear at other junctures as moved and highly admiring of such "extremism" in resistance. The contradiction in question is not the product of inattention on the historian's part, nor on the conflict of undigested sources, but of his doubled affect.[12] More than occasionally, we find Josephus admiring even the most extreme forms of resistance.[13] Sometimes Josephus even ascribes these emotions of admiration to certain of the Roman leaders themselves (itself a mode of Josephan self-adjustment and key to interpretation, as I shall show presently). Thus, as Pompey is building (on the Sabbath) the earthworks with which to conquer Jerusalem and the Temple, Pompey, nonetheless:

> marveled much at the patient endurance of the Judaeans and in particular how without ceasing, enveloped in the midst of the missiles, they carried out the *thrēskeia*. Just as if the city had been occupied by deep peace, the daily sacrifices, the expiations, and all of *therapeia* were precisely fulfilled for God. And not even when the Temple was captured and they were being massacred around the altar did they desert the daily custom/laws [*nomima*] concerning the *thrēskeia*.

> τά τε ἄλλα τῆς καρτερίας τοὺς Ἰουδαίους ἀπεθαύμαζεν καὶ μάλιστα τοῦ μηδὲν παραλῦσαι τῆς θρησκείας ἐν μέσοις τοῖς βέλεσιν ἀνειλημένους· ὥσπερ γὰρ εἰρήνης βαθείας κατεχούσης τὴν πόλιν αἵ τε θυσίαι καθ' ἡμέραν καὶ οἱ ἐναγισμοὶ καὶ πᾶσα θεραπεία κατὰ τἀκριβὲς ἐξετελεῖτο τῷ θεῷ, καὶ οὐδὲ κατ' αὐτὴν τὴν ἅλωσιν περὶ τῷ βωμῷ φονευόμενοι τῶν καθ' ἡμέραν νομίμων εἰς τὴν θρησκείαν ἀπέστησαν [War 1.148].

In this passage, Josephus indicates nothing but admiration for these priests who without hope give up their lives to avoid negotiation with the enemy that would want them to cease and desist from the service of God in the temple. Pompey's affect is communicated by the unambiguous *apothaumazō*, "wondered, marveled at," even "was full of admiration for." *Thrēskeia* in both instances in this passage means the Temple service, and it is clearly a close correspondent of *therapeia*. This is Josephus seemingly unambivalently admiring the steadfastness, the extremism of the Judaean resistance and willingness to die for the Temple service. (I will reexamine this seeming unambivalence shortly.) Even the Roman, whom one would expect would consider this *superstitio*, overdone rigid fear of god, is moved here to admiration and wonder. On the basis of this passage, and the well-attested penchant of the Romans to admire bravery and steadfastness even in their enemies,[14] Josephus can hide his own deep sympathy for them behind such camouflage.

Josephus' stories of suicide rather than surrender of Jews to Romans exemplify this voice within Josephus as well. A fine example is Josephus' account of an old brigand in the Galilee, sacrificing his wife, children, and himself, rather than fall under the Herodian/Roman yoke. Even before the war against the Romans under Pompey, there were Jewish rebels against Herod, the usurping part-Jewish client king of the Romans. These rebels installed themselves with their families in seemingly impregnable hillside caves in the Galilee, but Herod outsmarted them:

> Yet did he at length make use of a contrivance that was subject to the utmost hazard; for he let down the hardiest of his men in chests, and set them at the mouths of the dens. Now these men slew the robbers and their families, and when they made resistance, they sent in fire upon them [and burnt them]; and as Herod was desirous of saving some of them, he had proclamation made, that they should come and deliver themselves up to him; but not one of them came willingly to him; and of those that were compelled to come, many preferred death to captivity. And here a certain old man, the father of seven children, whose children, together with their mother, desired him to give them leave to go out, upon the assurance and right hand that was offered them, slew them after the following manner: He ordered every one of them to go out, while he stood himself at the cave's mouth, and slew his sons one by one as each went out. Herod was near enough to see this sight, and his bowels of compassion were moved at it, and he stretched out his right hand to the old man, and besought him to spare his children; yet did not he relent at all upon what he said, but over and above reproached Herod on the lowness of his descent, and slew his wife as well as his children; and when he had thrown their dead bodies down the precipice, he at last threw himself down after them.

> τελευταῖον δ' ἐπινοίᾳ χρήσασθαι σφαλερωτάτη. τοὺς γοῦν ἀλκίμους καθιμῶν ἐν λάρναξιν ἐνίει τοῖς στομίοις, οἱ δὲ ἀπέσφαττόν τε αὐτοὺς σὺν γενεαῖς καὶ πῦρ ἐνίεσαν τοῖς ἀμυνομένοις. βουληθεὶς δὲ ἐξ αὐτῶν καὶ περισῶσαί τινας Ἡρώδης ἐκήρυξεν ἀναχωρεῖν πρὸς αὐτόν. τῶν δὲ ἐθελουσίως μὲν οὐδεὶς προσέθετο, καὶ τῶν βιαζομένων δὲ πολλοὶ τῆς αἰχμαλωσίας προείλοντο θάνατον.
> ἔνθα καὶ τῶν γηραιῶν τις ἑπτὰ παίδων πατὴρ μετὰ τῆς μητρὸς δεομένους τοὺς παῖδας ἐπιτρέψαι σφίσιν ἐξελθεῖν ἐπὶ δεξιᾷ κτείνει τρόπῳ τοιῷδε· καθ' ἕνα προϊέναι κελεύσας αὐτὸς ἵστατο ἐπὶ τὸ στόμιον καὶ τὸν ἀεὶ προϊόντα τῶν υἱῶν ἀπέσφαττεν. ἐξ ἀπόπτου δὲ Ἡρώδης ἐπιβλέπων τῷ τε πάθει συνείχετο καὶ τῷ πρεσβύτῃ δεξιὰν ὤρεγεν φείσασθαι τῶν τέκνων παρακαλῶν. ὁ δὲ πρὸς οὐδὲν ἐνδοὺς τῶν λεγομένων ἀλλὰ καὶ προσονειδίσας τὸν Ἡρώδην εἰς ταπεινότητα ἐπὶ τοῖς παισὶν ἀναιρεῖ καὶ τὴν γυναῖκα καὶ καταβαλὼν κατὰ τοῦ κρημνοῦ τοὺς νεκροὺς τελευταῖον ἑαυτὸν ἔρριψεν [War 1:311–13].

While our own values might clearly lead us to sympathy with the wife and children importuning their father to let them live, it seems clear enough that Josephus, torn as he might be, bears enormous admiration for those who prefer death for themselves and their families rather than submission to the thinly disguised Roman here. Lest this be taken as a simple tale of an obstreperous old thief simply not wanting to give in to any master, Josephus sends us the clue of his objection to Herod as unworthy king owing to his illegitimacy as ruler of the Judaeans. As Rajak says, this militance on Josephus' part makes his eventual change of heart all the more surprising and shocking (to us!), but in antiquity, what he had to answer for and explain away was more his former separatist militance than his latter-day capitulation to the inevitable.

JOSEPHUS AND THE *SICARII*

Josephus' affect with regard to the *sicarii* (knifers/Zealots) is, if anything, more ambivalent. In every sense possible, they are his sworn enemies, the very ones who caused the total destruction of Jerusalem, the Temple, and any semblance of organized Judaean life by not realizing the cost of their intransigence in the face of the implacable enemy to whom God had transferred his favor. Indeed, in the most famous moment of Zealot rhetoric, the speech of the leader El'azar proposing the famous murder/suicide pact, Josephus has him, as it were, conceding the point to Josephus:

> Maybe, indeed, we ought from the very first—when, having chosen to assert our liberty, we invariably experienced such hard treatment from one another, and still harder from our foes—to have sought after God's intention and to have recognized that the Judaean tribe, once beloved of him had been condemned.

> ἔδει μὲν γὰρ εὐθὺς ἴσως ἐξ ἀρχῆς, ὅτε τῆς ἐλευθερίας ἡμῖν ἀντιποιεῖσθαι θελήσασι πάντα καὶ παρ' ἀλλήλων ἀπέβαινε χαλεπὰ καὶ παρὰ τῶν πολεμίων χείρω, τῆς τοῦ θεοῦ γνώμης στοχάζεσθαι καὶ γινώσκειν, ὅτι τὸ πάλαι φίλον αὐτῷ φῦλον Ἰουδαίων κατέγνωστο·[War 7:327].

It is hard to imagine the intransigent Zealot uttering such sentiments of regret, but especially since they echo Josephus' own line so exactly, they must be laid at the historian's doorstep.

At one moment—indeed nearly everywhere—Josephus will refer to the madness of the *sicarii* attacking around Cyrene like a disease, Ἥψατο δὲ καὶ τῶν περὶ Κυρήνην πόλεων ἡ τῶν σικαρίων ἀπόνοια καθάπερ νόσος [War 7:437], and, at the next manage to express deep admiration, even wonder at their courage. It is truly remarkable to find him finding it in his heart to evince deep sympathy (and even esteem) for the very last of those same *sicarii* holed up in Alexandria after the final destruction. The council of elders of the Judaeans, realizing the danger to them, exposing—once again—the "madness [ἀπόνοια][15] of the *sicarii*," advises the Alexandrian Judaeans to deliver them up to the Romans and thus make peace with them, an eminently Josephan piece of wisdom. Then:

> Realizing the greatness of the danger, they obeyed the advice, and rushed with great haste upon the *sicarii* to seize them. Six hundred were caught immediately; and all that escaped into Egypt and Thebes, quickly being apprehended were brought back. There was not a person who was not amazed at the patience and madness/desperation, or should we call it strength of purpose, displayed by these victims. For under torture and maiming of the body contrived for the sole purpose of making them acknowledge Caesar as absolute ruler, not one submitted nor was brought even to the edge of speaking, but all, overcoming force, kept their purpose, as if anesthetized in their bodies, verily rejoicing in their souls at their tortures and the fire. But most of all, the spectators were astounded at the children in age, not one of which would be forced to call Caesar master. So far did the strength of their courage reign over the weakness of their bodies.

> συνιδόντες τοῦ κινδύνου τὸ μέγεθος ἐπείσθησαν τοῖς λεγομένοις, καὶ μετὰ πολλῆς ὁρμῆς ἐπὶ τοὺς σικαρίους ᾄξαντες συνήρπαζον αὐτούς. τῶν δ' ἑξακόσιοι μὲν εὐθὺς ἑάλωσαν, ὅσοι δ' εἰς

τὴν Αἴγυπτον καὶ τὰς ἐκεῖ Θήβας διέφυγον, οὐκ εἰς μακρὰν συλληφθέντες ἐπανήχθησαν. ἐφ'
ὧν οὐκ ἔστιν ὃς οὐ τὴν καρτερίαν καὶ τὴν εἴτε ἀπόνοιαν εἴτε τῆς γνώμης ἰσχὺν χρὴ λέγειν οὐ
κατεπλάγη· πάσης γὰρ ἐπ' αὐτοὺς βασάνου καὶ λύμης τῶν σωμάτων ἐπινοηθείσης ἐφ' ἓν
τοῦτο μόνον, ὅπως αὐτῶν Καίσαρα δεσπότην ὁμολογήσωσιν, οὐδεὶς ἐνέδωκεν οὐδὲ
ἐμέλλησεν εἰπεῖν, ἀλλὰ πάντες ὑπερτέραν τῆς ἀνάγκης τὴν αὐτῶν γνώμην διεφύλαξαν,
ὥσπερ ἀναισθήτοις σώμασι χαιρούσῃ μόνον οὐχὶ τῇ ψυχῇ τὰς βασάνους καὶ τὸ πῦρ
δεχόμενοι. μάλιστα δ' ἡ τῶν παίδων ἡλικία τοὺς θεωμένους ἐξέπληξεν· οὐδὲ γὰρ ἐκείνων τις
ἐξενικήθη Καίσαρα δεσπότην ἐξονομάσαι. τοσοῦτον ἄρα τῆς τῶν σωμάτων ἀσθενείας ἡ τῆς
τόλμης ἰσχὺς ἐπεκράτει [War 7:415–19].

Josephus is almost beside himself with his own ambivalence here. At one moment, he is, as usual, sure that the purpose of the *sicarii* is always and only madness; but at the very next moment, he is not sure whether to call it madness or refer to it with much more admiring adjectives; and the end, especially the pathos of the children finds him full of respect for them. These moments of apparent esteem for the most zealous of the rebels are all inscribed, I would remind once more, at such time as Josephus is already in Rome, already the client of Vespasian and Titus. They are all the more indicative, I would suggest, of the complexities of his mental state, *as manifest in the text*, however precisely one is inclined to interpret that state. The impassioned preceding speech of Josephus in favor of abandoning the war goes directly counter to the texts I have just shown. If here he admires the priests who serve at the altar as they are being killed, the rebel who sacrifices his children to the lost cause, the final Zealot holdouts that will not give up or give in, there he counsels surrender to the Romans since it is clear that they will win. Rome is God's tool to scourge Israel for her sins, but God does not desire, according to this second Josephan voice, dead martyred priests but rather living Judaeans who will recognize his rule through the Romans. Josephus, of course, made his own personal choice based on this latter counsel, having failed to persuade the other rebels of the justice of his argument. What is remarkable is to what extent he allows the position of the rebel, rejectionist, "extremist" to shine through as well.

Thinking with Empson's seventh type of ambiguity, one can sharply delineate a moment in Josephus' text in which such directly contradictory affects are communicated in one and the same linguistic forms. The story is one of a Passover in Jerusalem very early in the insurrection. Multitudes had come in from the countryside for the festal sacrifices but some, "had united in the temple, securing provisions for the civil strife" (ἐν τῷ ἱερῷ συνειστήκεσαν τροφὴν τῇ στάσει ποριζόμενοι [War 2.10]). The Roman ruler became anxious and sent in a cohort secretly to subdue the leaders of the rebels; the Judaean crowd became incensed and destroyed most of the cohort: "After that, as if nothing *deinos* had happened, they turned back to offering sacrifice. To Archelaus, the rabble [*to plēthos*] appeared no longer restrainable without carnage, and so he let loose his entire army on them." ἔπειθ' οἱ μὲν ὡς μηδενὸς δεινοῦ γεγονότος ἐτρέποντο πρὸς θυσίαν· οὐ μὴν Ἀρχελάῳ δίχα φόνου καθεκτὸν ἔτι τὸ πλῆθος ἐφαίνετο, τὴν δὲ στρατιὰν ἐπαφίησιν αὐτοῖς ὅλην. Noting that *deinos* is ambiguous in Greek (something like *terrible* in French), moving easily between "terrible, awful; awesome, wonderful," Mason remarks: "Does he mean to blame the rebels for returning to sacrifice after killing, or obliquely to recognize the casual heroism of the Judaean citizenry, who could so calmly return to worship after dispatching a professional military cohort?"[16] As I have earlier analyzed Josephus' "divided mind," I could claim a precise example of the seventh type of ambiguity of Empson's account.

Much to the point of the discussion in the context of this book, the repeated narratives of conspiracy and planning for the rebellion during the festivals bespeak no division whatever between "religion" and "politics." It would be hard to imagine those very radical forces fighting for the liberty of Judaean cult violating the sanctity of that very cult if they did not understand their organizing for the rebellion as part and parcel of the defense of the cult itself.

Such exploitation of the ambiguity built into *thrēskeia* is not confined to the Jewish historian. Thus Dio Cassius (160 C.E.–230 C.E.) in the third century uses *thrēskeia* to refer to the ardors of the "others": in this case, the Jews, in a way that also emphasizes the excessiveness [*perissotata*] of their practice:

> This was the course of events at that time in Palestine; for this is the name that has been given from of old to the whole country [*ethnos*] extending from Phoenicia to Egypt along the inner sea.[17] They have also another name that they have acquired: the country has been named Judaea and the people themselves Judaeans. I do not know how this title came to be given to them, but it applies also to all the rest of mankind, although living in other countries [*alloethneis*], who emulate their *nomina*. This class [*genos*] exists even among the Romans, and though often repressed has increased to a very great extent and has won its way to the right of freedom in its observances. They are distinguished from the rest of mankind in practically every detail of life, and especially by the fact that they do not honor the other gods, but extremely revere [*ischurōs sebousin*] one particular one. They never had any statue of him even in Jerusalem itself, but believing him to be ineffable and formless, they *thrēskeuousi* him in the most excessive [fashion] [*perissotata*] of any people [37.17.3–4].[18]

The meaning of the term *thrēskeuousi* here is something on the order of, "they devote themselves to him," "perform veneration to him." Note especially that the element of extravagance, too-muchness is here too in the neighborhood of *thrēskeia*. In point of fact, in the usage here, *perissotata* recalls that of Herodotus with reference to the Egyptians—*Theosebees de perissōs eontes malista pantōn anthrōpōn*—where it is hardly complimentary. The term most frequently in Greek has even more negative connotations of excessiveness, superfluity, and even uselessness. On the other hand, it can also be used in a more (if ambivalent) complimentary sense, *viz.*, in Euripides, Hippolytos, line 948: σὺ δὴ θεοῖσιν ὡς περισσὸς ὢν ἀνὴρ ξύνει "Are you the man who is joined with the gods beyond [*perissos*] others?" Considering the context, one would be inclined to see some sarcastic intent even here, but surely not in the following from Aristotle: Of one who seeks knowledge, he says, "If the poets are indeed right and god is by nature jealous, then it is likely that with respect to this one thing [knowledge] he would be most jealous and most unfortunate would be those who are *perittoi* [in knowledge]" (εἰ δὴ λέγουσί τι οἱ ποιηταὶ καὶ πέφυκε φθονεῖν τὸ θεῖον, ἐπὶ τούτου συμβῆναι μάλιστα εἰκὸς καὶ δυστυχεῖς εἶναι πάντας τοὺς περιττούς [Metaphysics 1982–83]). Nonetheless, and allowing for this ambiguity, one would imagine that the dominant tone for Dio is the "bad sense," as LSJ terms it.

In another remarkable passage in Dio, this sense of the excessiveness of the practices of the Jews is brought out even more explicitly but with a detectable measure of ambivalence as well, using indeed another one of Josephus' ambiguity-words as well:

Many and terrible/wonderful [*deinos*] things had the Jews done to the Romans, for the *genos* is relentless when aroused to anger, but they suffered much more themselves. The first of them to be captured were those who were defending the temple of their god, and then the rest on the day then called the day of Kronos.[19] And so surpassing/excessive [*periēn*] were they in their *thrēskeia* that the first set of prisoners, those who had been subdued along with the temple, begged permission from Sosius, when the day of Saturn came round again, and went up into the temple and there performed all the customary rites, together with the rest of the people [49.22.4].[20]

Although it seems to me that Stern somewhat stacks the deck here by translating *periēn* simply as "excessive," nonetheless it would seem that an air of ambivalence hovers over this text as well. I would suggest "surpassing/excessive," but I am *not* suggesting that I would choose between the senses were I able, but rather that both of these senses are present in Greek. The Roman is both contemptuous of this extravagant piety that leads the Judaeans to their doom and, at the same time, marvels at them. The ambivalences of *thrēskeia*, *deinos*, *periēn* all flutter in the air, allowing a kind of ambiguity of evaluation that is missed entirely when translated univocally.

It is vital to remember once more that as much as Josephus is telling a story of before he came to Rome, he is always writing in and from Rome. Tessa Rajak has sensitively adumbrated this important point: namely, that Josephus is always writing "after the fact."[21] This means, *inter alia*, that we have very little access through his texts to his mind at the time of the events of the War itself, when he was a leader of the rebel forces. At other points, Rajak seems to underplay her own insight, taking, for instance, Josephus' highly critical account of the reasons for the war as having represented his opinions and affects even at the beginning of the war itself and not, as seems at least possible, inflected by his latter-day negotiatory, or even apologetic, stance. Thus sometimes in her book, the responsibility for war is laid by Josephus at the door of bad procurators who have cruelly provoked the Jews, on the one hand, and wild, extreme Judaeans on the other (exonerating the Emperors and Josephus' class of Judaeans entirely), the implication being that Josephus himself had never really identified with the war.[22] This implication seems at best not necessary, and at worst counterintuitive. Rajak helps make this point herself. Referring to Josephus' usage of words like *lēstai* (brigands), she writes, "[I]t is quite probable that Josephus deployed those words and not others partly because they were the ones which happened to spring readily to mind and looked appropriate to a Greek history. They can hardly have had close Aramaic equivalents: in what terms he would have spoken of the rebels in Jerusalem during the revolt itself we cannot know."[23] We cannot, therefore, determine from Josephus' use of the words "bandits" or "brigands" to refer to the rebels that that is the way he would have seen them then. It is similarly difficult, if not impossible, to suss out precisely how Josephus felt about the war when he was a part of it, thinking in Judaean as it were. This does not constitute a claim, however, that one can be assured that he identified with the war at that time either, as many scholars have thought. I would prefer to imagine him as of divided mind throughout with more or less inclination to one or the other side depending on his circumstances. Rajak critically paraphrases one commonly held view: "Josephus is, then, a man who assisted his former enemy and was paid for it. His views could well have been determined by his situation in court circles in the imperial capital, where, after the failure of the revolt, he wrote his historical works. His uniqueness, it might be suggested, disqualifies him from being a witness to much beyond his own psychology."[24] There is no question but that Rajak is right to discredit this simplistic view; there is little reason to assume, *a priori*, that having been a general in the rebellion implies full identification with it any more than Thucydides' Nicias was identified with the Sicilian expedition, even then, but neither is such a possibility to be excluded *a priori*. Josephus, moreover, certainly is a vitally important witness to much more than his own psychology. There remains, nonetheless, very tantalizing evidence in his writing for a divided mind, which is itself, I reckon, also important historical testimony.

Thrēskeia, *Ambiguity, and* Dissimulatio

Josephus' "divided mind," however, provides only a partial explanation for his self-contradictions; there seems to be much more to it, his necessity for self-protective coloring in the conditions of Flavian Rome. Shadi Bartsch's striking discussion of Tacitus' *Dialogus de Oratoribus* may serve as a good backdrop for the more complex case—not, I hasten to clarify, more complex than Tacitus but than many other accounts of Josephus—that I hope to be making in this chapter. Tacitus ostensibly has written in this text an explanation for why the quality of oratory has gone down so much "in the present day:" that is, after the transition from the Republic to the Empire. In good Platonic or Ciceronian form, Tacitus responds to this query from a friend by (re)producing a dialogue on that very topic that he had heard in his youth, some 20 years earlier. A certain poet (and orator) Maternus has just recited a controversial and dangerous play that he wrote on the subject of Cato: dangerous because it implies praise of the Republic over the Empire. His friends Secundus and Aper have come with young Tacitus tagging along with them to convince him not to behave so recklessly. The conversation then consists of three debates.

I won't go into great length on this here, but the important point is that some sharp contradictions exist in the text. First, while Tacitus presents it as a text that explains why oratory is on the decline, the first dialogue is entirely on the subject of poetry, defending its dignity over that of oratory. Second, there is a direct contradiction between two of the dialogues. As Bartsch herself has well outlined it: "Maternus, however, who seems to be similarly at risk for *his* work about yet another Republican-hero-turned-ideological-figurehead—Cato—uses his closing speech in this dialogue to praise the political conditions of the present and the emperor himself even as he outlines in it his own reasons for the decline of contemporary oratory. And this second speech clashes not only with the implicit stance that must belong to any author of a *Cato* but also with the explicit content of Maternus' first speech in defense of poetry."[25] Bartsch goes on to outline various methods that have been used to reduce these contradictions, arguing however that, "These contradictions, long an obstacle to a complete understanding of the *Dialogus*, are not to be decried or eliminated through compromise. Rather, they function as signposts for readers of the *Dialogus*; pinpointing attention upon themselves, they establish their own clash as the locus of meaning."[26] Bartsch's reading successfully dismisses scholarly interpretations that ascribe the contradictions to the "riven soul of the poet, torn between a longing for the artistic and political freedom of the republic and an appreciation of the peace of the present" (Maternus), the riven soul of the historian (Tacitus), "the author's incorporation of two different historical periods into a single dialogue," or to the nature of the dialogue form itself.[27] Instead of all these reductive options, Bartsch produces a brilliant reading in which, going beyond critics who have argued that Maternus' speech in praise of Vespasian is ironic, shows that while some audiences might read the praise-speech as sincere, others will realize that the very presence of the ironic praise-speech—with the possibility of reading it unironically—is precisely the proof of the thesis of the text: namely, that honest speech, that jewel of the republic, is impossible now under the Emperors.[28] Remembering that Josephus was writing at exactly the same period as Tacitus, under the same emperors, and, *mutatis mutandis*, with similar dangers and perils facing him, especially when one remembers that the *Antiquities* was written under the monster, Domitian, I will keep Bartsch's distinctions in the background of my analysis of his own version of doublespeak (as I hypothesize it in his work).

Mason has taken us a big leap forward in articulating the situation of Josephus in Rome. Having observed the terrible tensions inflicting intellectuals in Flavian Rome, Mason in his paper on figured speech and irony in Josephus, elucidates the ironic situation of a client of the Flavians writing a history in which he "undermines, albeit in the nicest way, the Flavian presentation of this conflict [the Jewish War]."[29] Where the Flavians portrayed the Jewish War—quite naturally—as a great triumph for Rome and its generals, Josephus was insistent on reading it as God's punishment of the Jews for their sins and Rome as the mere instrument of his wrath. That is, even Josephus' own capitulation, as it were, to the Romans can (and will) be given two readings: Titus', in which Roman force put down a rebellious and strong subject state; and Josephus', in which Rome was a tool of God and the defeat of the Judaeans was pre-ordained as a punishment for them. Josephus' account of the war is a Judaean story told by a Jerusalem aristocrat from a Judaean vantage point on history, one informed by prophetic themes and interpretations; and at the same time, it is a story of accommodation to the Romans. Mason goes on in his long and closely reasoned essay to establish and interpret various modes of Josephan irony in all his works.

Irony, however, as Mason himself notes, is not enough to explain all Josephus' figured speech. As much as we have learned from Mason, to my taste, irony per se—especially not the detached romantic irony of which Mason speaks—is not quite the rubric for reading Josephus. As Bartsch has put it with respect to the Tacitus text, "a more informative concept than 'irony' for what Maternus is doing in offering a praise that asks not to be taken only at face value is that of 'doublespeak.'"[30] And she goes on to write of Tacitus and Juvenal: "[P]raise and criticism thus coexist in a volatile alliance, ready to emerge from the crucible of reception as pure panegyric or pure irony, depending on the nature of the audience.... And since the question is yielded up to the audience in this way, it seems clear that what is going on in *Satire* 7, as in Tacitus' *Dialogus*, is not merely irony, but doublespeak, meant to have different meanings for different audiences."[31]

The virtue of doublespeak, then, as Bartsch lays it out, "is precisely its capacity to engage both the public and the hidden transcripts *at the same time and with the same words*."[32] One must remember, too, that such doublespeak has not only been practiced but also theorized in Josephus' world. It seems most plausible to ascribe the use of the doublespeak posited here to Josephus' attempts at applying the sort of advice suggested by his near-contemporary, the rhetor Quintilian: "For we may speak against the tyrants in question as openly as we please without loss of effect, provided always that what we say is susceptible of a different interpretation, since it is only danger to ourselves, and not offense to them, that we have to avoid. And if the danger can be avoided by any ambiguity of expression, the speaker's cunning will meet with universal approbation" [Institutio Oratoria 9:67–68 in Loeb translation]. Quintilian is being very subtle here. It is expected that the tyrant will recognize what is going on, not that he will be fooled. (One is not trying to avoid offense but execution.) If the tyrant calls the rhetor on the offense, he exposes himself to ridicule, as if to say, "Of course, Quintilian, when you praised me ambiguously, you meant to damn me," confessing thereby that he deems himself unworthy of the praise.[33] This kind of ambiguity doesn't work by deceiving the tyrant but by trapping him in a dilemma. An excellent example of this is analyzed by Bartsch. Pliny the Younger, in a court case, cited a precedent that had been decided by a judge now exiled for treason. His opposing attorney, a former lackey for Nero and now for Domitian, endeavors to embarrass him by asking him what his opinion is of the traitor, to which he replies, "'You ask me what I think,' I said; 'but for my part, I don't consider it right to ask such a thing about someone on whom sentence has been passed.' He fell silent; as for me, I was heaped with praise and congratulations, since I had neither marred my reputation by some reply that would have been expedient but shameful, nor snared myself in the nooses of so insidious an interrogation" (*Epistulae* 1.5.7).[34] As Bartsch makes clear, Regulus, the opposing attorney, cannot respond to the falsity of the message without indicting himself. He cannot indicate that he thinks that Pliny really has doubts about the indictment of Modestus without somehow allowing the thought that it is he who has such doubts. Bartsch remarks on this that, "[H]is response operated on two levels at the same time. It conformed to the public 'truth' about the exiled Modestus ('a traitor') and yet it avoided by its ambiguity, the taint of an outright endorsement of that truth—*a responsum inhonestum*."[35]

Josephus, too, may have been speaking to more than one audience at the same time. I wish to suggest, with all the epistemological caution proposed by Bartsch in play, that one of the ways of interpreting Josephus' ambiguous language is as precisely such "doublespeak." For example, his use of *thrēskeia* could be taken as signaling to the Roman readership disapproval of Judaean behavior, while to a Judaean audience, it might have signaled precisely the opposite effect, thus conforming nicely to Bartsch's description: "[I]t pointed through its very evasiveness to the existence of another current of opinion on the exiled senator, one that the listening audience had no difficulty recognizing."[36]

This mode of explanation itself divides into two subheadings: According to one, Josephus is sending a double message: one to the Jews who read his works, and one to the Romans who might be reading. The second sub-explanation is a bit more complex. According to this second mode of explanation, this is a more internal process: That is, Josephus says something that he takes to be true intending it, however, to be misunderstood by the audience but maintaining his integrity (analogous perhaps to the Jesuits in England swearing that they were not Catholics *con reservatio*) regardless of whether there is another audience to detect what he is doing. This interpretation brings it closer, perhaps, to what Vasily Rudich has named "self-adjustment." Of the Julio-Claudian period, Rudich has written, "[T]he intellectual and psychological landscape of that period was fraught with mental anguish, confused and discordant attitudes, and inconsistent behavior encapsulated in each individual's quest for self-adjustment."[37] Deciding between these alternatives—that is, whether Josephus writes with two different audiences in mind (doublespeak) or whether his ambiguity is meant to mask an internally held opinion while maintaining some measure of integrity, self-adjustment—depends on decisions that the reader/interpreter makes on controversial questions as to Josephus and his audience, decisions that I will not attempt to make here in this context.

Whether doublespeak or self-adjustment, at any rate, one of the modes of introducing the "ambiguity of expression" recommended by Quintilian is via the use of words that are, themselves, ambiguous in denotation or connotation, evoking *avant la lettre*, as it were, Empson's seventh type. In his commentary on the *War*, Mason calls our attention to how Josephus can use words that "occupy" ambiguous semantic "space" to produce what Mason names a sort of "Romantic ironic" effect in his discourse, detaching himself, as it were, from "full sincerity" with regard to the text. Mason's main example is, as I show earlier herein, Josephus' occasional use of the adjective *deinos*=terrible, awful; awesome, wonderful to "maintain his narrator's distance." Accepting his account, I shall nonetheless attempt here to interpret it slightly differently, sensing, as I do, that romantic irony and detachment are not quite tonally right for Josephus. My hypothesis is that this ambiguity is occasioned by the exigencies of Josephus' life in Flavian Rome, more than by "narrator's distance"—in other words, that Josephus is recording two possible and opposite reactions to this event: one for his Roman hosts and one for a hypothetical "Judaean" audience. Alternatively, as I have just allowed, the "other" audience being not an audience of actual Judaeans but of Josephus himself: one message for the outside, one for the inside.

Here is a lovely example of how much double-meaning Josephus can convey with a word. Some Judaean bandits having plundered a Roman official, Cumanus sends soldiers to arrest the head men of the villages, as they had not prevented the banditry (as they were required to do). While this was happening:

> . . . Then one of the soldiers, having found the sacred Law [*ton hieron nomon*] in a certain village, ripped up the volume and tossed it into a fire. And the Judaeans, as if their entire countryside had been incinerated, were devastated: as if being drawn together by some engine [*organon*], namely *deisidaimonia*, by one proclamation,[38] they all ran together to Cumanus in Caesarea, begging that he not leave unpunished the one who had thus

committed outrage against God and their Law. He [Cumanus] deemed it best, since the mob was not resting unless it found satisfaction, to bring forward the soldier. He directed that he be led off to his death through the middle of those who were laying the charges. And the Judaeans withdrew.[39]

This is a rich and clear example of doublespeak, via the word *deisidaimonia*. Mason translates *deisidaimonia* as "reverence for the divine," but notes as well "or 'superstition'. Greek δεισιδαιμονία has various possible connotations." One need not decide between these two meanings here as the correct one but only note this deep ambiguity—akin to the one claimed by me for *thrēskeia*—thus capturing perfectly the ambiguity of the Josephan phrase. It is important to note that while *deisidaimonia* generally has distinctly negative connotations, matching fairly closely Latin *superstitio*, as shown in Chapter 8, "Imagine No *Thrēskeia*: The Task of the Untranslator," it is also fairly well attested in a positive sense, "fearing god." Its range of meanings thus overlaps that of *thrēskeia* fairly exactly.

For an example of *deisidaimonia* used in an entirely positive sense, we need look no further than Aristotle [Politics 1314b-1315a]:

And further [the king] must appear always to be pre-eminently zealous in matters having to do with the gods (for people are less afraid of suffering illegal things from [the ruler], if they think their ruler *deisidaimōn* and taking thought of the gods, and they plot against him less since he has the gods as his allies), though he must not display foolishness [*abelteria*] in these things [matters having to do with the gods].

ἔτι δὲ τὰ πρὸς τοὺς θεοὺς φαίνεσθαι ἀεὶ σπουδάζοντα διαφερόντως (ἧττόν τε γὰρ φοβοῦνται τὸ παθεῖν τι παράνομον ὑπὸ τῶν τοιούτων, ἐὰν δεισιδαίμονα νομίζωσιν εἶναι τὸν ἄρχοντα καὶ φροντίζειν τῶν θεῶν, καὶ ἐπιβουλεύουσιν ἧττον ὡς συμμάχους ἔχοντι καὶ τοὺς θεούς,) δεῖ δὲ ἄνευ ἀβελτερίας φαίνεσθαι τοιοῦτον.

One could not ask for a clearer case. Not only is *deisidaimōn* plainly marked as a desirable quality for the ruler here, but it is exactly opposed to *abelteria*, or foolishness. It is clear from this passage, at any rate, that to be *deisidaimōn* is not to be foolish [*abelteria*]; indeed, the ruler must be *deisidaimōn* without manifesting foolishness. It is thus clear that *deisidaimōn* here means very much what "god-fearing" means in English, thus strongly supporting the suggestion that Josephus exploits it for its double meaning, just as I have argued earlier for *deinos*. Surely one reader could take him as referring to the silly superstition of the Jews, while another might understand their impressive god-fearing qualities.

This example concerns, to be sure, the adjective, *deisidaimōn*, but one can also observe the noun in this sense, in for instance, Diodorus Siculus 11.89.8, describing a place in Sicily in which there were highly sacralized sulphurous springs and apparently boiling geysers:

And so great is the *deisidaimonia* of this shrine, that men who have disputes, when, for instance, they are being prevailed upon by a person of prominence, have their claims adjudicated through the examination of the oaths.

μεγάλης δ' οὔσης δεισιδαιμονίας, οἱ τὰς ἀμφισβητήσεις ἔχοντες, ὅταν ὑπό τινος ὑπεροχῆς κατισχύωνται, τῇ διὰ τῶν ὅρκων τούτων ἀνακρίσει κρίνονται.

Diodorus is claiming that the power of the deities of the shrine is such that people's oaths are taken as determining cases since no one would dare to swear falsely in such a place. It will be seen that *deisidaimonia* is quite close here to its etymological sense of fear of the spirits but also clearly has none of the negative connotations that the word so frequently carries of useless, paralyzing, harmful fearfulness, of superstitiousness. Diodorus goes on to indicate that this sacred precinct has also been designated from time immemorial as a sanctuary for slaves fleeing from cruel masters who may only regain their slaves by swearing an oath to treat the slave appropriately from now on. And then:

> And nobody, of <all> those who have given to their slaves this surety, is recorded as <ever> having transgressed (i.e., broken their pledge). To such a degree their *deisidaimonia* with respect to the gods makes those oath-swearers faithful towards <even> their slaves.[40]

> καὶ οὐδεὶς ἱστορεῖται τῶν δεδωκότων τοῖς οἰκέταις πίστιν ταύτην παραβάς· οὕτω γὰρ ἡ τῶν θεῶν δεισιδαιμονία τοὺς ὀμόσαντας πρὸς τοὺς δούλους πιστοὺς ποιεῖ.

The fear of the gods of that place is such that anyone who swears an oath by those gods keeps her oath. It is crucial to note here that this is not only control top-down, as it were, a way to keep the slaves and less powerful in check by their fear of the gods. In both of the Diodoran cases, it is the power of the powerful that is checked by this *deisidaimonia* against their weaker antagonists, whether plaintiffs or slaves. Clearly *deisidaimonia* here is a good thing, securing good results and, apparently, well justified. Diodorus certainly seems to imply at any rate that he respects the sacred power of the place.

Another very revealing instance may be found at Polybius 6.56.6–7:

> It seems to me that the greatest difference for the better of the Roman commonwealth is in their handling of the gods. And it seems to me that that which is reproached among other humans is that which keeps the Roman affairs together, namely the *deisidaimonia*.

> Μεγίστην δέ μοι δοκεῖ διαφορὰν ἔχειν τὸ Ῥωμαίων πολίτευμα πρὸς βέλτιον ἐν τῇ περὶ θεῶν διαλήψει. καί μοι δοκεῖ τὸ παρὰ τοῖς ἄλλοις ἀνθρώποις ὀνειδιζόμενον, τοῦτο συνέχειν τὰ Ῥωμαίων πράγματα, λέγω δὲ τὴν δεισιδαιμονίαν.

To be sure, Polybius remarks here that the *deisidaimonia* of which he speaks is reproached by other ethnic groups, but for the Romans, it is nonetheless clearly marked by him from the Roman perspective as entirely positive.[41]

I do need to note, however, that the negatively marked meaning "superstition" is by far the more common one for *deisidaimonia*. Mason's correct observation thus sets up a double or ambivalent reading here, drawn by reverence of the divine or by "superstition": It's all in the reading. Similarly, "as if their entire countryside had been incinerated" could be taken as a positive description of their great devotion and zeal, or, as Rajak would have it, "showing that his sympathy for his pious compatriots had its limits."[42] My point is not that Rajak is incorrect in her interpretation but rather that two (contradictory) interpretations are encoded in the same words. To my taste, the thrust of the rhetoric of this passage is to approve of the steadfastness and fidelity of these Judaeans, not to discountenance them. At the same time, I propose a measure of rhetorical ambiguity reflecting to be encoded in

Josephus' language here as well, allowing for Rajak's reading as well. This reinforces the sense of Josephus' capacity for ambiguous speech that conveys double and contradictory meanings, *à la* Quintilian. Josephus is more than capable of exploiting this ambiguity.

Building on the preceding semantic analysis, I would suggest *thrēskeia* as another word full of ambiguous possibilities for Josephus to exploit, for (as shown in the previous chapters of this book), most often in Greek literature before Josephus, it means something closely akin to the meaning of *deisidaimonia*—while in epigraphy (virtually only attested in Thrace and Bithynia), it means only "cult," as in the "cult of Apollo," for instance. I have hypothesized there that *thrēskeia* is a native, perhaps Thracian, word from the East to mean "cult"; but when used by western writers, it is taken to indicate the alleged wildness and "superstitio" of northeastern practices, much like how "magic" functions in Greek (or for that matter in English), with respect to Persian practice. This positive epigraphic use of *thrēskeia*, I suggest, provides an explanation for its availability in the sense of "our own cult" to Josephus as well. I don't mean to suggest, of course, that Josephus "got" the word in this sense from inscriptions, but presumably it was available in eastern forms of *koinē*. To be sure, in his accommodation to the Romans of explaining the Judaeans to a Roman audience and portraying them in a positive light, Josephus tends to use *thrēskeia* in the positively marked sense of "our" cult, our worship. Shades, however, of a darker, pejorative sense also haunt the text, making it available to him as well for the "seventh type of ambiguity"—or as, once again, Bartsch has named the practice of doublespeak: "a discourse that plays on the slippery slope of praise and blame."[43] Josephus can exploit, I suggest, this double meaning to perform his double agency.

There is another point to be made, moreover. As I show in the previous chapter, the aspect of *thrēskeia* most often negatively marked is excessive zeal, overwrought and useless commitment. For Josephus, however, it seems, such zeal, marked frequently by non-Jewish writers as excessive and deplorable, is commendable. Hence, he generally uses *thrēskeia* in ways that are neutral or positively marked. At the same time, it appears that other connotations were not dead for him, especially when he is giving the voice of the Other. Josephus, by mobilizing this ambiguity, can allude to the ways that the others observe the Jews as well. In this way, to paraphrase Dickens, he does the Empire in different voices. He writes, that is, as a Judaean referring to their "zeal," "fervency," "ardor" as well as service of the Judaeans, but he can allude, I hypothesize, to the more negatively marked usages of the word as well: perhaps, "perfervidity." It is not the semantics of the word that have shifted—or better put, are different—but the ideation that can be mobilized with respect to those semantics [cf. "queer"]. What might be excess to the Roman (with overtones of superiority) is for the Flavian-Judaean, superiority (with overtones of excess). But, I suggest, he mobilizes those very overtones to produce two voices, and it is his own ambivalence that one can hear as well. Both voices are his. He writes, after all, as a Roman as well, addressing an elite Flavian audience in Rome, who undoubtedly perceive Jewish practice as unnecessary, excessive, and dangerous.[44] The ambiguous reference to *thrēskeia* that I have shown as either highly admirable zeal or contemptible hyper-scrupulosity reflects more deeply running currents of ambivalence in Josephus with respect to the practices themselves. Imagine the complexities of Josephus in Flavian Rome presenting the deliberations and conflicts in Jerusalem before the war. Josephus' doublespeak is more than just a game of self-preservation, physical and mental/moral: It is, I suggest, also a reflex of his doubled identity.

Here is a particularly rich moment of such ambiguity from the *Jewish War*. Gaius Caesar (Caligula) has sent the legate of Syria and extremely distinguished Roman ex-consul, Petronius, to Jerusalem to set up statues of the emperor in the Temple of Jerusalem because he considers himself a god and wishes to be called by that name [2. 184]. Unsurprisingly, this is not acceptable to the Jews:

> Having mustered in the plain at Ptolemais, Judaeans with women and children kept imploring Petronius, first for the sake of their ancestral laws [*hoi patrioi nomoi*] then for their own sakes. . . . But while they were putting forward the law and the ancestral custom [*ho nomos kai to patrion ethos*], and how it would not be lawful to place any representation of God—let alone of a man—in the shrine itself or even in some ordinary place in the countryside, Petronius, replying, declared, "But surely in my case, is not the law of *my* master to be guarded? For after transgressing it and sparing you, I shall rightly perish. The one who sent me, and not I, will make war with you; I myself, just like you, am under orders." At this, the rabble shouted that they were ready to suffer everything for the sake of the law. After he had quelled their outburst, Petronius said, "Will you then make war on Caesar?" The Judaeans declared that they offered sacrifice twice a day for Caesar and the Roman people, but if he wants to set up the images, he will need first to offer up as a sacrifice the entire nation of Judaeans—and they presented themselves ready for the butchery, children and wives included. Amazement and sympathy went into Petronius at these [words], both for the *anuperblētos thrēskeia* of the men and for their ready, disposition [*hetoimon parastēma*] toward death (War 2 192–98).

Ἰουδαῖοι δὲ μετὰ γυναικῶν καὶ τέκνων ἀθροισθέντες εἰς τὸ πεδίον τὸ πρὸς Πτολεμαΐδι καθικέτευον τὸν Πετρώνιον ὑπὲρ τῶν πατρίων νόμων πρῶτον, ἔπειτα ὑπὲρ αὐτῶν. ὁ δὲ πρός τε τὸ πλῆθος καὶ τὰς δεήσεις ἐνδοὺς τοὺς μὲν ἀνδριάντας καὶ τὰς στρατιὰς ἐν Πτολεμαΐδι λείπει, προελθὼν δὲ εἰς τὴν Γαλιλαίαν καὶ συγκαλέσας τό τε πλῆθος καὶ τοὺς γνωρίμους πάντας εἰς Τιβεριάδα τήν τε Ῥωμαίων διεξῄει δύναμιν καὶ τὰς Καίσαρος ἀπειλάς, ἔτι δὲ τὴν ἀξίωσιν ἀπέφαινεν ἀγνώμονα· πάντων γὰρ τῶν ὑποτεταγμένων ἐθνῶν κατὰ πόλιν συγκαθιδρυκότων τοῖς ἄλλοις θεοῖς καὶ τὰς Καίσαρος εἰκόνας τὸ μόνους ἐκείνους ἀντιτάσσεσθαι πρὸς τοῦτο σχεδὸν ἀφισταμένων εἶναι καὶ μεθ' ὕβρεως. Τῶν δὲ τὸν νόμον καὶ τὸ πάτριον ἔθος προτεινομένων καὶ ὡς οὐδὲ θεοῦ τι δείκηλον, οὐχ ὅπως ἀνδρός, οὐ κατὰ τὸν ναὸν μόνον ἀλλ' οὐδὲ ἐν εἰκαίῳ τινὶ τόπῳ τῆς χώρας θέσθαι θεμιτὸν εἴη, ὑπολαβὼν ὁ Πετρώνιος "ἀλλὰ μὴν καὶ ἐμοὶ φυλακτέος ὁ τοὐμοῦ δεσπότου νόμος," ἔφη·"παραβὰς γὰρ αὐτὸν καὶ φεισάμενος ὑμῶν ἀπολοῦμαι δικαίως. πολεμήσει δ' ὑμᾶς ὁ πέμψας με καὶ οὐκ ἐγώ· καὶ γὰρ αὐτός, ὥσπερ ὑμεῖς, ἐπιτάσσομαι." πρὸς ταῦτα τὸ πλῆθος πάντ' ἐβόα πρὸ τοῦ νόμου πάσχειν ἑτοίμως ἔχειν. καταστείλας δ' αὐτῶν ὁ Πετρώνιος τὴν βοήν, "πολεμήσετε," εἶπεν, "ἄρα Καίσαρι;" καὶ Ἰουδαῖοι περὶ μὲν Καίσαρος καὶ τοῦ δήμου τῶν Ῥωμαίων δὶς τῆς ἡμέρας θύειν ἔφασαν, εἰ δὲ βούλεται τὰς εἰκόνας ἐγκαθιδρύειν, πρότερον αὐτὸν δεῖν ἅπαν τὸ Ἰουδαίων ἔθνος προθύσασθαι· παρέχειν δὲ σφᾶς αὐτοὺς ἑτοίμους εἰς τὴν σφαγὴν ἅμα

τέκνοις καὶ γυναιξίν. ἐπὶ τούτοις θαῦμα καὶ οἶκτος εἰσῄει τὸν Πετρώνιον τῆς τε
ἀνυπερβλήτου θρησκείας τῶν ἀνδρῶν καὶ τοῦ πρὸς θάνατον ἑτοίμου παραστήματος.

The words left in Greek transliteration here are all equivocal: *Parastēma* "standing beside" is actually very similar to "ecstasy" (Greek *ekstasis*: standing outside) in etymology and can mean both "desperate courage" or "exaltation" with all the possible affective nuances of both. It was those elements, already subsisting in the lexicon (by which I mean the intertext, as it were, the already used usages of the word *thrēskeia*) that rendered it so appealing for Josephus as a way to turn the blame of Jewish *superstitio* into praise of Jewish militant commitment. The ironic effects here are similar to ones that Wayne Booth has found in Mark Twain: "Throughout *Huckleberry Finn* Huck's version of his motives and feelings differs considerably from the one we reconstruct; the story that Mark Twain tells us is consequently quite different from the story that Huck thinks he is telling."[45] Similarly, the story that Josephus tells us is quite different from the story that Petronius thinks he is telling—except, of course, that one can't be sure what story Josephus is telling. This is perhaps closest to the kind of irony discussed by Northrup Frye, "[W]henever a reader is not sure what the author's attitude is or what his own is supposed to be, we have irony with relatively little satire."[46] As noted already, the primary sense of *anuperblētos thrēskeia* has to be read as "insuperable devotion" (Mason's choice) or ardor. However, given, as well in my view, the available negative connotations of *thrēskeia*, as so clearly manifested in 4 Maccabees,[47] this could be given a pejorative interpretation as well.

As such, the "insuperable" here could also carry connotations in the eyes of the Roman of excessive, fanatical devotion. Which is it: positively marked fervor or negative perfervidity? In this light, one could also question whether "sympathy" with a positive valence or "pity" with its more negative marking is the best rendering here of *oiktos*, and in any case, the same ambiguity obtains. On the one hand, the text could be read simply as commending a vaunted Roman virtue on the part of Petronius: "According to the emperor Claudius, 'It had pleased the ancestors to show as much forbearance to a suppliant as they showed persistence against a foe' (Tacitus, *Annales* 12.20)."[48] On the other hand, it could be read as genuine admiration for the virtue of the Judaeans. Both are available interpretations and both work (differently) for Josephus' purposes.

On this passage, Mason has already remarked:

> Josephus' language here (ἑτοίμου παραστήματος) has a studied ambiguity, reflecting the legate's viewpoint. . . . As this high Roman official observes the remarkable determination of the natives, he may (in the story) feel both admiration and annoyance.[49]

Mason further notes that:

> Like the purity of δεισιδαιμονία that overcame Pilate at 2.174 (in connection with the same issue of images [see immediately following here]), the unconquerable—or stubborn (ἀνυπέρβλητος)—θρησκεία that astonishes Petronius here can be understood as either virtuous or contemptible: either cultus/ritual/worship or vain superstitious practice. Josephus leaves Petronius' assessment artfully ambiguous, especially through the evocation of both amazement and pity (2.198).[50]

My only addition to this insight of Mason would be to add that it is not only the intra-diegetic ambivalence of the legate that is encoded here but also Josephus' own as well. The best argument for this is in the immediate sequel where *apraktoi*, in Mason's words, "sustains the ambiguity: It could mean that the Judaeans left "intractable, unyielding," or as Mason himself translates and defends, "unsuccessful." Here, surely, the ambiguity is extra-diegetic, authorial, and not within the legate's affect but in the author's voice and ambivalence, supporting our account of Josephan doublespeak.

Supporting this interpretation (of ambiguity in the usage of *thrēskeia*), is a highly parallel (and very famous) story in which another Roman figure is astonished at the willingness of the Jews to die in order that their ancestral mores not be violated. I refer to the narrative of Pilate's attempt to move the legionary standards into Jerusalem:

> Having been sent into Judaea as procurator by Tiberius, Pilate, by cover of night, introduced into Jerusalem Caesar's images, called "legionary standards." After daybreak, this raised a big tumult among the Judaeans. For those nearby were shocked at the sight, because their laws [*nomoi*] had been trodden under foot, for they do not deem it appropriate to place a representation in the city. And in addition to the wrath of those in the city, the people from outside the city streamed together in close order.[51] Rushing to Pilate in Caesarea, they were approaching him as suppliants to carry out the standards from Jerusalem and to guard *ta patria* [those ancestral things, the customs, the *nomoi*] for them. Pilate refusing, they prostrated themselves around his house and for five days and nights alike endured motionless. On the next day, Pilate sat on the platform in the great stadium and calling the crowd as one who would be willing to answer them truthfully, gave the soldiers a sign by arrangement to encircle the Judaeans with weapons. The phalanx being arrayed around three-deep, the Judaeans were speechless at the unexpected sight. Pilate then said that he would cut them down if they would not receive the images of Caesar favorably; he nodded to the soldiers to bare their swords. The Judaeans, for their part, just as if by preconcerted signal, fell down and bent their necks, crying that they were ready to do away with themselves, rather than transgress the law. Exceedingly amazed by their untempered *deisidaimonia*,[52] Pilate ordered to immediately carry out the standards from Jerusalem.

> Πεμφθεὶς δὲ εἰς Ἰουδαίαν ἐπίτροπος ὑπὸ Τιβερίου Πιλᾶτος νύκτωρ κεκαλυμμένας εἰς Ἱεροσόλυμα εἰσκομίζει τὰς Καίσαρος εἰκόνας, αἳ σημαῖαι καλοῦνται. τοῦτο μεθ' ἡμέραν μεγίστην ταραχὴν ἤγειρεν Ἰουδαίοις· οἵ τε γὰρ ἐγγὺς πρὸς τὴν ὄψιν ἐξεπλάγησαν ὡς πεπατημένων αὐτοῖς τῶν νόμων, οὐδὲν γὰρ ἀξιοῦσιν ἐν τῇ πόλει δείκηλον τίθεσθαι, καὶ πρὸς τὴν ἀγανάκτησιν τῶν κατὰ τὴν πόλιν ἄθρους ὁ ἐκ τῆς χώρας λαὸς συνέρρευσεν. ὁρμήσαντες δὲ πρὸς Πιλᾶτον εἰς Καισάρειαν ἱκέτευον ἐξενεγκεῖν ἐξ Ἱεροσολύμων τὰς σημαίας καὶ τηρεῖν αὐτοῖς τὰ πάτρια. Πιλάτου δὲ ἀρνουμένου περὶ τὴν οἰκίαν πρηνεῖς καταπεσόντες ἐπὶ πέντε ἡμέρας καὶ νύκτας ἴσας ἀκίνητοι διεκαρτέρουν. Τῇ δ' ἑξῆς ὁ Πιλᾶτος καθίσας ἐπὶ βήματος ἐν τῷ μεγάλῳ σταδίῳ καὶ προσκαλεσάμενος τὸ πλῆθος ὡς ἀποκρίνασθαι δῆθεν αὐτοῖς θέλων, δίδωσιν τοῖς στρατιώταις σημεῖον ἐκ συντάγματος κυκλώσασθαι τοὺς Ἰουδαίους ἐν τοῖς ὅπλοις. περιστάσης δὲ τριστιχεὶ τῆς φάλαγγος Ἰουδαῖοι μὲν ἀχανεῖς ἦσαν πρὸς τὸ ἀδόκητον τῆς ὄψεως, Πιλᾶτος δὲ κατακόψειν εἰπὼν αὐτούς, εἰ μὴ προσδέξαιντο τὰς Καίσαρος εἰκόνας, γυμνοῦν τὰ ξίφη τοῖς στρατιώταις ἔνευσεν. οἱ δὲ Ἰουδαῖοι καθάπερ ἐκ συνθήματος ἀθρόοι καταπεσόντες καὶ τοὺς αὐχένας παρακλίναντες ἑτοίμους ἀναιρεῖν σφᾶς

ἐβόων μᾶλλον ἢ τὸν νόμον παραβῆναι. ὑπερθαυμάσας δὲ ὁ Πιλᾶτος τὸ τῆς δεισιδαιμονίας ἄκρατον ἐκκομίσαι μὲν αὐτίκα τὰς σημαίας Ἱεροσολύμων κελεύει.

Once again, there are marvelous verbal ambiguities in this passage that, on my reading, represent a profound level of ambivalence in Josephus' writing. First, noting that Josephus uses here *deisidaimonia* instead of the *thrēskeia* of the nearly parallel narrative of Petronius, one needs to inquire why. I would suggest that while, as I have shown, *thrēskeia* can have for Josephus generally more positive senses than it had in earlier (and even contemporary) authors, *deisidaimonia* more generally functions negatively, something like our modern "superstition," as I show in Chapter 8, "Imagine No *Thrēskeia*: The Task of the Untranslator." *Deisidaimonia*, however, can carry, rarely but certainly, positive connotations as well, as I show earlier in this chapter, thus setting up an ambiguity in Josephus' text. As Mason remarks of *deisidaimonia*, "at 2.230 (the only other occurrence in War), the word describes the apparently virtuous Judaean reaction to a Roman soldier's burning of the sacred law, unless it should be understood, as it were, in quotation marks there. So it remains unclear—perhaps artfully so—whether the word should reflect Pilate's negative judgment on this foreign 'superstition' or whether the word itself should take a less pejorative sense here."[53] Moreover, *akraton* also can either refer positively to the purity of their devotion or to the unalloyed, untempered quality of their anxiety.[54] The narrative, even more effectively than in the Petronius episode, thus wavers or oscillates between two readings: one in which Pilate is moved at the devotion of the Judaeans and gives into them willingly; and another in which he is simply nonplussed at their stubborn scruples and gives up. Josephus, as is his wont, simply leaves us suspended between two readings and thus two valuations of the Judaean position.[55]

On the one hand, by using the equivocal word, Josephus can simultaneously convey Pilate's judgment of the Judaeans while leaving room for an entirely different judgment on the part of Judaeans themselves who could "read" *deisidaimonia* in its less frequent, but nonetheless extant, more positive senses. On the other hand, Josephus himself through this equivocation can represent his own doubled judgment of the Judaean behavior, his own admiration for their steadfastness in defense of the Torah and his (ultimate) contempt for this as self-destructive stubbornness in one and the same sentence, through one and the same word. It is important to remember that Josephus could have used here an unambiguously positive term such as *eusebeia* or *theosebeia* if he simply wanted to convey their "reverence for the divine." The choice of *deisidaimonia* is, therefore, highly marked and artful indeed. Again, these two valuations could be located within Pilate's fictive consciousness as it were, or between a "Roman" and a "Judaean" reading of the situation—or, most attractively, within "Josephus," as the implied author, the Josephus who, as we have seen, admired the last of the Zealots holding out to the very last man and the Josephus who despised the rebels as brigands at one and the same time.

If one imagines that Josephus has a "religion"—a sphere set apart from the equally anachronistic "politics"—then one simply cannot see (or perhaps more modestly put, it is much more difficult to see) the range of nuance and ambiguity encoded in words like *thrēskeia*. Nor will it do, as I have claimed repeatedly, to say something on the order of we know that the Romans, Judaeans, whomever had nothing that corresponds to the modern folks' sense of "religion," but we'll use the term anyway, and use it, moreover, to translate some ancient Roman and Greek words (an option that is still very much alive for some scholars).

A Glance at the Future: *Thrēskeia* and the Literature of Apologetic, First to Third Centuries C.E.

Similarly to what is found in Tertullian for *religio*, in literary contexts that can be classified broadly as apologetic in nature, one shall be able to see quite a different usage of *thrēskeia* than the equivocation of Josephus or the negatively tinged ones of most other Greek writers, including Judaeo-Greek.

Thrēskeia *among the Apologists*

Earlier, in Chapter 9, "The *Thrēskeia* of the Judaeans: Josephus and The New Testament," I showed that for Philo, *thrēskeia* usually expresses his own negative affect toward excessive or otherwise negatively marked cultic observance, matching up, therein, with both the negative connotations of the word found in other contemporaneous writers and with the strong *Tendenz* toward moderation in most Greek writers. This is not, however, always the case, even in Philo.

Having observed that in Philo, *thrēskeia* is generally used in pejorative contexts to refer to the practices of others, or even (as I have shown, too) to external observance without the "soul," I want, then, to point to a significant exception. In another Philonic text, however, in an explicitly apologetic context, *thrēskeia* is used in a significantly different sense: one that will foreshadow—for very good reasons—usages generally to be found only a couple of centuries later:

Was our temple the first to receive sacrifices on behalf of Gaius's reign, only in order that it should be the first and only one to have its ancestral *thrēskeia* taken away from it?

πρῶτον τὸ ἡμέτερον ἱερὸν ἐδέξατο τὰς ὑπὲρ τῆς ἀρχῆς Γαΐου θυσίας, ἵνα πρῶτον ἢ καὶ μόνον ἀφαιρεθῇ τῆς θρησκείας τὸ πάτριον; [De legatione 232].

Similarly to what has been observed with respect to Tertullian earlier in this book, for Philo as well, some writings are in an apologetic mode with respect to the Empire, and others are more pugnaciously resistant. In this apologetic context, we see something not seen before, or not as clearly: namely, the association of the same noun *thrēskeia* for both Jewish and non-Jewish cult with the implication that the Jewish one should be not less well treated than those of the others in the Empire.

Another instance from Philo is also found in De legatione, *The Embassy to Gaius*:

In, then, the twenty-three years during which he was Emperor, with respect to the Temple, he maintained the *thrēskeia* that had been handed down from ancient times and neither destroyed nor disturbed any part of it.

ἐν γοῦν τρισὶ καὶ εἴκοσιν ἔτεσιν οἷς αὐτοκράτωρ ἐγένετο τὴν κατὰ τὸ ἱερὸν ἐκ μηκίστων χρόνων παραδεδομένην θρησκείαν ἐτήρησεν, οὐδὲν αὐτῆς παραλύσας ἢ παρακινήσας μέρος [De legatione 298].

There is no possible sense that could be adduced here for *thrēskeia* other than the Temple cult. In general, one might say that the usage of *thrēskeia* in Philo refers primarily to cultic activity, to the organized cult of the Temple, and is in semantic opposition to inner feelings or emotions of piety. These two, cultic acts and piety, together form *therapeia*. *Thrēskeia* is also used of the cult of the Jews especially in apologetic contexts in which that very cult is not being vaunted as superior to others but claiming its place in the world of ignored or tolerated cults on the part of the Emperor and the Empire. As Elaine Pagels has sharply seen with respect to this very text, "Even in an empire in which *politics* and *religion* seemed inextricably intertwined, then, some Jews found ways to untwist these strands and open the way for what later generations would call separation of church and state."[1] While I am inclined to take the last statement as an overstatement, the insight that the naming of a *thrēskeia* among others belongs to the realm of apologetic seems sound and strong. In my view, moreover, we cannot speak of an intertwining of "politics" and "religion" as if these were pre-existent entities that had happened to get mixed up with each other. Not so much a calling for separation of church and state, it is rather, a plea that the Judaean cult be afforded the same dignity and rights that all other cults were within the Empire.[2] Nonetheless with these caveats, it remains the case that Pagels has made a significant point, one that will help to see and make other distinctions shortly.

As I discuss in the introduction of this book, Timothy Fitzgerald presents a nuanced interpretation of the emergence of certain aspects of the modern concept of religion within a particular kind of social context: namely, a theology of ecumenism ("world religions") in the late-nineteenth and early-twentieth centuries.[3] I would supplement his compelling work by observing that certain aspects of the ecumenical project belong to an early modernity a couple of centuries before the emergence of "world religions": namely, in the period after the Peace of Westphalia when Protestant and Catholic princes were trying to figure out a way to end the endless wars of religion.

What I would suggest at this juncture is that such emergences are not one-time and linear developments but rather that the impulse to separate something religion-like from other aspects of a polity emerges in similar social conditions in the past as well, among them the formation of a Christian community within the pagan Roman Empire. *Thrēskeia* thus develops something of what will be defined as "religion" in apologetic contexts, by which I mean specific rhetorical contexts in which "toleration" for cultic difference is being extended or requested, precisely to indicate that these differences do not threaten the powers that be. This same process can be found among the Greek Christian apologists of the second century. In the second century, a group of Christian writers set out explicitly to defend Christianity from the attacks of its enemies.[4] The sociopolitical context of their writing is thus comparable, *grosso modo*, to that of Philo's *Legatio*, and indeed, frequently enough, these "apologies" are also addressed, at least nominally, to the Emperor. Fascinatingly, it is in this context that one can clearly see *thrēskeia* emerging in the sense of a grouping for cultic purposes: that is, one of a set of such possible cultic groupings. This does not happen in all the writers of this group, but studying the others as well will help clarify the catachresis, the terminological lack that explains best the development in meaning that *thrēskeia* undergoes as well.

Let me begin by observing that the first impulse to produce a word that means "religion" as a sphere separate from "politics" comes precisely from this apologetic moment.[5] As Pagels has recently written of Justin Martyr, one of the first authors of such apologies, "Yet because Justin still hoped to find a way for people like himself to live peaceably under imperial rule, he sometimes changed his tone and addressed the emperors with cautious respect. What he wanted to do, after all, was revolutionary. In a world in which patriotism, family piety, and religious devotion were inseparable, Justin boldly tried to drive a wedge between what I call *politics* and *religion*—and so, to create the possibility of a *secular* relationship to government."[6] Recognizing clearly here (as not in the earlier quote) that "religion" and "politics" are modern terminology, Pagels clearly makes the point that the very necessity for a term that means "religion" as separated from "politics" is precisely a product of a particular historical condition and refers to a certain kind of response to that situation. As opposed to Christians who considered "Christianity" to be an entirely alternate mode of government entirely standing in opposition to the Roman order (e.g., Tertullian), these apologists produced a separation between what they called their "religion"—for the moment, by whatever word—and the political order, such that Christians could play a full role in the latter without compromising the former. "Religion" and thus the necessity for a word to name it were invented under those circumstances and those alone, as I will try now to show.

Theophilus of Antioch, second-century apologist, deploys several words within this semantic field. He uses, not surprisingly, words that carry the overtones of fear, such as, "And the names of the gods you say you *sebesthai* are the names of dead human beings" [Ad Aut., I, 9] "Καὶ τὰ μὲν ὀνόματα ὧν φὴς σέβεσθαι θεῶν ὀνόματά ἐστιν νεκρῶν ἀνθρώπων."[7]

This usage occurs several times. He also makes use of *theosebeia* [lit. god-fear]: "Some time ago we had a discussion, O excellent Autolycus, and when you asked me who my God is and briefly lent your ears to my discourse, I set forth the nature of my *theosebeia* to you" [Book II, 1].[8] Grant translates here "religion," but it would seem that the more literal fear of God would be more precise as well as less anachronistic.[9] It is in this same context that one first encounters *thrēskeia* in this author as well:

> I wish to provide to you through the present treatise a more accurate proof concerning the pointless labour and pointless *thrēskeia* in which you are held fast.

> πλὴν βούλομαί σοι καὶ νῦν διὰ τοῦδε τοῦ συγγράμματος ἀκριβέστερον ἐπιδεῖξαι τὴν ματαιοπονίαν καὶ ματαίαν θρησκείαν ἐν ᾗ κατέχῃ [ad loc.].

Now on the one hand, the sense of *thrēskeia* here parallels with his own *theosebeia*, so one might be tempted, as Grant clearly was, to give "religion" here again. On the other hand, that option for translation obscures the simple fact that Theophilus has chosen different words here, and I don't believe that we are dealing with stylistic variation.[10]

Since there are two "pointless" or "vain" things brought together here—the labor and the *thrēskeia*—trying to think those together might be helpful in achieving more precision here. The first seems to refer to actual work done, as can be shown comparatively. Strabo, for instance, uses this rare compound to indicate the effort that went into building a particularly unappealing temple in Egypt:

> There is also a building with a great number of pillars, as at Memphis, in the barbaric style; for, except the magnitude and number and rows of pillars, there is nothing pleasing nor worth writing about, but rather a display of labour wasted.

> ἔστι δέ τις καὶ πολύστυλος οἶκος, καθάπερ ἐν Μέμφει, βαρβαρικὴν ἔχων τὴν κατασκευήν· πλὴν γὰρ τοῦ μεγάλων εἶναι καὶ πολλῶν καὶ πολυστίχων τῶν στύλων οὐδὲν ἔχει χαρίεν οὐδὲ γραφικόν, ἀλλὰ ματαιοπονίαν ἐμφαίνει μᾶλλον.[11]

It would seem then that *mataioponia* refers to vain physical effort, such as in the case of Theophilus, the effort involved in making the idols; and the vain *thrēskeia* would be then the cult of those very idols, contrasted by Theophilus with his own *theosebeia*. This interpretation is borne out by the continuation in which Theophilus explicitly remarks the waste involved in the work of all the artisans who "construct gods." Theophilus can also use *proskuneō*, "to bow down to," as well; interestingly enough, he explicitly distinguishes between this verb of which only God is worthy and *timaō* "to honor," frequently used with respect to divinity in other Greek writers but here used with respect to the non-divine—by his lights—Emperor.[12] Theophilus goes on to use this verb as well as the verb form derived from *thrēskeia* to refer to the activity of Autolycus and his associates with respect to their gods as well,[13] but seems to reserve the latter term only for non-Christian cult, while his own is described by fear-terms, such as *eusebeia, theosebeia*.

The point that he uses *thrēskeia* to refer to non-Christian cults can be supported by the second instance of *thrēskeia* in the same author. After mentioning that Hesiod talks nonsense and contradicts himself in various ways, Theophilus writes: "not to mention the Egyptian demons (or foolish men) recorded by Apollonides surnamed Horapias in his book entitled *Semenouthi* and in the rest of his histories concerning the Egyptian *thrēskeia* and their kings [ad loc.]." Although this is a strange sentence in its context—it's not quite clear, for instance, what Apollonides is doing in a screed against Hesiod, nor why *thrēskeia* goes together with kings—nonetheless, it would seem that the "foolish" and "useless" cult of the Egyptians are being referenced.

A further example of this distinction can be found in the same work, where Theophilus writes:

> The divine law forbids not only *proskunein* to idols but also to the heavenly elements, the sun, the moon, and the other stars, but also *thrēskeuein* the heaven, the earth, the sea, the springs, or the rivers. Rather one must *latreuein* only the true God and maker of the universe. . . .

> Ὁ μὲν οὖν θεῖος νόμος οὐ μόνον κωλεύει τὸ εἰδώλοις προσκυνεῖν, ἀλλὰ καὶ τοῖς στοιχείοις, ἡλίῳ σελήνῃ ἢ τοῖς λοιποῖς ἄστροις, ἀλλ᾽ οὔτε τῷ οὐρανῷ οὔτε γῇ οὔτε θαλάσσῃ ἢ πηγαῖς ἢ ποταμοῖς θρησκεύειν, ἀλλ᾽ ἢ μόνῳ τῷ ὄντως θεῷ καὶ ποιητῇ τῶν ὅλων χρὴ λατρύειν. . . . [11.35].[14]

To the false gods, one performs forbidden *thrēskeia*, but to the true God, *latreia*. Once again, I see clear distinction between the verbs used for the forms of service that Theophilus condemns and the one form of which he approves.

Another apologetic epistle from roughly the same period makes clearer the terminological difficulties in which these early Christian writers were caught in trying to articulate what they were. In the text known as the Letter to Diognetus, there is quite a bit of discussion of what precisely this new collective is. Several of the target words already discussed here appear in the very incipit of the letter in which the writer (an anonymous second-century Christian) explains the reason for its writing:

> Since I perceive you, most excellent Diognetus, exceedingly zealous to learn the *theosebeia* of the Christians, and making very clear and careful inquiry about them—both who is the god in whom they trust and how they are *thrēskeuontes* him, so that all disdain the world and despise death, and neither account those to be gods who are esteemed as such by the Greeks, nor observe the *deisidaimonia* of the Jews; and what is the affection which they have for one another; and why it is that this new *genos* [class of people] or mode of living has entered into the world now, and not formerly. . . .

> Ἐπειδὴ ὁρῶ, κράτιστε Διόγνητε, ὑπερεσπουδακότα σε τὴν θεοσέβειαν τῶν Χριστιανῶν μαθεῖν καὶ πάνυ σαφῶς καὶ ἐπιμελῶς πυνθανόμενον περὶ αὐτῶν, τίνι τε θεῷ πεποιθότες καὶ πῶς θρησκεύοντες αὐτὸν τόν τε κόσμον ὑπερορῶσι πάντες καὶ θανάτου καταφρονοῦσι καὶ οὔτε τοὺς νομιζομένους ὑπὸ τῶν Ἑλλήνων θεοὺς λογίζονται οὔτε τὴν Ἰουδαίων δεισιδαιμονίαν φυλάσσουσι, καὶ τίνα τὴν φιλοστοργίαν ἔχουσι πρὸς ἀλλήλους, καὶ τί δή ποτε καινὸν τοῦτο γένος ἢ ἐπιτήδευμα εἰσῆλθεν εἰς τὸν βίον νῦν καὶ οὐ πρότερον.[15]

The very first thing that I wish to observe about this passage is that the author himself does not know what Christians are. He does not know whether he is a member of a new *genos*, race of people, or whether his own group should just be identified as a way of life.

This uncertainty about what "we" are, I suppose, has been one of the important catalysts in the semantic move of *thrēskeia* in the direction of "Church" in the Durkheimian sense. Second, this development in the meaning of *thrēskeia* clearly has not yet taken place for two reasons: (1) Had it taken place, he would not have needed the equivocation at the end of the quotation that I just mentioned; and (2) to the extent that it is not semantically equivalent but coordinated with *theosebeia*, which is not, therefore, subsumed within it, the meaning of "religion" or "Church" is not yet there. Just from this context, I would suggest that *theosebeia* means more or less literally what it says—reverence for the deity—*pōs thrēskeuontes auton* means "how they serve him," while *deisidaimonia* refers here to the excessive scrupulosity of the Jews in their practices of the Torah, especially it seems to the Sabbath, for which see also Diog. IV.1. Meecham remarks that this is one of the first uses of the word *thrēskeuo* with respect to Christians by Christians.[16] Just a couple of sentences further, moreover, I find the author writing of those whom Diognetus and his fellows call gods, "τούτοις δουλεύετε τούτοις προσκυνεῖτε, those to whom you are slaves, those to whom you bow down" (II.5). I am not necessarily insisting that *proskuneō* is always to be taken in its literal and most concrete sense, but "worship" is far too pallid a word.

In the next section of the letter, the author turns to the subject of the Jews, and their practices giving us another rich set of terminology:

> In the next place, I suppose that you are especially anxious to hear why they (the Christians) do not *theosebein* in the same manner as the Jews. The Jews indeed, if, on the one hand, they abstain from the *latreia* described above, rightly deem that they *sebein* the one god of the universe and think of him as master; but if, on the other hand, they offer this *thrēskeia* to him in like fashion to those already mentioned, they go utterly astray. For whereas the Greeks furnish an example of foolishness, by making offerings to images void of sense and hearing, the Jews ought rather to consider it folly, not *theosebeia*, in thinking that they are offering these things to God as though He were in need of them.

> 1. Ἑξῆς δὲ περὶ τοῦ μὴ κατὰ τὰ αὐτὰ Ἰουδαίοις θεοσεβεῖν αὐτοὺς οἶμαι σε μάλιστα ποθεῖν ἀκοῦσαι. 2. Ἰουδαῖοι τοίνυν, εἰ μὲν ἀπέχονται ταύτης τῆς προειρημένης λατρείας, καλῶς θεὸν ἕνα τῶν πάντων σέβειν καὶ δεσπότην ἀξιοῦσι φρονεῖν· εἰ δὲ τοῖς προειρημένοις ὁμοιοτρόπως τὴν θρησκείαν προσάγουσιν αὐτῷ ταύτην, διαμαρτάνουσιν. 3. ἃ γὰρ τοῖς ἀναισθήτοις καὶ κωφοῖς προσφέροντες οἱ Ἕλληνες ἀφροσύνης δεῖγμα παρέχουσι, ταῦθ' οὗτοι καθάπερ προσδεομένῳ τῷ θεῷ λογιζόμενοι παρέχειν μωρίαν εἰκὸς μᾶλλον ἡγοῖντ' ἄν, οὐ θεοσέβειαν [III.1–3].[17]

The Jews worship the right god, indeed, but they worship that god in the wrong way: They worship as the idolators do. They perform acts that are foolish and unnecessary. What they do is *thrēskeia* and not *theosebeia*. It simply will not do, therefore, to go on translating all of these words as "worship" as even the redoubtable Lightfoot does. I see clearly here, as I have intimated already, that *thrēskeia* and *theosebeia* are not quite the same thing. The Jews mistakenly engage in what they believe to be *theosebeia* by performing *thrēskeia*. The latter must, then, be cult, service. Insofar as it is "offered" or "furnished" to god and referred to as that which he does not need, it is clear that it is the sacrificial cult of the Temple to which the author of the epistle refers. Since they do what is foolish and not necessary, once again the odor of the theatrical attends their actions. This point is borne out further in the sequel where it is detailed that it is of the sacrifices that he speaks, and they are labeled with the epithets of "fatuity, deceit, and pride." Once more, note that what the author is denying is that this is *theosebeia* while calling it *thrēskeia*.

Further support for the notion that *theosebeia* means something more than "piety" or "cult," comes from a further passage in the same author, in which, continuing his screed against the Jews, he writes:

> Well then, I think that you have learned sufficiently that Christians are right in keeping aloof from the general fatuity and deceit and from the meddlesomeness and pride of the Jews, but as regards the mystery of their (the Christians') own *theosebeia*, do not expect to be able to learn this from man.

> τῆς μὲν οὖν κοινῆς εἰκαιότητος καὶ ἀπάτης καὶ τῆς Ἰουδαίων πολυπραγμοσύνης καὶ ἀλαζονείας ὡς ὀρθῶς ἀπέχονται Χριστιανοί, ἀρκούντως σε νομίζω μεμαθηκέναι· τὸ δὲ τῆς ἰδίας αὐτῶν θεοσεβείας μυστήριον μὴ προσδοκήσῃς δύνασθαι παρὰ ἀνθρώπου μαθεῖν [4.6].[18]

Theosebeia includes cultic service, as I have shown, and also a *mystērion*. It is contrasted twice by words that mean "folly" or "nonsense."

The sequel to this statement about the *mystērion* of their *theosebeia*, perhaps the most famous passage in the epistle of Diognetus, is the one that most clearly articulates the conditions under which eventually (not too long after), the word *thrēskeia* would expand and shift its meaning:

> 5:1 For Christians are distinguished from the rest of men neither by country nor by language nor by customs. For nowhere do they dwell in cities of their own; they do not use some altered form of speech, or practice a singular mode of life.[19] This lore of theirs has not been discovered by any design and thought of prying men, nor do they champion a mere human doctrine, as some men do. But while they dwell in both Greek and barbarian cities each as his lot was cast, and follow the customs of the land in dress and food and the other matters of living, they show forth the remarkable and admittedly strange order of their own citizenship. They live in fatherlands of their own, but as aliens; they share in all things as citizens, and they suffer all things as strangers. Every foreign land is their fatherland, and every fatherland a foreign land.[20]

> 1. Χριστιανοὶ γὰρ οὔτε γῇ οὔτε φωνῇ οὔτε ἔθεσι διακεκριμένοι τῶν λοιπῶν εἰσιν ἀνθρώπων. 2. οὔτε γάρ που πόλεις ἰδίας κατοικοῦσι οὔτε διαλέκτῳ τινὶ παρηλλαγμένῃ χρῶνται οὔτε βίον παράσημον ἀσκοῦσιν. 3. οὐ μὴν ἐπινοίᾳ τινὶ καὶ φροντίδι πολυπραγμόνων ἀνθρώπων μάθημα τοῦτ' αὐτοῖς ἐστιν εὑρημένον, οὐδὲ δόγματος ἀνθρωπίνου προεστᾶσιν, ὥσπερ ἔνιοι. 4. κατοικοῦντες δὲ πόλεις Ἑλληνίδας τε καὶ βαρβάρους, ὡς ἕκαστος ἐκληρώθη, καὶ τοῖς ἐγχωρίοις ἔθεσιν ἀκολουθοῦντες ἔν τε ἐσθῆτι καὶ διαίτῃ καὶ τῷ λοιπῷ βίῳ θαυμαστὴν καὶ ὁμολογουμένως παράδοξον ἐνδείκνυνται τὴν κατάστασιν τῆς ἑαυτῶν πολιτείας. 5. πατρίδας οἰκοῦσιν ἰδίας, ἀλλ' ὡς οἰκοῦσιν ἰδίας, ἀλλ' ὡς πάροικοι· μετέχουσι πάντων ὡς πολῖται, καὶ πάνθ' ὑπομένουσιν ὡς ξένοι· πᾶσα ξένη πατρίς ἐστιν αὐτῶν, καὶ πᾶσα πατρὶς ξένη.

This is, indeed, a beautiful exposition of the condition of Christians. In contrast to Diaspora Judaeans who have (at that time at least, as it were) two homelands, Christians have none: They are also not defined by genealogy. The question that arises, however, is what one calls such a grouping of people, such a collective. None, it would seem, of the existent categories will work. A catachresis is produced. He attempts to solve this problem by analogizing the world to a body and the Christians to the soul of that body, and then, "The soul which is invisible is guarded in the body which is visible: so Christians are recognized as being in the world, and yet their *theosebeia* remains invisible" (6:4). If I understand him correctly here, he is saying that outwardly, Christians belong to the world:—that is, they are Greeks, Romans, Persians, Judaeans; but inwardly, in their *theosebeia*, they form a collective but one that is invisible to the world. Eventually the word *thrēskeia* will be adopted to name that invisible, other-worldly, connection. Notwithstanding, then, the evident fact that for the author of the Epistle to Diognetus, the word *thrēskeia* had not significantly shifted its meaning from earlier usages, *grosso modo*, one can still thus observe the conditions that would eventually foster such a shift.

The earliest example of *thrēskeia* in the sense of an institution or the name of a collective and not a practice of which I know is from the Bishop of Sardis, Melito, writing at about the same time as the Epistle to Diognetus to none other than Marcus Aurelius:

> For the philosophy current with us flourished in the first instance among barbarians; and, when it afterwards bloomed among your nations, during the mighty reign of your ancestor Augustus, it came to be exceedingly auspicious and good for your reign. For from that time the Roman power has risen to greatness and radiance. To this power you have come as the desired successor; and such you will be, together with your son, if you protect [*phulassōn*] that philosophy which has grown up with your rule [like a foster brother] and been a joint ruler with Augustus; to which also your ancestors paid honor along with the other *thrēskeiai*.

> Ἡ γὰρ καθ' ἡμᾶς φιλοσοφία πρότερον μὲν ἐν βαρβάροις ἤκμασεν, ἐπανθήσασα δὲ τοῖς σοῖς ἔθνεσιν κατὰ τὴν Αὐγούστου τοῦ σοῦ προγόνου μεγάλην ἀρχήν, ἐγενήθη μάλιστα τῇ σῇ βασιλείᾳ αἴσιον ἀγαθόν. Ἔκτοτε γὰρ εἰς μέγα καὶ λαμπρὸν τὸ Ῥωμαίων ηὐξήθη κράτος· οὗ σὺ διάδοχος εὐκταῖος γέγονάς τε καὶ ἔσῃ μετὰ τοῦ παιδός, φυλάσσων τῆς βασιλείας τὴν σύντροφον καὶ συναρξαμένην Αὐγούστῳ φιλοσοφίαν, ἣν καὶ οἱ πρόγονοί σου πρὸς ταῖς ἄλλαις θρησκείαις ἐτίμησαν [Melito Fragmenta 1.3].

Melito seems still to be struggling somewhat for a name with which to name Christianity as a category. As I see, he twice within this extract refers to it as a philosophy but then finally hits on *thrēskeia* as a name for what it is among others of its kind, protected by the Emperor. His usage here is similar to that observed earlier in Philo's apology to Gaius. For the Christian writer, however, this is more of a semantic shift given that there is no Christian sacrificial cult. This is the most common later usage of this term: that is, in the apologetic context of a desire for a particular, nondominant group to be considered part of an imperial polity. It is then that the notion of a "religion," separate from imperial government, the familial, the economic becomes necessary.

The category of Christian writers called Apologists are not all the same, not at all. Indeed, the category per se is a difficult one. It is in the apologists properly so-called who are attempting to persuade the powers that be to treat the Christians favorably among their other subjects that one begins to find *thrēskeia* being used more or less (or at any rate, shading toward) the sense of a group having certain ideas in a certain way and practicing in a certain way owing to their ideas, but others of the group known as Apologists are doing something entirely different. Instead of seeking a home for Christians within the Greco-Roman world and the Roman Empire, they are attacking that world and all its works (as in Tertullian's separatist or attack mode that was exposed in Chapter 7, "Precarious Integration: Managing the Fears of the Romans"). Robert Grant already has made this differentiation, writing, "There is a great gulf fixed between the conciliatory petitions to Marcus Aurelius from Christians in 176 and the bitterly antagonistic essay of Tatian addressed to 'the Greeks' within the next year or so. Apollinarus, Melito, and Athenagoras offered adulation, while Tatian denounced almost every aspect of Greco-Roman culture and religion in his *Oration Against the Greeks*."[21] Regardless of whether I accept Grant's somewhat apologetic explanation for this difference, it remains nonetheless the case that these are very different types of rhetoric. Not surprisingly, in Tatian, one does *not* find *thrēskeia* in the afore-mentioned acceptation of a cultic group among other such groups but only as a name for the cult of demons (*daimones*):

> Demons are seen also by "psychic" men, for at times they show themselves to men, in order to be thought important, or even to do them some harm as enemies, nursing intentions against them like bad friends, or providing to those like them incitements towards their *thrēskeia*.

> Βλέπονται δὲ καὶ ὑπὸ τῶν ψυχικῶν οἱ δαίμονες, ἔσθ' ὅτε τοῖς ἀνθρώποις ἑαυτοὺς ἐκείνων δεικνύντων, ἵνα τε νομισθῶσιν εἶναί τινες ἢ καί τι βλάψωσι καθάπερ πολεμίους, φίλοι κακοὶ τὴν γνώμην ὑπάρχοντες, ἢ τῆς εἰς αὐτοὺς θρησκείας τοῖς ὁμοίοις αὐτοῖς τὰς ἀφορμὰς παράσχωσιν.[22]

It is entirely clear here that *thrēskeia* has an entirely negative sense, as I have shown it in earlier Greek usage and in near contemporaries such as Plutarch. It is virtually certain that Tatian would not have used it to refer to his own belief system or ritual practice at all. This point is even stronger when one examines the second instance of the usage of *thrēskeia* in this writer:

> Therefore when I had seen those things and had taken part in the mysteries and had scrutinized all of the *thrēskeiai* which through the female-males and the male-females are organized . . .

> Ταῦτ' οὖν ἰδών, ἔτι δὲ καὶ μυστηρίων μεταλαβὼν καὶ τὰς παρὰ πᾶσι θρησκείας δοκιμάσας διὰ θηλυδριῶν καὶ ἀνδρογύνων συνισταμένας,[23]

Notwithstanding the fact that I can't distinguish between female-males and male-females (unless the former refers just to sexual practice and the latter to genital morphology),[24] it is clear that these are deeply negative terms for Tatian. *Thrēskeia* seems, therefore, once more, even more explicitly, to be entirely negatively marked in this writer, whom one might style more of an antagonist than an apologist.

It is precisely the apologetic context of such otherwise diverse writers as Philo and Melito—according to my hypothesis—that leads to the disembedding of *thrēskeia* as a separate sphere of life and practice and as one of a number of such available (which is not to say freely choosable, of course).[25] It is for the apologist—not the antagonist—that the positive sense of *thrēskeia* as but one member of a class is necessary, providing an important key to its emergence in modernity as well, but this is a story for another day.

Conclusion: What You Find When You Stop Looking for What Isn't There

Our readers will surely have noticed two "I's" in this book: two speakers with distinct voices but a perhaps surprising degree of agreement in substance between them. This book is the product of the confluence of two projects that we were working on respectively about five years ago. Barton was studying the Roman sacrificial system (to which she will now return), and Boyarin was tracing the genealogy of "Judaism" (to which he will now return). At a certain point, reading each other's early drafts, we realized that the propaedeutic for both projects was similar: a close study of the ancient Latin and Greek terms later taken to mean "religion" was a necessary foundation for both our projects. Barton, a Roman historian, took on the Latin work. She had long wrestled with the meanings of *religio* in republican and imperial Latin. (Her enormous additional task for this book would be reading all of Tertullian.) Boyarin, a Talmudist, by default of having no Latin, took on responsibility for analyzing the Greek material, including (as he did not realize at the beginning) reading virtually all of Josephus in Greek. There followed several years of reading, research, constant discussion, and lively disputation until the theses of this book came together. The goal that we had in mind from the beginning was that this would not be a book with two voices, in the sense of two opinions that agree to disagree, but rather that we would talk and think over every point until, having taken into consideration the arguments of the other, we had attuned our views to a stage at which we could both be satisfied. We succeeded in that goal; whether we have succeeded in any other, we leave to readers to decide.

Many scholars by now have contested the use of "religion" as an analytic category for the study of cultures other than the modern West. Some of these have already been discussed, and there are others to add to the discussion, notably the new books by Jason Ananda Josephson and Severin Fowles.[1] In fact, such studies multiply by the day. We have tried to contribute to this conversation in two ways: (1) by detailed and lengthy philological studies of the two most prominent words in the so-called classical languages that are the etyma of modern European words for religion; namely, *religio* and *thrēskeia*; and (2) by exploring through case studies of crucial figures, one writing in Latin and one writing in Greek, how much can be discovered about their cultural and intellectual worlds by refusing to separate off a category they would not have recognized, that "product of the scholar's study": "religion." We have extended the very brief studies of these words in Latin and Greek offered by Nongbri[2] and others. This lexical work has demonstrated conclusively what others have surmised: Translating *religio* or *thrēskeia* by "religion" obscures more than it reveals. Our extended studies have yielded further fruit in that we have found in these words whole cultural systems very different from our own systems of borders, boundaries, and binaries.

Common to both ancient Greek and Latin cultures, if more easily discernible in the Latin, is a sense that the median is the ideal and deviations from it in either direction[3]—too much or too little—are problematic and dangerous. And so too much *religio* is *superstitio*, while *thrēskeia*, like *deisidaimonia*, is, very frequently, the marker of inordinate fear of or enthusiasm for gods. This attraction to balance and measure seems to be the case even for many Greek-writing Jewish authors as well, notably Philo, the most prominent of all. (On the whole, Latin *religio* is less theocentric than Greek *thrēskeia*, but will be pushed in that direction by those Latin writers familiar with and allured by Greek thought.)

Our two semantic studies, then, have revealed a similar cultural anxiety with regard to "extreme" behaviors and emotional states, a mistrust of intemperance. In the Roman case, both the *religiosi* and the *superstitiosi* display too much emotion, too much fear, and too much ardor with respect to their *religiones* (and later to their gods); while in much of its Greek usage, *thrēskeia* is the passion and nervous fear of the *deisidaimon*, and carries meanings close to the negative forms of *religio* and *superstitio* in Latin.

In the works of Tertullian—the first important Latin writer to translate Christian ideas into Latin—and Josephus—the Judaean writer who gives us perhaps the richest insights into the culture of first-century Iudaioi—we see the tensions and contradictions that occur with the introduction of a set of values encouraging, even demanding, excess: ferocity, fidelity, fear, devotion, and love. Both have to wring their words from worlds with opposing values. In this light, it is easier to understand Josephus' frequent usage of *thrēskeia* to positively mark Judean fervor and devotion, even while allowing his Roman readers to process it pejoratively as fanaticism. In Josephus' thought, two cultural systems that would seem to be in inexorable contradiction are rendered somehow compatible and/or—their contradictions obfuscated—by utilizing the equivocal term *thrēskeia*. In comparison, Tertullian could not imagine a negative Christian *religio*, however extreme. (By the late-third and early-fourth centuries, Lactantius would write that it was impossible to have too much *religio* [*Institutiones divinae* 4.28.7].)

Comparing Tertullian and Josephus, our major case studies for this book, we found that both were responding to the Emperor of Rome. By focusing on the actual terms used by these thinkers to describe their worlds rather than superimposing on them structures drawn from another time and place, such as "religion," we can, we suggest, compare them more adequately. Their strategies were different, but also from one point of view, surprisingly the same. Both often envisaged perfected worlds (often both cosmic and social *politeiai* or *imperia*) in which it would be impossible, as well as undesirable, to set off one sphere or aspect of the polity for "religion" and another for "politics."[4] For Josephus, the Torah served as the constitution of the *ethnos/politeia*, which he triumphantly claimed, most manifestly in *Contra Apionem*, to be superior to those of both Athens and Sparta. Similarly (but differently), Tertullian imagined his *disciplina, his religio* (under Ciceronian influence), as a complete rival and replacement for the Roman Empire, his god as rival and replacement for the Roman emperor.[5]

At the same time, we hope to have shown another concurrent development in the history of *thrēskeia* and *religio*. In a particular genre of writing, known as "apologetic," the author (usually portraying himself as addressing the Emperor directly) attempts to negotiate a safe space for his or her group within the Empire. One of the available "apologetic" strategies was to divide off something called *religio* or *thrēskeia* from its general usage as part and parcel of an entire cultural system and mark it as a distinct and complementary realm to that of the Roman Empire, thus anticipating in some ways, modern usage of "religion" as something different from and not necessarily in conflict with the "political." When used in this sense, the words (as is frequently the case now) were meant to indicate that one could be different with respect to *religio/thrēskeia* and remain a good citizen, a loyal subject of the Emperor. Again, this usage appears in the Greek and Latin "apologists" for Christianity while remaining spectacularly absent from other writings of those who renounced the Roman *imperator* and his domination. Tertullian, in his fleeting "apologetic" or "negotiatory" moods, was willing to present Christians as a benign fellowship separated out from the wider culture only by their particularly stringent *disciplina* and *religiones.* But in his rebellious and "segregationist" writings, *religio* meant something very different: a total top-down, through-the-looking-glass governing system with an army of fervid soldiers and a King God poised to defeat and displace the Roman Emperor.

Where Tertullian and Josephus differ is in the strategies they adopted in their "apologetic" or "accomodationist" mode. Josephus never declares himself an intractable opponent of Rome and its works but reveals and conceals his resistance through equivocation. Tertullian prefers to present himself most often as an intractable opponent of the emperor, in a war until the end with "the devil and his pomps."

Tessa Rajak has written: "There is nothing more difficult, in writing about the Palestine of this period, than to form an adequate conception of the relation between *religion* and other spheres of life" [emphasis ours].[6] Perhaps, we would suggest, the difficulty lies in the fact that there is no such distinction made by the people in the culture, certainly not Josephus. Rajak quotes Josephus: "We were proceeding with the ordinary service and engaged in prayer, when Jesus rose and began to question us about the furniture and uncoined silver. . . ." (Bellum Iudaicum 295; Thackeray translation).[7] Josephus remarks that most of the planning for the rebellion took place at the festivals. So much for separate spheres! Similarly, for the Romans, the language and behaviors of the sacrificial system were interwoven into every aspect of life. Every oath, every contract, every birth and every battle, every meal and every pile of dung were in the same web of life.

Thinking of "religion" frequently sunders what, in the ancient world, ought to be thought together. And so we have tried to do both close analysis of the texts and broad comparative work on ancient ideas and behaviors while abstaining from at least one set of occluding and anachronistic abstractions. We hope our efforts have revealed some things that might be hard to see otherwise.

ACKNOWLEDGMENTS

We feel keenly the loss of Helen Tartar, a fine and inspiring editor and so much more than an editor. She encouraged us to write this book and offered intellectual aid and comfort throughout. We, like myriad others, are deeply saddened that she wasn't able to see it published. Helen can never be replaced, but we are grateful to her successor, Richard Morrison, for continuing her work.

The authors wish to acknowledge gratefully the following teachers, friends, and colleagues who have read portions of this book and commented helpfully, critically, and encouragingly: Erich Gruen, Susan Harvey, Karen King, Donald Mastronarde, Steven Mason, Jason Moralee, Brent Nongbri, James Porter, Tessa Rajak, Mark Roblee, Christopher Whitton, and the members of the Five College Late Antique Seminar.

Sections of the book have been offered as lectures by one or the other of us at Brown University, Cornell University, Syracuse University, Models of Piety Group, UC Berkeley; and the conference "Senses, Affect, and the Imagination in Late Antiquity" at Colgate University. The work was enhanced at all these settings.

INTRODUCTION: WHAT YOU CAN SEE WHEN YOU STOP LOOKING FOR WHAT ISN'T THERE

1. Cited as a personal communication in Brent Nongbri, *Before Religion: A History of a Modern Concept* (New Haven, Conn.: Yale University Press, 2013), 156.

2. The "we" in this introduction (when it is not all of us, writers and readers) comprises authors Barton and Boyarin. Later chapters are written in the first-person singular to reflect the writerly voice of the prime author of the chapter. All chapters manifest one combined scholarly voice. The introduction and conclusion are composed by two writerly voices so intertwined as to justify the "we."

3. Nongbri, *Before Religion*, 158–59.

4. Nongbri, *Before Religion*, 159.

5. C. P. Jones, "Ἔθνος and γένος in Herodotus," *Classical Quarterly* n.s. 46 (1996), 315–20, 316. Jones' short article is an exemplary instance of how a lexical study ought to be conducted.

6. The usual approach to lexicographical semantics is to define a word, to discover its "essence"—the overlying abstract concept that generates all the specific instances of its usage. This approach could be termed "metaphorical," while ours traces the connections of one meaning to another without assuming a common check list of characteristics that will fit all instantiations of the word. We have relied to some degree on Wittgenstein's notion of "family resemblances." ("Family resemblance" referred simply to the fact that a human biological family may look like each other without any one feature being constitutive of that similarity, but person A may have red hair, hazel eyes, and a large nose; person B has brown hair, brown eyes, and a large nose; and person C has brown hair, brown eyes, and a small nose. C and A do not share any of the characteristics, but when put together, A, B, and C can be picked out as members of the family owing to the similarity of both A and C to B. The "clues" will usually be more subtle, distinctive, and manifold. For an excellent exposition of this theory and its descendent, prototype semantics, see Chana Kronfeld, *On the Margins of Modernism: Decentering Literary Dynamics*, Contraversions [Berkeley: University of California Press, 1996], 27–28.)

7. "*Die Wortgeschichte, wenn sie sich zu einer Geschichte der Begriffe vertieft, kann uns noch immer reichen Aufschluß über Probleme geben, denen wir auf keinem anderen Wege nahe kommen können.*" Cited in Willem Cornelis van Unnik and Pieter Willem van der Horst, *Das Selbstverständnis der jüdischen Diaspora in der hellenistisch-römischen Zeit*, Arbeiten zur Geschichte des antiken Judentums und des Urchristentums 17 (Leiden; New York: Brill, 1993), 68.

8. Smith, "Trading Places," *Relating Religion: Essays in the Study of Religion* (Chicago: The University of Chicago Press, 2004), 215–29, 221–22. Emphasis original.

9. Norman Holland, "Unity, identity, text, self," *Proceedings of the Modern Language Association* 90 (1975), 813–22, 816.

10. Nongbri, *Before Religion*, 3.

11. Fitzgerald, *The Ideology of Religious Studies* (New York: Oxford University Press, 2000), 82.

12. Much like the disaggregation/aggregation that has produced "sexuality," this aggregation has a specific history—one that can be traced not to a unique moment of origin perhaps but to beginnings nonetheless. Note that Foucault's history of sexuality is analogous conceptually to our "imagine no religion," in that in both instances the scholar is being asked to pay attention to the fact that what has appeared to be a timeless universal is a specific construction of a particular society. The Foucauldian connections of this enterprise are signaled both in Talal Asad's title, *Genealogies of Religion: Discipline and Reasons of Power in Christianity and Islam* (Baltimore: Johns Hopkins University Press, 1993) and Nongbri's *Before Religion*.

13. We are eschewing here the usual "believed in," as that concept is itself very culture-specific.

14. Daniel Dubuisson, *The Western Construction of Religion: Myths, Knowledge, and Ideology*, trans. William Sayers (Baltimore: Johns Hopkins University Press, 2003), 12.

15. Nongbri, *Before Religion*, 4.

16. Fitzgerald, *The Ideology of Religious Studies*, 24.

17. In his own necessarily very brief accounts of the trouble caused by imposing translations drawn from an entirely different culture on the terms of ancient Greek and Latin, Nongbri provides, moreover, an elegant and compelling example: namely, the words that are frequently translated by "piety" in renderings of Greek and Latin. As he remarks, "[T]o be sure, ancient people had words to describe the proper reverence of the gods, but these terms were not what modern people would describe as strictly 'religious.' They formed part of the vocabulary of social relations more generally." Nongbri rehearses in this instance the case of *eusebeia* ["good fear"], the normal Greek word for "piety," and remarks that this term is not restricted in any way to relations between humans and divine objects but "to hierarchical social protocols of all sorts." As he points out, Plato describes the rewards for those who practice *eusebeia* and consequent punishments for those who display *asebeia* "to gods and parents."

18. "*Religion, Religions, Religious,*" Critical Terms for Religious Studies, ed. Mark C. Taylor (Chicago: The University of Chicago Press, 1998), 269–84, 280

19. Smith, "The Topography of the Sacred," *Relating Religion: Essays in the Study of Religion* (Chicago: The University of Chicago Press, 2004), 101–116, 106.

20. We are not claiming, not at all, that the "external" observer can never see things that are occluded from the member of the culture itself. Any given culture makes distinctions that are not articulated (that are tacit, that "go without saying") and makes categories and distinctions that do not operate "on the ground." (For instance, informants might tell an ethnographer that we do not marry first cousins but only second cousins—and then the ethnographer discovers many first-cousin marriages.) Such discrepancies are well known to ethnographers, but this hardly marks an opposition between subjective and objective or insiders' and outsiders' perspectives. One would have to demonstrate *in either case* on the basis of the same kind of evidence whether a distinction or category is operative within the culture.

21. Smith, "The Topography of the Sacred," 106.

22. Fitzgerald, *The Ideology of Religious Studies*, 9.

23. It is somewhat startling to find Fitzgerald, in the second half of his book, marking ritual, politics, and soteriology, as his *replacement* terms for "religion." Unless we have very much mistaken him, the latter two categories are precisely ones that he interrogates and problematizes in the first half. (See the explicit critique of "soteriology" at p. 16.) Furthermore, he tends to meld "Judaism" into Christianity in the form of the Judaeo-Christian, which quite misses the point that Jewry is one of the non-western collectives upon which the idea of religion has been foisted—if fairly willingly (L. Batnitzky, *How Judaism Became a Religion: An Introduction to Modern Jewish Thought* [Princeton: Princeton University Press, 2011]). Benson Saler repeats this gesture by insisting on substituting "Western" for Talal Asad's "Christian" (Benson Saler, *Conceptualizing*

Religion: Immanent Anthropologists, Transcendent Natives, and Unbounded Categories, Studies in the History of Religions 56 [Leiden; New York: Brill, 1993], 96).

24. Emile Durkheim, *The Elementary Forms of Religious Life*, trans. Carol Cosman, abridged with an introduction and notes by Mark S. Cladis, Oxford World's Classics (Oxford: New York: Oxford University Press, 2001), 59.

25. As Nongbri remarks, "Because of the pervasive use of the word 'religion' in the cultures of the modern Western world . . . we already intuitively know what 'religion' is before we even try to define it: religion is anything that sufficiently resembles modern Protestant Christianity." Durkheim defines "religion" in terms of "practices," with the pride of place, however, given to "faith" or "beliefs": "The individuals . . . feel themselves united to each other by the simple fact that they have a common faith." Secondly, Durkhein translates his definition into a definition of a "Church" as a group of people united precisely by their ideas about the sacred and their practices. He seeks to incorporate a group called the "Hebrews" under this rubric by suggesting that sometimes a people constitutes a Church. Ironically enough for this scion of a great rabbinic family, every single one of these definitions is a product of Christianity and Christianity alone, and indeed Durkheim's very definition of the religion of the so-called Hebrews as a Church is drawn from Christian renditions of Jewry.

26. Saler, *Conceptualizing Religion*, 82–83.

27. Dumont, *Homo Hierarchicus: an Essay on the Caste System*, trans. Mark Sainsbury, The Nature of Human Society Series (Chicago: The University of Chicago Press, 1970).

28. Oral communication of Stanley Kurz, quoted in Saler, *Conceptualizing Religion*, 82.

29. Wittgenstein, *Philosophical Investigations*, trans. G. E. M. Anscombe (New York: Macmillan, 1958), 4.

30. Wittgenstein, *Philosophical Investigations*, 8.

31. For a good and concise description of these views, see Nongbri, *Before Religion*, 1–3.

32. Asad, *Genealogies*.

33. "The first model to be discarded is that of 'religion' itself. The crippling ambiguities of the term have been demonstrated by Wilfred Cantwell Smith. Only the establishment of Christendom in the fourth century created the conditions which make the typical modern use of the word historically realistic," E. A. Judge, *Social Distinctives of the Christians in the First Century: Pivotal Essays*, ed. David M. Scholer (Peabody, Mass: Hendrickson Publishers, 2008), 130. We tend to agree *grosso modo* with this perspective adding only that some other factors, *viz.* Cicero's use of *religio* (see Chapter 2) also rendered the modern developments possible.

34. Fitzgerald, *The Ideology of Religious Studies*.

35. Nongbri, *Before Religion*, 6.

36. Wilfred Cantwell Smith, *The Meaning and End of Religion: A New Approach to the Religious Traditions of Mankind*, foreword by John Hick (New York: Macmillan, 1962); T. Asad, *Genealogies*.

37. Nongbri, *Before Religion*.

38. Nongbri, *Before Religion*, 7.

39. Very many scholars writing and speaking of "religion" avoid the problem of definition (and thus the need to examine their own presuppositions) by simply using the category as axiomatic. Thus they avoid the quicksand into which anthropologists have driven that word by including all sacralizing and desecrating behaviors. When loosened from its Christian moorings, the interpretations given to the word "religion" have drifted toward every direction of the compass. However *none* of these additional definitions cover the same ground as Roman *religio*.

We can refer to a few important titles: Henri Bouillard, "La Formation du concept de religion en Occident," *Humanisme et foi chrétienne. Mélanges scientifiques du centenaire de l'institut catholique de Paris*, eds. Charles Kannengiesser and Yves Marchasson (Paris: Éditions Beauchesne, 1967), 451–61; Smith, *The Meaning and End of Religion*; Michel Despland, *La Religion en occident: évolution des idées et du vécu* (Montreal: Fides, 1977); Ernst Feil, *Religio: die Geschichte eines neuzeitlichen Grundbegriffs vom Frühchristentum bis zur Reformation* (Göttingen: Vandenhoeck & Ruprecht, 1986); Benson Saler, *"Religio* and the Definition of Religion," *Cultural Anthropology* 2 (1987) 395–99; id., *Conceptualizing Religion;* Asad, *Genealogies;* Smith, "Religion, Religions, Religious"; Nongbri, *Before Religion.*

40. Nongbri himself, however, engages in the same sort of self-contradiction when he assents to J. Z. Smith's approach, approvingly citing Smith's comment that, "It is the very distance and difference of religion as a second-order category that gives it cognitive power." Jonathan Z. Smith, *Relating Religion: Essays in the Study of Religion* (Chicago: The University of Chicago Press, 2004), 208.

41. Fitzgerald, *The Ideology of Religious Studies,* 4.

1. *RELIGIO* WITHOUT "RELIGION"

1. "Religion in the Roman Empire," in *Experiencing Rome: Culture, Identity and Power in the Roman Empire,"* ed. Janet Huskinson (London: Routledge, 2000), 245–75, 246.

2. My work on Roman emotions, especially the emotions of "honor," has served as the foundation for my study of the Roman *religiones.* It will be immediately apparent that I am indebted, as well, to anthropologists and historians who have been influenced by the study of the relationship of pre-state systems to state systems. There are too many to name, but I would give special mention to Karl Meuli, Ake Hultkrantz, Valerio Valeri, Godfrey Lienhardt, and Walter Burkert.

3. *Pudor,* the Roman "sense of shame," was an acute and inhibiting sensitivity to the eyes and opinions of others. The word embraced both the inhibiting emotions that discouraged the transgressions of boundaries and the "shame" that acted as the punishment for transgressions. I have discussed Roman notions of *pudor* at length in Carlin Barton, *Roman Honor* (Berkeley: University of California Press, 2003).

4. Although the word *religio* will have metamorphosed and become greatly restricted over the centuries, Augustine can still lament in the early fifth century that the word, like *pietas* and *cultus,* was not sufficiently restricted to observances directed at the one god; not sufficiently god-centered and restricted. He states that it was not just the ignorant, but also the learned who were wont to say that *religio* ought to be observed in dealing with relationships, affinities, and bonds of every sort: that *religio* is the observance of a variety of duties and obligations in human relations. (. . . *Latina loquendi consuetudine, non imperitorum, verum etiam doctissimorum, et cognationibus humanis atque adfinitatibus et quibusque necessitudinibus dicitur exhibenda religio . . . observantia propinquitatis humanae [Civitas dei* 10.1].)

5. For the movement from *honor* to *honestas,* the movement from situational to codified and formalized responses, see *Roman Honor* , esp. pp. 270–28. *Honor/honos*—which was always potentially transgressive—became "honesty," which was never transgressive.

6. For example, Mommsen: "Roman religion in its pure, unhampered, and thoroughly national character" (*History of Rome,* trans. William Dickson, vol. 1 [New York, 1886], 239). Cumont: *"Subordonnée à la politique, elle [la religion des Romains] cherche avant tout par la stricte exécution de pratiques appropriées à assurer à l'État la protection des dieux ou à détourner les effets de leur malveillance"* (*Les Religions orientales dans le paganisme romain,* Paris, 1906, 36). "Roman religion, properly speaking, comprised the public cults or the city of Rome and its citizens. Budding out from this model, as it were, were the cultic practices of various notionally autonomous citizen groups. . . ." (Greg Woolf, "Divinity and Power in Ancient Rome," in *Religion and Power,* ed. Nicole Brisch, Chicago [2008], 243–59, 249).

7. "*L'Originalité du vocabulaire religieux Latin,*" *Rites, Cultes, Dieux de Rome,* Paris, 1979, 30–53, 37 = *Revue Belge de Philologie et d'histoire* 49 (1971), 31–54.

8. There could be domestic or family, popular or folk versions of these institutions, but it was the city-state (or kingdom) that provided the model. It is as if they internalized the Platonic model of the equivalence of the city-state with the moral economy of the individual.

9. Very many scholars writing and speaking of "religion" avoid the problem of definition (and thus the need to examine their own presuppositions) by simply using the category as axiomatic. Thus they avoid the quicksand into which anthropologists have driven that word by including all sacralizing and desecrating behaviors. When loosened from its Christian moorings, the interpretations given to the word "religion" have drifted toward every direction of the compass. However *none* of these additional definitions cover the same ground as Roman *religio*. For the literature on the definitions and history of definitions of "religion," see the Introduction to this book. Here I can refer to a few important titles: Bouillard, op. cit.; William Cantwell Smith, *The Meaning and End of Religion*, Minneapolis, 1962; Michel Despland, *La Religion en occident; évolution des idées et du vécu*, Montreal, 1977; Ernst Feil, *Religio: die Geschichte eines neuzeitlichen Grundbegriffs vom Frühchristentum bis zur Reformation*, Göttingen, 1986; Benson Saler, "*Religio* and the Definition of Religion," *Cultural Anthropology* 2 (1987): 395–99; *Conceptualizing Religion*, New York/Oxford, 2000 [1993]; Talal Asad, *Genealogies of Religion*, Baltimore/London, 1993; Johnathan Z. Smith, "Religion, Religions, Religious," *Critical Terms for Religious Studies*, ed. Mark C. Taylor, Chicago, 1998, 269–84; Brent Nongbri, *Before Religion*, New Haven, 2013.]

10. Schilling, "Le Romain de la fin de la république et du début de l'empire en face de la religion," *Antiquité Classique* 41 (1972): 540–557, 541.

11. Howe, "The *religio* of Lucretius," *Classical Journal* 52 (1957): 329–33, 329.

12. Bouillard, "La Formation du concept de religion en Occident," *Humanisme et foi chrétienne. Mélanges scientifiques du centenaire de l'institut catholique de Paris* (Paris: Éditions Beauchesne, Belles Lettres, 1967), 451–61, esp. 453–54.

13. Despland, *La Religion en occident*, 23–40.

14. Fugier, *Recherches sur l'expression du sacré dans la langue Latine* (Paris: Éditions Beauchesne, Belles Lettres, 1963), 176–79.

15. Leibeschuetz, *Continuity and Change in Roman Religion* (Oxford: Clarendon Press, 1979), 10+n. 1.

16. Shield, *Roman Religion*, 23.

17. Ando, "Religion, Law and Knowledge," 1–2.

18. Irmscher, "Der Terminus *religio* und seine antiken Entsprechungen im philologischen und religionsgeschichtlichen Vergleich," in *The Notion of "Religion" in Comparative Research*, ed. Ugo Bianchi.; Selected Proceedings of the XVIth Congress of the International Association for the History of Religions Rome, 1994, 62–73.

19. "Vocabulaire Religieux" 41. Cf. Franz Altheim, *A History of Roman Religion*, trans. Harold Mattingly (New York: E. P. Dutton, 1937), 181, 270; L. Troiani: "La Religione e Cicerone," *Rivista Storica Italiana* (1984): 920–52, 923.

20. . . . *in perorando cohortabatur ut meminissem me et Cottam esse et pontificem; quod eo credo valebat, ut opiniones quas a maioribus accepimus de dis inmortalibus, sacra caerimonias religionesque defenderem. Ego vero eas defendam semper semperque defendi, nec me ex ea opinione quam a maioribus accepi de cultu deorum inmortalium ullius umquam oratio aut docti aut indocti movebit. Sed cum de religione agitur, Ti. Coruncanium P. Scipionem P. Scaevolam, pontifices maximos, non Zenonem aut Cleanthen aut Chrysippum sequor, habeoque C. Laelium augurem eundemque sapientem, quem potius audiam dicentem de religione in illa oratione nobili quam quemquam principem Stoicorum.*

21. The oration of Laelius that Cicero's Cotta praises here and in *De divinatione* is the one that the former delivered in 143 B.C.E. when he strongly opposed the proposal of C. Licinius Crassus to allow vacant seats in the priestly colleges to be filled by popular elections.

22. For Émile Benveniste, "religion" should be an instituton with a distinct sphere (*Le Vocabulaire des institutions indo-européens*, vol. II (Paris, 1969): 266. It is set apart. Cicero occasionally applies *religio* to places and things and activities set apart in cultures other than the Roman;

e.g., Cicero, *In Verrem* 2.4.94+111 [70 B.C.E.]. The statue of Apollo is called *beneficium Africani, religionem domesticam, ornamentum urbi* (ibid. 2.4.93)

23. *Quod in imperita multitudine est vitiosissimum, varietas et inconstantia et crebra tamquam tempestatum sic sententiarum commutatio, hoc tu ad hos transferas, quos ab inconstantia gravitas, a libidinosa sententia certum et definitum ius religionum, vetustas exemplorum, auctoritas litterarum monumentorumque deterret?*

24. The enemies of the republic and those who violate the laws of gods and men are sometimes visited with eternal punishment by Cicero's gods. Cf. Cicero, *In Catilinam* 1.33; *De republica* 6.26.29.

25. See C. Barton, "Being in the Eyes; Shame and Sight in Ancient Rome," in *The Roman Gaze*, ed. David Fredrick (Baltimore, Md.: Johns Hopkins University Press, 2002), 216–35.

26. For an exhaustive treatment of the very relevant Latin notions of *disciplina*, see Otto Mauch, *Der lateinische Begriff Disciplina*, diss. Freiburg, 1941, esp. 14–82. I will be dealing extensively with the concept of discipline in the chapters herein (4–7) on the Christian Tertullian.

27. "Cicero and Divination: The Formulation of a Latin Discourse," *Journal of Roman Studies* 76 (1986): 33–46, 36; cf. 45–46.

28. Graydon F. Snyder remarks that "extensive, forcible literary discussion regarding a sign would necessarily imply an attempt to alter its meaning. One thinks, for example, of Tertullian discussion of the crown symbol" (*De corona* 14.15) (*Ante Pacem*; *Archaeological Evidence of Church Life Before Constantine* (Macon, Geo.: Mercer University Press, 2003) [1985]).

It is important to note that there were no attempts to define or to abstract and generalize concerning Roman *religio* or the *respublica* apart from the philosophical works of Cicero and Varro. It was the very process of generalizing and abstracting that constituted Cicero's *ratio religionis* (*De natura deorum* 3.2.6), and that created covering categories of analysis such as *religio* and *superstitio*.

29. The ancient systems of bargaining and reciprocity that gave rise to the Latin notion of *religio* will live on almost unchanged in the cult of the dead even in post-Constantinian Empire with its superstructure of Christian ideology.

30. "*Religio* und *Superstitio*," 92. Cf. Ando, "Introduction: Religion, Law and Knowledge in Classical Rome," in *Roman Religion*, ed. Ando (Edinburgh, UK: Edinburgh University Press, 2003), 1–15, 2.

31. "*Religio/Superstitio*: historique d'une subversion et d'un retournement." *Revue de l'Histoire des Religions* 208 (1991): 367.

32. *Religion und Philosophie bei den Romern* (Berlin: Franckhische Verlagshandlung, 1866), 9.

33. Editor of the *Oxford Latin Dictionary* (1982).

34. Gaston Boissier, *La Religion Romaine d'Auguste aux Antonins*, vol. I (Paris: Hachette, 1900): 21; Warde Fowler, "The Latin History of the Word *Religio*," *Third International Congress for the History of Religions* (Oxford: Clarendon Press, 1908), 169–175; Georges Dumézil, *Les dieux des Indo-Européens* (Paris: Presses Universitaires, 1952), 130; Otto, "*Religio* und *Superstitio*," *Aufsätze zur Römischen Religionsgeschichte*, Meisenheim am Glan, 1975, 92–130 = *Archiv für Religionswissenschaft* 12 (1909): 532–54 and 14 (1911): 406–22, 534+537; Benveniste, *Le Vocabulaire des institutions indo-européennes*, vol. II (Paris: Éditions de Minuit, 1969), 270–72. The treatment of *religio* in the *Oxford Latin Dictionary* (1982) is a great improvement in complexity over Lewis and Short's Latin dictionary, but it is to be remarked that its focus is still overwhelmingly on Cicero and later authors.

35. Stanley Pease, *M. Tulli Ciceronis De Natura Deorum*, vol. II (New York: Arno, 1979), 574.

36. Kätzler, "*Religio*. Versuch einer Worterklärung," *Jahresbericht des bischöflichen Gymnasiums Paulinum in Schwaz* 20 (1952–1953): 2–18, 2–4. For more on the inhibiting aspects of Roman *religio*, see M. Kobbert, *De verborum religio atque religiosus usu apud Romanos* (1910), 42–48; R. Mulder, *De conscientiae notione quae et qualis fuerit Romanis* (Leiden: E. J. Brill (1908), 51–61; F. de Visscher,

Le Droit des tombeaux romains (Milan: Giuffré, 1963), 45; Benveniste, *Vocabulaire*, esp. 270; R. Schilling, "*Vocabulaire religieux Latin*," esp. 39–43.

37. Sabbatucci, "*Sacer*," *Studi e materiali di storia delle religioni* 23 (1951–1952): 91–101, 99.

38. Wissowa, *Religion und Kultus der Römer* (Munich: C. H. Beck, 1902), 318.

39. A. Ernout and A. Meillet, *Dictionnaire Étymologique de la Langue Latine*, 4th ed., (Paris: Klincksieck, 1985 [1932]), 569.

40. Bayet, *Histoire politique et psychologique de la religion romaine* (Paris: Pavot, 1969), 59.

41. Schilling, "*Vocabulaire religieux*," p. 94.

42. Belayche, "Religious Actors in Daily Life," *A Companion to Roman Religion*, ed. Jörg Rupke (Oxford: Blackwell, 2007), 275–91, 279.

43. Fugier, *Expression du sacré*, 177; J. Sheid, *An Introduction to Roman Religion*, trans. Janet Lloyd (Bloomington: Indiana University Press, 2003), 22–23; Rüpke, art. "Religion: Roman," *Brill's New Pauly*, vol. 12 (Leiden/Boston: Brill, 2008), col. 490; Turcan, *Religion Romaine*, vol. 2: *Le culte* (Leiden/New York: Brill, 1988), 3–4. For many scholars of the nineteenth and early twentieth century, it was exactly the protomonotheism or proto-Christianity that they found most praiseworthy in Cicero. For Eli Burriss, for example, Cicero's greatest value was his commitment to "a Divine Power not unlike our own God." He begins with a Ciceronian definition of "religion" that has all the elements of nineteenth and early twentieth century "religion": (1) "the acknowledgment of a Being superior to man; (2) the necessity of coming into right relations with that Being through proper ceremonies; (3) a feeling of regard for the Being thus worshipped—a definition which should satisfy the most exacting" ("Cicero and the Religion of His Day," *The Classical Journal* 21 [1926]: 524–32, 524, 527–28).

44. "By this bond of piety we are tied and fastened to God; whence *religio* takes its name, not, as Cicero interpreted, from *relegendo*. . . ." (*Hoc vinculo pietatis obstricti deo et religati sumus; unde ipsa religio nomen accepit, non ut Cicero interpretatus est, a relegendo . . . [Divinae institutiones 4.28]*). Compare Isidore's version: "*Religio* is so called because through it we bind (*religare*) by the chain of service our souls to the one God for the purpose of divine worship" (*Etymologiae 8.2*). Interestingly, Isidore also links *religio* to *relegere*, interpreting *relegere* as the equivalent of *eligere*, *religio* of *eligio*.

45. Liebeschuetz, *Continuity and Change in Roman Religion* (Oxford: Clarendon Press, 1979), 60; cf. "The Religious Position of Livy's History," *Journal of Roman Studies* 57 (1967): 45–55, 46 n. 11, 48 n. 46. "During the Republic Roman religious belief was based on rigorous observance: it had no emotional heart or set of prescribed beliefs" (Keay, *Roman Spain* [Berkeley: University of California Press, 1988] 145). "In Rome, people had always steered clear of imagination and the surge of emotions in religious matters . . ." (Robert Turcan, *The Gods of Ancient Rome* [New York: Routledge, 2001], 11). "In the Roman religion . . . [t]he only religious requirement was the strict observance of rituals, and all manifestation of emotion was excluded from the religious domain" (M. Linder, and J. Scheid, "Quand croire c'est faire. Le problème de la croyance dans la Rome ancienne," *Archives de Sciences Sociales des Religions* 81 [1993]: 47–62, 47).

46. Mommsen, *The History of Rome*, trans. William Purdie Dickson (New York, 1886, vol. I), 224. "True religion is, first of all, closeness to God. Every religious ceremony is but empty make-believe if the faithful who participate in it do not feel that thirst for the Absolute, that anxious desire to enter into personal contact with the Mysterious Being who is hidden behind appearances" (André-Jean Festugière, *Personal Religion Among the Greeks* [Berkeley: University of California Press, 1954], 1). For Festugière, the "religious man" was filled with love and longing for, and dependence on "a Being who exists in all perfection and splendor."

47. Cumont, *The Oriental Religions in Roman Paganism*, trans. Grant Showerman (Chicago: Open Court, 1911), 28–29. The last two passages are mentioned at the beginning of Warde Fowler's *The Religious Experience of the Roman People* (London: Macmillan, 1911), 2–3 and appear again in John Scheid's *An Introduction to Roman Religion*, trans. Janet Lloyd (Bloomington: Indiana University Press, 2003), 7.

48. "Those who [in contrast to the *superstitiosi*] carefully reviewed and so to speak retraced all that had to do with the cult of the gods were called *religiosi* from *relegere*." (*Qui omnia quae ad cultum deorum pertinerent diligenter retractarent et tamquam relegerent, <hi> sunt dicti religiosi, ex religendo*.) I believe that Cicero, in conceiving this etymology, was responding to the common associations of *religio* with "reasoning" and "having second thoughts." [Compare Cicero's derivation of *lex* from *legere* (*De legibus* 1.6.19, 2.5.11).] See Benveniste, op. cit. 268, 271–72. Those who subscribe to this etymology sometimes point out the opposition between *relegere* and *neglegere* (e.g., Benveniste, op. cit. 271; Altheim, *History of Roman Religion* (New York: E. P. Dulton), 355; Carl Koch, *Religio; Studien zu Kult und Glauben der Römer* (Nurenberg: H. Carl, 1960), 100; P. Boyancé, *La Religion de Virgile* (Paris: Presses Universitaires, 1963), 73; Fugier, *Expression du sacré*, 176–77; cf. Varro, *Antiquitates Rerum Divinarum* 1 frag. 2a Cardauns = Augustine, *De civitate dei* 6.2; Fugier, *Expression du sacré* 178 + n. 72. The first-century c.e. legal scholar Masurius Sabinus offered still another etymology, deriving *religio* from *relinquere*, reckoning that "*religio-sum est quod propter sanctitatem aliquam remotum ac sepositum a nobis . . .*" (Aulus Gellius 4.9.8). Macrobius attributes this same etymology to Servius Sulpicius—perhaps Servius Sulpicius Rufus, the legal scholar and friend of Cicero (3.3.8).

49. Sachot ("*Religio/Superstitio*," 365) points out that the only other author apart from Cicero linking *religio* to *relegere* was Nigidius Figulus, the same who explained *religiosus* as "being *bound* by an extreme and *supersitiosa religio*" (Gellius, *Noctes Atticae* 4.9.2). [I will return to this passage in another context.] For surveys of the problems created by the various etymologies of *religio* surviving from ancient Latin sources, see Otto, "*Religio und Superstitio*," *Archiv für Religionswis-senschaft* vol. 12 (1909), 533; vol. 14 (1911), 406; Ernout et Meillet, *Dictionnaire*, 569; Benveniste, *Vocabulaire* vol. II, 268; Kätzler, "*Religio*," 2; Henry Toomey Wilt, *Religio; A Semantic Study of the Pre-Christian Use of the Terms Religio and Religiosus*, diss. Columbia University, 1954, esp. 1–30, 124–28; G. Lieberg, "Considerazioni sull'etimologia e sul significato de *religio*," *Rivista di Filologia e di Istruzione Classica* 102 (1974), 34–57; Lawrence A. Springer, "The Role of *religio, solvo* and *ratio* in Lucretius," *Classical World* 71 (1977), 55–61 esp. 57 n. 17; Hubert Petersmann, "Εὐσέβεια, θρησκεία et *religio*," *Lingua et Religio* (Göttingen: Vanderhoeck & Ruprecht, 2007), 48–56; Axel Bergmann, *Die 'Grundbedeutung' des lateinischen Wortes Religio* (Marburg: Diagonal-Verlag, 1998). There is neither enough evidence to decide between the possibilities, nor is it necessary to do so. Ancient etymologies are often most useful as evidence of the types of mental and verbal associa-tions made by their authors. The Latin etymologies made by modern scholars are often as revealing of their prejudices as the ancient.

50. See Wilt's excellent discussion of this and the following passage of Plautus (*Religio* 54–60), a discussion vitiated by his insistence that every instance of *religio* be translated in accordance with Greek *alego*, "having regard for." That *religio* implies paying attention (as Altheim frequently observed in his *History of Roman Religion*) is certainly correct, but *religio* embraces many emotions and behaviors that are not sufficiently covered by Altheim and Wilt's "attention." Wilt observes, correctly, that Charinus has been in difficulties from which he has again and again tried to free himself. He is tense and alert. The whole section begins with the words "*qui me revocat?*" (867). "The whole tone of this passage is one of checking, restraining and persuading. Charinus intends to do one thing but is persuaded by Eutychus to do the opposite. (. . .) The words and phrases that Eutychus uses effect a restraining and a stopping, a looking back, a reconsidering and a going back by Charinus to the direction opposite in which he was first going. (. . .) [*Religio* seems] "something like a restraint arising from the commands '*huc respice*' '*revortere*' '*huc prosperes*' '*cape versoriam*' '*recipe te*' and '*huc*' and '*hic*' which are repeated several times" (*Religio*, 56–57).

51. *obiecere religionem.*

52. *Iratus Flacco dixit M. Lurco. . . . Nihil dixit quod laederet eum, cum cuperet; impediebat enim religio; tamen id quod dixit quanto pudore, quo tremore et pallore dixit!*

53. *Ibi cum velut saeptos montium altitudo teneret Gallos circumspectarentque quanam per iucta caelo iuga in alium orbem terrarum transirent, religio etiam tenuit quod allatum est advenas quaerentes agrum ab Saluum gente oppugnari.* "The praetors set out for their assignments [208 B.C.E.], but *religio* detained the consuls because, when a number of prodigies were announced, they did not easily obtain favorable indications (*litationes*)." (*Praetores in provincias profecti; consules religio tenebat, quod prodigiis aliquot nuntiatis non facile litabant.*

54. It is the restraint, the stopping before something or someone *set apart* that caused *religio* to be associated with things, persons, places and times that were highly sacralized. Indeed, nothing could be sacralized without *religio*. "It is a common custom for the *religiosi* among travelers, when they come upon some grove (*lucus*) or sacred place (*locus sanctus*), to ask for a favor (*votum postulare*), offer up a piece of fruit, and sit down for a while. (. . .) For the traveler can find no fitter motives for a *religiosus* pause/delay (*religiosam moram*) than an altar decked with flowers, or a grotto shaded with foliage, or an oak loaded with horns, or a beech crowned with skins, or even a consecrated (*consecratus*) and enclosed hillock, or a trunk chiseled into the form of an image, or a turf redolent of libation, or a stone bedewed with ointment" (Apuleius, *Florida* 1.1).

55. See the upcoming discussion of "taboo."

56. For example, "Learned men . . . subject everything to a minute and scrupulous inquiry" (*minutius et scrupulosius scrutantur omnia* [Quintilian, *Institutio oratoria* 5.14.28]).

57. "Those bound by their oaths ought to issue judgments with more *religio*" (*qui iurati statuere maiore cum religione et diligentia debuerunt* [Cicero, *Pro Cluentio* 43.121]). For the connection of *religio* with "scruples," see especially Fowler, "The Latin History of the Word *religio*," 170; Benveniste, *Vocabulaire* vol. II, 269–71; Boyancé, *Religion de Virgile*, 73; Sachot, "*Religio/Superstitio*," 366–67, 370.

58. *The Other Greeks; The Family Farm and the Agrarian Roots of Western Civilization*, (New York: Free Press, 1995), 72, 136–37. Hanson's account of the endless anxious cautiousness and necessary self-reliance of the small farmer is acute and rich in detail. Cf. 43, 47–90, 138–67. Hanson talks about the "utilitarianism" of the small farmer: "utilitarianism in the sense of doing everything he can do to preserve his small farm from the disasters, natural and man-induced, that daily threatened his existence" (ibid., 134). The wives and children, like the slaves, the wagon, the livestock and the dog were all precious tools (ibid., 134–35). I would add that the gods were also, in this universe, unashamedly instrumental. Hanson, in his detailed descriptions of Greek farming life, repeatedly emphasizes notions of balancing, maintaining the mean that was also central to the life of Roman farmers who lived in a world of carefully apportioned limited "goods" (e.g., 166–67, cf. 108–10).

59. Hanson, op. cit., 156. Plato spoke of "the fears of farmers" (*Leges* 10.906E); cf. Hanson, op. cit., 162. For the nervousness, distrustful, diffident alertness, fearfulness, and duplicity of the peasant farmer and their justifications, see George M. Foster, "Peasant Character and Personality," 296–323, and Michael Maccoby, "Love and Authority: A Study of Mexican Villagers," 336–46 (both in *Peasant Society; A Reader*, Jack M. Potter, May N. Diaz and George M. Foster [Boston: Little Brown, 1967]). This nervous anxiety and the reasons for it are brilliantly depicted in Akira Kurasawa's film "*Seven Samurai*" (1957).

60. Hanson, op. cit., 176.

61. The priests and magistrates of the state will try, over time, to maximize the dependency and powerlessness of the citizens and so focus, limit, and direct their attention and energies. Hanson: "Never have I encountered a farmer who could believe long (and many have wished to, as I can attest) in big government, centralized control, benign bureaucracy" (*The Other Greeks*, 31). "The net result of bureaucratization was the creation of vulnerable dependence and a restriction of agricultural expertise" (loc. cit.). The farmer tended to be as careful and conservative as possible, relying on the maintenance and repetition of hitherto successful behaviors and rites.

62. "Artisans and peasants, whose *res* and *fides* are in their hands." (*opifices agrestesque omnes, quorum res fidesque in manibus sitae erant* [Sallust, *Bellum Iugurthunum* 73.6].)

63. E. R. Dodds, talking about the life of the ancient Greek farmer says, "It is a pattern of anxiety punctuated by relief" ("The Religion of the Ordinary Man in Classical Greece," in *The Ancient Concept of Progress and Other Essays* [Oxford: Clarendon Press, 1973], 140–55, 146; cf. all of 146–52).

64. Turcan, *Religion Romaine*, 3–4.

65. Occasionally, *religiosus* is used to describe someone whose actions are characterized by this scrupulous care and attention. "In worshipping we raise our right hand to our lips and turn around our whole body, the Gauls considering it more *religiosus* to turn to the left." (*In adorando dextram ad osculum referimus totumque corpus circumagimus, quod in laevum fecisse Galliae religiosus credunt* [Pliny, *Naturalis Historia* 28.5.25].)

66. Another (unfortunately corrupt and restored) passage of Accius preserved in Nonius (566 Lindsay) seems to reflect the identity of *religio* and "scruple": "Now Calchas, make an end of/put a limit to your *religio*. Cease to delay the army; do not hinder me from going home with your awful/ill-boding sign." (*Nunc, Calcha, finem religionum fac, desiste exercitum morari nec me ab domuitione arcere tuo obsceno omine* [*Astyanax* fr. 136–37, Warmington].)

67. We might say "with a clear conscience," but *conscientia* is still overwhelmingly "guilt" in the republic. Cf. Barton, *Roman Honor*, passim esp. 280–81, 284.

68. **Davos:** *Mysis, nunc opus est tua mihi ad hanc rem exprompta malitia atque astutia.*

Mysis: *Quidnam incepturu's?*
Davos: *Accipe a me hunc ocius atque ante nostram ianuam adpone.*
Mysis: *Obsecro, humine?*
Davos: *Ex ara hinc sume verbenas tibi atque eas substerne.*
Mysis: *Quam ob rem id tute non facis?*
Davos: *Quia, si forte opus sit ad erum iurato mihi non adposisse, ut liquido possim.*
Mysis: *Intellego:nova nunc religio in te istaec incessit. cedo!*

69. **Simo:** *Ne istam multimodis tuam inveniri gaudeo.*
Pamphilus: *Credo, pater.*
Chremes: *At scrupulus mi etiam unus restat.*
Pamphilus: *In malum rem ut dignus es cum tua religione, odium: nodum in scirpo quaeris.*

70. Sargeaunt's trans.: "I have scruples about owning that I haven't a penny."

71. *Admirationem deinde auxit signo receptui dato adeo tranquilla serenitas reddita ut velut numine aliquo defensa castra oppugnare iterum religio fuerit.*

72. In Livy's story of the *devotio* of Publius Decius Mus (8.9), the soldiers of Decius' faltering wing, "their spirits freed from *religio*," are able to fight with renewed vigor. We do not know what caused them to soldiers of Decius' wing to be hesitant in their encounter with the Latins (most probably that they were fighting with bad omens), but the expiatory sacrifice of their general freed them from fear and hesitation.

73. *Iam ante in eo religio civitatis apparuerat quod cum in publico deesset aurum, ex quo summa pactae mercedis Gallis confieret, a matronis conlatum acceperant ut sacro auro abstineretur.*

74. "When, in friendship, requests are submitted that are not *honesta*, let *religio* (scrupulousness/honor) and *fides* take precedence over [the obligations of] friendship." (*Cum . . . in amicitia, quae honesta non sunt, postulantabuntur, religio et fides anteponature amicitiae* [Cicero, *De officiis* 3.10.46].) "And yet, while we should never persecute the innocent, we need not consider it an offense against our sense of honor/scrupulousness (*religioni nocentem*) to undertake on occasion the defense of a guilty person, provided he is not infamously depraved and *impium*." (*Nec tamen, ut hoc fugiendum est, item est habendum religioni nocentem aliquando modo ne nefarium impiumque* [Cicero, *De* officiis 2.14.51].) Cf. Livy 5.13.4–8.

75. *Incessit dein religio quonam in templo locandum foret donum quod pro valetudine Augustae equites Romani voverant equestri Fortunae: nam etsi delubra eius deae multa in urbe, nullum tamen tali cognomento erat. Repertum est aedem esse apud Antium quae sic nuncuparetur cuntasque caeremonias Italicis in oppidis templaque et numinum effigies iuris atque imperii Romani esse. Ita donum apud Antium statuitur.* Apuleius still has something he calls a *religiosum scrupulum*, but he is already operating in a new thought world (*Metamorphoses* 11.26–27).

76. *Antequam digrediamur a Scythia, religio est praeterire quaenam peculiares sint ferae Scythiae.*

77. On *religio* and taboo, see especially Kobbert, "*Religio*," 53; Otto, "*Religio und Superstitio*," 418–20; Warde Fowler, "The Latin History of the Word *religio*," 169–75. On the notion of taboo, see Valerio Valeri, *The Forest of Taboos* (Madison, Wisc.: University of Wisconsin Press, 2000), esp. xxii and n. 1; 43–112; Sigmund Freud, *Totem and Taboo*, vol 13. of *The Standard Edition of the Complete Psychological Works of Sigmund Freud*, ed. and trans. James Strachey (London: Hogarth Press, 1958); Franz Steiner, *Taboo* (Harmondsworth: Penguin, 1967 [1956]); E. M. Zuesse, "Taboo and the Divine Order," *Journal of the American Academy of Religion* 42(3), (1974): 482–504; A. R. Radcliffe-Brown, "Taboo" in *Structure and Function in Primitive Society* (New York: Free Press, 1965), 133–52.

78. *Salinum cum sale in mensa ponere figulis religioni habetur.*

79. *Iam tanta religio est sepulchrorum, ut extra sacra et gentem inferri fas negent esse. . . .*

80. According to Cicero's Pythagoras, "Men feel most full of *religio* (awe, hesitation, restraint) when they are in temples" (*De legibus* 2.10.26). Linking the emotion of *religio* to the temple and so to the gods will enable Cicero to describe awe *of the gods* as *religio*.

81. *Miror audere atque religione non teneri, statuas deorum, exempla eorum facierum, signa domi pro supellectile statuere* (=H. Malcovati, *Oratorum Romanorum Fragmenta⁴*, vol. I [Turin: Paravia, 1976 (1930)] fr. 71).

82. *Creati censores C. Sulpicius Camerinus Sp. Postumius Regillensis, coeptaque iam res morte Postumi, quia collegam suffici censori religio erat. Igitur cum Sulpicius abdicasset se magistratu censores alii vitio creati non gesserunt magistratum; tertios creari velut dis non accipientibus in eum annum censuram religiosum fuit.*

83. *Fuere qui profiscenti Othoni moras religionemque nondum conditorum ancilium adferrent.*

84. *Equo Dialem flaminem vehi religio est. Item religio est "classem procinctam" extra pomerium (. . .) Locum in quo bustum est numquam ingreditur, mortuum numquam attigit; funus tamen exequi non est religio.* Gellius uses *religio est* as synonymoua for *nefas*, *fas non est*, *ius non est*, and *licitum non est*.

85. *Religio id est metus ab eo quod mentem religet dicta religio.* Again Servius: *omnis religio sit timoris* (*Ad Aeneidem* 12.139). Servius, *ad Aeneidem* 2.715: "*Religione patrum*" timore; *et est reciprocum. Sic Terentius: "nam mihi nihil esse, religio est dicere," id est metus; item Vergilius contra* (7.60): "*multosque metu servata per annos.*" *Connexa enim sunt timor et religio ut Statius: "primus in orbe deos fecit timor.*" Cf. Lucretius' *timefactae religiones* (*De rerum natura* 2.44).

86. =H. Meyer, *Oratorum Romanorum Fragmenta* (Turin), 1842, 62 =Henricus Iordan ed., *M. Catonis praeter librum de re rustica quae exstant* (Stuttgart: Teubner, 1967 [1860]), 60.

87. For example, Cicero, *De officiis* 2.1.2. Schilling remarks on "*la difficulté qu'éprouvaient les Anciens à distinguer le contenu* objectif [emphasis in original] *de ses incidences subjectives: quand ils traitaient de* la réalité [emphasis mine] *ils songaient au concept de ligare, quand ils évoquaient l'aspect psychologiqe de la* religio *et du* religiosus, *ils se réferaient à* relegere . . ." (95–96).

88. *magnam vim, magnam necessitatem, magnam possidet religionem paternus maternus sanguis; ex quo si qua macula concepta est, non modo elui non potest, verum usque eo permanat ad animam, ut summus furor atque amentia consequatur.*

89. Both *pathos* and *adfectus* could mean the emotion or the words that evoked that emotion. Cf. Macrobius, *Saturnalia* 4.2.4: *pathos est et in hoc versu.*

90. For example, Cicero, *De officiis* 1.42.150–51; cf. 1.8.28. *Veritas* can be the feeling of sureness, confidence, security and whatever gives one that feeling, both the emotion and the

actions, things, ideas eliciting that emotion. Cicero, *De officiis* 1.7.23: "The foundation of *iustitia* is *fides*—that is, *constantia* and *veritas* (sincerity, firmness, dependability) with regard to one's word and one's contracts. Therefore we dare to follow the Stoics who diligently inquire into the derivation of words and accept their notion (although it may seem a bit rude to some) that *fides* is so called because what is affirmed is effected." (*Fundamentum autem est iustitiae fides, id est dictorum conventorumque constantia et veritas. Ex quo, quamquam hoc videbitur fortasse cuipiam durius, tamen audeamus imitari Stoicos, qui studiose exquirunt, unde verba sint ducta, credeamus, quia fiat, quod dictum est, appelatam fidem.*) In *De inventione* 2.22.65 + 2.53.161, Cicero listed *veritas* among the emotions that bound and obliged: "The law of nature is something which is implanted in us not by opinion, but by a kind of innate instinct; it includes *religio, pietas, gratia, vindicatio, observantia* and *veritas.*" (*As naturae quidem ius esse, quod nobis non opinio, sed quaedam innata vis adferat, ut religionem, pietate, gratiam, vindicationem, observantiam, veritatem.*) He goes on (in 2.22.66 + 2.53.161) to explain each of these emotions: "*veritas* . . . by which we take care that nothing could do anything but confirm . . . ." (*veritatem, per quam damus operam, ne quid aliter quam confirmaverimus fiat aut factum aut futurum sit* [2.22.66].)

91. *Religio* as the word for a stricture, bond or obligation, treaty or oath is so frequent in the civil war period and after that I can only give a sample of citation: Cicero, *De natura deorum* 2.3.8; *De inventione* 2.55.168; *Pro Balbo* 5.12; 15.34; *De domo suo* 15.41, 51.107; *De legibus* 2.7.15; *Philippicae* 1.6.13; Caesar, *De bello civile* 1.11, 1.67; Seneca, *Epistulae* 95.35; Pliny, *Naturalis Historia* 25.11.30; 30.14.42.

92. *Hac evolsa scrobem repleri vario genere frugum religio est ac terrae piamentum.*

93. The "chicken and egg" dispute between Otto and Kobbert over which came first—the numinous object or the emotions of fear and reverence (Otto, "*Religio* und *Superstitio*," 95; Kobbert, "*Religio*," 2) is, in part, a result of the mirrored values in ancient Roman *religio*. But whether modern scholars emphasize the primacy of the emotions of respect or fear or the object of that respect or fear depends, necessarily, on the degree to which they want to give an independent and original existence to "The Numinous," "The Transcendent," or "God." Otto believed that *religio* arose from the fear inspired by the "numinous" object. Kobbert believed that the emotions were ascribed to the object. Our "religion" (as opposed to Roman *religio*) demands the prior existence and ascendency, if not transcendency, of the object of devotion and obedience.

94. Apulieus writing in the 160's c.e. in *De deo socratis* 148 remarks, in speaking of the *daemones* to whom humans render cultic rites: "Hence, as a consequence of the different attentions/careful observances [of rules, practices] of *religiones* and the various offerings of *sacra*, we should believe that there are some of this class of *divi* who take pleasure in the various sacrifices, ceremonies, and rites which take place by night or day, publicly or secretly, with comparative joy or sorrow." (*Unde etiam religionum diversis observationibus et sacrorum variis suppliciis fides inpertienda est. et sunt nonnulli ex hoc divorum numero, qui nocturnis vel diurnis, promptis vel occultis, laetioribus ver tristioribus hostiis vel caerimoniis vel ritibus gaudeant.*) Apuleius here links *religiones* with *observationes*. Latin *observatio* includes observing, paying attention to, watching as a precaution, keeping an eye on, careful punctiliousness, deferential attention, and practice.

95. *Scelus* was the violation of a *religio* or "taboo," a wicked or accursed act, a crime *and* the curse or misfortune resulting from the transgression. The *vicus sceleratus*, for example, was the road where Tullia, daughter of Servius Tullius, drove over her father's corpse (Varro, *De Lingua Latina* 5.159; Livy 1.48.7; Ovid, *Fasti* 6.609; Hyginus, *Fabulae* 255; Paulus Festus 451 Lindsay). The *campus sceleratus* was the place near the Colline Gate where unchaste Vestals were buried alive (Livy 8.15.8; Paulus/Festus 449 Lindsay). The *porta scelerata* was a name for the *Porta Carmentalis* through which the 300 Fabii marched to their doom in 477 b.c.e. (Paulus/Festus 451 Lindsay; Silius Italicus, *Punica,* 7.48; Florus 1.6 [1.12.1]). The camp in which Claudius Drusus died was afterwards the *castra scelerata* (Suetonius, *Claudius* 1.3). Among the miserable and accursed parents were the *Mater Scelerata* (*Corpus Inscriptionum Latinarum* 6.15160) and the *Parentes Scelerati* (*Corpus Inscriptionum Latinarum* 6.35769).

96. For *haerere . . . religionem*, see Cicero, *De divinatione* 1.30: *ut peccatum haereat . . . in eo qui non obtemperarit*; *Pro Quincto Roscio* 17; *religione civitatem obstrinxisse* (*De oratore* 2.66.268).

97. *Ambulatio postes nemo umquam tenuit in dedicando: simulacrum autem aut aram si dedicasti, sine religione loco moveri potest.* Cf. Cicero, *In Verrem* 2.4.51.113.

98. Examples of similar uses of *religio* in Livy: 9.8.6+14; 9.9.3; 25.1.6–12, 27.37.1–5, 36.1.1–5, 40.47.8. Muldor points out that respect for bonds was not incompatible with the feeling of a pure or free "conscience"; it was only the crossing of the boundaries that made a Roman *conscius*: "*Ut capra, vinculo alligata, id fere non sentit, pascens, quatenus vinculum permittit, tum vero, cum terminos excedit, sentit, sic etiam Romani cohibentes sese certis legibus finibus, . . . vinculorum sibi non conscii erant, tum vero, cum terminos excedebant, religione impediebatur*" (*De Conscientiae notione* 57 n. 3).

99. *Ac ne qua religio deum impune contaminaretur, monimentum, quod libertus eius e lapidibus templo Capitolini Iovis destinatis filio exstruxerat, diruit per milites ossaque et reliquias quae inerant mari mersit.* For *religio* as guilt, see especially Wilt, *Religio*, 85.

100. *Homo sacer is est quem populus iudicavit ob maleficium.*

101. According to Livy, the plebs in 449 sanctioned a law to the effect that the "head" (i.e., life) of whoever should harm the tribune of the plebs, the plebeian aediles, or the decemviral judges would be "sacred" to Jupiter and that his wealth would be sold at the temple of Ceres, Liber, and Libera. (*ut . . . eius caput Iovi sacrum esset, familia ad aedem Cereris Liberi Liberaque venum iret* [Livy 3.55.7; cf. Dionysius 2.10.3].) Cf. C. Barton, "Between the Axe and the Altar: The Relationship of Sacrifices and Executions in Ancient Rome" (in preparation). Like the treaty-breaker, the slave or dependent son, the domesticated animal who transgressed was liable to *noxae deditio*, being handed over to the one offended ([*caper*] *noxae tibi deditus hostis . . . Bacche*). Ovid has the gods, beginning with Ceres, avenging the crimes committed by animals against the vegetation under their protection ([*Ceres*] *ulta suas opes*). The gods require the execution/sacrifice of the pigs who damage or threaten the grain of Ceres (*sus dederat poenas*) and the goats who gnaw at the vines of Liber/Bacchus. The pig and the goat deserve their deaths (*merita caede*), but, Ovid asks, what crime did the ox or the lamb commit? (*Fasti* 349–62).

102. Warde Fowler, "The Original Meaning of the Word *Sacer*," *Journal of Roman Studies* 1 (1911), 57–63; H. Bennett, "*Sacer Esto*," *Transactions and Proceedings of the American Philological Association* 61 (1930), 5–18; A. Ernout and A. Meillet, art. "*sacer*," *Dictionnaire étymologique de la langue Latine*, 585–87, 586; D. Sabbatucci, "*Sacer*," *Studi e materiali di storia delle religioni* 23 (1951/1952), 91–101; Joël Le Gall, *Recherches sur le culte du Tibre* (Paris: Presses Universitaires, 1953), esp. Chapter VII ("In Tiberim"), 83–95; Fugier, *Recherches*, 224–39.

103. But notice the notion of contagious guilt. Gracchus' *religio* might infect the whole of the Roman people.

104. Phrases meaning freedom or release from *religio* (*religione solvere, levare*, or *liberare*) occur often in Livy. For example, 9.8.6 *exsolvamus religione populum*; 9.8.14: *exsolvi religione populum*; 39.16.7: *religione liberare*.

105. *Praedo . . . qui cum fana spoliasset, deinde aram aliquam in littore deserto somniis stimulatis aut religione aliqua consecraret, . . . horreret animo, cum divinum numen scelere violatum placare precibus cogeretur. . . .*

106. = *C. Lucilii carminum reliquiae*, ed. F. Marx, vol. I, 51.

107. Wissowa, *Religion und Kultus*, 187, believes that this passage refers to the days of the Parentalia in the second half of February.

108. *dum tamen haec fiunt, viduae cessate puellae:/(. . .)/ conde tuas, Hymenaee, faces et an ignibus atris/aufer!(. . .)/ di quoque templorum foribus celentur opertis./ ture vacent arae stentque sine ingen foci./ nunc animae tenues et corpora functa sepulcris/ errant, nunc posito pascitur umbra cibo.*

109. "The place deep within the temple of Vesta, fenced off with rushes, is called the *penus*, which is opened on designated days at the time of the Vestalia. Those days are considered

religiosi." (*<Penus v>ocatur locus intimus in aede Vestae tegetibus saeptus, qui certis diebus circa Vestalia aperitur. I dies religiosi habentur* [Festus, s.v. *"Penus,"* Lindsay, 296].)

110. *Maiores nostri funestiorem diem esse voluerunt Aliensis pugnae quam urbis captae, quod hoc malum ex illo: itaque alter religiosus etiamnunc dies, alter in vulgus ignotus.* The day which, by calendrical coincidence, marked both the defeat at the Cremera in 477 and the Roman defeat by the Gauls at Allia in 390 was still considered ill-omened and unsuitable for the performance of *caerimoniae publicae* in the late republic and early Empire (cf. Livy, 6.1 ff; Suetonius, *Vitellius* 11, Tacitus, *Historiae* 2.91).

111. Wissowa, *Religion und Kultus,* 376–77.

112. Gellius goes on to quote Cicero, *Ad Atticum* 9.5.2. According to Livy, "Some think that because Sulpicius, on the day after the ides of July, made a sacrifice that was not accepted by the gods (*non litasset*), and two days later, without having gained divine approval, exposed the Roman army to the enemy, that therefore *res divinae* were omitted also on the days after the several Ides and that afterwards it became traditional that the morrow after Kalends and Nones should likewise be avoided from the same *religio."* (*Quidem, quod postridie Idus Quintiles non litasset Sulpicius tribunus militum neque inventa pace deum post diem tertium obiectus hosti exercitus Romanus eset, etiam postridie Idus rebus divinis supersederi iussum; inde, ut postridie Kalendas quoque ac Nonas eadem religio esset, traditum putant* [6.1.12].) Here scruple, fear, and curse are all entailed.

113. *Tum de diebus religiosis agitari coeptum, diemque a.d. XV Kal. Sextiles, duplici clade insignem, quo die ad Cremeram Fabii caesi, quo deinde ad Alliam cum exito urbis foede pugnatum, a posteriore clade Alliensem appellarunt reique nullius publice privatimque agendae fecerunt.*

114. Compare the way in which, since the Early Modern Period, the beatification of a Catholic saint by the Vatican "authorizes," traditions made without reference to the will of the Pope. The history of the papal "ratification," "sanctification" of the "saints" is a close parallel to the developments I am trying to sketch out in this chapter. For appropriating or "high-jacking" the power to sanctify individual humans, see Kenneth L. Woodward, *Making Saints* (New York: Simon & Schuster, 1990); Anna L. Peterson, *Martyrdom and the Politics of Religion* (Albany: State University of New York Press, 1997).

115. See Chapter 2, "The Ciceronian Turn." Rüpke is wrong in ascribing the origins of *religio* to legal attributions of property. He is thinking of passages such as the following: "[The] many graves in that place [outside the Colline Gates] . . . were dug up; for the college of pontiffs decided that a place which was public property could not *privata religione obligari."* (*Sed cum multa in eo loco sepulchra fuissent, exarata sunt; statuit enim collegium locum publicum non potuisse privata religione obligari* [Cicero, *De legibus* 2.58].)

116. Negative sacralizing/execrating involved involuntary binding/sacralizing which cancelled the will, the *animus.*

117. These ideas are most beautifully articulated by Herbert Fingarette in his little book *Confucius, The Secular as Sacred* (New York: Harper & Row, 1972).

118. *Roman Religion,* 19.

119. *Religion Romaine,* vol. 2, 3.

120. Livy reports that the Roman senators were fearful to start a war with Antiochus in the year 191 B.C.E. They directed the consuls Publius Cornelius Scipio and Manius Acilius Glabrio to perform sacrifices and to offer prayers that the new war might turn out successfully for the senate and the Roman people. The sacrifices proved favorable, and the *haruspices* predicted that a victory and a triumph would be celebrated and that the boundaries of the Roman people would be enlarged. "When this had been reported, the *patres,* their spirits freed from *religio* (*solutis religione animis*), directed that the question should be put to the assembly, whether they wished the ordained war to be entered upon with King Antiochus and those who had followed his path. . . . (36.1.1–5)." Roman divination, personal and civic, taking the auspices, and inspecting the livers of victims, were actions not meant to block Roman will, but to regulate and guide it.

121. Cicero, *De haruspicum responsis* 18–19; *De natura deorum* 2.8; Valerius Maximus 1.1.8; Polybius 6.56–58; cf. Robert Muth, "Vom Wesen römischer *religio*," *Aufsteig und Neidergang der römischen Welt* II.16.1 (Berlin: W. de Gruyter, 1978), 290–354. esp. 290–98.

122. One can compare Roman *religio* with Greek *sebas*: the reverential awe that prevented one from transgressing, from doing something disgraceful.

123. *Qui exercitu lustrato cum Arretium versus castra movisset et contra Hannibalem legiones duceret et ipse et equus eius ante signum Iovis Statoris sine cause repente concidit, nec eam rem habuit religioni, obiecto signo, ut peritis videbatur, ne committeret proelium.* For *religionem habere* as "feeling inhibition, fear, anxiety," see also Aulus Gellius 4.6.10 (Gellius is quoting a passage from the fifth book of *De Pontificio Iure*).

124. *Archaic Roman Religion*, trans. Philip Krapp, vol. I (Baltimore: Johns Hopkins University Press, 1970) [1966]), 40.

125. *Vocabulaire* vol. 2, 267–73, esp. 279.

126. Still, in the fourth century, Donatus could gloss Terence's *Andria* (487:) "The *superstitiosi* are those who fear the gods too much" (*supersitiosi, qui deos nimis timent . . .*). While the word *superstitio* does not appear in Lucretius' epic poem, Servius remarks, "According to Lucretius, *superstitio* is a vain and excessive fear of things *superstantes*, that is, of things celestial and divine." (*Secundum Lucretium superstitio est superstantium rerum, i.e., caeslestium et divinarum, quae super nos stant, inanis et superfluus timor* [*Ad Aeneidem*. 8.187]). For *superstitio* as an excess of *religio*, see especially Otto, "*Religio* und *Superstitio*," 12 (1909), 532–54 and 14 (1911), 406–22; Benveniste, *Vocabulaire*, 272–75; Liebeschuetz, *Continuity and Change*, 117; Sachot, "*Religio/Superstitio*; Historique d'une subversion et d'un retournement," *Revue de l'Histoire des Religions* 208 (1991), 355–94, esp. 372–82. Compare Plutarch's vivid description of the debilitating terrors of *deisidaimonia* (*Moralia* 165D–168F), which he contrasts with ancestral *eusebeia*. See also Edwin Linkomies, "*Superstitio*," *Arctos* 7 (1931), 73–88; Denise Grodzynski, *Revue des Etudes Anciennes* 76 (1974), 36–60; Richard Gordon, "*Superstitio*, Superstition and Religious Repression in the Late Roman Republic and Principate," *The Religion of Fools?*, eds. S. A. Smith and Alan Knight, *Past and Present*, Supplement 3 (2008), 72–94.

127. *Sic uni cuique virtuti finitimum vitium reperietur . . . ut audacia quae fidentiae, pertinacia, quae perseverantiae finitima est, superstitio, quae religioni propinqua est. . . .*

128. Plautus, *Curculio* 397 (*superstitiosus . . . vera paraedicat*); *Rudens* 1139 (*aut supersititosa aut hariolast*). [Cassandra to her mother Hecuba:] "I have been sent to utter prophecies: Against my will Apollo drives me mad to the revelation of future ills." (*missa sum superstitiosis hariolationibus; nam me Apollo fatis fandis dementem invitam ciet* [Unknown author (possibly from Accius' *Hecuba* or Ennius' *Alexander*) quoted in Cicero, *De divinatione* 1.31.66].) "*O sancte Apollo*, you who possesses the undoubted navel of the world, from which the *superstitiosa saeva vox* first issued outdoors." (*O sancte Apollo qui umbilicum certum terrarum optines* [*obsides*], *unde superstitiosa primum saeva evasit vox foras.* [Unknown author (Ennius?), fragment of an unidentified tragedy apud Cicero, *De divinatione* 2.56.115 (= Warmington, *Fragments of Old Latin*)].) Jocelyn translates the second-century B.C.E. *superstitiosus* as "clairvoyant" and asserts that it could not have been used at that time as a near-synonym of *impudens* (shameless, brazen) (*The Tragedies of Ennius* [Cambridge: Cambridge University Press, 1969], 397). Cf. L. F. Janssen, "*Superstitio* and the Persecution of the Christians," *Vigiliae Christianae* 33 (1979), 131–59, 135. But at least once in Ennius, the *superstitiosi vates* are linked negatively with the *impudentes harioli* as people who do not know their own path yet point the way for others (*Telamon* fr. 332–26 Warmington). Cf. Cyril Bailey, *Lucretius, De Rerum Natura, Commentary*, Vol. II (Oxford: Clarendon Press, 1947), 609; Denise Grodzynski, "Superstitio," *Revue des Études Anciennes* 76 (1974), 36–60, 37. The early uses of *religiosus* and *superstitiosus* as synonymous in republican sources suggest that both were linked to a heightened or altered state of consciousness rather than being linked to the notion of "surviving" or "witnessing" as Benveniste surmised (*Le vocabulaire des institutions indo-européennes*, vol 2 273 ff.).

Benveniste was basing his conclusions on Cicero, *De natura deorum* 2.72, where Cicero combined the notion of excessive attention and anxiety with the notion of survival: "Those who pray all day long and make sacrifice for the survival of their children (*superstites essent*) are called *superstitiosi*." I think Walter Otto was closer to understanding the ancient Roman notion of *superstitio* when he compared it with Greek *ekstasis* ("*Religio* und *Superstitio*").

129. *Superstitio* as an excess of *religio* rather than the antithesis of *religio* is still occasionally met with in Christian sources. *Superstitio dicta est, ea quod superflua aut super istituta religionis observatio* (a fragment of the Donatist theologian Tyconius [d. ca. 400 C.E.] preserved in Beatus of Liebana, *In Apocalypsin commentaria* 297.33ff. [quoted by Michael Gaddis, *There is No Crime for Those Who have Christ* (Berkeley: University of Californa Press, 2005), 122 n. 79]). Compare Isidore's, "*superstitio dicta ea quod superflua aut superinstituta observatio*" (*Etymologiae* 8.3.6). Michele Salzman finds the word *superstitio* still being used as excessive *religio* in the third century C.E. by Christians and the fourth by non-Christians, and argues that imperial rescripts in the early third-to-fourth century deliberately employ *superstitio* in its two very different meanings as unnecessary/excessive and as unauthorized/illegitimate acts so that the purposefully ambiguous messages of the rescripts could be read differently in the West and in the East. She surmises that *superstitio* would still be read as excessive of superfluous *religio* in the West and as the opposite of *religio* in the East ("*Superstitio* in the Codex Theodosianus and the Persecution of Pagans," *Vigiliae Christianae* 41 [1987], 172–88, 174).

130. In his story of the Gallic sack, Livy's Gauls lose the advantage of their triumph by being "astonished" at the miracle of their victory (*Gallos . . . obstupefactos miraculum victoriae* [5.39.1]), at the deserted streets (*ipsa solitudine absterriti* [5.41.6]), and at the open doors and the sight of the impassive *seniores seated* like the statues of gods as they awaited impassively their deaths (5.41.8) and the audacity of Fabius Dorsuo (5.46.3).

131. *Sed ad Calvum . . . qui orator fuit cum litteris eruditior quam Curio tum etiam accuratius quoddam dicendi et exquisitius afferebat genus; quod quamquam scienter eleganterque tractabat, nimium tamen inquirens in se atque ipse sese observans metuensque ne vitiosum colligeret, etiam verum sanguinem deperdebat. Itaque eius oratio nimia religione attenuata. . . .*

132. *Tunc adeo fracti simul cum corpore sunt spiritus illi feroces, ut qui nihil ante ratus esset minus regium quam sacris dedere animum, repente omnibus magnis parvisque supersitionibus abnoxius degeret religionibusque etiam populum impleret. Ipsum regem tradunt volventem commentarios Numae, cum ibi quaedam occulta sollemnia sacrificia Iovi Elicio facta invenisset, operatum iis sacris se abdidisse; sed non rite initum aut curatum id sacrum esse, nec solum nullam ei oblatam caelestium speciem, sed ira Iovis sollicitati prava religione fulmine ictum cum domo conflagrasse.*

133. For example, Lucretius, *De rerum natura* 1.62–79: "Human life lay for all to see foully grovelling upon the ground, crushed beneath the weight of *religio* which displayed her head in the regions of heaven, threatening mortals from on high with horrible aspect. . . ." *Humana ante oculos foede / cum vita iaceret/ in terris oppressa gravi sub religion / quae caput a caeli regionibus ostendebat/ horribili super aspectu mortalibus instans, / religionum nodis animos exsolvere.*

134. *quod est bonorum pontificum, monete eum modum quemdam esse religionis. . . .*

135. W. Morel (*Fragmenta Poetarum Latinarum* [Stuttgart: Teubner], 1963 [1927], 6) and A. Bergmann (*Grundbedeutung*, 41–42) place this line among the *carmina vetustissima*.

136. Wilt points out that there are words ending in—*osus* "rich in" or "inclined to," which, while implying fullness, do not have a negative connotation: words such as *ingeniosus, formosus, speciosus* (48–52).

137. Caesar, *De bello Gallico* 6.16: "The whole nation of the Gauls is greatly devoted to *religiones*, and for that reason those who are smitten with the more grievous maladies and who are engaged in the perils of battle either sacrifice human victims or vow to do so, employing the Druids as ministers for such sacrifices. They believe, in effect, that unless for a man's life a man's

life be paid, the majesty of the immortal gods may not be appeased; and, in public, as in private life, they observe an ordinance of sacrifice of the same kind. Others use figures of immense size, whose limbs, woven out of twigs, they fill with living men and set on fire, and the men perish in a sheet of flame. They believe that the execution of those who have been caught in the act of theft or robbery or some crime is more pleasing to the immortal gods; but when the supply of such fails they resort to the execution even of the innocent." (*Natio est omnis Gallorum admodum dedita religionibus, atque ob eam causam, qui sunt adfecti gravioribus morbis quique in proeliis periculisque versantur, aut pro victimis homines immolant aut se immolaturos vovent administrisque ad eas sacrificia druidibus utuntur, quod, pro vita hominis nisi hominis vita reddatur, non posse deorum imortalium numen placari arbitrantur, publiceque eiusdem generis habent instituta sacrificia. Alii immani magnitudine simulaca habent, quorum contexta viminibus membra vivis hominibus complent; quibus succensis ciurcumventi flamma exanimantur homines. Supplicia eorum qui in furto aut in latrocinio aut aliqua noxia sint comprehensi gratiora dis immortalibus esse arbitrantur; sed, cum eius generis copia defecit, etiam ad innocentium supplicia descendunt.*)

138. It seems, in fact, Cicero himself who made this distinction. See Chapter 2, "The Ciceronian Turn."

139. *Maiores nostri superstitionem a religione separaverunt. Nam qui totos dies precabantur et immolabant ut sibi sui liberi superstites essent superstitiosi sunt appellati.* See Pease ad loc. and ad 2.148.

140. *Quo diutius trahebatur bellum et variabant secundae et adversaeque res non fortunam magis quam animos hominum, tanta religio, et ea magna ex parte externa, civitatem incessit ut aut homines aut dei repente alii viderentur facti. (. . .) Ubi potentius iam esse id malum apparuit quam ut minores per magistratus sedaretur, M. Aemilio praetori urbano negotium ab senatu datum est ut eis religionibus populum liberaret.*

141. This fixation, characteristic of all absolutes, will become positive in the *religio* of Tertullian.

142. For a wonderful description of the impotence caused by excessive *deisidaimonia*, see Plutarch, *De superstitione, Moralia* 165 B–F, 168C–169B.

143. *mures in aede Iovis aurum rosisse: adeo minimis etiam rebus prava religio inserit deos.* Cf. Livy 1.31.8; Nonius, 697, Lindsay.

144. *nihil enim in speciem fallacius quam prava religio. ubi deorum numen praetenditur sceleribus, subit animum timor, ne fraudibus humanis vindicandis divini iuris aliquid inmixtum violemus. hac vos religione innumerabilia decreta pontificum . . . liberant.*

145. "If anyone does anything whereby the light minds/spirits (*leves animi*) of men are terrified by *superstitio numinis*, the deified Marcus [Aurelius] wrote in a rescript that persons of this kind are to be relegated to an island." (*Si quis aliquid fecerit, quo leves hominum animi superstitione numinis terrentur, divus Marcus huiusmodi in insulam relegari rescripsit* [Herennius Modestinus (mid–third century C.E.), *De poenis* 1 = *Digesta* 48.19.30].)

146. *ut stultae et miserae omnes sumus religiosae, quom exponendam do illi, de digito anulum detraho. . . .* Note that Sargeaunt's translation ("with a woman's usual folly and miserable superstition") totally obscures the presence of the word *religio*. The unwillingness of modern translators to convey the negative senses of *religio* obscures the emotional economy of that concept.

147. *"certe nescio quid secreto velle loqui te aiebas mecum." "Memini bene, sed meliore tempore dicam; hodie tricesima sabbata; vin tu curtis Iudaeis oppedere?" "Nulla mihi," inquam "religio est." "At mi; sum paulo infirmior, unus multorum. Ignosces; alias loquar."*

148. The non-Christian Caecilius brands Christianity as shameful, a *prava religio* = *superstitio*, which has both the qualities of extreme shamelessness and extreme shame in Marcus Minucius Felix's *Octavius* 10.1 (cf. 8–10).

149. Heightened self-consciousness was generally negative in Roman thought, something one wanted to avoid or lessen as soon as possible.

150. Cicero, in his *De divinatione*, tries to steer a course between *anilis superstitio* and *impia neglegentia* (1.4.7). For more on the middle course, see *De divinatione* 2.148–49; Cicero, *De natura deorum* 1.122, 2.70–72.

2. THE CICERONIAN TURN

1. *Religio est quae superioris cuiusdam naturae, quam divinam vocant curam caerimoniamque adfert.*

2. *religione id est cultu deorum.*

3. The development of the centralized sacrificial system, as I will try to show elsewhere, is both the culmination and destruction of that system.

4. *Humana ante oculos foede cum vita iaceret / in terris oppressa gravi sub religione / quae caput a caeli regionibus ostendebat / horribili super aspectu mortalibus instans.*

5. *et quibus ille modis divom metus insinuarit / pectora, terrarum qui in orbi sancta tuetur / fana lacus lucos aras simulacraque divom.*

6. *Primus in orbe deos fecit timor, ardua caelo / fulmina cum caderent discussaque moenia flammis / atque ictus flagraret Athos.*

7. *Primus in orbe deos fecit timor.*

8. Cf. *De natura deorum* 2.28.72.

9. Compare the dangers of concentrated focus that the Romans association with fascination. The fixation of the attention of the Sabine guests on the spectacle of the Consualia allowed the Romans to seize their young women (Livy 1.9); Carlin Barton, *The Sorrows of the Ancient Romans: The Gladiator and the Monster* (Princeton: Princeton University Press, 1993), 85–106.

10. Compare Plutarch's descriptions of the debilitating terrors of *deisidaimonia*, which he contrasts with sensible and sane *eusebeia* (*De superstitione, Moralia* 165D–168F). See 169C, 164E–171F, esp. 168C–169A for the Jews' excessive fear of the gods and their resulting suicidal immobility on the Sabbath.

11. *"Iuppiter, ingentis qui das adimisque dolores," / mater ait pueri mensis iam quinque cubantis, / "frigida si puerum quartana reliquerit, illo / mane die, quo tu indicis ieiunia, nudus / in Tiberi stabit." Casus medicusve levarit / aegrum ex praecipiti, mater delira necabit / in gelida fixum ripa febremque reducet, / quone malo mentem concussa? Timore deorum.*

12. *Ille viriles sibi partes amputat, ille lacertos secat. Ubi iratos deos timent qui sic propitios merentur? Dii autem nullo debent coli genere, si hoc volunt. Tantus est perturbatae menti et sedibus suis pulsae furor ut sic dii placentur quem ad modum ne quidem homines saeviunt taeterrimi et in fabulas traditae crudelitatis. Tyranni laceraverunt aliquorum membra, neminem sua lacerare iusserunt. In regiae libidinis voluptatem castrati sunt quidam; sed nemo sibi ne vir esset, iubente domino manus adtulit. Se ipsi in templis contrucidant, vulneribus suis ac sanguine supplicant. Si cui intueri vacet, quae faciunt qaeque patiuntur, inveniet tam indecora honestis, tam indigna liberis, tam dissimilia sanis, ut nemo fuerit dubitaturus furere eos, si cum paucioribus furerent.*

13. *verum ubi vementi magis est commota metu mens, / consentire animam totam per membra videmus / sudoresque ita palloremque existere toto / corpore et infringi linguam vocemque aboriri, / caligare oculos, sonere auris, succidere artus, / denique concidere ex animi terrore videmus / saepe homines.* Cicero paints Publius Clodius as wavering, stuttering, all but paralyzed with anxiety and guilt (*De domo sua* 52.135; cf. 54.139).

14. The geologists' and biologists' notions of deep time, like the astronomers' notions of deep space can work, like Lucretius' universe of falling atoms, to free the human from the high anxiety that comes from a human's boundless desires, coupled with her inability to affect the world. It is hard to be terrified of global warming or nuclear war when one thinks in terms of billions of years. It can relieve fear to be utterly inconsequential and powerless. The Cynics also attempted to relieve anxiety by eliminating attachments and obligations and the shame and guilt that came with them.

15. Compare Caesar's description of the Celts in n. 137 above. After the sack of Rome by the Gauls in 387 B.C.E., according to Livy, the city was "then full of *religio* and, owing to the recent calamity even with leaders who were *supersitiosi* . . . ." (*In civitate plena religionum, tunc etiam ab recenti clade supersitiosis principus* . . . [6.5.6].) Similarly, in Livy 41.16.6 an accumulation of negative *religiones* filled the city with excessive anxiety to the tipping point at which *religio* became toxic, a form of terror producing paralysis or chaos. It was this extreme, dizzying and debilitating imbalance of *religio/superstitio* that tended to invert, in the way that too much shame tended to shamelessness or asceticism. It was the precipice from which one could make a Kierkegaardian leap into a set of emotions and behaviors that were the inversion and antithesis of Latin *religio*. Being "out of one's mind" could invert from being negative to positive, from *religio* as *superstitio* to *religio* as ecstasy, the self-overcoming submission to the hostile forces of the universe, as one would surrender to the victorious general and put oneself in the *dicio*, the *fides* of the forces which one could not control.

I have often discussed (and will again) the inversion of extremes in Roman thought. Virgil wrote of a tunic that was *squalens*, "squalid" with gold. This phrase, according to Aulus Gellius, was criticized because it was inappropriate to say *auro squalentem*, because "the brilliance and splendor of gold is quite opposed to the filth of squalor" (*nitoribus splendoribusque auri squaloris inluvies sit contraria* [*Noctes Atticae* 2.6.5]). The explanation Gellius offers was that *squalere* was applied to anything "overloaded and excessively crowded." (*quidquid igitur nimis inculcatum obsitumque aliqua re erat . . . id 'squalere' dicebatur* [ibid. 2.6.24].)

16. *Satricum urbem . . . igni concremarent; nec aliud tectum eius superfuit urbis, cum faces pariter sacris profanisque inicerent, quam matris Matutae templum; inde eos nec sua religio nec verecundia deum arcuisse dicitur sed vox horrenda edita templo cum tristibus minis ni nefandos ignes procul delubris amovissent.* Notice that *verecundia* and *religio* here are synonyms.

17. Compare Livy's description of a similar outbreak of such anxieties in 213 B.C.E. during the Hannibalic War (25.1.6–12). Cf. Warde Fowler, *Roman Essays and Interpretations* (Oxford: Clarendon Press, 1920), 9. For the aediles being trusted with such duties, see 3.55.13 and the note of R. M. Ogilvie, *A Commentary on Livy Books 1–5* (Oxford: Clarendon Press, 1965) *ad loc.* According to Ogilvie, the mission of the aediles whom he calls "primarily religious officers" was not, in this case, to suppress the newly instituted *ritus Graecus* of Apollo "but to ensure that the worship did not lead to extravagance and abuse." See also J. Bayet, *Histoire*, 144 ff. Jean Gagé, *Apollon Romain: essai sur le culte d'Apollon et le développement du "ritus Graecus" à Rome des origines à Augustus* (Paris: Boccard, 1955), 130–32.

18. *Nocturnaque proelia esse vitanda, quod perterritus miles in civili dissensione timori magis quam religioni consulere consuerit. At luce multum per se pudorem omnium oculis, multum etiam tribunorum militum et centurionum praesentiam afferre; quibus rebus coerceri milites et in officio contineri soleant.*

19. *nihil est enim illi principi deo, qui omnem mundum regit, quod quidem in terris fiat acceptius, quam concilia coetusque hominum iure sociati quae civitates appellantur.*

20. Cicero learned from Greek philosophy to project his desired goal from an axiomatic and unquestioned starting point.

21. Cf. *De inventione* 2.53.161; cf. *De haruspicum responsis* 19.

22. *Horum enim sententiae omnium non modo superstitionem tollunt in qua inest timor inanis deorum, sed etiam religionem quae deorum cultu pio continetur.* Cf. 2.28.71–72. Varro also has a notion of the positive fear of the gods (*Antiquitates Rerum Divinarum* 1 fr. 2a Cardauns = Augustine, *De civitate dei* 6.2; 1 fr. 18 Cardauns = Augustine, *De civitate dei* 4.31 with Cardauns' commentary ad. loc.). Servius attributes to Varro and the lawyer Ateius Capito (first century C.E.) the notion of the gods (such as the *dii manes*) being feared on account of their consecration (*deos qui propter sui consecrationem timentur, ut sunt dii manes* [*In Aeneidem* 5.45]). Servius goes so far as to attribute the etymology of *deus* to Greek *deos* (fear): *nam quod Graece δέος, Latine timor vocatur, inde deus dictus est, quod omnis religio sit timoris* (*Ad Aeneidem* 12.139). The non-Christian Caecilius in Minucius Felix (despite his own impersonal and Hellenized philosophy of nature and fortune) asserts that

atheists undermined "the fear and reverence by which mankind is governed:" "Let him be a Theodorus of Cyrene [late–fourth century B.C.E.] or an earlier Diagoras of Melos [late–fifth century B.C.E.] who both alike, by asserting that there were no gods, deeply undermined the fear and reverence by which mankind is governed." (*Sit licet ille Theodorus Cyrenaeus, vel qui prior Diagoras Melius, cui Atheon cognomen adposuit antiquitas, qui uterque nullos deos adseverando timorem omnem, quo humanitas regitur venerationemque penitus sustulerunt* [*Octavius* 8.2].)

23. Cf. *De inventione* 2.22.65; 2.53.160.

24. Beard makes the point that the dialog form that Cicero takes in his philosophical works allows him even a greater degree of distance and abstraction ("Cicero and Divination," 43–44).

25. Cf. Troiani, "La Religione e Cicerone," esp. 921–22.

26. Cicero was made augur in 53 B.C.E. by Pompey and Hortensius to fill the place on the college left vacant by the death of Crassus (2 Philippica 4).

27. *Conspicit inde sibi data Romulus esse priora, / auspicio regni stabilita scamna solumque* (= Ennius, *Annales* 1.90 Skutsch).

28. Festus attributes to the Augustan Aelius Gellius the following definition: "*religiosum* . . . is that which in not permitted for a man to do; so that if he should so act he will be seen to have acted against the will of the gods." (*religiosum esse Gallus Aelius ait quod homini facere non liceat, ut si id faciat contra deorum voluntatem videatur facere.*)

29. When King Tullus Hostilius himself engaged in excessive, distorted, twisted *religio* (*prava religio*), he was struck dead by Jupiter: "[The king] in turning over the commentaries of Numa discovered in them the record of certain sacrifices performed in honor of Jupiter Elicius, and devoted himself in secret to those rites; but the ceremony was improperly undertaken or performed, and not only was no divine manifestation granted him, but in consequence of the wrath of Jupiter, who was provoked by his *prava religio*, he was struck by a thunderbolt and consumed in the flames of his house" (Livy 1.31.8).

30. *Tu, Iuppiter, qui isdem, quibus haec urbs auspiciis a Romulo es constitutus, quem Statorem huius urbis atque imperi vere nominamus, hunc et huius socios a tuis ceterisque templis, a tectis urbis ac moenibus, a vita fortunisque civium omnium arcebis et homines bonorum inimicos, hostis patriae, latrones Italiae scelerum foedere inter se ac nefaria societate coniunctos aeternis suppliciis vivos mortuosque mactabis.*

31. *eorum animi, qui . . . deorum et hominum iura violaverunt, corporibus elapsi circum terram ipsam volutantur nec hunc in locum nisi multis exagitati saeculis revertuntur.* But consider his mockery of such notions in the *Tusculanae disputationes* (1.21.48).

32. Formalism compensates those who submit to it with another kind of power: It encourages and allows humans to interpret misfortunes as punishments. Humans often prefer to be guilty rather than powerless. Human guilt can be human power. The more intricate and impossible the laws, the more failure and mistakes are not only possibilities but inevitabilities, the easier it is to make all mishaps and disasters into the result of human error and failure and to make the ruling powers into benevolent, if punishing parents (like the abbot in Benedict's monastery). The greater the degree of formalism, the easier it is to interpret all negative events as part of the *potentia ordinata*. Interpreting misfortune as the result of human faults, as punishment for carelessness or transgressions, brings the uncontrollable forces of nature back into the world of human control. It is easy to see why Lucretius would offer the greatest challenge to Cicero's government.

33. *Cumque omnis populi Romani religio in sacra et in auspicia divisa sit, tertium adiunctum sit si quid praedictionis causa ex portentis et monstris Sibyllae interpretes haruspicesve monuerunt, harum ego religionum nullam umquam contemnendam putavi, mihique ita persuasi, Romulum auspiciis Numam sacris constitutis fundamenta iecisse nostrae civitatis, quae numquam profecto sine summa placatione deorum immortalium tanta esse potuisset. Habes Balbe quid Cotta quid pontifex sentiat. . . . A te enim philosopho rationem accipere debeo religionis, maioribus autem nostris etiam nulla ratione reddita credere.*

34. Cicero, *De divinatione* 1.58.132; cf. Tibullus 3.4.1–16 (on the vain terrors caused by dreams).

35. *Retinetur autem et ad opinionem vulgi et ad magnas utilitates rei publicae mos, religio, disciplina, ius augurum, collegi auctoritas.*

36. Compare Valerius Maximus writing in the early first century: "Our ancestors determined that fixed and formal annual ceremonies be regulated by the knowledge of the *pontifices*; that sanction for the good governance of affairs be marshaled by the observation of the *augures*." (*Maiores statas sollemnesque caerimonias pontificum scientia, bene gerendarum rerum auctoritates augurum observatione* [1.1.1a–b].)

37. It is given to the augurs and pontiffs to define, to "fix" the "sacred" and set borders between *religio* and *superstitio*. "*Qu'un accent se déplace, et l''exercise scupuleux des observances cultuelles' devient celui des 'observances reconnues légitimes': l'ordre pontifical s'instaure. (. . .) [L]es pontifes, en imprimant sur telle action ou tel objet le marque religiosus, ont sûrement contribué à aggraver, du poids de leur autorité, cette hésitation.(. . .) C'est assez dire que la discipline imposée par les pontifes au reste des citoyens tendait à objectiver en un empêchement extérieur aux consciences le sentiment de timidité éprouvé par le sujet. (. . .) religio s'imposant aux esprits . . . indique une prise de conscience effectuée sous le signe de la discipline*" (Fugier, *Expression du sacré*, 178–79).

38. A. Momigliano, "The Theological Efforts of the Roman Upper Classes in the First Century B.C.," *Classical Philology* 79 (1984): 199–211, 201.

39. For the influence of the language and philosophy of Cicero (and especially of *De natura deorum*) on Christians such as Tertullian, Minucius Felix, Lactantius, Arnobius, and Augustine, see Ilona Opelt, "Ciceros Schrift *De natura deorum* bei den lateinischen Kirchenvätern," *Antike und Abendland* 12 (1966), 141–55; Pease, "Introduction" to *De Natura Deorum*, 52–57; Bouillard, "Religion en Occident," 453; Andrew Dyck, "Introduction" to *Cicero, De natura deorum, Book I* (Cambridge: Cambridge University Press, 2003), 14–15.

40. *Roman Religion*, 23.

41. It was Cicero and the Latin writers who came after him, and not, as Maurice Sachot asserted, the Christians of the end of the second century C.E. who made the decisive "turn" in the meanings of *religio and superstitio* ("*Religio/Superstitio*," 363).

42. He uses *superstitiosus* as a term of insult (*superstitiosi vates impudentesque harioli* [*De divinatione* 1.58.132]) here quoting Ennius, *Telamon* fr. 332–36.

43. *Nam, ut vere loquamur, superstitio, fusa per gentis, oppressit omnium fere animos atque hominum imbecillitatem occupavit. (. . .) Multum enim et nobismet ipsis et nostris profuturi videbamur, si eam funditus sustulissemus. Nec vero—id enim diligenter intellegi volo—superstitione tollenda religio tollitur. Nam et maiorum instituta tueri sacris caerimoniisque retinendis sapientis est, et esse praestantem aliquam aeternamque naturam, et eam suspiciendam admirandamque hominum generi pulchritudo mundi ordoque rerum caelestium cogit confiteri.*

44. *Oppressa gravi sub religione* (Lucretius, *De rerum natura* 1.63). *Tantum religio potuit suadere malorum* (ibid. 1.101). Note that *religio* can still be used as the synonym for *superstitio* as late as Lactantius (*Divinae institutiones* 1.14.1).

45. Cf. *De divinatione* 1.4.7, 1.47.105, 2.7.19, 2.15.36, 2.68.141; *De natura deorum* 3.39.92; *Tusculanae disputationes* 1.21.48, 3.72; Joseph Mayor, *De natura deorum libri tres*, 3 vols. (Cambridge: Cambridge University Press, 1880), 1:152–53.

46. *Quotus igitur est quisque, qui somniis pareat, qui intellegat, qui meminerit? quam multi vero, qui contemnant eamque superstitionem imbecilli animi atque anilis putent!* For these aspects of Ciceronian *superstitio*, see especially Gordon, "Superstitio," 78–81, 87–88. For *vana superstitio*, see Vergil, *Aeneis* 8.187f. The non-Christian Caecilius in Minucius Felix argues for maintaining a healthy and hesitating doubt with regard to the mysteries of the universe; the declaring of certainty about the universe is the concomitant of the adoption of *anilis superstitio* and results in the destruction of *religio* (*Octavia* 13, esp. 13.5).

47. *Quid tibi necesse fuit anili superstitione, homo fanatice, sacrificium, quod alienae domi fieret, invisere? quae autem tanta mentis imbecillitas tenuit, ut non putares deos satis posse placari, nisi, etiam muliebribus religionibus te implicuisse?* Compare Cicero's attacks on Vatinius: "You who are accustomed to call yourself a Pythagorean and to conceal behind the name of a most learned man your monstrous and barbarian customs, what crookedness of mind possessed you, what frenzy so great? You have undertaken unheard-of *sacra*. You are accustomed both to call up the spirits of the dead with the entrails of boys and to increase (*mactare*) the powers of the infernal deities with the entrails of boys." (*Tu qui te Pythagoreum soles dicere et hominis doctissimi nomen tuis immanibus et barbaris moribus praetendere, quae te tanta pravitas mentis tenuerit, qui tantus furor, ut cum inaudita ac nefaria sacra susceperis, cum inferorum animas elicere, cum puerorum extis deos manes mactare soleas . . . [*In Vatinium* 6.14 (56 B.C.E.)].)

48. "Superstitio," 81.

49. *superstitiosos significari, qui inaniter semper verentur . . . nam religiosi sunt qui per reverentiam timent.*

50. *Religiosi dicuntur, qui faciendarum praetermittendarumque rerum divinarum secundum morem civitatis dilectum habent, nec se superstitionibus inplicant.*

51. *cum religiosum a superstitioso ea distinctione discernat, ut a superstitioso timeri deos, a religioso autem tantum vereri ut parentes, non ut hostes timeri. . . .*

52. Janssen, "Superstitio," 152; Maurice Sachot, "Comment le Christianisme est-il devenu religio," *Revue des Sciences Religieuses* 59 (1985), 95–118, 108; cf. 107.

53. *Utilis esse autem has opiniones quis neget, cum intellegat quam multa firmentur iure iurando, quantae saluti sint foederum religiones, quam multos divini supplici metus a scelere revocarit, quamque sancta sit societas civium inter ipsos diis inmortalibus interpositis tum iudicibus, tum testibus?* "You, *homo religiosus et sanctus* that you were, were reluctant to break the covenant . . ." (Cicero, *In Pisonem* 28 [56 B.C.E., ironically]). Cf. Plato, *Leges* 4.772D.

54. *Ut ordiar ab haruspicina, quam ego causa rei publicae, communisque religionis colendam censeo.*

55. For example, *Fragmentum Mediolanense* and *Fragmenta Cusana* of the *Pro Flacco*; *Pro Balbo* 5.12; *Epistulae ad Atticum* 1.16.4. Momigliano addressed the ways in which Nigidius Figulus, Varro, and Cicero refused to be restricted by the traditional ideas and practices of Roman cult in "Theological Efforts," 201, 204.

56. *Respublica* 2.377–78; 3.386–89, 4.439; *Leges* 10.889E.

57. Polybius (6.56.6–12; cf. 16.12.9–11) was the first to suggest that the *deisidaimonia* of the Romans was a tool of discipline effectively used by the government. The argument that the people are fickle, lawless, and irrational, and needed to be controlled by invisible terrors and rewards had and will continue to have a rich history. For the Greek tradition going back to Critias of Athens, see Mayor, *De Natura Deorum Libri Tres*, 1:221; Pease, *De Natura Deorum*, 513–14; F. W. Walbank, *A Historical Commentary on Polybius*, 3 vols. (Oxford: Clarendon Press, 1957), 1:741–42; Burkhart Cardauns, *M. Terentius Varro Antiquitates Rerum Divinarum, Teil II: Kommentar* (Mainz/Wiesbaden: Akademie der Wissenschaften und der Literatur, 1976 [1968]), 139.

58. "It is recorded that the learned pontiff Scaevola maintained that [the type of the gods of the philosophers] was not suited to city-states, because it included some superfluous doctrines and some also that it is harmful for the people to know." (*quod habeat aliqua supervacua, aliqua etiam quae obsit populis nosse.*) He would not transmit to the people the philosophical idea that their images of god are false (because the god has neither sex nor age nor bodily parts). "He [Mucius Scaevola] therefore considers it to be for the advantage of cities to be deceived *in religione.*" (*Expedire igitur existimat falli in religione civitates* [Augustine, *De civitate dei* 4.27].)

59. "There are many things that are *vera*, which to be popularly known (*vulgo scire*) is not useful. But indeed, there are other things that, even if false, should be considered otherwise if

they should be of helpful to the people" (*Antiquitates rerum divinarum* 1 fr. 21 Cardauns=Augustine, *De civitate dei* 4.27+31 with Cardauns' commentaries). Varro asserted that the philosophical debates with their dissenting opinions concerning the nature of the gods should be held in the schools behind closed doors and not in the forum. They are dangerous, as were the Greek mysteries (*Antiquitates* 1 fr. 8+21 Cardauns=Augustine, *De civitate dei* 4.27, 6.5). Varro also believed that it was "useful" (*utile*) even if false (*etiamsi falsum sit*) for *viri fortes* to believe they were begotten by the gods (*Antiquitates* 1 fr. 20 Cardauns=Augustine, *De civitate dei* 3.4).

60. *Quod vacua metu, cura, sollicitudine, periculo vita bonorum virorum sit; contra autem improbis semper aliqui scrupus in animis haereat.*

61. Predictably, it was exactly the frequent skeptical debunking of the Stoics, Epicureans, and the Romans' own cultic traditions by Cicero and other Romans educated in Greek thought that was used by Christians to attack the Romans' traditions. According to Lactantius, *totus liber tertius de natura deorum omnes funditus religiones evertit ac delet* (*Divinae institutiones* 1.17.4). Arnobius, writing at the beginning of the fourth century, tells us that in his day, there were *non-Christian* Romans who loathed and shunned Cicero's books *for their skepticism* and urged the senate to decree the destruction of "those writings by which the Christian *religio* was demonstrated and the *auctoritas* of antiquity counteracted." (*oportere statui per senatum aboleantur haec scripta quibus christiana religio comprobetur et vetustatis auctoritas opprimatur* [*Adversus Paganos* 3.7].)

62. "Cicero, a Hypocrite in Religion," *American Journal of Philology* 90 (1969), 304–12, 305.

63. Wissowa, *Religion und Kultus der Römer* (Munich: C.H. Beck, 1902). Wissowa devoted approximately 200 pages to describing the Roman gods. It was symptomatic of what he thought must be the central concern of ancient Roman "religion and cult."

64. This is not to say that Cicero credited even the auguries of the magistrates. "What wonder, then, if in auspices and every kind of divination weak minds should adopt *superstitiosa ista* and should be unable to discern the *verum*." (*Quid mirum igitur, si in auspiciis et in omni divinatione imbecilli animi superstitiosa ista concipiant, verum dispicere non possint?* [*De divinatione* 2.39.81].)

65. Momigliano, "Theological Efforts," 200. Momigliano also suggests that as Caesar began increasingly manipulating the cult to shore up his power and authority, Cicero, disabused, retreated increasingly into his philosophical skepticism ("Theological Efforts," 210–11).

66. Varro expressed strong preference for an abstract, non-iconic god (Augustine, *De civitate dei* 4.31)—perhaps modeled in part on his idea of the Hebrew god Iao (cf. Lydus, *De mensibus* [early–sixth century] 4.53). The more abstract, the more removed and set apart, the more hierarchical, the more fit to be channeled by the priestly authorities.

67. Keyes, "Original Elements in Cicero's Ideal Constitution," *American Journal of Philology* 42 (1921), 309–23, 309–12, pointed out that the third book of Cicero's *De legibus* contains the closest the Roman ever came to a written constitution: a document that is the result of a deliberate effort (rather than a consensus) to lay down once and for all a rigid body of coherent provisions for an imaginary future Roman republic (or a future benevolent despot willing to subject himself to the law?) by which the government might be firmly established and conducted. This constitution, of course covered *sacra*, *sacerdotes*, and *magistratus*.

68. The obsessive compulsive behavior that was the extreme can become the desirable norm; Stockholm Syndrome can cease to be a "syndrome."

3. PREFACE TO TERTULLIAN

1. Seneca, *Troades*, 438–812.
2. Apuleius, *Metamorphoses*, 9.39.
3. Both Seneca and Apuleius understood and deployed strategies that were not their preferred ones. Seneca was most often anything but a Stoic; Apuleius often anything but a Platonist. In the

words of Montaigne: "It has often seemed to me that even good authors are wrong to insist on fashioning a consistent and solid fabric out of us." (*Of the Inconsistency of our Actions*, trans. Donald Frame [Stanford: Stanford University Press, 1965]).

4. There were exceptions: (1) Tertullian expressed his strongest support for hierarchy within the *ecclesia* in Chapter 17.1 of *De baptismo* (in many ways, the most uncharacteristic of the treatises attributed to Tertullian); in it he reserved for the *summus sacerdos* the right to baptize (with provisions). (2) In *De ieiunia* (13.3), the *episcopus* was authorized to mandate fasts for the *universa plebs*. (3) In *De praescriptione haereticorum* (41.1–8), Tertullian (who claimed no office in his *ecclesia* apart from *doctor* [*Ad Martyras* 1.2]—a title he also attached to the apostles and the *Spiritus Sanctus* [*De praescriptione haereticorum* 8.14–15, 28.1])—attacked the "rebel" Marcionites for their insufficiently ordered and institutionalized *ecclesiae*. Elsewhere, Tertullian demonstrated very flexible notions of authority, sometimes assuming a sort of "priesthood of all believers": *De oratione* 18.3 (*nos sumus veri adoratores et veri sacerdotes*); *De exhortatione castitatis* 7.3 (*nonne et laici sacerdotes sumus?*). According to *De baptismo* (17.2–3), in the absence of the *summa sacerdos*, it was the right even for the *laici* to baptize (*etiam laicis ius est* [*baptizare*]). The principal hierarchical distinction that Tertullian insisted on maintaining was that of class: between the *ordo* and the *plebs*. "The *auctoritas* and *honor* of the *ecclesia* has established the difference between the *ordo* and the *plebs*" (*De exhortatione castitatis* 7.3–6). His fierce displacement of women from authority and responsibility in the *ecclesiae* (*De praescriptione haereticorum* 41.5, *De baptismo* 17.4–5) had to be modified under the influence of the New Prophecy, which gave great weight to the words of the female mediums of the Spiritus Sanctus (*De anima* 9.3–4, *Adversus Praxeas* 1.4, *De exhortatione castitatis* 10.5, *De resurrectione* 11.2). Outside of Tertullian's writings, the expansive role given to both women and prophecy at the expense of the magistrates of the *ecclesia* is evident in the *Passio Perpetuae*. In Saturus' vision of heaven (13), the *episcopus* Optatus and the presbyter Aspasius are made to throw themselves at the feet of the martyrs, begging them to heal the quarrels that have opened between the two of them.

5. *Ecclesia* appears as an abstraction in *De praescriptione haereticorum* 3.2–3, *De virginibus velandis* 2.2, and *De carne Christi* 4.2. *Mater ecclesia* appear in *Ad martyres* 1.1, *De anima* 43.10; cf. *Adversus Marcionem* 2.4.5, 3.5.4. Otherwise, *ecclesia* is used simply to refer to the local assembly of Christians (e.g., *De idololatria* 7.1, *Ad uxorem* 1.2.2).

6. For examples of Tertullian's ranking of sources of authority, see *De carne Christi* 1.3 and *De resurrectione carnis* 12.8. As it did for the authors of the *Passio Perpetuae*, the *spiritus sanctus* in its myriad of prophetic expressions usually ranked higher than the apostles, the bishops, and the scriptures, and provided the ultimate key for interpreting the latter. In his anti-heretical works, the apostles rank very high, but only when they agree with Tertullian's Holy Spirit. For instance, when in 1 Corinthians 27–28, Paul says, "You have been freed from a wife; seek not a wife. But if you shall marry, you will not sin," Tertullian declares that Paul is speaking "in accordance with his own counsel, not in accordance with divine precept" (*de consilio suo, non de divino praecepto* [*De exhortatione castitatis* 4.1]). Cf. 4.5: "In granting indulgence [to remarry], he [Paul] alleges the advice of a prudent man; in enjoining continence, he affirms the advice of the Holy Spirit." (*Cum veniam facit, hominis prudentis consilium allegat, cum continentiam indicit, spiritus sancti consilium affirmat*.)

7. For the erratic and interesting development of the notions of *hairesis* in early Greek Christian literature, see especially Alain Le Boulluec, *La notion d'hérésie dans la littérature grecque IIᵉ-IIIᵉ siècles* (Paris: Études Augustiniennes, 1985). The "orthodox church" that Frend saw in the Carthage of Tertullian's day (*Rise of Christianity* [Philadelphia: Fortress, 1984], 349–50) seems to me to be an anachronism; there is no evidence that the concept existed in Tertullian or that any authority structure existed with sufficient *auctoritas* to impose such distinctions. Tertullian knew that he was in possession of *veritas* and that anyone who disagreed with him was "heretical."

8. William Tabbernee (*Montanist Inscriptions and Testimonia: Epigraphic Sources Illustrating the History of Montanism* [Macon, Geo.: Mercer University Press, 1997], 54–55) expressed his doubts

that there had ever existed a separate "Montanist" congregation or that Tertullian left "the official church" to join such a group. Following the lead of Tabbernee, Laura Nasrallah, in her chapters on Tertullian in *An Ecstasy of Folly; Prophecy and Authority in Early Christianity* ([Cambridge, Mass.: Harvard University Press, 2003], 95–154) rejected the division of Tertullian's thought into "orthodox" versus "Montanist" phases, and instead based her analysis on "ideas of struggle and negotiation of identity in early Christianity" (100). Tertullian changes his mind (sometimes very wantonly) on very many topics, but I have found more evidence for continuity than for any sharp break in his thinking.

9. The most egregious examples: *Semen est sanguis Christianorum. Credo quia absurdum* (sic). *Quid ergo Athenis et Hierosolymis?*

10. I use the word "apologetic" advisedly. Tertullian may have been the first Christian to call a treatise an *Apologeticum* (or *Apologeticus*). The title *Apologia* given to two of Justin's works (which temporally preceded Tertullian's) "*ne sont pas authentiques*" (Louis Pautigny, *Justin, Apologies* [Paris: A. Picard, 1904], viii). It was only Eusebius of Caesarea, in the fourth century, who grouped under the broad category of *apologiai* the second-century writings of Tertullian, Quadratus, Aristides, Justin, Melito, Apolinarius, and Miltiades (the anti-Montanist) that were addressed to the Roman Emperors or their agents with the intention of exculpating the Christians from charges made against them or of explaining Christian ideas (*Historia Ecclesiastica* 2.2.4, 5.5.5, 4.3.1–3, 4.18.2, 4.26.1–2, 5.17.5). The creation of the "genre" of "apologetics" began with Eusebius and progressed with expanded collections of what seemed to the editors to be appropriate "apologetic works" in tenth-century Byzantium, seventeenth-century France, and nineteenth-century Germany. See especially Sara Parvis, "Justin Martyr and the Apologetic Tradition," in *Justin Martyr and His Worlds*, eds. Sara Parvis and Paul Foster (Minneapolis: Fortress Press, 2007), 115–127; Laura Nasrallah, *Christian Responses to Roman Art and Architecture* (Cambridge Cambridge University Press, 2010), ch. 1, "What is an Apology? Christian Apologies and the So-called Second Sophistic," 1–50 (with bibliography). Tertullian's *Apologeticum*, like Plato's, is alternately defensive and prosecutorial—sometimes very aggresively so.

11. Just how nebulous this "distinct" sphere still is can be shown by the fact that although in the United States, "churches" are granted major privileges and tax incentives, there is no "legal" definition of "religion"; the closest definition is that of a "church" in the tax code.

12. This is not to say that there are not many ironic statements in Tertullian (e.g., [famously] *credibile quia ineptum* [*De carne Christi* 5.4]), but he rarely makes consciously positive use of paradoxes. Irony is not paradox. Often the ironic statement is meant to invalidate or deny the possibility of paradox. For instance, when Tertullian says in *De idololatria* (15.8–10) that the Christian is prepared to be in complete obedience to magistrates, princes, and powers "as long as we keep at a distance from idolatry," he is speaking ironically, and will go on to insist that *all* engagement with non-Christians involved one in idolatry. (Thus he was actually denying the possibility of being both a Christian and a loyal subject to the Emperor.) He was speaking like the Roman warlord Marius when he swore to uphold the tribune Saturninus' plebiscite with the words, "I swear to obey the law providing it really is a law" (thereby indicating that he had no intention of obeying the law) (Plutarch, *Marius* 29.4). However self-contradictory and paradoxical Tertullian may appear *from my point of view*, Tertullian was committed to the necessity of a noncontradictory and abstract *veritas*.

13. "Integration, constituting or recognizing the oneness of anything, is not possible without differentiating it from other things" (Nancy Jay, "Sacrifice as Remedy for Having Been Born of Woman," in *Immaculate and Powerful. The Female Image and Social Reality*, eds. Clarissa Atkinson, C. Buchanan, and Margaret Miles [Boston: Beacon Press, 1985], 283–309, 295). The idea that there were no other gods "before" Yahweh presupposes the existence of other gods. "Paradoxically the implied existence of other gods is of fundamental importance to the basic idea of biblical monotheism. (. . .) In the same sense that the idea of the chosen people presupposes the existence of other

peoples, the idea of the 'one God' . . . presupposes the existence of other gods. (. . .) The idea of exclusivity—of God among the gods, of Israel among the nations, and of the unswerving truthfulness, loyalty, and incessant memory required of anyone wishing to remain within this exclusive relationship—implies the idea of difference, and the idea of difference implies plurality" (Jan Assman, *Of God and Gods* [Madison, Wisc.: University of Wisconsin Press, 2008], 3–4).

4. SEGREGATED BY A PERFECT FEAR

1. Quoted by Valerio Valeri, *Kingship and Sacrifice: Ritual and Society in Ancient Hawaii*, trans. Paula Wissing (Chicago: The University of Chicago Press, 1985), 24.

2. Valerio Valeri, *The Forest of Taboos: Morality, Hunting, and Identity among the Huaulu of the Moluccas* (Madison: University of Wisconsin Press, 2000), 53.

3. Tertullian's *fides* reflected only some aspects of what was, in ancient Latin, a complex and paradoxical set of reciprocal ideas that included both the fullness of power and its voluntary restraint. Latin *fides* could be used of the unfettered will, the *voluntas*, the fullness of power, the "discretion" of the victorious general over the conquered people, the patron or father over the family and client, the host over guest, the *creditor* over the *nexus*—which in turn (ideally) evoked the (voluntary) limitation or restraint of that power from within: that is, the voluntary restraint or inhibition of the will of the person with power. In response, the perception of such restraint elicited from others the feeling of certainty, trust ("confidence," "faith") in the person into whose discretion one had surrendered. The person of *fides*, in Roman tradition, was the person who could do harm but chose not to. Like *religio*, Latin *fides* was both a set of emotions and what evoked those emotions. For *fides* see Barton, *Roman Honor* passim esp. 142–58.

4. *Statim omnes pristini sensus retorpescunt, sanguis animi gelascit, caro spiritus exolescit. . . . Iam et ipsa mens sibi, quo vomat, quaerit, atque ita infirmitas, semel quae percussa est, sauciatam fidem vel in haeresin vel in saeculum expirat.* Socrates, confronted by his death, would not have been able to think clearly about the soul: "What could the *anima* of Socrates then contemplate with clarity? The sacred ship had returned, the hemlock drunk, death was now immanent; his spirit (*anima*) was, as one may suppose, naturally overwhelmed (*consternata*) at every emotion (*motus*)—or he would have been out of his mind" (*De anima* 1.1).

5. For the "soul-killing" Epicureans, see *De spectaculis* 30; cf. *De resurrectione carnis* 1.4, 2.1–2. In the latter passage, he includes the Sadducees and Marcionites—those who kill the soul by denying the resurrection.

6. *Verum ubi vementi magis est commota metu mens,/consentire animam totam per membra videmus/sudoresque ita palloremque existere toto/corpore et infringi linguam vocemque aboriri,/caligare oculos, sonere auris, succidere artus, denique concidere ex animi terrore videmus/saepe homines.*

7. For the paralysis and *stupor* caused by anxiety, fear, and shame, see Plautus, *Amphitruo* 333; Terence, *Phormio* 281–84; Horace, *Epodi* 7.16; Virgil, *Aeneis* 2.119–21; Livy 22.53.6, 9.1–11, 6.34.8, 29.12.15; Seneca, *Epistulae* 11.1; Barton, *Roman Honor*, 78–81, 84.

8. "'O Jupiter who gives and takes away sore afflictions,' cries the mother of a child that has been ill in bed for five long months, 'if the quartan chills leave my child, then on the morning of the day on which you appoint a fast he shall stand naked in the Tiber.' Should chance or the doctor raise the sick boy up from his peril, his crazy mother will kill him by planting him on the cold bank and bringing back his fever. What is the malady that has stricken her mind? *timor deorum*" (Horace, *Satirae* 2.3.288–95).

9. "The warrior's weapons fail him; another pays his vows to heaven and his own house falls and buries him in the act. Another slips from his coach and dashes out his eager soul. Make a fair reckoning, and you find shipwreck everywhere. You tell me that for those the water overwhelms there is no burial. As if it mattered how our perishable flesh comes to its end, by fire or water or the lapse of time. Whatever you may do, all these things achieve the same goal." (*Illum bellantem*

arma decipiunt, illum diis vota reddentem penatium suorum ruina sepelit. Ille vehiculo lapsus properantem spiritum excussit, cibus avidum strangulavit, abstinentem frugalitas. Si bene calculum ponas, ubique naufragium est [Satyricon 115].)

10. See Barton, *Roman Honor*, 78–84.

11. There were Romans who shared Tertullian's frustrated impatience. Seneca quotes a line from a poem by his friend Vagellius: "'If I must fall . . . I would prefer to fall from the sky.' I might say the same thing: If I must fall, let me fall with the world shattered, not because it is right to hope for a public disaster but because it is a great solace in dying to see that the earth too, is mortal" (*Quaestiones naturales* 6.2.9). "The only calm for me—if with me I see the universe overwhelmed in ruins; with me let all things pass away. It is sweet to drag others down when you are perishing" (Seneca, *Medea* 426). That such sentiments were already proverbial in Rome of the civil war period is suggested by Cicero: "We feel it wicked and inhuman for men to declare . . . that they care not if, when they themselves are dead, the universal conflagration ensues" (*De finibus* 3.64).

12. Cf. *De pudicitia* 9.9; 9.15. The devil's impatience sprang from his inability to tolerate his subjection to god and man (*De patientia* 5.5.6).

13. See Camus, *The Rebel: An Essay of Man in Revolt* (New York: Vintage Books, 1956 [1951]), 17; cf. Max Scheler, *Ressentiment*, trans. William W. Holdheim (New York: Free Press of Glencoe, 1961 [1910]).

14. *Civitas dei . . . dubitationem tamquam dementiam detestatur. (. . .) sine dubitatione ambulamus.* Seneca's Astyanax marched to his death *nec gradu segni puer* (*Troades* 1090); Polyxena progressed to her death: *non tulit retro gradum* (1151). "No step backward" was also, according to Inga Clendinnen, the motto of the Aztec Warrior: "The Cost of Courage in Aztec Society," *Past & Present* 107 (1985) 44–89, 61.

15. H. Musurillo, *The Acts of the Christian Martyrs* (Oxford: Oxford University Press, 1972), 86–89, 88.

16. *Mea quoque opinione quae sunt dubia, ut sunt, reliquenda sunt, nec, tot ac tantis viris deliberantibus, temere et audaciter in alteram partem ferenda sententia est, ne aut anilis inducatur superstitio aut omnis religio destruatur.*

Tertullian entertained the possibility of worshipping two gods: "If I saw before me two gods . . . [but] were I to worship both, I would be concerned lest excess of duty should be accounted *superstitio* and not *religio*." (*Ecce enim duos intuens deos . . . quid facerem? Si ambos colerem, vererer ne abundantia officii superstitio potius quam religio existimaretur [Adversus Marcionem* 1.5.4–5].) Here Tertullian fears excess of *officium* would turn *religio* to *superstitio*.

17. "In the conflict of certainties and uncertainties, of explicitness and obscurity, *fides* (here something like 'confidence') might be dissipated, *veritas* imperilled, and the *divinitas* himself branded as inconsistent." (. . . *incerta de certis et obscura de manifestis praeiudicari, vel ne inter discordiam certorum et incertorum, manifestorum et obscurorum fides dissipetur, veritas periclitetur, ipsa divinitas ut inconstans denotetur [De resurrectione carnis* 21.2].)

18. *Dicimus plenum primo perfectumque credendum iudicium dei, ut ultimum iam atque exinde perpetuum.*

19. Cf. *De spectaculis* 21–22. Tertullian attacked the *curiositas* and *scrupulositas* that led to excessive debate and inquiry. "'Seek and ye shall find' only applied to the doubting Jews and to the period before Jesus was clearly recognized as the Christ and Son of God" (*De praescriptione haereticorum* (8–11). "Seek and ye shall find" was the litany of the heretics, the *inimici veritatis* (ibid. 43.2). They were always advocating the search for something; in so doing they confessed that they still had no certainty, only doubt (*dubitatio*) (ibid. 14.6).

20. *Nobis curiositate opus non est post Christum Iesum nec inquisitione post evangelium. Cum credimus nihil desideramus ultra credere. Hoc enim prius credimus non esse quod ultra credere debeamus.*

21. *veritatis integritas . . . non inmutare sententiam nec variare iudicium. Non potest aliud esse, quod vere quidem est bonum seu malum. Omnia autem penes veritatem dei fixa sunt.* "In the conflict of

certainties and uncertainties, of explicitness and obscurity, confidence (*fides*) may be dissipated, *veritas* imperilled, and the Divinitas itself be branded as inconsistent." (. . . *incerta de certis et obscura de manifestis praeiudicari, vel ne inter discordiam certorum et incertorum, manifestorum et obscurorum fides dissipetur, veritas periclitetur, ipsa divinitas ut inconstans denotetur* [*De resurrectione carnis* 21.2].)

22. A "Brocken spectre" (German *Brockengespenst*), first observed in the Harz mountains, is the extraordinarily magnified shadow of the observer that can be, in a heavy mist, projected upon the upper surfaces of clouds opposite the sun onto a mountainside or cloud bank. The fall of the shadow on water droplets at varying distances from the eye easily confounds the depth perception of the viewer. The head of the magnificently magnified figure—of oneself—is often surrounded by a huge and magnificent glowing halo and rings of colored light.

23. *Apologeticum* 32.1.

24. Peter Berger and Thomas Luckman, *The Social Construction of Reality: A Treatise in the Sociology of Knowledge* (Garden City, N.Y.: Doubleday, 1967), 160.

25. Compare the words that Apuleius' Isis addressed Lucius: "Not your birth, nor even your position, [nor your fine education] has been of any help to you whatever. . . ." (*Metamorphoses* 11.15). The contradictory aspects of Tertullian's Christ are exactly his own: man and god, fleshly and spiritual, weak and exceedingly strong (*hominem et deum . . . hinc carneum, inde spiritalem, hinc infirmum, inde praefortem* [*De carne Christi* 5.7].)

26. *Neminem pudet, neminem paenitet. . . . Quid hoc mali est, quod naturalia mali non habet, timorem, pudorem tergiversationem, paenitentiam, deplorationem?* In Acts, the apostles' having been interrogated by the Sanhedrin, were released "rejoicing that they were worthy to be dishonored for the Name" (5.41). For a subtle and elegant discussion of notions of shame in the late antique sources, see Virginia Burrus, *Saving Shame; Martyrs, Saints and other Abject Subjects* (Philadelphia: University of Pennsylvania Press, 2007).

27. Tertullian was aware of and sometimes used Latin *religio* to express any careful and scrupulous attention inspired by *pudor*. The slave who behaved disrespectfully to his master was *irreligiosus* (*De ieiunio* 10.8). Christians who did not show reverence to the images or swear by the *genius* of the Emperor were labeled *irreligiosi* (*Ad nationes* 1.17). In the *Apologeticum*, he asked: "Where is the *religio*, where is the *veneratio* owed by you to your ancestors? In dress, habit of life, furniture, feeling and speech you have renounced your great-grandfathers!" (*Ubi religio, ubi veneratio maioribus debita a vobis? Habitu, victu, instructu, sensu, ipso denique sermone proavis renuntiastis* [6.9].) "Why need I say more of the *religio* and *pietas* of the Christians toward the Emperor?" (*Sed quid ego amplius de religione atque pietate Christiana in imperatorem?* [Ibid. 33.1].) Such reverent and dutiful attention might have been shown to the Christus of Marcion by the Jews if they had recognized him: "The Jews, certain that he who had come was an alien, not only rejected him as a stranger but even put him to death as an opponent, although they would beyond doubt have recognized him and treated him with all the dutiful attention of *religio* (*omne officium religionis*) if he had been their own." (*Iudaei certi et ipsi ali<en>um fuisse qui venit, non modo respuerint eum ut extraneum verum et interfecerint eum ut adversarium, agnituri sine dubio et omni officio religionis prosecuturi, si ipsorum fuisset* [*Adversus Marcionem* 3.4.2].)

28. *Sed et vulgus iam scit Christum hominem utique aliquem, qualem Iudaei iudicaverunt, quo facilius quis nos hominis cultores existimaverit. Verum neque de Christo erubescimus, cum sub nomine eius deputari et damnari iuvat. . . .*

29. 1 John 4.18.

30. *"Publicaris," inquit, "bonum tibi est;"* qui enim non publicatur in hominibus, publicatur in Domino. Ne confundaris; iustitia te producit in medium. Quid confunderis laudem ferens?*

31. For Athenagoras as an important influence on Tertullian, see J. H. Waszink, *"Pompa diaboli," Vigiliae Christianae* 1 (1947) 13–41.

32. Conversely, the Christians could not be honored by the Romans: "We reject your *honores et purpuras*" (*Octavius* 31.6).

33. It was very important for Tertullian that the dilemmas of Christ the human be his own and that the the the Spiritus Sanctus, the "prophetic engine" of Tertullian, be able to inhabit the living, embodied human being.

34. *Stulta mundi elegit deus, ut confundat sapientia* (*De carne Christi* 4.5 = 1 Corinthians 1.27).

35. In such cases, Tertullian resorted to the argument that God can do anything: "Should God be credited/believed by any other law than that he is believed to be able to do anything? (*non alia lege credendus est, quam ut omnia posse credatur?* [*De resurrectione carnis* 11.4; cf. 38.4; *Apologeticum* 48.6–7]).

36. For example, "When they say that what has undergone death is dead . . . then I must remember . . . that the wisdom of the world is foolishness" (*De resurrectione carnis* 3.3). It is not human but divine *ratio* which proves these convictions (ibid. 3.6; 5.1).

37. On the passage, see Eric Osborn, "Tertullian as Philospher and Roman," *Beihefte zur Zeitschrift für neutestamentliche Wissenschaft und die Kunde der älteren Kirche* 85 (1997) 231–47, 235–38.

38. Cf. *De carne Christi* 8.2 (*carnis ignominia*).

39. Meeks, speaking of the "convert": "The shift of effective reference group could go so far as to attempt to stand the larger society's measures of honor and shame on ther head, to attempt to 'nihilate' the power of those sanctions" (*The Origins of Christian Morality: The First Two Centuries* [New Haven, Conn.: Yale University Press, 1993] 48). For the "nihilation" of the former reference group of the "convert," see Peter Berger and Thomas Luckman. *The Social Construction of Reality: A Treatise in the Sociology of Knowledge* (Garden City, N.Y.: Doubleday, 1967), 159.

40. *Illuc sursum suspicientes Christiani manibus expansis, quia innocuis, capite nudo, quia non erubescimus.* In *Apologeticum* 23.15, the embarrassed demons and false gods blush out of fear of Tertullian's Christian exorcist, his Christ, his God of Judgment.

41. *Non posse suaviter vivi secundum Epicurum; Moralia* 1102B.

42. The Cynics, famously, made shamelessness their point of honor. "[The Cynics are so named] because the dog is a shameless animal, and they make a cult of shamelessness (*anaideia*), not as being beneath modesty (*aidos*)—but as superior to it" (*Scholion* on Aristotle, ed. Brandis, 23). "They [the Cynics] believe that shamelessness is freedom, being hated means they have been speaking frankly" (Aelius Aristides 3, "To Plato: In Defence of the Four" 666–71 in Charles A. Behr, *P. Aelius Aristides, The Complete Works*, 2 vols. [Leiden: Brill, 1986] 1:274–75). Tertullian lists the Cynic/Christian Peregrinus among the models, to be followed by Christians, of those who bravely and aggressively met death (*Ad martyras* 4). (For Lucian, on the other hand, Peregrinus' death was exactly the kind of arrogant and histrionic death abhorred by Marcus Aurelius.) "What he should have done," Lucian says, "was first await death patiently and not cut and run from life" (*Peregrinus* 21). While Tertullian did not name the Cynics explicitly, it seems to me that he was justifying Christian freedom to "talk back" to the Powers That Be on the basis of such freedom granted to the Cynics (*Ad nationes* 1.4.4). For parallel developments and possible direct inluences of the Cynic movement on Christianity, see especially F. Gerald Downing, *Cynics and Christian Origins* (Edinburgh: T & T Clark, 1992).

43. *Troades*, 1091–98.

44. The refusal to be shamed by those who could harm you was related to the notion of laughing in the face of the enemy. The fourth-century author Ammianus Marcellinus tells us that Simonides, condemned to death by burning, died bravely *"laughing amid the flames* in imitation of that other persecuted and illustrious philosopher (*philosophus clarus*) Peregrinus Proteus" (29.1.39).

45. *Qui enim non publicatur in hominibus, publicatur in Domino. Ne confundaris; iustitia te producit in medium. Quid confunderis laudem ferens?* (*De fuga* 9.4). Tertullian, speaking at length of the

mortifications of the suppliant sinner: ". . . while it abases the man, it raises him; while it covers him with squalor, it renders him more clean; while it accuses, it excuses; while it condemns it absolves. The less quarter you give yourself, the more, believe me, God will give you." (*Cum igitur provoluit hominem, magis relevat; cum squalidum facit, magis mundatum reddit; cum accusat, excusat; cum condemnat, absoluit: in quantum non peperceris tibi, in tantum tibi deus, crede, parcet* [*De paenitentia* 9.6].) For more on *exomologesis*, see *De oratione* 7. The defiant shamelessness of the Christian needed, like that of the gladiator, to be witnessed by his or her enemies.

46. *Angelus emissus est taliter alloquens: Daniel, homo es miserabilis, ne timueris, quoniam ex die prima, qua dedisti animam tuam recogitatui et humiliationi coram deo, exauditum est verbum tuum, et ego introivi verbo tuo. Ita xerophagiarum miseratio et humiliatio metum expellunt et aures dei advertunt et occultorum compotes faciunt.*

47. For example, *Passio Scillitanorum* 2. However, consider Tertullian's remarkable paeon to retribution (*talio*) in *Adversus Marcionem* 2.18.1.

48. In this aspect of Tertullian's thought, "turning the other cheek" did not imply that Tertullian had forgotten any of the insults or injuries which would, finally and inevitably, be avenged by his god. See Tertullian's juxtaposition of the command to "turn the other cheek" with the *lex talionis* (*Adversus Marcionem* 4.16). "It is in the interest of *disciplina* that injury should be avenged (*vindicari*). For it is only by fear of vengeance (*metu ultionis*) all iniquity is kept in check" (4.16.6; cf. 4.17.10). Finally, the self-restraint of the Christian is endurable because his god promises certain vengeance in the end.

49. *Nam omnis iniuria seu lingua seu manu incussa, cum patientiam offenderit eodem exitu dispungetur quo telum aliquod in petra constantissimae duritiae libratum et obtusum: concidet enim ibidem inrita opera et infructuosa et nonnumquam repercussum in eum qui emisit reciproco impetu saeviet. Nempe idcirco quis te laedit ut doleas, quia fructus laedentis in dolore laesi est: ergo cum fructum eius everteris non dolendo, ipse doleat necesse est amissione fructus sui; tunc tu non modo inlaesus ibis (quod enim solum tibi sufficit) sed insuper adversarii tui et frustratione oblectatus et dolore defensus.* This strategy was dear to the Roman Stoics of the Empire. Marcus Cato was, according to Seneca, struck while in the public bath by a man who failed to recognize him. "Later, when the man was apologizing, Cato said, 'I do not recall receiving a blow.' (. . .) Only a great soul can be superior to injury; the most humiliating kind of revenge is to have it appear that the man was not worth taking revenge upon. Many have taken slight injuries too deeply to heart in the act of revenging them. He is a great and noble man who acts the lordly wild beast that listens unconcernedly to the baying of tiny dogs" (*De ira* 2.32). Cf. *De vita beata* 27.3; *De constantia sapientis* 3.5, 6.8; Petronius, *Satyricon* 54.1; Marcus Aurelius 4.49.1; Barton, *Roman Honor*, 118–19; ead., "Savage Miracles: The Redemption of Lost Honor in Roman Society and the Sacrament of the Gladiator and the Martyr," *Representations* 45 (1994) 41–71.

50. Tertullian would shame the heretics who deny the flesh of Christ (*De carne Christi* 24.4). He would shame those who mock the Christian notion of bodily resurrection (*De resurrectione carnis* 1.2).

51. Cf. ibid. 2.4: "If they (the Iudaei) had *proximum diligerent, id est semet ipsos*. . . ." *Adversus Marcionem* 1.23.3–9: *inimicos quoque nostros et hoc nomine iam extraneos diligere iubeamur.* (He goes on to argue that the primary duty is to love "one's own," and only, by extension, those who are not "one's own.") Later in the *Adversus Marcionem*, he gives this edict the broadest possible interpretation while admitting two levels of its application—first toward *proximi*; and second, by extension, toward *extranei*, adding, "For who is there who is able to love stangers?" (*Quis enim poterit diligere extraneos?* 4.16.10–11).

52. In I John 4.7–21, the commandment to "love one another" was limited to fellow Christians (esp. 4.11, 4.20). For "the passionately sectarian love [of the Johanine Christian community] that binds members of the group exclusively to one another and the God they believe in,"

see Wayne A. Meeks, *The Origins of Christian Morality: The First Two Centuries* (New Haven, Conn.: Yale University Press, 1993, 61). The classical rabbinic version was "to love thy neighbor in the commandments." For the 20 or so "Christians for Christians" [third century c.e.] inscriptions from the upper Tembris Valley in Phrygia, see Elsa Gibson, "The 'Christians for Christians' inscriptions of Phrygia," *Harvard Theological Studies* 32 (Missoula, Mont: Scholars Press, 1978); Graydon F. Snyder, *Ante Pacem: Archaeological Evidence of Church Life Before Constantine* (Macon, Ga.: Mercer University Press, 2003 [1985], 241–42) entertains the idea that these inscriptions might reflect the kind of "public witness and encounter" mentality of Phrygian Montanists.

53. *Sed aliquis sustinet nostra nec obstrepit. Hoc est igitur delictum, quod gentiles nostra noverunt, quod sub conscientia iniustorum sumus, quod beneficium eorum est, si quid operamur.*

54. *Fides* is a word we shall meet often in Tertullian, most often as "fidelity." Tertullian's use of this word reflected only some aspects of what was, in ancient Latin, a delicate balancing system—a paradoxical set of reciprocal ideas that included both the fullness of power and its voluntary restraint. *Fides*, for Tertullian, was the antithesis of *haeresis*. "*Haereses* derive such strength as they have from the infirmities of individuals—having no strength whenever they encounter a really powerful *fides*." (*Non aliter haereses de quorundum infirmitatibus habent quod valent, nihil valentes si in bene valentem fidem incurrant* [*De praescriptione haereticorum* 2.8].) Heretics were *infideles, rebelli, desertores*. In many ways, for Tertullian, having an object of devotion was the means to the end of the emotion of fidelity. *Fides* was, for Tertullian, an emotional state—indeed, the ideal emotional state. *Fides* was its own reward. The *fidelis* did not doubt or hesitate. The excitement, the enthusiasm, the fearless fanaticism of *fides* was the greatest reward for the *disciplina* of the *fidelis*: it enthused; it filled with power. The willful self-restraint of Latin *fides* was expressed particularly in standing behind, being committed to one's "word" or oath. *Fides* in Tertullian could, on occasion, mean (as it did in older Latin texts), something akin to "accrediting" (and so, "trusting in") someone who has proven his or her *fides*.

In the vocabulary of Tertullian, the words that most often approached our notion of "faith" were the noun *fiducia* and the participle *confidens*: both expressed for Tertullian a feeling of obstinate certainty, often linked to his notion of *veritas* ("something firm").

55. *Fideles gentilium matrimonia subeuntes stupri reos constat esse et arcendos ab omni communicatione fraternitatis, ex litteris apostoli dicentis cum eiusmodi ne cibum quidem sumendum.* The sinner should be, like a leper, excluded from all contact and communication (*Adversus Marcionem* 4.9.3).

56. The Roman general, in the Republic, preferred to think of the *hostis* as a worthy opponent, and often adopted the defeated as his *clientes*, taking their name as his *cognomen*. But in the civil war period, the enemy was thoroughly "demonized." See, for example, Cicero's descriptions of his enemies Lucius Piso and Publius Clodius: "With these furies and firebrands, yes, with these pernicious portents who brought all but pestilence upon this empire" (*De haruspicum responsis* 4 [56 b.c.e.]). Cf. *De domo sua* [57 b.c.e.] 3.5+7, 8.21, 9.23, 10.26, 18.48, 27.72, 37.99, 40.105, 41.107, 44.115, 47.124, 48.126, 52.133, 54.139, 9.23.

57. Berger and Luckman, *Social Construction of Reality*, 159.

58. For Tertullian, "heretical" Christians were to be shunned as much—or even more—than non-Christians. For a parallel "raising of fences and safeguards" and the institution of Jewish ultra-orthodoxy as a response to the challenge of Jewish reform movements and "secularism," see Benjamin Brown, "The Two Faces of Religious Radicalism: Orthodox Zealotry and 'Holy Sinning' in Nineteenth-Century Hasidism in Hungary and Galicia," *The Journal of Religion* 93 (2013) 341–74.

59. For the poem in English, see *The Poetry of Yehuda Amichai*, ed. Robert Alter (New York: FSG [2015], 15).

60. For Perpetua's rejection of *misericordia* and *pietas* for the living, see *Passio* 5+6. The one object of her compassion seems to be her dead brother. [Note: *Misericordia* was an old word; *humanitas* was Ciceronian; *compassio* a new word.]

61. The *misericordia* of God did not play a major role in Tertullian's thought apart from *Adversus Marcionem* 2.17.1–3, where attention to God's mercy hardly counterbalances Tertullian's interest in his god's judgmental severity.

62. Speaking against those who believed that God shared in Jesus' sufferings, Tertullian asserts that to say that Jesus was accursed or suffering is not blasphemy—but to say that God the Father suffered would be blasphemy: "Therefore the Father *nec compassus est* with the son. (. . .) What does it mean to suffer with another (*compati*) than to suffer (*pati*)? He [God] is incapable of suffering in company with another (*incompassibilis*); otherwise, if he can suffer with another (*compassibilis*), he is of course capable of suffering (*passibilis*)." (*Ergo nec compassus est Pater Filio.* (. . .) *Quid est enim compati quam cum alio pati? Porro si impassibilis Pater, utique et incompassibilis; utique si compassibilis, utique passibilis* [*Adversus Praxean* 29.4–5].)

63. The late–fourth century C.E. grammarian Flavius Charisius, tracing the development of pity from *pietas*, records several lines that Warmington attributed to an ancient Latin poet: "Have you no *misericoridia* (*nihil commiserescit*) for the misfortune of men, for mine? Suppose I am a newcomer. Are you not moved by the solemn aid due to the name of brother, by the name of *pietas*?" (*Te nihil/ hominum fortunae, nihil commiserescit meae? / Finge advenam esse; nihil fraterni nominis/sollemne auxilium et nomen pietatis movet?* [*Corpus Glossariorum Latinorum* 1.280, 13K= *Remains* of Old Latin, 2:618–19, lines 110–13].) The convergence of *pietas* and *misericordia* seems to have occurred, however, principally in the imperial period. "*[À] l'époque impériale apparaît le sens de 'pitié'*" (Ernout and Meillet, *Dictionnaire*, s.v. *pius*, p. 510; cf. Edward B. Stevens, "Topics of Pity in the Poetry of the Roman Republic," *American Journal of Philology* 62 [1941] 426–40, 426–27). In Apuleius' *Metamorphoses*, the kidnapped girl asks *pietas* of the "mother" of the brigands who has only just horrified her by declaring that the robbers would ignore her tears and burn her alive: "Terrified by her words, the girl kissed the old woman's hands. '*Parce mi parens*,' she begged, 'and mindful of human *pietas* (*pietatis humanae memor*) help me a little in my harsh misfortune. You have had much experience in your long life and I do not think *miseratio* has totally dried up in that honorable grey head of yours.'" (*Tali puella sermone deterrita manuque eius exosculata.* "*Parce*," inquit "*mi parens, et durissimo casui meo pietatis humanae memor subsiste paululum. Nec enim, ut reor, aevo longiore maturae tibi in ista sancta canitie miseratio prorsus exaruit*" [4.26].) The development of these associations between *pietas* and *misericordia* can be grasped in the words of Apuleius' Lucius (at his public mock trial): "When I had finished this speech my tears welled up again and I stretched out my hands in supplication, sorrowfully begging now one group in the name of public *misericordia*, and now another for love of their own dear children." (*Porrectisque in preces manibus per publicam misericordiam, per pignorum caritatem maestus tunc hos, tunc illos deprecabor* [*Metamorphoses* 3.7].) Domitian, according to Suetonius, could frame his death sentences as clemency by first condemning "traitors" to brutal public beatings and then begging the senate to allow him to grant the accused the choice of his own death: "Permit me, *patres conscripti*, to gain by your *pietas* a favor which I know I shall obtain with difficulty, namely that you should indulge the condemned with the free choice in the manner of their death." (*Permittite, patres conscripti, a pietate vestra impetrari, quod scio me difficulter impetraturum, ut damnatis liberum mortis arbitrium indulgeatis.* . . . [*Domitianus* 11.3].)

64. *Quamvis enim placida et tranquilla, quam nec coniugis fletus statim viduae nec liberorum conspectus exinde pupillorum lege pietatis inflexerat, vel in hoc tamen mota, ne moveretur, ipsa constantia concussa est adversus inconstantiae concussionem.*

65. "[T]here is a chest (*arcus*) of a sort. . . . Once a month every man brings some modest coin . . . as a voluntary offering. You might call them the trust funds of *pietas*. For they are not spent upon banquets nor drinking parties nor thankless eating houses; but to feed the poor and to

bury them, for boys and girls who lack property and parents, and then for slaves grown old and shipwrecked mariners; and any who may be in mines, islands or prisons—provided that it is for the sake of God's *secta*, those who have become the wards/pensioners of their confession." (*Etiam si quod arcae genus est, non de honoraria summa quasi redemptae religionis congregatur. Modicam unusquisque stipem menstrua die . . . sponte confert. Haec quasi deposita pietatis sunt. Nam inde non epulis nec potaculis nec ingratis voratrinis dispensatur, sed egenis alendis humandisque et pueris ac puellis re ac parentibs destitutis, iamque domesticis senibus, item naufragis, et si qui in metallis, et si qui in insulis vel in custodiis, dumtaxat ex causa dei sectae, alumni confessionis suae fiunt* [Tertullian, *Apologeticum* 39.5–6].) The expenses of the *agape* are in the name of *pietas* (*Apologeticum* 39.16). One of the few acts that authorize the Christian woman to appear in public is to visit Christians who are debilitated (*De cultu feminarum* 2.11.1–2).

66. *Apologeticum* 36.4, 37.1; *Ad Scapulum* 1.3; Minucius Felix, *Octavius* 31.8 (*odisse non novimus*).

67. Musurillo, *Acts*, 86–89.

68. Christians do not feel free to hate or curse anyone: "God . . . forbids us to hate even with cause, when he bids us to love our enemies. God does not allow us to curse even with cause, when he teaches us to bless those who curse us." (*Deus certe etiam cum causa prohibet odisse, qui inimicos diligi iubet; deus etiam cum causa maledicere non sinit, qui maledicentes benedici praecipit"* [*De spectaculis* 16].) Cf. Athenagoras, *Legatio* 11; *Didache* 1.3, 2.7.

69. Compare the important role that the hatred of God plays in Lactantius, *De ira dei* 5.

70. For example, *De idololatria* 4.5, 9.6; *Scorpiace* 1.9; *De ieiunio* 1.5. (Here it is the Christian *psychici* who are anathematizing Tertullian.) In this self-contradiction, Tertullian is no different from the authors of the Gospels. Cf. Matthew 21.18–19; Mark 10.11–15, 11.12–22; Luke 9.5, 10.10–12; Acts 18.6. See the collection of Coptic Christian curses collected by Marvin W. Meyer and Richard Smith, *Ancient Christian Magic* (Princeton: Princeton University Press, 1999 [1994]), 183–273.

71. For another extended depiction of the glories of the Last Day, see *De resurrectione carnis* 25.

72. Division within the family was part of the common stock of eschatological motives. Mark 13.12; Matthew 12.49–53; Luke 12.49–53; Gospel of Thomas 55, 42.25–28; 101, 49.32–50.1. Interestingly, Tertullian, in his long theodicy in the *Adversus Marcionem* (2.15.1–2), justifies God's punishing of children for their fathers' crimes; it worked as a deterrent, "for surely any man will be more concerned for his children's safety than his own." (*Quis enim non magis filiorum salutem quam suam curet?* [2.14.1].) Here, inherited guilt would seem to make the man with children better able to face judgment day!

73. Cf. 1 Timothy 4.15.

74. *Quid si, quod diximus damnum, lucrum senties? Per continentiam enim negotiaberis magnam substantiam sanctitatis, parsimonia carnis spiritum adquires. Recogitemus enim ipsam conscientiam nostram, quam alium se homo sentiat, cum forte a sua femina cessat. Spiritaliter sapit: si orationem facit ad dominum, prope est caelo; si scripturis incumbit, totus illic est; si psalmam canit, placet sibi; si daemonem adiurat, confidit sibi* (10.1–2).

75. *Nam et quod nostrum videtur alienum est: nihil enim nostrum quoniam dei [sunt] omnia, cuius ipsi quoque nos [sumus]. Itaque si damno adfecti inpatienter senserimus, non de nostro amissum dolentes adfines cupiditatis deprehendemur: alienum quaerimus cum alienum amissum aegre sustinemus. Qui damni impatientia concitatur terrena caelestibus anteponendo, de proximo in deum peccat.*

76. There was an important ideological logic in Augustus' laws dictating that the Romans should be married and produce children. These *pignora*, hostages, discouraged rebellious and suicidal behavior. Seneca's writings are filled with stories of children and elderly parents acting as hostages of the tyrant and procuring the cooperation of the adults: Consider Astyanax in Seneca's *Troades*, Pastor's son in *De Ira*, Hercules' father in the *Hercules Furens*, Seneca's own father. The greatest example in Latin literature of the terror caused by the desire to protect a child was that instilled in Aeneas by his child and his father.

77. Cyprian, like Tertullian, insisted upon the necessity of putting one's loyalty to the Christian community before one's *res* or *parentes* (*De lapsis* 11–12). It was the failure of the *lapsi* to do this that caused them to break their oath and their bonds to Christ, to become *negatores*.

78. Tertullian quotes Matthew (10.16) on families breaking up on account of a member's commitment to Jesus. Cf. *De carne Christi* 7.13.

79. Christians took no care for things like food or clothing (or any of the other "worldly desires," such as spouses and families (*Ad uxorem* 1.4.7; cf. *De oratione* 6.3). In his address "To My Wife," Tertullian quotes Paul (1 Corinthians 7.34): "The unmarried woman . . . thinks about the things of the Lord. . . . But she who is married is solicitous . . . how she may please her husband" (*Ad uxorem* 1.3.6; cf. 2.3.4–2.4; *De exhortatione castitatis* 9.1).

80. *status fidei* here seems to combine the notions of standing firm, taking a position, and drawing the line.

81. *Non admittit status fidei allegationem necessitatis. (. . .) Nam et ad sacrificandum et directo negandum necessitate quis premitur tormentorum sive poenarum. Tamen nec illi necessitati disciplina conivet, quia potior est necessitas timendae negationis et obeundi martyrii quam evadendae passionis et implendi officii. [7] Ceterum subvertit totam substantiam sacramenti causatio eiusmodi. . . .*

82. *"vivere ergo habes?" Quid tibi cum deo est, si tuis legibus vivis?*

83. Tacitus' description of the foraging Fenni in the *Germania* (however disappointingly brief) is the only Roman text that I know of that describes, however briefly, a hunter–gatherer society with any seriousness. These ungoverned foragers are surpassing strange to this ultra-urbanite; he is aghast at their poverty and is confused by their equality—even while he envies them their independence. *"They have no need to ask for anything,"* and it is this that gives them freedom from both hope and fear. "The Fenni live in a state of astonishing wildness and loathsome poverty: no arms, no horses, no household; wild plants for their food, skins for their clothing, the ground for their beds. Their only power is in their arrows; for want of iron they tip them with sharp bone. Hunting is the support of the women as well as the men, for they accompany the men freely and claim their share of the spoil; nor have their infants any shelter against the wild beasts and rain except the covering afforded by a few intertwined branches. To these huts the young men return; these are the asylum of age. And yet they think it happier to live this way than to groan over field labor, to be encumbered with the building of houses, and to be forever involving their own and their neighbors' wealth in hope and fear. Untroubled in their relations with other men, untroubled in their relations with the gods, they have achieved something very difficult: they have no need to ask for anything" (*Germania* 46).

84. *Praesume, oro te, nihil tibi opus esse, si domino appareas, immo omnia habere, si habeas dominum.* The Christians were competing with the Cynics to see how much they could live without.

85. *The Complete Poems of Emily Dickinson* (Boston/Toronto: Little, Brown & Co., 1951, no. 985).

86. Compare the images of stripping down to a nakedness devoid of shame in the Gospel of Thomas (37, 39.29–40.1; 21a, 36.33–37.5). When the ultra-cosmopolitan lover of death, Yukio Mishima (the Japanese Peregrinus Proteus), converted in his middle age to being an ultra-nationalist and supporter of the divine Emperor, he led his own militia, practiced asceticism, and demonstrated of his sincerity with his final theatrical *seppuku*.

87. All displays of splendor and majesty were, for Tertullian, the parades of the devil. J. H. Waszink particularly associates these displays with those in what seemed, for Tertullian, their most spectacular form, the Roman circus ("*Pompa diaboli*," esp. 31–34).

88. For the New Prophecy movement, see the prologue to the *Passio Perpetuae* (1) and the dreams and visions contained within; Cecil M. Robeck, Jr., *Prophecy in Carthage: Perpetua, Tertullian, and Cyprian* (Cleveland: Pilgrim, 1992); Nasrallah, *Ecstasy of Folly*; William Tabbernee, *Prophets and Gravestones: An Imaginative History of Montanists and Other Early Christians* (Peabody, Mass:

Hendrickson, 2009). Tertullian rejected the even more extreme rigor of the "Marcionites" and other "Enkratites" (who rejected marriage outright). Was it jealousy?—a clinging to life?

89. *Sunt qui existimant Christianos, expeditum morti genus, ad hanc obstinationem abdicatione voluptatum erudiri, quo facilius vitam contemnant amputatis quasi retinaculis eius nec desiderent quam iam supervacuam sibi fecerunt.*

90. When we order a sibling whom we have pinned in an armlock to, "Say 'uncle'!", the word "uncle" is a nonsense word—anything at all can be and is substituted for it. What signaled submission was that the defeated lost their "word"; they become ventriloquists' dummies. See Barton, *Roman Honor*, 133–58, esp. 150. For Tertullian, it was not *what* but *that* one swore by the *genius* of the Emperor, but that in doing so one succumbed to the will of the imperial magistrate. For a very useful discussion of the notion of swearing by the *genius* of the emperor, see G. W. Clarke, *The Octavius of Marcus Minucius Felix* (New York: Newman, 1974), 329.

91. If you want to be a *domini discipulus*, you must take up distress and your cross (*angustias et cruciatus tuos*) and follow the *dominus* (*De idololatria* 12.2). The Christian model of surrender into the *fides* of God was the surrender of the defeated into the *fides* of the Roman imperator.

92. *illos nunquam magis detriumphamus quam cum pro fidei obstinatione damnamur.*

93. Probably the Emperor Severus who associated to himself in imperial power first his son Caracalla in 198 and then his younger son Geta in 208 C.E.

94. *Adhibetur quidam illic magis dei miles ceteris constantior fratribus, qui se duobus dominis servire posse praesumpserant, solus liber capite, coronamento in manu otioso. Vulgato iam et ista disciplina Christiano, relucebat.*

95. *Statim tribunus: 'Cur,' inquit, 'tam diversus habitus?' Negavit ille sibi cum ceteris licere. Causas expostulatus 'Christianus sum' respondit. O militem gloriosum in deo! Suffragia exinde, et res apud acta et reus ad praefectos. Ibidem gravissimas paenulas posuit, relevari auspicatus, speculatoriam morosissimam de pedibus absolvit, terrae sanctae insistere incipiens, gladium nec dominicae defensioni necessarium reddidit, laurea de manu caruit: et nunc rufatus sanguinis sui spe, calceatus de evangelii paratura, succinctus acutiore verbo dei ac totus de apostolo armatus, ut de martyrii candida laurea melius coronandus donativum Christi in carcere expectat.*

96. In Chapter 15 of *De corona*, Tertullian imagines all the crowns handed out by *their* King. (Much of his imagery is coming from the Apocalypse of John.) In 15.1, he quotes: "You also be faithful unto death, and fight the good fight, whose crown the apostle feels so justly confident has been set aside for him" [2 Timothy 4.8]. (*Esto et tu fidelis ad mortem, decerta et tu bonum agonem, cuius coronam et apostolus repositam sibi merito confidit.*) Cf. *Scorpiace* 13.10: "I have fought the good fight, I have finished my course, I have kept *fides*; there is set aside for me the crown which the *dominus* will give me on that day." (*agonem bonum decertavi, cursum consummavi, fidem custodivi; superest corona, quam mihi dominus illa die reddet.*) Cf. *De cultu feminarum* 2.3.3; Minucius Felix, *Octavius* 38.4. "How happy is the *ecclesia*, on which apostles poured forth all their teachings along with their blood! (. . .) where Paul wins his crown in a death like John [the Baptist's]." (*Ista quam felix ecclesia cui totam doctrinam apostoli cum sanguine suo profuderunt, . . . ubi Paulus Iohannis exitu coronatur, ubi apostolus Iohannes* [*De praescriptione haereticorum* 36.3–4].) "Some ferocity has already arrayed with a crown the *fides* of martyrs." (*aliqua atrocitas fidem martyrum coronavit* [*Scorpiace* 1.5].) "He who had called [the Christians] to salvation has been pleased to summon them to glory also, that they who were rejoicing in consequence of their deliverance may be in transports when they are crowned likewise." (*Amavit, qui vocaverat in salutem, invitare ad gloriam, ut qui gaudeamus liberati, exultemus coronati* [*Scorpiace* 6.2].) Cf. *De fuga in persecutione* 1.5. Compare the concluding line in some versions of the account of the Scillitan martyrs: "And so they all together were crowned (*coronati*) with martyrdom; and they reign (*regnant*) with the Father and the Son and the Holy Ghost, for ever and ever. Amen." (J. Armitage Robinson, ed., *Texts and Studies: Contributions to Biblical and Patristic Literature* 2 [Cambridge: Cambridge University Press, 1891] 18.1). Note:

This line does not appear in the edition of Musurillo. Cyprian's *confessores* reject the *corona diaboli* and await the *dei corona* (*De lapsis* 2; cf. 10).

97. *"les préceptes, la règle que le maître impose à l'élève,"* (H. I. Marrou, *"Doctrina* et *disciplina* dans la langue des Pères de l'Eglise," *Archivum Latinitatis Medii Aevi* 9 [1934]: 5–25: 10). Occasionally, Tertullian uses *disciplina* to mean the governing strictures or the rules or laws by which any group operates, just as we would talk about "scholarly disciplines." See, for example, *De idololatria* 9.3, where he talks about the *magorum religio*.

98. Compare *De idololatria* 14.5; *De corona* 10.8–10; *De resurrectione carnis* 21. 3. There are times, in Tertullian, where *superstitio* is still an excess. Marcion and his followers have an excessive *askēsis*. The Jews have an excess of laws. Seneca in his *Epistulae* 95.35 compared philosophy with the military in much the way that Tertullian compared Christianity with the military and advocated a sort a fanatical *superstitio* for philosophy: ". . . so it is with those whom you would bring to the happy life; the first foundations must be laid, and virtue worked into these men. Let them be held by a sort of *superstitio*; let them love her; let them desire to live with her and refuse to live without her." (*Prima fundamenta iacienda sunt et insinuanda virtus. Huius quadam superstitione teneantur; hanc ament; cum hac vivere velint, sine hac nolint.*)

99. Cyprian the Carthaginian bishop also showed a fondness for the word *disciplina* but prefered *fides* even to *disciplina*. For the committed authoritarian administrator of the Christian Empire, obedience and loyalty counted more than willfulness. *Disciplina* was mainly for the officials of the *ecclesia*, *fides* (both fidelity and trust) for the obedient subject in Cyprian's mind.

100. For wonderful descriptions of the complex strategies of Roman orators, see the remarks of Cicero, *De oratore* 1.221 and especially those of Titus Castricius as reported by Aulus Gellius, *Noctes Atticae* 1.6.4. See the illuminating discussion of Tacitus, *De Oratoribus* in Shadi Bartsch, *Actors in the Audience: Theatricality and Doublespeak from Nero to Hadrian* (Cambridge, Mass.: Harvard University Press, 1994).

101. The ideals of *integritas* and *simplicitas*, the desire to be all of a piece, could not be satisfied by the various roles and role-playing of the ancient *religiones*.

102. *"Doctrina* et *disciplina,"* 11. Cf. Vegetius, *Epitoma rei militaris* 2.3; 2.9; 3.1+10 etc.

103. Cf. *Adversus Marcionem* 4.1.5–7.

104. See *De resurrectione* 2.11 (the *rudes* and *simplices*—often wavering in their *fides* and in need of instruction); the *vulgi ignorantia* (ibid. 3.4). *Adversus Praxean passim*; *Scorpiace* 1.5–8; *De fuga* passim. For the *episcopus* mandating fasts for the *universa plebs*, *De ieiunia* 13.3. "The *auctoritas* and *honor* of the *ecclesia* has established the difference between the *ordo* and the *plebs*" (*De exhortatione castitatis* 7.3–6). (*Laicus*, "of the people" is the Latin transliteration of the Greek.) The increased emphasis on and necessity for indoctrination drove a wedge between the thought world of the *doctus* and the *indoctus*. It made the "peasant" or "rustic" who did not know of or did not accept the artificially simplified and structured ideological universe of the *doctus* the equivalent of "stupid." The *docti* prided themselves on reasoning deductively, on using abstractions, on having access to *veritas*, on privileged knowledge—all things that they did not have in the world of Homeric Greece or the earlier Roman republic. For the contempt of the Christian *docti* for the *plebs*, see Ramsay MacMullen, *Christianizing the Roman Empire* A.D. *100–400* (New Haven, Conn.: Yale University Press, 1984), 32 and nn. 21–24.

5. SEGREGATED BY A PERFECT FEAR. THE TERRIBLE WAR BAND OF THE ANTI-EMPEROR:
THE *CONIURATIO* AND THE *SACRAMENTUM*

1. *Inscriptiones Graecae* 12 Supplement, ed. F. Hiller von Gaertringen (Berlin: De Gruyter, 1939) 98–99, 99; trans. Ramsay MacMullen, *Paganism and Christianity 100–425 CE: A Sourcebook* (Minneapolis: Fortress, 1992) 53–54, 54.

2. *Octavius*, 207. "We want to point to the possibility that *the new religious community changes into a coniuratio* and becomes a danger for the ancient community from which it has come" (emphases mine) (Àgnes A. Nagy, "*Superstitio* et *Coniuratio*," *Numen* 49 [2002]: 178–92.)

3. The word *coniuratio* appears in Roman literature at least as early as Terence [d. 157 B.C.E.] (*Hecyra* 198).

4. The spoken oath was, in Roman thought, much more powerful than any written contract. "Our ancestors desired that there should be no tighter chain for fastening *fides* than the oath." (*Nullum enim vinculum ad adstringendam fidem iureiurando maiores arctius esse voluerunt* [Cicero, *De oratore* 3.31.111].) *Religio* could be the scrupulousness and sense of obligation produced by the oath: "The strongest bond of the military is *religio* and love for the *signa* and the *nefas* of desertion; . . . other duties can easily be demanded of him and trusts given to him when once the oath has been administered." (*primum militiae vinculum est religio et signorum amor et deserendi nefas* [Seneca, *Epistulae* 95.35]). For *religio* as the oath, see also Caesar, *Bellum civile* 1.67; Cicero, *Pro Balbo* 5.12.

5. Cf. Thomas N. Habinek, *The Politics of Latin Literature* (Princeton: Princeton University Press, 1998), 76–81.

6. See Livy's description of the oath taken by Publius Cornelius Scipio (Africanus) with his sword raised at Canusium to fortify the stricken and despairing survivors of Cannae in 116 B.C.E. (Livy 22.53.6).

7. The state administered the simple *sacramentum* that the soldiers would assemble at the bidding of the consul and not depart until bidden (*iussu consulum conventuros neque iniussu abituros*) (cf. Servius, *Commentarius ad Aeneidem* 7.614+8.1; Isidorus, *Etymologiae* 9.3.53). According to Hans Ulrich Instinsky, the soldiers might add to this oath their voluntary *coniuratio*, "Schwurszene und Coniuratio," *Jahrbuch für Numismatik und Geldgeschichte* 14 (1964): 83–88. Using the same evidence, Jochen Bleicken distinguished the *legitima militia*, which was inaugurated by the *sacramentum* (sworn individually before an authorized magistrate) and a *coniuratio*, which was a way of quickly organizing an armed force in cases of a *tumultus*, in which case the collective oath was not necessarily before or to an authorized magistrate (Servius, *Commentarius ad Aeneidem* 7.614+8.1; Isidorus, *Etymologiae* 9.3.53; cf. Livy 45.2.1; "*Coniuratio*: Die Schwurszene auf den Münzen und Gemmen der römischen Republik," *Jahrbuch für Numismatik und Geldgeschichte* 13 [1963]: 51–70; Jerzy Linderski, "Aphrodisias and the *Res Gestae*," *Journal of Roman Studies* 74 [1984]: 74–80, 76).

8. "*Coniuratio*," 57.

9. "[In] the communities of the archaic Greco-Roman world . . . [t]here was no question of *religion* providing the individual or group with a system of power of adherence, alternative to that of the city, the tribe or the family. (. . .) [I]f we consider the situation of the Greeks and Romans who lived in city-states . . . we can say that their *religious loyalty* was essentially to the city's gods and goddesses, not to any *religious commitment* of their own choice" [emphases mine] (John North, "The Development of Religious Pluralism," in *The Jews Among Pagans and Christians*, eds. Judith Lieu, John North and Tessa Rajak [New York: Routledge, 1992], 174–93, 177.) Although North states that "in some sense all groups in the pagan world were *religious* since they all involved some degree of cultic and ritual activity" (p. 177), he comes very close to asserting the inappropriateness of words like "religion" and "paganism" outside of and before the third-century Christian context: "[T]he *pagans*, before their competition with Christianity, had no *religion* at all in the sense in which that word in normally used today" (p. 187). But North was not willing to make the "leap" and continued to use both those words insistently—and on limiting his attention to other "religious" phenomena. If he had persisted, he might have seen that early Christian communities were more like *coniurationes* than local family, tribal, or city cults. North, like Arthur Darby Nock, saw commitment to, "conversion" to Christianity in the ancient world as unique "among religions" because it bound together disparate peoples in an

alternative to the "religion" embedded in the city-state. "It was A. D. Nock . . . who first grasped a profound distinction between the *religious* life of the Empire and that of earlier centuries. The basic contribution of his *Conversion* was the insight that in the conversions of St Paul and St Augustine we meet a new type of conversion that could not have happened in the world of pagan religions" (p. 175). Again, his argument makes sense only if one limits comparisons of Christianity with local family, village, and state cultic associations. Cf. A. D. Nock, *Conversion: The Old and the New in Religion from Alexander the Great to Augustine of Hippo* (London: Oxford University Press, 1933).

10. Livy 1.59.1.

11. There are many parallels between the creation of a parallel and/or counter-government by the plebs and by the early Christians.

12. The (plebeian) founder of the plebeian government was ascribed the very same name as the (patrician) founder of the senatorial Republic: Lucius Iunius Brutus. Note the competitive mirroring of the stories of the plebeian rebels with those of their enemy patricians. The stories of Marcus Manlius Capitolinus, Spurius Maelius, and Spurius Cassius were the plebeian answers to the stories of Mucius Scaevola, Atilius Regulus. The story of the plebeian Verginia was the answer to the story of the patrician Lucretia. Similarly, Christian heroes were often explicitly the rivals of Mucius Scaevola, Regulus, and Lucretia.

13. If the modern thinker's goal is actually to understand how the Greeks or Romans thought, felt, and behaved it is not helpful, in reading this passage, to separate out or from one another a "religion" and/or a "politics." These categories are not useful heuristic devises—far from it.

14. In Roman oaths (as in Roman confessions), when one person repeated the formula dictated by another, the person dictating the oath established his or her superior authority to the person who did not speak in his or her own voice. In that way, the oath could be used simultaneously to establish agreements and covenantal relations and distinctions in rank, to establish both forms of equality and submission.

15. *Iuravit in mea verba tota Italia sponte sua et me belli quo vici ad Actium ducem depoposcit. Iuraverunt in eadem verba provinciae Galliae Hispaniae Africa Sicilia Sardinia* (*Res gestae divi Augusti* 25.2); cf. Suetonius, *Augustus* 17.2. Dio (50.6.2ff.) asserts that both forces in the civil war between Anthony and Octavian were bound by oaths.

16. Emphasis mine. *Res Gestae Divi Augusti* (London: Oxford University Press, 1967), 68–69; cf. V. Ehrenberg and A. H. M. Jones, *Documents Illustrating the Reigns of Augustus and Tiberius*, 2nd ed. (Oxford: Clarendon Press, 1955), 145–46, no. 315 (the oath of Gangra 3 B.C.E.); Robert Sherk, *The Roman Empire: Augustus to Hadrian* (Cambridge, UK: Cambridge University Press, 1988), 31; T. B. Mitford, "A Cypriot Oath of Allegiance to Tiberius," *Journal of Roman Studies* 50 (1960): 75–79; Ronald Syme, *The Roman Revolution* (Oxford: Clarendon Press, 1939), 288 n. 3; P. Herrmann, *Der römische Kaisereid* (Göttingen: Vandenhoeck & Ruprecht, 1968), 123–26. Brunt and Moore emphasize that the formula of the oath varied as did the names of the gods called as witnesses. They describe this oath as a "religious" tie (p. 68). They are right only if they are speaking of the ancient Roman notion of *religio* as a bond or oath.

17. Cinna's oath to Sulla in 88 B.C.E. (Plutarch, *Sulla* 10.6); the oath to Catiline in 63 B.C.E. (Sallust, *Catilina* 22.1); to Antony in 44 B.C.E. (Appian, *Bellum civile* 3.46+58; Dio 45.13.5). For a general discussion of the notion of *coniuratio*, see Victoria Emma Pagán, *Conspiracy Narratives in Roman History* (Austin: University of Texas Press, 2004), 10–14.

18. The assemblies, oath-takings (*coniurationes*), and speeches of the Italiotes were reported to the meetings of the senators. (*Eorum* [*Italicorum*] *coetus coniurationesque et orationes in consiliis principum referuntur* [Livy, *Epitome* 71].)

19. Emphasis mine. Lily Ross Taylor remarks: "If, as I believe, this oath is genuine, it is clear that Drusus was building a very powerful body of followers among the Italians, who were then more numerous by far than the Roman citizens. There was some basis for the nobles' fear that

Drusus was striving for personal supremacy" (*Party Politics in the Age of Caesar* [Berkeley: University of California Press, 1949], 36–37, 45, 197 n. 40, 198 n. 67; 199 n. 69).

20. See H. A. Grueber, *Coins of the Roman Republic in the British Museum*, 3 vols. (London: British Museum, 1910), 2:329.

21. C. H. V. Sutherland, *Roman Coins* (London: Barrie & Jenkins, 1974), 65, no. 94. (Corfinum) (=Grueber, *Coins*, Social War no. 3).

22. See Anton von Premerstein, *Vom Werden und Wesen des Prinzipats* (*Abhandlungen der Bayerischen Akademie der Wissenschaften*, Philosophisch-historische Abteilung, N.F. 15 Munich: Beck, 1937), 27ff.

23. For the Pisonian *coniuratio* aimed at Nero in 65 c.e., see Tacitus, *Annales* 15.48.1.

24. Porcius Latro, *Declamatio in Catilinam* 19=XII Tables 26 (C.G. Bruns, *Fontes Iuris Romani Antiqui* [Tübingen: I.C.B. Mohr, 1909], 34).

25. See the charts in Robert M. Grant, *Greek Apologists of the Second Century* (Philadelphia: Westminster, 1988), 203–04; id., "Pliny and the Christians," *Harvard Theological Review* 44 (1948): 273–74, 273; Steve Benko, "Pagan Criticisms of Christianity," *Aufstieg und Niedergang der römischen Welt* 2.23.2 (Berlin; New York: W. de Gruyter, 1980), 1066–72; R. L. Wilken, *The Christians as the Romans Saw Them* (New Haven; London: Yale University Press, 1984); North, "The Development of Religious Pluralism," 181–86; Nagy, "*Superstitio* et *Coniuratio*," 178–92; Allen Brent, *A Political History of Early Christianity* (London: T & T Clark, 2009), 35–37.

26. Allen Brent asserts that, "The suppression of the Dionysiacs had been because they were considered to be practicing magical rites that would threaten the *pax deorum*. . . . It was this threat that constituted it as a *coniuratio*" (*Political History*, 69–72; cf. 35–37). Brent made much use of this notion in *The Imperial Cult and the Development of Church Order: Concepts and Images of Authority in Paganism* (Leiden; Boston: Brill, 1999, 17–72. Alas the notion of the *pax deorum* is, like "religion," a product of the scholar's study. Ste. Croix found in the disturbance of the *pax deorum* the principal explanation for the hostility of the Roman governing class to the Christians who refused to honor the gods ("Why Were the Early Christians Persecuted?" *Past & Present* 26 [1963]: 6–38, 29). But the Roman concept of the *pax*, formulated by Livy (6.41 fin. and Virgil 4.56 and 10.31) did not mean what it does to us. There was no general or normal state of covenant or contract between the gods and humans. Roman *pax* was the settlement imposed by the victor on the defeated. It was only beginning in Augustan propaganda that the *pax* imposed by Octavian at the end of the civil war gained—or rather given—its "pacific" associations even while the danger and threat of coercion remained in the background, as in the Ara Pacis and the *Res gestae* (where the lurking threat is still discernible). See Carlin Barton, "The Price of Peace in Ancient Rome," in *War and Peace in the Ancient World*, ed. Kurt A. Raaflaub (Malden, Mass; Oxford: Blackwell, 2007), 226–55. Brent omits many aspects of this movement that would have been the object of the attention of the Roman senatorial authorities. The whole modern debate over whether Jesus was a violent revolutionary, an apocalyptic prophet, a wisdom teacher, a wonder-worker or magician, misses the point that the Romans would not have perceived *any* of these possibilities as exclusive of the others, nor any as being "more religious than political" and therefore more benign.

27. "As regards their number, if I say that there are many thousands of them, you cannot help but be terrified, unless I shall at once add to that who and of what sort they are. First, then, a great part of them are women, and they are the source of this mischief; then there are males (*mares* [notice, not *viri*]) very like the women, debauched and debauchers (*stuprati et constuperatores*), fanatical (*fanatici*—a word that implied possession, enthusiasm, inspiration), with senses stupefied (*attoniti*) by wakefulness, wine, noise and shouts at night. The movement thus far has no strength, but it has an immense source of strength in that they grow more numerous every day" (39.15.8–10).

28. The *senatus consultum de Bacchanalibus* (ed. C.G. Bruns, *Fontes*, 164–166 = *Inscriptiones Latinae Selectae* 18).

29. The senators repeatedly iterated the possibility of the cultivation of Dionysus *provided* that devotees applied to the senate and met in small numbers with the permission of the senate (op cit. lines 4–6, 8–9, 15–22).

30. See the accounts of Diodorus Siculus preserved in Photios and Constantine Porphyrogennetos (34/35.2.1–3.11); cf. Florus 2.7.1–8.

31. For the Second Sicilian Slave War, see Diodorus Siculus 36.3.1–10.2 = Photios, *Bibliotheca* 387–90. The great social uprisings of the ancient Mediterranean were often feared as contagious proselytizing movements. Consider the response that Plutarch attributes to the other Peloponnesians to the reform movements of the Spartan Kings Agis and Cleomenes. A modern American might think of the state's reactions to separatist prophetic leaders like Jim Jones and David Koresh. For the role of the prophet in Native American resistance movements, see John Sugden, *Tecumseh: A Life* (New York: Henry Holt and Co., 1998) and Lee Irwin, *Coming Down From Above: Prophecy, Resistance and Renewal in Native American Religions* (Norman: University of Oklahoma Press, 2008).

32. Cf. Dio Cassius 37.30.3; Florus 4.1; Plutarch, *Cicero* 10.4; Tertullian, *Apologeticus* 9.9. For the way the language of the sacrificial system saturated all descriptions of the civil wars, see Barton, "Bending the Wheel of Sacrifice" (in preparation).

33. Compare the terrifying human sacrifices that were used to create the elite fighting force of the Samnites, the "Linen Legion" (Livy 10.38.2–13).

34. Many have made the point that—at least until the mid–third century—attacks on Christians were often initiated from the streets rather than the basilicas (de Ste. Croix, "Why Were the Early Christians Persecuted?" 7, 15, 26.)

35. Tacitus describes the forces that met the Roman consul Suetonius Paulinus (in command of Britain from 58 C.E.), when he attacked the island of Mona (Anglesey): "A circle of Druids, lifting their hands to heaven and showering imprecations, struck the troops with such awe at the extraordinary spectacle that, as though their limbs were paralyzed, they exposed their bodies to wounds without an attempt at movement. Then, reassured by their general, and inciting each other never to flinch before a band of females and fanatics (*agmen fanaticum*), they charged behind the standards, cut down all who met them, and enveloped the enemy in his own flames. The next step was to install a garrison among the conquered population, and to demolish the groves consecrated to their savage cults" (*Annales* 14.30).

36. The Romans had a long history of appropriating their enemies' gods. From the earliest days of the Republic, they had a formal ceremony of "calling out" (*evocatio*) of their enemy's gods (and offering them more scrupulous care at Rome). Just so, the Persian Cyrus "turned" the Babylonian Marduk: In the Akkadian text of the famous "Cyrus Cylinder" written shortly after his conquest of Babylon in October of 539 B.C.E., Cyrus' scribes addressed the Babylonian people claiming that their high god "Marduk, the great lord . . . ordered him to march against his city of Babylon. (. . .) Happily they greeted him [Cyrus] as a master through whose help they had come to life from death and had been spared damage and disaster, and they worshipped his name" (trans. A. Leo Oppenheim in J. B. Pritchard, *Ancient Near Eastern Texts Relating to the Old Testament*, 3rd ed. [Princeton: Princeton University Press, 1969], 315–16). See Bruce Lincoln, "Apocalyptic Temporality and Politics in the Ancient World," in *The Encyclopedia of Apocalypticism*, ed. John J. Collins, 3 vols. (London, 2004), 1:457–75.

37. Much later, in the Theodosian code (9.16, 16.10), while all soothsaying and sacrificial rites were forbidden to the subjects of the Empire, Constantine still permitted the harmless rites of peasants to effect healings, predict the weather, and so on (16.3).

38. When, in his ideal republic, Cicero gave to the state magistrate-priests the job of intruding into and being the arbiters of even the most private *sacra*, he was more worried about the state being able to control the people than the gods: "[For] without the assistance of those in charge of the public *sacra*, the people may not satisfy a *privata religio*; for the people's constant need for the

advice and authority of the aristocracy helps to hold the state together." (*Sine eis, qui sacris publice praesint, religioni privatae satis facere non possint; continet enim rem publicam consilio et auctoritate optimatium semper populum indigere* [*De legibus* 2.12].)

39. For Judas of Galilee (also known as Judas of Gamala), see Josephus, *Bellum Iudaicum* 2.118, 2.433, 7.253; *Antiquitates* 18.3–9, 18.23; *Acts of the Apostles* 5.36–37; Richard A. Horsley with John S. Hanson, *Bandits, Prophets and Messiahs* (San Francisco: Harper & Row, 1988), esp. 190–237; Christians emphasized that they paid their taxes (Matthew 22.21; cf. Mark 12.14; Luke 20.21; *Gospel of Thomas* 100; *Passio Scillitanorum* 6; Tertullian *De idololatria* 15.3; [figuratively in *Adversus Marcionem* 4.38.3; *De corona* 12.4]). See further discussion on these matters in Chapter 11, "A Jewish Actor in the Audience: Josephan Doublespeak."

40. Similarly, Perpetua and her fellow catechumens were not baptized until they had been arrested by the Roman authorities (*Passio* 3.5). Binding individuals from infancy enabled a kind of Christian citizenship/"subjectship" and brought Christianity closer to the model of both the king/subject and master–slave relationship, as did infant circumcision, which, like the branding of slaves, brought Judaism into this realm. Both allegiance to and obedience to the Christian governmental/ecclesiastical hierarchy then lost aspects of its ferocious voluntary quality (although total loyalty was still demanded). See Jonathan Boyarin and Daniel Boyarin, "Self-Exposure as Theory: The Double Mark of the Male Jew," in *Rhetorics of Self-Making*, ed. Debbora Battaglia (Berkeley: University of California Press, 1995), 16–42.

41. The oath of the Chinese Communist Party: "It is my will to join the Communist Party of China, uphold the Party's program, observe the provisions of the Party constitution, fulfill a Party member's duties, carry out the Party's decisions, strictly observe Party discipline, guard Party secrets, be loyal to the Party, work hard, *fight for communism throughout my life, be ready at all times to sacrifice my all for the Party and the people, and never betray the Party*" (Lawrence Sullivan, *Historical Dictionary of the Chinese Communist Party* [Lanham, Md: Scarecrow Press], 183 [emphasis mine]).

42. According to the author of the *Letter of Diognetus*, Christians did not differ from non-Christians either in land or speech or custom; they dwelt in their own *patriai* as "sojourners"/"resident aliens" (*paroikoi*) and strangers (*xenoi*). Still, miraculously, they had established their own *politeia*; they were citizens of heaven (5.1–6.2). For more discussion of this document, see Chapter 12, "A Glance at the Future: *Thrēskeia* and the Literature of Apologetic, First to Third Centuries C.E."

43. For the baptismal oath as a rejection of "the devil, his angels and his pomps," see also *De spectaculis* 24; *De anima* 35.3; *De idololatria* 6.1–2; *De corona* 3.2–3, 13.7; *De paenitentia* 5.7; *De cultu feminarum* 2.4. [Note: This fierce anti-Roman oath is missing from his more "apologetic" works.] A version of this oath formed part of the ordination of Hippolytus (170–236 CE) (R. H. Connolly, *The So-Called Egyptian Church Order* [Cambridge: Cambridge University Press, 1916], 184). The devil's angels were, of course, the "fallen angels" of Genesis (6.1–4) and 1 Enoch (8.1–3, 10.4–12, 12.4, 54.3–5; 2 Peter 2,4; Jude 6; Tertullian, *De cultu feminarum* 1.2.1; 1.3. Justin's angels were appointed by God to care for the humans "but transgressed their appointment . . . and afterwards subdued the human race to themselves through . . . fear" (Justin, *Apologia* 2.5). For demonology in the Roman Imperial period, see Elaine Pagels, "Christian Apologists and 'The Fall of the Angels': An Attack on Roman Imperial Power?" *Harvard Theological Review* 78 (1985): 301–25; J. Danielou, *The Origins of Latin Christianity*, trans. D. Smith and J. A. Baker (Philadelphia: Westminster, 1977), 405–18; Frederick E. Brenk, "In the Light of the Moon: Demonology in the Early Imperial Period," *Aufstieg und Niedergang der römischen Welt* 2.16.3 (Berlin; New York: W. de Gruyter, 1986), 2068–145; Neil Forsyth, *The Old Enemy: Satan and the Combat Myth* (Princeton: Princeton University Press, 1987), chapters 8, 9, 12–24, esp. 156–66, 219–381; Annette Yoshiko Reed, *Fallen Angels and the History of Judaism and Christianity: The Reception of Enochic Literature* (Cambridge: Cambridge University Press, 2005).

44. *De Baptismo* contained several passages that seemed so anomalous to me that I first suspected that either it was not written by Tertullian, or that it was subsequently modified or interpolated. The absence of any reference to the *sacramentum* is the most striking of those anomalies, but Chapter 17 also contains the only passages in the work of Tertullian enthusiastically ratifying the ecclesiastical hierarchy. It is possible that in this work, as in *De anima*, when Tertullian is actually playing the role of the philosopher (which is one of his consiliatory roles), he does not want to highlight the clearly rebellious and thinly veiled anti-Roman *sacramentum*.

45. Herbert Musurillo, for example, translates the opening words of the *Passio Perpetuae*— *vetera fidei exempla*—as "deeds recounted about *the faith*" rather than "examples of fidelity." Such a translation is unfaithful. Compare the translation "history of your religion" for what should be "story of your piety," in 4 Maccabees as discussed in Chapter 9, "The *Threskeia* of the Judaeans: Josephus and the New Testament."

46. Greek *pistis* came closer to our notion of "faith" as trust (e.g., Athenagoras, *Legatio* 7.3). Tertullian used *fides* to translate Greek *pistis* very frequently when translating or commenting on Greek texts as in book four of the *Adversus Marcionem*, which is an anti-Marcionite commentary on Luke's gospel (e.g., 2.2.6).

47. See Barton, "Savage Miracles." It is hard to exaggerate the importance, for Christians, of the image of themselves as soldiers of Christ from Paul on. See Adolf von Harnack, *The Mission and Expansion of Christianity in the First Three Centuries*, trans. James Moffatt, 2 vols. (London: Williams and Norgate, 1908), 1:414–416; id. *Militia Christi: The Christian Religion and the Military in the First Three Centuries*, trans. D. I. Gracie (Philadelphia: Fortress, 1981), ch. 1. For the association of the notion of the *sacramentum* with the soldier's oath, see J. de Ghellinck, *Pour l'histoire du mot* sacramentum (Louvain; Paris: E. Campion, 1924); F. J. Dölger, "*Sacramentum militiae*," *Antike und Christentum* 2 (1930): 268–80.

48. See the parallel of the Christian Roman soldier's choice of the book above the sword and his fatal decision to "hold to God" in Eusebius, *Historia* 7.15.

49. This stripping down resembled the impulse of the cosmopolitan relativist to find covering laws or abstractions.

50. The hatred of dissidents and heretics that one finds Tertullian, as in Paul and Augustine and Luther, arose in part because they wanted a simplified, purified existence and felt disappointed at the confusion, complexity, and strife that *others* introduced. Like Paul and Augustine and Luther, Tertullian felt that by breaking away, he might be *the* authoritative figure in his group.

51. *Huic sacramento militans ab hostibus provocor. Par sum illis, nisi illis manus dedero. Hoc defendo depugno in acie, vulneror, concidor, occidor. Quis hunc militi suo exitum voluit, nisi qui tali sacramento eum consignavit?*

52. For H. Rahner, the *pompa* of Tertullian's *sacramentum* was the Roman tyrant's *pompa triumphalis* ("*Pompa diaboli*; Ein Beitrag zur Bedeutungsgeschichte des Wortes πομπή—*pompa* in der urchristlichen Taufliturgie," *Zeitschrift für Katholische Theologie* 55 [1931]: 239–73, 245, 256). While J. H. Waszink and J. C. M. Van Winden think that "the devil and his angels" represent "the powers of evil in their totality" (*Tertullianus, De Idololatria* [Leiden: Brill, 1987], 135), for Tertullian, "evil" and "this (Roman) *saeculum*" are not separable concepts.

53. The "sign of God" (*signum dei*) marked on their forehead was the *seal*, the sign of the *sacramentum* that set apart the *milites Christi* (*De lapsis* 2).

54. See Judith Hallett, "*Perusinae glandes* and the Changing Image of Augustus," *American Journal of Ancient History* 2 (1977): 151–71.

55. Tertullian, like Paul and Josephus, often ascribed the power of the Romans to their own god. At the same time, illogically, Tertullian's hatred of Rome was expressed in his hatred of the devil "prince of the world" (*Apologeticum* 22.2). (For the domination of the devil in this *saeculum*,

see, e.g., *De spectaculis* 8: *totum saeculum satanas et angeli ipsius repleverunt.*) It is ironic that Tertullian's arch-enemy Marcion's hatred of Rome was expressed in his opposition to the god of the Hebrew scriptures who "had the hearts of kings in his hands." Lampe points out that in apocalyptic literature (e.g., 1 Enoch 85–90), mythical persons, tormenting angels had become transparent figures for the political authorities (*From Paul to Valentinus: Christians at Rome in the First Two Centuries*, trans. Michael Steinhauser [Minneapolis: Fortress, 2003], 248 n. 48).

56. Cf. 20.5, 23.1–5; Matthew 5.34.

57. "To have left the field and survived one's chief, this means lifelong infamy and shame: to defend and protect him, to devote one's own feats even to his gratification, this is the gist of their allegiance: the chief fights for victory, but the retainers for the chief" (Tacitus, *Germania* 13–14).

58. *Praescribitur mihi . . . ne alium [deum] adorem aut quo modo venerer praeter unicum illum, qui ita mandat, quem et iubeor timere, ne ab eo deserar, et de omni substantia deligere, ut pro eo moriar.* [5] *Huic sacramento militans ab hostibus provocor. (. . .) Hoc defendo depugno in acie, vulneror, concidor, occidor. Quis hunc militi suo exitum voluit, nisi qui tali sacramento eum consignavit?* "[Our] wrestling," he declares, "is not against flesh and blood, but against the world's powers, against the spirits of malice" (*adversus mundi potestates, adversus spiritalia malitiae*). It is right for us to make our stand against these not by flesh and blood, but by *fides* and *spiritus*" (*De ieiunio* 17.8).

59. Latin text: Musurillo, *Acts*, 86–89. For the oath by the genius of the Emperor, see also the "Martyrdom of Polycarp" 9.2 and the *Martyrdom of Apollonius* 3.

60. Consider the deeply affecting stories of the young Canadian Terry Fox, who when stricken with bone cancer, determined to run across Canada after having his leg amputated (and died in the attempt in 1981), or the American teenager Ben Comen, who although afflicted with cerebral palsy, took up cross-country running (2008).

61. Cf. *De cultu feminarum* 2.13.4–7. "We must have the ability to endure pain to such an extent that they lose the ability to inflict it. This and this alone will break them in the end" (Leon Uris, *Trinity* [Garden City, N.Y.: Doubleday, 1976], 466). Tim Pat Coogan, writing on the Blanket Protest and the even more ferocious Filthy Protest that preceded the Irish Republican Army's hunger strikes in Maze/Long Kesh prison in 1980–1981: "There was an element of taunting in the psychological battle: for every hardship the prisoners had inflicted on [the prison guards] they were prepared to inflict a hardship of at least equal severity on themselves, thus devaluing the system's power to intimidate them. Their willingness to deprive themselves undermined the authority of the regime to do so. Whatever debasement or humiliation the regime might impose on them in the form of punishment was nothing compared to what they were prepared to impose on themselves. . . ." (*On the Blanket* [Dublin: Ward River, 1980], 22–23). Pedraig O'Malley [writing of the subsequent hunger strikes:] "A hunger strike was an instrument of last resort to which the prisoners turned *to prevent a sense of impotence* from taking hold. (. . .) *A hunger strike would allow them to take action on their own behalf, to empower themselves, to see themselves as something other than victims*" [emphases mine] (*Biting at the Grave: The Irish Hunger Strikes and the Politics of Despair* [Boston: Beacon Press, 1990], 28–29).

62. *Meditemur duriora, et non sentiemus; relinquamus laetiora, et non desiderabimus. Stemus expeditae ad omnem vim, nihil habentes quod relinquere timeamus. Retinacula ista sunt spei nostrae.*

63. *. . . indicentes omnem* ταπεινοφρόνησιν, *cum carcer ediscendus et fames ac sitis exercendae et tam inediae quam anxii victus tolerantia usurpanda sit, ut in carcerem talis introeat Christianus, qualis inde prodisset, non poenam illic passurus, sed disciplinam, nec saeculi tormenta, sed sua officia, eoque fidentior processurus ad certamen e custodia abusus nihil habens carnis, sic ut nec habeant tormenta materiam, cum sola et arida sit cute loricatus, et contra ungulas corneus, praemisso iam sanguinis suco tamquam animae impedimentis, properante iam et ipsa, quae iam saepe ieiunans mortem de proximo norit.*

64. This "strategy" of submission, of willing not to will, so dear to the Roman Stoics, is most elaborately laid out by Tertullian in *De exhortatione castitatis* 1–4.

65. Guy G. Stroumsa, in *The End of Sacrifice: Religious Transformations in Late Antiquity* (trans. Susan Emanuel [Chicago: The University of Chicago Press, 2009, 23–24]), remarks: "Michel Foucault has proposed seeing the Christian attitude toward the self (referring especially to the writings of John Cassian, hence to Eastern monasticism as it was propagated in the West) as a will to suppress the self, to annihilate it, or at least to integrate it within a much larger framework. (. . .) He saw that the accent placed on the human person as an independent monad, alone responsible (24)—and responsible only—for the care of itself, is not found among Christians. But," Stroumsa argues, "his insistence on the limitation, even the suppression, of the self among Christian thinkers of Late Antiquity leads us along a false path. For it is not a *limitation* but indeed an *enlargement* of the person that the Christian thinkers achieve" (23–24). I would argue slightly differently: The suppression of the self was the *necessary precondition* for the enlargement of the self. As in ancient Indian Upanishadic tradition or Chinese Taoism, the feeling of being small, powerless, and entrapped can cause one to adopt a strategy of being everything, of being one with "The All"; one has only to stop resisting and attune one's will to that of the Powers That Be.

66. "Shall he [i.e., the Christian in military service to the Emperor] keep *stationes* (watches/vigils/fasts) for others more than for Christ, or shall he do it on the Lord's Day, when he does not even do it for Christ himself?" (*Iam et stationes aut aliis magis faciet quam Christo, aut et dominico die, quando nec Christo?* [*De corona* 11.3].) "For even soldiers, though never unmindful of their *sacramentum*, yet pay a greater deference to *stationes*." (*Nam et milites numquam immemores sacramenti magis stationibus parent* [*De ieiunio* 10.7].)

67. The sun stayed dark as a *lugubre officium* for the dead Christ.

68. In *Slavery as Salvation* (New Haven, Conn.: Yale University Press, 1990), Dale B. Martin points out that the slave partakes of the status and prestige of the master and, as agent of the master, is authorized by and speaks with the master's voice. And so claiming the status of "slave of god" could be a way of authorizing one's own words and actions. The authority of the writings (the *instrumenta*) of the apostles was derived directly from their work being a task imposed by God himself (*munus ab ipso domino impositum*) (*Adversus Marcionem* 4.2.1). For Tertullian, the Christian slave was to his *dominus* as Christ was to God in John's Gospel—deriving his warrant to speak and act from the summit of the chain of being (cf. *Adversus Marcionem* 3.2.1–2). The chain of authority in Tertullian caused his *ecclesia* to resemble the household of the Roman grandee of Plautus or Lucian with its elaborate pecking orders more than a community in which everyone was equal before God. In Tertullian's kingdom the last would be first—but there would be a sort of "dictatorship of the proletariat" with a strict hierarchical chain of command.

69. For Christians as "slaves of God," see, for example, *Ad uxorem* 1.4.2, 1.5.3; 2.3.1, 2.6.1; *De spectaculis* 1, 20, 24; *Apologeticum* 23.15; 30.5; *De idololatria* 13.2, 17.2, 18.5+8; *De fuga in persecutione* 1.3, 11.1; *De anima* 47.2, 51.6; *De cultu feminarum* 2.1.1; *De paenitentia* 4.1–4, 6.15; *De patientia* 10.4–6, 11.4; cf. Matthew 11.29.

70. *Dominus* is another of the Latin words that have been given a particular positive and "euphemized" ring by English translators. *Dominus* was the Latin word for the slave owner in relation to his slave. It was a word used to honor another when one wanted to emphasize one's extreme submissiveness and obedience (for example, by the Roman love poet to his mistress). It was early used to address Augustus, who knew how dangerously provocative a title it was and forbade its being used (Suetonius, *Augustus* 53). *Dominus* is usually translated as "Lord," which suggests in English a somewhat more benign figure to whom one owes loyalty and obedience because of his higher position by birth in the social hierarchy Hrothgar's *hlaford*.

71. *Igitur si probos quosque servos et bonae mentis pro ingenio dominico conversari videmus—siquidem artificium promerendi obsequium est, obsequii vero disciplina morigera subiectio est, quanto magis nos secundum dominum moratos inveniri oportet, servos scilicet dei vivi, cuius iudicium in suos non in compede aut pilleo vertitur sed in aeternitate aut poenae aut salutis? Cui severitati declinandae*

*vel liberalitati invitandae tanta obsequii diligentia opus est quanta sunt ipsa quae aut severitas commina-
tur aut liberalitas pollicetur. Et tamen nos non de hominibus modo servitute subnixis vel quolibet alio iure
debitoribus obsequii verum etiam de pecudibus, etiam de bestiis oboedientiam exprimimus intellegentes
usibus nostris eas a domino provisas traditasque. Meliora ergo nobis erunt in obsequii disciplina quae nobis
deus subdit? . . . nos qui soli subditi sumus, domino scilicet, auscultare dubitamus?* Tertullian arguing
against marrying outside the community of Christians: "Even among the *nationes* do not all the
strictest *domini* and those most tenacious of *disciplina* forbid their own slaves from marrying out of
their house? (. . .) Are terrestrial *disciplinae* to be kept more strictly than celestial prescripts?"
(*Nonne etiam penes nationes severissimi quique domini et disciplinae tenacissimi servis suis foras nubere
interdicunt? (. . .) Severiores habebuntur terrenae disciplinae caelestibus praescriptis. . . . ?* [*Ad uxorem*
2.8.1–2].)

72. *Paeniteat amasse quae deus non amat, quando ne nos quidem ipsi servulis nostris ea, quibus
offendimur, nosse permittimus: obsequii enim ratio in similitudine animorum constituta est.*

73. *Multis et variis exanclatis laboribus magnisque Fortunae tempestatibus et maximis actus procellis,
ad portum Quietis et aram Misericordiae tandem, Luci venisti. Nec tibi natales ac ne dignitas quidem, vel
ipsa qua flores usquam doctrina profuit. . . . Sed utcumque Fortunae caecitas, dum te pessimis periculis
discruciat, ad religiosam istam beatitudinem improvida produxit malitia. Eat nunc et summo furore
saeviat et crudelitati suae materiem quaerat aliam; nam in eos quorum sibi vitas in servitium deae
nostrae maiestas vindicavit non habet locum casus infestus. (. . .) Videant irreligiosi, videant et errorem
suum recognoscant. En ecce pristinis aerumnis absolutus Isidis magnae providentia gaudens Lucius de sua
Fortuna triumphat. Quo tamen tutior sis atque munitior da nomen sanctae huic militiae, cuius non olim
sacramento etiam rogabaris, teque iam nunc obsequio religionis nostrae dedica et ministerii iugum subi
voluntarium. Nam cum coeperis deae servire, tunc magis senties fructum tuae libertatis.* Compare also
the reply of the imperial *doulos* Euelpistus, who when interrogated by Rusticus (ca. 163–168 c.e.),
replied that he had been "freed by Christ" ("The Acts of Justin and Companions," Recension B,
4.2, in Musurillo, *Acts*, 50–51).

74. *Plane memineris et penita mente conditum semper tenebis mihi reliqua vitae tuae curricula
adusque terminos ultimi spiritus vadata.*

75. For the Hebrew Prophets advertising themselves as slaves, see Martin, *Slavery*, 55 and 198
nn. 3 + 14.

76. Cf. Cyprian, *Epistulae* 30.6.3.

77. "The [Roman] army proved successful in its ability to control the natural fear in the lives
of the soldiers. *Disciplina* certainly contributed to this ability, but ritual behavior also served to
dissipate the unconscious impulse of fear. (. . .) [The elaborate ritual life of the camps]
transform[ed] vague and general feelings of anxiety into specific fears of actual threats, and then
moving to eliminate those threats. . . ." (John Helgeland, "Roman Army Religion," *Aufstieg und
Niedergang der römischen Welt* II.16.2 [Berlin; New York: W. de Gruyter, 1978], 1470–1541, 1501).

78. Alas, we have lost Tertullian's treatise *De exstasi* in which, according to Jerome (*De viris
illustribus* 40), Tertullian defended the New Prophecy against attack.

79. Compare Minucius Felix: "It is natural to hate those whom you fear" (*naturale est enim et
odisse quem timeas*) (*Octavius* 27.8); Cicero (quoting Ennius): "Those whom they fear, they hate,
and whomever one hates, he seeks to destroy." (*quem metuunt oderunt, quem quisque odit, perisse
expetit* [*De officiis* 2.7.23].)

80. *Provocati ad sacrificiandum obstruimus gradum pro fide conscientiae nostrae, qua certi sumus ad
quos ista perveniant officia. . . . Sed quidam dementiam existimant, quod cum possimus et sacrificare in
praesenti et inlaesi abire manente apud animum proposito, obstinationem saluti praeferamus.* Clearly, not
every Christian shared Tertullian's priorities!

81. For Christians "despising their degradation," see Tacitus, *Annales* 15.44; Minucius Felix,
Octavius 9–10; Cyprian, *De lapsis* 12 (quoting Mark 10.29); Celsus in Origen, *Contra Celsum* 8.2.
See Barton, *Roman Honor*, 88–130.

82. *neque enim dubitabam, qualecumque esset quod faterentur, pertinaciam certe et inflexibilem obstinationem debere puniri.*

83. According to a press release of the Islamic Society of Boston, April 22, 2013, the rebellious Chechen Moslem Tamerlan Tsarnaev, shortly before setting a bomb at the finish line of the Boston Marathon on April 15, 2013, expressed in his mosque outrage at the willingness of his fellow American Muslims to respect American holidays such as the Fourth of July and Thanksgiving or to honor Martin Luther King, Jr.

84. *Honorem Caesari quasi Caesari, timorem autem Deo* (*Passio Scillitanorum* ed. Musurillo, *Acts*, 9). Compare the answer of Justin to the Prefect Quintus Iunius Rusticus [urban prefect between 163 and 168] in the "Martyrdom of Justin and Companions" Recension 2+6 (ed. Musurillo, *Acts*, 55+61); Tatian, *Oratio ad Graecos* 4.2.

85. Tertullian's god sees into the mind and thoughts of men and judges them: "The Lord has declared that sins are committed in the mind and in the consciousness. (*Et bene, quod in animo et conscientia delinqui dominus dixit.*) If concupiscence (*concupiscentia*) or malice (*malitia*) rises into the heart of a man (*in cor hominis ascenderit*), these are reckoned as a deed (*pro facto teneri*)" (*De idololatria* 23.2). For God as a constant witness and judge not only of one's behavior but even one's most hidden thoughts, see also Minucius Felix, *Octavius* 10.5, 32.8–33.1, 35.6; the *Pastor Hermae* (*Visio* 1 1.8–9, 2.4). Cyprian, even more than Tertullian, will instill a terror of a god who sees every secret infraction of body or mind (e.g., *De lapsis* 24–27).

The idea of enlisting the gods as thought police had been advocated in Greek thought. Xenophon's Socrates had kept his companions from impiety and injustice "not only when they were seen by men, but even in solitude; since they ever felt that no deed of theirs could at any time escape the gods" (*Memorabilia* 1.4.19). Similarly, Plutarch felt that a more powerful and dangerous eye needed to be turned on humans than that of their neighbor. Cf. Critias (ca. 480–403 B.C.E.) (fragment of the satiric play "Sisyphus") = Hermann Diels, *Die Fragmente der Vorsokratiker*, 2nd ed., 3 vols. (Berlin: Weidmann, 1907) 3:620–622, frag. B 25 (English trans.: Kathleen Freeman, *Ancilla to the Pre-Socratic Philosophers* [Cambridge, Mass.: Harvard University Press, 1978], frag. 25, 157–58).

86. The use of *verus* as a modifier indicates that Tertullian means to shift the meaning of *religio* and *obsequium*.

87. *Ceterum quotus quisque meminerit religionis occupatis memoriae locis, impeditis sapientiae membris. Nemo ita ut decet, ita ut par est, ita ut utile est, recordabitur dei eo in tempore, quo ipsum sibi hominem excidere sollemne est. Omnem disciplinam victus aut occidit aut vulnerat.*

88. Compare the protagonist of Jonathan Swift's poem "The Lady's Dressing Room" (1732), who deliberately pries into his mistress' dirty chamber pot in order to reduce her to dirt in his own mind.

89. The *fascinum* protected against fascination, stupefaction, and envy by inspiring *religio*, shame, and inhibition. For example, the *fascinum* protected the Roman infant and the Roman *triumphator* with *religio* (cf. Varro, *De lingua Latina* 7.97; Pliny, *Naturalis historia* 28.7.39). For the reciprocal physics of fascination, see Barton, *Sorrows of the Ancient Romans*, 85–175. Tertullian's Christians also drive away envy and evil by spitting and blowing and making the sign of the cross; see *De corona* 3.4; *Ad uxorem* 2.5.2; William Le Saint, *Tertullian, Treatises on Marriage and Remarriage* (New York: Newman, 1951), 129.

90. For the Saturnalia from the Saturnalia, see Barton, *Sorrows of the Ancient Romans*, 72, 76, 162–64, 172–73.

91. Compare, famously, Socrates' "little inner voice"—his personal *daimonion*.

92. "[Christ] reminds them [his disciples] that they should not fear those who only kill the body . . . but that they must consecrate their fear (*metum consecrandum*) to him rather who has the power to kill both body and soul, and destroy them in hell (*Gehenna*). Who are these slayers of

the body only—but the governors and kings—mere men." (. . . *monet non eos timendos, qui solum corpus occidant, animam autem interficere non valeant, sed illi potius metum consecrandum, qui et corpus et animam occidere et perdere possit in gehennam. Quinam hi solius corporis interemptores, nisi praesides et reges . . . homines.*)

93. "Donata said: 'Honor to Caesar as Caesar—but fear to God.'" (*Honorem Caesari quasi Caesari; timorem autem deo* [*Passio sanctorum Scillitanorum* 8+9, ed. Musurillo, *Acts*, 86–89]).

94. *Praescribitur mihi . . . ne alium* [*deum*] *adorem aut quo modo venerer praeter unicum illum, qui ita mandat, quem et iubeor timere, ne ab eo deserar, et de omni substantia deligere, ut pro eo moriar.* "We Christians should prefer to die in battle under our beloved *imperator Christus* than survive by fleeing the confrontation with our evil enemy" (*De fuga* 10.1–2).

95. It did not matter to Tertullian who was on the Roman throne. The notion of a Christian Roman Emperor would have seemed like an oxymoron to him. To a Roman historian like myself, the sanctification of Christians of Constantine (over, say, Antoninus Pius or Marcus Aurelius) seems cruelly perverse. How would Tertullian have felt about Constantine? "The empire had never had on the throne a man given to such bloodthirsty violence as Constantine" (MacMullen, *Christianizing the Roman Empire*, 50).

96. Cf. Basil (fourth century C.E.) *Epistulae* 164: "The blood of martyrs watered the church and reared up many times as many champions of piety."

97. *Multi apud vos ad tolerantiam doloris et mortis hortantur ut Cicero in Tusculanis, ut Seneca in Fortuitis, ut Diogenes, ut Pyrrhon, ut Callinicus. Nec tamen tantos inveniunt verba discipulos quantos Christiani factis docendo. Ipsa illa obstinatio, quam exprobratis, magistra est. Quis enim non contemplatione eius concutitur ad requirendum quid intus in re sit? Quis non, ubi requisivit, accedit?*

98. In Livy's history, Titus Manlius Torquatus endeavored to shame the survivors of Cannae: "Fifty thousand of your countrymen and allies on that very day lay around you slain. If so many examples of courage did not inspire you [to die] nothing will" (Livy 22.60.14).

99. Compare Ignatius of Antioch writing in eager expectation of his execution (very early–second century C.E.). "I write to you while living, desiring to die. My passion has been crucified . . . instead there is living water which is speaking in me, saying to me from within . . . 'Come to the Father'" (*Epistula ad Romanos* 7). Compare the address of Jesus to the cross in the fragmentary "Gospel of the Savior": "O cross, do not be afraid! I am rich. I will fill you with my wealth, [I] will mount you, O cross. [I] will be [hung] upon you (. . .) [Do not] weep, O [cross], but rather [rejoice] and recognize [your] Lord as he [is coming toward] you. . . ." (Stephen Emmel, "The Recently Published Gospel of the Savior; Righting the Order of Pages and Events," *Harvard Theological Review* 95 (2002): 45–72; Bart Ehrman, *Lost Scriptures: Books That Did Not Make It into the New Testament* (Oxford; New York: Oxford University Press, 2003), 52–56. Compare the gladiator's *amor mortis* (Barton, *Sorrows*, ch. 1.)

100. *Sed quando Deus magis creditur, nisi cum magis timetur, nisi in tempore persecutionis? Ecclesia in attonito est; tunc et fides in expeditione sollicitior et disciplinatior in ieiuniis et stationibus,* [*et*] *in orationibus et humilitate, in alterutra diligentia et dilectione, in sanctitate et sobrietate: non enim vacatur nisi timori et spei. Adeo et ex hoc ipso ostenditur nobis non posse diabolo deputari eam, quae meliores efficit Dei servos.*

101. *Sic et agonem intellegi capit persecutionem. A quo certamen edicitur, nisi a quo corona et praemia proponuntur? Legis edictum agonis istius in Apocalypsi, quibus praemiis ad victoriam invitet, vel maxime illos, qui proprie vicerint in persecutione, vincendo luctati re vera non adversus carnem et sanguinem, sed adversus spiritalia nequitiae. Ita agnosces ad eundem agonithetam pertinere certaminis arbitrium, qui invitat ad praemium.*

102. *In certaminis nomine deus nobis martyria proposuisset, per quae cum adversario experiremur. . . .* (. . .) *Evulsum enim hominem de diaboli gula per fidem iam et per virtutem inculcatorem eius voluit efficere, ne solummodo evasisset, verum etiam evicisset inimicum.*

103. Cf. John 16.8, 33; 18.28–19.16; 12.31.

104. *Times hominem, Christiane, quem timeri oportet ab angelis, siquidem angelos iudicaturus es; quem timeri oportet a demoniis, siquidem et in daemonas accepisti potestatem; quem timeri oportet ab universo mundo, siquidem et in te mundus iudicatur.* For men superior to and judging angels, see also *Adversus Marcionem* 2.9.7.

105. "All this *dominatio et potestas* derives its force from the *nominatio Christi* and the reminder of what they (the demons/gods of the non-Christians) expect to come upon them from God by the *arbitrium Christi.* They are afraid of Christ in God and God in Christ. . . ." (*Omnis haec nostra in illos dominatio et potestas de nominatione Christi valet et de commemoratione eorum quae sibi a deo per arbitrum Christum imminentia exspectant. Christum timentes in deo et deum in Christo, subiciuntur servis dei et Christi. Ita de contactu deque afflatu nostro, contemplatione et repraesentatione ignis illius correpti, etiam de corporibus nostro imperio excedunt inviti et dolentes et vobis praesentibus erubescentes.*)

106. Notice that Tertullian did not claim that Christians were filling up the farms or country-side. Again, Tertullian's is an emphatically urban world.

107. *Si enim et hostes exertos, non tantum vindices occultos agere vellemus, deesset nobis vis numerorum et copiarum?* (. . .) *Hesterni sumus, et orbem iam et vestra omnia implevimus urbes, insulas, castella, municipia, conciliabula, castra ipsa, tribus, decurias, palatium, senatum, forum; sola vobis reliquimus templa. Cui bello non idonei, non prompti fuissemus, etiam impares copiis, qui tam libenter trucidamur, si non apud istam disciplinam magis occidi liceret quam occidere?*

108. *Nam licet subiecta sit nobis tota vis daemonum et eiusmodi spirituum, ut nequam tamen servi metui nonnumquam contumaciam miscent, et laedere gestiunt quos alias verentur. Odium enim etiam timor spirat. Praeterquam et desperata condicio eorum ex praedamnatione solatium reputat fruendae interim malignitatis de poenae mora. Et tamen adprehensi subiguntur et condicioni suae succidunt, et quos de longinquo oppugnant, de proximo obsecrant. Itaque cum vice rebellantium ergastulorum sive carcerum vel metallorum vel hoc genus poenalis servitutis erumpunt adversus nos, in quorum potestate sunt, certi et impares se esse et hoc magis perditos.*

109. Compare the way in which "the Powers of the World," Satan and his minions, fathers of the giants on earth, are depicted as rebels in 1 Enoch. And compare the words of the fifth-century Pseudo-Augustinian treatise *Altercatio ecclesiae et synagogae* (*Corpus Christianorum, Series Latina* 69A 26, 27, 37+38): "I used to possess sheep and cattle, you an army. And so it is that although I am the lesser and poorer and you greater and richer, you are in decline, subjugated by me, destined to serve a lesser people" (quoted by Leslie Dossey, *Peasant and Empire in Christian North Africa* [Berkeley: University of California Press, 2010], 101). The "imperial synagogue" in this text is, as Dossey points out, the Roman Empire.

110. For Jews as *aemuli: Apologeticum* 7.3; *De testimonio animae* 1.1; *De praescriptione haereticorum* 40.2–4. Tertullian states, categorically, that envy (*livor*) cannot be ascribed to his god (*De resurrectione* 21.6). Tertullian's generalized projected envy perhaps tells us less about the motivations of the devils and non-Christians than his own motivations.

111. *Ego imperium huius saeculi non cognosco; sed magis illi deo servio quem nemo hominum vidit nec videre his oculis potest, furtum non feci, sed siquid emero teloneum reddo quia cognosco domnum meum imperatorem regum et omnium gentium.*

112. Tertullian's notion of sovereignty required that he constantly compare his god with the human king. "In almost every particular the world of the gods is . . . a projection of terrestrial conditions" (Thorkild Jacobsen, "Primitive Democracy in Ancient Mesopotamia," in *Toward the Image of Tammuz and Other Essays in Mesopotamian History and Culture*, ed. W. L. Moran [Cambridge, Mass.: Harvard University Press, 1970], 164.) "The earthly reality preceded and served as the basis for speculation about the divine. Thus, in cases where common imagery is shared by God and the king, I assume that human imagery has been projected upon God rather than vice-versa," Marc Zvi Brettler, *God is King: Understanding an Israelite Metaphor* (Sheffield: JSOT Press, 1989), 15, cf. 23. This dependence was repeatedly emphasized by A. M. Hocart in *Kings and*

Councillors: An Essay in the Comparative Anatomy of Human Society (Chicago: The University of Chicago Press, 1970 [1936]).

113. For a brilliant analysis of the making, the sacralization of a king—in this case, the King of Apuapem—see Michele Gilbert, "The person of the king: ritual and power in a Ghanian state," in *Rituals of Royalty; Power and Ceremonial in Traditional Societies*, eds. D. Cannadine and S. Price (Cambridge: Cambridge University Press, 1987), 298–330. The video of the crowning of George VI (available on a YouTube video) is also wonderfully illustrative.

114. *Nusquam facilius proficitur quam in castris rebellium ubi ipsum esse illic promereri est. Itaque alius hodie episcopus, cras alius; hodie diaconus qui cras lector; hodie presbyter qui cras laicus. Nam et laicis sacerdotalia munera iniungunt.*

115. Cf., for example, M. Terentius Varro, *Antiquitates Rerum Divinarum*, ed. Cardauns, vol. 1, frag. 7; with vol. 2, 139–43; cf. Tertullian, *Ad nationes* 2.1.9–11; Minucius Felix, *Octavius* 23.5–24.8; Augustine, *De civitate dei* 6.6, cf. 4.27. (See the additional sources cited by Cardauns, 2:140.) The absence of self-criticism, paradoxically, makes Tertullian seem more arrogant than the despised Romans. (For an exception, see *De patientia* 1.1.)

116. "Bronze statues set by gateways display the right hands thinned away by the frequent kissing/touching of those who greet them and those who pass by." (. . . *tum portas propter aena/signa manus dextras ostendunt adtenuari/saepe salutantum tactu praeterque meantum* [Lucretius, *De rerum natura* 1.316–18].)

6. GOVERNED BY A PERFECT FEAR

1. Trans. R. Travers Herford, *Pirke Aboth* (New York: Jewish Institute of Religion, 1945), 64.

2. For Seneca, the Golden Age was brought to an end by the loss of moderation (*modus*) and the introduction of excess (*luxuria*) (*Epistulae* 90.14–19).

3. For Plutarch, the absence of fear and hope leaves one open to the charge of "atheism" (1100C, 1101B). Cf. Lactantius, *De ira dei* 4; *Clementine Recognitions* (uncertain date, probably fourth century) 4.31.

4. Berger and Luckman, *Social Construction of Reality*, 164.

5. Compare Paul as god's *oikonomos* in Dale C. Martin, *Slavery as Salvation*, (New Haven, Conn.: Yale University Press, 1990), 50–85.

6. Ovid's description of the terrified and terrifying inhabitants of Tomis who do not even farm (*Tristia* 3.10.67–76) was, like Tertullian's description of Marcion's Scythia, designed less to inform than to evoke the horror of his cosmopolitan readers.

7. Kings and king gods, projected far into the past (Romulus, Numa, Theseus, Moses, the Yellow King, etc.) are, in large part, projections of people who have long lived in, or were subject to, or had to resist hierarchical cultures. Seneca projects a version of the king back into the remotest times: "[T]he first men and those who sprang from them, still unspoiled, followed nature, having one man as both their leader and their law, entrusting themselves to the control of one better than themselves. For nature has the habit of subjecting the weaker to the stronger. Even among the dumb animals those which are either biggest or fiercest hold sway. It is no weakling bull that leads the herd; it is the one that has beaten the other males by his might and his muscle" (*Epistulae* 90.4). For kingship retrojected, see also Sallust, *Bellum Catilinae* 2.1.

8. Lucretius, writing during the civil wars of the Republic, imagined the situation for humans that led to the creation of the state: "For the race of men, tired of living in violence, was fainting from its feuds, and so they were readier of their own will to submit to statutes and strict rules of law." (*nam genus humanum, defessum vi colere aevom,/ex inimicitiis languebat; quo magis ipsum/sponte sua cecidit sub leges artaque iura* [*De rerum natura* 5.1145].) Whether humans started off in good order and then suffered a long downward slide, or began in disorder and were saved only by the king or god who put an end to the chaos, often depended on whether humans were conceived as

possessing any capacity for or mechanisms of autonomy and *self*-government. For these scenarios in all their infinite varieties and elaborations, see Arthur O. Lovejoy and George Boas, *Primitivism and Related Ideas in Antiquity* (Baltimore: Johns Hopkins University Press, 1935).

9. There is an eloquent description of the ways in which systems of reciprocity are discovered, imbibed, and practiced by young children at the beginning of G. W. Tromp's *Payback: The Logic of Retribution in Melanesian Religions* (Cambridge, UK: Cambridge University Press, 1994), 2 [with bibliography]. For shame in children, see Barton, *Roman Honor The Fire in the Bones* (Berkeley: University of California Press, 2003), 11.

10. See especially the arguments in *Adversus Marcionem* 1.25–28; 4.8.7–8, 4.15.6. The Marcionites boasted that they did not fear their god (1.27.3; 4.8.7).

In 1.25.7, Tertullian lists *ira, discordia, odium, dedignatio, indignatio, bilis, nolentia,* and *offensa* as the *sensus et affectus, the motus animi* (1.26.1) necessarily accompanying the will and desire of his god. In 2.16.1, *ira, aemulatio,* and *saevitia* are elements of the *bona severitas* of God. *Ira, exasperatio* (2.16.6–7); cf. 4.8.7; *De anima* 18.10–11; *Scorpiace* 4.

11. *Si enim neque aemulatur neque irascitur neque damnat neque vexat, utpote qui nec iudicem praestat, non invenio quomodo illi disciplinarum ratio consistat. . . .* "An act forbidden without the threat of retribution is tacitly permitted." (*Tacite permissum est quod sine ultione prohibetur (Adversus Marcionem* [1.26.3].) "To every one of his decisions and laws he owes a sanction, to establish its authority and the necessity of obedience. (. . .) God can only be completely good if he is the enemy of the bad, so as to put his love of the good into action by hatred of the bad, and discharge his wardship of the good by the overthrowing of the bad." (*quod qualicunque sententiae suae et legi debeat vindictam in auctoritatem et obsequii necessitatem. (. . .) et quidem deo optimo, qui non alias plene bonus sit, nisi mali aemulus, uti boni amorem odio mali exerceat et boni tutelam expugnatione mali impleat* [*Adversus Marcionem* 1.26.5].) See all of *Adversus Marcionem* 2.13 (*timor iudici ad bonum non ad malum confert* [2.13.2]). "Would not all men take the easy course if there was nothing to fear? Even though we stand in terror of the Creator's fearsome threatenings, even so we are not easily wrenched away from evil. What if there were no threatenings?" (2.13.3).

12. Psalm 110.10; Proverbs 1.7.

13. Here again, Tertullian uses *religiosus* in one of its ancient senses: "scrupulous."

14. *Negant deum timendum: itaque libera sunt omnia et soluta. Ubi autem deus non timetur nisi ubi non est? ubi deus non est, nec veritas ulla est; ubi veritas nulla est merito et talis disciplina est. At ubi deus, ibi metus in deum qui est initium sapientiae. Ubi metus in deum, ibi gravitas honesta et diligentia attonita et cura sollicita, et adlectio explorata et communicatio deliberata et promotio emerita et subiectio religiosa et apparitio devota et processio modesta et ecclesia unita et dei omnia.* [cf. the pseudo-Cyprian *Adversus Judaeos*].

15. Cf. *Adversus Marcionem* 2.16.3.

16. *Sunt qui etsi deum, non negent, dispectorem plane et arbitrum et iudicem non putent, in quo utique nos maxime reiciunt, qui ad istam disciplinam metu praedicati iudicii transvolamus, sic deum honorantes, dum curis observationis et molestiis animadversionis absoluunt, cui ne iram quidem adscribunt. Nam si deus, inquiunt, irascitur, corruptibilis et passionalis est: porro quod patitur quodque corrumpitur, etiam interitum potest capere, quem deus non capit.* (. . .) The passage continues: "But if the soul is divine or God-given, it doubtless knows its giver; and if it knows him, it undoubtedly fears him too, and especially as having been by him so amply endowed. Has it no fear of him who it desires to be propitious, rather than angry? Whence, then, the soul's natural fear of God, if God cannot be angry? How is there any dread of him whom nothing offends? What is feared but anger? Whence comes anger but from observing what is done? What leads to watchful oversight, but judgment in prospect? Whence is judgment but from power? To whom does supreme authority and power belong but to God alone?" (*Si enim anima aut divina aut a deo data est, sine dubio datorem suum novit, et si novit, utique et timet et tantum postremo ad auctorem. An non timet quem magis propitium velit quam iratum? Unde igitur naturalis timor animae in deum, si deus non*

novit irasci? Quomodo timetur nisi ira? Unde ira nisi ex animadversione? Unde animadversio nisi de iudicio? Unde iudicium nisi de potestate? Cuius potestas summa, nisi dei solius?)

17. "There is no certain work where the reward is uncertain. There is no real *timor* when the peril is doubtful." (*Nullum opus certum est mercedis incertae, nullus timor iustus est periculi dubii* [*De resurrectione carnis* 21.4].)

18. Tertullian's use of the title *pontifex maximus* was not meant to be reverent; the *episcopus episcoporum* and the *psychici* had become, in Tertullian's mind, mimics and collaborators with the daemonic forces ruling the Empire.

19. For Tertullian equating Marcion with the Epicureans: *Adversus Marcionem* 1.1.1, 1.25.3–5, 2.16.2, 4.15.2; *De resurrectione carnis* 2.1. For the moral dangers of feeling secure, see *De cultu feminarum* 2.2.2–3.

20. Cf. *Adversus Marcionem* 2.11.2.

21. In one of his most philosophical treatises, *De anima*, Tertullian makes no objection to Plato's concept of god as invisible, incapable of delineation, uniform, supreme, rational and intellectual (24.1). In this case, he objects only to attributing those same qualities to the fallible human soul. A great deal has been written on the great intellectual debt owed by educated Greek and Latin Christians to the Greek philosophers. I can refer to only a tiny selection of these works: E. Zeller, *Die Entwicklung des Monotheismus bei den Griechen* (Stuttgart: Franckhische Verlagshandlung, 1862); W. Jaeger, *The Theology of the Early Greek Philosophers* (London; New York: Oxford University Press, 1947); Michael Frede, "Monotheism and Pagan Philosophy in Later Antiquity," in *Pagan Monotheism in Late Antiquity*, eds. Polymnia Athanassiadi and Michael Frede (Oxford: Clarendon Press, 1999), 41–67.

22. See the extended arguments to this effect in Lactantius' *De ira dei*. God instituted an intense "legal discipline" in order that humans might never for an instant be unoccupied with thoughts of God (*Adversus Marcionem* 2.19.1, 3).

23. The notion of the benign god was adopted also by the author of the "Gospel of Truth" (ed. Harold W. Attridge, *Nag Hammadi Codex I (The Jung Codex)* [Leiden: Brill, 1985], 82–117 [English translation in Ehrman, *Lost Scriptures*, 45–51]). Similarly, the highly abstract, intellectualized god of cosmopolitan Greek and Latin philosophers was often depicted as apathetic or anger-free (cf. Cicero, *De officiis* 3.28.102; *De natura deorum* 3.38.91; Seneca, *De ira* 2.27.2).

24. Robert McL. Wilson makes the point that the strategy of internalized withdrawal employed by many Gnostics made externally imposed systems of ethics irrelevant ("Gnosticism," *Religious Diversity in the Greco-Roman World*, eds. Dan Cohn-Sherbok and John M. Court [Sheffield: Sheffield Academic Press, 2001], 164–81, 179). In fact, *anomia* and self-discipline are quite compatible, as the ancient Roman *religiones* demonstrated, and as Marcion, many Cynics, and Epicureans have shown. "[T]hus far," as Kurt Rudolph observed, "no libertine writings have appeared even among the plentiful Nag Hammadi texts" (*Gnosis: The Nature and History of Gnosticism* [New York: Harper, 1987 (1977)], 255–57, 254). Tertullian was aware of and embarrassed by the belief that the celibate Marcionites were stricter in sexual matters even than he was.

25. The clearest and most powerful statement that I know of the way in which an "anomic morality" can be built on compassion is Albert Camus' "Letters to a German Friend" (*Resistance, Rebellion and Death*, trans. J. O'Brien [New York: Knopf, 1960 (1948)], 1–32). The origin of Camus' morality was not fear of a punishing god but the desire, finally, not to be alone—which desire encouraged him to posit, when looking in the eyes of another that another was looking back at him—another not altogether unlike himself and capable of the same depth of suffering. His morality was based on a deliberate willingness to be sensitive to the eyes of others, a deliberate willingness to be vulnerable, a willingness to risk being shamed by the eyes of others.

26. It is Tertullian's desire for a righteous and cruel purity that led von Harnack to sympathize with Tertullian's *bête noire*, Marcion. "What is the enemy of the good is that compulsory, acquired and self-satisfied 'righteousness' that knows no more of love . . . and that oscillates

between fear and a haughtily virtuous behavior. . . ." (*Marcion, The Gospel of the Alien God*, trans. J. E. Steely and L. D. Bierma [Eugene, Oreg: Wipf & Stock, 2007], 140).

27. Cf. *Adversus Marcionem* 1.11.4. Tertullian, like many Christian writers, considered the ideas of Euhemerus of Messene a great resource and ally. In the *Sacra Historia* of Euhemerus (late–fourth century B.C.E., translated into Latin by the poet Ennius), he asserted that the gods were distinguished dead men or kings. The notion that gods were divinized humans would not have disturbed the ancestor-worshipping Romans. The Romans did not find either "human" or "dead" incompatible with their notion of *divinitas*. Tertullian, like Minucius Felix, either does not—or pretends not—to understand the powerful role of sacralized humans and ancestor worship in Roman life. (It was not the divinizing of the *human* but the *crucified criminal* that scandalized the Romans.) At the same time, Tertullian and other Christians who insistently quoted Euhemerus had to tread carefully when they come to divinizing the human Jesus. For the use of Euhemerus by the Christian writers, see, for example, Minucius Felix, *Octavius* 20.5–6; 21.1–2, 9–12; Aristides, *Apologia* 7; Athenagoras, *Legatio* 28; Theophilus, *Ad Autolycum* 1.9–10, 2.2–3.

28. *Siquidem maiore formidine et callidiore timiditate Caesarem observatis quam ipsum de Olympo Iovem.* (. . .) *adeo et in isto inreligiosi erga deos vestros deprehendemini, cum plus timoris humano dominio dicatis. Citius denique apud vos per omnes deos quam per unum genium Caesaris peieratur.*

29. *Sic eorum numen vocant, ad imagines supplicant. Genium, id est daemonem, implorant, et est eis tutius per Iovis genium peierare quam regis.* Compare the use of statues of the emperor as asylums, which, according to Philostratus, were "more dreaded at that time" [i.e., the time of Apollonius of Tyana, late–second century C.E.] and more inviolable than the Zeus of Olympia." He goes on to say that a master who struck a slave clutching a silver drachma of Tiberius was considered guilty of *asebeia* (*asebēsai tuptēsas*) (Philostratus, *Life of Apollonius of Tyana* [ca. 217 C.E.] 1.15).

30. In Josephus' story of the attempt by Caligula to install his statue in the temple at Jerusalem (*Bellum Iudaicum* 2.184–187, 192–203; cf. *Antiquitates* 17.240–262), the Jews beg Petronius, the governor of Syria, not to cause offense to the "laws of their fathers." The response of the governor Petronius was to warn them concerning the might of the Romans and the menaces of the Emperor and to warn them, "I too must obey the law of my master" (195). For further discussion of this important passage, see Chapter 11, "A Jewish Actor in the Audience: Josephan Doublespeak." See the colorful stories of the paralyzing terror and punishing anguish of *conscientia* of those who, not sufficiently fearing the *ira Dei*, but instead fearing the anger of the Emperor, submitted to the command of the Emperor Decian to sacrifice, in Cyprian (*De lapsis* 24–26).

31. There were closely paralleled developments in ancient Indian thought: Human self-governing though *dharma* (without *danda*, the infliction of punishment) in a sort of positive state of nature (*arajaka*) was rejected by the *brahman* priests and *kshatriya* warrior class in favor of a divine and authoritative kingship. The "state of nature" had become the Hobbesian war of all against all (*matsyanyaya*). See the famous *Shantiparva* (*parva* 12 of the *Mahabharata*), especially sections 67+68. "If there were no king on earth for holding the rod of punishment the strong would have oppressed the weak after the manner of fishes in the water" (*Shantiparva* 67.16f.) In the words of Arjuna, "The wise have designated the rod of punishment as righteousness itself. . . . If punishment were done away with in this world, creatures would soon be destroyed" (ibid. 15.2, 15.30). See Charles Drekmeier, *Kingship and Community in Early India* (Stanford: Stanford University Press, 1962), 129–46; S. J. Tambiah, *World Conqueror and World Renouncer: A Study of Buddhism and Polity in Thailand against a Historical Background* (Cambridge: Cambridge University Press, 1976), 23–27. See also John Spellman, *Political Theory of Ancient India: A Study of Kingship from the Earliest Times to circa a.d. 300* (Oxford: Clarendon Press, 1964), esp. 23–25. Similar developments of thought can be traced in ancient China culminating in the development of an elaborate theory of the necessity for the king and his punishments especially in "Legalist" thought.

See, for example, Mark Edward Lewis, *Sanctioned Violence in Early China* (Albany: State University of New York Press, 1990), esp. 195–98.

32. *Recogitate ea etiam pro brevitate supplicii cuiuslibet, non tamen ultra mortem remansuri.*

33. *Nullus timor iustus est periculi dubii; et merces autem et periculum in resurrectionis pendet eventu.* Cf. *De resurrectione carnis* 28.4.

34. *Sed quanta auctoritas legum humanarum, cum illas et evadere homini contingat et plerumque in admissis delitescenti, et aliquando contemnere ex voluntate vel necessitate delinquenti?*

35. Cf. Cicero: *iam doloris medicamenta illa Epicurea tamquam de narthecio proment: 'si gravis, brevis, si longus, levis'* (*De finibus* 2.7.22).

36. Already in the time of Tiberius, the emperor was making the kind of movements towards centralized uniform jurisdiction over the cultic life of the Empire that they had begun to assert already in the second-century B.C.E. over Roman land in Italy. Beginning in 23 C.E., the Emperors began adjudicating the rights of asylum to Greek temples (Tacitus, *Annales* 4.14). Requesting that the Emperor adjudicate the claims of individual towns to build imperial temples had similar effects (ibid. 4.55–56).

37. Compare the *politeuma* in Paul, Philippians 3.20.

38. For Christians constituting a *natio* or *genus*, see, for example, *Adversus Iudaeos* 1.4, 5.1; *De spectaculis* 1; *Ad nationes* 1.8.1; *Apologeticum* 37.10; *Scorpiace* 10.10.

39. Tertullian aimed for exactly what Hugo Rahner called "the unhealthy amalgam of religion and politics" (*Church and State in Early Christianity*, trans. L. D. Davis [San Francisco: Ignatius Press, 1992 (1961)], 8).

40. See the discussion of Allen Brent on the notion of Christianity as a contra-culture, depending on the norms of the society even while inverting them (*Imperial Cult*, 11–16). Cf. Alistair Stewert-Sykes, "Ordination Rites and Patronage Systems in Third-Century Africa," *Vigiliae Christianae* 56 (2002): 115–30, 115+129. Brent shows a keen appreciation of this hostile mirroring of the Roman Empire by those who, like "John the Seer" longed for its replacement by a Kingdom of God. See his *A Political History of Early Christianity* (London: T & T Clark, 2009), 158–66. (Brent is one of innumerable scholars who continue to use "political" and "religious" as distinct categories even while those categories are continually undermined by their own research and analysis.)

41. The Christianization of Virgil's *imperium sine fine* will appear again in Prudentius, *Contra Symmachum* 1.506ff., esp. 541–43; cf. Robert Markus, *Saeculum: History and Society in the Theology of St. Augustine* (Cambridge: Cambridge University Press, 2007 [1970], 28).

42. The "narcissism of minor differences" is a Freudian phrase. For Freud, this "setting apart" facilitated group coherence by directing aggression to the nonconforming others. See *Group Psychology and the Analysis of the Ego* (1921): *Standard Edition* 18:101; "The Taboo of Virginity" (1918); ibid., 11:199; *Civilization and Its Discontents*, trans. James Strachey (New York: W. W. Norton, 1962), 61.

43. Cf. *De oratione* 15.1–2.

44. Anton Blok, in "The Narcissism of Minor Differences" (*Honour and Violence* [Cambridge; Malden, Mass: Polity, 2001], 115–136) discusses the ways in which the leveling or disturbance of local hierarchies of domination or prestige aggravate minor distinctions to the point of hatred and violence between (to name just a few of his many thoughtful examples) European Christians and assimilated Jews, the Hutu and Tutsi, the Dinka and Nuer, the Sinhalene and Tamil.

45. The "idolatry" that Tertullian rails against: the sacrifices, idols, incense, splendid temples, and so on *would be acceptable* if the acts and objects had been sacralized by (the *right* or *true*) Christians. The (*right* or *true*) Christians sacralize the *right* god, the *right* royal family, the *right* hierarchy, the *right* marriage, and so forth. The Tertullianic position on sacralizing was that *who* was sacralizing was the critical issue: enabling Christians, when they ceased to be rebels (who sacralized by stripping down) and had sufficient freedom to sacralize by decorating up, to

appropriate the signs and behaviors of "idolatry," such as altars, temples filled with silver and gold, incense, statues, vestments, and so forth. After one has defaced the enemies' temple, one can consecrate one's own temple on its ruins.

46. In any complex hierarchical society, nothing is more fiercely fought over than the right of sacralizing and desecrating. Modern American debates on abortion and gay marriage are, at heart, debates over *who* gets to sacralize the foetus, the bond, and so forth.

47. *Audaciam existimo de bono divini praecepti disputare; neque enim quia bonum est, idcirco auscultare debemus, sed quia deus praecepit: ad exhibitionem obsequii prior est maiestas divinae potestatis, prior est auctoritas imperantis quam utilitas servientis.*

48. Compare Tertullian's argument on animal sacrifice: "Nor should anyone find fault with the burdensome expense of sacrifices and the troublesome scrupulosities of services and oblations [detailed in the Hebrew scriptures]. . . . Rather, one should perceive [in the prescriptions for sacrifice] that industry by which God wished to attach a people prone to idolatry and transgression to his own *religio* by duties of the same sort in which the *superstitio* of the *saeculum* was engaged." (*Sacrificiorum quoque onera et operationum et oblationum negotiosas scrupulositates nemo reprehendat. . . . Sed illam dei industriam sentiat qua populum pronum in idololatriam et transgressionem eiusmodi officiis religioni suae voluit adstringere quibus superstitio saeculi agebatur* [*Adversus Marcionem* 2.18.3].) It was not the sacrificing or what was sacrificed so much as who sacrificed and who received the augmentation of the sacrifice that made all the difference.

49. He goes on to list many of the ways in which non-Christian rules and rites seem to mockingly imitate those of the Christians. Cf. *Apologeticum* 7.3; *De testimonio animae* 1.1.

50. ". . . to fear the lord your god, to walk in all his ways, and to love him, and to serve the lord your god with all your heart and soul" (Deuteronomy 10.12). Freud talks of "the excess of anxious worry which is said to be the cause of the taboo ceremonial" (*Totem and Taboo: Resemblances between the Psychic Lives of Savages and Neurotics*, trans. A. A. Brill [New York: Vintage, 1946 (1913)], 66). He went on to relate this to the careful treatment that one renders the taboo person (the king, for example) with "excessive tenderness" [Strachey's trans: "excessive solicitude"]. On love of god, the king, the father: "[This excessive solicitude] occurs wherever, besides the predominant tenderness, there exists a contrary but unconscious stream of hostility, that is to say, wherever the typical case of an ambivalent affective attitude is realized. The hostility is then cried down by an excessive increase of tenderness ["solicitude"] which is expressed as anxiety and becomes compulsive because otherwise it would not suffice for its task of keeping the unconscious opposition in a state of repression. . . . Applied to the treatment of privileged persons this theory of an ambivalent feeling would reveal that their veneration, their very deification, is opposed in the unconscious by an intense hostile tendency, so that, as we had expected, the situation of an ambivalent feeling is here realized. The distrust which certainly seems to contribute to the motivation of the royal taboo, would be another direct manifestation of the same unconscious hostility."

51. 1 John 3.16.

52. The Roman love poets, who to scholars of "religion" might seem light years away from Tertullian, used many of the same strategies: (1) rebellion against the state; denial of the moral authority of the emperors and the laws of the state; (2) unwillingness to be shamed by the broader society; (3) total focus on the beloved; (4) identification of the poet as slave of the beloved; (5) extended use of military metaphors; (6) willingness to suffer pain, humiliation and death on behalf of the beloved. And, like Tertullian, the Roman love poets existed in a world filled with spells, curses, sorcerers, and magicians.

53. Cf. 1 Thessalonians 4.3. The hoplite phalanx as depicted by the Spartan Tyrtaeus, was the pinnacle of this phenomenon, the community composed of interchangeable parts. If one man fell, another literally stepped into his place. It not only was bearable but exalting if one embraced self-destruction, like the Spartan hoplite—something that Archilochus was not willing to do.

54. [*Paenitentiam*] *ita amplexare ut naufragus alicuius tabulae fidem. Haec te peccatorum fluctibus mersum prolevabit et in portum divinae clementiae protelabit. Rape occasionem inopinatae felicitatis, ut ille tu nihil quondam penes dominum nisi stilla situlae et areae pulvis et vasculum figuli arbor exinde fias, illa arbor quae penes aquas seritur et in foliis perennat et tempore suo fructus agit quae non ignem, non securem videbit.* Tertullian protests against the claims of the "Jewish proselyte" that God accounted the *gentes* (i.e., non-Jewish Christians) as less than a drop in a bucket, as dust on the threshing floor in the *Adversus Iudaeos* 1.3. (For these metaphors, see Psalms 1.3, 2.9; Jeremiah 17.7–8; Isaiah 40.15; Daniel 2.35; Matthew 3.10+12; Luke 23.31; Revelations 2.27.)

55. "Killing the kids" was always the ultimate psychological test enabling this strategy. An example of this phenomenon is the story from the admittedly much later *Apophthegmata patrum* (fifth century and later) about the monk, who having abandoned his children to join the monastery (an excellent example of an alternative government/*religio*), misses them but returns to find all but one of them dead. He is then instructed by the abbot to throw the surviving child in the furnace, which he does [Nau, "Histoires des solitaires . . ." #295]. Seneca, although he would have liked to liberate himself from all the dangerous and debilitating attachments that could cause one fear and grief, cannot do so. Consider his outburst in the story of Cambyses and Praexaspes, and his profound and poignant depiction of Andromache attempting to save Astyanax. She is the antithesis of the "Mother of the Nation" in 4 Maccabees.

56. "There is no following wind for a man without a port." Caecilius, in Minucius Felix *Octavius*, attributed the degeneration of the *saeculum*, in part, to the Christians (9). But Tertullian had ready to hand, in refuting this position, the long tradition of self-criticism of both the Romans and the Jews.

57. Tertullian was like Lisa Cohen, the angry and alienated heroine of Kenneth Lonergan's movie *Margaret* (2011). Compassion and guilt were the enemies that threatened to overcome the purity that protected but also alienated her.

7. PRECARIOUS INTEGRATION. MANAGING THE FEARS OF THE ROMANS: TERTULLIAN ON TENTERHOOKS

1. There is an uncharacteristic rhapsodic passage on the renewal of light and nature in *De resurrectione carnis* 12, but it served only as a metaphor and argument for the return of life to the *human* body.

2. For the implications of the urban nature of Paul and the "Imperial Mission" after him, see especially Wayne A. Meeks, *The First Urban Christians: The Social World of the Apostle Paul* (New Haven, Conn.: Yale University Press, 1983) and *The Origins of Christian Morality: The First Two Centuries* (New Haven, Conn.: Yale University Press, 1993). Meeks (like Frend and MacMullen, especially in *The Second Church: Popular Christianity A. D. 200–400* [Atlanta: Society of Biblical Literature, 2009]) is exceptionally sensitive to the profound ambiguities and conflicts necessarily present in the relationship not only of communities of followers of Jesus but of other "subcultures" in the cities of the Roman Empire. There were, to be sure, Christians in the villages. The "Scillitan" Christians seem to have come from a small town and the author of the *Pastor Hermae* has a (strangely surrealistic) rural landscape.

3. Tertullian's contempt for all nonhuman creatures runs throughout his works. He rejects the concept of metempsychosis because: "All creatures are the slaves of man, all are his subjects, all his dependents. If by and by he is to become one of these creatures, he is by such a change debased and degraded" (*De anima* 33.9).

4. *De fuga* 12.2; *De patientia* 3.7; *Adversus Marcionem* 3.7.1.

5. Allen Brent has done much, in his work, to establish the mirroring of Christian and Roman *imperia* (*The Imperial Cult and the Development of Church Order: Concepts and Images of Authority in Paganism* [Leiden; Boston: Brill, 1999], esp. 73ff.).

6. I cannot emphasize enough that Latin had no way to distinguish a "politics" from a "religion," and Latin notions of "sacred" and "profane" did not map onto later Christian notions. *Pace* Durkheim, Benveniste, Hubert, and Mauss, sacred and profane were, in Roman thought, relative and reversible terms. A place that was framed and set apart—for example, a temple (*fanum*) was sacred relative to what was before or outside the boundary (*profanum*)—but the thing that was *profanum* (before or outside the *fanum*) might, in turn, be enclosed within another sacred boundary: for instance, that of the physical or psychological walls of the city (the *moenia*, the *pomerium*, etc.) What might be outside the sacred frame in one perspective could be within the frame in another. And what was outside the *fanum*, by its proximity to the *fanum*, could be associated with, rather than opposed to, what was inside, in the way the suburbs were related to the *urbs* or the altar to the temple. ("*Profanum* 'being before the sanctuary'," Varro explains, "applies to something that is in front of the sanctuary and joined to it; from this, anything in the sacrifice . . . is called '*profanatum*' 'brought before the sanctuary, dedicated'" (*De lingua latina* 6.54). *Profanare* could be used as a synonym for *sacrificare*. Similarly, *sanctitas* had no particular relationship to—and certainly no opposition to—the notion of the *saeculum* or *mundus*. See Mishna Kelim 1:6–9 for similar relativism among the Rabbis.

7. *Paganus* appears twice, in Tertullian's *De pallio* 4 and *De corona* 11.4, where it has the meaning, common in Imperial Latin, of "civilian" as opposed to "enlisted in the military": "When a man has taken up the *fides* and has been sealed (*signata* [i.e., has taken the oath of loyalty]) either it [his *fides*=oath] must straightaway be deserted—as is done by many—or all kinds of quibbling must take place lest something opposed by god should be committed which is not permitted outside the military service, or, finally, that those sufferings must be endured on behalf of God which the *fides pagana* equally stipulates/consigns." (*Dum tamen suscepta fide atque signata aut deserendum statim sit, ut a multis actum, aut omnibus modis cavillandum, ne quid adversus deum committatur, quae nec extra militiam permittuntur, aut novissime, perpetiendum pro deo, quod aeque fides pagana condixit.*) On the contrast between the *paganus* as civilian and the *miles* as enlisted soldier, see, for example, Pliny, *Epistulae* 7.25, 10.86b; Tacitus, *Historiae* 1.53, 3.43; Suetonius, *Augustus* 27; *Galba* 19; Juvenal 16.33; Quintus Cervidius Scaevola [second half of second century C.E.] *Digesta* 35.2.96; Aemilius Macer [early–third century C.E.] *Digesta* 48.19.14; Vegetius, *Epitoma rei militaris* 2.23; Theodore Zahn, "Paganus," *Neue Kirchliche Zeitschrift* 10 (1899): 18–44; von Harnack, *Mission and Expansion of Christianity*, 1:416–18; Einer Löfstedt, *Late Latin* (Oslo: Aschehoug, 1959), 75–78; Christine Mohrmann, "Quelques Traits Charactéristiques du Latin des Chrétiens," in *Études sur le Latin des Chrétiens* 2 vols. (Rome: Edizioni di storia e letteratura, 1961), 1:21–50, 27–28; Martin Heimgartner, "Paganus," *Brill's New Pauly* 10, ed. M. Landfester et al. (Leiden; Boston: Brill, 2007), 338–39. "*Pagani* were civilians who had not enlisted through baptism as soldiers of Christ against the powers of Satan" (Robin Lane Fox, *Pagans and Christians* [New York: Knopf, 1986], 30–31). The first appearance of the word *paganus* with the meaning non-Christian was in the fourth century and became accepted usage only with Augustine; it appears with that meaning in an inscription from the early fourth century (*Corpus Inscriptionum Latinarum* X² 7112); its first appearance in an imperial decree with the meaning of non-Christian is in a rescript of Valentinian (370 C.E.) in the *Codex Theodosianus* 16.2.18. In everyday colloquial usage, it remained either "civilian" or "rustic." Garth Fowden attributes to "the lazy cunning of Christian apologists," the term "pagan" to describe non-Christians in a review of Lane Fox's *Pagans and Christians* in the *Journal of Roman Studies* 78 (1988): 176; see also David Frankfurter, *Religion in Roman Egypt: Assimilation and Resistance* (Princeton: Princeton University Press, 1998), 33.

8. For example, *De resurrectione carnis* 22.2 (Tertullian yearning for the *saeculi huius occasus*).

9. For the *saecula saeculorum*, see also *Passio Perpetuae* 11.

10. Compare *saeculum* in Cyprian's translation of Mark 10.29: "'There is no man,' he said, 'that leaves house, or land, or parents, siblings, or wife, or children on account of the kingdom of

God, who will not receive seven-fold even in this time, but in the age to come (*in saeculo venturo*) life everlasting.'" ('*Nemo est,*' inquit, '*qui relinquat domum aut agrum aut parentes aut fratres aut uxorem aut filios propter regnum Dei et non recipiat septies tantum in isto tempore, in saeculo autem venturo vitam aeternam*' [*De lapsis* 12].) "The *saeculum* is God's, the *saecularia* are the devil's" (*saeculum dei est, saecularia autem diaboli* [Tertullian, *De spectaculis* 15].)

11. Time, for Tertullian, was endlessly malleable, an *ouroboros* that could smoothly turn back onto itself. Past history and future eschatology were often mirror images. Tertullian similarly constructed his arguments: Every path led to and through to his desired end. As in scripture, "things future are set down as if they had already taken place . . . in God's sight there is no distinction of tense, since with him eternity itself controls a condition in which all tenses are alike" (*Adversus Marcionem* 3.5.2–4). Tertullian's time, like his god, could justify the status quo or justify its overthrow; it could authorize either *antiquitas* or *novitas*. For conceiving time in this manner, see Berger and Luckman, *Social Construction of Reality* (Garden City, N.Y.: Doubleday, 1967), 159–60. For the very flexible relationship of past and future in prophecy, see also Justin [ca.100–ca.165 C.E.], *Dialogus cum Tryphone* 114; Irenaeus [ca.130–ca.200 C.E.] *Demonstratio* 67.

12. For examples of the *spiritalis* and *prophetica* meaning of the scriptures (*lex*), see *Adversus Marcionem* 2.19.1, 21.2, 23.1. Compare the interpretive strategies of the authors of the Qumran *Pesharim* who understood the ancient prophets to be predicting what was happening in their own and future time (James Vanderkam and Peter Flint, *The Meaning of the Dead Sea Scrolls* [New York: Harper Collins, 2002], 221–22).

13. Even when in his books against Marcion, he engaged in a long defense of the Israelite god, Tertullian was vexed to provide justifications for the divine rules and behaviors that he felt had been abrogated or superseded. See, for instance, his justifications for the dietary laws and for animal sacrifices (2.18).

14. The great majority of the human race was ignorant even of the name of Moses, let alone his writings (*Adversus Marcionem* 1.10.2).

15. The soldiers, like Josephus, were aware that a few rebels could bring destruction on many. In a late antique story about two rabbis who lived in the time of Hadrian, Rabbi Yose expressed the danger of provoking the Romans: "When Rabbi Yose the son of Kisma became ill, Rabbi Ḥanina the son of Teradion went to visit him. He said to him: 'Ḥanina, my brother, don't you know that this nation [Rome] was set to rule over us by Heaven, and it has destroyed His house, and burned His temple, and killed His saints, and destroyed His goodly things, and still it exists, and I have heard that you gather crowds together in public, with a Scroll of the Torah in your lap, and you sit and teach!' He [Ḥanina] said to him, 'From Heaven they will have mercy.' He [Yose] said to him, 'I say logical things to you, and you answer me: "From Heaven [they] will have mercy!"' "I will be surprised if they do not burn you and the Scroll of the Torah with you"'" (*Avoda Zara* 17).

16. *ut de abrupto et praecipiti et mori cupido, qui de habitu interrogatus nomini negotium fecerit, solus scilicet fortis inter tot fratres commilitones, solus Christianus. Plane superest, ut etiam martyria recusare meditentur qui prophetias eiusdem spiritus sancti respuerunt. Musitant denique tam bonam et longam pacem periclitari sibi. Nec dubito quosdam <secundum> scripturas emigrare, sarcinas expedire, fugae accingi de civitate in civitatem. Nullam enim aliam evangelii memoriam curant. Novi et pastores eorum in pace leones, et in proelio cervos.*

17. *Christians and Their Many Identities in Late Antiquity, North Africa 200–450 CE* (Ithaca, N.Y.; London: Cornell University Press, 2012), ch. 1+2. As John North points out, those who joined the movement brought with them the totality of their experience outside the movement ("The Development of Religious Pluralism," in *The Jews Among Pagans and Christians*, eds. by Judith Lieu, John North, and Tessa Rajak, 174–93. [New York: Routledge, 1992], 176). Graydon Snyder, *Ante Pacem: Archaeological Evidence of Church Life Before Constantine* (Macon, Ga.: Mercer University Press, 2003 [1985]), and (addressing a slightly later period) MacMullen (*The Second Church*) show the

persistence, and even domination of family and ancestor cult on the local level. For the deeper integration of Christians into the Roman world than would have pleased Tertullian, see Philip A. Harland, *Associations, Synagogues, and Congregations: Claiming a Place in Ancient Mediterranean Society* (Minneapolis: Fortress, 2003), esp. 184ff.

18. For Christians modeling themselves on the gladiators of the Roman arena, see Barton, *Sorrows of the Ancient Romans* (Chapters 1 and 2) and ead., "Savage Miracles."

19. Timothy Barnes, in *Tertullian: A Historical and Literary Study* (Oxford: Clarendon Press [1971], 3–29) does all that is humanly possible to squeeze biographical particulars from the stone of Tertullian's abstract universe. Tertullian, in his writings, chose to hide almost every detail of his life. I agree with Barnes in rejecting Jerome's characterization of Tertullian as a *presbyter*. But, regardless of whether he was a practicing advocate, he had been highly trained in rhetoric and law.

20. See especially Peter Brown, *Body and Society: Men, Women, and Sexual Renunciation in Early Christianity* (New York: Columbia University Press, 1988).

21. Even when he is speaking as a heresy-hunter to a small number of other educated Christians, he nevertheless expected them to be impressed, affected, and responsive to traditions of the Greco-Roman culture around him.

22. Bruce Lincoln nicely explains the appeal of apocalypticism to "sectors of society that have lost power, prestige, wealth, confidence, and or security . . . displaced elites, marginal intellectuals, those deprived of patrons, peoples in exile, and classes threatened with structural obsolescence" ("Apocalyptic Temporality and Politics in the Ancient World," in *The Encyclopedia of Apocalypticism*, ed. John J. Collins, 3 vols. [London: Continuum, 2004] 1:457–75, 468).

23. Tertullian's movement (like that of the Bolsheviks, Maoists, and early Muslims) will intensify and tighten the centralizing, hierarchizing processes that they first undermined. Although complex cultures are fragile "houses of cards" and can crumble easily and quickly, they usually form up again according to the same pattern, often with more determined and ferociously violent hierarchies.

24. *Domitiani vero natura praeceps in iram . . . moderatione tamen prudentiaque Agricolae leniebatur, quia non contumacia neque inani iactatione libertatis famam fatumque provocabat. Sciant quibus moris est inlicita mirari, posse etiam sub malis principibus magnos viros esse, obsequiumque ac modestiam, si industria ac vigor adsint, eo laudis excedere, quo plerique per abrupta sed in nullum rei publicae usum ambitiosa morte inclaruerunt.* Compare Martial: "In that you follow the teachings of the great Thrasea and the consummate Cato . . . and yet do not throw yourself on drawn swords, you are, Decianus, doing what I want you to do. I do not wish to praise the man who redeems his honor by a facile shedding of his blood—but the man who can do so without dying" (1.8).

25. I use the phrase "apologetic mode" with caveats mentioned in Chapter 3, "Preface to Tertullian."

26. "*Orthodox* Christians felt towards heretics much as *pagans* felt towards them," de Ste. Croix, "Why were the Early Christians persecuted?" *Past & Present* 26 (1963), 26.

27. *Natura veneranda est, non erubescenda. Concubitum libido, non condicio foedavit. Excessus, non status est impudicus, siquidem benedictus status apud deum: crescite et in multitudinem proficite, excessus vero maledictus, adulteria et stupra et lupanaria* (*De anima* 27.4). This embrace of moderation appears as well when he is reacting to what he considers the excessive rigor and asceticism of the Marcionites (*Adversus Marcionem* 1.29).

28. It is this negotiatory thinking that motivates the complex rhetorical strategies of Tertullian mapped by Robert Sider (*Ancient Rhetoric and the Art of Tertullian* [London: Oxford University Press, 1971]) and Laura Nasrallah (*Ecstasy of Folly* [Cambridge, Mass.: Harvard University Press, 2003]). The Romans of the Imperial period, as Shadi Bartsch has demonstrated, had to perform the same complex negotiations (*Actors in the Audience* [Cambridge, Mass.: Harvard University Press, 1994]). For the strategies of Seneca and Lucan in dealing with the acute

insecurities of living close to the center, see also C. Barton, *Vis mortua: Irreconcilable Patterns of Thought in the Literature of the Neronian Period* (Berkeley: University of California, diss., 1985).

29. *Ecclēsia* was adopted by Greek-speaking Christians of the Eastern Empire, an ordinary word for the assembly of the Greek town, thereby avoiding words for their movement that would imply open resistance (rejecting *synagōgē*, which had come to be associated with the restive Jews). See Brent, *Political History*, 202–3.

30. *De spectaculis* 1, *Adversus Iudaeos* 1.4.

31. *Ad nationes* 1.8.11.

32. *Adversus Iudaeos* 1.4, 5.1.

33. *Ad nationes* 1.3, 1.4.6+11, 1.7.8, 1.10.1; *Apologeticum* 2.18–19, 5.2, 17.5, 21.2+26; *De idololatria* 14.1–2; *Scorpiace* 10.9+14; *De corona* 1.4, 11.4.

34. *Apologeticum* 21.26.

35. While Steve Mason is aware of the problematical nature of the word "religion," in his otherwise wonderfully useful and perceptive article, "Jews, Judaeans, Judaizing, Judaism: Problems of Categorization in Ancient History," *Journal for the Study of Judaism* 38 (2007): 457–512, he seems mistakenly to attribute to Tertullian the formation of the conception of Christianity as a "belief system" or a "faith" "forcefully rejecting resisting categories for Christianity" (p. 472) and "able to jettison earlier attempts at accommodating their faith to existing categories . . . [not] admitting the definitive state of established forms" (p. 476). He seems to me to attribute to Tertullian the formation of a conception of a "faith" (a word that modern translators employ as a synonym for "religion"). Mason makes Tertullian a thinker who simply discards the past to arrive at a new formulation of Christianity as *sui generis* (pp. 472, 476). The Tertullian I have found is ever in the midst of his search for ways of conceptualizing what he is as a Christian and has very varied attitudes toward the old and the new.

36. For the central role of *disciplina* in Tertullian and in other early Latin Christian writers, see Marrou, "*Doctrina* et *disciplina* dans la langue des Pères de l'Eglise" (*Archivum Latinitatis Medii Aevi* 9 [1934]), V. Morel, "Le développement de la *disciplina* sous l'action du Saint Esprit chez Tertullien," *Revue de l'histoire ecclésiastique* 35 (1935): 243–65; id., "*Disciplina*: le mot et l'idée representée par lui dans les oeuvres de Tertullien," *Revue de l'histoire ecclésiastique* 40 (1944/45): 5–46; W. Dürig, "*Disciplina*. Eine Studie zum Bedeutungsumfang des Wortes in der Sprache der Liturgie und der Väter," *Sacris Erudiri* 4 (1952): 245–79; P. G. Van Der Nat, "Tertullianea," *Vigiliae Christianae* 18 (1964): 129–43, 134–36.

37. Famously: "What has Athens to do with Jerusalem? What concord is there between the Academy and the Church?—between heretics and Christians? Our instruction (*institutio*) comes from '*the Porch of Solomon*' [Acts 3.5—the "Stoa," where the apostles taught] (. . .) Away with all attempts to produce a mottled *Christianismus* of Stoic, Platonic and dialectic composition! There is no need of *curiositas* after Christ Jesus, no inquisition after the gospel! When we believe (*credimus*) we have no need to believe anything further. When we believe in this to begin with, there is nothing additional we should believe." (*Quid ergo Athenis et Hierosolymis? quid academiae et ecclesiae? quid haereticis et christianis? Nostra institutio de porticu Solomonis est . . . Viderint qui Stoicum et Platonicum et dialecticum christianismum protulerunt. Nobis curiositate opus non est post Christum Iesum nec inquisitione post evangelium. Cum credimus nihil desideramus ultra credere. Hoc enim prius credimus non esse quod ultra credere debeamus* [*De praescriptione haereticorum* 7.9–13].) "Our knowledge of god comes to us from the prophets and from Christ, not from the philosophers or Epicurus." (*Deum nos a prophetis et a Christo, non a philosophis nec ab Epicuro erudimur* [*Adversus Marcionem* 2.16.2].) For Greek philosophy inspiring *haereses*, see *De anima* 3.1, 18.4, 23.5; *Adversus Marcionem* 1.13.3; *Adversus Hermogenem* 1.3. See the perceptive remarks of Laura Nasrallah on the complex rhetorical strategies of Tertullian's *De anima* ("Tertullian the Philosopher, Tertullian the Antiphilosopher," in *Ecstasy of Folly*, 101–10).

38. *Et tamen philosophis patet libertas transgrediendi a vobis in sectam et auctorem et suum nomen, nec quisquam illis odium movet, cum in mores ritus cultus victusque vestros palam et publice omnem eloquii amaritudinem elatrent, cum legum contemptu, sine respectu personarum ut quidam etiam in principes ipsos libertatem suam impune iaculentur.*

39. *Sed dum unicuique manifestatur veritas nostra, interim incredulitas, dum de bono sectae huius obducitur, . . . non utique divinum negotium existimat, sed magis philosophiae genus. Eadem, inquit, et philosophi monent atque profitentur: innocentiam, iustitiam, patientiam, sobrietatem, pudicitiam. Cur, ergo quibus comparamur de disciplina, non proinde illis adaequamur ad licentiam impunitatemque disciplinae? (. . .) Quis enim philosophum sacrificare aut deierare aut lucernas meridie vanas proferre conpellit? Quin immo et deos vestros palam destruunt et superstitiones vestras commentariis quoque accusant laudantibus vobis. Plerique etiam in principes latrant sustinentibus vobis, et facilius statuis et salariis remunerantur quam ad bestias pronuntiantur.* Not surprisingly, in his apologetic or negotiatory mode, Tertullian's tirades against the *haereses* (that would have been interpreted by non-Christians as conflicts between philosophical sects or schools [*haireseis*]) are all but invisible.

40. In the *praedicatio* of the *discipuli*, the latter might be suspected of seeking glory (*gloriae studium*) if the *auctoritas* of their teacher (*magister*) did not back them up. In this case, the *apostoli* were supported by the *auctoritas* of Christ, "which made the *discipuli* into *magistri*" (*Adversus Marcionem* 4.2.1).

41. *Ego iam illi etiam divinae sectae ac disciplinae commercium confero. Gaude pallium et exsulta! Melior iam te philosophia dignata est ex quo Christianum vestire coepisti.*

42. Note, as will be shown in Chapter 12, "A Glance at the Future: *Thrēskeia* and the Literature of Apologetic, First to Third Centuries C.E.," that at about the same time as Tertullian, Christian apologists (and before them Philo, the Jew) were using *thrēskeia* to make similar arguments.

43. *Colat alius deum, alius Iovem, alius ad caelum manus supplices tendat, alius ad aram Fidei, alius, si hoc putatis, nubes numeret orans, alius lacunaria, alius suam animam deo suo voveat, alius hirci. Videte enim ne et hoc ad inreligiositatis elogium concurrat, adimere libertatem religionis et interdicere optionem divinitatis, ut non liceat mihi colere quem velim, sed cogar colere quem nolim. Nemo se ab invito coli volet, ne homo quidem.*

44. *Atque adeo et Aegyptiis permissa est tam vanae superstitionis potestas avibus et bestiis consecrandis et capite damnandis qui aliquem huiusmodi deum occiderint.*

45. Cf. Minucius Felix 21.9.

46. For this kind of list of *sacrorum ritus*, see also Minucius Felix 6.1; Athenagoras, *Legatio* 1.14; Justin, *Apologia* 1.24.

47. This will be extensively documented in Chapter 12, "A Glance at the Future: *Thrēskeia* and the Literature of Apologetic, First to Third Centuries C.E.," but for now, consider *First Clement* 62.1–2 and its early Latin translation.

"We have now written to you, brethren, sufficiently touching the things which befit our *religio/thrēskeia*, and are most useful for those wishing eternal life and to proceed justly and *pie/ eusebōs*. For we have touched on every aspect of *fides* and *paenitentia* and sobriety/self-control and *patientia*. . . ."

Περὶ μὲν τῶν ἀνηκόντων τῇ θρησκείᾳ ἡμῶν καὶ τῶν ὠφελιμωτάτων εἰς ἐνάρετον βίον τοῖς θέλουσιν εὐσεβῶς καὶ δικαίως διευθύνειν, ἱκανῶς ἐπεστείλαμεν ὑμῖν, ἄνδρες ἀδελφοί. περὶ γὰρ πίστεως καὶ μετανοίας καὶ γνησίας ἀγάπης καὶ ἐγκρατείας καὶ σωφροσύνης καὶ ὑπομονῆς πάντα τόπον ἐψηλαφήσαμεν . . .

De his quae pertinent ad religionem nostram, et quae utilia sunt his qui perpetuam vitam volunt pie et iuste incedere, sufficienter scripsimus vobis, viri fratres. Nam de fide et paenitentia et sobrietate et patientia omnem locum tractavimus . . .

Compare James 1.26–27:

"Whoever claims to be *religiosus/thrēskos* but fails to keep a tight rein on the tongue but, rather, deceiving his own heart, that person's *religio/thrēskeia* is worthless. Pure unspoiled *religio/ thrēskeia*, in the eyes of God the Father is this: coming to the help of orphans and widows in their hardships, and keeping oneself uncontaminated by the world."

Εἴ τις δοκεῖ θρησκὸς εἶναι, μὴ χαλιναγωγῶν γλῶσσαν αὐτοῦ ἀλλὰ ἀπατῶν καρδίαν αὐτοῦ, τούτου μάταιος ἡ θρησκεία. θρησκεία καθαρὰ καὶ ἀμίαντος παρὰ τῷ θεῷ καὶ πατρὶ αὕτη ἐστίν, ἐπισκέπτεσθαι ὀρφανοὺς καὶ χήρας ἐν τῇ θλίψει αὐτῶν, ἄσπιλον ἑαυτὸν τηρεῖν ἀπὸ τοῦ κόσμου.

Vulgatus: *Si quis autem putat se religiosum esse, non refrenans linguam suam, sed seducens cor suum, huius vana est religio. [27] Religio munda et immaculata apud Deum et Patrem, haec est: visitare pupillos et viduas in tribulatione eorum, et immaculatum se custodire ab hoc saeculo.*

Observe, in this quote, the notion of discipline and attention to obligations. He who cannot restrain his tongue, who is not self-controlled, his *thrēskeia/religio* is in vain.

48. This figure, he tells us, had ass' ears, and was dressed in a toga with a book, having a hoof for one of its feet. Tertullian (*Apologeticum* 16.1) makes it sound as if non-Christians thought that the Christians' god had the head of an ass.

49. According to Allen Brent, Luke-Acts, Clement, Justin, Tatian, Athenagoras, and Tertullian "sought to establish the foundations for a *legal argument* for the recognition of the Christian *cultus* as a so-called *religio licita*, though the validity of the concept in Roman law has been questioned. (. . .) if the characteristic of a *religio illicita* is that it is no true *religio* but a degenerate *superstitio* and, on the example of the Bacchanalian riot, a threat to public order, morality and the civil peace" (*Imperial Cult*, 8). I would argue that any conceptual means of legalizing a "religion" was absent. G. E. M. de Ste. Croix was correct in concluding that the governor's right of *cognitio* involved broad discretionary powers only limited by specific imperial directives ("Why were the Early Christians Persecuted?", esp. 14–17). It was Tertullian and not the Romans who first expressed the notion of an authorized or legitimate *religio/disciplina*. *Secta . . . religio certe licita* was Tertullian's own colloquial expression for a tolerated cult.

50. The Romans thought in terms of *fas* and *nefas* (verbally "permitted" or "forbidden") and *iustus* (something permitted within a particular sphere).

51. Daniel 3.12–4.

52. 1 Peter 2.13.

53. See *Ad nationes* 1.10.29, 1.17.6; *Apologeticum* 10.1, 21.13, 24.3–4, 28.1, 33–34, 35.1+4; *De idololatria* 12.5, 15, 18; *De corona* 13.9; *Scorpiace* 8.6–7, 14.3.

54. *Rex enim etsi summum magnum est in suo solio usque ad deum, tamen infra deum, comparatus autem ad deum excidet iam de summo magno. . . .*

55. "[Hierarchy] is none other than the conscious form of reference of the parts to the whole in the system." (Louis Dumont, *Homo Hierarchicus An Essay on the Caste System*, translated by Mark Sainsbury [Chicago: The University of Chicago Press, 1970] 65.) "To adopt a value is to introduce hierarchy," (ibid. p. 20). "[W]here we condemn and exclude, India hierarchizes and includes" (ibid. p. 431 n. 14). The Romans, with their hierarchies of infinite statuses, were like the ancient Indians, highly stratified but inclusive; there was room for everyone in the endlessly elaborated Roman hierarchy. The early Christians were more like the Athenians, who with their democracy were much more exclusive. For the Athenians one was either in or out—either one had the fullness of citizenship or nothing at all.

56. The gods of non-Christians are given various degrees of existential reality. Like Plato, Tertullian's world had two dimensions: Like Plato, he vacillated between conceiving the desired world as real and the rejected as unreal, or one as simply more real and the other less real. The vacillations in Tertullian between these two "realities" are maddeningly frequent and unexamined,

but the dichotomy of more real/less real at least allowed for the less real some experiential authority.

57. Neither the Romans nor the Christians were afraid of the gods but only the humans. Sorcerers were attacked—not the gods of sorcerers.

58. Origen, exercising similar caution, attacked the worship only of the kings of Egypt, Persia, and the Greeks (*Contra Celsum* 8.6). The avoidance by the persecuted subject of *direct* attack on the tyrant/oppressor/master is so universal as to hardly need examples. One has only to think of Seneca's plays, and books like Daniel, John the Seer's *Apocalypsis*, Verdi's *Rigoletto*, the Christian hymns of American slaves.

59. The reader might well ask: How can one separate such a story into "secular" and "sacred" "religion" and "politics"? It would be impossible. The stories of the Gracchi are filled with sacrificial imagery and languages, and a sacrifice to the two champions of the people was instituted by the plebs after their death (Plutarch, *Gaius Gracchus* 18).

60. Robert Grant, in the first chapter of his *Greek Apologists of the Second Century* ("The Background of Christian Apologetics" [Philadelphia: Westminster, 1988, 1–18]), does an excellent job of articulating the kinds of statements and images that were generally NOT found in "apologetic," including military metaphors, "martyrdom," prophecy, messianism, and teleological apocalyptic.

61. *Apologeticum* 43.1, cf. 21.17, 23.1+12, 25.12; *De idololatria* 9.1–4; *De praescriptione haereticorum* 43; *De pudicitia* 5.11; *De spectaculis* 2; *Ad uxorem* 2.5.2; *De anima* 28.5, 57.7; *De carne Christi* 2.1.

62. Cf. Augustine, *De civitate dei* 10.1. Latin *cultus*, like Greek *therapeia*, indicated the attention, the scrupulous care that one paid to anything that one valued. But English "worship" is usually reserved for gods and kings. We think it is a sort of comic exaggeration when applied to plants and animals. Similarly, we assume that something "sacred" is associated with gods, whereas Latin *sacer* could be *anything* set apart to blessed or cursed, further decorated up or stripped down, sacralized or desecrated.

63. *Nonne conceditis de aestimatione communi aliquem esse sublimiorem et potentiorem, velut principem mundi perfectae potentiae et maiestatis? Nam et sic plerique disponunt divinitatem, ut imperium summae dominationis esse penes unum, (. . .) [appellatio] dei ita ut imperatoris in aliquo principe. . . .*

64. Cf. *Adversus Marcionem* 1.10.2.

65. Cf. especially *De resurrectione carnis* 3.1–2; *Adversus Marcionem* 1.3.2–3; 1.10. While elsewhere, the wisdom of the world was foolishness, in his negotiatory mode Tertullian preferred to start his arguments from premises to which "everyone can agree" (*De resurrectione carnis* 2.7 ff.). It is easy to identify the most fragile points in Tertullian's arguments by the appearance of some version of "all men, by nature, agree. . . ." The proposition that is in dispute becomes axiomatic, Tertullian's version of the "Platonic Turn" ("Of course, Socrates, how could it be otherwise?"). His imaginary opponents confess to the opposite position from the one they are ostensibly arguing. This kind of argumentation ("Begging the question" *petitio principii*) allowed Tertullian to make the propositions that he could *not* prove into the indisputable of his arguments, allowed him to make generalizations deductively rather than inductively.

66. *Sed et Victorias adoratis, cum in tropaeis cruces intestina sint tropaeorum. Religio Romanorum tota castrensis signa veneratur, signa iurat, signa omnibus deis praeponit. Omnes illi imaginum suggestus in signis monilia crucum sunt; siphara illa vexillorum et cantabrorum stolae crucum sunt. . . . Noluistis incultas et nudas cruces consecrare.* Constantine (with the help of Eusebius) will be able to present the cross to his soldiers as the *tropaeum* of the cross, a trophy and sign of victory (Eusebius, *Vita Constantini* 28; cf. 37.1 with the commentary by Averil Cameron and Stuart Hall on this passage [*Eusebius, Life of Constantine* (Oxford: Clarendon Press, 1999), 207–08]).

67. Cf. 2 Thessalonians 2.6–8.

68. *Est et alia maior necessitas nobis orandi pro imperatoribus, etiam pro omni statu imperii rebusque Romanis, qui vim maximam universo orbi imminentem ipsamque clausulam saeculi acerbitates horrendas*

comminantem Romani imperii commeatu scimus retardari. Itaque nolumus experiri, et dum precamur differri, Romanae diuturnitati favemus.

69. *Nos vero ieiuniis aridi et omni continentia expressi, ab omni vitae fruge dilati, in sacco et cinere volutantes invidia caelum tundimus, deum tangimus, et cum misericordiam extorserimus, Iuppiter honoratur!* Cf. *Apologeticum* 38.9–10, 39.1–6, 43.2, 46.5; *De pallio* 5.5.

70. *Falsa nunc sint quae tuemur et merito praesumptio, attamen necessaria; inepta, attamen utilia; siquidem meliores fieri coguntur qui eis credunt, metu aeterni supplicii et spe aeterni refrigerii. Itaque non expedit falsa dici nec inepta haberi quae expedit vera praesumi. Nullo titulo damnari licet omnino quae prosunt. In vobis itaque praesumptio est haec ipsa quae damnat utilia. Proinde nec inepta esse possunt; certe etsi falsa et inepta, nulli tamen noxia. Nam et multis aliis similia quibus nullas poenas inrogatis, vanis et fabulosis, inaccusatis et inpunitis, ut innoxiis.*

71. Marcus Aurelius—the "healthy eye" of the good king, like that of physician—should be able to look at everything (10.35).

8. IMAGINE NO *THRĒSKEIA*: THE TASK OF THE UNTRANSLATOR

1. This development will be considered by me in future work (in progress).

2. Dale B. Martin, *Inventing Superstition: From the Hippocratics to the Christians* (Cambridge, Mass.; London: Harvard University Press, 2004).

3. Carlin Barton, "The Price of Peace in Ancient Rome," in Kurt A. Raaflaub, ed., *War and Peace in the Ancient World* (Oxford: Blackwell [2007], pp. 245–55).

4. Surely not "believes in." As Conrad Leyser has recently written, "As recent work by Stefan Esders and Andrew Marsham has shown, to understand 'faith' in the late ancient world, we need to begin with the oaths of loyalty sworn by soldiers to their generals. *Fides* in this sense was a fearsome obligation, having precious little to do with modern interiorized notions of religious belief" [TLS December 21 and 28, 2012, p. 1; see also discussion of *fides* in chapters above, *passim*]. When *nomizō* is used with gods and belief it has to do with what a person believes about the gods, not believing in them, thus 'θεὸν νομίζουσι εἶναι τὸ πῦρ' Hdt.3.16, 'believes that fire is a god.'"

5. Were I tempted to suggest that *thrēskeia* is, as it were, unmarked and conclude that only the *periergos* marks its negativity, I would have to grant the same to *deisidaimonia* and conclude that only foreign ones are to be avoided, but this is patently not the case. Conclude rather that *deisidaimonia* here is indicted as foreign and *thrēskeia* as *periergos*.

6. Temkin writes "superstition."

7. Soranus of Ephesus, *Soranus' Gynecology*, translated with an introduction by Owsei Temkin, the assistance of Nicholson J. Eastman, Ludwig Edelstein, and Alan F. Guttmacher (Baltimore; London: Johns Hopkins University Press, 1991), 7. Of course, I have untranslated both Greek terms.

8. Cf. text from Virgil's Georgica 3.454–456, discussed in Chapter 1, "*Religio* Without 'Religion,'" where the farmer is instructed that a sheep's ulcer must be lanced, not prayed over.

9. This bell-like clarity is, however, not carried out through the semantic map, and this is precisely my point.

10. Theophrastus, *The Characters of Theophrastus*, newly ed. and trans. J. M. Edmonds. Herodes, et al., Loeb Classical Library (Cambridge, Mass.: Harvard University Press; London: W. Heinemann, 1929), 79–80.

11. In later Christian Latin, *religio* is not defined as in Cicero as the practices that are useful and appropriate for maintaining Roman solidarity and social order, but as the belief in that which is true, that is, as sanctioned by an authoritatively and ultimately legally produced ecumenical orthodoxy. Beard, North, and Price support this point:
"*Religio* is worship of the true god, *superstitio* of a false" [*Religio veri dei cultus est, superstitio falsi*, 4.28.11.], as the Christian Lactantius remarked in the early–fourth century A.D.—so asserting that

alien practices and gods were not merely inferior to his own, but actually bogus. The traditional Roman distinction seems to have made no such assumption about truth and falsehood: When Romans in the early empire debated the nature of *religio* and *superstitio*, they were discussing instead different *forms* of human relations with the gods. This is captured in Seneca's formulation that '*religio* honours the gods, *superstitio* wrongs them'" (Mary Beard, John A. North, and S. R. F. Price, *Religions of Rome* [Cambridge: Cambridge University Press, 1998], 216). See earlier Maurice Sachot: "Dans la bouche de chrétien *religio* renvoie désormais non plus seulement à pratiques et à des institutions individuelles, familiales ou civiles, mais aussi et avant tout à un rapport absolu à la vérité" (Sachot, "Comment le Christianisme," 97). This should almost surely be connected up with other semantic shifts in Latin as well, notably the shift in the meaning of *verus* itself (Carlin A. Barton, "The 'Moment of Truth' in Ancient Rome: Honor and Embodiment in a Contest Culture," *Stanford Humanities Review* 6 [1998]: 16–30).

12. With thanks to Karen King for this figure.

13. Perrin [see next note] gives here "superstitious," in the ancient sense of exorbitant ardor (even to a true god).

14. The translation here modifies that of Bernadotte Perrin, *Plutarch's Lives. Vol. 7, Demosthenes and Cicero; Alexander and Caesar*, with an English translation by Bernadotte Perrin, Loeb Classical Library (London: Heinemann; Cambridge, Mass.: Harvard University Press, 1919), 227–29. While Plutarch presents this narrative as only one version of the origins of Alexander, it nonetheless remains the case that his parenthetical etymology for *thrēskeia* is his own opinion about that word and not part of the cited narrative, as noted by Perrin correctly.

15. Joseph Christiaan Antonius van Herten, *Thrēskeia Eulabeia Hiketēs. [Bijdrage Tot de Kennis der Religieuze Terminologie in Het Grieksch]* (University of Amsterdam: diss., 1934) 7. English translation of Greek text, Daniel Boyarin.

16. The context is a bit more charged than "ethnographic," pace Nongbri, *Before Religion*, 35. Herodotus, here, is, after all, using this text to justify his account of the borders of Egypt, not to present ethnographic material. Cf. Laurence Foschia, "Le Nom du culte, θρησκεία et ses derives à l'epoque imperiale," *L'Hellénisme d'époque romaine: nouveaux documents, nouvelles approches (Ier s. a. C. - IIIe s. p. C.). Actes du Colloque international à la memoire de Louis Robert, Paris, 7–8 juillet 2000* (Paris: De Boccard, 2004), 15–35, who translates here "cultic regulation." I have learned much from this essay even though my interpretations are sometimes divergent from hers.

17. Cf. Josephus Ant. 1:166 for this topos about the Egyptians. See Foschia, *"Le Nom du culte,"* 19–20 for discussion of the particularized usage of *thrēskeutēs* for devotees of Egyptian cults, a usage that might find its explanation with regard to this topos of the extra, even the excessive piety of such devotees.

18. Foschia observes that it was probably an Ionian term which reappears with the beginning of the Empire, Foschia, *"Le Nom du culte,"* 15.

19. Fritz Graf, *Magic in the Ancient World*, trans. Franklin Philip (Cambridge, Mass.: Harvard University Press, 1997), 46. He connects it, as well, at least historically with shamanism.

20. Graf, *Magic in the Ancient World*, 49. See also pp. 21, 22, and 26–28 there.

21. www.holyfamilycounseling.org

22. Frances Pownall, "Aristodemos (104)," *Brill's New Jacoby*, ed. Ian Worthington (Leiden: Brill, 2013). Although the editor of Aristodemos in Brill's New Jacoby, Frances Pownall translates "because of their religious beliefs," there is absolutely no warrant for the translation.

23. B. P. Reardon, ed., *Collected Ancient Greek Novels* (Berkeley: University of California Press, 1989), 109 [translation modified].

24. van Herten, *Thrēskeia*, 8.

25. Personal communication October 11, 2013, Prof. Nikolaos Papazarkadas. See also Benveniste, *Vocabulaire*, 2:266.

26. Louis Robert, *Études épigraphiques et philologiques*, École pratique des hautes études. Bibliothèque. Sciences historiques et philologiques (Paris: Librairie Ancienne Honoré Champion, 1938), 226–35. See too, Foschia, *"Le Nom du culte,"* 16.

27. Wilhelm Dittenberger, *Sylloge Inscriptionum Graecarum, a Guilelmo Dittenbergero Condita et Aucta, Nunc Tertium Edita.* (Leipzig: S. Hirzel, 1915–1924).

28. Foschia, *"Le Nom du culte,"* 17.

29. van Herten, *Thrēskeia*, 4–5.

30. For the frequent positive association of *eusebeia* and *thrēskeia* in these inscriptions, see Foschia, *"Le Nom du culte,"* 18–19.

31. van Herten, *Thrēskeia*, 6.

32. For θεραπεύειν as general word for service of god, see inter alia, Josephus Ant. 1:267–8.

33. Cf. "The use of θρησκεύω with regard to a human comes as no surprise, when one assumes that it conveys the attitude of the concubines towards the Persian queen, to whom they pay tribute as to a higher power," van Herten, *Thrēskeia*, 8.

34. See Émile Benveniste, "Remarks on the Function of Language in Freudian Theory," *Problems in General Linguistics*, trans. Mary Elizabeth Meek, Miami Linguistics Series 8 (Coral Gables, Fla.: University of Miami Press, 1971), 65–75.

9. THE *THRĒSKEIA* OF THE JUDAEANS: JOSEPHUS AND THE NEW TESTAMENT

1. Considering that Hebrew has the same figure of speech in which "bowing down" signifies all manners of veneration, it is even possible that the usage of the Septuagint has had an impact here on Josephan Jewish Greek, as well.

2. See earlier discussion in the introduction to the Tertullian chapters.

3. For a similar usage of this collocation in referring to the rules of the Torah observed by the Judaeans/Jews, see War 2.220: They kept the nation peaceful by not disturbing the customs of the country [οἳ μηδὲν παρακινοῦντες τῶν ἐπιχωρίων ἐθῶν ἐν εἰρήνῃ τὸ ἔθνος διεφύλαξαν].

4. Begg's text here is erroneous, as he gives "they were not unwilling to disbelieve this," thus rendering the passage unintelligible as well as false to the Greek. This is almost surely a simply mechanical error that I point out only in aid of readers.

5. Similar usages can be found at Ant. 4:312 (with transgressing again),

6. αἵρεσις as "sect" of the Jews, as in Pharisees, Essenes, and Sadducees is commonplace in Josephus, as is "philosophies." On this, see James A. Montgomery, "The Religion of Flavius Josephus," *Jewish Quarterly Review*, NS 11.3 (1921): 277–305, 280.

7. "Wanton violence" or "insolence" is also possible here. Once again, it is not a matter of determining the correct translation but of recognizing the multiple overtones of the word.

8. Translation following J. J. Collins in James H. Charlesworth, *The Old Testament Pseudepigrapha* (Garden City, N.Y.: Doubleday, 1985), 427, substituting *thrēskeia* for Collins' "worship."

9. "to require (a person) to do or refrain from doing (some act)."

10. Of which, dictionary.com remarks: "Sanction has two nearly opposite meanings: to sanction can be to approve of something, but it can also mean to punish, or speak harshly to. Likewise, a sanction can be a punishment or approval."

11. Nat. an. X 28. Aelian, *[De Natura Animalium]: On the Characteristics of Animals*, with an English translation by A. F. Scholfield. Volume 2, Books VI–XI (London: Heinemann, 1959).

12. Pyrrhon. Hyp. III 220. Sextus Empiricus, *Sextus Empiricus: Vol. 1, Outlines of Pyrrhonism*, with an English translation by R. G. Bury (London: Heinemann, 1933), 472, translation here Boyarin.

13. Herodian, *History of the Empire*, with an English translation by C. R. Whittaker, Loeb Classical Library, 2 vols. (Cambridge, Mass: Harvard University Press, 1969–1970), 1:325.

14. Herodian, *History of the Empire*, 1:334.

15. Herodian, *History of the Empire*, 1:374.

16. Herodian, *History of the Empire*, 1:418.

17. Herodian, *History of the Empire*, 2:23.

18. Wittgenstein, *Philosophical Investigations*, 7.

19. All Philo texts according to *TLG*; translation Boyarin.

20. Philo, as is well known, does not reject the "outer" performances of Jewish practice and writes sharply against those who do.

21. This is consistent with Philo's definition of *therapeia* as given earlier as a motion of the soul, as well as with his discussion of the *Therapeutai* in his famous *De vita contemplativa* (David Winston, "Philo and the Contemplative Life," *Jewish Spirituality from the Bible Through the Middle Ages*, ed. Arthur Green, *World Spirituality: An Encyclopedic History of the Religious Quest* 13 [New York: Crossroad, 1988], 198–231.) He seems to be saying that the reward/prize for the athletic activity of self-purification is a kind of mystic state which he calls *therapeia*, which is, as he said in the passage quoted above, the only true service of God.

22. For dating tending toward the first century c.e., see D. A. deSilva, *4 Maccabees* (Leiden; Boston: Brill, 2006), xvii.

23. See James Pasto, "The Origin, Expansion and Impact of the Hasmoneans in Light of Comparative Ethnographic Studies (and Outside of its Nineteenth-Century Context)," *Second Temple Studies III: Studies in Politics, Class and Material Culture*, eds. P. R. Davies and J. M. Halligan (London; New York: Sheffield Academic Press, 2002), 166–201, 173–74, 190.

24. deSilva, *4 Maccabees*, 129–30, emphasis added.

25. The question arises why deSilva translates against his own interpretation. The answer to this conundrum seems to be that deSilva was imagining a culture, perhaps all cultures in his imagination, that had a word/concept "religion" *a priori*, and thus "religion" had to go in as his translation of *thrēskeia* even when manifestly, and as he himself acknowledges openly, the word signifies nothing of the kind. This is an example of what one might call deductive rather than inductive lexicography.

10. JOSEPHUS WITHOUT JUDAISM: *NOMOS, EUSEBEIA, THRĒSKEIA*

1. This point is not uncontroversial.

2. For the structure of his new name, see Werner Eck, "Flavius Iosephus, nicht Iosephus Flavius," *Scripta Classica Israelica* 19 (2000): 281–83.

3. The important exception being the views expressed by Mason in his commentaries which, however, have to be gathered from among his notes. The views developed here owe much to Mason.

4. Flavius Josephus, *Judaean War 2*, translation and commentary by Steve Mason, Josephus, Flavius. Works. English. 2000, vol. 1B (Leiden: Brill, 2008), 30, n. 260. My translations of War 2 throughout are all based closely on Mason's with modifications as I have seen fit or necessary. Similarly, I have followed other translators from Mason's Brill series, Begg and Spilsbury, Feldman, and Barclay where they are available. Where only Thackeray (Loeb) is available, I have made my own translations from scratch, as his, while elegant, are far too loose for my philological purposes here.

5. Mason in Josephus, *Judaean War 2*, 30, n. 260.

6. Mason ms.

7. Lest this seem a straw man here, as it ought to, let me just note that the question of translating *thrēskeia* as "religion" or not is very much a live one in Josephan scholarly circles as of the writing of this book. The point will not be belabored herein.

8. *War* 2.119–166; *Ant.* 13.171–173; 18.12–25; *Life* 10–12.

9. Tessa Rajak, *Josephus*, Classical Life and Letters (London: Duckworth, 1983), 10.

10. Rajak, "Justus of Tiberias," *The Classical Quarterly*, NS 23, no. 2 (1973): 347–48.

11. See Barclay's note:

Josephus had portrayed the Judaean laws as the Mosaic "constitution" in Antiquities book 4, but here returns to that task with different emphases. (see Rajak 2002, 195–218) (Josephus, *Against Apion*, ed. Steve Mason, trans. and commentary by John Barclay, Josephus Flavius Works. English. 2000 [Leiden: Brill, 2007], ad loc.).

12. This is not rule by priests, as shown by Barclay in Josephus, *Against Apion*, 262 n. 638. Josephus has a perfectly good other word for rule by priests—"aristocracy"—or he might have used the etymologically perfect *hierarchia*: literally, rule of priests! As Barclay remarks, the first rule of semantics is that the meaning of words is derived from their context, not from a lexicon!

13. Eusebius reads "laws" not "words" here, but in any case, as mentioned, so is it glossed in the next sentence by Josephus, so even without emending the text, that is the sense (Barclay). As Copeland remarks, "[T]he Nomos concept was quite prominent and bore universal connotations both in the Bible and in Greek thought, and because Law and Word were intimately related in both contexts," E. Luther Copeland, "Nomos as a Medium of Revelation—Paralleling Logos—in Ante-Nicene Christianity," *Studia Theologica* 27 (1973): 51–61, 51–52.

14. For this dualism within rabbinic culture, see:

Rabbi Tarfon and the Elders were reclining in the upper room of the House of Natza in Lydda and the following question was asked of them: Which is greater: Is study greater or the deed? Rabbi Tarfon responded and said: the deed is greater. Rabbi Akiva responded and said: study is greater. All then responded and said: study is greater, as it conduces to the deed [TB Kiddushin:40b].

וכבר היה רבי טרפון וזקנים מסובין בעלית בית נתזה בלוד. נשאלה שאילה זו בפניהם: תלמוד גדול או מעשה

גדול? נענה רבי טרפון ואמר: מעשה גדול. נענה רבי עקיבא ואמר: תלמוד גדול. נענו כולם ואמרו: תלמוד

גדול, שהתלמוד מביא לידי מעשה.

15. Josephus, *Against Apion*, 267, n. 677, citing *Ant. rom.* 2.28.

16. Cf. Barclay in Josephus, *Against Apion*, 282 n. 794.

17. Cf. Steve Mason, "Jews, Judaeans, Judaizing, Judaism," 463. Incidentally, another lexeme that can be used in this context is *paratropē*, as in τῆς παρατροπῆς τῶν πατρίων ἐθῶν at Ant. 5:101–02.

18. My synchronic semantic conclusion about Josephus' usage is thus quite close to that of Mason mentioned earlier even if my causal explanation is quite divergent.

19. Typically, Thackeray gives here "the worship," but it is very hard to see how one transgresses worship!

20. These are variants between the manuscripts.

21. On some of the semantic complexities of *hosios/hosia* in Greek, see Robert Parker, *Miasma: Pollution and Purification in Early Greek Religion* (Oxford: Clarendon Press, 1983), 322–23, 330, 338. It seems to function in opposition to both "sacred," and, therefore forbidden, and also to "impure," and, therefore, forbidden.

22. Caleb Smith, *The Oracle and the Curse: A Poetics of Justice from the Revolution to the Civil War* (Cambridge, Mass.: Harvard University Press, 2013), 10.

23. In saying this, I make no claim as to the intended or still less the actual audience of the works.

24. Rajak, *Josephus*, 64.

25. For an excellent discussion of the collocation of *thrēskeia* and *eusebeia* in epigraphic material, see Laurence Foschia, "*Nom du culte*," 18–19.

26. See "Our triumph over them is never greater than when we are condemned on account of our faithful *obstinatio*" (*Apologeticum* 27.7). To which one should compare *obstinatio* as a *charge* that Romans bring against Christians, *Ad nationes* 1.17.

27. Note the relation between the lawgiver and God here.

28. Josephus, *Against Apion*, 296–97.

29. Translation modified from Flavius Josephus, *Judaean Antiquities 1–4*, trans. Louis H. Feldman (Boston: Brill, 2004).

30. Within this single passage, Feldman translates *thrēskeia* once as worship and twice as piety, which does, indeed, capture the semantic movement from an inner disposition to an outer expression, but not, I think, quite precisely enough.

31. For a much later culture in which enthusiasm was deemed a disorder, see Smith, *The Oracle and the Curse*, 22–24.

32. This extended study of Josephan semantics leads us in a very different direction than that of Foschia, "*Nom du culte*," passim, who seems to regard the eventual concatenation of the emotional sense (piety) and the practical (cult) as being a product of the Romanization of the eastern Empire, rather than the "Orientalization" of the eastern Empire!

33. For the morphology and syntax of the participle used in this way, see Josephus, *Judaean War* 2, 263, n. 3150.

34. Mason's "paramount commitment" works just as well although I find his addition of "devotional" otiose here (cf. Tertullian's "sabbati religio," "reverence for the Sabbath," *Against the Jews* 4.6).

35. Mason's observation that at this time they were violating two truces, as it were, is incisive and compelling. They slaughtered soldiers to whom they had pledged safe conduct and violated the Sabbath all in one fell swoop. The verb carries both senses, another example of Josephus' brilliance as well.

36. Josephus, *Judaean War* 2, 30.

11. A JEWISH ACTOR IN THE AUDIENCE: JOSEPHAN DOUBLESPEAK

1. Shadi Bartsch, *Actors in the Audience: Theatricality and Doublespeak from Nero to Hadrian*. (Cambridge, Mass.: Harvard University Press, 1994), 68–69.

2. Hannah M. Cotton and Werner Eck, "Josephus' Roman Audience: Josephus and the Roman Elites," *Flavius Josephus and Flavian Rome*, eds. Jonathan Edmondson, Steve Mason, and James Rives (Oxford, New York: Oxford University Press, 2005), 37–52, 37.

3. Steve Mason quite convinces at least this writer that Josephus' implied audience (or even first real audience) is entirely a Roman one although one that could incorporate other elite Roman Jews as well: Steve Mason, "Of Audience and Meaning: Reading Josephus' *Bellum Judaicum* in the Context of a Flavian Audience," in *Josephus and Jewish History in Flavian Rome and Beyond*, eds. Joseph Sievers and Gaia Lembi (Leiden: Brill; Biggleswade: Extenza Turpin, 2005), 71–100; Steve Mason, "Josephus, Publication, and Audiences: A Response," *Zutot* 8 (2011): 81–94; (cf. however, Cotton and Eck, "Josephus' Roman Audience"). I would add, moreover, that Josephus himself as Judaean would be part of his Roman-Judaean audience as well, as it were; more simply said: He is writing to and for himself as well. See too on the question of audience, Tessa Rajak, *Josephus*, Classical Life and Letters (London: Duckworth, 1983), 152.

4. Tessa Rajak, "Justus of Tiberias," *The Classical Quarterly*, NS 23.2 (1973): 345–68, 352.

5. See the excellent Timothy Fitzgerald, *The Ideology of Religious Studies*, discussed in the introduction of this book.

6. William Empson, *Seven Types of Ambiguity* (London: The Hogarth Press, 1991), 192.

7. It needs to be noted, upfront, that many of the examples that I have found for this analysis have been treated as well by Steve Mason as noted later. My contribution here is to the particular interpretation of these passages within Josephus, somewhat modulated (for good or for ill) from that of Mason himself. I would like to thank Prof. Mason for generously reading more than one

draft of this piece and immeasurably improving it, although, I suspect, he will continue to disagree to greater or lesser degree.

8. William Empson, *Seven Types of Ambiguity* (London: The Hogarth Press, 1991), 192.

9. J. Laplanche and J. B. Pontalis, *The Language of Psycho-Analysis*, trans. Donald Nicholson-Smith, Introd. by Daniel Lagache (New York: W. W. Norton, 1973), 138.

10. To be sure, Bartsch rejects such a possibility for accounting for self-contradiction in Juvenal, writing, "Let us cast Juvenal . . . in the mold of a man of mixed feelings or limited tact, and all difficulties fade" (*Actors in the Audience*, 129), of course rejecting this "easy" solution to a crux in Juvenal's writing. She may very well be right with respect to Juvenal, but this does not preclude, however, the possibility that any other given author is indeed a man with mixed feelings. I, too, reject mechanistic solutions that would attribute the contradictions to different sources and any other reductive moves of that sort.

11. I think it is not inapposite to compare here Thucydides on the Melian Dialogue where the Athenians refer to the uselessness of the Melians pressing claims for justice because clearly the Athenians have been adorned with power.

12. For a very perspicacious account of earlier attempts to make sense of contradictions in Josephus, see Steve Mason, *Flavius Josephus on the Pharisees: A Composition-Critical Study*, Studia Post-Biblica 39 (Leiden; New York: Brill, 1991), 18–53. Although Mason is focusing on a different (albeit related) problem, his critique of earlier scholarship holds for this one as well.

13. It is not inapposite to remember here that when Josephus is later accused of misconduct during the War, at least one of the charges brought against him by Justus of Tiberias is that he fomented the revolt there and brought disaster on his people (Rajak, "Justus of Tiberias," 347). This, of course, is not probative in itself, but it is suggestive, at least, that Josephus' earlier position was indeed a militant one. This point is supported also by Rajak's own testimony that one of the objectives of Josephus' later writing, *The Life*, is "to justify what might have appeared to be an excess of anti-Roman zeal," (*Josephus*, 152). Thus Rajak writes:

> The 'revelations' fall under several heads. First, and most fundamental, that Josephus was personally responsible for the revolt of the Galilee in general, and of Tiberias in particular (V. 341). This is the charge which Josephus rebuts by pointing to the great militancy of the Tiberians after his own departure (350). It is in retaliation that he maintains that Justus was wholly responsible for all the disasters (41). This dispute lies behind much of the debate: Justus must have pointed to many occasions on which in his view Josephus had aided and abetted the extremists. This of course turned Josephus' eventual desertion into an even more shocking act; but we do not know how far his desertion was emphasized by Justus. It would also make Josephus suspect in the eyes of his Roman patrons; but we may doubt both whether they would have read Justus' book, and whether they would have cared. The charge can most readily be understood if it is seen as appealing to men with a more intimate fear and hatred of Zealots: the more prosperous Jews of the cities would constitute such a readership. It is, of course, the same readers, with the same assumptions, to whom Josephus addresses his reply. Their criticisms of Josephus would have been the opposite of those directed at him in modern times ("Justus of Tiberias," 355).

In modern times, Rajak is saying that Josephus is attacked as a Benedict Arnold (and especially despised by Zionists); in his own times, it seems that it was his earlier commitment to the Revolt that was more assailable by Judaeans of his class and background. It may well be that Josephus already during the war itself was playing a double-game, as Rajak argues ("Justus of Tiberias," 353), but the texts that I cite shortly suggest strongly that part of his own inner double-game involved a moment of strong and not extinguished approbation of the militants as well even to the bitter end! As Rajak herself writes in another place, "he was unexpectedly enthusiastic about, for example, the heroes of Masada" (Rajak, *Josephus*, 107).

14. Barton, "Savage Miracles."

15. Interestingly enough, this word can also be used as a synonym for *stasis*, civil strife. See LSJ, ad loc.

16. Flavius Josephus, *Judaean War* 2, 13, n. 85; Flavius Josephus, *Life of Josephus*, ed. and trans. with commentary by Steve Mason (Leiden: Brill, 2000), 72–73, nn. 499, 506.

17. For the different senses of ἔθνος, see C. P. Jones, "ἔθνος and γένος in Herodotus." See also, "In scores of passages, Polybius identifies a territory according to those who inhabit it, e.g., the Nucarians. Polybius identifies no fewer than eighteen ἔθνη, and there is no indication that he uses any other criteria for the use of the term other than territory." Michael L. Satlow, "Jew or Judean," in *The One Who Sows Bountifully: Essays in Honor of Stanley K. Stowers*, eds. Caroline Johnson Hodge, Saul M. Olyan, Daniel Ullucci, Emma Wasserman, Brown Judaic Studies (Providence, R.I.: Brown University, Program in Judaic Studies, 2013), 165–75.

18. ταῦτα μὲν τότε ἐν τῇ Παλαιστίνῃ ἐγένετο· οὕτω γὰρ τὸ σύμπαν ἔθνος, ὅσον ἀπὸ τῆς Φοινίκης μέχρι τῆς Αἰγύπτου παρὰ τὴν θάλασσαν τὴν ἔσω παρήκει, ἀπὸ παλαιοῦ κέκληται. ἔχουσι δὲ καὶ ἕτερον ὄνομα ἐπίκτητον ἥ τε γὰρ χώρα Ἰουδαία καὶ αὐτοὶ Ἰουδαῖοι ὠνομάδαται· ἡ δὲ ἐπίκλησις αὕτη ἐκείνοις μὲν οὐκ οἶδ' ὅθεν ἤρξατο γενέσθαι, φέρει δὲ καὶ ἐπὶ τοὺς ἄλλους ἀνθρώπους ὅσοι τὰ νόμιμα αὐτῶν, καίπερ ἀλλοεθνεῖς ὄντες, ζηλοῦσι. καὶ ἔστι καὶ παρὰ τοῖς Ῥωμαίοις τὸ γένος τοῦτο, κολουσθὲν <μὲν> πολλάκις, αὐξηθὲν δὲ ἐπὶ πλεῖστον, ὥστε καὶ ἐς παρρησίαν τῆς νομίσεως ἐκνικῆσαι. κεχωρίδαται δὲ ἀπὸ τῶν λοιπῶν ἀνθρώπων ἔς τε τἆλλα τὰ περὶ τὴν δίαιταν πάνθ' ὡς εἰπεῖν, καὶ μάλισθ' ὅτι τῶν μὲν ἄλλων θεῶν οὐδένα τιμῶσιν, ἕνα δέ τινα ἰσχυρῶς σέβουσιν. οὐδ' ἄγαλμα οὐδὲν <οὐδ'> ἐν αὐτοῖς ποτε τοῖς Ἱεροσολύμοις ἔσχον, ἄρρητον δὲ δὴ καὶ ἀειδῆ αὐτὸν νομίζοντες εἶναι περισσότατα ἀνθρώπων θρησκεύουσι.

This passage is frequently cited as evidence that "Judaism" is a "religion" for Dio given that he explicitly remarks that people of other "races" who observe its rites are called "Jews." In a forthcoming publication, *Judaism: A Genealogy*, Boyarin will attempt to show that this is a misreading of Dio.

19. =Saturn: hence, Saturday.

20. [4] πολλὰ μὲν δὴ καὶ δεινὰ καὶ οἱ Ἰουδαῖοι τοὺς Ῥωμαίους ἔδρασαν· τὸ γάρ τοι γένος αὐτῶν θυμωθὲν πικρότατόν ἐστι, πολλῷ δὲ δὴ πλείω αὐτοὶ ἔπαθον. ἑάλωσαν μὲν γὰρ πρότεροι μὲν οἱ ὑπὲρ τοῦ τεμένους τοῦ θεοῦ ἀμυνόμενοι, ἔπειτα δὲ καὶ οἱ ἄλλοι ἐν τῇ τοῦ Κρόνου καὶ τότε ἡμέρα ὠνομασμένῃ. καὶ τοσοῦτόν γε τῆς θρησκείας αὐτοῖς περιῆν ὥστε τοὺς προτέρους τοὺς μετὰ τοῦ ἱεροῦ χειρωθέντας παραιτήσασθαί τε τὸν Σόσσιον, ἐπειδὴ ἡμέρα αὖθις ἡ τοῦ Κρόνου ἐνέστη, καὶ ἀνελθόντας ἐς αὐτὸ πάντα μετὰ τῶν λοιπῶν τὰ νομιζόμενα ποιῆσαι [49,22]. Menachem Stern, *Greek and Latin Authors on Jews and Judaism* (Jerusalem: Israel Academy of Sciences, 1980), 360–62.

21. Rajak, *Josephus*, 65–66.

22. Rajak, *Josephus*, 78.

23. Rajak, *Josephus*, 86.

24. Rajak, *Josephus*, 106.

25. Bartsch, *Actors in the Audience*, 106.

26. Bartsch, *Actors in the Audience*, 107.

27. Bartsch, *Actors in the Audience*, 112.

28. Bartsch, *Actors in the Audience*, 115.

29. Steve Mason, "Figured Speech and Irony in T. Flavius Josephus," in *Josephus, Judea, and Christian Origins: Methods and Categories*, ed. Steve Mason (Peabody, Mass: Hendrickson, 2009), 69–102, 79.

30. Bartsch, *Actors in the Audience*, 115.

31. Bartsch, *Actors in the Audience*, 145–46.

32. Bartsch, *Actors in the Audience*, 156, emphasis original.

33. See Bartsch, *Actors in the Audience*, 161.

34. As translated and cited in Bartsch, *Actors in the Audience*, 63–64.

35. Bartsch, *Actors in the Audience*, 64.

36. Bartsch, *Actors in the Audience*, 64.

37. Vasily Rudich, *Political Dissidence Under Nero: The Price of Dissimulation* (New York: Routledge, 1993), xxii.

38. Here is an example of Josephus' use of martial metaphors for Judaean action; they are drawn, at least arguably, as by an engine of war, by a proclamation of war.

39. Κουμανὸς δὲ περιπέμψας τοὺς ἐκ τῶν πλησίον κωμῶν δεσμώτας ἐκέλευσεν ἀνάγεσθαι πρὸς αὐτόν, ἐπικαλῶν ὅτι μὴ διώξαντες τοὺς λῃστὰς συλλάβοιεν. ἔνθα τῶν στρατιωτῶν τις εὑρὼν ἔν τινι κώμῃ τὸν ἱερὸν νόμον διέρρηξέν τε τὸ βιβλίον καὶ εἰς πῦρ κατέβαλεν.

Ἰουδαῖοι δὲ ὡς ὅλης αὐτοῖς τῆς χώρας καταφλεγείσης συνεχύθησαν, καὶ καθάπερ ὀργάνῳ τινὶ τῇ δεισιδαιμονίᾳ συνελκόμενοι πρὸς ἓν κήρυγμα πάντες εἰς Καισάρειαν ἐπὶ Κουμανὸν συνέδραμον ἱκετεύοντες τὸν οὕτως εἰς τὸν θεὸν καὶ τὸν νόμον αὐτῶν ἐξυβρίσαντα μὴ περιιδεῖν ἀτιμώρητον. ὁ δέ, οὐ γὰρ ἠρέμει τὸ πλῆθος, εἰ μὴ τύχοι παραμυθίας, ἠξίου τε προάγειν τὸν στρατιώτην καὶ διὰ μέσων τῶν αἰτιωμένων ἀπαχθῆναι τὴν ἐπὶ θανάτῳ κελεύει. καὶ Ἰουδαῖοι μὲν ἀνεχώρουν [War 2.229–31].

40. I have been helped in the translation of this (to me) tricky passage by my colleague Prof. Mark Griffith.

41. Interestingly, examination of the context suggests that Polybius is using *deisidaimonia* in the sense that Cicero will invent for *religio* because he argues that it is the *deisidaimonia* that keeps the common people in check. LSJ s.v. δεισιδαιμονία lists other such "positive" usages of the word.

42. Rajak, *Josephus*, 70.

43. Bartsch, *Actors in the Audience*, 169.

44. Mason, "Of Audience and Meaning."

45. Wayne C. Booth, *A Rhetoric of Irony* (Chicago; London: The University of Chicago Press, 1974), 141.

46. Northrop Frye, *Anatomy of Criticism: Four Essays* (Princeton: Princeton University Press, 1957), 223.

47. See Boyarin, *Genealogy*, forthcoming.

48. Barton, "The Price of Peace in Ancient Rome," 250.

49. Josephus, *Judaean War* 2, 265, n. 1248.

50. Josephus, *Judaean War* 2, n. 1246.

51. Following Mason here, it is as if the Judaean crowd is being ironically compared with the army Josephus, *Judaean War* 2, 142, n. 1068.

52. A kind of "religio" on Pilate's part.

53. Josephus, *Judaean War* 2, 2. 174, n. 1096. See my earlier discussion in this chapter of this passage.

54. Or, as Simon Goldhill has remarked, (p.c.) can call up associations with *akrasia*, lack of control, dissoluteness.

55. See similar judgment of Josephus, *Judaean War* 2, 145, n. 196.

12. A GLANCE AT THE FUTURE: *THRĒSKEIA* AND THE LITERATURE OF APOLOGETIC, FIRST TO THIRD CENTURIES C.E.

1. Elaine Pagels, *Revelations: Visions, Prophecy, and Politics in the Book of Revelation* (New York: Viking, 2012), 110.

2. I intend in future work to pursue this matter further into a discussion of the use of *thrēskeia* and *religio* in the Edict of Milan.

3. Timothy Fitzgerald, *The Ideology of Religious Studies* (New York: Oxford University Press, 2000).

4. For the latest scholarly thought about this category and its problems, see Sara Parvis, "Justin Martyr and the Apologetic Tradition," in *Justin Martyr and His Worlds*, eds. Sara Parvis and Paul Foster (Minneapolis: Fortress, 2007), 115–27. The conclusions reached there would only support the argument here.

5. It is worth noting that that Ciceronian notion of government with god at the top, then the king, then the hierarchy all the way down, which he derives from Plato and names *religio*, seems never to appear with a name and certainly never to be called *thrēskeia* in Greek.

6. Pagels, *Revelations*, 108–9. See Justin Martyr, *The First and Second Apologies*, trans. L. W. Barnard, *Ancient Christian Writers: The Works of the Fathers in Translation* 56 (Mahwah, N.J.: Paulist Press, 1997).

7. Theophilus of Antioch, *Ad Autolycum*, ed. and trans. Robert M. Grant, Oxford Early Christian Texts (Oxford: Clarendon Press, 1970), 14.

8. Theophilus of Antioch and Grant, *Ad Autolycum*, 23.

9. For θεοσεβεῖς as devotees of the Christian (Jewish) God, see too, 11:30 Theophilus of Antioch and Grant, *Ad Autolycum*, 74. For non-Christian "vain" service to gods, Theophilus uses λατρεύει. Grant translates both by "worship." It is, of course, this usage that gives us εἰδωλολατρεία as well. See, for example, 11:34 Theophilus of Antioch and Grant, *Ad Autolycum*, 84.

10. This parallels the usage in 4 Maccabees in which the Gentile characters refer to Judaic practice as *thrēskeia*, while the Judaic characters refer to it as *eusebeia*.

11. Strabo, *Strabonis Geographica*, ed. Augustus Meineke, Bibliotheca Scriptorum Graecorum et Romanorum Teubneriana (Leipzig: Teubner, 1877), 17.1.28.

12. Theophilus of Antioch and Grant, *Ad Autolycum*, 15. This verb is used as well with respect to "idols" by Theophilus (11:35, Theophilus of Antioch and Grant, *Ad Autolycum*, 84). Once again, the translation just gives us "worship."

13. Strabo and Meineke, *Strabonis Geographica*, 23.

14. Theophilus of Antioch and Grant, *Ad Autolycum*, 84.

15. Henry G. Meecham, *The Epistle to Diognetus: The Greek Text with Introduction, Translation and Notes* (Manchester, UK: Manchester University Press, 1949), 74–75.

16. Meecham, *Epistle to Diognetus*, 93.

17. Meecham, *Epistle to Diognetus*, 76–77.

18. Meecham, *Epistle to Diognetus*, 78–79.

19. It is perhaps worth noting that at about the same time, Trypho in Justin's dialogue is making this statement precisely as a charge against Christians.

20. Meecham, *Epistle to Diognetus*, 81.

21. Grant, *Greek Apologists*, 112.

22. Tatian, *Oratio Ad Graecos and Fragments*, ed. and trans. Molly Whittaker, Oxford Early Christian Texts (Oxford: Clarendon Press, 1982), 32.

23. Tatian, *Oratio Ad Graecos and Fragments*, 53.

24. Cf. Aristotle Historia animalium 631b16-18, γίνονται δὲ καὶ θηλυδρίαι ἐκ γενετῆς τῶν ὀρνίθων τινὲς οὕτως ὥστε καὶ ὑπομένειν τοὺς ἐπιχειροῦντας ὀχεύειν, "some birds are *thēludriai* from birth, so as even to submit to (males) who attempt to mount them." Tatian may, however, be simply aggregating synonyms for general sexual aberrance. I am grateful to Michael Zellman-Rohrer for this observation and for other help of a philological nature.

25. This is as much the case in the other two instances in which Ptolemy uses the word as well. In both cases, it is collocated with the priestly *logos*.

CONCLUSION: WHAT YOU FIND WHEN YOU STOP LOOKING FOR WHAT ISN'T THERE

1. Jason Ananda Josephson, *The Invention of Religion in Japan* (Chicago: The University of Chicago Press, 2012); Severin M. Fowles, *An Archaeology of Doings: Secularism and the Study of Pueblo Religion* (Santa Fe: School for Advanced Research Press, 2013).

2. Brent Nongbri, *Before Religion: A History of a Modern Concept* (New Haven, Conn.: Yale University Press, 2013).

3. Barton will be writing extensively on the "balancing system" in Roman culture and beyond elsewhere.

4. Steve Mason was right to claim that Josephus was often concerned to describe the Judaeans to his readers as one *ethnos* among the others that make up the Hellenistic-Roman world. Steve Mason, "Jews, Judaeans, Judaizing, Judaism: Problems of Categorization in Ancient History," *Journal for the Study of Judaism* xxxviii 4–5 (2007): 457–512 and passim throughout his Josephus commentaries.

5. The Roman love poets, who to scholars of "religion" might seem light years away from Tertullian, used many of the same strategies: (1) rebellion against the state; (2) denial of the moral authority of the emperors and the laws of the state; (3) unwillingness to be shamed by the broader society; (4) total focus on the beloved; (5) identification of the poet as slave of the beloved; (6) extended use of military metaphors; (7) willingness to suffer pain, humiliation, and death on behalf of the beloved. And, like Tertullian, the Roman love poets existed in a world filled with spells, curses, sorcerers, and magicians. Altogether, it would seem, that is only through this angle of vision that we could perceive how close Tertullian is to Lucan, the Roman love poets, or Cicero in so much of his world view.

6. Tessa Rajak, *Josephus*, Classical Life and Letters (London: Duckworth, 1983), 10.

7. Tessa Rajak, "Justus of Tiberias," *The Classical Quarterly*, NS 23, no. 2 (1973): 347–48.

Aelian. *De Natura Animalium: On the Characteristics of Animals*, edited and translated by A. F. Scholfield. Volume 2, Books VI–XI. London: Heinemann, 1959.

Altheim, Franz. *A History of Roman Religion*, translated by Harold Mattingly. New York: E.P. Dutton, 1937.

Ando, Clifford. "Introduction: Religion, Law and Knowledge in Classical Rome." In *Roman Religion*, ed. id., 1–15. Edinburgh: Edinburgh University Press, 2003.

Asad, Talal. *Genealogies of Religion: Discipline and Reasons of Power in Christianity and Islam.* Baltimore, Md.: Johns Hopkins University Press, 1993.

Assmann, Jan. *Of God and Gods.* Madison, Wisc.: University of Wisconsin Press, 2008.

Attridge, Harold W. *Nag Hammadi Codex I (The Jung Codex).* Leiden: Brill, 1985, 82–117.

Bailey, Cyril. *Lucretius, De Rerum Natura, Commentary*, 3 vols. Oxford: Clarendon Press, 1947.

Barnes, Timothy. *Tertullian: A Historical and Literary Study.* Oxford: Clarendon Press, 1971.

Barton, Carlin A. *Vis mortua: Irreconcilable Patterns of Thought in the Literature of the Neronian Period.* Berkeley: University of California, diss., 1985.

———. *The Sorrows of the Ancient Romans: The Gladiator and the Monster.* Princeton: Princeton University Press, 1993.

———. "Savage Miracles: The Redemption of Lost Honor in Roman Society and the Sacrament of the Gladiator and the Martyr." *Representations* 45 (1994): 41–71.

———. "The 'Moment of Truth' in Ancient Rome: Honor and Embodiment in a Contest Culture." *Stanford Humanities Review* 6 (1998): 16–30.

———. "Being in the Eyes; Shame and Sight in Ancient Rome." In *The Roman Gaze: Vision, Power, and the Body*, edited by David Fredrick, 216–35. Baltimore, Md.: Johns Hopkins University Press, 2002.

———. *Roman Honor: The Fire in the Bones.* Berkeley: University of California Press, 2003.

———. "The Price of Peace in Ancient Rome." In *War and Peace in the Ancient World*, edited by Kurt A. Raaflaub, 226–55. Malden, Mass.; Oxford: Blackwell, 2007.

Bartsch, Shadi. *Actors in the Audience: Theatricality and Doublespeak from Nero to Hadrian.* Cambridge, Mass.: Harvard University Press, 1994.

Batnitzky, L. *How Judaism Became a Religion: An Introduction to Modern Jewish Thought.* Princeton, N.J.: Princeton University Press, 2011.

Bayet, Jean. *Histoire politique et psychologique de la religion romaine.* Paris: Payot, 1969.

Beard, Mary. "Cicero and Divination: The Formulation of a Latin Discourse." *Journal of Roman Studies* 76 (1986): 33–46.

Beard, Mary, John A. North, and S. R. F. Price. *Religions of Rome.* Cambridge; N.Y.: Cambridge University Press, 1998.

Behr, Charles A. *P. Aelius Aristides, The Complete Works*, 2 vols. Leiden: Brill, 1986.

Belayche, Nicole. "Religious Actors in Daily Life." In *A Companion to Roman Religion*, edited by Jörg Rüpke, 275–91. Malden, Mass.: Blackwell, 2007.

Benko, Steve. "Pagan Criticisms of Christianity." In *Aufstieg und Niedergang der römischen Welt* 2.23.2, 1066–1072. Berlin; New York: W. de Gruyter, 1980.

II. Bennett, H. *"Sacer esto."* *Transactions and Proceedings of the American Philological Association* 61 (1930): 5–18.

Benveniste, Émile. *Le Vocabulaire des Institutions Indo-européens*, 2 vols. Paris: Éditions de Minuit, 1969.

―――. "Remarks on the Function of Language in Freudian Theory." In *Problems in General Linguistics*, translated by Mary Elizabeth Meek, Miami Linguistics Series 8, 65–75. Coral Gables, Fla: University of Miami Press, 1971.

Berger, Peter, and Thomas Luckman. *The Social Construction of Reality: A Treatise in the Sociology of Knowledge*. Garden City, N.Y.: Doubleday, 1967.

Bergmann, Axel. *Die "Grundbedeutung" des lateinischen Wortes Religio*. Marburg, Germany: Diagonal-Verlag, 1998.

Bleicken, Jochen. *"Coniuratio*: Die Schwurszene auf den Münzen und Gemmen der römischehn Republik." *Jahrbuch für Numismatik und Geldgeschichte* 13 (1963): 51–70.

Blok, Anton. *Honour and Violence*. Cambridge; Malden, Mass.: Polity, 2001.

Boissier, Gaston. *La Religion romaine d'Auguste aux Antonins*, 2 vols. Paris: Hachette, 1900.

Booth, Wayne C. *A Rhetoric of Irony*. Chicago; London: The University of Chicago Press, 1974.

Bouillard, Henri. "La Formation du concept de religion en Occident." In *Humanisme et foi chrétienne. Mélanges scientifiques du centenaire de l'institut catholique de Paris*, edited by Charles Kannengiesser and Yves Marchasson, 451–61. Paris: Éditions Beauchesne, 1967.

Boyancé, P. *La Religion de Virgile*. Paris: Presses Universitaires, 1963.

Boyarin, Jonathan, and Daniel Boyarin. "Self-Exposure as Theory: The Double Mark of the Male Jew." In *Rhetorics of Self-Making*, edited by Debbora Battaglia, 116–42. Berkeley: University of California Press, 1995.

Brenk, Frederick E. "In the Light of the Moon: Demonology in the Early Imperial Period." In *Aufstieg und Niedergang der römischen Welt* 2.16.3, 2068-45. Berlin; New York: W. de Gruyter, 1986.

Brent, Allen. *The Imperial Cult and the Development of Church Order: Concepts and Images of Authority in Paganism*. Leiden; Boston: Brill, 1999.

―――. *A Political History of Early Christianity*. London: T & T Clark, 2009.

Brettler, Marc Zvi. *God is King: Understanding an Israelite Metaphor*. Sheffield: JSOT Press, 1989.

Brown, Benjamin. "The Two Faces of Religious Radicalism: Orthodox Zealotry and 'Holy Sinning' in Nineteenth-Century Hasidism in Hungary and Galicia." *The Journal of Religion* 93 (2013): 341–74.

Brown, Peter. *Body and Society: Men, Women, and Sexual Renunciation in Early Christianity*. New York: Columbia University Press, 1988.

Bruns, C. G. *Fontes Iuris Romani Antiqui*. Tübingen: I.C.B. Mohr, 1909.

Brunt, P. A., and J. M. Moore. *Res Gestae Divi Augusti*. London: Oxford University Press, 1967.

Burriss, Eli. "Cicero and the Religion of His Day." *The Classical Journal* 21 (1926): 524–32.

Burrus, Virginia. *Saving Shame: Martyrs, Saints and Other Abject Subjects*. Philadelphia: University of Pennsylvania Press, 2007.

Cameron, Averil, and Stuart Hall. *Eusebius, Life of Constantine*. Oxford: Clarendon Press, 1999.

Camus, Albert. *The Rebel: An Essay of Man in Revolt*. New York: Vintage Books, 1956 [1951].

―――. *Resistance, Rebellion and Death*, translated by J. O'Brien. New York: Knopf, 1960 [1948].

Cardauns, Burkhart. *M. Terentius Varro Antiquitates Rerum Divinarum*, 2 vols. (*Teil I: Die Fragmente; Teil II: Kommentar*). Mainz/Wiesbaden: Akademie der Wissenschaften und der Literatur, 1976 [1968].

Clarke, G. W. *The Octavius of Marcus Minucius Felix*. New York: Newman, 1974.

Clendinnen, Inga. "The Cost of Courage in Aztec Society." *Past & Present* 107 (1985): 44–89.

Collins, J. J. "Sybilline Oracles." In James H. Charlesworth, *The Old Testament Pseudepigrapha*. Garden City, N.Y.: Doubleday, 1985.

Connolly, R. H. *The So-Called Egyptian Church Order*. Cambridge: Cambridge University Press, 1916.

Coogan, Tim Pat. *On the Blanket*. Dublin: Ward River, 1980.

Copeland, E. Luther. "Nomos as a Medium of Revelation—Paralleling Logos—in Ante-Nicene Christianity." *Studia Theologica* 27 (1973): 51–61.

Cotton, Hannah M., and Werner Eck. In "Josephus' Roman Audience: Josephus and the Roman Elites," *Flavius Josephus and Flavian Rome*, edited by Jonathan Edmondson, Steve Mason, and James Rives, 37–52. Oxford; New York: Oxford University Press, 2005.

Cumont, Franz. *Les Religions orientales dans le paganisme romain*. Paris: E. Leroux, 1906.

———. *The Oriental Religions in Roman Paganism*, translated by Grant Showerman. Chicago: Open Court, 1911.

Danielou, J. *The Origins of Latin Christianity*, translated by D. Smith and J. A. Baker. Philadelphia: Westminster, 1977.

de Ghellinck, J. *Pour l'histoire du mot* sacramentum. Louvain; Paris: E. Campion, 1924.

de Ste. Croix, G. E. M. "Why Were the Early Christians Persecuted?" *Past & Present* 26 (1963): 6–38.

de Visscher, F. *Le Droit des tombeaux romains*. Milan: Giuffré, 1963.

deSilva, D. A. *4 Maccabees*. Leiden; Boston: Brill, 2006.

Despland, Michel. *La Religion en occident: évolution des idées et du vécu*. Montreal: Fides, 1977.

Diels, Hermann. *Die Fragmente der Vorsokratiker*, 2nd ed., 3 vols. Berlin: Weidmann, 1907.

Dittenberger, Wilhelm. *Sylloge Inscriptionum Graecarum, a Guilelmo Dittenbergero Condita et Aucta, Nunc Tertium Edita*. Leipzig: S. Hirzel, 1915–24.

Dodds, E. R. "The Religion of the Ordinary Man in Classical Greece." In *The Ancient Concept of Progress and Other Essays*. Oxford: Clarendon Press, 1973, 140–55.

Dölger, F. J. "*Sacramentum militiae*." *Antike und Christentum* 2 (1930): 268–80.

Dossey, Leslie. *Peasant and Empire in Christian North Africa*. Berkeley: University of California Press, 2010.

Downing, F. Gerald. *Cynics and Christian Origins*. Edinburgh: T & T Clark, 1992.

Drekmeier, Charles. *Kingship and Community in Early India*. Stanford, Calif.: Stanford University Press, 1962.

Dubuisson, Daniel. *The Western Construction of Religion: Myths, Knowledge, and Ideology*, translated by William Sayers. Baltimore, Md.: Johns Hopkins University Press, 2003.

Dumézil, Georges. *Les dieux des Indo-Européens*. Paris: Presses Universitaires, 1952.

———. *Archaic Roman Religion*, translated by Philip Krapp, 2 vols. Baltimore, Md.: Johns Hopkins University Press, 1970 [1966].

Dumont, Louis. *Homo Hierarchicus; An Essay on the Caste System*, translated by Mark Sainsbury, The Nature of Human Society Series. Chicago: The University of Chicago Press, 1970.

Dürig, W. "*Disciplina*. Eine Studie zum Bedeutungsumfang des Wortes in der Sprache der Liturgie und der Väter." *Sacris Erudiri* 4 (1952): 245–79.

Durkheim, Emile. *The Elementary Forms of Religious Life*, translated by Carol Cosman, abridged with an introduction and notes by Mark S. Cladis, Oxford World's Classics. Oxford; New York: Oxford University Press, 2001.

Dyck, Andrew. *Cicero, De natura deorum, Book I*. Cambridge, Mass.: Cambridge University Press, 2003.

Ehrenberg, V. and A. H. M. Jones. *Documents Illustrating the Reigns of Augustus and Tiberius*, 2nd ed. Oxford: Clarendon Press, 1955.

Ehrman, Bart. *Lost Scriptures: Books That Did Not Make It into the New Testament*. Oxford; New York: Oxford University Press, 2003.

Emmel, Stephen. "The Recently Published Gospel of the Savior: Righting the Order of Pages and Events." *Harvard Theological Review* 95 (2002): 45–72.

Empiricus, Sextus. *Sextus Empiricus: Vol. 1, Outlines of Pyrrhonism*, translated by R. G. Bury. London: Heinemann, 1933.

Empson, William. *Seven Types of Ambiguity*. London: The Hogarth Press, 1991.

Ernout, A. and A. Meillet. *Dictionnaire Étymologique de la Langue Latine*, 4th ed. Paris: Klincksieck, 1985 [1932].

Feil, Ernst. Religio: *die Geschichte eines neuzeitlichen Grundbegriffs vom Frühchristentum bis zur Reformation*. Göttingen: Vandenhoeck & Ruprecht, 1986.

Fingarette, Herbert. *Confucius: The Secular as Sacred*. New York: Harper & Row, 1972.

Fitzgerald, Timothy. *The Ideology of Religious Studies*. New York: Oxford University Press, 2000.

Forsyth, Neil. *The Old Enemy: Satan and the Combat Myth*. Princeton, N.J.: Princeton University Press, 1987.

Foschia, Laurence. "Le Nom du culte, θρησκεία et ses derives à l'epoque imperiale." In *L'Hellénisme d'époque romaine: nouveaux documents, nouvelles approches (Ier s. a. C. - IIIe s. p. C.)*, 15–35. *Actes du Colloque international à la memoire de Louis Robert, Paris, 7–8 juillet 2000*. Paris: De Boccard, 2004.

Foster, George M. "Peasant Character and Personality." In *Peasant Society: A Reader*, edited by Jack M. Potter, May N. Diaz, and George M. Foster, 296–323. Boston: Little, Brown, 1967.

Fowler, Warde. "The Latin History of the Word *Religio*," *Third International Congress for the History of Religions*. Oxford: Clarendon Press, 1908, 169–75.

———. *The Religious Experience of the Roman People*. London: Macmillan, 1911.

———. "The Original Meaning of the Word *Sacer*." *Journal of Roman Studies* 1 (1911): 57–63.

———. *Roman Essays and Interpretations*. Oxford: Clarendon Press, 1920.

Fowles, Severin M. *An Archaeology of Doings: Secularism and the Study of Pueblo Religion*. Santa Fe, N.M.: School for Advanced Research Press, 2013.

Fox, Robin Lane. *Pagans and Christians*. New York: Knopf, 1986.

Frankfurter, David. *Religion in Roman Egypt: Assimilation and Resistance*. Princeton: Princeton University Press, 1998.

Frede, Michael. "Monotheism and Pagan Philosophy in Later Antiquity." In *Pagan Monotheism in Late Antiquity*, edited by Polymnia Athanassiadi and Michael Frede, 41–67. Oxford: Clarendon Press, 1999.

Freeman, Kathleen. *Ancilla to the Pre-Socratic Philosophers*. Cambridge, Mass.: Harvard University Press, 1978.

Frend, W. H. C. *The Rise of Christianity*. Philadelphia: Fortress, 1984.

Freud, Sigmund. *Totem and Taboo: Resemblances between the Psychic Lives of Savages and Neurotics*, translated by A. A. Brill. New York: Vintage, 1946 [1913].

———. *The Standard Edition of the Complete Psychological Works of Sigmund Freud*, edited and translated by James Strachey, 24 vols. London: Hogarth Press, 1953–1974.

———. *Civilization and Its Discontents*, translated by James Strachey. New York: W.W. Norton, 1962.

Frye, Northrop. *Anatomy of Criticism: Four Essays*. Princeton, N.J.: Princeton University Press, 1957.

Fugier, Huguette. *Recherches sur l'expression du sacré dans la langue latine*. Paris: Belles Lettres, 1963.

Gaddis, Michael. *There Is No Crime for Those Who Have Christ*. Berkeley: University of California Press, 2005.

Gagé, Jean. *Apollon Romain: essai sur le culte d'Apollon et le développement du "ritus Graecus" à Rome des origines à Augustus*. Paris: Boccard, 1955.

Gibson, Elsa. "The 'Christians for Christians' inscriptions of Phrygia," *Harvard Theological Studies* 32. Missoula, Mont: Scholars Press, 1978.

Gilbert, Michele. "The person of the king: ritual and power in a Ghanian state." In *Rituals of Royalty; Power and Ceremonial in Traditional Societies*, edited by D. Cannadine and S. Price. Cambridge: Cambridge University Press, 1987.

Glare, P. G. W. *Oxford Latin Dictionary*. Oxford: Clarendon Press, 1982.

Gordon, Richard. "*Superstitio*, Superstition and Religious Repression in the Late Roman Republic and Principate." In *The Religion of Fools?*, edited by. S. A. Smith and Alan Knight. *Past and Present*, Suppl. 3 (2008): 72–94.

Graf, Fritz. *Magic in the Ancient World*, translated by Franklin Philip. Cambridge, Mass.: Harvard University Press, 1997.

Grant, Robert M. "Pliny and the Christians." *Harvard Theological Review* 44 (1948): 273–74.

———. *Greek Apologists of the Second Century*. Philadelphia: Westminster, 1988.

Grodzynski, Denise. "*Superstitio*." *Revue des Études Anciennes* 76 (1974): 36–60.

Grueber, H. A. *Coins of the Roman Republic in the British Museum*, 3 vols. London: British Museum, 1910.

Habinek, Thomas N. *The Politics of Latin Literature*. Princeton, N.J.: Princeton University Press, 1998.

Hallett, Judith. "*Perusinae glandes* and the Changing Image of Augustus." *American Journal of Ancient History* 2 (1977): 151–71.

Hanson, Victor David. *The Other Greeks: The Family Farm and the Agrarian Roots of Western Civilization*. New York: Free Press, 1995.

Harland, Philip A. *Associations, Synagogues, and Congregations: Claiming a Place in Ancient Mediterranean Society*. Minneapolis: Fortress, 2003.

Heibges, Ursula. "Cicero, a Hypocrite in Religion." *American Journal of Philology* 90 (1969): 304–12.

Heimgartner, Martin. "Paganus," *Brill's New Pauly* 10, edited by M. Landfester et al., 338–39. Leiden; Boston: Brill, 2007.

Helgeland, John. "Roman Army Religion." In *Aufstieg und Niedergang der römischen Welt* 2.16.2, 1470–1541. Berlin; New York: W. de Gruyter, 1978.

Herford, R. Travers. *Pirke Aboth*. New York: Jewish Institute of Religion, 1945.

Herodian, *History of the Empire*, translated by C. R. Whittaker, Loeb Classical Library, 2 vols. Cambridge, Mass.: Harvard University Press, 1969–1970)

Herrmann, P. *Der römische Kaisereid*. Göttingen: Vandenhoeck & Ruprecht, 1968.

Hocart, A. M. *Kings and Councillors: An Essay in the Comparative Anatomy of Human Society*. Chicago: The University of Chicago Press, 1970 [1936].

Holland, Norman. "Unity, identity, text, self." *Proceedings of the Modern Language Association* 90 (1975): 813–22, 816.

Horsley, Richard A., with John S. Hanson. *Bandits, Prophets and Messiahs*. San Francisco: Harper & Row, 1988.

Howe, Herbert M. "The *religio* of Lucretius." *Classical Journal* 52 (1957): 329–33.

Instinsky, Hans Ulrich. "Schwurszene und *Coniuratio*." *Jahrbuch für Numismatik und Geldgeschichte* 14 (1964): 83–88.

Iordan, Henricus. *M. Catonis praeter librum de re rustica quae exstant*. Stuttgart: Teubner, 1967 [1860].

Irmscher, Johannes. "Der Terminus *religio* und seine antiken Entsprechungen im philologischen und religionsgeschichtlichen Vergleich." In *The Notion of "Religion" in Comparative Research*, Selected Proceedings of the XVIth Congress of the International Association for the History of Religions, Rome, 1990, edited by Ugo Bianchi, 62–73. Rome: L'Erma, 1994.

Irwin, Lee. *Coming Down from Above: Prophecy, Resistance and Renewal in Native American Religions.* Norman, Okla.: University of Oklahoma Press, 2008.

Jacobsen, Thorkild. "Primitive Democracy in Ancient Mesopotamia." In *Toward the Image of Tammuz and Other Essays in Mesopotamian History and Culture,* edited by W. L. Moran. Cambridge, Mass.: Harvard University Press, 1970.

Jaeger, W. *The Theology of the Early Greek Philosophers.* London; New York: Oxford University Press, 1947.

Janssen, L. F. "*Superstitio* and the Persecution of the Christians." *Vigiliae Christianae* 33 (1979): 131–59.

Jay, Nancy. "Sacrifice as Remedy for Having Been Born of Woman." In *Immaculate and Powerful. The Female Image and Social Reality,* edited by Clarissa Atkinson, C. Buchanan, and Margaret Miles, 283–309. Boston: Beacon Press, 1985.

Jocelyn, H. D. *The Tragedies of Ennius.* Cambridge: Cambridge University Press, 1969.

Jones, C. P. "Ἔθνος and γένος in Herodotus." *Classical Quarterly* n.s. 46 (1996): 315–20.

Josephus, Flavius. *Life of Josephus,* edited and translated by Steve Mason. Leiden: Brill, 2000.

———. *Judaean Antiquities 1–4,* translated by Louis H. Feldman. Boston: Brill, 2004.

———. *Judaean War 2,* translated by Steve Mason, *Josephus, Flavius. Works. English.* vol. 1B. Leiden: Brill, 2008.

Judge, E. A. *Social Distinctives of the Christians in the First Century: Pivotal Essays,* edited by David M. Scholer. Peabody, Mass.: Hendrickson Publishers, 2008.

Justin Martyr. *The First and Second Apologies,* translated by L. W. Barnard, Ancient Christian Writers: The Works of the Fathers in Translation, 56. Mahwah, N.J.: Paulist Press, 1997.

Kätzler, J. B. "*Religio*. Versuch einer Worterklärung." *Jahresbericht des bischöflichen Gymnasiums Paulinum in Schwaz* 20 (1952–53): 2–18.

Keay, S. J. *Roman Spain.* Berkeley: University of California Press, 1988.

Keyes, Clinton Walker. "Original Elements in Cicero's Ideal Constitution." *American Journal of Philology* 42 (1921): 309–23.

Kobbert, M. *De verborum religio atque religiosus usu apud Romanos.* Königsberg: Harungiana, 1910.

Koch, Carl. *Religio: Studien zu Kult und Glauben der Römer.* Nuremberg: H. Carl, 1960.

Kronfeld, Chana. *On the Margins of Modernism: Decentering Literary Dynamics.* Berkeley: University of California Press, 1996.

Lampe, P. *From Paul to Valentinus: Christians at Rome in the First Two Centuries,* translated by Michael Steinhauser. Minneapolis: Fortress, 2003.

Le Boulluec, Alain. *La notion d'hérésie dans la littérature grecque IIe–IIIe siècles.* Paris: Études Augustiniennes, 1985.

Le Gall, Joël. *Recherches sur le culte du Tibre.* Paris: Presses Universitaires, 1953.

Le Saint, William. *Tertullian, Treatises on Marriage and Remarriage.* New York: Newman, 1951.

Lewis, Mark Edward. *Sanctioned Violence in Early China.* Albany, N.Y.: State University of New York Press, 1990.

Lieberg, G. "Considerazioni sull'etimologia e sul significato de *religio*." *Rivista di Filologia e di Istruzione Classica* 102 (1974): 34–57.

Liebeschuetz, J. H. W. G. "The Religious Position of Livy's History." *Journal of Roman Studies* 57 (1967): 45–55.

———. *Continuity and Change in Roman Religion.* Oxford: Clarendon Press, 1979.

Lincoln, Bruce. "Apocalyptic Temporality and Politics in the Ancient World." In *The Encyclopedia of Apocalypticism,* edited by John J. Collins, 3 vols, 1:457–75. London: Continuum, 2004.

Linder, M., and J. Scheid, "Quand croire c'est faire. Le problème de la croyance dans la Rome ancienne." *Archives de Sciences Sociales des Religions* 81 (1993): 47–62.

Linderski, Jerzy. "Aphrodisias and the *Res Gestae*." *Journal of Roman Studies* 74 (1984): 74–80.

Linkomies, Edwin. "*Superstitio*." *Arctos* 7 (1931): 73–88.

Löfstedt, Einer. *Late Latin.* Oslo: Aschehoug, 1959.

Lovejoy, Arthur O., and George Boas. *Primitivism and Related Ideas in Antiquity.* Baltimore: Johns Hopkins University Press, 1935.

Maccoby, Michael. "Love and Authority: A Study of Mexican Villagers." In *Peasant Society; A Reader,* edited by Jack M. Potter, May N. Diaz, and George M. Foster, 336–46. Boston: Little, Brown, 1967.

MacMullen, Ramsay. *Christianizing the Roman Empire A.D. 100–400.* New Haven, Conn.: Yale University Press, 1984.

———. *Paganism and Christianity 100–425 C. E.: A Sourcebook.* Minneapolis: Fortress, 1992.

———. *The Second Church: Popular Christianity A.D. 200–400.* Atlanta: Society of Biblical Literature, 2009.

Malcovati, H. *Oratorum Romanorum Fragmenta,* 4th ed., vol. 1. Turin: Paravia 1976 [1930].

Markus, Robert. *Saeculum: History and Society in the Theology of St. Augustine.* Cambridge: Cambridge University Press, 2007 [1970].

Marrou, H. I. "*Doctrina* et *disciplina* dans la langue des Pères de l'Eglise." *Archivum Latinitatis Medii Aevi* 9 (1934): 5–25.

Martin, Dale B. *Slavery as Salvation: The Metaphor of Slavery in Pauline Christianity.* New Haven, Conn.: Yale University Press, 1990.

———. *Inventing Superstition: From the Hippocratics to the Christians.* Cambridge, Mass.; London: Harvard University Press, 2004.

Marx, F. *C. Lucilii carminum reliquiae,* 2 vols. Leipzig: Teubner, 1904–1905.

Mason, Steve. *Flavius Josephus on the Pharisees: A Composition-Critical Study,* Studia Post-Biblica 39. Leiden; New York: Brill, 1991.

———. "Of Audience and Meaning: Reading Josephus' *Bellum Judaicum* in the Context of a Flavian Audience." In *Josephus and Jewish History in Flavian Rome and Beyond,* edited by Joseph Sievers and Gaia Lembi, 71–100. Leiden: Brill; Biggleswade: Extenza Turpin, 2005.

———. "Jews, Judaeans, Judaizing, Judaism: Problems of Categorization in Ancient History." *Journal for the Study of Judaism* 38 (2007): 457–512.

———. "Figured Speech and Irony in T. Flavius Josephus." In *Josephus, Judea, and Christian Origins: Methods and Categories,* edited by Steve Mason, 69–102. Peabody, Mass.: Hendrickson, 2009.

———. "Josephus, Publication, and Audiences: A Response." *Zutot* 8 (2011): 81–94.

Mauch, Otto. *Der lateinische Begriff Disciplina.* Freiburg, Germany: diss., 1941.

Mayor, Joseph. *De natura deorum libri tres,* 3 vols. Cambridge: Cambridge University Press, 1880.

Meecham, Henry G. *The Epistle to Diognetus: The Greek Text with Introduction, Translation and Notes.* Manchester, UK: Manchester University Press, 1949.

Meeks, Wayne A. *The First Urban Christians: The Social World of the Apostle Paul.* New Haven, Conn.: Yale University Press, 1983.

———. *The Origins of Christian Morality: The First Two Centuries.* New Haven, Conn.: Yale University Press, 1993.

Meyer, H. *Oratorum Romanorum Fragmenta.* Turin: Orelli, Fuesslini et soc., 1842.

Meyer, Marvin W. and Richard Smith, *Ancient Christian Magic.* Princeton: Princeton University Press, 1999 [1994].

Mitford, T. B. "A Cypriot Oath of Allegiance to Tiberius." *Journal of Roman Studies* 50 (1960): 75–79.

Mohrmann, Christine. "Quelques Traits Charactéristiques du Latin des Chrétiens." In *Études sur le Latin des Chrétiens* 2 vols, 1:21–50. Rome: Edizioni di storia e letteratura, 1961.

Momigliano, A. "The Theological Efforts of the Roman Upper Classes in the First Century B.C." *Classical Philology* 79 (1984): 199–211.

Mommsen, Theodor. *History of Rome*, translated by William Dickson, 4 vols. New York: E.P. Dutton, 1886.

Montgomery, James A. "The Religion of Flavius Josephus." *Jewish Quarterly Review, NS* 11.3 (1921): 277–305.

Morel, V. "Le développement de la *disciplina* sous l'action du Saint Esprit chez Tertullien." *Revue de l'histoire ecclésiastique* 35 (1935): 243–65.

———. "*Disciplina*: le mot et l'idée representée par lui dans les oeuvres de Tertullien." *Revue de l'histoire ecclésiastique* 40 (1944/45): 5–46.

Morel, W. *Fragmenta Poetarum Latinarum*. Stuttgart: Teubner, 1963 [1927].

Mulder, R. *De conscientiae notione quae et qualis fuerit Romanis*. Leiden: Brill, 1908.

Muth, Robert. "Vom Wesen römischer *religio*." In *Aufstieg und Niedergang der römischen Welt* 2.16.1, 290–354. Berlin: W. de Gruyter, 1978.

Nagy, Àgnes A. "*Superstitio* et *Coniuratio*." *Numen* 49 (2002): 178–92.

Nasrallah, Laura. *An Ecstasy of Folly: Prophecy and Authority in Early Christianity*. Cambridge, Mass.: Harvard University Press, 2003.

———. *Christian Responses to Roman Art and Architecture*. Cambridge: Cambridge University Press, 2010.

Nock, A. D. *Conversion: The Old and the New in Religion from Alexander the Great to Augustine of Hippo*. London: Oxford University Press, 1933.

Nongbri, Brent. *Before Religion: A History of a Modern Concept*. New Haven, Conn.: Yale University Press, 2013.

North, John. "The Development of Religious Pluralism." In *The Jews Among Pagans and Christians*, edited by Judith Lieu, John North, and Tessa Rajak, 174–93. New York: Routledge, 1992.

Ogilvie, R. M. *A Commentary on Livy Books 1–5*. Oxford: Clarendon Press, 1965.

O'Malley, Pedraig. *Biting at the Grave: The Irish Hunger Strikes and the Politics of Despair*. Boston: Beacon Press, 1990.

Opelt, Ilona. "Ciceros Schrift *De natura deorum* bei den lateinischen Kirchenvätern." *Antike und Abendland* 12 (1966): 141–55.

Osborn, Eric. "Tertullian as Philosopher and Roman." *Beihefte zur Zeitschrift für neutestamentliche Wissenschaft und die Kunde der älteren Kirche* 85 (1997): 231–47.

Otto, W. F. "*Religio* und *Superstitio*." In *Aufsätze zur Römischen Religionsgeschichte*, ed. id. (Meisenheim am Glan: Hain, 1975) 92–130=*Archiv für Religonswissenschaft* 12 (1909): 532–54 and 14 (1911): 406–22, 534+537.

Pagán, Victoria Emma. *Conspiracy Narratives in Roman History*. Austin: University of Texas Press, 2004.

Pagels, Elaine. "Christian Apologists and 'The Fall of the Angels': An Attack on Roman Imperial Power?" *Harvard Theological Review* 78 (1985): 301–25.

———. *Revelations: Visions, Prophecy, and Politics in the Book of Revelation*. New York: Viking, 2012.

Parker, Robert. *Miasma: Pollution and Purification in Early Greek Religion*. Oxford: Clarendon Press, 1983.

Parvis, Sara. "Justin Martyr and the Apologetic Tradition." In *Justin Martyr and His Worlds*, edited by Sara Parvis and Paul Foster, 115–27. Minneapolis: Fortress, 2007.

Pasto, James. "The Origin, Expansion and Impact of the Hasmoneans in Light of Comparative Ethnographic Studies (and Outside of its Nineteenth-Century Context)." In *Second Temple Studies III: Studies in Politics, Class and Material Culture*, edited by P. R. Davies and J. M. Halligan, 166–201. London; New York: Sheffield Academic Press, 2002.

Pautigny, Louis. *Justin, Apologies*. Paris: A. Picard, 1904.

Pease, Arthus Stanley. *M. Tulli Ciceronis De Natura Deorum*, 2 vols. New York: Arno, 1979.

Perrin, Bernadotte. *Plutarch's Lives. Vol. 7, Demosthenes and Cicero; Alexander and Caesar*, translated by Bernadotte Perrin, Loeb Classical Library. London: Heinemann; Cambridge, Mass.: Harvard University Press, 1919.

Petersmann, Hubert. "Εὐσέβεια, θρησκεία et *religio*." In *Lingua et Religio: ausgewählte kleine Schriften zur antiken Religionsgeschichte auf sprachtwissenschaftlicher Grund*, edited by Hubert Petersmann and Bernd Hessen, 48–56. Göttingen, Germany: Vanderhoeck & Ruprecht, 2007.

Peterson, Anna L. *Martyrdom and the Politics of Religion*. Albany, N.Y.: State University of New York Press, 1997.

Pownall, Frances. "Aristodemos (104)." In *Brill's New Jacoby*, edited by Ian Worthington. Leiden: Brill, 2013.

Pritchard, J. B. *Ancient Near Eastern Texts Relating to the Old Testament*, 3rd ed. Princeton, Mass.: Princeton University Press, 1969.

Radcliffe-Brown, A.R. "Taboo." In *Structure and Function in Primitive Society*, 133–52. New York: Free Press, 1965.

Rahner, Hugo. "*Pompa diaboli*; Ein Beitrag zur Bedeutungsgeschichte des Wortes πομπή—*pompa* in der urchristlichen Taufliturgie." *Zeitschrift für Katholische Theologie* 55 (1931): 239–73.

———. *Church and State in Early Christianity*, translated by L. D. Davis. San Francisco: Ignatius Press, 1992 [1961].

Rajak, Tessa. "Justus of Tiberias." *The Classical Quarterly*, NS 23.2 (1973): 345–68.

———. *Josephus*, Classical Life and Letters. London: Duckworth, 1983.

Reardon, B. P., ed. *Collected Ancient Greek Novels*. Berkeley: University of California Press, 1989.

Rebillard, E. *Christians and Their Many Identities in Late Antiquity, North Africa 200–450 C.E.* Ithaca, N.Y.; London: Cornell University Press, 2012.

Reed, Anette Yoshiko. *Fallen Angels and the History of Judaism and Christianity: The Reception of Enochic Literature*. Cambridge, Mass.: Cambridge University Press, 2005.

Rives, James. "Religion in the Roman Empire." In *Experiencing Rome: Culture, Identity and Power in the Roman Empire*, edited by Janet Huskinson, 245–75. London; New York: Routledge, 2000.

Robeck Jr., Cecil M. *Prophecy in Carthage: Perpetua, Tertullian, and Cyprian*. Cleveland, Ohio: Pilgrim, 1992.

Robert, Louis. "*Études épigraphiques et philologiques*." In École pratique des hautes études, 226–35. Bibliothèque. Sciences historiques et philologiques. Paris: Librairie Ancienne Honoré Champion, 1938.

Robinson, J. Armitage, ed. *Texts and Studies: Contributions to Biblical and Patristic Literature 2*. Cambridge, Mass.: Cambridge University Press, 1891.

Rudich, Vasily. *Political Dissidence Under Nero: The Price of Dissimulation*. New York: Routledge, 1993.

Rudolph, Kurt. *Gnosis: The Nature and History of Gnosticism*. New York: Harper, 1987 [1977].

Rüpke, Jörg. "Religion: Roman." In *Brill's New Pauly*, vol. 12, col. 490. Leiden; Boston: Brill, 2008.

Sabbatucci, Dario. "*Sacer.*" *Studi e materiali di storia delle religioni* 23 (1951–52): 91–101.

Sachot, Maurice. "Comment le Christianisme est-il devenu *religio*." *Revue des Sciences Religieuses* 59 (1985): 95–118.

———. "*Religio/Superstitio*: historique d'une subversion et d'un retournement." *Revue de l'Histoire des Religions* 208 (1991): 355–94.

Saler, Benson. "*Religio* and the Definition of Religion." *Cultural Anthropology* 2 (1987): 395–99.

———. *Conceptualizing Religion: Immanent Anthropologists, Transcendent Natives, and Unbounded Categories*, Studies in the History of Religions, vol. 56. Leiden; New York: Brill, 1993.

Salzman, Michele. "*Superstitio* in the Codex Theodosianus and the Persecution of Pagans." *Vigiliae Christianae* 41 (1987): 172–88.

Satlow, Michael L. "Jew or Judean." In *The One who Sows Bountifully: Essays in Honor of Stanley K. Stowers*, edited by Caroline Johnson Hodge, Saul M. Olyan, Daniel Ullucci, and Emma Wasserman, Brown Judaic Studies, 165–75. Providence, R.I.: Brown University, Program in Judaic Studies, 2013.

Scheid, John. *An Introduction to Roman Religion*, translated by Janet Lloyd. Bloomington, Ind.: Indiana University Press, 2003.

Scheler, Max. *Ressentiment*, translated by William W. Holdheim. New York: Free Press of Glencoe, 1961 [1910].

Schilling, Robert. "Le Romain de la fin de la république et du début de l'empire en face de la religion." *Antiquité Classique* 41 (1972): 540–57.

———. "L'Originalité du vocabulaire religieux Latin." In *Rites, Cultes, Dieux de Rome*, 30–53. Paris: Klincksieck, 1979 [= *Revue Belge de philologie et d'histoire* 49 (1971) 31–54].

Sherk, Robert. *The Roman Empire: Augustus to Hadrian*. Cambridge: Cambridge University Press, 1988.

Sider, Robert. *Ancient Rhetoric and the Art of Tertullian*. London: Oxford University Press, 1971.

Smith, Caleb. *The Oracle and the Curse: A Poetics of Justice from the Revolution to the Civil War*. Cambridge, Mass.: Harvard University Press, 2013.

Smith, Jonathan Z. "Religion, Religions, Religious." In *Critical Terms for Religious Studies*, edited by Mark C. Taylor, 269–284. Chicago: The University of Chicago Press, 1998.

———. *Relating Religion: Essays in the Study of Religion*. Chicago: The University of Chicago Press, 2004.

———. "The Topography of the Sacred." In *Relating Religion: Essays in the Study of Religion*, 101–16. Chicago: The University of Chicago Press, 2004.

———. "Trading Places." In *Relating Religion: Essays in the Study of Religion*, 215–29. Chicago: The University of Chicago Press, 2004.

Smith, Wilfred Cantwell. *The Meaning and End of Religion: A New Approach to the Religious Traditions of Mankind*, foreword by John Hick. New York: Macmillan, 1962.

Snyder, Graydon F. *Ante Pacem: Archaeological Evidence of Church Life Before Constantine*. Macon, Ga.: Mercer University Press, 2003 [1985].

Soranus of Ephesus. *Soranus' Gynecology*, translated by Owsei Temkin, Nicholson J. Eastman, Ludwig Edelstein, and Alan F. Guttmacher. Baltimore; London: Johns Hopkins University Press, 1991.

Spellman, John. *Political Theory of Ancient India: A Study of Kingship from the Earliest Times to circa* A.D. 300. Oxford: Clarendon Press, 1964.

Springer, Lawrence A. "The Role of *religio, solvo* and *ratio* in Lucretius." *Classical World* 71 (1977): 55–61.

Steiner, Franz. *Taboo*. Harmondsworth, UK: Penguin, 1967 [1956].

Stern, Menachem. *Greek and Latin Authors on Jews and Judaism*. Jerusalem: Israel Academy of Sciences, 1980.

Stevens, Edward B. "Topics of Pity in the Poetry of the Roman Republic." *American Journal of Philology* 62 (1941): 426–40.

Stewert-Sykes, Alistair. "Ordination Rites and Patronage Systems in Third-Century Africa." *Vigiliae Christianae* 56 (2002): 115–30.

Strabo. *Strabonis Geographica*, edited by Augustus Meineke, Bibliotheca Scriptorum Graecorum et Romanorum Teubneriana. Leipzig, Germany: Teubner, 1877.

Stroumsa, Guy G. *The End of Sacrifice: Religious Transformations in Late Antiquity*, translated by Susan Emanuel. Chicago: The University of Chicago Press, 2009.

Sugden, John. *Tecumseh: A Life*. New York: Henry Holt and Co., 1998.

Sullivan, Lawrence. *Historical Dictionary of the Chinese Communist Party*. Lanham, Md.: Scarecrow Press.

Sutherland, C. H. V. *Roman Coins*. London: Barrie & Jenkins, 1974.

Tabbernee, William. *Montanist Inscriptions and Testimonia: Epigraphic Sources Illustrating the History of Montanism*. Macon, Ga.: Mercer University Press, 1997.

———. *Prophets and Gravestones: An Imaginative History of Montanists and Other Early Christians*. Peabody, Mass.: Hendrickson, 2009.

Tambiah, S. J. *World Conqueror and World Renouncer: A Study of Buddhism and Polity in Thailand against a Historical Background*. Cambridge: Cambridge University Press, 1976.

Tatian. *Oratio Ad Graecos and Fragments*, edited and translated by Molly Whittaker, Oxford Early Christian Texts. Oxford: Clarendon Press, 1982.

Taylor, Lily Ross. *Party Politics in the Age of Caesar*. Berkeley: University of California Press, 1949.

Theophilus of Antioch. *Ad Autolycum*, edited and translated by Robert M. Grant, Oxford Early Christian Texts. Oxford: Clarendon Press, 1970.

Theophrastus. *The Characters of Theophrastus*, edited and translated by J. M. Edmonds, Loeb Classical Library. Cambridge, Mass.: Harvard University Press; London: W. Heinemann, 1929.

Troiani, L. "La Religione e Cicerone." *Rivista Storica Italiana* (1984): 920–52.

Tromp, G. W. *Payback: The Logic of Retribution in Melanesian Religions*. Cambridge: Cambridge University Press, 1994.

Turcan, Robert. *Religion Romaine*, 2 vols. Leiden; New York: Brill, 1988.

———. *The Gods of Ancient Rome*. New York: Routledge, 2001.

Uris, Leon. *Trinity*. Garden City, N.Y.: Doubleday, 1976.

Valeri, Valerio. *Kingship and Sacrifice: Ritual and Society in Ancient Hawaii*, translated by Paula Wissing. Chicago: The University of Chicago Press, 1985.

———. *The Forest of Taboos: Morality, Hunting, and Identity among the Huaulu of the Moluccas*. Madison, Wisc.: University of Wisconsin Press, 2000.

Van Der Nat, P. G. "Tertullianea." *Vigiliae Christianae* 18 (1964): 129–43.

van Herten, Joseph Christiaan Antonius. *Thrēskeia Eulabeia Hiketēs. [Bijdrage Tot de Kennis der Religieuze Terminologie in Het Grieksch]*. Amsterdam: diss., 1934.

van Unnik, Willem Cornelis, and Pieter Willem van der Horst, *Das Selbstverständnis der jüdischen Diaspora in der hellenistisch-römischen Zeit*, Arbeiten zur Geschichte des antiken Judentums und des Urchristentums 17. Leiden; New York: Brill, 1993.

Vanderkam, James and Peter Flint. *The Meaning of the Dead Sea Scrolls*. New York: HarperCollins, 2002.

von Gaertringen, F. Hiller, ed. *Inscriptiones Graecae* 12 Suppl. Berlin: G. Reimer, 1939.

von Harnack, Adolf. *The Mission and Expansion of Christianity in the First Three Centuries*, translated by James Moffatt, 2 vols. London: Williams and Norgate, 1908.

———. *Militia Christi: The Christian Religion and the Military in the First Three Centuries*, translated by D. I. Gracie. Philadelphia: Fortress, 1981.

———. *Marcion, The Gospel of the Alien God*, translated by J. E. Steely and L. D. Bierma. Eugene, Oreg.: Wipf & Stock, 2007.

von Premerstein, Anton. *Vom Werden und Wesen des Prinzipats [Abhandlungen der Bayerischen Akademie der Wissenschaften*, Philosophisch-historische Abteilung, N.F. 15]. Munich: Beck, 1937.

Walbank, F. W. *A Historical Commentary on Polybius*, 3 vols. Oxford: Clarendon Press, 1957.

Warmington, E. H. *Remains of Old Latin*, 4 vols. Cambridge, Mass.: Harvard University Press, 1935–1940.

Waszink, J. H. "*Pompa diaboli*." *Vigiliae Christianae* 1 (1947): 13–41.

Waszink, J. H., and J. C. M. Van Winden. *Tertullianus, De Idololatria*. Leiden: Brill, 1987.

Wilken, R. L. *The Christians as the Romans Saw Them*. New Haven; London: Yale University Press, 1984.

Wilson, Robert McL. "Gnosticism." In *Religious Diversity in the Greco-Roman World*, edited by Dan Cohn-Sherbok and John M. Court, 164–81. Sheffield: Sheffield Academic Press, 2001.

Wilt, Henry Toomey. Religio: *A Semantic Study of the Pre-Christian Use of the Terms* Religio *and* Religiosus. New York: diss., Columbia University, 1954.

Winston, David. "Philo and the Contemplative Life." In *Jewish Spirituality from the Bible Through the Middle Ages*, edited by Arthur Green, 198–231. *World Spirituality: An Encyclopedic History of the Religious Quest* 13. New York: Crossroad, 1988.

Wissowa, Georg. *Religion und Kultus der Römer.* Munich: C.H. Beck, 1902.

Wittgenstein, Ludwig. *Philosophical Investigations*, translated by G. E. M. Anscombe. New York: Macmillan, 1958.

Woodward, Kenneth L. *Making Saints.* New York: Simon & Schuster, 1990.

Woolf, Greg. "Divinity and Power in Ancient Rome." In *Religion and Power: Divine Kingship in the Ancient World and Beyond*, edited by Nicole Brisch, 243–59. Chicago: Oriental Institute, 2008.

Zahn, Theodore. *"Paganus." Neue Kirchliche Zeitschrift* 10 (1899): 18–44.

Zeller, E. *Die Entwicklung des Monotheismus bei den Griechen.* Stuttgart: Franckhische Verlagshandlung, 1862.

———. *Religion und Philosophie bei den Römern.* Berlin: C.G. Lüderitz, 1866.

Zuesse, E. M. "Taboo and the Divine Order." *Journal of the American Academy of Religion* 42.3 (1974): 482–504.

284n30; *'avoda*, 158; balancing *thrēskeia*,
172–74; complexity of *thrēskeia*, 157; contradictions in, 285n12; cultic associations of
thrēskeia, 135–36, 194; *deisidaimonia*, 171;
deisidaimonia versus *thrēskeia*, 198–99;
doublespeak and, 189–92; inner conflict,
178–79; *Jewish War*, 179–88, 195–96; Judaean
laws, 159–60; martial metaphors, 287n38;
misconduct charges, 285n13; Moses as
lawgiver, 161–62; multiple audiences, 190–92;
nomos/nomoi, 156; occurrences of *thrēskeia*,
156–57; philosophies, 157; positive uses of
thrēskeia, 135–36; religion and, 156; religious
versus secular use of *thrēskeia*, 138; on
resistance, 182–83; *sicarii* and, 184–88;
theocracy, 160; Torah, 161–62; *Torah*, 158–59;
Torah and, 156; Torah and *thrēskeia*, 164–66,
168–69; writing after the fact, 187; on the
Zealots, 180–84
Judaean Antiquities, thrēskeia, nomos and, 163–64
Judaean-Greek, *thrēskeia*, negative context,
141–43
Judaeans: devotion to practice, 149–50; *eusebeia*,
150–51
Judge, Edwin, 1

kingship/monarchical rule, 107; divine king,
Cicero and, 51; government, 97; hopes for,
103–4; retrojected, 265n7; *rex regum*, 113.
See also Emperor

law. See *nomos*/tradition/law
Lienhardt, Godfrey, 220n2
love, fear and, 102–3; love one another, 246n52;
Roman love poets, 270n52, 289n5
loyalty. See *fides*

magia/goēteia/"magic," 130
martyr/martyres: Perpetua, 65; as euphemism for
rebelli, 108; voluntary death, 92, 263n99
Mason, Steve, 282nn3,4, 284n30; ambiguity in
Josephus, 185, 191; *anuperblētos thrēskeia*, 196;
apraktio, 197; Christianity as belief system,
Tertullian, 275n35; *deisidaimonia*, 192–93;
figured speech in Josephus, 189; *hosios*, 174;
philosophies in Josephus, 157; *thrēskeia* in
Josephus, 156–58
mataioponia, 203
Meuli, Karl, 220n2
miles Christi/Christian Soldier/*miles sacratus*,
71–73, 80–83, 86, 106, 252n98, 258n47; and
annealing opposition/*antiperistasis*, 86, 106
misericordia, 67, 248nn60–61; *pietas* and, 248n63.
See also *compassio*/compassion

Mishna Kelim, 138–39
Momigliano, 239n65
Montanists, 241n8
morality, 32, 38, 96, 88–89, *anomia*, 267nn24–25;
Gnostics and, 267n24; *pudor*, 38; Torah, 162.
See also *askesis*; *disciplina*; government; *pudor*

necessary lies, 117
New Prophecy, 57, 98
nomos/tradition/law, conflicting, 112, 136–37,
150; and deeds, 160–61; *dei disciplina*, 112–13;
for interaction with gods, 46; Josephus, 156,
158–59; *politeuma* and, 159; sacralization, 100;
thrēskeia, 128–32; *thrēskeia* as, 163–67; *thrēskeia*
comparison, 175–77; Torah and, 160–63;
versus words, 283n13
Nongbri, Brent, 4–5, 9, 218n17

oaths: Chinese Communist Party, 257n41;
Christian, Pliny and, 82; of Christian soldiers,
81–83; *coniuratio*, 75; to Drusus, 77; *fides
christiana*, 79–80; as a form of idolatry for
Tertullian, 82; of loyalty, 76–77; *religio* as oath,
75; Roman, 254n14; *sacramentum*, 75, 77;
spoken, 253n4; Tertullian's baptismal oaths,
79–82, 257nn40,43
obedience/submission, 174; versus *religio*, 42
obstinatio, 91–92, 283n26. See also *contumacia/
obstinatio* and fear
'orayta, 158
Otto, Walter, 19, 228n93

paganus, "pagan," 253n9, 272n7
Pagels, Elaine, 201–2
paranomeō, 165
parastēmia, 196
patientia, 61
pax, 71, *pax deorum*, 255n26
periēn, 187
periergos, 125, 279n5
perissotata, 186
Philo Judaeus: *De legatione*, 201; *eusebeia*, 126–27;
Special Laws, 126–27; *thrēskeia*, 142–43, 200–1;
thrēskeia and cultic activity, 201; *thrēskeia* in,
147–48
pietas, 31, 47–48, 67–68; *misericordia* and
pity as, 248n63; offerings, 248n65; *pudor*
and, 31
pious falsehood. See necessary lies
"politics" and religion, 202, 272n6
profanum, 139, 272n6
prophetae, 57
proskunein, 203, 281n1; *thrēskeia* and, 136
psychici, 67